Network 4

Student's Book & Workbook

Paul Radley

With:
Elizabeth Sharman
Jacqueline Walkden

OXFORD
UNIVERSITY PRESS

Contents

Unit	Functions	Vocabulary	Grammar	
1 Family life p.9	Talking about family Talking about possessions (1)	Family	Verb *be* and Prepositions of place (1) Possessive *'s* Verb *have got* *a/an, any, How many...?*	
2 Free time p.17	Talking about sports and free-time activities Expressing likes and dislikes	Sports Free-time activities (1)	Present simple (1) Verbs + *-ing* Personal pronouns *play, go, do* *So do I. / Neither do I.* (Functions on film)	
p.25 Functions on film — Agreeing and disagreeing 🎥				
3 Everyday life p.27	Talking about daily routine Telling the time Talking about lifestyle	Daily routine The time Free-time activities (2) (Word builder +)	Present simple (2) • Adverbs of frequency Expressions of frequency Prepositions of time *at, on, in* Expressions with *have*	
4 School life p.35	Talking about school Talking about temporary actions Talking about your life at the moment	School subjects	Present continuous (1)+(2) Present continuous or Present simple? *Let's..., Shall we...,* *How about / Do you fancy... ?* (Functions on film)	
p.43 Functions on film — Making suggestions 🎥				
5 Difficult days p.45	Talking about dates Talking about ability Making arrangements	Ordinal numbers Months and dates Abilities (Word builder +)	*can* • Ability Present continuous (3) • The future Present simple (3) • The future	
6 In town p.53	Talking about places in your town Asking for and giving directions	Places in a town City adjectives (Word builder +)	Prepositions of place (2) (Word builder) *there is/are + some/any* The Imperative Prepositions and adverbs of movement *Could...?* (Functions on film)	
p.61 Functions on film — At the Tourist Information Centre 🎥				
7 Let's eat! p.63	Talking about your favourite food Talking about quantities Talking about diet Talking about your town	Food and drink Food quantities and containers (Word builder +) Shops (Word builder +)	Countable and uncountable nouns (Word builder) *some/any* *much/many, a lot of/lots of* *(a) little (bit of) / (a) few* *too much/many, (not) enough*	
8 Take a break p.71	Talking about holidays Talking about the past	Holidays (1)	Past simple • Verb *be* *be born* Past time expressions Prepositions of place (3) • *in, at* Past simple • Regular and irregular verbs (affirmative and negative forms) *will* and *would like* (Functions on film)	
p.79 Functions on film — Eating out 🎥				

2

Contents

Welcome to Network

Ciascuna unità dello *Student's Book* contiene:

Word builder

Presenta il nuovo lessico dell'unità.

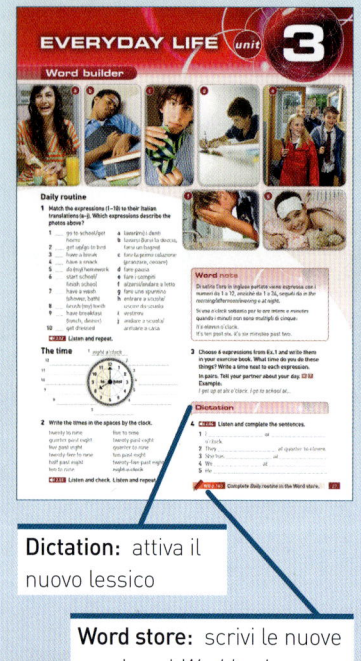

Dictation: attiva il nuovo lessico

Word store: scrivi le nuove parole nel *Workbook*

Presentation and practice

5 diversi *photostory* con i teenager, ciascuno ambientato in una delle capitali del Regno Unito.

Grammar: presenta la grammatica usando frasi dal dialogo

Word builder + Estende il lessico delle unità precedenti

Pronunciation: pratica la tua pronuncia

Word recall: riattiva il lessico della pagina *Word builder*

Real talk: espressioni colloquiali dal dialogo

Grammar note: informazioni su ulteriori funzioni grammaticali

Fast finishers! Esercizi che puoi fare se finisci prima

Speaking: metti in pratica il nuovo linguaggio

⚠ Note per aiutarti a evitare errori tipici

What do you think? Esprimi la tua opinione sui personaggi e sugli avvenimenti del *photostory*

Skills and culture

Argomenti attuali per imparare di più sul Regno Unito. Sviluppi le tue abilità di *reading, listening, speaking e writing.*

 2.20 Audio registrato sull'audio CD dello studente (Vedi pag.302 per l'elenco delle tracce)

Study skills: efficaci strategie di apprendimento nelle 4 abilità

Exam icons: attività per KET **K**, PET **P** and Trinity **T**

Grammar • stop and check

Riassunto della grammatica dell'unità con esercizi di consolidamento.

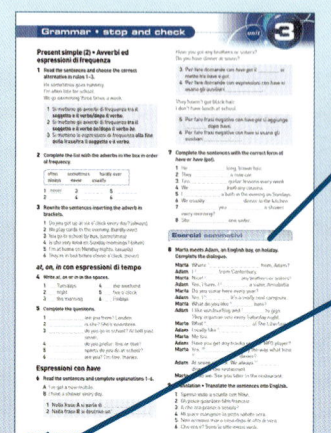

Esercizi sommativi: tutto il linguaggio dell'unità e delle unità precedenti

Workbook: vai al *Workbook* per spiegazioni grammaticali, il *Word store* e ulteriori esercizi

Dopo ogni due unità:

Functions on film

Linguaggio autentico per situazioni di vita quotidiana.

VIDEO
Guarda il video clip del dialogo su *My Digital Book*

Say it right! Fai il dialogo per parlare in modo più sciolto

Culture network

Leggi il testo su un aspetto della civiltà britannica e confrontarlo con la tua esperienza.

Did you know? Fatti culturali interessanti

VIDEO
Network video Guarda il video clip che estende il tema di *Culture network* su *My Digital Book*

Com'è organizzato *My Digital Book*

Books

• **Più di un libro:**
Starter, *Student's Book & Workbook*, *Digital Reader* con audio: *Emma* (Jane Austen)

• Facilmente navigabile tra i diversi 'libri' e le diverse sezioni

• Facilmente navigabile tra una pagina e l'altra

Tool Box

• Zoom
• Pagina intera (Reset zoom)
• Cancella
• Cancellare lo schermo
• Pennarello
• Evidenziatore
• Aggiungere note
• Aggiungere sito
• Tendine schermo
• Illumina

Resources

• *Culture Video Activity Book*
• Alfabeto
• Numeri
• Simboli fonetici
• *Wordlist* con audio per ogni unità
• Lista dei verbi irregolari con audio
• Guida alla pronuncia e guida alla punteggiatura con audio
• Cartine
• Lezioni CLIL
• Attività con il dizionario
• Schede di Recupero
• Accesso a un *practice test* online per il *Cambridge English: Preliminary (PET) for Schools*
• Oxford 3000™
• *Help file*
• ...e altre risorse per *Network*

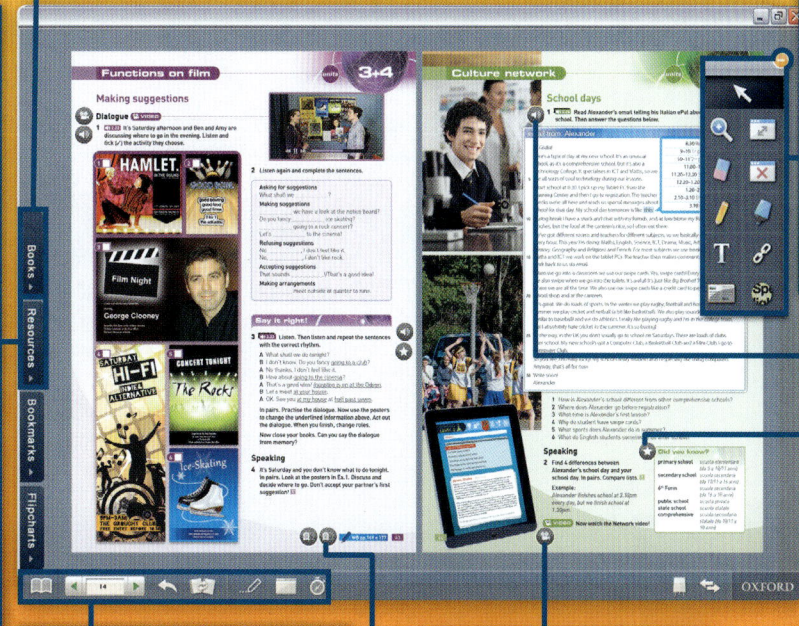

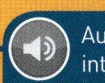
Audio integrato

Attività interattive integrate con correzione automatica

Navigation tool bar

• Navigabile tra i diversi 'libri' e le diverse sezioni
• Passaggio a una nuova pagina
• Visione della pagina singola o doppia
• Timer

Filmati DVD integrati

Rimando al *Workbook* per ulteriori attività

Espansioni online a:
www.oup.com/elt/networkitaly

The British Isles

N

Over 1000m
500 - 1000 m
200 - 500m
100 - 200m
Under 100m
Below sea level

Units 6–10
Hannah from Belfast

Units 11–15
Sam from Edinburgh

Units 1–5
Oliver from London

Orkney Islands
Mainland
Sanday
Stronsay
Hoy
S. Ronaldsay
Kirkwall

Unst
Yell
Foula
Mainland
Bressay
Lerwick
Sumburgh Head
Shetland Islands

Butt of Lewis
Cape Wrath
Pentland Firth
John o'Groats
Wick
Stornoway
Lewis
North Minch
Ullapool
Harris
North Uist
Grimsay
Uig
Skye
South Uist
Barra
Little Minch
Rhum
Mull
Inner Hebrides
Jura
Islay

Hebrides
Outer Hebrides

North West Highlands
Moray Firth
Fraserburgh
Loch Ness
Inverness
Cairngorms
Aberdeen
Ben Macdhui
Grampian Mountains
Montrose
Fort William
Ben Nevis
SCOTLAND
Dundee
Oban
Perth
Loch Lomond
Stirling
Firth of Forth
Glasgow
EDINBURGH
Kilmarnock
Southern Uplands
Cheviot Hills

North Atlantic Ocean

Malin Head
Giant's Causeway
Campbeltown
Arran
Firth of Clyde
Aran Island
Rossan Point
Londonderry
Antrim Hills
Donegal
Omagh
Stranraer
Solway Firth
Carlisle
Dumfries
HADRIAN'S WALL
Newcastle-upon-Tyne
Gateshead
Sunderland
Erris Head
Enniskillen
Sligo
Lough Neagh
BELFAST
NORTHERN IRELAND
Slieve Donard
Lough Conn
Achill Head
Achill Island
Dundalk
Lough Mask
Dundalk Bay
Douglas
Isle of Man
Lake District
Scafell Pike
Grasmere
Morecambe Bay
Middlesbrough
North Yorkshire Moors
Scarborough
Lancaster
Yorkshire Dales
Filey Bay
Flamborough Head

REPUBLIC OF IRELAND
Lough Derg
DUBLIN
Irish Sea
Holyhead
Leeds
York
Hull
Galway
Aran Islands
Wicklow Mountains
Wicklow
Wicklow Head
Anglesey
Caernarfon Bay
Colwyn Bay
Chester
Liverpool
Manchester
Salford
Bolton
Sheffield
Peak District
Stoke-on-Trent
Grimsby
Spurn Head
Lincolnshire Wolds
Yorkshire Wolds

North Sea

Loop Head
Limerick
Tralee Bay
Tralee
Killarney
Carrauntuohill
Bray Head
Cork
Bantry Bay
Bantry
Mizen Head
Old Head of Kinsale
Cork Harbour
Rosslare
Waterford
Fishguard
St. George's Channel
St. David's Head
Aberystwyth
Cardigan Bay
Cambrian Mts.
WALES
Derby
Stafford
Nottingham
Leicester
Birmingham
Coventry
Northampton
ENGLAND
Norwich
The Broads
Cambridge
Ipswich
Colchester
Orford Ness
The Naze
The Wash
The Fens
Welland
Stratford-upon-Avon
Oxford
Cotswold Hills
Chiltern Hills
Reading
Watford
LONDON
Greenwich
Thames Estuary
North Downs
Canterbury
South Foreland
Dover

Milford Haven
Carmarthen Bay
Newport
CARDIFF
Bristol
Bath
STONEHENGE
Bristol Channel
Lundy
Brecon Beacons
Salisbury Plain
Windsor
Medway
South Downs
Dungeness
Glastonbury
Southampton
Portsmouth
Brighton
Beachy Head
New Forest
Bournemouth
Selsey Bill
Isle of Wight
Newquay
Bodmin Moor
Dartmoor
Exeter
Lyme Bay
Portland Bill
Plymouth
Land's End
Penzance
Lizard Point
Isles of Scilly
Start Point

English Channel

Alderney
Channel Islands
Guernsey
Sark
Jersey

FAMILY LIFE

Word builder

Louise
grandmother
(grandma) **&** **Tom**
grandfather
(grandad)

Paul
father (dad) **&** **Tanya**
mother (mum)

Me **&** **Chris**
brother

Meg
auntie **&** **Tony**
uncle

Alice
cousin **&** **Tim**
cousin

Family

1 🔊 **1.24** Oliver Leigh, from London, is describing his family. Look at the photos. Listen and read.

1 Right, this is my grandma. Her name's Louise. And that's my grandad, Tom.

2 Now, these are my parents. This is my dad. His name's Paul. And this is my mum. Her name's Tanya.

3 This is me and my brother, Chris.

4 And here's my Auntie Meg. She's my mum's sister. That's Uncle Tony. So, I am Auntie Meg and Uncle Tony's nephew.

5 They've got a daughter and a son, Alice and Tim, who are my cousins – Alice and Tim are my parents' niece and nephew.

2 Translate the words into Italian.

1 husband/wife _marito/moglie_

2 grandmother (grandma)/grandfather (grandad)
_____

3 father (dad)/mother (mum) _____
4 brother/sister _____
5 aunt (auntie)/uncle _____
6 cousin _____
7 niece/nephew _____
8 parents _____
9 son/daughter _____

🔊 **1.25** Now listen and repeat.

Word note

father/mother-in-law	*suocero/suocera*
brother/sister-in-law	*cognato/cognata*
stepfather/stepdad	*patrigno*
stepmother/stepmum	*matrigna*
stepbrother	*fratellastro*
stepsister	*sorellastra*
only child	*figlio/a unico/a*

Speaking • My family

3 Write the names of 6 members of your family. In pairs. Ask and answer questions. **T**

Example:
A Who's Laura?
B Laura's my auntie.

Dictation

4 🔊 **1.26** Listen and complete the sentences.

1 This is my _____ and that's my _____.
2 Alan's my _____ and Chloe's my _____.
3 Where's _____? He's with _____ in the garden.
4 Teresa's my _____ and _____ Sonya is her _____.
5 My _____ are from Scotland.

WB p.147 Complete *Family* in the Word store.

Where are my headphones?

1 🔊 **1.27** It's Saturday and Oliver's got a diving competition. What's Oliver's girlfriend's name? Listen and read.

1
Where are you, Mum? Are you upstairs?

No, I'm not. I'm in the kitchen.

Can you help me, please? I'm late for the competition. Where are my headphones?

They're probably under your bed, **as usual**.

2
No, Mum. They aren't under my bed.

Are they under Chris's bed?

No, they aren't. Oh, here they are. They're on the floor behind the chair.

3
Hi. How are you, Katie?

I'm fine thanks, Chris.

4
Oliver, Katie's here.

Hi, Katie.

Oliver. **You're so messy!**

And **you're boring**. Er… Where *is* my swimming bag?

5
I remember now! It's in your parents' car, Katie. **Give them a ring**, quick! The competition starts in half an hour…

But they're in Edinburgh this weekend.

Comprehension check

2 Match the people or the objects (1–4) to 4 of the places (a–f).

1 ___ Mum
2 ___ Oliver's headphones
3 ___ Oliver's bag
4 ___ Katie's parents

a in Katie's parents' car
b behind the chair
c in Edinburgh
d under Chris's bed
e on the bed
f in the kitchen

Real talk

as usual	come al solito
You're so messy!	Sei così disordinato!
You're boring	Sei noioso
Give them a ring	Chiamali

What do you think?

1 Is Oliver really messy, in your opinion?
2 Are you messy or tidy?

Grammar

Verbo *be* e preposizioni di luogo (1)

Forma interrogativa	Forma affermativa e negativa
Where are you?	I'm/I'm not **in** the kitchen.
Where's my bag?	It's/It isn't **under** the desk.
Where are they?	They're/They aren't **behind** the chair.

Forma interrogativa	Risposte brevi
Are you upstairs?	Yes, I am./No, I'm not.
Is my book **on** the desk?	Yes, it is./No, it isn't.
Are they friends?	Yes, they are./No, they aren't.

Nell'inglese parlato si usa di solito la forma contratta del verbo.

Non si usa mai la forma contratta nelle risposte brevi affermative.

 **WB p.146**

Grammar check

3 Match the questions (1–8) to the answers (a–h).

1 _c_ Where's my pen?
2 ___ Where are you from?
3 ___ Is she a student?
4 ___ Are you French?
5 ___ Where are the books?
6 ___ Are you in the kitchen?
7 ___ Where are you?
8 ___ Is he English?

a No, I'm not. I'm upstairs.
b They're behind the desk.
c It's under the bed.
d No, we aren't.
e Yes, he is.
f I'm in my room.
g No, she isn't.
h I'm from Canterbury.

Grammar note

Per indicare possesso si usa il **genitivo sassone** dei sostantivi:

Chris**'s** bed
Oliver**'s** brother — sostantivo singolare: +'s
Katie**'s** parents
her parents**'** car — sostantivo plurale che termina in -s: +'
the children**'s** school — sostantivo plurale irregolare: +'s

Con più di un possessore, il genitivo sassone si usa solo con l'ultimo: Peter and Kim**'s** school.

 **WB p.146**

Grammar check

4 Add the possessive 's or ' to complete the sentences.

1 It's Mary_'s_ stereo.
2 It's Mr Jones___ house.
3 It's my parents___ digital camera.
4 They're Mr Davis___ DVDs.
5 They're the boys___ rollerblades.
6 It's Paul___ laptop.
7 They're my cousins___ books.
8 They're Molly___ sunglasses.

Pronunciation • *th* (voiced and unvoiced)

5a 🔊 **1.28** Listen to the pronunciation of *th*.

/ð/ the   /θ/ think

5b 🔊 **1.29** Listen and write the words in the correct column.

thank you	they	that	Thursday
three	thing	there	bath
this	then	think	these

/ð/ (voiced *th*)	/θ/ (unvoiced *th*)

🔊 **1.30** Listen and check. Listen and repeat.

Speaking • Where are Oliver's sunglasses?

6 Find 4 personal possessions (e.g. headphones, stereo, etc.) on p.10 and memorize where they are. In pairs. A: ask and answer questions. B: cover p.10. 🇹

Example:
A Where's Oliver's skateboard?
B It's behind the chair.
A No, it isn't behind the chair. It's on the floor!

Speaking • Possessions

7 🔊 **1.31** Listen to Lucy and match the names to the possessions.

1 ___ Ethan
2 ___ Chloe
3 ___ Nathan
4 ___ Lucy's parents
5 ___ Linda and Tom
6 ___ Holly
7 ___ Chris
8 ___ Rebecca

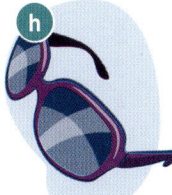

In pairs. Ask and answer questions. 🇹

Example:
A Is that Holly's laptop?
B No, it isn't. It's Ethan's laptop.

Now write 8 sentences.

1 *It's Ethan's laptop.*

Have you got a girlfriend?

1 🔊 **1.32** Oliver wins the diving competition. He's in the café at the swimming pool. Are Katie and Grace friends? Listen and read.

Grace Who's that?
Amy His name's Oliver, I think.
Grace He's gorgeous! Has he got a girlfriend?
Amy Yes, he has. Her name's...
Grace Oh, **who cares!** He hasn't got his girlfriend with him now.

Grace Well done, Oliver! Great dives!
Oliver Oh, er... thanks, er...
Grace Grace! Grace Holt. So, what's the secret of your success?
Oliver Well, I've got a good trainer.
Grace You're too modest! **Fancy a drink?**
Oliver Erm, OK. Let's sit here...

Oliver I don't believe it! *Another* message from my brother. He's got a new mobile. Have you got any brothers or sisters?
Grace No, I haven't. I'm **an only child.**
Oliver Lucky you!
Grace I haven't even got any cousins. Or a boyfriend... Have you got a girlfriend?
Oliver Yes, I have, but...
Katie But what, Oliver?
Oliver But... Hi, Katie. This is Grace.
Katie Hello, Grace. Nice to meet you.

Comprehension check

2 True or false? Write T or F. Correct the false sentences. 🄺

1 ___ Grace and Amy are Oliver's friends.
2 ___ Oliver's good at diving.
3 ___ Oliver isn't very modest.
4 ___ Oliver's pleased to get the message from his brother.
5 ___ Grace hasn't got any brothers or sisters.
6 ___ Katie's angry with Oliver.

Real talk

Who cares!	Che importa!
Fancy a drink?	Ti va qualcosa da bere?
an only child	figlia unica
Lucky you!	Beata te!

What do you think?

1 Is Katie *really* pleased to meet Grace?
2 Who do you prefer, Katie or Grace?

Grammar

Verbo *have got*

Forma affermativa
I/You/We/They**'ve got** a cousin.
He/She/It**'s got** a brother.

Forma negativa
I/You/We/They **haven't got** any cousins.
He/She/It **hasn't got** any brothers or sisters.

Forma interrogativa e risposte brevi
Have I/you/we/they **got** any brothers or sisters?
Yes, I/you/we/they **have./No,** I/you/we/they **haven't.**

Has he/she/it **got** a phone?
Yes, he/she/it **has./No,** he/she/it **hasn't.**

Nell'inglese parlato si usa di solito la forma contratta. Non si usa mai la forma contratta nelle risposte brevi affermative.

 **WB p.147**

Grammar check

3 Complete the sentences with the correct form of *have got*.

1 *Have you got* a mobile?
  Yes, I _____.
2 Oliver _____ a car. (not)
3 _____ a sister?
  Yes, he _____.
4 His uncle _____ a fantastic motorbike.
5 They _____ a computer. (not)
6 _____ an MP3 player?
  No, they _____.

Word recall Family

4 Write the English translations.

1 nonna/nonno _____
2 suocero/suocera _____
3 padre/madre _____
4 fratello/sorella _____
5 figlio/figlia _____
6 zio/zia _____
7 cugino/cugina _____
8 nipote (m)/nipote (f) _____
9 marito/moglie _____
10 figlio/a unico/a _____
11 fratellastro/sorellastra _____

Grammar note

Nelle frasi negative e interrogative con *have got* si usa *any* davanti ai sostantivi plurali:
Have you got **any** brothers or sisters?
Hai fratelli o sorelle?
I haven't got **any** friends.
Non ho amici.

Nelle domande su sostantivi plurali si usa *how many*.
How many brothers and sisters have you got?

 **WB p.147**

Speaking • Personal profile

5 In pairs. Ask questions about your partner and his/her family.
  Ask about: age, family, friends, boyfriends/girlfriends, interests, pets, possessions, jobs. K T

  Example:
  A Have you got any brothers or sisters?
  B Yes, I've got a sister.
  A How old is she?
  B She's twenty.

Luke's got a sister

6 🔊 **1.33** Luke and his friend are writing a family tree for homework. Listen and complete the table. K

	Relationship	Name	Age
1		Cindy	
2	stepdad	Mike	
3		Ann	44
4		Tina	
5	uncle	Trevor	
6	cousin	David	
7		Jake	22
8		Jill	

In pairs. Ask and answer questions to check your answers.

Example:
A How many brothers and sisters has Luke got?
B He's got one sister.
A What's her name?
B Her name's...

Fast finishers!

Write 8 sentences about Luke's family.

Reading

1 Before you read • In pairs. Ask and answer the questions.

1 Are names important? Why?
2 What are your favourite boys' and girls' names?
3 Are your favourite names Italian or from a different country?
4 Have you got a nickname?

2 🔊 1.34 While you read • Read the text and tick (✓) the names which are mentioned.

Ann ___	James ___	Brian ___	Boris ___
Apple ___	Peaches ___	Ewan ___	Gladys ___
Ryan ___	Sophie ___	Rebecca ___	Cameron ___
Eric ___	Winona ___	Elizabeth ___	Norman ___

Are you happy with your name?

What's the origin of your name? Is it your grandad's or grandma's name? Or is it a pop star's or actor's name? Is it traditional or modern? Very **common** or rare?

hello my name is ???

In the UK at the moment the top names for 16-year-olds are Tom for boys, and Rebecca for girls. There are lots of traditional names in Scotland, Ireland and Wales: for example, Cameron (for a boy) in Scotland, Sinead in Ireland, and Tegan (for a girl) in Wales. Some Welsh names 5 are impossible for non Welsh-speakers to pronounce! But British parents often choose the name of their favourite pop stars, actors or sportspeople, such as Ewan, after the Scottish actor Ewan McGregor, or Theo, after the footballer 10 Theo Walcott.

Famous people often choose very bizarre names for their children, sometimes naming them after fruit, **flowers** and cities! Here are some of our favourites: Peaches (Bob Geldof's daughter), Chanel (Francesco Totti's daughter), 15 Apple (Gwyneth Paltrow's daughter), Sunday Rose (Nicole Kidman's daughter), Brooklyn, Romeo and Cruz (the Beckhams' sons).

In some European countries, for example Germany and Italy, it's illegal to give your child a strange or ridiculous 20 name. Recently, an Italian mother and father wanted the name 'Bottom'* for their baby boy. Fortunately for the baby, the court **refused** permission and the boy's name is now Giorgio.

How important are names? Some people think that your 25 name determines the level of success in your life. A **survey** in the UK revealed that people called 'James' and 'Elizabeth' are **successful** but people called 'Lisa' and 'Brian' aren't very successful at all. But **don't worry** if your name is 'Brian', 'Lisa' or even 'Bottom'! It is legally possible to change it!

*Sedere, fondoschiena

Apple & Gwyneth Paltrow

Peaches & Bob Geldof

Brooklyn, Romeo, Cruz & David Beckham

3 Vocabulary • Look at the words in bold in the text. Match them to their Italian translations.

1 ___ common   a sondaggio
2 ___ flowers   b rifiutò
3 ___ refused   c non preoccuparti
4 ___ survey   e fiori
5 ___ successful   f persona che riesce bene
6 ___ don't worry   in quello che fa
                    g diffuso

4 Comprehension check • Complete the sentences with the correct names.

1 _____ and _____ are the most popular names for 16-year-olds in the UK.
2 _____, _____ and _____ are traditional Scottish, Irish and Welsh names.
3 _____ is a famous Scottish actor.
4 _____'s daughter's name is Sunday Rose.
5 Men called _____ are often successful.
6 Women called _____ are often unsuccessful.

Speaking

5 In pairs. Ask and answer the questions. 🅣

1 Which are your favourite names in the text?
2 Are 'Peaches' and 'Apple' nice names?
3 In your opinion, is it true that a person's success depends on his/her name? Why?/Why not?
4 In your opinion, are there any 'successful' or 'unsuccessful' Italian names?

Listening

6 Read the Study skills. Then do Ex.7.

> ### Study skills
>
> #### How to listen
>
> 1 Leggi le istruzioni dell'esercizio con cura per sapere quello che devi fare esattamente.
>
> 2 Sembra ovvio, ma è molto importante non parlare o fare rumore durante l'ascolto. Né tu né i tuoi compagni riuscireste a sentire la registrazione.
>
> 3 La prima volta che ascolti, non scrivere niente. Cerca di capire il senso globale per poi cercare di capire i particolari più dettagliati durante il secondo o terzo ascolto.

Chanel &
Francesco Totti

7 🔊 1.35 Listen to Jack and Isabel talking about their families. Choose the correct alternative.

Jack

1 There are **four/five** people in Jack's family.
2 Jack's sister's **fifteen/ten**.
3 Jack's mum's **forty/thirty**.
4 Jack's dad's name is **Wyndham/Wyndell**.
5 The name means **friend/strong**.
6 Jack's mum likes the actor Jack **Nicholson/Black**.

Isabel

7 There are **two/three** people in Isabel's family.
8 Isabel's aunt's name is **Frances/Florence**.
9 Isabel's dad is from **Germany/France**.
10 Isabel's cousin's name is **Victoria/Mel**.
11 Isabel's cousin's got a lot of **computer games/DVDs**.
12 Isabel's dad likes **Roxy Music/The Beatles**.

Writing

8 Write a short text (60–80 words) about your family using the verbs *be* and *have got*. Include this information: 🅣

• your name and where you're from
• your family's names, ages and what they do
• a description of your family's names. Are they traditional or modern? Do they have a special meaning?

Begin like this:

My name's (Francesco) and I'm (sixteen) years old. I'm from (Arezzo) in (Italy).

Verbo *be* e preposizioni di luogo (1)

1 Read the sentences and complete rules 1–5 with the words from the box.

Hi! I'm John.
I'm not from England.
She isn't a student.
They aren't English.
Are you American? Yes, I am.

interrogativa	not	contratta (x2)
n't	am	verbo

1 Nell'inglese parlato si usa spesso la forma _____ del verbo.
2 Per formare la forma negativa di *is/are* si aggiunge _____/_____ .
3 Invece per formare la forma negativa di ____ si usa solo *not*.
4 Alla forma _____ si invertono il _____ e il soggetto.
5 Nelle risposte brevi affermative non si usa la forma _____ .

2 Answer the questions using short answers.

1 Are you English? _____
2 Is your father a doctor? _____
3 Are you fifteen years old? _____
4 Is your English teacher Italian? _____
5 Are your parents English? _____

3 Rewrite the sentences as questions.

1 You're from Australia.
2 It's under the bed.
3 They're in your class.
4 I'm very good-looking.
5 We're late for school.
6 Harry's house is behind the swimming pool.

Now write the sentences in the negative.

Genitivo sassone

4 Add ' or 's to complete the sentences.

1 My parents___ bedroom's upstairs.
2 My cousin___ name's Ed.
3 Her friends___ names are Betty and Sam.
4 This is the women___ toilet.
5 Mr Thomas___ book's on the floor.
6 The children___ bikes are in the garden.

Verbo *have got* + *any*

5 Read the sentences and answer questions 1–5.

I've got a laptop and he's got a games console.
Have you got any DVDs? Yes, I have.
Have you got a brother? No, I haven't.
He hasn't got any friends.

1 Quali sono le due forme contratte della forma affermativa di *have got*?
_____
2 Nelle risposte brevi affermative con *have got* si può usare la forma contratta? _____
3 Si include *got* nella risposta breve? _____
4 Che cosa si aggiunge a *have* e *has* per fare la forma negativa? _____
5 Si usa *any* con i sostantivi singolari?
_____

6 Complete the questions with *a*, *an* or *any*. Then write the short answers.

1 Have you got __a__ mobile? ✓ *Yes, I have.*
2 Has Oliver got _____ sister? ✗
3 Have they got _____ pets? ✗
4 Has Jessica got _____ children? ✓
5 Have you got _____ cousins? ✗
6 Have Oliver and Katie got _____ computer? ✓

7 Rewrite the sentences so they are true for you.

1 I've got two brothers. *I haven't got any brothers.*
2 I haven't got any sisters.
3 My father's got a bicycle.
4 My mum's got blonde hair.
5 I've got three mobile phones.
6 I haven't got an MP3 player.
7 We haven't got any pets.
8 My auntie and uncle have got a Ferrari.

Esercizi sommativi

8 Read the dialogue and choose the correct alternative.

Boy Hi. What [1]'s/are your name?
Girl My name [2]am/'s Richelle.
Boy That's an interesting name.
Girl Yes, I [3]'s/'m from France. I'm in the UK for a mountain bike race.
Boy Have you got [4]any/a sponsors?
Girl Yes, I [5]'ve/have. My dad [6]'s/s' company is my sponsor. [7]Has/Have you got a bike?
Boy Yes, I [8]has/have. Actually, it's my brother [9]'s/s bike. It's over there. [10]Are/Is your parents here?
Girl Yes, they [11]'re/are. That's my parent [12]s'/'s camper van over there. Come and meet them.
Boy OK.

9 Translation • Translate the sentences into English.

1 Il cellulare è per terra.
2 Ho due nonni e una nonna.
3 Quanti cugini avete?
4 La mia borsa è dietro di te.
5 Questo è lo scooter di mio zio.

FREE TIME

Word builder

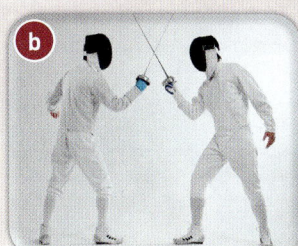

a b c d e

f g h

Sports

1 Match the sports (1–8) to the photos (a–h).

1. ___ play football
2. ___ go mountain biking
3. ___ go swimming
4. ___ play basketball
5. ___ play volleyball
6. ___ go rollerblading
7. ___ go snowboarding
8. ___ do fencing

🔊 **1.36** Listen and repeat.

Now add 2 of your favourite sports:

1 _____ 2 _____

Speaking • Are you good at swimming?

2 What sports are you good at? In pairs. Ask and answer questions. **K** **T**

Example:

A Are you good at swimming?
B Yes, I am. I'm quite/very/really good at it.
No, I'm not.

Free-time activities (1)

3 Match the activities (1–8) to the photos (i–p).

1. ___ listen to music
2. ___ go out with friends
3. ___ use the Internet
4. ___ play computer games
5. ___ watch TV/DVDs
6. ___ text/phone friends
7. ___ play the guitar/the piano/the drums
8. ___ go shopping

🔊 **1.37** Listen and repeat.

Now add 2 of your favourite free-time activities:

1 _____
2 _____

Speaking • My favourite free-time activities

4 Look at the free-time activities in Ex.3. Number them in order of preference.
In pairs. Compare your lists.

Example:

A For number 1 I've got 'text friends'. For number 2 I've got 'use the Internet'. What about you?

Dictation

5 🔊 **1.38** Listen to 5 teenagers talking about their free-time activities. Complete the sentences.

1. I play _____.
2. I _____ in my free time.
3. I _____ and I _____ in my free time.
4. In _____? I _____
and I _____.
5. I _____ free time really, but I _____ a lot.

k l m

i j n o p

WB p.153 Complete *Sports* and *Free-time activities (1)* in the Word store. **17**

Do you play the guitar?

1 🔊 1.39 Oliver and Katie are in the park. Why isn't Katie happy with Oliver? Listen and read.

Katie Hey, they're really good! Who's the singer?
Oliver His name's Ethan.
Katie Does he go to your school?
Oliver Yes, he does. And the guitarist's name is Lucy.
Katie Do they do concerts, too?
Oliver Yes, they do. Come on. I'll introduce you.
Hi, you guys!
Ethan Hello, Oliver.
Oliver This is Katie.
Katie Hi. You're *really* good!
Lucy Thanks. We practise a lot.
Ethan Yeah, we're pretty serious about music. We want to get a recording contract, so we practise every evening.
Oliver Every evening! You don't go out very much, then.
Lucy We don't stay at home *every* night – we go out with our friends at the weekend.
Katie Ignore him! He's jealous. He doesn't play any instruments. Do you play the guitar, Ethan?
Ethan Yes, I do.

Lucy *And* he plays the piano.
Ethan Not very well, though. Do you play anything, Katie?
Katie No, I don't, but I like music and I go to a lot of concerts. I usually go on my own because Oliver goes diving at weekends. Every weekend. He's obsessed with diving!
Lucy That's probably why he's good at it.
Oliver Thanks, Lucy.

Comprehension check

2 Complete the sentences with the correct names.
1 _____ and _____ play the guitar.
2 _____ plays the piano.
3 _____ and _____ don't play any instruments.
4 _____ goes to a lot of concerts.
5 _____ goes diving every weekend.

What do you think?

1 Is Oliver jealous of Ethan and Lucy in your opinion?
2 Are you obsessed with music? Do you sing or play the guitar?

Grammar

Present simple (1)

Forma affermativa
I/You/We/They **like** music.
She/He/It **plays** the piano.

Forma negativa
I/You/We/They **don't stay** at home.
She/He/It **doesn't play** any instruments.

Forma interrogativa e risposte brevi
Do I/you/we/they **play** any instruments?
Yes, I/you/we/they **do.**   **No,** I/you/we/they **don't.**

Does he/she/it **go** to your school?
Yes, he/she/it **does.**   **No,** he/she/it **doesn't.**

Per le variazioni ortografiche della terza persona singolare vedi p.152.

WB p.152

Grammar check

3 Complete the sentences with the correct Present simple form of the verbs in brackets.

1 _____ you _____ computer games? No, I _____. (like)
2 They _____ DVDs. (watch)
3 _____ she _____ out with her friends? Yes, she _____. (go)
4 Katie _____ her friends after dinner. (text)
5 We _____ to the cinema at weekends. We stay at home. (not go)
6 I _____ to music on my MP3 player. (listen)
7 He _____ his friends. He texts them. (not phone)
8 She _____ the guitar in a band. (play)
9 _____ they _____ the Internet? Yes, they _____. (use)
10 She _____ to parties every weekend. (go)

Word recall Free-time activities

4 Write the name of a free-time activity for each word in the box.

| listen | Internet | out with friends | guitar |
| shopping | computer | watch | text |

listen to music _____   _____

_____   _____

_____   _____

_____

What do they do?

5 🔊 1.40 Listen to 4 teenagers talking about their free-time activities. Tick (✓) the activities that they do.

	Thomas	Molly	Alex and Amy
listen to music			
play an instrument			
watch DVDs			
use the Internet			
go shopping			
go out with friends			

In pairs. Ask and answer questions to check your answers.

Example:
A What does Thomas do in his free time?
B He watches DVDs.

Pronunciation • *do*

6a 🔊 1.41 Listen to the pronunciation of *do*.

1 (stressed)   Yes, I **do**. /duː/
2 (not stressed) **Do** they know? /də/

6b 🔊 1.42 Listen and write 1 or 2.

A Do they go out with their friends? ____
B Do Jack and Emily like hip hop? Yes, they **do**. ____/____

🔊 1.43 Listen and check. Listen and repeat.

Speaking • Free-time questionnaire

7 Write complete questions.

1 what/sports/you/do?
_____

2 you and your friends/cinema?
_____

3 you/play/computer games?
_____

4 you/chat/online?
_____

5 you/go out/weekends?
_____

6 what other things/you/do/free time?
_____

Now add 2 more questions.

In pairs. Take turns to ask and answer the questions. 🅣

Example:
A What sports do you do?
B I play basketball and I go swimming.

Fast finishers!

Write a paragraph about your partner's free-time activities (40 words).

I really love diving

1 🔊 1.44 Oliver's in a sports shop in London. What do Oliver and Sophie have in common? Listen and read.

Comprehension check

2 True or false? Write T or F. Correct the false sentences. 🄺

1 ___ Sophie and Oliver like The Script.
2 ___ Sophie's sister likes diving.
3 ___ Oliver likes running.
4 ___ Oliver and Sophie like playing tennis.
5 ___ Sophie likes going to concerts.
6 ___ Sophie's mum phones Sophie.

Real talk

going to gigs	andare ai concerti
I've got to go	Devo andare
By the way	A proposito

What do you think?

1 Why do you think Oliver likes Sophie?
2 Do you ever meet new people when you're out?

Grammar

Verbi + -ing

Forma interrogativa
What **do** you **like doing**?
Does she **like watching** DVDs?

Forma affermativa	Forma negativa
I quite **like running**.	I **don't like playing** tennis.
She **loves playing** tennis.	She **doesn't like playing** volleyball.
She **hates/can't stand doing** karate.	

I verbi di opinione, per esempio *like*, *love*, *hate* e *can't stand* sono seguiti dal verbo alla forma in -*ing*.

Vedi p.152 per le variazioni ortografiche per l'aggiunta di -*ing*.

Si possono usare *really* e *quite* per modificare il significato dei verbi. *Really* intensifica il significato mentre *quite* indebolisce il significato leggermente.

 **WB p.152**

Grammar check

3 Write complete sentences.

1 I/can't stand/play computer games.
2 She/hate/go shopping.
3 They/not really like/play football.
4 I/love/listen to music.
5 We/really like/watch films on TV.
6 He/not like/use Internet.
7 You/really love/go mountain biking.
8 I/quite like/do karate.

Word recall Sports

4 Complete the expressions.

1 p*lay* f*ootball*
2 g_____ mo_____ _____g
3 g_____ sw_____
4 p_____ b_____
5 p_____ v_____
6 g_____ ro_____
7 g_____ sn_____
8 d_____ f_____

Speaking • What have we got in common?

5 Make a note of 3 things that you like doing and 3 things that you don't like doing. Use *quite/really like*, *love*, *don't like* and *hate/can't stand*.

In pairs. Ask and answer questions. What have you got in common? K T

Example:
A What do you like doing?
B I really love playing basketball.
A Me too!/Oh, I hate it!

Now write a short paragraph about your partner's likes and dislikes (40 words).

Grammar note

Osserva i pronomi personali complemento:
She likes **me**.
I love **you**.
I really like **Oliver**. → I really like **him**.
I really like **Sophie**. → I really like **her**.
I hate **football**. → I hate **it**.
They like **you, Kim and me**. → They like **us**.
I really like **dogs**. → I really like **them**.

 **WB p.153**

6 Rewrite the sentences using a pronoun.

1 She quite likes **you and Tony**.
2 We really like **Will Smith**.
3 He loves **horror films**.
4 They like **my sister and me**.
5 I can't stand **that film**.
6 Martin really likes **Lady Gaga**.

Speaking • Give your opinion!

7 Match the words (1–8) to the photos (a–h).

1 ___ popcorn
2 ___ Leona Lewis
3 ___ Keira Knightley
4 ___ coffee
5 ___ Robert Pattinson
6 ___ Jonas Brothers
7 ___ Sonohra
8 ___ designer clothes

In pairs. Ask and answer questions. T

Example:
A What do you think of popcorn?
B I hate it. Do you like it?

Reading

1 Before you read • In pairs. Ask and answer the questions.

1 What sports do you do at school?
2 Are you a member of a sports club?
3 Do you play a musical instrument?
4 Do you do any unusual free-time activities?

2 🔊 1.45 While you read • *My passion!* is a website about people's favourite free-time activities. Read the blogs and complete the table. K

Name	Passion
Jade	
Jed	
Luke	
Ellie	

MY PASSION!

a JADE

"My name's Jade. I'm eighteen years old and I'm passionate about street dancing. Street dancing is a **mixture** of different dance styles and gymnastics. **Basically**,
5 people play music in the street and dance. It's brilliant to dance or just watch. It's for boys and girls and it's completely free. You don't need any experience of dancing or gymnastics when you start. You just watch
10 other people and learn. I go street dancing every weekend with my friends."

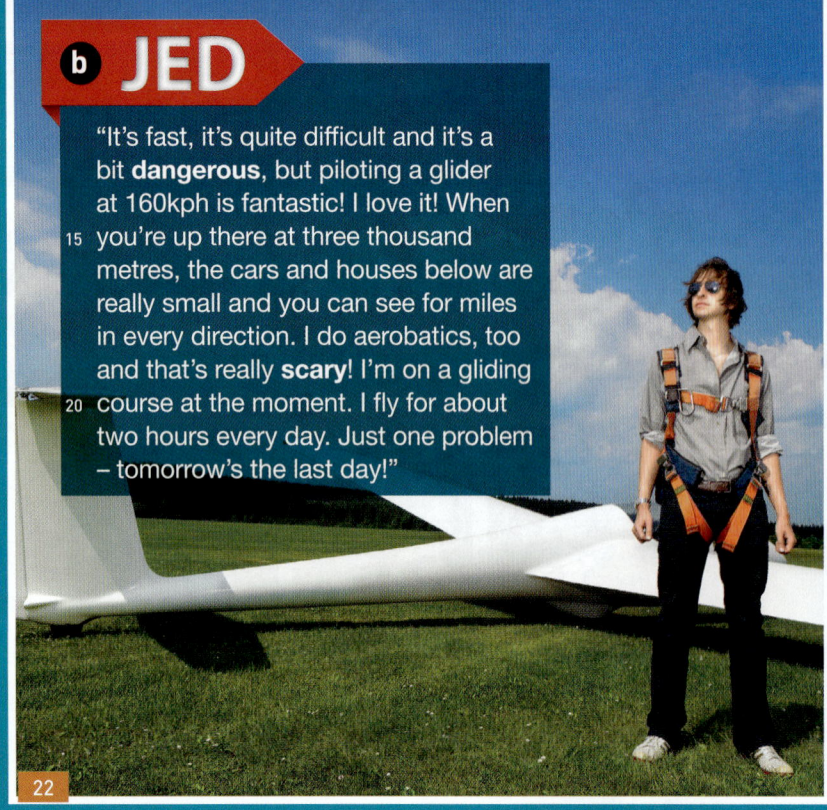

b JED

"It's fast, it's quite difficult and it's a bit **dangerous**, but piloting a glider at 160kph is fantastic! I love it! When
15 you're up there at three thousand metres, the cars and houses below are really small and you can see for miles in every direction. I do aerobatics, too and that's really **scary**! I'm on a gliding
20 course at the moment. I fly for about two hours every day. Just one problem – tomorrow's the last day!"

c LUKE

"I love painting big pictures on **walls**. It's really satisfying when you finish a painting.
25 I'm lucky because our **town council** gives us a big wall where we can do graffiti legally. I'm sometimes a bit **worried** before I start a new painting, but when I start, I immediately forget my nerves. I really love
30 telling stories with my art – I think it makes it more interesting. My inspiration comes from my life at home, at school and from things I see on the Internet."

3 Comprehension check • Match the sentences (1–8) to the blogs (a–d).

1 ___ This person makes things for her family and friends.
2 ___ This activity is dangerous.
3 ___ This person is sometimes anxious before starting.
4 ___ Music is an essential part of this activity.
5 ___ This person goes to lessons every week.
6 ___ You sometimes feel excited and sometimes frightened when you do this.
7 ___ You don't pay anything to do these activities.
8 ___ This person likes telling stories.

4 Vocabulary • Match the translation to the words in bold in the blogs.

a ¹in pratica _____   ²un miscuglio _____
b ³che fa paura _____   ⁴pericoloso _____
c ⁵comune _____   ⁶preoccupato/teso _____
   ⁷muri _____
d ⁸argento _____   ⁹collane _____
   ¹⁰principalmente _____

Speaking

5 In pairs. Ask and answer the questions. **T**

1 Which activity on the *My passion!* website do you like best? Why?
2 Which activities don't you like? Why not?
3 What's your passion?

Listening

6 Match the sports (1–6) to the pictures (a–f).

1 ___ basketball ___   4 ___ tennis ___
2 ___ dance ___   5 ___ football ___
3 ___ cycling ___   6 ___ weight training ___

🔊 **1.46** Listen to Amelia and Callum talking to a local radio reporter about sport. Which of the sports above do they mention? Write A (Amelia) or C (Callum) after the sports.

Listen again. What are their favourite sports?

Callum _____   Amelia _____

Writing

7 Lewis is your new Internet penfriend. Read his email.

---
email from: Lewis

Hi!
My name's Lewis Holmes and I live in Blackpool. In the winter I play football and I also go swimming. Football is OK, but I really love swimming. In the summer I do athletics. I love it. Running's my favourite sport and I take part in competitions in the local athletics team. I run the 400 metres. I think it's really exciting! I also like going mountain biking and I love going out with my mates. What sports do you do?
Bye for now,
Lewis

Now write a reply. Tell Lewis about your favourite free-time activities (60–80 words). **T**

d **ELLIE**

35 "My sister, Mia, and I love making jewellery. We make **necklaces** and rings from **silver**. We go to evening classes in jewellery-making every Friday. We make it **mainly** for members of our family. My mum really likes my necklaces. She always wears them on
40 special occasions. I also give my jewellery to my friends for their birthdays. I like making jewellery for myself, too. It's cool to wear original things."

Present simple (1)

1 Read the sentences and complete rules 1–4.

They play computer games.
She likes Madonna.
I don't play the guitar.
He doesn't play the piano.
Do you play basketball? Yes, I do.
Does he watch films? No, he doesn't.

> **1 Forma affermativa:**
> *I/You/We/They* + forma base del verbo
> *He/She/It* + forma base del verbo + _____
> **2 Forma negativa:**
> *I/You/We/They* + _____ + forma base del verbo
> *He/She/It* + _____ + forma base del verbo
> **3 Forma interrogativa:**
> _____ + *I/you/we/they* + forma base del verbo +?
> *Does* + _____ + forma base del verbo +?
> **4 Risposte brevi:**
> *Yes/No,* + *I/you/we/they* + _____.
> *Yes/No,* + *he/she/it* + _____.

2 Write short answers to these questions.

1 Do you watch TV? ✗
2 Does Katie go out with her friends? ✗
3 Do James and Amy go sailing? ✓
4 Do I play rugby? ✗
5 Does Tony like school? ✓
6 Rob and Anna, do you go to gigs? ✗

3 Rewrite the sentences as questions.

1 You play basketball. *Do you play basketball?*
2 He likes Brad Pitt.
3 They go out with their friends.
4 Maria plays the drums.
5 We watch DVDs in the evening.
6 Arjan goes swimming.

Now write the sentences in the negative.

1 *You don't play basketball.*

Verbi + *-ing*

4 Read the sentence and complete the rule.

He loves going to the cinema.

> I verbi *like*, *love*, *hate* e *can't stand* sono seguiti dal
> _____ + *-ing*.

5 Complete the sentences about free-time activities.

1 I love _____
2 I like _____
3 I quite like _____
4 I don't like _____
5 I can't stand/hate _____

Pronomi personali complemento

6 Complete the table.

Pronomi	
soggetto	**complemento**
I	1
you	2
he	3
she	4
it	5
we	6
you	7
they	8

7 Match the questions (1–5) to the answers (a–e).

1 ___ Do you like Tom Cruise?
2 ___ What do you think of Angelina Jolie?
3 ___ Do they like you and me?
4 ___ Do you like horror films?
5 ___ Do you like dancing?

a No, I don't like them.
b No, I don't. I can't stand him.
c Yes, I do. I really like it.
d I love her.
e Yes, they do. They like us a lot.

Esercizio sommativo

8 You meet Tom at a party. Follow the instructions and write the dialogue in your exercise book.

You [1] Chiedi a Tom che cosa gli piace fare nel tempo libero.

Tom [2] Risponde che gli piace andare al cinema e leggere. Ti chiede se ti piace ascoltare la musica.

You [3] Rispondi di sì.

Tom [4] Ti chiede se ti piacciono i Gorillaz.

You [5] Rispondi che non ti piacciono molto.

Tom [6] Ti chiede se hai fratelli o sorelle.

You [7] Rispondi che hai una sorella e che è alla festa anche lei.

Tom [8] Ti chiede che cosa piace fare a tua sorella nel tempo libero.

You [9] Rispondi che le piace ballare.

Tom [10] Risponde 'fantastico' e ti dice che piace ballare anche a lui. Ti chiede dov'è tua sorella.

You [11] Rispondi che è nel salotto.

Tom [12] Ti saluta.

You [13] Rispondi.

Agreeing and disagreeing

Dialogue 🎬 VIDEO

1 🔊 1.47 Dan and Charlotte are 2 American students at a college in the UK. Listen to them doing the *Are you an Anglophile?* Quiz. Write D (Dan) or C (Charlotte) for their answers.

ARE YOU AN ANGLOPHILE?

Do you like...

1 British food?
YES: NO:

2 the Royal Family?
YES: NO:

3 tea?
YES: NO:

4 British fashion?
YES: NO:

5 British music?
YES: NO:

6 British football teams?
YES: NO:

7 British films?
YES: NO:

8 British cars?
YES: NO:

Say it right!

2 🔊 1.48 Listen. Then listen and repeat the sentences with the correct rhythm.

1 A Do you like Harry Potter films?
  B Yes, I do.
  A So do I. I love them.

2 A Do you like the Royal Family?
  B No, I don't.
  A Neither do I. I'm not really interested in them.

3 A Do you like James Bond?
  B No, I don't.
  A Oh, I do. He's so cool.

4 A Do you like tea?
  B Yes, I do. I like it with lemon and sugar.
  A Oh, I don't. It's horrible.

In pairs. Practise the 4 dialogues. When you finish, change roles.

Grammar note

Per dimostrare accordo/disaccordo con un'affermazione al *Present simple* si può dire:
Agree: So do I./Neither do I. = *Anch'io./Neanch'io.*
Disagree: Oh, I do./Oh, I don't. = *Io sì./Io no.*
A me sì./A me no.

✏️ **WB p.153**

Speaking

3 In pairs. Do the anglophile quiz. Agree and disagree and give reasons. **T**
Now check the key below to see if you're an anglophile!

KEY (1 point for every 'yes' answer)

7–8 points You're the perfect anglophile. Go and live in the UK now!

3–6 points You quite like the UK, but you prefer your own country really.

0–2 points Oh dear! Don't go and live in the UK!

Favourite London places

1 🔊 1.49 Jamie is a London student. Read the post he wrote about London for the student exchange website . Then answer the questions below.

1 Why is it a good idea to book tickets for the London Eye online?
2 Which park has a zoo in it?
3 Where do tourists go to see their favourite stars?
4 Where can you see all of London?
5 What's the name of a good park to see modern art in central London?

2 Look at the map of central London and choose a place to visit. Find out about your place on the Internet and write a short description like Jamie's. 🇹

📹 **VIDEO** Now watch the Network video!

My London

Hi! My name's Jamie and I'm from Battersea in the west of London. I love London. Here are three of my favourite places in the city. Enjoy!

The London Eye

When you come to London, visit the London Eye. Please! It's fantastic! Its
5 32 capsules carry about 10,000 people every day. Each capsule holds a maximum of 25 people, so they're pretty big. The wheel's 135 metres high and it takes about half an hour to do a complete turn. At the top of the wheel there's a 360 degree panoramic view of the city – amazing. It's
10 best to book your tickets online because there are always long queues, and don't forget your camera!

Hyde Park

London's famous for its beautiful parks. The main ones are Green Park, St James's Park, Regent's
15 Park and Hyde Park. These are very near the centre of London and there are lots more in the suburbs, including Hampstead Heath, where you can generally spot a celebrity or two – I saw Hugh Grant the other day! Richmond Park is great and full of wildlife, and Regent's Park even has a zoo in it! My
20 favourite park is Hyde Park. They often exhibit weird and wonderful sculptures and modern art in the park and there's a lake in the middle. If you go, hire a boat and go for a trip on the lake.

Madame Tussauds

Madame Tussauds is really bizarre! It's full of
25 perfect wax models of famous people from the past and present. These include royalty, sportspeople, actors and singers: people like Queen Elizabeth II, David Beckham, Leonardo Di Caprio and Justin Bieber. There are also lots of music stars like Amy Winehouse, Michael Jackson, Elvis Presley and Lady Gaga. Everybody
30 looks so real! My favourite part is the Chamber of Horrors with its collection of psychotic killers. It's really scary!

Word builder

 **A**  **B**  **C**  **D**  **E**

Daily routine

1 Match the expressions (1–10) to their Italian translations (a–j). Which expressions describe the photos (A–G) above?

1 ___ go to school/get home
2 ___ get up/go to bed
3 ___ have a break
4 ___ have a snack
5 ___ do (my) homework
6 ___ start school/finish school
7 ___ have a wash (shower, bath)
8 ___ brush (my) teeth
9 ___ have breakfast (lunch, dinner)
10 ___ get dressed

a lavar(mi) i denti
b lavarsi (farsi la doccia, farsi un bagno)
c fare la prima colazione (pranzare, cenare)
d fare pausa
e fare i compiti
f alzarsi/andare a letto
g fare uno spuntino
h entrare a scuola/uscire da scuola
i vestirmi
j andare a scuola/arrivare a casa

 **F**  **G**

🔊 **2.02** Listen and repeat.

Word note

Di solito l'ora in inglese parlato viene espressa con i numeri da 1 a 12, anziché da 1 a 24, seguiti da _in the morning/afternoon/evening_ e _at night_.

Si usa _o'clock_ soltanto per le ore intere e _minutes_ quando i minuti non sono multipli di cinque:
It's eleven o'clock.
It's ten past six. It's six minutes past two.

The time

¹ _eight o'clock_

12 _____
11 _____
10 _____
9 _____
8 _____

2 _____
3 _____
4 _____
5 _____
6 _____
7 _____

(clock face: 12 11 10 9 8 7 6 5 4 3 2 1, "to" "past")

2 Write the times in the spaces by the clock.

twenty to nine
quarter past eight
five past eight
twenty-five to nine
half past eight
ten to nine

five to nine
twenty past eight
quarter to nine
ten past eight
twenty-five past eight
~~eight o'clock~~

🔊 **2.03** Listen and check. Listen and repeat.

3 Choose 6 expressions from Ex.1 and write them in your exercise book. What time do you do these things? Write a time next to each expression.

In pairs. Tell your partner about your day. **K T**
Example:
I get up at six o'clock. I go to school at...

Dictation

4 🔊 **2.04** Listen and complete the sentences.

1 I _____ at _____ o'clock.
2 They _____ at quarter to eleven.
3 She has _____ at _____.
4 We _____ at _____.
5 He _____.

✏️ **WB p.163** Complete _Daily routine_ in the Word store.

27

We never go out on Saturday nights!

1 🔊 2.05 It's Saturday night. Oliver and Katie are at Oliver's house. Does Chris agree with Oliver or with Katie? Listen and read.

Katie Let's go out tonight.

Oliver Sorry, Katie, but I've got a competition tomorrow morning.

Katie Oh, Oliver! I'm fed up. We hardly ever go out on Saturday nights!

Oliver That's not true! Besides, you often go out with your friends on Saturdays.

Katie Yes, I do, because I don't like staying at home and watching TV on Saturday nights.

Oliver But you know that I usually have diving competitions on Sundays and I need to go to bed early.

Katie Diving! Diving! That's all you think about. You never think about me!

Oliver Oh, come on, Katie. You know that's not true.

Katie What? On Sunday you've got competitions. On Monday you're usually tired and you've often got homework to do because you haven't got time at the weekend. You always go training on Tuesday, and on Wednesday you usually do more homework. On Thursday, training again, and on Friday... Well, on Friday we *sometimes* go out. Sometimes...

Chris Yes, she's right, Oliver. You *are* a bit selfish.

Oliver Chris! Go away! It's got nothing to do with you.

Katie Thanks, Chris! You see, Oliver?

Comprehension check

2 Answer the questions.

1 Why is Katie angry?
2 Who does Katie often go out with on Saturday nights?
3 What does Oliver do on Sundays?
4 Why doesn't he want to go out on Mondays?
5 What does he do on Wednesdays?
6 When do Oliver and Katie sometimes go out?

Real talk

I'm fed up	Sono stufa
Besides,...	E comunque,...
Come on!	Dai!
It's got nothing to do with you	Non ti riguarda

What do you think?

1 Who's right, Oliver or Katie, in your opinion?
2 Do you ever argue with your friends? What about?

Grammar

Present simple (2) • Avverbi di frequenza

0% You **never** think about me.
10% I **hardly ever** go out on Saturday nights.
40% We **sometimes** go out on Friday.
60% You **often** go out with your friends.
90% I **usually** have competitions on Sundays.
100% You **always** go training on Tuesday.

Si mette l'avverbio di frequenza tra il soggetto e il verbo, tranne quando si tratta del verbo *be*:

You're **usually** tired on Monday.
I'm **often** late for school.

 **WB p.162**

Grammar check

3 Write the sentences in the correct order.

1 plays she weekend tennis at usually the
2 school after I am tired often
3 with never out they parents go their
4 you do the always in TV evening watch?
5 for late we're sometimes school
6 homework does hardly his Nathan ever
7 play you football never
8 always after Chloe football plays school

Grammar note

1 Di solito si mettono le **espressioni di frequenza** alla fine della frase.
He goes out with his friends **every weekend**.
I usually go running **three times a week**.
She visits her grandma **every month**.

2 Nota quando si usano le **preposizioni** *at, on, in*.
at: con le ore e con alcune espressioni di tempo
at five o'clock, at the weekend, at night
on: con i giorni
on Tuesday, on Monday morning
in: con i mesi e con le fasi del giorno
in October, in the evening

 **WB pp.162–163**

 once (~~one time~~)
twice (~~two times~~)
three times, four times, five times...

Word builder + Free-time activities (2)

4 Match the activities (1–6) to the pictures (a–f).

1 ___ go for a ride
2 ___ have a chat
3 ___ go for a walk
4 ___ go dancing
5 ___ rent a DVD
6 ___ hang around with friends

 **WB p.163** Complete *Free-time activities* in the Word store.

Speaking • Who is it?

5 Choose a person in your class that you know well. Make notes about his/her physical appearance (height, hair colour) and free-time activities (What?, When?, How often?).

In pairs. A: describe your person.
            B: guess the person's identity.

Example:
A He's very tall. He's got long, brown hair. He usually plays football at the weekend.
B It's Federico.
A That's right.

When you finish, change roles.

My free time

6 Complete the sentences about what you do in your free time. 🔲

I always *go swimming on Saturdays.*

1 I always _____
2 I usually _____
3 I often _____
4 I sometimes _____
5 I hardly ever _____
6 I never _____

In pairs. Read your sentences. What have you got in common?

Fast finishers!

Write 6 sentences about the person you described in Ex.5.

When does he have a rest?

1 🔊 **2.06** Jay Johnson is a competitor in *Wow-Factor*, a TV talent contest. Does Jay like the other performers? Listen and read.

Network Magazine reporter Annie Hughes interviews:

★ Jay Johnson ★

JAY JOHNSON is in the *Wow-Factor* bootcamp*. It's an incredible house – it's got 18 bedrooms and a jacuzzi, but he doesn't have time to use it. He's one of 24 contestants in the house and their
5 daily schedule is manic. Jay gets up really early and goes to bed very late, seven days a week. When does he have a rest? Never!

We met Jay after a rehearsal this morning.

NETWORK: So, Jay, do you have time to eat?
10 **JAY:** Yes, of course I do!
NETWORK: What time do you have breakfast?
JAY: I have breakfast very early, at six o'clock.
NETWORK: Six o'clock! That is early!

After breakfast Jay has two hours of singing
15 lessons, and then he learns dance routines all morning. Jay doesn't have lunch because he's too busy. He just has a snack. In the afternoons he practises for the group dance and does interviews. Does he have fun? Yes, he does!

JAY: I have dinner with the other performers at seven
20 o'clock. It's the only time we relax. The other contestants are really funny – we have a good laugh! Then after dinner we have more rehearsals.

Life's very hard in the *Wow-Factor* bootcamp, but Jay says **it's worth it** because he desperately wants to be a
25 professional singer. He's **under pressure** because this is the crucial stage of the competition. One bad performance and he's on the bus home!

*campo di addestramento

Comprehension check

2 True or false? Write T or F. Correct the false sentences. **K**

1 ___ Jay Johnson's got lots of free time in the bootcamp.
2 ___ Jay gets up before six o'clock.
3 ___ Jay has singing lessons all morning.
4 ___ Jay doesn't eat at lunchtime.
5 ___ Jay has dinner at seven o'clock.
6 ___ Jay doesn't like working hard.

Real talk

It's worth it.	Ne vale la pena.
under pressure	sotto pressione

What do you think?

1 Does the bootcamp seem hard to you?
2 Has Jay got a chance of winning, in your opinion?
3 Do you think that 'overnight success' is a bad thing?

Grammar

Espressioni con *have*

Forma affermativa
I **have** breakfast very early.
He **has** singing lessons.

Forma negativa
I **don't have** lunch.
He **doesn't have** a rest.

Forma interrogativa
Do you **have** time to eat?
Does he **have** fun?
What time do you **have breakfast**?
When does he **have a rest**?

Si usa *have* con certe espressioni per descrivere azioni.
Si usa *have got* solo per parlare di possesso.

Con il verbo *have* si usano gli ausiliari *do/does/don't/doesn't* nelle forme negativa e interrogativa.

 **WB p.163**

Grammar check

3 Do these sentences describe actions or possession? Write A o P.

1 _A_ I have dinner at eight o'clock.
2 ___ They've got a new teacher.
3 ___ She's got long hair.
4 ___ We have lunch at twelve o'clock.
5 ___ I have a bath in the morning.
6 ___ You've got blue eyes.
7 ___ He has singing lessons.
8 ___ They have a break at ten o'clock.

Now rewrite the sentences in the negative and interrogative.

1 *I don't have dinner at eight o'clock.*
  Do you have dinner at eight o'clock?

Word recall Daily routine and time

4 Daily routine • Don't look at Ex.1 on p.27. How many phrases can you remember for each of these verbs?

1 go _____
2 get _____
3 have _____
4 do _____
5 finish _____
6 brush _____
7 start _____

Time • In pairs. A: say a time in Italian. B: say it in English.

After 5 times, change roles.

 Si usano *am (ante meridiem)* e *pm (post meridiem)* negli orari e nell'inglese scritto.

Pronunciation • *-s, -es*

5a 2.07 Listen to the pronunciation of the final *-(e)s*.

1 finish**es** /ɪz/   2 start**s** /s/   3 go**es** /z/

5b 2.08 Listen. Which category do these words belong to? Write 1, 2 or 3.

___ gets   ___ has   ___ likes
___ brushes   ___ uses   ___ texts
___ washes   ___ plays   ___ listens

2.09 Listen and check. Listen and repeat.

Jay's day

6 2.10 Listen to Jay talking in detail about a typical day in the *Wow-Factor* bootcamp. Write the times next to the activities.

1 get up _____
2 have a shower _____
3 have breakfast _____
4 have singing lessons _____
5 have a break _____
6 have lunch _____
7 practise for the group dance _____
8 do an interview _____
9 have dinner _____
10 go to bed _____

In pairs. Ask and answer questions about Jay's day.
A: ask about 1–5 above. B: ask about 6–10.

Example:
A What time does Jay get up?
B He gets up at…

Speaking • My Saturday

7 Prepare a description of your typical Saturday. List 8 activities you do: 6 true and 2 false.

In pairs. A: describe your Saturday. B: listen and guess which 2 things aren't true. T

Example:
A I get up at six o'clock.
B That's not true!
A Yes, you're right. I get up at…

When you finish, change roles.

Reading

1 Before you read • In your opinion, who are the speakers in these 6 statements? Write **A (adults)** or **T (teenagers)**.

1 ___ 'The teen years are the best years of your life.'
2 ___ 'Most teenagers don't do what their parents want them to.'
3 ___ 'A lot of teenagers take drugs.'
4 ___ 'Teenagers like hanging around together.'
5 ___ 'Teenagers need rules at home.'
6 ___ 'Parents don't really understand teenagers.'

In pairs. Discuss the statements. Are they true?

2 While you read • Read the *Network Magazine* article and choose the correct title A, B or C.

A A day in the life of a teenager
B The problems of being a teenager
C Why I hate being a teenager

3 🔊 **2.11** Listen and check.

Spencer Morgan, a 16-year-old from Oldham, talks to *Network* about being a teenager today.

'When I walk down the street with a group of my mates, people often think we're **troublemakers**. We're quite noisy, we **mess around** and maybe they don't like our clothes. People cross the road when
5 they see us. Why? I suppose they think we want trouble, when most of the time we just want to buy a burger. But that's just part of being a 16-year-old these days.
Many people have a stereotypical idea of teenagers.
10 Most of the time it's completely untrue and unfair. I think I'm a typical teenager – I like **hanging around** with my friends, but we're not criminals. I play the guitar in a band, I like going to parties and I don't always **obey** my parents.
15 And like most teenagers, I want to be somebody in life. I want to be successful. I worry about my future and I work hard at school. However, I also know I'm lucky because my mum and my dad always

encourage me to do well and they always **set limits**.
20 They let me go out in the week, but I have to be home at 11 pm.
I know some people of my age get into trouble, but in my school they're a minority. Some boys drink and smoke after school, but I don't go out with them
25 because I don't want to **waste** my life. Most of the young people who get into trouble don't have good role models. As a result, they often **lose their way**, but they need help, not criticism. Good parents are strict but loving at the same time.
30 Most teenagers like using their time to do useful things. For example, at the moment my schoolfriends and I are **raising money** to help to build a school in Kenya. You never hear about the good things teenagers do – just the bad things.
35 So when you see me and my friends in the street, don't cross the road or ignore us. We're quite nice, really!'

4 Read the Study skills. Then do Ex.5.

5 Vocabulary • Look at the words in bold in the text. What do they mean? Write a translation.

1 troublemakers   _____

2 mess around   _____

3 hang around   _____

4 obey   _____

5 set limits   _____

6 waste   _____

7 lose their way   _____

8 raise money   _____

6 Comprehension check • Answer the questions.

1 Why do people cross the road when they see Spencer and his friends?

2 How does Spencer describe typical teenagers?

3 Is Spencer ambitious?

4 Why has Spencer got good parents, in his opinion?

5 Why doesn't Spencer hang out with the boys who smoke and drink?

6 What example does Spencer give of teenagers doing something good?

Speaking

7 In pairs. Ask and answer the questions. **T**

1 Do you think your parents have a good or bad opinion of teenagers? Why?

2 What do teenagers do in your town on Saturday night?

3 Do you go out in the evenings during the week?

4 Are your parents strict?

Listening

8  **2.12** Listen to three teenagers talking about where they live. Match the people (1–3) to the places (a–e). **K**

1 ___ William
2 ___ Chloe
3 ___ Rebecca

a Edinburgh
b London
c Cardiff
d Southstoke
e Newcastle

Listen again and choose the correct alternative.

1 William lives in a small village near Bath/Bristol.

2 William says that life in the village is **boring/exciting**.

3 The last **bus/train** home is at ten o'clock.

4 Chloe goes **ice skating/dancing** on Saturday nights.

5 She enjoys herself, but it's **expensive/tiring**.

6 Chloe's **boyfriend/dad** takes her home at twelve o'clock.

7 Rebecca doesn't do much because she **has got exams/hasn't got any money**.

8 Rebecca and her boyfriend like going to the **theatre/concerts**.

Writing

9 Answer the questions to write a short text about going out at the weekend in Italy (60–80 words). **T**

- What nights do you usually go out?
- Who do you go out with?
- What time do you go out?
- What do you wear?
- Where do you go?
- How much do you spend?

Present simple (2) • Avverbi ed espressioni di frequenza

1 Read the sentences and choose the correct alternative in rules 1–3.

He sometimes goes running.
I'm often late for school.
We go swimming three times a week.

> 1 Si mettono gli avverbi di frequenza **tra il soggetto e il verbo/dopo il verbo**.
> 2 Si mettono gli avverbi di frequenza **tra il soggetto e il verbo** be/dopo il verbo be.
> 3 Si mettono le espressioni di frequenza **alla fine della frase/tra il soggetto e il verbo**.

2 Complete the list with the adverbs in the box in order of frequency.

> | often | sometimes | hardly ever |
> |---|---|---|
> | always | ~~never~~ | usually |

1 _never_   3 _____   5 _____
2 _____   4 _____   6 _____

3 Rewrite the sentences inserting the adverb in brackets.

1 Do you get up at six o'clock every day? (always)
2 We play cards in the evening. (hardly ever)
3 You go to school by bus. (sometimes)
4 Is she very tired on Sunday mornings? (often)
5 I'm at home on Monday nights. (usually)
6 They're in bed before eleven o'clock. (never)

at, on, in con espressioni di tempo

4 Write at, on or in in the spaces.

1 ___ Tuesdays   4 ___ the weekend
2 ___ night   5 ___ five o'clock
3 ___ the morning   6 ___ Fridays

5 Complete the questions.

1 _____ are you from? London.
2 _____ is she? She's seventeen.
3 _____ do you go to school? At half past seven.
4 _____ do you prefer: this or that?
5 _____ sports do you do at school?
6 _____ are you? I'm fine, thanks.

Espressioni con have

6 Read the sentences and complete explanations 1–6.

A I've got a new mobile.
B I have a shower every day.

> 1 Nella frase A si parla di _____.
> 2 Nella frase B si descrive un' _____.

Have you got any brothers or sisters?
Do you have dinner at seven?

> 3 Per fare domande con *have got* il _____ si mette tra *have* e *got*.
> 4 Per fare domande con *have* si usano gli ausiliari _____.

They haven't got black hair.
I don't have lunch at school.

> 5 Per fare frasi negative con *have got* si aggiunge _____ dopo *have*.
> 6 Per fare frasi negative con *have* si usano gli ausiliari _____.

7 Complete the sentences with the correct form of *have* or *have got*.

1 He _____ long, brown hair.
2 They _____ a new car.
3 Tim _____ guitar lessons every week.
4 We _____ (not) any cousins.
5 I _____ a bath in the evening on Sundays.
6 We usually _____ dinner in the kitchen.
7 _____ you _____ a shower every morning?
8 She _____ one sister.

Esercizi sommativi

8 Marta meets Adam, an English boy, on holiday. Complete the dialogue.

Marta Where ¹_____ from, Adam?
Adam I ²_____ from Canterbury.
Marta Nice! ³_____ any brothers or sisters?
Adam Yes, I have. I ⁴_____ a sister, Annabella.
Marta Do you come here every year?
Adam Yes, I ⁵_____. It's a really cool campsite.
Marta What do you like ⁶_____ here?
Adam I like windsurfing and ⁷_____ to gigs. They organise one every Saturday night.
Marta What ⁸_____ of The Libertines?
Adam I really like ⁹_____.
Marta Me too.
Adam Have you got any tracks on your MP3 player?
Marta Yes, ¹⁰_____. By the way, what time ¹¹_____ dinner?
Adam At seven o'clock. We always ¹²_____ dinner in the restaurant.
Marta So do we. See you later in the restaurant.

9 Translation • Translate the sentences into English.

1 Spesso vado a scuola con Mike.
2 Gli piace guardare film francesi.
3 A che ora pranzi a scuola?
4 Mi piace mangiare la pizza sabato sera.
5 Non arrivano mai a casa dopo le otto di sera.
6 Che ora è? Sono le otto meno venti.

SCHOOL LIFE

Word builder

Chemistry

Geography

School subjects

1 🔊 **2.13** Listen and repeat. Then complete the mind map with the school subjects in the box.

Spanish	Physics	football	Latin
~~Maths~~	Italian	swimming	Greek
Biology	French	History	volleyball
English	Chemistry	Geography	German
basketball	Citizenship	~~IT (Information Technology)~~	
RE (Religious Education)			

IT (Information Technology)

IT (Information Technology)

Maths

LANGUAGES

SCIENCE

SCHOOL SUBJECTS

PE (PHYSICAL EDUCATION)

HUMANITIES

Speaking • My favourite subjects

2 Look at the list of subjects in Ex.1. In pairs. Do you like the same subjects? **K** **T**

Example:
A Do you like Maths?
B Yes, I do. It's interesting.
A So do I. Do you like…

Dictation

3 🔊 **2.14** Listen and complete the sentences.

1 On Monday mornings _____
_____.
2 French is _____.
3 Do they _____?
4 At _____.
5 On Friday mornings _____
_____.

WB p.169 Complete *School subjects* in the Word store.

35

I'm waiting for the bus

1 🔊 **2.15** It's nine o'clock on Monday morning. Where do you think Oliver is? Tick (✓) a picture. Listen and read to check your answer.

Oliver Oh, hi, Mum. What's the matter?

Mum Nothing. Everything's fine. Where are you?

Oliver I'm on my way to school.

Mum Right. Are you walking to school?

Oliver No, I'm not. I never walk to school. You know that! I'm waiting for the bus, but it's late again.

Mum Oh dear! And it's raining, too. Er... What's that terrible noise?

Oliver That's Jack and Arjan.

Mum What are they doing? Are they arguing?

Oliver No, they aren't. They're checking their homework. Why all the questions, Mum?

Mum No reason... I can hear a guitar. Is Dan playing the guitar at the bus stop?

Oliver No, he isn't! Gemma's listening to music on her phone. Mum, I've got to go. I'm getting on the bus now.

Mum Come off it, Oliver. You aren't getting on the bus!

Oliver What do you mean?

Mum Oliver, I'm sitting in the car outside the café. Look out of the window. Now tell me why you aren't at school, please!

Real talk

What's the matter?	Che c'è?
Come off it	Smettila

Comprehension check

2 Answer the questions.

1. Is Oliver walking to school?
2. Is Oliver waiting for the bus?
3. Is it true the bus is late?
4. Where's Oliver?
5. Where's Oliver's mum?

What do you think?

1. Is Oliver's mum really angry with him?
2. Do you ever miss school without permission?

Grammar

Present continuous (1)

Forma affermativa
I**'m getting** on the bus.
She**'s listening** to music.
We**'re checking** our homework.

Forma negativa
I**'m not walking** to school.
It **isn't raining**.
We **aren't getting** on the bus.

Forma interrogativa
Are you **walking** to school?
Is he **playing** the guitar?
Are you **arguing**?
What **are** they **doing**?

Risposte brevi
Yes, I **am./No**, I'm **not**.
Yes, he **is./No**, he **isn't**.
Yes, we **are./No**, we **aren't**.

Si usa il *Present continuous* per parlare di azioni in corso nel momento in cui si parla.

WB p.168

Grammar check

3 Write complete sentences.

1 what/you/do? I/do/my homework
   What are you doing? I'm doing my homework.
2 what/Edith/do? she/write/email/Betty
3 you/have lunch? yes/we
4 they/not go/leisure centre
5 why/he/ride/bike/to work? they/repair/his car
6 Rebecca/Martha/watch/video? no
7 he/not/do/his homework
8 she/watch/documentary? yes

Speaking • What are they doing?

4 Look at the pictures. What are these people doing? Write sentences.

1 *He's drinking tea.*
2 _____
3 _____
4 _____
5 _____
6 _____
7 _____
8 _____

In pairs. Ask and answer questions to check your answers.

Example:
A Is he drinking coffee?
B No, he isn't. He's...

5 Choose the correct alternative.

1 I always get/'m always getting to school at half past eight.
2 He's listening/listens to music at the moment.
3 We often go/'re often going out for lunch.
4 I'm having/have coffee at the moment.
5 They're always spending/always spend their holidays in Spain.
6 You're never coming/never come home early.
7 She isn't here. She's playing/plays tennis in the park.
8 We're in the library and we study/'re studying hard for our exams.

Grammar note

Osserva la differenza fra queste due frasi:
Sorry – are you watching TV? Ring me later!
I always watch TV after school.

Il *Present continuous* si usa per descrivere un'azione in corso nel momento in cui si parla.

Il *Present simple* si usa per descrivere un'azione abituale. In inglese non si usa il *Present simple* per un'azione in corso di svolgimento.
What are you doing? (~~What do you do?~~)
I'm watching a film.

WB pp.168–169

Fast finishers!

Imagine what these people are doing at the moment: the President, Shakira, Brad Pitt, Federica Pellegrini and Jessica Alba. Write 5 sentences (50 words).

He isn't concentrating in class

1 🔊 **2.16** Oliver's mum asks to talk to Mr Slater, one of Oliver's teachers. Why is Oliver worried about his dad? Listen and read.

Mum	I'm sorry to bother you, Mr Slater. It's just that I'm worried about Oliver. Is he coming to all his lessons?
Mr Slater	No, he isn't. He's missing a lot of lessons and there's another problem. He isn't concentrating in class. In fact, he's doing very badly in Maths and Physics.
Mum	Oh dear. I'm quite surprised because he does at least two hours' homework every day.
Mr Slater	Well, that's good to hear. Oliver often looks very tired. I know he's in the local diving team. Is he training very hard?
Mum	Yes, he is, actually. He loves diving. He does his homework and then goes to the pool every night.
Mr Slater	Every night? And is he going out a lot with his friends, too?
Mum	Well, no, he isn't. He hasn't got time during the week. He sometimes goes out on Friday nights, but never on Saturdays. Is he getting on OK with the other kids?

Mr Slater	Yes, he is. In fact, he's very popular.
Mum	Oh, good. Well, maybe he's worried about his dad.
Mr Slater	His dad?
Mum	Yes. He's having problems at work at the moment.
Mr Slater	I see…

Comprehension check

2 True or false? Write T or F. Correct the false sentences. 🄺

1 ___ Oliver isn't going to some of his lessons.
2 ___ Oliver's doing well in Maths and Physics.
3 ___ Oliver's training very hard at the moment.
4 ___ Oliver's classmates don't like Oliver.
5 ___ Oliver goes out a lot with his friends at weekends.
6 ___ Oliver's dad hasn't got a job.

Real talk

I'm sorry to bother you	Mi dispiace disturbarLa
It's just that…	È solo che…
Is he getting on OK with…?	Va d'accordo con…?
I see	Ho capito

What do you think?

1 Do you think Oliver is a good student?
2 Do you talk to your parents about school?

Grammar

Present continuous (2)

He's **having** problems at work.
He **isn't concentrating** in class.
Is he **going** out a lot with his friends? **No**, he **isn't**.

Il *Present continuous* si può usare anche per parlare di un'azione temporanea di una certa durata ma che non è necessariamente in corso di svolgimento nel momento in cui si parla.

Come in italiano, certi verbi (i verbi di stato) di solito non si usano al *Present continuous*:
I know he's in the diving team.
(I'm knowing he's in the diving team.)

Alcuni dei verbi di stato più frequenti sono: *know*, *want*, *like/hate*, *understand*, *believe*, *have got* e *be*.

 **WB pp.168–169**

Grammar check

3 Look at the sentences. Write TS (temporary situation) or N (now).

1 _N_ I can't answer the phone. I'm having a bath.
2 ___ They're in the dining room. They're eating.
3 ___ We're finding Geography very difficult this year.
4 ___ He's studying a lot with Mark these days.
5 ___ I'm doing my homework now.
6 ___ He's reading a book in the garden.
7 ___ Mia's doing a lot of sport this term.
8 ___ I'm not sleeping very well this week.

Word recall) School subjects

4 Write a list of subjects for each category: Humanities, Science, PE, Languages.

In groups of 3 or 4. Compare your lists.

Pronunciation • -n, -m, -ng

5a 2.17 Listen to the pronunciation of *-n, -m, -ng*:

1 win /n/
2 him /m/
3 doing /ŋ/

5b 2.18 Listen to the sentences.

1 She's tall and thi**n**.
2 He's talki**ng** to hi**m** o**n** the pho**n**e.
3 I'm doi**ng** my ho**m**ework i**n** the garde**n**.

Listen and repeat.

Progress at school

6 2.19 Harry is talking to his Aunt Emily about his school work. Listen and write the names of the subjects that you hear.

1 _____
2 _____
3 _____
4 _____
5 _____

Listen again and complete the questions that Aunt Emily asks Harry.

1 _____ at school these days?
2 _____ in History at the moment?
3 What are you studying _____?
4 What other subjects _____?
5 _____ any other languages?
6 _____ PE?

In pairs. Ask and answer the questions about Harry.

Example:
A How's Harry doing at school these days?
B He's...

Speaking • My life now

7 In pairs. Ask and answer questions about your life at the moment. Ask about school, sport, free-time activities, and friends and family. T

Example:
A How's school at the moment?
B I'm doing OK at school at the moment...

B What sports are you doing at the moment?
A I'm playing a lot of volleyball.

Reading

1 Before you read • Look at the list of places to visit on a school trip. Tick (✓) the places you would like to visit.

1 ___ a museum
2 ___ a castle
3 ___ a famous Italian city (Venice, Florence, etc)
4 ___ a different country
5 ___ a nature reserve
6 ___ an art gallery
7 ___ an outdoor activity centre
8 ___ a theme park (e.g. *Gardaland*)

In pairs. Compare your answers. Give reasons.

2 🔊 **2.20** While you read • Read this website review of a school trip to the Science Museum in London. Find and write the correct number in the spaces.

1 The number of galleries in the museum. _____
2 The number of the first Apollo spacecraft which orbited the moon. _____
3 The number of inventions in the 'Making the Modern World' gallery. _____
4 The number of floors in the museum. _____
5 The total number of things in the museum. _____
6 The number of experiments in the Launch Pad section. _____

3 Vocabulary • Underline 6 words in the website review that you don't know.

1 Guess the meaning from the context and write a translation.
2 Check your answers in the glossary.

4 Comprehension check • True or false? Write T or F. Correct the false sentences. **K**

1 ___ The Science Museum is near a London Underground station.
2 ___ It's possible to visit the 46 galleries of the museum in a day.
3 ___ It's expensive to get into the museum.
4 ___ The writer's favourite part of the museum is the Launch Pad.
5 ___ The toilet is one of the top 150 inventions for humanity.
6 ___ The exhibitions in the Antenna gallery are the same all year.
7 ___ Tickets for the IMAX cinema are free.
8 ___ The writer intends to visit the museum again.

APOLLO 10

THE BEST THINGS IN LIFE ARE FREE!

The Science Museum in London is incredible! Apparently there are more than 300,000 objects in the museum. There are a total of 46 galleries on seven floors so you can't see everything in a day. You can find out about the
5 history of the Western world through science, technology and medicine. The best stuff is in the six interactive galleries, and I also love the IMAX cinema and the Virtual Voyages motion-ride simulator. It's all so much FUN!

WHAT TO SEE MY TOP FOUR FAVOURITES ARE:

1 ▶ THE LAUNCH PAD

There are about 50 interactive experiments here. In my
10 opinion, this is the best part of the museum. I love 'Icy Bodies', where you see frozen particles of carbon dioxide race across a pool of water as they turn into gas. The 'Watch Water Freeze' is brilliant, too. You look through a special lens and see the amazing colours of water as it forms ice crystals.

2 ▶ MAKING THE MODERN WORLD

15 This gallery's got 150 inventions which changed the world, including the first steam engine, the first computer, Apollo 10 (which orbited the Moon) and even the first toilet!

3 ▶ ANTENNA

This bit of the museum is all about science today so they often change the exhibitions. At the moment
20 they're showing an exhibition about the effect of air transport on the environment. There's also a 'robots playground' where you can interact with real working robots! Last of all, there's the 'Oceanlab camera'. It takes photos
25 of fish 8 kilometres below the surface of the sea. Amazing!

Speaking

5 Look at the list of important inventions in the Science Museum. Put them in order of importance. Write numbers in the spaces. (1 = very important)

___ the toilet   ___ Apollo 10   ___ the steam engine
___ the first computer   ___ robots   ___ deep sea cameras

In pairs. Compare your lists. Give reasons for your choices. T

Example:

A My number one is the toilet. It's a necessary thing that everyone uses every day.

Listening

6 🔊 **2.21** Look at the photos. Listen and tick (✓) the 2 places that Charlie and Abigail are visiting on their school trips. K

Listen again and choose the correct alternative.

1 Stonehenge is **5,000/6,000** years old.
2 The stones are near the village of **Aylesbury/Amesbury**.
3 Some of the stones weigh **40/4** tonnes.
4 The summer solstice is the **longest/shortest** day of the summer.
5 Abigail is staying at a **youth hostel/campsite** in the Lake District.
6 Today she's doing **an astronomy/a meteorology** experiment.
7 She is climbing the **Old Man/Old Woman** of Coniston.
8 The mountain is **8,000/800** metres high.

Writing

7 Imagine you're on a school trip. Write a postcard to a friend (60–80 words). Include this information: T

- a greeting (Hi, Hello, etc)
- the weather (good/bad, hot/cold...)
- the place you are visiting
- where you're staying
- where you're writing the postcard
- an ending (See you, Bye now, etc)

DEEP SEA (IMAX)

4 > THE IMAX CINEMA

This is quite expensive, but the films are fantastic! They're in 3D, so you feel like you're taking part in the action. The films include *Deep Sea*, *Space*
30 *Station* and *Dinosaurs Alive*. My favourite is *Deep Sea*, because I love seeing the incredible creatures that exist at the bottom of the ocean. There's lots more to see at the Science Museum, too. In fact, it's so good that I want to go back
35 there again and again – I'm lucky it's free!

GENERAL INFORMATION

The museum's a 10-minute walk from South Kensington tube station on the District line. Loads of buses stop near the Science Museum, including the 14, 49, 70 and 74.
40 Best of all, it's free to get in! You only pay for special exhibitions, the IMAX cinema and to use the motion-ride simulators.

Present continuous (1) e (2)

1 Read the sentences and answer questions 1–5 below.

a I'm getting on the bus.
b Oliver's training very hard these days.
c What are you doing?
d She isn't listening to music.

1 Come si ottiene la forma affermativa del *Present continuous*?
Con il _____ del verbo *be* + _____.
2 Come si ottiene la forma interrogativa?
Si invertono il _____ e il _____.
3 Come si ottiene la forma negativa?
Si aggiunge _____ al verbo *be*.
4 Abbina le frasi a–d qui sopra alla descrizione corretta:
___ un'azione in corso nel momento in cui si parla.
___ un'azione temporanea che si svolge in questo periodo anche se non necessariamente in questo momento.
5 Quali di queste espressioni si usano con il *Present continuous*?
1 ___ at the moment 3 ___ usually
2 ___ these days   4 ___ now

2 Write *Yes/No* questions and short answers using the Present continuous.

1 Samantha/the newspaper? ✗
Is Samantha reading the newspaper? No, she isn't.
2 James and Mary/a break? ✓
3 you/a bath? ✓
4 Lisa and Nick/tennis? ✗
5 Rob/his Maths homework? ✓
6 Rebecca/a DVD? ✗
7 you and Steve/a good time? ✓
8 Mark/karate? ✗

3 Write questions for these answers.

1 I'm reading a book by J.K.Rowling.
What are you reading?
2 They're watching a film about Elvis.
3 She's eating a sandwich.
4 I'm studying Physics.
5 We're listening to Ligabue.
6 I'm buying a magazine.

4 Answer the questions.

1 What are you doing?
_____
2 What's your mum/dad doing?
_____
3 Where are you sitting?
_____
4 What are you studying in History this week?
_____
5 Are you enjoying school these days? Why?/Why not?
_____

Present continuous o Present simple?

5 Read the sentences and complete explanations 1–2 with the correct tense.

I'm getting dressed at the moment.
I get dressed at half past seven every morning.

1 Si usa il _____ per parlare di azioni in corso.
2 Si usa il _____ per parlare di dati di fatto e azioni abituali.

6 Correct the mistake in each sentence. Be careful! 3 sentences are correct.

1 I'm spending a month in England.
2 Harry doesn't enjoy his holiday in France. The weather's terrible!
3 Wait a minute! I have a shower.
4 They never go to bed early.
5 We listen to music at the moment.
6 I get up at six o'clock every day.
7 She's never having lunch at school.
8 She doesn't do the shopping at the moment.

Esercizi sommativi

7 Complete Abigail's email with the correct form of the verbs in brackets.

email from: Abigail

Hi, Holly!
I [1]_____ (write) this email in bed at the hostel in Coniston. My friends, Alice and Nicole, [2]_____ (be) in the room with me, but they [3]_____ (sleep). I [4]_____ (enjoy) this school trip. It's excellent! We [5]_____ (get up) early every day, we [6]_____ (have) breakfast and then we [7]_____ (go) walking. All day! I [8]_____ (get) very fit! We usually [9]_____ (get) back to the hostel at about 5pm. The weather's very changeable. Sometimes it's awful but today it [10]_____ (not rain) and it's quite hot. See you on Saturday!
Love, Abigail

8 Translation • Translate the sentences into English.

1 Che cosa stai facendo? Sto giocando a pallone.
2 Mio zio sta usando il suo computer.
3 Che cosa fai? Sono un'insegnante.
4 Sto bevendo una tazza di thè.
5 Dove vai a scuola? Vado a scuola a Bristol.
6 Ho lezione di chitarra ogni mercoledì.
7 A lei non piace ascoltare la musica rock.
8 Dove vai? Sto andando in palestra.

Making suggestions

Dialogue 🎥 VIDEO

1 🔊 **2.22** It's Saturday afternoon and Ben and Amy are discussing where to go in the evening. Listen and tick (✓) the activity they choose.

2 🔊 **2.22** Listen again and complete the sentences.

Asking for suggestions
What shall we _____?

Making suggestions
_____ we have a look at the notice board?
Do you fancy _____ ice skating?
_____ going to a rock concert?
Let's _____ to the cinema!

Refusing suggestions
No _____, I don't feel like it.
No, _____, I don't like rock.

Accepting suggestions
That sounds _____!/That's a good idea!

Making arrangements
_____ meet outside at quarter to nine.

Say it right!

3 🔊 **2.23** Listen. Then listen and repeat the sentences with the correct rhythm.

A What shall we do tonight?
B I don't know. Do you fancy <u>going to a club</u>?
A No thanks, I don't feel like it.
B How about <u>going to the cinema</u>?
A That's a good idea! <u>*Inception* is on at the Odeon</u>.
B Let's meet <u>at your house</u>.
A OK. See you <u>at my house</u> at <u>half past seven</u>.

In pairs. Practise the dialogue. Now use the posters to change the underlined information above. Act out the dialogue. When you finish, change roles.

Now close your books. Can you say the dialogue from memory?

Speaking

4 It's Saturday and you don't know what to do tonight. In pairs. Look at the posters in Ex.1. Discuss and decide where to go. Don't accept your partner's first suggestion! **T**

School days

1  Read Alexander's email telling his Italian ePal about his new school. Then answer the questions below.

email from: Alexander

Hi Giulia!

Here's a typical day at my new school. It's an unusual school, as it's a comprehensive school, but it's also a Technology College. It specialises in ICT and Maths, so we
5 use all sorts of cool technology during our lessons.

I start school at 8.30. I pick up my tablet PC from the Learning Centre and then I go to registration. The teacher checks we're all here and reads us special messages about school for that day. My school day tomorrow is like this:

8.30	Registration
9–10	1st period: Maths
10–11	2nd period: Physics
11.00–11.20	Break
11.20–12.20	3rd period: English
12.20–1.20	4th period: ICT
1.20–2.10	Lunch
2.10–3.10	5th period: French
3.10	Home!!!!

10 During break I have a snack and chat with my friends, and at lunchtime my friends bring packed lunches, but the food at the canteen's nice, so I often eat there.

We've got different rooms and teachers for different subjects, so we basically change rooms every hour. This year I'm doing: Maths, English, Science, ICT, Drama, Music, Art, PE, Humanities (History, Geography and Religion) and French. For most subjects we use books, but for Science,
15 Maths and ICT we work on the tablet PCs. The teacher then makes comments and sends our work back to us via email.

When we go into a classroom we use our swipe cards. Yes, swipe cards! Every student's got one. We also swipe when we go into the toilets. It's awful! It's just like *Big Brother*! The teachers know where we are all the time. We also use our swipe cards like a credit card to pay for snacks at the
20 school shop and at the canteen.

PE's great. We do loads of sports. In the winter we play rugby, football and hockey, and in the summer we play cricket and netball (a bit like basketball). We also play rounders sometimes (it's similar to baseball) and we do athletics. I really like playing rugby and I'm in the college team, but I absolutely hate cricket in the summer. It's so boring!

25 By the way, in the UK you don't usually go to school on Saturdays. There are loads of clubs after school. My new school's got a Computer Club, a Basketball Club and a Film Club. I go to Computer Club.

So you see, I'm really lucky! My school's really modern and I especially like using computers. Anyway, that's all for now.

30 Write soon!
Alexander

1 How is Alexander's school different from other comprehensive schools?
2 Where does Alexander go before registration?
3 What time is Alexander's first lesson?
4 Why do students have swipe cards?
5 What sports do they play in summer?
6 What do English students sometimes do after school?

Speaking

2 Find 4 differences between Alexander's school day and your school day. In pairs. Compare lists. **T**

Example:
Alexander finishes school at 3.10pm every day, but we finish school at 1.30pm.

VIDEO Now watch the Network video!

Did you know?

primary school	*scuola elementare (da 5 a 11 anni)*
secondary school	*scuola secondaria (da 11 a 16 anni)*
6th Form	*scuola secondaria (da 16 a 18 anni)*
public school	*scuola privata*
state school	*scuola statale*
comprehensive	*scuola secondaria statale non selettiva (a differenza dei Grammar school che sono a numero chiuso)*

DIFFICULT DAYS (unit) 5

Word builder

Ordinal numbers

1 Write the ordinal numbers in full using the words in the box.

ninth   sixth   sixteenth   tenth   seventh   twelfth   fifth   first
twentieth   eighth   second   fourth   third   thirteenth   eleventh

1st _____	6th _____	11th _____
2nd _____	7th _____	12th _____
3rd _____	8th _____	13th _____
4th _____	9th _____	16th _____
5th _____	10th _____	20th _____

🔊 **2.25** Listen and repeat.

2 Complete the numbers in column A with -st, -nd, -rd, or -th. Then complete column B with the ordinal numbers in full.

A	B	A	B
17___	_____	24___	_____-_____
18___	_____	25___	_____-_____
19___	_____	26___	_____-_____
20___	*twentieth*	27___	_____-_____
21___	twenty-_____	28___	_____-_____
22___	twenty-_____	29___	_____-_____
23___	_____-_____	30___	_____

🔊 **2.26** Listen and repeat.

Months

3 Write the months in the correct order in your exercise book.

April	December	August	February	November	May
January	July		October	March	June	September

🔊 **2.27** Listen and repeat.

4 Match the dates (1–6) to the festivals below (a–f).

1 ___ 14th February   3 ___ 1st May   5 ___ 5th November
2 ___ 1st April   4 ___ 31st October   6 ___ 31st December

🔊 **2.28** Listen and check. Listen and repeat.

Word note

Si scrive:
3rd January/January 3rd
Si dice:
the third of January/January the third
My birthday's on the third of January.

Speaking • Birthdays

5 Close your books.
A: say a cardinal number between 1 and 30.
B: say the corresponding ordinal number.

6 Ask 4 people in the class when their birthdays are. Write down their answers. **T**

A When's your birthday, Paolo?
B It's on the twelfth of April.

Find out:
- Are there 2 people with the same birthday?
- Whose birthday is next?
- Is it anyone's birthday today?
- Is anyone's birthday on 29th February?
- Is anyone's birthday on Christmas Day?

Dictation

7 🔊 **2.29** Listen and complete the sentences. Write the numbers in words.

1 My birthday's on the _____
   of _____.
2 My _____ birthday's on _____.
3 _____ the date today? It's _____.
4 _____ the match? _____.
5 The _____.

a New Year's Eve

d Valentine's Day

b Bonfire Night

e May Day

c April Fool's Day

f Hallowe'en

✏ **WB p.179** Complete *Ordinal numbers*, *Months* and *Dates* in the Word store.

Presentation and practice

Can you play an instrument?

1 🔊 **2.30** Katie and Oliver are at Katie's house. Why are they arguing? Listen and read.

1 Oh, hi... Sorry, Ethan. I can't talk now... OK... Bye.

Ethan? Why's *he* phoning you?

2 Why not? He's a friend and... Well, he's very talented.

Yes, I know. He can sing really well, he can play the guitar *and* he can play the piano.

Oh, Oliver. He's just a friend.

3 Anyway, I don't know what you've got in common with him. Can *you* play the guitar?

No, I can't. You know that.

Besides, he's going out with Lucy.

No, he isn't. Not any more.

4 Oh, now I understand.

No, you don't. You're just jealous.

What do you expect? You know I can't play any instruments and I'm hopeless at singing, too.

5 Don't be pathetic!

Well, if that's the way you feel, I'm off!

Oh, Oliver! Don't go...

Comprehension check

2 Complete the sentences with the correct names.

1 _____ phones _____ .
2 _____'s good at playing instruments and singing.
3 _____ isn't going out with _____ any more.
4 _____'s jealous of _____ .
5 _____ isn't good at singing.
6 _____ gets angry and leaves.

Real talk

Don't be pathetic! Non fare il patetico!
I'm off! Me ne vado!

What do you think?

1 Is Oliver's jealousy justified in your opinion?
2 Are you a jealous person?

Grammar

can • Abilità

Forma affermativa
I/You/He/She/We/They **can** sing really well.

Forma negativa
I/You/He/She/We/They **can't** play any instruments.

Forma interrogativa
Can I/you/he/she/we/they play the guitar?

Risposte brevi
Yes, I/you/he/she/we/they **can**.
No, I/you/he/she/we/they **can't**.

Si usano (*not*)… *at all*, (*not*)… *very well*, *quite well*, *very well*, *really well* per descrivere il livello di abilità.

Per parlare di abilità si usano anche espressioni come *I'm good/brilliant/hopeless at…* + verbo in -*ing*.

 **WB p.178**

⚠ Dopo il verbo *can* si usa la forma base del verbo senza *to*.
I can speak French. (~~I can to speak French.~~)

Grammar check

3 Complete the sentences with *can* or *can't*.

1 I _____ play the trumpet very well. I'm in a band.
2 She _____ speak French. In fact, she's hopeless at all languages.
3 _____ you ski? Yes, I _____.
4 Max _____ ride a horse well. He sometimes takes part in competitions.
5 I _____ ride a motorbike, but I want to learn.
6 _____ they play tennis? No, they _____.
7 Katie _____ rollerblade very well. She's an expert.
8 My brother _____ cook really well. He makes fantastic curry.

Word builder + Abilities

4 Write the names of the activities. Use a dictionary to help you.

1 *speak French*

 WB p.179 Complete *Abilities* in the Word store.

Pronunciation • *can*, *can't*

5a 🔊 **2.31** Listen to the pronunciation of *can* and *can't*.

a can /kæn/   b can /kən/   c can't /kɑːnt/

5b 🔊 **2.32** Listen and write a, b or c.

1 ___*a*___ / _____   3 _____ / _____
2 _____   4 _____

🔊 **2.33** Listen and check. Listen and repeat.

Daniel's family

6 🔊 **2.34** Daniel's talking about his family. Listen and tick (✓) the things they *can* do.

	Mum	Dad	David	Chloe	Rebecca
speak Spanish					
ride a horse					
play tennis					
play football					
swim					
ski					
sing					
run					

In pairs. Ask and answer questions about Daniel's family.
A Can his mum speak Spanish?
B Yes, she can.

Speaking • Yes, I can!

7 Look at the activities in Ex.4. Write 3 sentences about things you can and can't do.

I can play the piano quite well, but I can't sing.

What can your partner do? In pairs. Ask and answer questions. Give as much information as possible. **T**

Example:
A Can you play the piano?
B Yes, I can – quite well. I have lessons twice a week.

He's having an interview at three o'clock

1 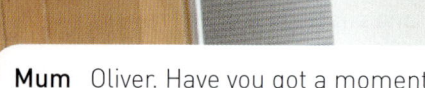 🔊 2.35 Oliver's mum's got some bad news for him. Why does Oliver get upset? Listen and read.

Mum	Oliver. Have you got a moment?
Oliver	Not really, Mum. I'm meeting Arjan.
Mum	When are you meeting him?
Oliver	In half an hour, so I can't talk now.
Mum	Actually, Oliver, it's important. Your dad's company's making him redundant. Friday's his last day at work.
Oliver	I don't believe it! So what happens now?
Mum	Well, we're thinking of moving to Bristol. There are more jobs for him there.
Oliver	But I've got all my friends here! What about my diving?
Mum	I know it's difficult for you, Oliver. It's difficult for us, too. Anyway, he's having an interview at three o'clock this afternoon in Bristol.
Oliver	You must be joking!
Mum	Oliver, wait! Oh dear!

Later that afternoon...

Dad	Hello! I've got the job!
Mum	Oh, that's fantastic news! When do you start?
Dad	In two weeks' time.
Mum	Wow – that's very soon.
Dad	Listen, I can't talk now. My train leaves at five.
Mum	What time does it get to Paddington?
Dad	It gets to Paddington at... **hang on**... seven o'clock.
Mum	OK. See you later!

Real talk

Actually,...	A dire il vero,...
That's fantastic news!	Che bella notizia!
Hang on	Aspetta un attimo
See you later!	Ci vediamo dopo!

Comprehension check

2 Answer the questions.

1 Why doesn't Oliver want to talk to his mum?
2 Why is Oliver's dad having an interview?
3 What time is Oliver's dad's interview?
4 Why doesn't Oliver want to move?

What do you think?

1 Is Oliver selfish to want to stay in London?
2 Do you like the idea of moving to another city?

Grammar

Present continuous (3) • Il futuro

When **are** you **meeting** him?
He**'s having** an interview at three o'clock.

Si usa il *Present continuous* per il futuro quando si tratta di appuntamenti o di un programma stabilito. Si usano spesso queste espressioni di tempo futuro con il *Present continuous*:

at five o'clock, tonight
this afternoon/evening
tomorrow morning/afternoon/evening
next week/Sunday/weekend
in two days' time
on Saturday (morning)/16th April

Present simple (3) • Il futuro

What times **does** the train **get** to Paddington?
It **gets** to Paddington at seven o'clock.

Si usa il *Present simple* per il futuro quando si tratta di orari.

 **WB pp.178–179**

Grammar check

3 Complete the sentences with the Present simple or the Present continuous of the verbs in brackets.

1 _____ the film _____ at nine o'clock?
  Yes, it _____. (start)
2 Where _____ you _____ Nathan?
  I _____ him at the library. (meet)
3 She _____ the dentist at eleven today. (see)
4 The plane _____ at nine. (leave)
5 When _____ the supermarket _____ ?
  It _____ at eight. (open)
6 We _____ rugby next Saturday morning. (play)

 Che fai stasera? = What are you doing tonight?
~~(What do you do tonight?)~~

Word recall Dates

4 Write down 5 dates in the spaces (1–5). In pairs.
A: say your dates. B: write A's dates down.
When you finish, change roles.

My dates	My partner's dates
1 _____	_____
2 _____	_____
3 _____	_____
4 _____	_____
5 _____	_____

Compare dates. Has your partner got them right?

Basketball match dates

5 🔊 **2.36** The Stratford Strollers is a basketball team. The trainer's giving the players the dates of their matches. Listen and write the dates.

Bristol Bombers	_____
Leeds Lions	_____
Street Stars	_____
Fordham Fleet	_____
Didcot Devils	_____

In pairs. Check your answers. Ask and answer questions.

A When are they playing the Bristol Bombers?
B They're playing them on...

Speaking • Excuses!

6 In pairs. A: imagine you really like B. Ask questions to find out when B is free next week. B: A wants to go out with you next week, but you don't want to go. Find an excuse for every day of next week. **T**

Example:
A What are you doing on Sunday night?
B I'm washing my hair.

When you finish, change roles.

Fast finishers!

Next weekend you can do anything that you like. Write 6 sentences about your arrangements.

On Saturday morning I'm having breakfast in bed at half past ten.

Speaking

1 In pairs. Ask and answer the questions. **P** **T**

1 What type of music do you like?
2 Do you listen to music every day?
3 Do you go and see live bands?
4 List your favourite 3 bands/singers in order.
5 What band/singer is the class's favourite?

Reading

2 Read the Study skills. Then do Ex.3.

Study skills

Predicting content

Se hai già un'idea del contenuto di un testo prima di leggerlo, sarà più facile capirlo. Per avere un'idea del contenuto puoi leggere il titolo dell'articolo e guardare le foto che lo accompagnano. Qualche volta ci sono anche delle frasi che riassumono il contenuto di ogni capoverso. Leggile prima di cominciare una lettura più dettagliata.

3 Before you read • Look at photos a, b and c. Where are the people? What are they doing? Read the title of the article and the paragraph headings. What's the article about?

🔊 **2.37** Now read the article and check your answer.

4 Vocabulary • Look at the words in bold in the article. Match them to their Italian translations.

1 ___ buskers
2 ___ homeless
3 ___ perform
4 ___ pitches
5 ___ fine
6 ___ less
7 ___ range
8 ___ audience

a gamma
b meno
c postazioni
d pubblico
e suonatori ambulanti
f esibirsi
g senzatetto
h multa

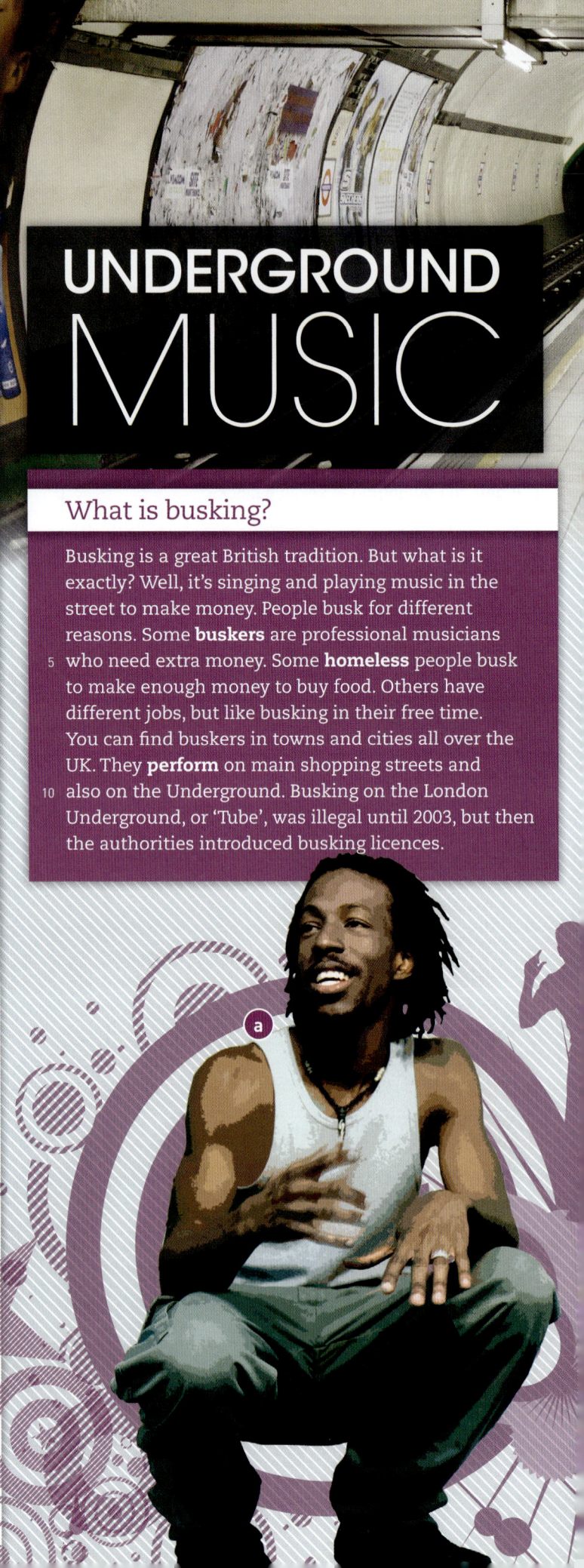

UNDERGROUND MUSIC

What is busking?

Busking is a great British tradition. But what is it exactly? Well, it's singing and playing music in the street to make money. People busk for different reasons. Some **buskers** are professional musicians
5 who need extra money. Some **homeless** people busk to make enough money to buy food. Others have different jobs, but like busking in their free time. You can find buskers in towns and cities all over the UK. They **perform** on main shopping streets and
10 also on the Underground. Busking on the London Underground, or 'Tube', was illegal until 2003, but then the authorities introduced busking licences.

How to busk on the Tube

To busk on the Tube you need to audition before applying for a licence, which costs £20 a year. There
15 are only 300 licensed buskers on the Tube and competition is tough. Out of the 400 auditions every year, about 75% of applicants are successful. They can then perform in designated places (**'pitches'**) for two-hour sessions every day. Some people busk illegally
20 on the Tube, but they risk getting a £100 **fine**.

How much do they earn?

A good busker can make £50 a day, but many buskers earn a lot **less**. The quality of music on the Tube is very high these days – you can watch people playing a **range** of instruments, from the guitar to the harp,
25 saxophone or accordion.

Are buskers usually men or women?

For every female busker there are three male buskers. One woman busker is 21-year-old Jessica Lawton. She's a rapper.

'I like singing in front of
30 a live **audience**. I work a couple of days a week in a shop, but I just love singing. I don't make much money, but when people
35 stop to listen to me, it's a good feeling!'

5 Comprehension check • Complete the table with numbers from the article.

£20	the cost of a busking licence for the Tube
	the number of licensed buskers
	the number of auditions for pitches on the Underground every year
	the fine for illegal busking
	the sum of money a good busker makes every day
	Jessica Lawton's age
	the number of days she works in a shop

Listening

6 🔊 **2.38** Listen to this *Network Magazine* interview with a busker. Tick (✓) the questions you hear.

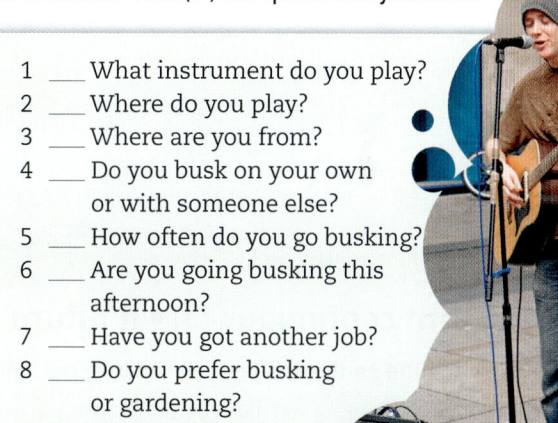

1 ___ What instrument do you play?
2 ___ Where do you play?
3 ___ Where are you from?
4 ___ Do you busk on your own or with someone else?
5 ___ How often do you go busking?
6 ___ Are you going busking this afternoon?
7 ___ Have you got another job?
8 ___ Do you prefer busking or gardening?
9 ___ Do you make a lot of money?
10 ___ What are the good and bad things about busking?

Listen again and write down Kiaran's answers.

In pairs. Compare answers.

Writing

7 You're going to a concert with some friends. Post a message on your social network page (60–80 words). Include the answers to these questions: 🅿 🆃

- Who are you going with?
- What band are you seeing?
- When is the concert?
- What time does it start?
- Where are you meeting?
- How do you feel about going?

can • Abilità

1 Read the sentences and choose the correct alternative in rules 1–2.

I can play the piano, but I can't sing very well.
Can you speak German? No, I can't.

> 1 *Can* è seguito dalla forma base del verbo con/senza *to*.
> 2 Si ottiene la forma interrogativa invertendo il soggetto e *can*/usando l'ausiliare *do*.

2 Write questions for these answers using *can*.

1 _____
Yes, I can. I really like singing.
2 _____
No, they can't. In fact, they haven't got a computer.
3 _____
Yes, she can. She's a skiing champion.
4 _____
No, I can't. I don't like horses.
5 _____
No, we can't. And there's no swimming pool here.
6 _____
Yes, he can. His dad's German.

Present continuous (3) • Il futuro

3 Match the sentences (a–b) to the descriptions (1–2).

a She's meeting her friends at six o'clock.
b I'm playing a fantastic video game.

> 1 _____ Questa frase si riferisce al presente.
> 2 _____ Questa frase si riferisce al futuro.

Now write the English for these future time expressions.

domani ¹_____
la settimana prossima ²_____
stasera ³_____/_____
fra due giorni ⁴_____
domani mattina ⁵_____
giovedì prossimo ⁶_____

4 Write sentences using the Present continuous.

1 What/you/do/this evening?
_____
2 We/play volleyball/tomorrow afternoon.
_____
3 I/not go to school/tomorrow.
_____
4 He/have lunch/with his dad/at one o'clock.
_____
5 Where/they/spend the weekend?
_____

6 You/leave/on the six o'clock train.
_____

Present simple (3) • Il futuro

5 Read the sentences and choose the correct alternative in the rule.

The bus leaves at ten past three.
The film starts at half past eight.

> Il *Present simple* si può usare per parlare del futuro quando si tratta di **progetti prestabiliti/orari**.

Present simple o Present continuous?

6 Complete the sentences with the Present continuous or the Present simple of the verbs in brackets.

1 The supermarket _____ (close) at half past eight.
2 She _____ (visit) her cousin next Saturday afternoon.
3 I _____ (go) to the theatre this evening.
4 The coach _____ (arrive) in Edinburgh at ten o'clock.
5 They _____ (have) a karate lesson at six today.
6 He _____ (work) at home tomorrow.
7 The museum _____ (open) at nine o'clock.
8 My interview _____ (start) at quarter past two.

Dates (Word builder)

7 Complete the rule.

> Per dire la data si usano le parole _____ e _____ che non compaiono nella data scritta. Per esempio, 3/11 si dice _____ *third* _____ *November*.

8 Write the dates in words.

1 15/9 *the fifteenth of September*
2 5/2 _____
3 9/4 _____
4 2/12 _____
5 4/6 _____
6 12/3 _____

Esercizio sommativo

9 Translation • Translate the sentences into English.

1 Sai suonare il pianoforte? Sì.
2 La corriera arriva alle sei.
3 Domani sera esco a mangiare con Roberto.
4 Il mio compleanno è il 12 dicembre.
5 Giochi a basket sabato prossimo? No.
6 Lunedì prossimo vado dal dentista.
7 Sanno giocare molto bene a pallavolo.
8 Quando vai in Grecia? Vado il 6 gennaio.

IN TOWN

Word builder

Places in a town

1 Translate the words into Italian.

1 restaurant _____
2 park _____
3 shopping centre _____
4 stadium _____
5 (train) station _____
6 café _____
7 hospital _____
8 tourist information centre _____
9 takeaway _____
10 post office _____
11 bank _____
12 supermarket _____
13 market _____
14 bus/coach station _____

◄)) 2.39 Listen and repeat.

Preposizioni di luogo (2)

2 Look at the pictures above and match the beginnings (1–6) to the endings (a–f).

1 __ The town hall is   4 __ The clothes shop is
2 __ The bus stop is   5 __ The car park is
3 __ The newsagent's is   6 __ The chemist's is

a **in** Langton Road.   d **opposite** the library.
b **next to** the shoe shop. e **in front of** the church.
c **behind** the leisure   f **on the corner of** Smith
   centre.   Street and George Street.

◄)) 2.40 Listen and check. Listen and repeat.

⚠ Let's meet **in front of** the cinema =
Troviamoci davanti all'ingresso del cinema.
The café is **opposite** the cinema =
Il bar è fronte al cinema. (sul lato opposto della strada).

Speaking • My town

3 In pairs. Ask questions about the town or area where you live. Use the words in Ex.1 and Ex.2. **T**

Example:
A Where's the station?
B It's opposite the supermarket.

Dictation

4 **◄)) 2.41** Listen and complete the sentences.

1 Let's meet _____ the _____.
2 The Italian _____ is _____
   Kings _____.
3 Where's the _____, please?
   It's _____.
4 I really like the shoes in that _____
   _____.

There are some great clubs in Belfast!

1 🔊 2.42 Hannah's replying to an email from her Australian cousin, Ryan. What 2 questions did Ryan ask Hannah in his email? Listen and read.

Getting ready to go out with my friends!

Compose

Attachments: places_to_go_in_Belfast.doc

Hi Ryan,

Thanks for your message. You want to know more about Belfast, then? Well, it's a fantastic city because there are lots of things to do. There are some great clubs, pubs and restaurants on the Golden Mile (a street between Belfast City Hall and Queen's University), and there are lots of good music venues in the city, too. One of them is a big theatre, the Grand Opera House. Then there's the Empire Music Hall and Custom House Square – that's my favourite. I go there a lot because there are often free concerts. You can find out lots about the city on the Internet. **Check out** the links in the attachment.

Mind you, I don't actually live in the centre of Belfast. I live in South Belfast. It's OK, but there isn't much to do here. There isn't a leisure centre near me and there aren't any good clubs for teenagers. **I bet** there are loads of good clubs in Sydney! When I go out with my friends in the evening, we always catch the bus to the centre. I can't wait for you to see the centre – it's brilliant! I can show you the fantastic night life. **I'm dying to see you!**
Write soon,
Hannah

P.S. Are there any nice girls in Belfast? Yes, there are!

Real talk

Check out	Dai un'occhiata a
Mind you,...	Però,.../Detto questo,...
I bet	Scommetto che
I'm dying to see you!	Non vedo l'ora di vederti!

Comprehension check

2 True or false? Write T or F. Correct the false sentences. P

1 ___ Belfast is a good place if you like live music.
2 ___ Hannah lives in the city centre.
3 ___ There's a lot to do in South Belfast.
4 ___ Hannah often goes to the leisure centre in South Belfast.

What do you think?

1 Does Belfast sound like an interesting city?
2 What do you like doing when you visit new cities?
3 What do you prefer: living in the city centre or in the suburbs?

Grammar

there is/are + some/any

Forma affermativa
There's a big theatre.
There are some great clubs.

Forma negativa
There isn't a leisure centre.
There aren't any good clubs.

Forma interrogativa	Risposte brevi
Is there a university?	Yes, there is./No, there isn't.
Are there any clubs?	Yes, there are./No, there aren't.

there's (*there is*) = c'è   *there are* = ci sono

Si usa *some* con sostantivi plurali nelle frasi affermative.

Si usa *any* con sostantivi plurali nelle frasi interrogative e negative.

✏ **WB p.184**

Grammar check

3 Complete the sentences with the correct form of *there's/there are* and *some* or *any* (where necessary).

1 _____ nice shops in your town?
  Yes, _____.
2 Unfortunately, _____ a cinema in my village.
3 Yes, _____ good students in my class.
4 _____ a library near your house?
  Yes, _____.
5 _____ good cafés in Basingstoke?
  No, _____.
6 _____ a chemist's in the High Street?
  No, _____.
7 _____ a fantastic new pizzeria in town. I'm going tomorrow.
8 _____ Italian restaurants in Slapton. It's a shame!

Word recall ⟩ Places in a town

4 Where can you get these things? Write the names of the places.

1 train ticket _____
2 jumper _____
3 pair of shoes _____
4 bottle of medicine _____
5 food shopping _____
6 cup of coffee _____
7 plate of spaghetti _____
8 football match programme _____
9 a newspaper _____
10 town map _____

Can you remember any other places in a town?

Speaking • Places in a town

5 Look at the places in Ex.1 & Ex.2 on p.53 for 2 minutes. Then close your books.
In pairs. A: tell your partner the first 2 letters of a place in a town. B: say the place.

Example:
A C, H...
B Chemist's.

After 5 places, change roles.

Pronunciation • Silent -r

6a 🔊 **2.43** Listen to the 2 different pronunciations of -r.

(pronounced) great

(silent) market

6b 🔊 **2.44** Listen and underline -r when it's pronounced.

1 My car's in front of the church.
2 He's at the tourist information centre.
3 We're French and they're German.
4 The Russian café's in Richmond Road.

🔊 **2.45** Listen and check. Listen and repeat.

Speaking • Is there a bank near here?

7 In pairs. Look at the map on p.57 for 2 minutes. Try to remember where the shops and buildings are.
A: close your book.
B: ask 5 questions about the places on the map.
A: answer with as much information as possible.

Example:
B Are there any pubs?
A Yes, there are. There are three pubs.
B Where are they?
A There's one in Queens Road...

After 5 questions, change roles.

Speaking • My town

8 In pairs. Ask and answer questions about the places in your town. T

Example:
A Where is the post office?
B It's in via Mazzini, opposite the market.

After 3 questions, change roles.

My town

9 What does your town have to offer? Write a brief description of your town (50 words).

How do I get to the library?

1 🔊 2.46 Hannah's waiting for the bus. Why's the woman angry at the end? Listen and read.

1

Woman Excuse me. How do I get to the library?

Hannah Er... Oh, yes. I know... Go straight on **as far as** the traffic lights and then turn left.

Woman OK... left at the traffic lights.

Hannah Then go down Ashley Avenue and take the first left. Turn left again when you get to the end, and the library's at the end of that road on the right. Don't worry! **You can't miss it.**

Woman OK. **I think I've got that.** Thanks!

Here are the traffic lights. Turn left here...

Good! This is Ashley Avenue. Take the first turning on the left here.

ASHLEY AV

Real talk

as far as	fino a
You can't miss it	Non può sbagliarsi
I think I've got that	Credo di aver capito

So, the library's at the end on the right. but... That's the bus stop again! And there's that girl again!

Oops! It's that woman again.

I'm really sorry!

Comprehension check

2 Answer the questions.

1 Where does the woman want to go?
2 Is Hannah sure of the directions she gives?
3 Does the woman find Ashley Avenue?
4 Is the woman happy at the end?

What do you think?

1 How do you think Hannah feels when she sees the woman again?
2 Are you good at giving directions?

Grammar

L'imperativo

Forma affermativa	Forma negativa
Turn left at the traffic lights.	**Don't** worry.

L'imperativo si ottiene con la forma base del verbo e senza pronome personale.

Per costruire la forma negativa, si mette *don't* prima del verbo.

 **WB pp.184–185**

Grammar check

3 Complete the sentences using the correct form of the verbs in the box.

take	go	cross	go	turn	tell

1 _____ straight on as far as the pub.
2 _____ right at the post office.
3 _____ to bed late. You've got school tomorrow.
4 _____ Lisa about the party! It's a secret!
5 _____ the road at the traffic lights.
6 _____ a break for five minutes.

4 Match the phrases (1–7) to their Italian translations (a–g).

1 ___ Go down/along Walton Street   a Attraversa il parco
2 ___ Turn left/right (at)   b Vai dritto (fino a)
3 ___ Go straight on (as far as)   c Passa sotto/sopra il ponte
4 ___ Go across the car park   d Gira a sinistra/destra (a)
5 ___ Go through the park   e Percorri Walton Street
6 ___ Go past the café   f Attraversa il parcheggio
7 ___ Go under/over the bridge   g Vai oltre il bar

🔊 **2.47** Listen and repeat.

⚠️ Turn right at the bridge. (~~Turn on the right at the bridge.~~)

Speaking • Giving directions

5 🔊 **2.48** Listen to the 2 conversations. Start from 'You are here' and follow the directions on the map below. Where do the 2 people want to go?

1 _____
2 _____

In pairs. Start from 'You are here'.
A: give your partner directions to a place on the map.
B: follow A's directions and point to the place on the map. **T**

Example:
A Go over the bridge and then go straight on. Take the second turning on the left and go over the bridge. Where are you?
B At the Leisure Centre.

When you finish, change roles.

Fast finishers!

Write directions to get from your house to your school or from your school to another place in town (50 words).

Listening

1 🔊 2.49 Zoe, Tom and Melanie are talking about their favourite city. Listen and match each person to the city (a–e) he/she describes.

1 Zoe ___   2 Tom ___   3 Melanie ___

a Dublin
b Edinburgh
c Bristol
d Cardiff
e Belfast

Word builder + City adjectives

2 Match the adjectives (1–10) to their translations (a–j).

1 ___ interesting	a diverso
2 ___ exciting	b bellissimo
3 ___ friendly	c civile
4 ___ civilized	d interessante
5 ___ beautiful	e meraviglioso
6 ___ modern	f elettrizzante
7 ___ different	g fantastico
8 ___ fantastic	h amichevole
9 ___ lively	i moderno
10 ___ wonderful	j vivace

Listen again. Which adjectives describe each city?

✏️ **WB p.185** Complete *City adjectives* in the Word store.

Speaking

3 Look at the photos and your notes. In pairs. Discuss and decide which city to visit next weekend. **P**

Example:
A Which city do you like?
B I like Bristol because it's…

Which is the most popular city in your class?

Writing

4 Imagine you are visiting a city in Ex.1 next weekend. Write an email to a friend (60–80 words). Include this information: **P T**

• tell him/her what you are doing at the weekend
• invite your friend to come with you
• describe the city and what you want to do there
• ask your friend to email or phone you soon

Reading

5 Before you read • When you visit a city, what do you want to see and do? Put the following in order of preference (1–6).

A ___ historic buildings (castles, cathedrals, etc.)
B ___ zoos
C ___ parks and gardens
D ___ shopping streets and markets
E ___ bars and clubs
F ___ special attractions

6 🔊 3.02 While you read • Read the text about Belfast. Are any of the places in Ex.5 mentioned in the text?

7 Vocabulary • Look at the words in bold in the text. What do they mean? Write a translation.

1 top floor _____
2 oldest _____
3 was built _____
4 throughout _____
5 yourself _____
6 sank _____
7 former _____
8 cellar _____

8 Comprehension check • Read the information and write a word or expression in each space.

1 _____ A famous ship that you can visit.
2 _____ A place where you can buy old clothes.
3 _____ A place where you get a good view of the city.
4 _____ You can go dancing here.
5 _____ You can make something nice to eat here.
6 _____ You can watch sport here.
7 _____ A famous engineer.
8 _____ You can watch a match on TV here.

Five Good Reasons To Visit Belfast

This is a great time of year to visit Belfast, so here are five good reasons to visit the city!

1 Odyssey Arena and W5

Odyssey Arena is a fantastic modern sports and entertainment centre situated in Titanic Quarter beside the River Lagan. At the Arena you can see concerts and ice hockey matches with the Belfast
5 Giants team. Odyssey is also home to W5, an exciting interactive science and discovery centre. From the **top floor** there are spectacular views over the city.

2 St George's Market

St George's Market is one of Belfast's **oldest**
10 attractions. It **was built** between 1890 and 1896 and is one of the best markets in the UK and Ireland. There is the Friday Variety Market (6am–1pm) where you can buy food and antique clothes, and the City Food and Garden Market on Saturdays
15 (9am–3pm). There are also events **throughout** the year, including food festivals, exhibitions, music concerts and fashion shows.

3 Choc-o-bloc

For all chocolate-lovers! At Choc-o-bloc they demonstrate how to make delicious
20 novelty chocolate bars with a simple step-by-step process. You don't just watch what they do, you can make the chocolate bars **yourself**. And you can take home (or eat!) the chocolate you make.
Admission: £6 (1 hour session)

4 *Titanic* Tours Belfast

25 Susie Millar, the *Titanic* Tours Belfast guide, is the great-granddaughter of Thomas Millar, an engineer who worked on the construction of the *Titanic*. Thomas was on the ship when
30 it **sank** in April 1912. Susie's tours are informative and very interesting. On the tour you visit the key sites in the construction of the *Titanic* and
35 you also visit the *SS Nomadic*. This ship took first class passengers to the *Titanic*.
Tours cost £25 per adult.

5 Night life

There are some fantastic places for live music in Belfast. Our favourite is The Empire Music Hall. This
40 is a multi-level bar in a **former** church in the historic centre of the city. In the **cellar** you can eat, drink and watch soccer and rugby matches on big-screen TVs. Upstairs at weekends, there are live bands. There are also comedy nights, dance nights and traditional Irish
45 music nights.
It's open every day from 8.30 pm to 2 am.

Preposizioni di luogo (2)

1 Write complete sentences putting the prepositions in English.

1 bus stop/bank (davanti a)
The bus stop is in front of the bank.

2 supermarket/Ham Road/Martin Street (fa angolo con)

3 shoe shop/clothes shop (accanto a)

4 leisure centre/shopping centre (dietro)

5 pub/Red Lion Street (in)

6 swimming pool/train station (di fronte a)

there is/are

2 Read the sentences and complete the explanation.

There's a clothes shop in Richmond Road.
There are three takeaways in my town.

> In italiano *there is/there are* equivalgono a
> _____/_____.

3 Choose the correct alternative.

1 **There are/They are** three banks in Twickenham.
2 **There is/It is** the first road on the right.
3 **There are/They're** from Liverpool, in the north-west of England.
4 **Are there/Is there** any good restaurants in Kingston?
5 'Diva'? **There's/It's** a very good club.
6 **There's/It's** a new Ferrari in the car park.
7 **Is there/Is it** a shoe shop on Hill Street?
8 **There aren't/They aren't** any nice boys in my class.

some/any

4 Read the sentences and complete rules 1–2.

There are some good actors in this film.
There aren't any bad actors.
Are there any takeways in your town?

> 1 Si usa _____ con sostantivi plurali nelle frasi affermative.
> 2 Si usa _____ con sostantivi plurali nelle frasi interrogative e negative.

5 Complete the sentences with *some* or *any*.

1 There aren't _____ exercise books on the table.
2 Are there _____ good games on that website?
3 There aren't _____ live bands at that club.
4 There are _____ interesting people at this party.

5 Are there _____ good films on at the cinema?
6 There are _____ fantastic photos in the exhibition.

L'imperativo

6 Use the words to write the directions.

1 park/the/across/walk

2 the/on/straight/station/go/as far as

3 leisure/go/centre/the/past

4 right/pub/turn/the/at

5 bridge/over/the/go

6 Marchmont/down/Road/go

7 car/through/park/the/go

8 the/post/turn/office/left/after

Esercizi sommativi

7 Complete the dialogue between Lia and Max.

Lia   I [1]_____ to the dentist's tomorrow.
Max   Really? Poor you!
Lia   Thanks. [2]_____ do I get there?
Max   It's very easy. Go [3]_____ Williams Street, [4]_____ over the bridge. [5]_____ the second turning on the right and [6]_____ past the bus station. Then take the first left and it's [7]_____ the right, opposite the café.
Lia   OK. I've got that.
Max   What [8]_____ your appointment?
Lia   [9]_____ at quarter past ten.
Max   Do you [10]_____ going for lunch afterwards?
Lia   Yes, that [11]_____ nice.
Max   [12]_____ meet for lunch at twelve o'clock.
Lia   Good idea! Where [13]_____ we meet?
Max   Let's meet in front of the café [14]_____ the dentist's.
Lia   OK. [15]_____ you tomorrow then.

8 Translation • Translate the sentences into English.

1 Gira a destra dopo il semaforo.
2 Vai sempre dritto fino alla chiesa.
3 L'edicola è a sinistra dopo il bar.
4 Non ci sono ristoranti buoni nella mia città.
5 Il negozio di scarpe è di fronte al ristorante cinese.
6 Ci sono studenti tedeschi nella tua classe?
7 Ci sono dei gruppi musicali italiani veramente bravi.
8 La fermata dell'autobus è davanti al municipio.

At the Tourist Information Centre

Dialogue 🎥 VIDEO

1 🔊 **3.03** Rick's visiting Oxford for the first time. He goes to the Tourist Information Centre. Listen and complete the sentences with the phrases in the box.

Can I have	Are there any
Could you recommend	How much

Woman	Hello.
Rick	Hello. ¹_____ a good, cheap place to stay, please?
Woman	Yes, there's a really good youth hostel on Botley Road.
Rick	²_____ is it?
Woman	It's only £11.95 a night.
Rick	Thanks. ³_____ a map of Oxford, please?
Woman	Yes, of course. Here you are.
Rick	⁴_____ places to eat near the hostel?
Woman	Yes, there's the George pub.
Rick	OK. Thanks for your help.
Woman	You're welcome.

Listen again and repeat.

Say it right!

2 🔊 **3.04** Listen. Then listen and repeat the sentences with the correct rhythm.

1 **A** Could you recommend a restaurant, please?
   B Yes, there's Gino's in Smith Street.

2 **A** Are there any hotels near here?
   B Yes, there's a good hotel in Richmond Road.

3 **A** Can I have some information about things to do here?
   B Yes, here's our *What's on* leaflet.

In pairs. Practise the 3 dialogues. When you finish, change roles.

Now close your books. Can you say the dialogues from memory?

Tourist Information ℹ️

Speaking

3 In pairs.
A: you are a tourist. Ask for information about accommodation and food in Leeds.
B: you work at the Tourist Information Centre in Leeds. Read the information and answer A's questions.

Leeds

Accommodation:
Traveller's Hotel, Vicar Lane – £19

Food in Vicar Lane:
New Jumbo Restaurant, 3 Indian restaurants

When you finish, change roles:
B: you are a tourist. Ask for information about accommodation and food in Brighton.
A: you work at the Tourist Information Centre in Brighton. Read the information and answer B's questions.

Brighton

Accommodation:
Journeys Hostel, Richmond Place – £10.95

Food in Richmond Place:
Planet India,
Jack and Linda Mills' Fish and Chip Shop

Northern Ireland

1 🔊 **3.05** Read the text. Then answer the questions below.

Giant's Causeway

Ballygally Castle

George Best

My Country

Northern Ireland is part of the United Kingdom. It covers an area of 14,120 km^2 and its total population is 1,613,800 – only 122 people per km^2! Almost 46% of the total population of Northern Ireland is under 30 years old! This makes it an exciting and lively place.

5 The countryside is incredibly beautiful. There aren't any really high mountains, but the hills are lovely and very green because it rains a lot here.

The Northern Irish accent is very distinct and there are lots of words which you only hear in Northern Ireland. For example, we
10 say, 'Bout ye' for 'How's it going?' and we call a child 'a wean'. In Belfast, 'Northern Ireland' is pronounced 'Norn Iron'!

Tourism is very important for us. Lots of tourists visit the spectacular coastline of the Giant's Causeway in County Antrim, and the capital city, Belfast, is obviously also very popular. There is
15 also a great live music scene and it's a lovely place to go fishing (in the lakes and the sea) or walking.

Northern Ireland is full of castles, including the beautiful Dunluce Castle, on the coast of County Antrim. The oldest occupied castle in Ireland is Killyleagh Castle, built in the 13th century. A very
20 popular castle, Ballygally Castle, is now a hotel. It's in the seaside town of Ballygally and is very famous because it's got a very lively ghost! James Shaw built the castle in 1625 and his wife, Lady Isobel Shaw, committed suicide there. Apparently, she knocks on doors of the hotel rooms at night and then disappears! Very scary!

25 Some very famous people come from Northern Ireland, such as the author of the *Chronicles of Narnia*, C.S.Lewis. His stories are now also really good films. Other famous people include the brilliant footballer George Best, the actors Kenneth Branagh and Liam Neeson, and Gary Lightbody, the singer with the excellent
30 band, Snow Patrol.

1 What's the population of Northern Ireland?
2 What's an important industry for the Northern Irish economy?
3 How do you say *Come va?* in Northern Irish?
4 Where can you see a ghost?
5 What is C.S.Lewis famous for?

Speaking

2 In pairs. Ask and answer the questions. **P T**

1 Do you like the *Chronicles of Narnia*?
2 Do you prefer reading books or going to the cinema?
3 Who are your favourite authors?
4 What's your favourite film?

Did you know?

The biggest group of immigrants to Northern Ireland are the Polish. There are 30,000 Poles in the country, so Polish is the second language spoken after English!

📹 **VIDEO** Now watch the Network video!

LET'S EAT!

Word builder

Food and drink

1 Match the words (1–12) to the pictures (a–l).

1 ___ peas	5 ___ apples	9 ___ bread
2 ___ salt	6 ___ oranges	10 ___ vinegar
3 ___ wine	7 ___ chicken	11 ___ potatoes
4 ___ oil	8 ___ pepper	12 ___ mineral water

🔊 **3.06** Listen and repeat.

2 Complete the mind map with the words in the box.

courgettes	beer	beef	pasta
tomatoes	pears	cakes	lamb
seafood	~~rice~~	lettuce	pork
green beans	biscuits	milk	butter
carrots	veal	eggs	coke
orange juice	cheese	salmon	

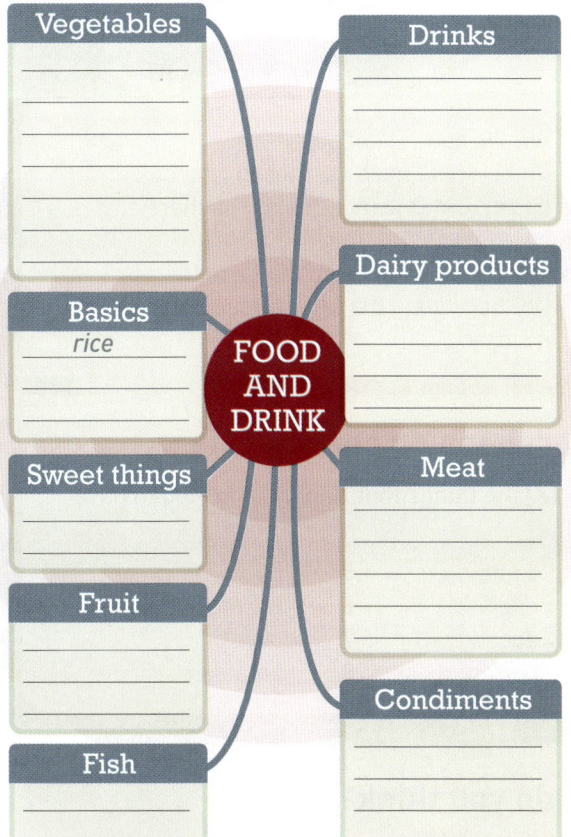

Vegetables

Drinks

Dairy products

Basics
rice

FOOD AND DRINK

Sweet things

Meat

Fruit

Fish

Condiments

🔊 **3.07** Now add the items of food in Ex.1. Listen and repeat.

Grammar note

Si chiamano *countable* (numerabili) i nomi di cose che si possono contare: *one egg, two eggs*.

Si chiamano *uncountable* (non numerabili) i nomi di cose (come le sostanze) che non si possono contare: *water*.

Alcuni sostantivi possono essere sia numerabili, che non numerabili:

I bought two chickens for dinner. (= numerabile)
Do you want some chicken? (= non numerabile)

✏️ **WB p.194**

3 Write the words from Ex.2 under these 3 headings in your exercise book.

Countable   Uncountable   Countable and uncountable

Speaking • My favourite food

4 Tick (✓) 6 things in Ex.1 and Ex.2 that you like eating or drinking. In pairs. Ask questions to find out your partner's favourite food and drink. **T**

Example:
A Do you like chicken?
B Yes, I do. I think it's delicious./No, I don't. I think it's disgusting.

Dictation

5 🔊 **3.08** Listen and complete the sentences.

1 I like _____.
2 I _____ like _____ or _____ very much.
3 _____ and _____ are _____ for you.
4 I eat fresh _____ like _____ and _____ every day.
5 I _____ drink _____ with my meals.

✏️ **WB p.195** Complete *Food and drink* in the Word store.

How much pasta have we got?

1 🔊 3.09 Hannah and her friend, Megan, are spending a weekend camping near Derry in Northern Ireland. What do they decide to cook for dinner? Listen and read.

Hannah	Let's start cooking then. What shall we make?
Megan	I don't know. **What do you fancy?**
Hannah	I don't know, but **I'm starving.**
Megan	How about spaghetti carbonara?
Hannah	OK. So we need pasta, eggs, cheese and bacon. How much pasta have we got?
Megan	I can't remember. There's a bag with some food in it over there.
Hannah	We've got lots of pasta. We've got two packets.
Megan	Good. And are there any eggs?
Hannah	Yes, there are. We've got three.
Megan	Three. That's fine. Is there any Parmesan cheese?
Hannah	No, there isn't.
Megan	OK. What about bacon? How much bacon have we got?
Hannah	Ah! We haven't got any.
Megan	Right, so we need Parmesan cheese and bacon. Oh! **One more thing** – is there any olive oil?
Hannah	Yes, there is. We've got half a bottle.
Megan	OK. Let's go to the village shop before it closes.

Comprehension check

2 Tick (✓) the things that Hannah and Megan have got.

1 ___ pasta   5 ___ bacon
2 ___ apples   6 ___ Parmesan cheese
3 ___ eggs   7 ___ olive oil
4 ___ butter   8 ___ potatoes

Real talk

What do you fancy?	Che cosa ti va?
I'm starving	Sto morendo di fame
One more thing	Un'ultima cosa

What do you think?

1 Is spaghetti carbonara a good meal to cook when you're camping?
2 What can you cook?

Grammar

some/any

Per parlare di quantità indefinite si usano *some* e *any* sia con i sostantivi numerabili che con quelli non numerabili.

Are there **any** eggs?
There are **some** eggs./There aren't **any** eggs.
Is there **any** water?
There's **some** water./There isn't **any** water.

much/many, a lot of/lots of

Per informarsi sulla quantità si usa *How much* con i sostantivi non numerabili, e *How many* con quelli numerabili.

How much water have we got?
How many eggs have we got?

Si usano *much* (+ sostantivi non numerabili) e *many* (+ sostantivi numerabili) nelle frasi negative.

We haven't got **many** eggs.
We haven't got **much** water.

Si usano *a lot of/lots of* nelle frasi affermative e interrogative sia con i sostantivi numerabili che con quelli non numerabili.

We've got **a lot of/lots of** eggs/water.

 **WB p.194**

Grammar check

3 Choose the correct alternative. NB In one case both alternatives are correct!

1 I haven't got **much/many** new DVDs.
2 Is there **any/much** orange juice in that carton?
3 How **much/many** money have you got?
Not **much/many**.
4 How **many/much** students are there in your class?
5 Gemma hasn't got **much/some** time for lunch.
6 I've got **any/some** bananas.
7 He's got **a lot of/many** pasta.
8 The supermarket's got **any/some** salmon, but it hasn't got **some/any** tuna.
9 Belfast has got **some/any** fantastic night life.
10 They haven't got **much/many** friends.

Grammar note

C'è una differenza tra *(very) little* e *a little*. Lo stesso vale per *(very) few* e *a few*:

1 *little/a little* + sostantivi non numerabili
We've got *little* milk. (*little* = poco)
We've got *a little* milk. (*a little* = un po')

2 *few/a few* + sostantivi numerabili
We've got *few* eggs. (*few* = poche)
We've got *a few* eggs. (*a few* = alcune)

Spesso *little* e *few* vengono preceduti da *very*.
Di solito si usa *a little bit of* anzichè *a little*.

 **WB p.194**

4 Complete the sentences with *very little, a little, very few* or *a few*.

1 The party wasn't very good. _____ people came.
2 Great! There are _____ biscuits left.
3 Oh dear. There's _____ water in the fridge.
4 She's lucky. She's got _____ very good friends.
5 I've got _____ cash in my wallet, but not much.
6 The students in this class work hard and _____ of them fail their exams.

Word recall Food and drink

5 Write items of food and drink for these colours.

yellow | white | green | orange | red

bananas

Pronunciation • /ə/ *a, an, some*

6 🔊 3.10 Listen to the schwa /ə/ sound in these sentences. Then listen and repeat.

1 I've got **a** new bike.
2 He's **an** engineer.
3 There are s**o**me apples.

Word builder +
Food quantities and containers

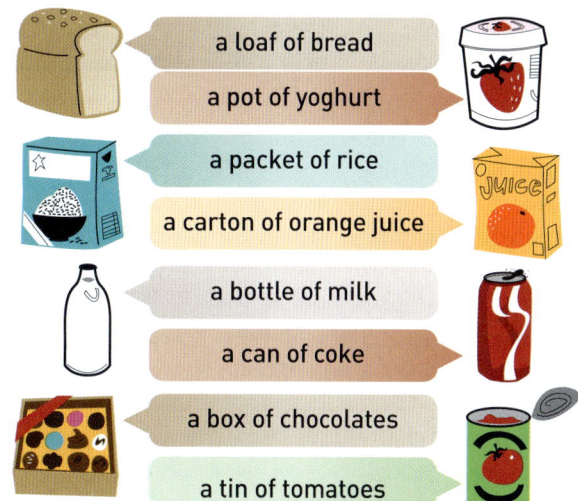

a loaf of bread
a pot of yoghurt
a packet of rice
a carton of orange juice
a bottle of milk
a can of coke
a box of chocolates
a tin of tomatoes

7 Translate the phrases into Italian.

WB p.195 Complete *Food quantities and containers* in the Word store.

Speaking • Oliver's leaving party

8 🔊 3.11 Oliver's getting ready to leave London. He's at the supermarket, but can't find his shopping list. He phones his mum. Listen and write the food that they've got. Then listen again and write the food they need. In pairs. Ask and answer to check your answers.

Example:
A How much pasta have they got?
B They've got 3 packets.
A How much pasta do they need?

There aren't enough young people

1 🔊 **3.12** It's raining now and the girls are deciding what to do. Are they enjoying their holiday? Listen and read.

Hannah This is really nice pasta, Megan!

Megan Thanks. Is there enough salt in it?

Hannah Yeah, it's fine.

Megan **Shame about the weather**, though.

Hannah Yeah, camping's really awful when the weather's like this.

Megan The campsite's not very good either.

Hannah Oh, it's not that bad. **What's wrong with it?**

Megan Well, there aren't enough showers and there's too much noise from the main road.

Hannah **You're right there.** And there are too many spiders.

Megan And it's too far from the village. You need a car, really.

Hannah But it's a nice walk.

Megan In the rain?

Hannah **Good point.**

Megan And there isn't enough to do in the village. There aren't enough young people.

Hannah Do you mean, 'not enough boys'? It's only a village.

Megan I know. But it's a really boring one. There's absolutely no nightlife.

Hannah Well, what do you want to do, then?

Megan Let's go to Derry. There are lots of bars and a few nightclubs there. We can get a room in a B&B.

Hannah Mmm… It *is* raining very hard. OK… let's pack up the tent.

Comprehension check

2 Answer the questions.

1 Are Hannah and Megan enjoying their pasta?
2 What's wrong with the campsite, in Megan's opinion?
3 What's wrong with the village, in Megan's opinion?
4 What do they decide to do in the end? Why?

Real talk

Shame about the weather	Peccato per il tempo
What's wrong with it?	Che cosa ha che non va?
You're right there	Hai proprio ragione
Good point	È vero

What do you think?

1 Who's a more positive person, Megan or Hannah?
2 In your opinion, do they do the right thing?
3 Do you like camping holidays? Why?/Why not?

Grammar

too much/many

Sostantivi non numerabili:
There's **too much** noise. (= troppo)

Sostantivi numerabili:
There are **too many** spiders. (= troppi)

(not) enough

There**'s enough** food for four people.
There **are enough** shops in my town.
There **aren't enough** people.
There **isn't enough** time.
(*not*) *enough* = (non) abbastanza

WB pp.194–195

Grammar check

3 Complete the sentences with *too much/many* or *enough*.

1 There are _____ supermarkets and not enough small shops.
2 I haven't got _____ money to go out.
3 There isn't _____ pasta for three people.
4 I never have _____ time to do my homework.
5 There are _____ students in my class. There are 40 of us!
6 He's eating _____ chocolate these days – it isn't healthy!
7 There aren't _____ good clothes shops in my town.
8 _____ sugar is bad for you.

Speaking • Our diets

4 Write down what you eat on a typical weekday and on a typical day at the weekend. In pairs. Look at your partner's diet and discuss.

Example:
You eat enough fruit, but you don't eat enough vegetables and you eat too much chocolate at the weekend!

Word builder + Shops

5 Match the shops (1–6) to the pictures (a–f).

1 bookshop
2 electrical goods shop
3 service station
4 hairdresser's
5 baker's
6 greengrocer's

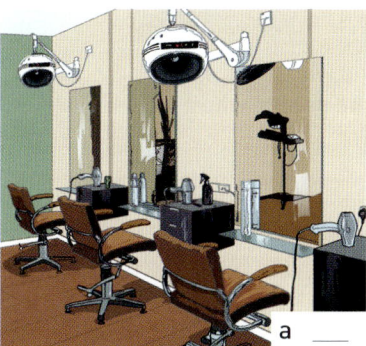
a ____

b ____

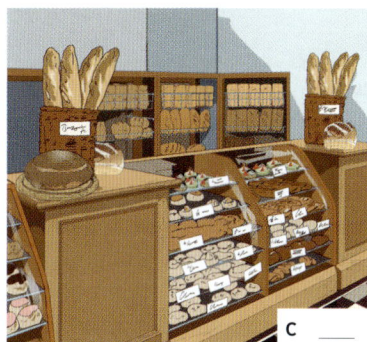
c ____

d ____

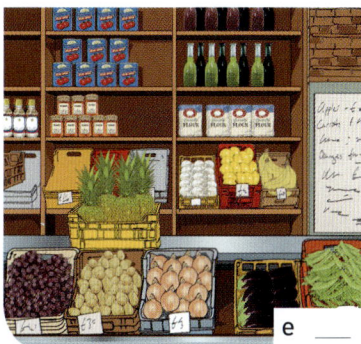
e ____

f ____

WB p.195 Complete *Shops* in the Word store.

Speaking • Problems with my town

6 Read the sentences. Are they true for your town? In pairs. Give your opinions. **T**

1 There aren't enough good cafés or takeaways in my town.
2 There are too many cars and not enough buses.
3 There are too many banks and not enough clothes shops.
4 There are too many supermarkets and not enough Internet cafés.
5 There are too many expensive restaurants.

Fast finishers!

Write a short paragraph about your diet (50 words).

Reading

1 Before you read • In pairs. Ask and answer the questions. **P** **T**

1 What do you have for breakfast?
2 Do you think you have a healthy breakfast?
3 Do you have breakfast with the rest of your family?
4 What do you think British people have for breakfast?

2 🔊 **3.13** While you read • Read the web page. Write the names and nationalities of the people who replied to Emma.

3 Vocabulary • Look at the highlighted words on the web page and match them to their Italian translations.

1 leggero _____
2 alghe essiccate _____
3 bacche _____
4 cetrioli sottaceto _____
5 bomboloni _____
6 poco sana _____

FOOD online

- **HOME**
- **PROFILE**
- **ARTICLES**
- **RECIPES**
- **BLOGS**
- **FORUM**
- **CONTACT**

BIZARRE BREAKFASTS!

posted by EMMA_UK at 11.06AM

My name's Emma and I'm taking a gap year this year. I'm curious to know what people eat for breakfast in the countries I'm going to visit. Foreigners often think that in Britain we eat a full English breakfast every morning. That's eggs, bacon,
5 sausages, fried bread, mushrooms and baked beans with a cup of tea. Can you imagine eating that every day? In fact, we usually eat a bowl of cereal or a slice of toast and juice, tea or coffee. In the winter some people eat porridge. You only get 'traditional' breakfasts when you go to a B&B or a hotel. But
10 what about breakfast in your country? Write and tell me!

Hi Emma! Here in the States we often have a very unhealthy breakfast (but it's delicious too!). We have donuts, fried eggs, hash browns (made of potatoes) with ketchup, cereal, orange juice, pancakes with syrup, or giant blueberry muffins. And of course we
15 drink a lot of coffee too.

TOM

In Japan, a traditional breakfast consists of hot rice, miso soup, grilled fish, tofu or eggs, dried seaweed ('nori'), and tsukudani (small fish and shellfish boiled in soy sauce and sugar). It's incredibly light and healthy, but these days lots of Japanese
20 teenagers prefer western-style breakfasts or Japanese-style fast food like rice balls. For Japanese teenagers, fast = good! Bye!

ETSUO

Some Russians like coffee for breakfast, but strong hot tea is more popular. We also eat different types of bread (black bread is traditional), blini (a sort of pancake), sausages, fried eggs, and
25 gherkins. Cereal is very common, especially for children. People eat it with a soft cheese similar to ricotta cheese ('tvorog'). Come and taste it! Love from Mila

MILA

I hope you come to Brazil, Emma. We've got very good breakfasts here. We have excellent black coffee, milk and white cheese. We
30 drink a lot of fresh juices (especially orange, guava, mango and passion fruit). We also drink a juice made of acai berries – it's very good for you! Another popular drink is coconut water. It's rich in potassium and it's delicious. Have a good trip!

MARIANA

4 Comprehension check • Complete the table.

Breakfast food and drink		
Country	Food	Drink
Britain		
USA		
Japan		
Russia		
Brazil		

IMAGES

full English breakfast

American breakfast

Japanese breakfast

Brazilian breakfast

Writing

5 Post a reply to Emma about breakfast in Italy. Include information on regional differences and also breakfasts on special occasions (60–80 words). **T**

Listening

6 🔊 **3.14** Listen to Olivia and Joseph discussing fast food. Who is for and who is against fast food?
For: _____
Against: _____

Listen again and tick (✓) the two things below that Olivia and Joseph mention.

1

2

3

LITTER

4
£1

5

Speaking

7 Read the Study skills. Then do Ex.8.

8 In pairs. A: argue against fast food. B: defend fast food. Use the arguments you heard in Ex.6 to help you. **P T**

Sostantivi numerabili e non numerabili

1 Complete explanations 1–3 with *countable* and *uncountable*.

> 1 I sostantivi che si possono contare cioè che possono essere sia singolari che plurali (per esempio: *eggs*, *apples*, *carrots*) si chiamano _____ e costituiscono la maggior parte dei sostantivi inglesi.
> 2 I sostantivi che non si possono contare e che non hanno la forma plurale (per esempio: *milk*, *bread*, *butter*) si chiamano _____.
> 3 C'è un terzo gruppo di sostantivi (per esempio: *coffee*, *chicken*, *chocolate*) che possono essere sia _____ che _____.

2 Write three words for each category below.

Countable: _____/_____/_____
Uncountable: _____/_____/_____
Countable and uncountable: _____
_____/_____

much/many, a lot of/lots of

3 Read the sentences and answer questions 1–3.

There isn't much rice in this packet.
How many apples do you need? I need three.
We've got lots of friends.
Have you got lots of homework?

> 1 Con quali sostantivi si usa *much*? _____
> 2 Con quali sostantivi si usa *many*? _____
> 3 Con quali sostantivi si usa *a lot of/lots of*?
> _____

4 Write questions using *How much* or *How many*. Then write answers which are true for you. Use *(not) much*, *(not) many* or *a lot of/lots of*.

1 free time/you/have got?
_____
_____
2 housework/you/do every week?
_____
_____
3 books/you/own?
_____
_____
4 snacks/you/eat/every day?
_____
_____
5 TV/you/watch?
_____
_____
6 cinemas/there/be/in your town?
_____
_____

(a) little/(a) few

5 Rewrite the sentences using *a little*, *a few*, *(very) little* or *(very) few*.

1 There aren't many biscuits – we need some more.
There are _____
2 He's busy, but he's got 20 minutes now to see you. (time) _____
3 They haven't got much sun in Siberia.
_____
4 I don't get many birthday presents but I get some.
_____
5 I've only got two friends. I prefer to be alone.
_____
6 The classroom is almost full. There isn't much room.
_____

too much/many, (not) enough

6 Read the sentences and complete rules 1–3.

I've got too much homework today.
There are too many people at this party.
I haven't got enough money to go out.
We've got enough pasta for dinner.

> 1 Si usano _____ e _____ per parlare di un eccesso di qualcosa.
> 2 Si usa _____ per parlare di una mancanza di qualcosa.
> 3 Si usa _____ per dire che c'è una quantità sufficiente di qualcosa.

7 Choose the correct alternative.

1 She hasn't got **enough/too much** time to go out.
2 There are **too much/too many** pubs in this town.
3 He's eating **too much/too many** cake.
4 There's **too much/enough** diesel in the car to get home.
5 I don't drink **enough/too many** water.
6 There aren't **enough/too much** parks in our town.
7 **Too much/Too many** cakes are bad for you.
8 I've got **enough/much** money to buy a scooter.

Esercizio sommativo

8 Translation • Translate the sentences into English.

1 Quante persone vanno alla festa stasera?
2 Quanti soldi ha Irene?
3 Ci sono pochissimi studenti a scuola oggi.
4 Abbiamo bisogno di uova.
5 Non hanno abbastanza tempo.
6 Quanto latte bevi per colazione?
7 Non bere troppo caffè.
8 C'è un po' di formaggio nel frigo.

Word builder

Holidays (1)

1 Write the words and phrases in the box under the correct headings below.

clean	stay in a B&B	go to the seaside	go by plane	tiring	go by ferry
go to the beach	stay in a hotel	stay on a campsite	boring	go sightseeing	dirty
delicious	disgusting	go on an adventure holiday	relaxing	go to clubs	do water sports
go by car	exciting	go to the Alps/Dolomites	eat out	go by train	go by coach

Types of holiday	Accommodation	Transport	Activities	Opinion adjectives

🔊 **3.15** Listen and repeat.

Speaking • My ideal holiday

2 Invent your ideal holiday. Choose words from the table in Ex.1. Consider these questions.

- Are you going with your family or with your friends?
- Are you staying in Italy or going abroad?
- Do you want to eat in restaurants or cook your own food?
- What month are you going?

In pairs. Describe your ideal holiday and discuss your choices. T

A I'm going to the seaside and I'm staying in a hotel.

B Mmm… I don't like going to the seaside. There are too many people.

Dictation

3 🔊 **3.16** Listen and complete the sentences.

1 _____ year I go to the _____ and I stay in a _____.

2 I _____ every evening and go to _____.

3 We _____ or go _____ _____.

4 The _____ in this _____ is _____.

5 Travelling _____ is _____.

6 When I _____, I _____.

✏️ **WB p.201** Complete *Holidays (1)* in the Word store.   **71**

He was OK yesterday

1 🔊 3.17 It's Friday night and Hannah and her friends, Megan and Razim, are in Belfast city centre. Who are they waiting for and why is he late? Listen and read.

Megan This is a really cool place.

Hannah Yes, Mario, the owner, was born in Rome. He makes great pizzas.

Razim Where were you yesterday afternoon, Hannah? You weren't at school. Were you ill?

Hannah No, I wasn't. I was at the dentist's.

Razim Lucky you – Geography was really boring!

Megan Oh, look! A text from Elliott. He says he's coming, but he's not feeling very well.

Hannah Poor thing. He was OK yesterday.

Razim He's always tired. He spends too much time at the gym.

Hannah Yes, he's obsessed with his appearance.

Megan Here he comes.

Hannah Hey, Elliott! You look awful! What's the matter?

Elliott Oh, it's nothing. I'm just a bit tired, that's all.

Razim Right, we're ready to order. What do you want, Elliott?

Elliott Actually, I'm not that hungry. I'll have a salad.

Razim Just a salad? OK.

Hannah Now, Elliott. Tell us about your exchange trip to France.

Real talk

Poor thing	Poverino
Here he comes	Eccolo
I'll have...	Prendo...

Comprehension check

2 Choose the correct alternative.

1 Hannah and her friends are in a **bar/restaurant**.
2 The owner of the restaurant **lives in/comes from** Italy.
3 Hannah **was/wasn't** at school yesterday afternoon.
4 Hannah was at the **doctor's/dentist's**.
5 Elliott was **ill/all right** yesterday.
6 Elliott orders a **pizza/salad**.

What do you think?

1 What do you think is wrong with Elliott?
2 Is it possible to do too much exercise?
3 How often do you do sport?

Grammar

Past simple • Verbo *be*

Forma affermativa
I/He/She/It **was** at the dentist's.
You/We/They **were** at the doctor's.

Forma negativa
I/He/She/It **wasn't** at school.
You/We/They **weren't** at school.

Forma interrogativa e risposte brevi
Was she ill? **Yes**, she **was**./**No**, she **wasn't**.
Were they ill? **Yes**, they **were**./
                              No, they **weren't**.

Where **was** he last night?
Where **were** we yesterday afternoon?

to be born = nascere
I was born in Rome. *Sono nato a Roma.*
She was born in March. *È nata a marzo.*

 **WB p.200**

Word note

Col *Past simple* si usano **espressioni di tempo passato**, come:
an hour/a week/a month **ago**
last week/month/year
last Wednesday/night
yesterday morning/afternoon/evening

Grammar check

3 Rewrite the sentences in the Past simple with the past time expression in brackets.

1 We're at home this evening.
   (yesterday evening)
2 She's ill this week.
   (last week)
3 Are you tired today? Yes, I am.
   (yesterday)
4 They aren't at school this morning.
   (last Tuesday)
5 Where are you? I'm at the cinema.
   (last night)
6 Is he at work this afternoon? Yes, he is.
   (yesterday afternoon)
7 Are they at the shopping centre? No, they aren't. (last Sunday)
8 I'm not in England this month.
   (last month)

Speaking • Were they born in Jamaica?

4 Where were the people below born?
In pairs. Ask and answer the questions.

Example:
A Were the Williams sisters born in Jamaica?
B No, they weren't. They were born in the USA.

1 Venus and Serena Williams   Jamaica/USA?
2 Arctic Monkeys   Scotland/England?
3 Colin Farrell   USA/Ireland?
4 Jessica Alba   Brazil/USA?
5 Albert Einstein   Poland/Germany?
6 Russell Crowe   Australia/New Zealand?
7 Madonna   Italy/USA?
8 Lewis Hamilton   UK/Nigeria?
9 The Jonas Brothers   USA/England?
10 Keanu Reeves   USA/Lebanon?

Word note

Osserva le **preposizioni di luogo**.

in (the)

in town	in the centre (of town)
in Exeter	in the car
in bed	in the kitchen/garden

at (the)

at school	at the party/disco
at home	at the airport
at work	at the shops
at church	at the swimming pool/beach
at university	at the cinema/theatre

Speaking • Where were they?

5 In pairs. Look at the table. Ask and answer questions.

Where	was were	your sister your brother your best friend your teacher you your friends your parents	an hour ago? at 6.30 this morning? last night? at 7.30 last Tuesday night? at 3 o'clock yesterday? yesterday morning? last Saturday?

Example:
A Where was your brother at 6.30 this morning?
B He was at home in the kitchen./I haven't got any brothers.

Where did you go?

1 🔊 3.18 Hannah, Megan and Razim ask Elliott about his school exchange trip to France. What towns did Elliott see in France? Listen and read.

Megan How did you get on in France, Elliott?

Elliott Really well, thanks. It was great!

Razim Where did you go?

Elliott I went to Cannes, in the South of France. It's a really beautiful town and the weather was great.

Megan What did you do?

Elliott I went to school, of course. And then at weekends I went to the beach. I didn't go sightseeing very much because it was really hot.

Hannah Sounds great!

Elliott Yes, and I went away for a weekend with Luca and his family. We went to Marseilles.

Hannah Really? What did you see there?

Elliott We saw the old port and the cathedral, and there was an amazing clothes market. I bought these jeans there.

Megan Nice! Where did you stay? In a hotel?

Elliott No, we didn't stay in a hotel because Luca's auntie lives in Marseilles, so we stayed with her.

Razim What was Luca like?

Elliott He was really nice. We got on very well. He's coming to England next year.

Hannah That's good. Oh look, here's our food.

Comprehension check

2 Tick (✓) the things that Elliott did in France.

1 ___ He went to school.
2 ___ He went sightseeing a lot.
3 ___ He went to the beach.
4 ___ He met a nice French girl.
5 ___ He saw the cathedral in Marseilles.
6 ___ He argued with his French friend.

Real talk

How did you get on...?	Come è andata...?
What was Luca like?	Com'era Luca?

What do you think?

1 Did Elliott have a good time in France?
2 Would you like to go on a school exchange to the UK?
3 What sort of problems can happen on an exchange?

Grammar

Past simple • Verbi regolari e irregolari

Forma affermativa

<u>Regolari</u>

He **stayed** with his auntie.

La forma affermativa del *Past simple* dei verbi regolari è uguale per tutte le persone e si ottiene così:
forma base + *-ed*

<u>Irregolari</u>

He **went** to Cannes.

Alcuni verbi di uso comune sono irregolari. Per esempio: *go – went, see – saw, do – did, eat – ate, buy – bought, leave – left, get – got*
Osserva la lista di verbi irregolari a pp.286–287.

Forma interrogativa	Forma negativa
Where **did** you **stay**?	I **didn't stay** in a hotel.
Where **did** you **go**?	I **didn't go** sightseeing.

Le forme negative e interrogative sono uguali sia per i verbi regolari che irregolari.

WB pp.200–201

Grammar check

3 Write questions for these answers.

1 I went to the seaside. (Where?)
2 We played beach volleyball. (What?)
3 They ate pasta and they drank mineral water. (What?)
4 She left for school at half past seven. (What time?)
5 He stayed in a hotel. (Where?)
6 We saw Jane last week. (Who?)
7 I visited London when I was ten. (When?)
8 They travelled to Athens by coach. (How?)

Now rewrite the sentences in the negative.

Word recall) Holidays

4 In pairs. Play this chain game.

1 A: say a type of holiday.
2 B: repeat A's type of holiday and add a holiday word/phrase.
3 A: repeat the words and add a holiday word/phrase.

A go to the Alps
B go to the Alps – stay on a campsite
A go to the Alps – stay on a campsite – exciting

You win if your partner forgets any of the sequence of words or if he/she can't think of a new word or phrase.

Pronunciation • -ed

5a 🔊 **3.19** Listen to the three ways of saying *-ed*.

/ɪd/ visit**ed**   /t/ finish**ed**   /d/ play**ed**

La desinenza *-ed* del *Past simple* dei verbi regolari si pronuncia:

/ɪd/ dopo i suoni /d/, /t/;
/t/ dopo i suoni /f/, /k/, /p/, /s/, /ʃ/, /tʃ/;
/d/ in tutti gli altri casi.

5b 🔊 **3.20** Listen and write /ɪd/, /t/ or /d/.

a ___ The train **stopped** at Crewe.
b ___ She **phoned** a travel agency this morning.
c ___ They **wanted** to see the London Eye.

🔊 **3.21** Listen and check. Listen and repeat.

Speaking • My favourite holiday

6 Think of your favourite holiday. Make notes under these headings: **P T**

1 Destination	5 Accommodation
2 Time of year	6 Activities
3 Travelling companions	7 Food
4 Transport	8 Opinion

In pairs. Ask and answer questions.

Example:
A Where did you go?   B I went to Spain.

Speaking • Travellers

7 Look at the 3 people in the photos. They all love travelling.

1 Choose a person and invent a profile for him/her (name, age, hobbies...)
2 Imagine what his/her last holiday was like. Use the headings in Ex.6 to help you.
3 In pairs. Take turns to interview your partner about his/her person's last holiday.

Begin like this:
A Which person is it? What's his/her name?
B Right, it's photo 2. His name's...

Fast finishers!

Write a short paragraph about your holiday in Ex.6 (50 words).

Speaking

1 In pairs. Ask and answer the questions. 🅣

1 Have you got fair or dark skin?
2 Do you tan easily?
3 Do you go sunbathing when you're on holiday?
4 Do you ever go to a tanning centre?
5 Do you think that having a suntan is important?
6 What are the dangers of sunbathing?

Listening

2 🔊 **3.22** A *Network* reporter is talking to a dermatologist about suntans. Listen and choose the correct alternative.

1 Suntans became popular in the **1920s/1930s**.
2 People with suntans were usually **poor/rich**.
3 Sunbathing became more popular with the arrival of the **bikini/package holiday**.
4 In the 1940s and 1950s, the media said that sunbathing was **good/dangerous** for you.
5 The number of different skin cancers increased in the **1980s/1990s**.
6 People started getting skin cancer because they started **sunbathing/swimming** for longer periods of time.
7 Sunbeds **are/aren't** dangerous.
8 Dr Stevens suggests that people protect their skin with suncreams and wear **sunglasses/hats**.

Reading

3 Before you read • Do you agree or disagree with these statements? Write A (agree), D (disagree) or NS (not sure) in the spaces.

1 ___ I'm happy with my physical appearance.
2 ___ People at school are popular because of their personality, not their appearance.
3 ___ I'd like to have cosmetic surgery one day.
4 ___ It's important to be thin.
5 ___ There's nothing wrong with being a bit fat.
6 ___ When you're fit, you feel good about yourself.

In pairs. Compare and discuss your answers.

4 🔊 **3.23** While you read • Read the article and write the headings (A–E) above the paragraphs (1–5).

A How to be happy
B Teens think about plastic surgery
C Joseph's story
D The illusion of perfection
E Eating problems

MIRROR MIRROR

1 _____

Young people are becoming obsessed with all aspects of their appearance. More than 27% of 10 and 11-year-old girls in the UK say that they aren't happy with the way they look. Almost 30% of girls
5 under 16 said they would like plastic surgery to improve their appearance in the future.

2 _____

And it's not just girls who are obsessed. When Joseph was 12, he was an excellent footballer and runner. He was very proud of his body, but as he
10 got older, he wanted to be fitter and fitter, so he started to eat less and exercise more. Joseph lost a lot of weight and became angry and aggressive. His mum took him to the doctor's and the doctor sent him to a specialist in eating disorders. Thanks
15 to his treatment, Joseph sorted out his problems and feels good about himself again.

3 _____

Why do people like Joseph suffer from eating disorders? Well, eating disorders are often a reaction to trauma or stress. In other cases it's a question of self-image, that is, how you
20 see yourself. People sometimes diet because they think they are too fat, even though their weight is quite normal. They don't feel satisfied with their own body. When this dissatisfaction becomes an obsession, they can become ill.

4 _____

Some people think there are other causes for this
25 obsession with physical appearance. A lot of people say it's the fault of the media: TV, Internet, magazines and newspapers. The people we see in the media are often 'perfect'. TV and film stars are usually slim, with perfect hair, skin, bodies, and teeth. This is, in fact, an illusion
30 – digital image manipulation on computers means that people's imperfections disappear with the click of a mouse. Stars also have lots of money, so people – especially young people – make the mistake of thinking that a perfect appearance + money = happiness.

5 _____

35 Self-esteem is the basis for happiness. You need to accept the parts of yourself that you can't change, and have realistic goals about what you can change. Eating well and regular exercise improve your self-esteem because they help you to feel more positive. Being positive about yourself,
40 and learning to accept and like yourself, is much more important than trying to look like your favourite star!

5 Vocabulary • Underline 6 words in the article that you don't know.

1 Guess the meaning from the context and write a translation.
2 Check your answers in the glossary.

6 Comprehension check • True or false? Write T or F. Correct the false sentences. **P**

1 ___ The majority of girls under 16 in the UK want plastic surgery.
2 ___ Joseph became ill because he didn't eat enough.
3 ___ Joseph is healthy now.
4 ___ People who diet sometimes get ill.
5 ___ Some people think the media causes low self-esteem.
6 ___ Young people sometimes want to look like famous people.
7 ___ Money and good looks always make people happy.
8 ___ Good self-esteem depends on accepting yourself as you are.

Writing

7 Write a description of your best friend (60–80 words). Include this information: **T**

- personal information (age, family, etc)
- physical appearance (hair, eyes, build)
- how he/she feels about his/her appearance

My best friend's name is Roberto. He...

Past simple • Verbo *be*

1 Read the sentences and complete rules 1–6.

I was at school yesterday.
She wasn't at home last night.
Where were they yesterday?
Were you at the match yesterday? Yes, I was.
She was born in London.

> 1 Il *Past simple* di *am* e *is* è _____.
> 2 Il *Past simple* di *are* è _____.
> 3 Per fare una frase negativa al *Past simple* si aggiunge _____ a *was* e *were*.
> 4 Per fare una domanda al *Past simple* si invertono _____ e _____.
> 5 A quali tempi verbali equivale il *Past simple* in italiano? _____.
> 6 Come si traduce 'nascere' in inglese? _____.

2 Complete the sentences with the Past simple of *be*.

1 Where _____ Oliver last night? He _____ at the swimming pool.
2 We _____ in the Dolomites last weekend.
3 I _____ born in Madrid.
4 You _____ at the party last Saturday. _____ you ill?
5 They _____ at the airport at six o'clock. They weren't late.
6 _____ you in bed at six o'clock this morning? Yes, I _____.
7 I _____ at home on Sunday. I was at the stadium.
8 Where _____ you born? Germany.

3 Put the past time expressions in the correct order. Write a number (1–8) in each space.

___ last night   ___ last month
___ last weekend   _1_ an hour ago
___ last year   ___ yesterday afternoon
___ yesterday morning   ___ at six o'clock this morning

Past simple • Verbi regolari e irregolari

4 Read the sentences and answer questions 1–4.

Where did you go on holiday?
I went to Mexico.
We stayed in a big hotel.
They didn't play football yesterday.

> 1 Che cosa si aggiunge alla forma base di un verbo regolare per formare il *Past simple*? _____
> 2 Esistono regole per la formazione del *Past simple* dei verbi irregolari? _____
> 3 Quale ausiliare si usa per formare domande al *Past simple*? _____
> 4 E per fare frasi negative? _____

5 Write the Past simple of these verbs.

1 start _____   5 eat _____
2 go _____   6 play _____
3 see _____   7 buy _____
4 visit _____   8 have _____

6 Rewrite these sentences in the Past simple.

1 She buys a new mobile every year.
2 I eat pizza for dinner.
3 She doesn't see them a lot.
4 Where do we play football?
5 When do you go mountain biking?
6 They don't have lunch at school.

Esercizi sommativi

7 Complete the dialogue between Jim and Mel with the correct tense of the verbs in the box.

do (x2)	have got	spend	call
stay	go (x4)	see	get	be

Jim What [1]_____ last night?
Mel I [2]_____ to a concert with my friend, Marta.
Jim Who did you see?
Mel I [3]_____ a band from Leeds called Zimba.
Jim Great! What time did you get home?
Mel I [4]_____ home at half past twelve.
Jim [5]_____ you tired?
Mel Yes, I am. But I [6]_____ to school on Saturdays, so it doesn't matter.
Jim What are you doing tomorrow?
Mel I [7]_____ my homework first and then I [8]_____ to the cinema with Tom. What about you?
Jim I [9]_____ at home tomorrow. I [10]_____ any money because I [11]_____ it all last weekend when I [12]_____ away with the basketball club.
Mel I see! Anyway, I've got to go now! My mum [13]_____ me because dinner's ready.

8 Translation • Translate the sentences into English.

1 La settimana scorsa ero in Francia.
2 Le mie cugine sono nate in Grecia.
3 Ieri sera sono andato in palestra.
4 Hanno mangiato pasta a pranzo oggi.
5 Abbiamo visitato un museo quando eravamo in gita scolastica.
6 Sono uscita da casa alle sette stamattina.
7 Maria ha passato lo scorso weekend a Roma.
8 Mio fratello non è andato all'università.

Eating out

1 Look at the menu. Check any unknown words in the glossary.

the PuRPLe ZEBRA Restaurant

LuNch MeNu £7.50*

ONE 'STARTER' & ONE 'MAIN'

STaRTeRS

carrot & coriander soup

'hot' cheesy garlic bread

mains

salmon fishcakes

simply pasta 'margherita'

grilled half chicken

all mains served with fries or salad

dRINKS

sparkling /still mineral water

coke/diet coke

fresh orange juice

service charge not included

SeRVeD 11am - 2PM

Dialogue

2 3.24 Listen to Amy and Ben ordering food. Write A (Amy) or B (Ben) on the menu next to the food and drink that they choose.

Say it right!

3 3.25 Listen. Then listen and repeat the sentences with the correct rhythm.

Waitress	Hello. Are you ready to order?
Jim	Yes, I'll have the soup for my starter, please.
Waitress	OK. What would you like for your main course?
Jim	I'd like salmon fishcakes with fries, please.
Waitress	And what would you like to drink?
Jim	Sparkling mineral water, please.
Later...	
Jim	Could I have the bill, please?
Waitress	Yes, of course.

In pairs. Practise the dialogue. When you finish, change roles.

Now close your books. Can you say the dialogue from memory?

Grammar note

Si usa *I'll* (*I will*) per decisioni non premeditate, prese nel momento in cui si parla.

soggetto + *will* + forma base

I'll have the soup, please. *Prendo la minestra, grazie.*

WB p.201

Speaking

4 In pairs. A: you're the waiter/waitress. B: you're the customer. You're very hungry.

Act out the dialogue, using the menu in Ex.1. When you finish, change roles.

Global food

1 Match the types of restaurants (1–6) to the photos (a–f).

1 ___ Indian   3 ___ Chinese   5 ___ Italian
2 ___ Thai   4 ___ Japanese   6 ___ Mexican

2 Which restaurants do you think are most popular in the UK? Match the names from Ex.1 to the number of restaurants.

1 _____ 9,500   3 _____ 5,000   5 _____ 750
2 _____ 7,500   4 _____ 370   6 _____ 205

> **Did you know?**
>
> 49% of UK adults often eat Chinese food and 39% eat Indian food.

3 🔊 **3.26** Read the text. Then answer the questions below.

Ethnic food & immigration

When you look at the statistics, there's an enormous number of ethnic restaurants in the UK. But why is this? Well, the simple answer is because Britain once had colonies all over the world. It was also a centre for world trade, so seamen often came to Britain and small immigrant communities
5 grew up in the main ports.

India was a British colony for many years, and the British also occupied part of China. Indian immigration to Britain began in the 1880s, but it was in the 1950s that Indians and other ethnic minorities started coming to the country in large numbers. Why? Because it was possible to earn more money working in
10 Britain than in India. Another reason is that long-distance travel became cheaper at that time. Now there are over a million Indians and almost 750,000 Pakistanis in the UK, which explains why there is an Indian restaurant on every high street and why it's one of the nation's favourite cuisines. There are also around 250,000 Chinese people and just over 100,000 Italians. The first Italian restaurant opened in London
15 in 1936 and now there are more than 5,000. And yes, it's true that some of them sell American-style deep-fried pizza and pronounce bruschetta 'bruscetta,' but you can find a good authentic pizza in the big cities, and possibly even a good coffee, too...

1 Why has Britain got so many immigrants?
2 Where did immigrants live when they first came to Britain?
3 Why did people come to Britain in the 1950s?
4 What's the largest group of immigrants in the UK?
5 What's the difference between Italian restaurants in Italy and some Italian restaurants in the UK?

> **Did you know?**
>
> The first Chinese restaurant in the UK opened in London in 1908.

Speaking

4 In pairs. Ask and answer the questions. 🅿 🆃

1 Do you ever go to non-Italian restaurants in Italy? Which kind?
2 What's your favourite non-Italian dish?
3 Which of the restaurants on this page would you like to try?

📹 **VIDEO**   Now watch the Network video!

CONNECT

Word builder

The media

1 Complete the mind map with the words in the box.
Some words can be in more than one box.

documentary	chat show	reality show	newspaper	magazine	film	book
social network site	sitcom	the news	cartoon	advert	soap	email
sports programme	comic	talent show	quiz show	blog	wiki	

THE INTERNET

t_____n_____   b_____   f_____

s_____n_____s_____

e_____

a_____

w_____

PRINTED MEDIA

m_____   b_____

n_____

c_____

a_____

THE MEDIA

TELEVISION (TV)

r_____s_____

d_____

c_____s_____

f_____

t_____n_____

s_____

s_____

t_____s_____

a_____

s_____p_____

c_____

q_____s_____

3.27 Listen and repeat.

Speaking • Media habits

2 In pairs. Use words from Ex.1 and ask and answer
questions about your media habits. **P T**

Example:
A How often do you use the Internet?
B I use the Internet every day.
A What websites do you usually go on?
B I usually go on social network sites.

Dictation

3 **3.28** Listen and complete the sentences.

1 I _____ a _____ every day.
2 I _____ watch _____. I don't like them.
3 _____ are OK, but I prefer
_____ and _____.
4 Last _____ we _____ a _____.
5 She chats with her _____ on a _____
_____ site every _____.

Did you see Luke yesterday?

1 ◀◉ 3.29 Hannah and Megan meet in a café in the centre on Sunday morning. Who's Luke? Listen and read.

Megan Hi, Hannah. Are you OK?
Hannah Yes, I'm fine. A bit tired, though. I stayed up to watch the final of *Wow-Factor* last night. Did you watch it?
Megan No, I didn't. Did Jay Johnson win?
Hannah Yes, he did. I was so pleased! He was definitely the best.
Megan Yes, definitely. Did he sing *Still in my heart*?
Hannah No, he didn't. He sang a new song, but I can't remember the name. Hey! Did you see Luke yesterday?
Megan Yes, I did. I saw him at the skatepark.
Hannah And?
Megan Well, he was with his friends, so I couldn't really talk to him...
Hannah Shame! Did they speak to you?
Megan No, they didn't, so I didn't hang around. It was embarrassing. Anyway, did I tell you about next weekend?

Hannah No, you didn't. What's happening next weekend?
Megan I'm having a party at my house.
Hannah Excellent! And I can guess who you're inviting!

Comprehension check

2 **True or false? Write T or F. Correct the false sentences.** P

1 ___ Megan is tired because she stayed up to watch TV.
2 ___ Jay Johnson won the *Wow-Factor* competition.
3 ___ Hannah and Megan think Jay was the best competitor.
4 ___ Luke was alone at the skatepark.
5 ___ Megan spoke to Luke.
6 ___ Megan intends to invite Luke to her party.

Real talk

definitely the best	decisamente il migliore
I didn't hang around	non sono rimasta

What do you think?

1 Do you think that Luke knows that Megan is interested in him?
2 Why didn't Megan speak to Luke at the skatepark?
3 When you like someone, what do you do to get to know him/her?

Grammar

Past simple • Forma interrogativa e risposte brevi

Forma interrogativa
Did I/you/he/she/it/we/they **watch** the *Wow-Factor*?

Risposte brevi
Yes, I/you/he/she/it/we/they **did**.
No, I/you/he/she/it/we/they **didn't**.

 **WB p.210**

Grammar check

3 Write a question and short answer for each sentence.

1 I saw Mark yesterday.
   Did you see Mark yesterday? Yes, I did.
2 They didn't go to the party.
3 She didn't have lunch at school.
4 They didn't enjoy the concert.
5 I read a newspaper yesterday.
6 We didn't have any homework last Friday.
7 They went to a basketball match this morning.
8 He didn't come home late.

Word recall The media

4 In pairs. Look at the words in Ex.1 on p.81.
   A: choose a category.
   B: close your book. Say the words in that category.

   When you finish, change roles.

Speaking • My media habits

5 In pairs. Ask and answer questions about yesterday using the ideas below. Give as much information as possible. Make a note of your partner's answers. **T**

1 read a newspaper, book or magazine?
2 use a social network site?
3 watch TV?
4 chat with your friends?
5 watch a film?
6 use the Internet?
7 listen to music?
8 watch the news (on TV or the Internet)?

Example:
A Did you read a newspaper yesterday?
B Yes, I did.
A Which newspaper did you read?
B I read *Gazzetta dello Sport*.
A Was it interesting?
B Yes, it was. I read an article about Lionel Messi.

What did you do?

6 🔊 **3.30** Listen to Nathan and Zoe and underline the mistake in the information in each sentence.

1 Zoe went to a concert at the stadium on Tuesday night. _____
2 She saw the Sixth Street Band. _____
3 The tickets cost £50. _____
4 Nathan went to a friend's house and watched a film. _____
5 It was a science fiction film. _____
6 The title of the film was *Reds*. _____
7 Nathan bought the DVD. _____
8 Nathan had bad dreams after he watched the film. _____

Listen again and write the correct information in the spaces. In pairs. Check your answers.

Example:
A Did Zoe go to a concert at the stadium on Tuesday night?
B No, she didn't. She went on...

Fast finishers!

Write 5 sentences about your partner based on the results of the questions in Ex.5.

Michele used the Internet last night. He emailed some friends and watched a film.

I couldn't understand anything!

1 🔊 3.31 Elliott and Razim are talking in the gym after school. Where's Razim from? Listen and read.

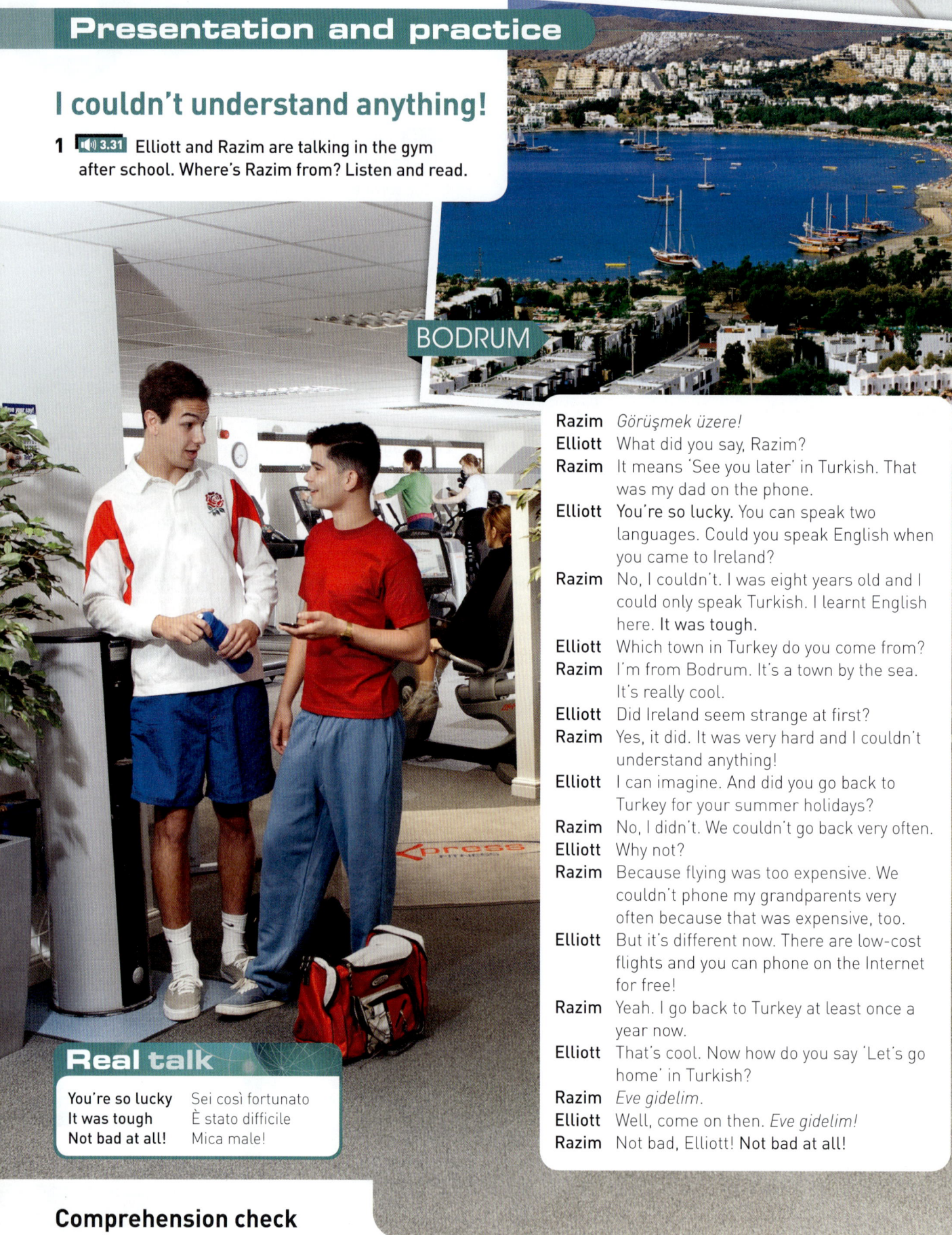

BODRUM

Razim	*Görüşmek üzere!*
Elliott	What did you say, Razim?
Razim	It means 'See you later' in Turkish. That was my dad on the phone.
Elliott	**You're so lucky.** You can speak two languages. Could you speak English when you came to Ireland?
Razim	No, I couldn't. I was eight years old and I could only speak Turkish. I learnt English here. **It was tough.**
Elliott	Which town in Turkey do you come from?
Razim	I'm from Bodrum. It's a town by the sea. It's really cool.
Elliott	Did Ireland seem strange at first?
Razim	Yes, it did. It was very hard and I couldn't understand anything!
Elliott	I can imagine. And did you go back to Turkey for your summer holidays?
Razim	No, I didn't. We couldn't go back very often.
Elliott	Why not?
Razim	Because flying was too expensive. We couldn't phone my grandparents very often because that was expensive, too.
Elliott	But it's different now. There are low-cost flights and you can phone on the Internet for free!
Razim	Yeah. I go back to Turkey at least once a year now.
Elliott	That's cool. Now how do you say 'Let's go home' in Turkish?
Razim	*Eve gidelim.*
Elliott	Well, come on then. *Eve gidelim!*
Razim	Not bad, Elliott! **Not bad at all!**

Real talk

You're so lucky	Sei così fortunato
It was tough	È stato difficile
Not bad at all!	Mica male!

Comprehension check

2 Answer the questions.

1 What language does Razim speak with his father?
2 What language could Razim speak when he was eight?
3 Why was life difficult for Razim when he first arrived in Northern Ireland?
4 Why didn't Razim go back to Turkey very often?
5 How often does Razim go back now?

What do you think?

1 What things do you think Razim found strange when he went to Northern Ireland?
2 What are the advantages of being able to speak two languages?
3 Would you like to go and live in another country?

Grammar

could • Abilità e possibilità

Forma affermativa
I/you/he/she/it/we/they **could** speak Turkish.

Forma negativa
I/you/he/she/it/we/they **couldn't** understand English.

Forma interrogativa e risposte brevi
Could I/you/he/she/it/we/they **speak** English?
Yes, I/you/he/she/it/we/they **could**.
No, I/you/he/she/it/we/they **couldn't**.

Si usa *could* per parlare di abilità al passato.
Could you speak English when you came to England?

Si usa *could* anche per esprimere possibilità
e impossibilità al passato.
I couldn't go back to Turkey very often.

WB pp.210-211

Grammar check

3 Rewrite these sentences in the past using the expression in brackets.

1 Can you speak English? Yes, I can. (2 years ago)
   Could you speak English 2 years ago? Yes, I could.
2 I can't play football. (when I was six)
3 They can walk to school every day. (when they went to junior school)
4 Can she read very well? No, she can't. (3 years ago)
5 Can we buy clothes online? Yes, you can. (in 1999)
6 Can you ride a bike? No, I can't. (when you were four)

Grammar note

A differenza dell'italiano, in inglese una domanda può concludersi con una preposizione:
Where do you come **from**?
(From where do you come?)

What are you waiting **for**?
(For what are you waiting?)

WB p.211

⚠ **listen to**
I like listening to music. (I like listening music.)

4 Write questions for these answers.

1 I like listening to rock music. (What type)
2 I'm waiting for my friend. (Who)
3 He comes from London. (Where)
4 She's looking at a website. (What)
5 I'm thinking about the holidays. (What)
6 He's looking for his English book. (What)
7 I'm going to the beach with my sister. (Who)
8 They're talking to their teacher. (Who)

Pronunciation • Silent -*l*

5a 🔊 **3.32** Listen to the -*l* sound:

told /təʊld/ (pronounced)   could /kʊd/ (silent)

5b 🔊 **3.33** Listen and underline the words where -*l* is silent:

walk   old   sold   talk   would   belt

🔊 **3.34** Listen and check. Listen and repeat.

Speaking • Progress

6 Guess which of these things people could do in 1990 in the UK. Put a tick (✓) or a cross (✗) in the spaces.

1 ___ record TV programmes
2 ___ watch films in 3D
3 ___ navigate using GPS
4 ___ send and receive emails
5 ___ send and receive text messages
6 ___ read newspapers on the computer
7 ___ take photos with a mobile
8 ___ listen to music on a portable cassette player
9 ___ buy things on the Internet
10 ___ watch TV on a mobile

Ask and answer questions to compare answers. 🅣

Example:
A Could they record TV programmes in 1990?
B Yes, they could.
A I agree.

🔊 **3.35** Listen and check your answers.

Speaking • When I was eight...

7 Write 3 things that you could do when you were 8 years old and 3 things that you couldn't. Include 2 things which are not true!

In pairs. A: read your first sentence. B: say if it's true or not. Then ask B the same question.

Example:
A I could ride a bike when I was eight.
B I think that's probably true.
A Yes, you're right. Could you ride a bike when you were eight?
B No, I couldn't.

Reading

1 Before you read • In pairs. Ask and answer the questions. **T**

1 Does technology dominate your life?
2 What are the advantages and disadvantages of a hi-tech life?
3 What things can you do now that your parents couldn't do when they were your age?
4 And your grandparents?

2 🔊 3.36 While you read • Read the text and write which year each paragraph describes (1950, 1980 or 2010) in the spaces above each one (1–3).

3 Vocabulary • Look at the words in bold in the text. Match them to their Italian translations.

1 ___ interactive whiteboards
2 ___ broadband
3 ___ landline
4 ___ phone box
5 ___ entertainment

a cabina telefonica
b lavagne interattive multimediali
c intrattenimento
d telefono fisso
e banda larga

Techno Transformation

1

Life was fast and very hi-tech. In the UK, technology was present in almost every aspect of a teenager's life. At school, students used computer labs and laptops. They watched DVDs and had lessons using
5 **interactive whiteboards**. Students depended on the Internet to do homework – they rarely used libraries as a resource for study. Technology dominated their free time, too. The mobile phone was an essential accessory for listening to music, watching TV, surfing
10 the Internet, communicating with friends (by text message and phone), accessing social networks, and even reading the newspaper. At home, most families had at least one computer and a **broadband** Internet connection. Widescreen high definition TVs were
15 standard, but many people preferred to watch TV online. People still bought newspapers to read about world events, but online TV and newspapers were very popular, too.

2

At this time there was less technology in schools.
20 There were language labs, video recorders and TVs, and a few computers, but usually for the teachers. Above all, there was no Internet, so students couldn't do their homework without using books. Mobile phones were very expensive and not very
25 common. You couldn't simply phone your friends or text them when you wanted to. You phoned them from the **landline** at home or from a public **phone box**. At home, families usually had a colour TV with a video cassette recorder. People listened to the
30 radio or music on a stereo, which played cassettes or vinyl records. Teenagers often listened to music on a portable cassette player. People watched the news on TV and listened to the radio. Most families bought a newspaper every day.

4 Comprehension check • Complete the table with information from the text.

	Paragraph 1: Year _____	Paragraph 2: Year _____	Paragraph 3: Year _____
Technology in schools		*Language labs*	
Personal communication			
Home entertainment			
Access to the news			

Speaking

5 In pairs. Ask and answer the questions. **P T**

1 How do you access the news?
2 Do you ever read newspapers?
3 Which sections of the newspaper (online or printed) do you always read? Why?
4 Which sections do you never read? Why not?
5 Do you believe what you see and read in the news? Why?/Why not?

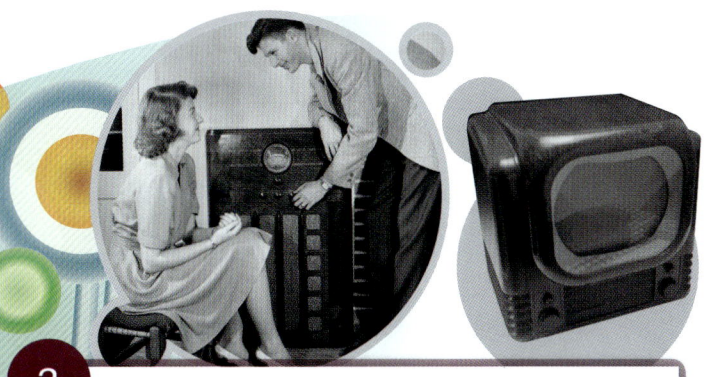

3

_____

35 Go back to this time and the differences are dramatic! There was no technology in school at all. Students occasionally listened to special programmes for schools on the radio, but that was all. Everything else was books, books and more
40 books. And the books were usually black and white and were passed from generation to generation of students. The differences outside school were even more extreme. Most families didn't have a phone. People went to one another's houses instead. For
45 **entertainment** at home, people listened to music on the radio. People also listened to the news on the radio or read the newspaper. Very few people had a television and they were black and white and the picture was very poor quality. Reading was
50 very popular. In their free time, teenagers went out dancing, went to the cinema, to youth clubs or read at home.

Listening

6 🔊 **3.37** In the UK there are often 'joke' news items on April 1st, April Fool's Day. Listen to the 3 news items. Decide if you think each item is genuine (✓) or a joke (✗).

Read the summaries of the 3 news items and complete them with the words from the box. Then listen again and check.

days	hundreds	Useful Networks
~~marathon~~	50p	Birmingham
SNIFF	digital	find
maintenance costs		
Houses of Parliament		

1 A Japanese athlete is running a ¹ _marathon_ for 26 ² _____ because of a translator's mistake. At the moment he is running towards ³ _____.

2 ¹ _____ of people protested outside the ² _____ because they are intending to install a ³ _____ clock face on Big Ben to reduce high ⁴ _____ .

3 ¹ _____, a technology company, is selling an application called ² _____ for use on mobile phones. It costs ³ _____ to ⁴ _____ people on social networks.

Writing

7 Read the Study skills. Then do Ex.8.

Study skills

Linking words: _and, so that, but, because_

1 Si usa _and_ per unire due frasi.
   He came into the room and he turned on the television.

2 Si usa _so that_ per parlare dello scopo di un'azione.
   I took my umbrella with me so that I didn't get wet.

3 Si usa _but_ per contrapporre due idee diverse.
   I like Italian food, but I don't like pasta very much.

4 Si usa _because_ per spiegare il motivo di qualcosa.
   He was late for school because he missed the bus.

8 Look at these sentences from a newspaper article. Complete the sentences with the correct linking word: _and, so that, but, because_.

1 Thousands of people went to fast food restaurants to ask for the new burger _____ they believed the advert.
2 It said that the ingredients were in a special position _____ left-handed people could eat it more easily.
3 According to the advert, the new burger was for left-handed people, _____ it explained exactly why it was special.
4 On April 1st 1998, an American fast food shop published an advert for a new hamburger, _____ the hamburger didn't actually exist!

Now put the sentences (1–4) in the correct order and think of a headline for the article.

Past simple • Forma interrogativa e risposte brevi

1 Read the sentences and complete rules 1–2.

Did you listen to music last night? Yes, I did.
Did they see the match last Saturday? No, they didn't.

> 1 **Forma interrogativa:**
> _____ + soggetto + _____?
> 2 **Risposte brevi:** *Yes*, + soggetto + _____./
> _____ + _____ + *didn't*.

2 Reorder the words to make questions. Then write short answers.

1 concert Tuesday he to on night go did the? ✓

_____

2 Andy yesterday see she school at did? ✗

_____

3 win they did competition the? ✓

_____

4 bag house my I did leave your at? ✓

_____

5 a jacket market at did the you buy? ✗

_____

6 plane did she Paris by go to? ✗

_____

could • Abilità e possibilità

3 Read the sentences and complete rules 1–3.

I could speak French when I was five years old.
I couldn't walk to school because it was too far.
Could you write when you were four? No, I couldn't.

> 1 In italiano *could* si traduce sia con _____, sia con _____.
> 2 La forma negativa di *could* si fa aggiungendo _____.
> 3 Dopo *could* si usa _____ del verbo.

4 Use the words to write questions and short answers.

1 you/ski/primary school? (I, ✓)
 Could you ski when you were at primary school?
 Yes, I could.
2 she/read/four? (she, ✗)

_____

3 I/speak Italian/three? (you, ✓)

_____

4 they/walk to the beach/on holiday? (they, ✓)

_____

5 you/play the piano/eight? (I, ✗)

_____

6 he/see the sea from his hotel room/on holiday? (he, ✓)

_____

Verbi + preposizioni nelle domande

5 Write the questions in English.

1 Da dove vieni?
2 Che tipo di musica ascolti di solito?
3 Di che cosa avete parlato?
4 A che cosa stai pensando?
5 Che tipo di pizza hai chiesto?

6 Write questions for these answers.

1 _____
 My sister works for the government.
2 _____
 I'm thinking about my summer holidays.
3 _____
 That author wrote about Roman history.
4 _____
 They're talking about a boy.
5 _____
 We looked at an amazing car.
6 _____
 He's waiting for the bus.

Esercizi sommativi

7 Complete the dialogue between Al and Kim.

Al Where [1]_____ you go on holiday last year?
Kim I [2]_____ to the USA.
Al Who did you go [3]_____?
Kim Unfortunately my boyfriend [4]_____ come. He was ill at the last moment, so my friend, Amy and I [5]_____.
Al Did you [6]_____ a good time?
Kim Yes, I [7]_____.
Al Which cities did you visit?
Kim I [8]_____ New York and Washington.
Al [9]_____ you like the food?
Kim No, I [10]_____. Not really. But it [11]_____ bad.
Al [12]_____ you spend a lot of money?
Kim Yes, I did. I [13]_____ lots of clothes and souvenirs.
Al Sounds great!
Kim Yes, it [14]_____!

8 Translation • Translate the sentences into English.

1 Sapevo giocare a tennis quando avevo sei anni.
2 Potevi andare a scuola in bici quando abitavi a Roma? No.
3 Lei sapeva nuotare quando aveva dieci anni? Sì.
4 Non potevo tornare a casa in autobus perché non avevo soldi.
5 Hai scritto un'email a Jack ieri sera? No.
6 Con chi sei andato alla festa?
7 Hanno fatto i compiti ieri pomeriggio? Sì.
8 Per chi è questa torta?

PEOPLE

Word builder

Personality adjectives (1)

1 Match the adjectives (1–12) to their translations (a–l).

1 ___ selfish _____		**a** sensibile
2 ___ insecure _____		**b** interessante
3 ___ impulsive _____		**c** estroverso/a
4 ___ silly _____		**d** egoista
5 ___ easy-going _____		**e** intelligente
6 ___ outgoing _____		**f** allegro/a
7 ___ sensitive _____		**g** sciocco/a
8 ___ interesting _____		**h** insicuro/a
9 ___ decisive _____		**i** pigro/a
10 ___ cheerful _____		**j** impulsivo/a
11 ___ lazy _____		**k** calmo/a e rilassato/a
12 ___ clever _____		**l** deciso/a

Then write an opposite adjective from the box next to each adjective above.

> thick-skinned   shy   generous   sensible
> stupid   indecisive   grumpy   energetic
> cautious   confident   uptight   boring

◀)) 3.38 Listen and repeat.

> ⚠ Le seguenti parole sono *false friends*, cioè il loro significato non è quello che sembra.
> sensitive = *sensibile*
> sensible = *ragionevole/assennato*
> nervous = *ansioso/teso/preoccupato*
>   (*nervoso* = irritable)
> sympathetic = *comprensivo*
>   (*simpatico* = nice/friendly)

Speaking • Describing people

2 Look at the photos of the 6 people. Imagine what their personalities are like. Choose a person and think of a description. **T**
In pairs.
A: describe your person.
B: guess which person A is describing.

Example:
A I think this person is very outgoing and generous.
B Has this person got long, black hair?
A Yes.
B Is it photo A?
A Yes, it is!
B I agree with you. I think she's very cheerful.

When you finish, change roles.

Dictation

3 **◀)) 3.39** Listen and complete the sentences.

1 I'm quite _____ and a bit _____.
2 I don't like _____, _____ people.
3 His _____'s really _____
and _____.
4 My _____ is very _____, but he's
also _____.
5 My _____ very _____ and
_____, but he's _____.

 WB p.217 Complete *Personality adjectives (1)* in the Word store.   89

What happened?

1  It's Sunday morning, the day after the school disco. Hannah and Megan are at Hannah's house. Did Hannah have a good time at the disco? Listen and read.

Megan	So how many people went to the disco?
Hannah	About three hundred, apparently. Shame you couldn't go.
Megan	I know, but I felt really ill. Anyway what happened? Who did you dance with?
Hannah	Oh, **loads of people**. Elliott, Razim, Emmett...
Megan	Not with Luke, then?
Hannah	Er... no...
Megan	Why not?
Hannah	Well, erm..., he was with someone.

Megan	Oh no! Who danced with Luke, Hannah?
Hannah	Kelly.
Megan	What? Kelly! But she's awful – she's selfish and grumpy and...
Hannah	I know, I know, but don't forget she's also...
Megan	Gorgeous?
Hannah	Exactly! Apparently, they left after about an hour.
Megan	Who told you that?
Hannah	Elliott told me.
Megan	**I'm gutted!** Hi, Razim. What's the matter?
Razim	Oh, nothing. It's just that... See you later.
Hannah	**What's up with him?**
Megan	I don't know!

Comprehension check

2 Put the facts in order. Write 1, 2, 3... in the spaces.

- **A** ___ Elliott told Hannah about Luke and Kelly leaving.
- **B** ___ Razim came to see Hannah, but left immediately.
- **C** ___ Hannah saw Luke with Kelly.
- **D** ___ Luke and Kelly left the disco.
- **E** ___ Hannah went to the disco.
- **F** ___ Megan visited Hannah on Sunday to find out about the disco.

Real talk

loads of people	un sacco di gente
I'm gutted!	Sono distrutta!
What's up with him?	Che cos'ha?

What do you think?

1 How do you think Megan feels?
2 Why do you think Razim left immediately?
3 Are discos good places to meet new people?

Grammar

Subject and object questions

Who danced with Luke? (*Who* = soggetto)
Who did you dance with? (*Who* = complemento)

How many people went to the disco?
(*How many people* = soggetto)
How many people did you see?
(*How many people* = complemento)

What happened? (*What* = soggetto)
What did you do? (*What* = complemento)

Quando le parole interrogative (*Who*, *What*, *How many*) sono il soggetto della frase, non si usa mai l'ausiliare.

 **WB p.216**

Grammar check

3 Write questions for these answers.

1 Spielberg directed the film *Schindler's List*. (Who?)
2 I met my friend Alex on Saturday night. (Who?)
3 My dad met me at the station. (Who?)
4 2,000 people ran the marathon. (How many?)
5 I saw a hundred people at the concert. (How many?)
6 An electrical problem caused the fire at the factory. (What?)
7 I had cereal and toast for breakfast. (What?)
8 Frank Whittle invented the jet engine. (Who?)

Pronunciation • -o

4a 🔊 **3.41** Listen to the different pronunciations of -*o*:

wh**o** /uː/   w**o**man /ʊ/   g**o** /əʊ/
fr**o**m /ɒ/   w**o**men /ɪ/   c**o**me /ʌ/

4b 🔊 **3.42** Listen to these sentences.

1 That w**o**man s**o**metimes g**o**es to my sh**o**p.
2 Wh**o** is fr**o**m D**o**ver?
3 Th**o**se w**o**men are c**o**ming to the c**o**ncert.
4 D**o**n't w**o**rry, it's **o**nly m**o**ney!

🔊 **3.43** Listen and repeat.

Speaking • Razim's in love

5 Write the questions.

1 Who/look/depressed?
   Who looks depressed?
2 Who/Razim/like?
3 What/Razim/want to do?
4 Who/Megan/like?
5 Who/idiot?
6 Who/Luke/go out with?
7 What/Elliott/think?
8 What/Elliott/suggest?

🔊 **3.44** Now listen to Elliott and Razim. In pairs. Answer the questions.

Speaking • Culture Quiz

6 Choose the correct answers.

1 Which actor comes from the UK?
a Robert Pattinson
b Johnny Depp

2 Who wrote the play *Macbeth*?
a Charles Dickens
b William Shakespeare

3 Who wrote *The Lord of the Rings*?
a J.R.R.Tolkien
b J.K.Rowling

4 Who directed the film *Avatar*?
a James Cameron
b Steven Spielberg

5 Who was the first woman to win an Oscar for Best Director?
a Jodie Foster
b Kathryn Bigelow

6 Who's the lead singer in the band Muse?
a Matt Bellamy
b Will Champion

7 Which actor played Harry Potter in the films?
a Ewan McGregor
b Daniel Radcliffe

8 Who won Wimbledon in 2010?
a Roger Federer
b Rafael Nadal

In pairs. Ask and answer to check your answers. Then think of 4 more questions to ask your classmates.

What's Ryan like?

1 🔊 **3.45** Megan and Hannah are talking about Hannah's Australian cousin, Ryan. What have Ryan and Razim got in common? Listen and read.

Megan So when's your cousin Ryan coming to see you?

Hannah In about two weeks.

Megan What's he like?

Hannah It's difficult to say because I don't really know him. He seems outgoing and very confident, but quite sensitive, too. He's also pretty intelligent! And **he's a good laugh**.

Megan What does he like doing? In his free time, I mean.

Hannah He likes playing football and basketball. He's very fit.

Megan What does he look like?

Hannah He's very tall and he's got brown, wavy hair. He looks a bit like Razim, actually.

Megan Do you fancy Razim?

Hannah He's very nice, but no, I don't. Do *you* fancy him?

Megan Yes, I do, actually. A little bit. But he's not interested in me.

Hannah Oh, yes he is!

Megan What makes you think that?

Hannah Well, remember yesterday in the kitchen? I think Razim was upset when he heard us talking about Luke. That's why he went away.

Megan Oh! Yes, I see what you mean...

Comprehension check

2 Complete the sentences with the correct names.

1 _____ is coming to visit _____ in two weeks' time.
2 _____'s description of _____ is very positive.
3 _____ looks a bit like _____ .
4 _____ thinks that _____ isn't interested in her.
5 _____ says that _____ fancies _____ .
6 _____ heard _____ and _____ talking about Luke.

Real talk

He's a good laugh	È divertente
I mean	Voglio dire
Oh, yes he is!	Sì che lo è!
What makes you think that?	Cosa te lo fa pensare?

What do you think?

1 Do you think Ryan sounds nice?
2 Do you prefer Luke or Razim?
3 What do you think's going to happen next?

Grammar

be like vs. look like vs. like

What + am/is/are + like?
What's Ryan like?   He's outgoing and confident.
Si usa per chiedere com'è qualcuno di carattere.

What + do/does + soggetto + look like?
What does he look like?
He's very tall and he's got long, brown, wavy hair.
Si usa per chiedere com'è qualcuno fisicamente.

What + do/does + soggetto + like (doing)?
What does he like doing?
He likes playing football.
Si usa per chiedere che cosa piace o non piace (fare) a qualcuno.

 **WB p.216**

Grammar check

3 Write questions and answers.

1 Hannah? cheerful/sensible
   What's Hannah like? She's cheerful and sensible.
2 your sister? play the piano/running
3 you? a bit/indecisive/quite/easy-going
4 your boyfriend? tall/long/black/hair
5 you? read/listen to music
6 your mum and dad? mum/very easy-going/dad/a bit uptight
7 they? play rugby/skateboard
8 Zoe? short/blonde/hair/good-looking

Word recall Personality adjectives

4 Write 5 positive and 5 negative adjectives to describe a person's personality.

Then write words to describe a person's appearance under these headings (see *Starter Book*, Lesson F):

Hair
Length	Colour	Quality
long	brown	wavy

Appearance
beautiful

Height
tall

Build
slim

Word note

Nelle descrizioni dei capelli, la lunghezza viene sempre per prima:

lunghezza – colore – qualità
She's got short, brown, wavy hair.

oppure: lunghezza – qualità – colore
She's got short, wavy, brown hair.

Famous people

5 Look at the photos. Choose one person and write a brief description (20–30 words) of his/her appearance and personality. Don't say who it is.

Rihanna

Tom Cruise

Simona Ventura

Will Smith

In pairs. Read your partner's description and guess who it is. Do you agree with the description? Why?/ Why not?

Speaking • My parents

6 In pairs. Describe your mum or dad. **T**

Example:
A My dad's tall and slim, and he's got short, black, straight hair and blue eyes. He's quite good-looking. Sometimes he's a bit grumpy, but he's usually quite cheerful.
B My dad's very different from that. He's...

Fast finishers!

Write a brief description of the person your partner described in Ex.6 (20–30 words).

Reading

1 Before you read • In pairs. Ask and answer the questions. **T**

1 What colour do you like on bedroom walls?
2 And in a living room? Why?
3 What's a good colour for a new scooter?
4 What colours are in fashion for clothes at the moment? Do you like them?

2 **3.46** While you read • Tick (✓) the colour (1–5) that you like best. Read the text and guess which colour matches each description. Write the colours in the spaces.

A Question of Colour

Psychologists say that the colours we like are often an indication of our personality.
Which of these colours do you like best?
Does the description correspond to your personality?

A

You are outgoing and an extrovert. You are a very busy, energetic person who wants to live a full life. Sometimes you are a little bit aggressive and impulsive. You like doing very
5 energetic sports like football, basketball and volleyball. You like being happy, but sometimes you aren't, and this makes you confused and upset. You get bored easily. You make **judgements** about other people very quickly
10 and you express your opinions openly.

B

You are quite ambitious and want to have a successful life. This is the colour of idealism. You are very intelligent and use your intelligence well. You are sometimes a bit
15 distant from other people, but you are not shy. Sometimes you feel uncomfortable when you are with other people, but the situation never gets **out of control**. You like being alone and you like doing solitary sports like running or
20 swimming.

C

You are a very sensible and well-balanced person. You say what you think, you like your freedom and you have lots of friends. You belong to lots of
25 organizations and clubs. You like going to parties and you love food! You like to have enough money to spend. Other people's opinions of you are important. You want people to like you and you
30 really like being with other people.

D

You want a calm and **orderly** life. You don't like mess and your homework is probably very **neat** and tidy! You are quite shy and introspective, and you work and study hard.
35 You enjoy studying and you are probably very successful at school. Sometimes you can be a little bit selfish and opinionated, but you accept responsibility and orders from other people. You are quite sensitive,
40 but you have control of your emotions.

E

You are very **strong-willed**, even a little obstinate at times. You are very conscientious and people like you because you are **reliable** and stable.
45 You don't like wasting money. You are good at solving problems and you are very rational and sensible. You don't like superficial people and you are very perceptive in your relationships.
50 Now check your answers at the bottom of the page!

3 Vocabulary • Look at the words in the text in bold. What do they mean? Write a translation.

1 judgements _____
2 out of control _____
3 orderly _____
4 neat _____
5 strong-willed _____
6 reliable _____

4 Comprehension check • Complete the table for each colour.

Colour	Key adjectives
green	
brown	
red	
blue	
yellow	

Speaking

5 In pairs. Ask and answer the questions. **T**

1 Do you agree with the description of yourself in the text? Which parts in particular?
2 Is the description for a different colour more appropriate for you? Why?
3 In pairs. Write 3 adjectives to describe your personality and 3 to describe your partner's.

In pairs. Compare lists. Are they different?

Listening

6 **3.47** Listen to Clare talking about herself and her brother Toby. Then listen to Toby describing himself and Clare. Tick (✓) the adjectives you hear.

modest ___	shy ___	neat ___	impulsive ___
brilliant ___	selfish ___	silly ___	tidy ___
outgoing ___	energetic ___	boring ___	lazy ___
cheerful ___	uptight ___	confident ___	sensible ___
grumpy ___	nice ___	intelligent ___	

Listen again and complete the table with the adjectives in the box.

Clare's description of Clare	
Clare's description of Toby	
Toby's description of Toby	
Toby's description of Clare	

Writing

7 Write a description of yourself (80–100 words). Include this information: **T**

- your height/build/hair/eyes
- 3 positive and 3 negative aspects of your personality

Answers: A3 B5 C1 D4 E2

Subject and object questions

1 Read the sentences and choose the correct alternative in the rule.

How many students went to the lesson?
How many people did they invite?

> Quando la parola interrogativa è **soggetto/ complemento** della frase non si usa l'**ausiliare/ il verbo**.

2 Use the words to write questions.

1 Who/invite/to lunch? (I invited Harry.)
2 How many/people/be/on the bus? (There are 50.)
3 What/you/do/last night? (I stayed at home.)
4 Who/go/match/with you? (My brother went with me.)
5 How many/hamburgers/you/eat every day? (I eat 3.)
6 Who/play/the guitar/in that band? (Phil Acton plays the guitar.)
7 What/cause/the accident? (A fallen tree caused it.)
8 Who/give/them/the money? (Katie gave it to them.)

be like vs. *like* vs. *look like*

3 Read the questions and answers. Then complete rules 1–3.

What are Hannah and Megan like? They're both very nice.
What does Jim look like? He's short and slim.
What do you like doing at weekends? I like going out with friends.

> 1 Chiedere che cosa piace fare a qualcuno:
> What + _____ + soggetto + like _____?
> 2 Chiedere che aspetto fisico ha qualcuno:
> What + do/does + _____ + _____ like?
> 3 Chiedere che carattere ha qualcuno:
> What + _____ + _____ + like?

4 Match the questions (1–5) to answers (a–e).

1 ___ What's Simon like?
2 ___ Does Petra look like Simon?
3 ___ Does Petra like skiing?
4 ___ What does Simon look like?
5 ___ What does Simon like doing?

a Yes, she does. They've got the same colour hair and eyes.
b No, she doesn't. She can't stand it.
c He likes going out with his friends.
d He's very generous and easy-going.
e He's got short, brown hair and green eyes.

Ordine degli aggettivi

5 Read the sentences and answer questions 1–2.

I've got long, blonde, curly hair.
He's got short, straight, black hair.

1 Nelle descrizioni dei capelli, quale di questi aggettivi viene per primo: colore, qualità, lunghezza? _____
2 L'ordine degli altri due aggettivi è fisso o flessibile? _____

6 Write the sentences in the correct order.

1 brown sister's hair got short straight my
2 hair blue I've red eyes and short got curly
3 black got green long and eyes hair she's straight
4 shoulder-length mum's got blonde her hair

Esercizi sommativi

7 Complete the dialogue between Tom and Harry with questions using the words in brackets.

Tom   Hi, Harry! [1]_____ (you/ have) a good holiday?
Harry   Yes, I did. It was fantastic!
Tom   [2]_____ (who/you/go) with?
Harry   I went camping in Greece with my friends Nick and William.
Tom   [3]_____ (what/you/do) on holiday?
Harry   I ate lots of good food and saw lots of interesting places.
Tom   [4]_____ (who/cook) the food?
Harry   Nick. He's a really good cook!
Tom   I don't think I know Nick. [5]_____ (what/he/like)?
Harry   He's very generous and he's a good laugh too.
Tom   No, I mean, [6]_____ (what/ he/look/like)?
Harry   Oh, sorry! He's tall and he's got short, black hair.
Tom   Oh, yes. I remember him now. [7]_____ (when/you/get) home?
Harry   This morning at five o'clock.
Tom   Five o'clock! [8]_____ (who/ meet/you) at the airport?
Harry   My dad met us. I'm really tired. I'm going to bed now.
Tom   I can imagine. See you tomorrow.

8 Translation • Translate the sentences into English.

1 Com'è Maria? È molto simpatica.
2 Quante persone hai invitato alla tua festa di compleanno sabato scorso?
3 Quante persone ti hanno dato un regalo?
4 Che cosa è successo?
5 Che aspetto ha il tuo nuovo fidanzato?
6 Chi ti ha invitato a cena ieri sera?
7 A loro che cosa piace fare il fine settimana?
8 Sam è molto alto. Ha i capelli lunghi, biondi e lisci e gli occhi marroni.

At the Lost Property Office

Dialogue 📹 VIDEO

1 🔊 **3.48** Charlotte left her rucksack on a bus last Friday. It's Saturday morning and she's at the Lost Property Office. Listen and answer the questions.

1 Which bus was Charlotte on?

_____

2 Where did she get on the bus?

_____

3 Where did she get off?

_____

4 What was in her rucksack?

_____

5 Did she get her rucksack back?

_____

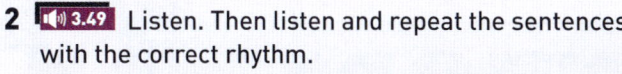

Say it right!

2 🔊 **3.49** Listen. Then listen and repeat the sentences with the correct rhythm.

Man	Good morning. Can I help you?
Girl	Yes. I left my <u>umbrella</u> on the <u>train</u> yesterday.
Man	Which <u>train</u> were you on?
Girl	I was on the <u>10.00 train</u> to <u>London</u>.
Man	And what does the <u>umbrella</u> look like?
Girl	It's a <u>big, blue umbrella with a black handle</u>.
Man	Just a minute. I'll have a look.
Man	I'm sorry. We haven't got your <u>umbrella</u> at the moment. Could you fill in this form, please?
Girl	OK. Here you are.
Man	Thanks. We'll be in touch.

In pairs. Practise the dialogue. When you finish, change roles.

Now close your books. Can you say the dialogue from memory?

Speaking

3 In pairs. Imagine you have lost something (a bag, a coat, a laptop, a phone). Change the information underlined in the dialogue in Ex.2 (object, means of transport, time). Act out the dialogue.

A You're the customer.
B You're the lost property office attendant.

When you finish, change roles.

Lost Property Form No.298

Address:
Mobile number:
Email address:
Date property was lost:
What was lost: Umbrella.
Colour of main item: Blue (black handle).
Further information:
... of travel: train.
... details: 10.00 to Lo...

A nation of inventors!

1 Inventions Quiz: When were these things invented?
Write the correct date under the photo (a–f).

| 1926 | 1989 | 1928 | 1823 | 1802 | 1871 |

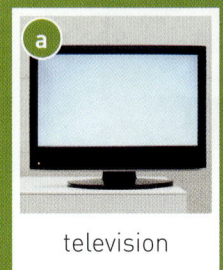
a
television
_____

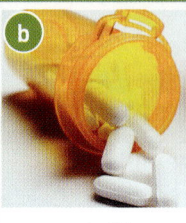
b
penicillin
_____

c
waterproof material
_____

d
World Wide Web
_____

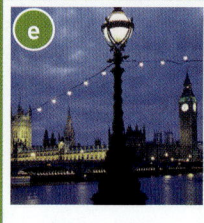
e
electric light
_____

f
penny-farthing
_____

2 What do all these inventors have in common?
Write the invention (a–f) next to the inventors.

1 ___ James Starley   3 ___ Tim Berners-Lee   5 ___ Humphry Davy
2 ___ Charles Macintosh 4 ___ John Logie Baird   6 ___ Alexander Fleming

Check your answers below.

> **Did you know?**
> About 80% of information on the World Wide Web is in English.

3 🔊 **4.02** Read the text. Then answer the questions below.

BRITISH INVENTORS

Britain is a nation of inventors! As you saw in the Quiz above, some of the most important inventions in the history of humanity came from Britain. Can you imagine a world without the Internet or television? Probably
5 not. And the tradition lives on. Here are two more inventors from the UK.

Kate Evans suffered from insomnia when she was a student. She designed a special light called the 'LightSleeper' to help her fall asleep.
10 Her <u>device</u> projects a white light onto the ceiling. When you look at it, your eyes follow the light and this relaxes your mind, helping you to fall asleep. It's so good that the government is considering
15 prescribing it for insomnia patients.

Emily Cummins was only 18 when she invented a fridge which works without electricity. She thought of the idea when she was working on
20 a school project. When she left school, she went to Africa and <u>perfected</u> her invention – a fridge which uses solar power to keep things cool. Just for the record, she also invented a water carrier, as lots of Africans have to carry water for long
25 distances every day. Back in the UK, she invented a toothpaste squeezer for people with arthritis.

| device | apparecchio |
| perfected | perfezionò |

1 Why did Kate Evans invent the LightSleeper?
2 Is the LightSleeper effective?
3 What did Emily Cummins invent?
4 Where did she finalize her invention?
5 What else did she invent?

Speaking

4 In pairs. Ask and answer the questions. **T**

1 Which invention on this page is the most important for you?
2 Are any modern inventions a bad thing for humanity? Which?
3 What invention(s) would you like to see in the future?

🎥 **VIDEO** Now watch the Network video!

Word builder

Clothes

1 Match the clothes (1–18) to the pictures (a–r).

1 ___ dress		10 ___ tracksuit	
2 ___ sweatshirt		11 ___ jumper	
3 ___ trainers		12 ___ coat	
4 ___ socks		13 ___ tights	
5 ___ boots		14 ___ cardigan	
6 ___ anorak		15 ___ scarf	
7 ___ skirt		16 ___ shoes	
8 ___ gloves		17 ___ hat	
9 ___ trousers		18 ___ shirt	

🔊 **4.03** Listen and repeat.

2 Translate the words into Italian.

1 shorts _____
2 T-shirt _____
3 sandals _____
4 swimming costume _____
5 jacket _____

🔊 **4.04** Listen and repeat.

Word note

Spesso si usa *a pair of* (= un paio di) con i sostantivi plurali:
socks/a pair of socks

3 Match the adjectives (1–9) to their translations (a–i).

1 ___ trendy	**a** economico
2 ___ smart	**b** comodo
3 ___ nice	**c** costoso
4 ___ boring	**d** fuori moda
5 ___ comfortable	**e** di moda
6 ___ expensive	**f** informale
7 ___ cheap	**g** banale
8 ___ old-fashioned	**h** carino
9 ___ casual	**i** elegante

Speaking • My clothes

4 In pairs. Ask and answer the questions. **T**

What do you wear...
1 when you go on a date with a new boyfriend or girlfriend?
2 when you go to school?
3 when you go out with your friends?
4 when you go on a summer holiday?
5 when it's very cold in winter?

⚠ I'm wearing a dress today. (~~I wear a dress~~)
Porto/Ho messo/Indosso un vestito oggi.

Dictation

5 🔊 **4.05** Listen and complete the sentences.

1 I like wearing _____ and _____.
2 Today I'm _____ a blue and _____.
3 I don't like _____.
   I prefer _____.
4 I wear _____, _____ when I go out _____.
5 At the beach I _____ and _____ or a _____.

✏ **WB p.227** Complete *Clothes* in the Word store.

99

They're more expensive

1 🔊 **4.06** Sam Mackenzie works in a sports shop in Edinburgh on Saturdays. His friends, Kali and Molly, are in the shop. Molly's buying some trainers. Where are the 2 pairs of trainers from? Listen and read.

Kali	Are they comfortable, Molly?
Molly	Yes, the black ones are more comfortable than the white ones.
Kali	Great! I think they're nicer than the white ones.
Molly	Mmm, but they're more expensive.
Sam	There's only £3 difference, but they're much better shoes. They're trendier than the others.
Molly	I can't make my mind up. I think they're a bit bigger than the white ones. Have you got the white ones in a larger size?
Sam	Yes, here you are.
Molly	That's better! These are fine. What do you think, Kali? Be honest.
Kali	They're OK, but they're not as nice as the others. And look! They're made in Indonesia.
Sam	What's the problem with that?
Kali	Well, we pay £60 for the trainers, but a lot of workers in factories in Indonesia earn a lot less than that a month. And they work 7 days a week. It's a rip-off for us, and I think it's wrong to buy them.
Molly	Yes, but all these trainers are the same. Look! Made in India, made in Vietnam, made in…
Sam	Actually, the black trainers are made in England. That's why they're more expensive. So, which trainers do you prefer, Molly?
Molly	I really don't know now…

Comprehension check

2 Answer the questions.

1 Which trainers are more expensive, the black pair or the white pair?
2 Which trainers does Sam prefer?
3 Which trainers does Kali prefer?
4 In Kali's opinion, why are the white trainers cheaper?

Real talk

I can't make my mind up	Non riesco a decidermi
Here you are	Ecco qua
Be honest	Dimmi la verità
It's a rip-off	Costa di più di quanto vale

What do you think?

1 Which trainers do you think Molly buys in the end?
2 What's more important to you when you're buying clothes, looks or comfort?
3 Do you ever think about where your clothes come from?

Grammar

Comparativo di maggioranza

Il comparativo di maggioranza si forma con l'aggettivo comparativo + *than*.
L'aggettivo comparativo si forma così:

1 Aggettivi monosillabi: + *-er/-r*
   (cheap) These trainers are **cheaper than** those trainers.
   (nice) They're **nicer than** the white pair.

2 Aggettivi monosillabi che terminano in vocale + consonante: si raddoppia la consonante + *-er*
   (big) They're a bit **bigger than** the white pair.

3 Aggettivi di 2 o più sillabe: *more* + aggettivo
   (comfortable) The black ones are **more comfortable than** the white pair.

4 Aggettivi bisillabi che terminano in *-er*, *-ow*, *-le*:
   + *-er*
   (clever) You're **cleverer than** me.

5 Aggettivi bisillabi che terminano in consonante + *-y*:
   si toglie la *-y*, + *-ier*
   (trendy) They're **trendier than** the others.

Alcuni aggettivi comparativi irregolari sono:
good – better   bad – worse   far – farther/further

Comparativo di uguaglianza e di minoranza

Per fare il comparativo di minoranza si usa:
not as + aggettivo + *as*
They are**n't as** nice **as** the others.
oppure:
less + aggettivo + *than*
They're **less** expensive **than** those shoes.

Per fare il comparativo di uguaglianza si usa:
as + aggettivo + *as*
We're **as** intelligent **as** them.

 **WB p.226**

Grammar check

3 Make comparisons using the adjectives in brackets.

1 my dad/me (tall) *My dad's taller than me.*
2 football/table tennis (exciting)
3 My parents' room/my room (tidy)
4 I/you (thin)
5 Norway/Italy (cold)
6 Indian food/Italian food (spicy)
7 sunny weather/rainy weather (good)
8 pollution in Milan/pollution in Orvieto (bad)

Now make comparisons using *not as... as*.

1 *I'm not as tall as my dad.*

Word note

Spesso si usa *much* prima di un aggettivo comparativo per intensificarne il significato.
Nick is much more intelligent than Dan.
Nick è molto più intelligente di Dan.

Per rendere meno forte il significato, si usa *a bit*.
This T-shirt is a bit smaller than the other.
Questa maglietta è un po' più piccola dell'altra.

Word recall Clothes

4 Choose an item of clothing that someone in the classroom is wearing. Write it down.
   In pairs. Take turns to guess your partner's item.

   Example:
   A Is it a smart skirt?
   B No, it isn't.
   A Is it a jacket?
   B Yes, it is.
   A Is it a casual, blue jacket?
   B Yes, it is.
   A It's Mario's jacket!

   When you finish, change roles.

Speaking • Comparing clothes

5 Look at the clothes in the pictures below.
   In pairs. Compare the clothes. T

   Example:
   A The beige trousers are more expensive than the jeans.
   B That's true! But the jeans are cooler than the beige trousers.
   A Yes, you're right.

Damian   Nathan   Emily   Rachel

The largest archipelago in the world

1 🔊 **4.07** Kali sends Sam an Internet link about Indonesia. What is the principal religion in Indonesia? Listen and read.

email from: Kali

Hi, Sam! **Seeing as you haven't got a clue about** Indonesia, where my parents are from, here's a link to a good website: www.travelblog/indonesia.

Indonesia

Indonesia is the largest archipelago (group of islands) in the world. Its 18,110 islands are in south-east Asia, but only 6,000 islands are inhabited. It's got a population of 230,000,000 and is the fourth biggest country in the world. It's also got the largest Muslim
5 population in the world – 86% of Indonesians are Muslim.

Indonesia's a fascinating country with an enormous range of fabulous wildlife, including Sumatran tigers, which can swim across rivers, orangutans, rhinoceroses, and amazing fruit bats that hang above your head in restaurants! There are monkeys everywhere. But the
10 most memorable of all animals is the terrifying Komodo dragon. It's the closest we can ever get to seeing a dinosaur…

There are also lots of sports activities on offer. Bali is the best place for water sports enthusiasts. You can go diving, snorkelling, surfing and fishing. Bali's got some of the longest beaches in the world. It's
15 the second most visited tourist destination in the world after Hawaii (in America). But tourists don't only come to Indonesia for the strange animals and the water sports. They also come because Indonesia has some of the most unusual and interesting dance and storytelling traditions in the world. And of course lots of tourists want to buy
20 some of the fantastic colourful clothes that Indonesians produce.

Indonesia is a tropical country, so it's got two seasons: the dry season from April to October, and the wet season from November to March. The dry season is the best time to visit. The worst time is the wet season – it's one of the wettest places in the world then!

25 Whatever time of year you visit Indonesia, you will always get **a warm welcome** – Indonesians are probably the friendliest people in the world!

Real talk

Seeing as…	Visto che…
You haven't got a clue about…	Non hai la più pallida idea di…
a warm welcome	un benvenuto caloroso

Comprehension check

2 True or false? Write T or F. Correct the false sentences. 🅿

1 ___ Indonesians don't live on all of the islands.
2 ___ Indonesia has a bigger population than Italy.
3 ___ Bali is a good place to go for a seaside holiday.
4 ___ Hawaii is one of the islands of Indonesia.
5 ___ June is a good time to visit Indonesia.

What do you think?

1 Do you think Indonesia sounds like a good place for a holiday?
2 Do you like the idea of going abroad or do you prefer to stay in Italy for your holidays?

Grammar

Superlativo relativo

Il superlativo relativo si forma con l'aggettivo superlativo preceduto da *the*.
L'aggettivo superlativo si forma così:

1 Aggettivi monosillabi: + *-est/-st*
   (long) **The longest** river is the Nile.
   (large) It's **the largest** archipelago in the world.

2 Aggettivi monosillabi che terminano in vocale + consonante: si raddoppia la consonante + *-est*
   (wet) **The wettest** place in the UK yesterday was Bath.

3 Aggettivi di 2 o più sillabe: *most* + aggettivo
   (comfortable) **The most interesting** place is Bali.

4 Aggettivi bisillabi che terminano in *-er, -ow, -le*:
   + *-est*
   (clever) She's the **cleverest student**.

5 Aggettivi bisillabi che terminano in consonante + *y*:
   si toglie la *-y*, + *-ier*

Alcuni aggettivi superlativi irregolari sono:
good – the best   bad – the worst
far – the farthest/the furthest

Per esprimere il superlativo relativo di minoranza, si usa *the least*.
It was **the least difficult** question in the test.
Era la domanda meno difficile del compito.

 **WB pp.226–227**

Grammar check

3 Complete the sentences with the superlative of the adjectives in the box.

| small   cheap   comfortable   hot   intelligent   funny |

1 We bought _____ sofa in the shop. Lovely!
2 Enrico is _____ boy in our class. He's a genius!
3 Vatican City is _____ country in Europe.
4 Catania is _____ city in Italy. It's often 38° there.
5 The Fiat Panda is one of _____ cars on the market.
6 Jim Carrey is one of _____ actors in the world. He always makes me laugh.

Pronunciation • Word stress

4a 🔊 **4.08** Listen to the stress in these words.

boring ●•   in**ter**esting ●••   ex**pen**sive •●•

4b 🔊 **4.09** Listen and mark the stressed syllable in these words.

exciting   old-fashioned   beautiful
different   unusual   trendy

🔊 **4.10** Listen and repeat.

Speaking • World records

5 Write questions about world geography.

1 high/mountain
   What's the highest mountain in the world?
2 long/river
3 populated/country
4 big/ocean
5 cold/place
6 big/continent
7 hot/place
8 large/lake

Word builder + Personality adjectives (2)

6 Match the words (1–6) to their Italian translations (a–f).

1 ___ talented   a giovane
2 ___ ugly   b divertente
3 ___ funny   c vecchio
4 ___ young   d di talento
5 ___ old   e carismatico
6 ___ charismatic   f brutto

✏️ **WB p.227** Complete *Personality adjectives (2)* in the Word store.

Speaking • Famous people

7 Complete the table with 2 names per category. Then write sentences using the adjectives from Ex.6. 🇹

Singer: *Rihanna/talented*
Rihanna's the most talented singer in the world.

| Singer/Group: |
| Politician: |
| Sportsperson: |
| Actor: |
| Other: |

In pairs. Read your sentences. Do you and your partner agree?

A I think Rihanna's the most talented singer in the world.
B Rihanna? Come on, she's not talented at all! I think Adele is much more talented.

Fast finishers!

Look at Ex.5 again. Write answers to questions 1, 2, 5, 7 and 8 with information about Italy.

The highest mountain in Italy is...

Reading

1 Before you read • Look at the names of the countries in the box. In pairs. Discuss the questions. 🔳

Republic of Congo	Luxembourg
Norway	Zimbabwe

1 Which are two of the richest and two of the poorest nations in the world?

2 The Republic of Congo and Zimbabwe are ex-colonies. Which countries once occupied them?

3 Why are some countries much poorer than others? List 3 reasons.

2 Read the Study skills. Then do Ex.3.

Study skills

Reading for specific information

Non è sempre necessario capire il significato di tutte le parole quando leggi un testo. Per esempio, quando leggi un testo sul risultato di una gara di MotoGP, probabilmente ti interessa sapere chi ha vinto, come si è piazzato il tuo pilota preferito e chi guida la classifica adesso. Probabilmente non ti interessano altre informazioni. Nell'esercizio che segue, devi concentrati soltanto sulle informazioni elencate. Non cercare di capire tutto l'articolo e non fermarti ad ogni vocabolo che non conosci.

3 🔊 4.11 While you read • Look at these names from the newspaper article. Read the article and match the names (1–7) to the descriptions (a–e).

1 ___ Vietnam

2 ___ Indonesia   **a** a famous person who supports fair trade

3 ___ Balthazar   **b** countries where they produce trainers

4 ___ USA   **c** places where people are criticizing shoe manufacturers

5 ___ The Fairtrade Foundation   **d** the name of an organization which helps workers

6 ___ Emma Watson   **e** the name of an Indonesian factory worker

7 ___ Europe

4 Vocabulary • Look at the words in bold in the article. Match them to their Italian translations.

1 equo   _____
2 pressione   _____
3 etichette   _____
4 (lavoro) straordinario   _____
5 stipendi più bassi   _____
6 trattano   _____

Topic of the week:

To buy or not to buy?

Do you wear trainers? Of course you do! Most teenagers wear trainers more than any other type of shoe.
5 But do you ever look at the **labels** on your trainers?

These days nearly all trainers are made in countries like
10 Vietnam and Indonesia. That's because global companies can pay the workers much **lower wages** than in Europe or the USA. This means the companies make a big profit when they sell the shoes in rich western countries. Let's take a
15 closer look at one of the countries where they make trainers.

Indonesia is a really wonderful place for a holiday, but everyday life is very difficult there because most Indonesians earn very little money. The legal
20 minimum wage in Jakarta is $122 a month, which isn't enough to buy food and clothes and pay the rent. And some people earn less than the minimum wage.

Balthazar is 17 years old and he works in a factory in
25 Jakarta, making trainers for a well-known American
company,

'I work 40 hours **overtime** a week, so I work about 80 hours a week altogether, but I only have just enough money to live on. And the supervisors in the factory **treat** us really badly.'

So is it all bad news for workers in developing countries? Fortunately not. Many people in the USA and Europe are putting **pressure** on western companies to improve workers' conditions in their
40 factories in developing countries. There are also organizations, selling products including food, clothes and cosmetics, which guarantee that the workers get a **fair** wage for their work.

One of these organizations is the Fairtrade
45 Foundation. Fair trade is about better prices, decent working conditions, local sustainability, and fair terms of trade for farmers and workers in the developing world. The UK is one of the world's most
50 important fair-trade markets. About 20% of coffee, and 20% of bananas sold in the UK are now fair-trade.

In 2010, Emma Watson, the actress who plays Hermione in the Harry Potter film series, started working with a fair-trade brand called *People Tree*.
55 She developed a line of fashionable clothes for teenagers called *Love from Emma*. The clothes come from Bangladesh, India and Nepal and the people who make the clothes get a fair wage for their work.

So next time you buy a pair of trainers or jeans, look
60 for the Fairtrade logo and make an ethical decision about what to buy!

5 **Comprehension check • Answer the questions.**

1 Why don't western manufacturers usually want to make trainers in their own countries?
2 Why is life difficult for most Indonesians?
3 What does Balthazar complain about?
4 What 2 things are some people in the West doing about unfair working conditions?
5 What does the Fairtrade Foundation do for workers in developing countries?
6 Who produces the clothes for Emma Watson's *Love from Emma* collection?

Speaking

6 **In pairs. Ask and answer the questions.** T

1 How much do you spend on clothes every month?
2 What's your most expensive item of clothing?
3 What's your favourite item of clothing? Why?
4 Where do you buy your clothes?
5 Do you ever buy your clothes on the Internet? Why?/Why not?
6 Did you know about fair-trade clothes?

Listening

7 **4.12** **Listen to George and Abigail discussing the questions in Ex.6. Who is more interested in clothes, George or Abigail?** _____

Listen again and choose the correct alternative. P

1 Abigail spends about £120/£20/£220 on clothes every month.
2 Abigail has got a part-time job in a **supermarket/ call centre/clothes shop**.
3 George spends about £120/£20/£220 on clothes every month.
4 George's most expensive item of clothing is a **coat/pair of trainers/jacket**.
5 Abigail's favourite dress cost £150/£100/£30.
6 George buys most of his clothes **at the market/ on the Internet/at outlet centres**.
7 George bought a pair of fair-trade **trainers/boots/ sandals** on the Internet.
8 Abigail doesn't buy many fair-trade clothes because she thinks they aren't very **cheap/ fashionable/nice**.

Writing

8 **Write a short text (80–100 words) about your clothes-shopping experiences. Use Ex.6 to help you. Also include information about:** T

- the most/least expensive shops in your area
- the most traditional/fashionable shops in your area

Comparativo di maggioranza, di uguaglianza e di minoranza

1 Read the sentences and complete rules 1–5.

This jacket is **warmer than** that jacket.
Orange juice is **nicer than** water.
Mexico City is **hotter than** London.
Your jacket was **more expensive than** my jacket.
John is **cleverer than** Dave.
My parents are **tidier than** me.
My jacket was **not as expensive as** your jacket.
My jacket was **less expensive than** your jacket.

> 1 Agli aggettivi monosillabi si aggiunge
> _____ o _____ all'aggettivo.
> 2 Agli aggettivi monosillabi che terminano in vocale + consonante , si raddoppia la _____ finale e si aggiunge _____.
> 3 Gli aggettivi di 2 o più sillabe sono preceduti da _____.
> 4 Agli aggettivi bisillabi che terminano in -er, -ow, -le si aggiunge _____.
> 5 Agli aggettivi di due sillabe che terminano in -y, si toglie la _____ e si aggiunge -ier.
> 6 Si forma il comparativo di minoranza usando *not as ...as* o _____ _____.

2 Write comparisons using the adjectives in brackets.

1 New York/Oxford (exciting)
2 Africa/India (big)
3 carrots/pizzas (tasty)
4 planes/trains (fast)
5 Johnny Depp/Jack Black (good-looking)
6 Maths tests/English tests (bad)
7 scooters/cars (expensive)
8 Mount Everest/Mont Blanc (high)

3 Complete the second sentence so it has the same meaning as the first.

1 His scooter is less expensive than your scooter.
His scooter isn't _____
2 Norway is less hot than Spain.
Spain's _____
3 Milan is less crowded than Tokyo.
Milan is _____
4 Italian is harder than English.
English isn't _____
5 Charlie Chaplin is less funny than Mr Bean.
Mr Bean _____

Superlativo relativo

4 Read the sentences and answer questions 1–6.

Mont Blanc is **the highest** mountain in Italy.
She's **the nicest** person in our school.
He's **the thinnest** boy in my class.
You're **the cleverest** student.

He's **the funniest** actor in the world.
This is **the most expensive** scooter in the shop.

> 1 Che cosa si premette agli aggettivi monosillabi? _____
> 2 Che cosa si aggiunge agli aggettivi monosillabi? _____ _____
> 3 Come si forma il superlativo relativo degli aggettivi monosillabi che terminano in vocale + consonante? _____
> 4 Che cosa si aggiunge agli aggettivi bisillabi che terminano in -er, -ow, -le? _____
> 5 Come si forma il superlativo relativo degli aggettivi bisillabi che terminano in -y?
> _____
> 6 Che cosa si premette agli aggettivi con 2 o più sillabe? _____

5 Complete the paragraph about Jakarta with the superlative of the adjectives in brackets.

Jakarta is the capital and [1]_____ (large) city in Indonesia. It is also [2]_____ (populated) city in south-east Asia. Jakarta is really a province which consists of five smaller cities – Central, West, South, East and North Jakarta. Central Jakarta is [3]_____ (small) city and is the political and administrative centre. You can find [4]_____ (famous) monuments here, including the Istiqlal Mosque. West Jakarta has [5]_____ (high) concentration of industry, while South Jakarta is [6]_____ (rich) part of the city, with lots of shopping centres and residential areas. Jakarta has a tropical climate. January is [7]_____ (wet) time of year, with an average monthly rainfall of 385mm. [8]_____ (dry) month of the year is July.

Esercizi sommativi

6 Follow the instructions and write the dialogue in your exercise book.

You	[1]Chiedi a Katie dov'era ieri.
Katie	[2]Di' che sei andata al nuovo centro commerciale.
You	[3]Chiedi che cosa ha comprato Katie.
Katie	[4]Di' che hai comprato due maglie.
You	[5]Chiedi se puoi vederle.
Katie	[6]Di' di sì. Chiedi quale preferisce.
You	[7]Di' che ti piace quella blu. Dì che è davvero carina.

7 Translation • Translate the sentences into English.

1 Marco è il ragazzo più alto della mia classe.
2 Londra è più grande di Roma.
3 Il Po non è lungo quanto il Nilo.
4 Ben Nevis è la montagna più alta del Regno Unito.
5 Usain Bolt era l'atleta più veloce del mondo nel 2010.
6 Qual è la città più grande d'Italia?

HELPING OUT

Word builder

UPSTAIRS

DOWNSTAIRS

OUTSIDE

Rooms and furniture

1 Look at the picture. Match the rooms (1–8) to the words.

___ bathroom   ___ garage   ___ bedroom   ___ dining room
___ living room   ___ garden   ___ kitchen   ___ study

🔊 **4.13** Listen and repeat.

2 Find this furniture in the house. Check the meanings in the glossary.

bed	table	desk	chair	armchair
sofa	bookcase	wardrobe	fridge	washing machine

🔊 **4.14** Listen and repeat.

In pairs. Ask and answer questions.

Example:
A Where's the washing machine?
B It's in the kitchen.

Housework

3 Match the jobs (1–11) to the activities in the house (a–k).

1 ___ do the washing
2 ___ do the ironing
3 ___ make (my) bed
4 ___ tidy (my) bedroom
5 ___ take out the rubbish
6 ___ do the washing-up
7 ___ clear the table
8 ___ cut the grass
9 ___ hoover (the living room)
10 ___ do the shopping
11 ___ feed the cat

🔊 **4.15** Listen and repeat.

> ⚠️ do the shopping = *fare la spesa (cibo, detersivi, ecc.)*
> go shopping = *fare compere, fare shopping (vestiti, ecc.)*

Speaking • My jobs

4 Who does the jobs in your house? In pairs. Ask and answer questions. **T**

Example:
A Who tidies the living room in your house?
B My mum and dad tidy the living room.

When you finish, change roles.

Dictation

5 🔊 **4.16** Listen and write the 5 sentences.

1 _____
2 _____
3 _____
4 _____
5 _____

WB p.233 Complete *Rooms and furniture* and *Housework* in the Word store.

It's mine!

1 🔊 **4.17** It's Monday morning and Sam and Kali are at school. Whose mobile was on the desk? Listen and read.

1 This is the right room, isn't it, Kali?

Yeah, we've got Maths now.

Whose mobile is that?

Oh, thanks. It's mine.

2 Hey! That mobile isn't yours. It's mine.

No, it isn't. It's an L55. It's mine. Get off!

Hey! Don't push me!

3 What's going on here? What are you fighting about, Daniel?

He took my mobile, sir.

Is that true, Sam?

No, it isn't. This is *my* mobile.

Now, come on. Whose mobile is it?

4 It's mine. Oh... Here's mine. It's in my pocket. That mobile *is* his. Sorry!

And I'm sorry, Sam, but we don't tolerate bullying here. Come with me...

Comprehension check

2 Complete the sentences with the correct names.

1 _____ saw a mobile on a desk in the classroom.
2 _____ and _____ argued about the mobile.
3 _____'s phone was in his pocket.
4 _____ apologised to Daniel.
5 _____ thinks Sam is a bully.

Real talk

Get off!	Giù le mani!/Vai via!
What's going on?	Che cosa sta succedendo?

What do you think?

1 Do you think Sam's a bully?
2 Is bullying a problem in your school?
3 What's the best treatment for bullies?

Grammar

Whose e i pronomi possessivi

Ci sono due modi di formulare la domanda con *whose*:

Whose mobile is that?
Whose is that mobile?

Non c'è nessuna differenza nel significato.

Alle domande con *whose* si risponde usando i pronomi possessivi o il genitivo sassone del possessore.

Whose mobile is that?

It's **mine**.	It's **ours**.
It's **yours**.	It's **theirs**.
It's **his**.	(It's **Oliver's**.)
It's **hers**.	

WB p.232

Grammar check

3 Write questions and answers.

1 whose/pen/this? (I)
Whose pen is this? It's mine.

2 whose/those/books? (she)
_____

3 whose/camera/it? (we)
_____

4 whose/this/pullover? (Jessica)
_____

5 whose/these/sunglasses? (he)
_____

6 whose/that/scooter? (Chris)
_____

7 whose/house/this? (Mark and Tom)
_____

8 whose/rollerblades/these? (I)
_____

Pronunciation • Silent *w-*

4a 🔊 **4.18** Listen. Notice the silent *w-* in these words.

whose /huːz/   write /raɪt/

4b 🔊 **4.19** Listen and underline the words with a silent *w-*.

1	walk	4	when
2	went	5	wrote
3	wrong	6	who

🔊 **4.20** Listen and check. Listen and repeat.

Speaking • Whose is it?

5 Match the people (1–6) to their possessions (a–f).

In pairs. Take turns to ask and answer questions.

Example:
A Whose is that jacket?
B I think it's his – number 3.
A Why?
B Because he looks very trendy.

Speaking • Whose pen is it?

6 Play this game:

1 Everyone give an object (a pencil, a book, a mobile...) to your teacher.
2 Your teacher puts the objects in a bag.
3 The teacher then takes an object out of the bag and asks questions.

Example:

Teacher	Whose pen is this?
Student	It's Francesca's.
Teacher	Is this MP3 player Edoardo's?
Student	No, it's mine!

Can I borrow £15?

1 🔊 **4.21** Sam and his dad are in the garage. What does Sam want from his dad? Listen and read.

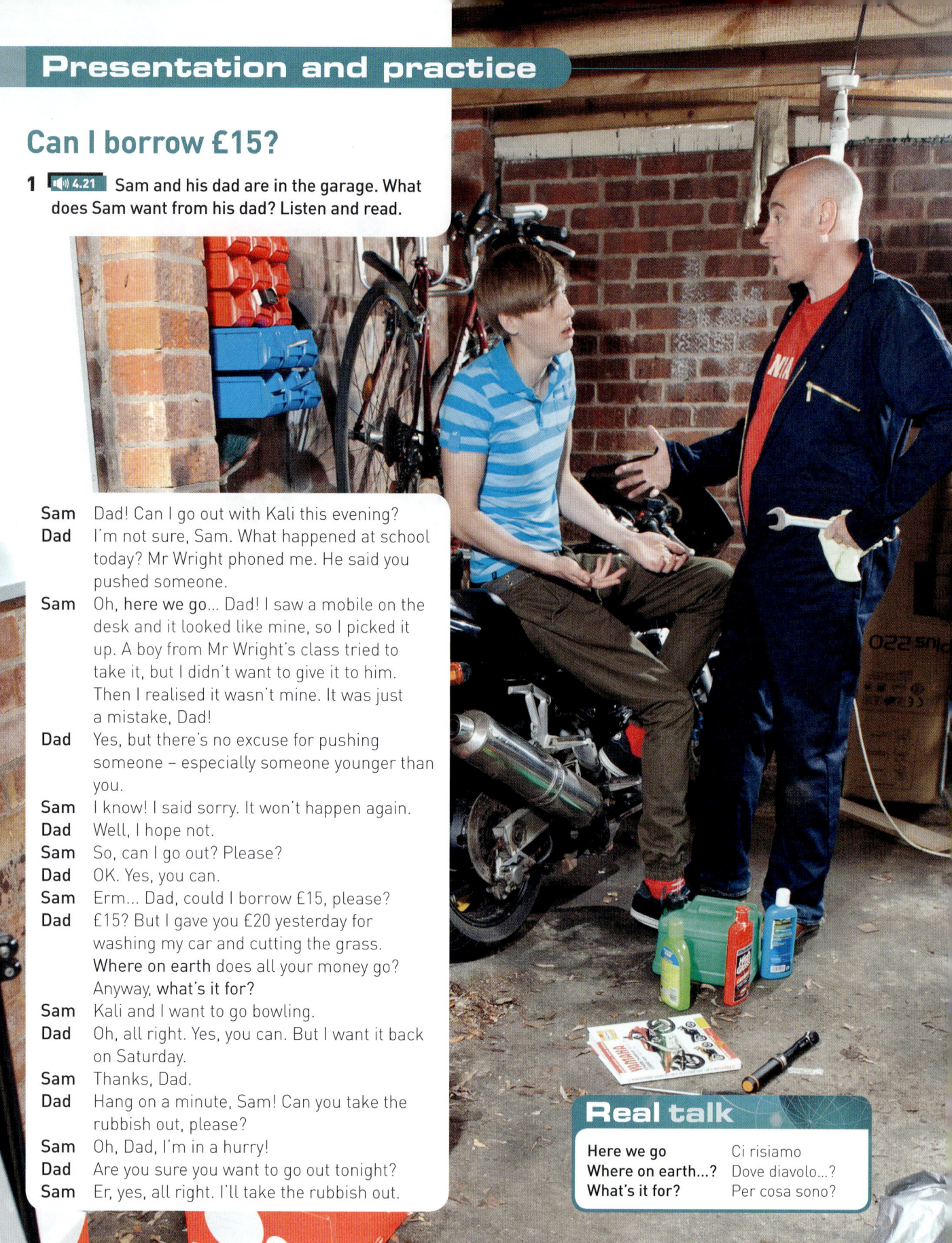

Sam Dad! Can I go out with Kali this evening?

Dad I'm not sure, Sam. What happened at school today? Mr Wright phoned me. He said you pushed someone.

Sam Oh, here we go... Dad! I saw a mobile on the desk and it looked like mine, so I picked it up. A boy from Mr Wright's class tried to take it, but I didn't want to give it to him. Then I realised it wasn't mine. It was just a mistake, Dad!

Dad Yes, but there's no excuse for pushing someone – especially someone younger than you.

Sam I know! I said sorry. It won't happen again.

Dad Well, I hope not.

Sam So, can I go out? Please?

Dad OK. Yes, you can.

Sam Erm... Dad, could I borrow £15, please?

Dad £15? But I gave you £20 yesterday for washing my car and cutting the grass. Where on earth does all your money go? Anyway, what's it for?

Sam Kali and I want to go bowling.

Dad Oh, all right. Yes, you can. But I want it back on Saturday.

Sam Thanks, Dad.

Dad Hang on a minute, Sam! Can you take the rubbish out, please?

Sam Oh, Dad, I'm in a hurry!

Dad Are you sure you want to go out tonight?

Sam Er, yes, all right. I'll take the rubbish out.

Real talk

Here we go	Ci risiamo
Where on earth...?	Dove diavolo...?
What's it for?	Per cosa sono?

Comprehension check

2 Choose the correct alternative.

1 Sam's **teacher/mother** phoned his dad about Sam's argument at school.
2 Sam's dad **accepts/doesn't accept** Sam's apology.
3 Sam asks his dad to **lend/give** him £15.
4 Sam's dad gave Sam **£15/£20** the day before.
5 In the end, Sam **agrees/refuses** to take the rubbish out.

What do you think?

1 Do you think that Sam's dad was strict enough?
2 Do you borrow money from your parents? Do you always pay it back?
3 Do you help your parents with the housework?

Grammar

Verbi modali • *can, could* e *may*

Chiedere un permesso

Informale

Can I go out, please?
Yes, you can./No, you can't./I suppose so.

Più cortese

Could I borrow £15, please?
Yes, OK./No, sorry, I gave you £20 yesterday.

Molto formale

May I go home early today, please?
Yes, you may./No, you may not.

Fare una richiesta

Molto informale

Can you take the rubbish out?
Yes, all right./Sorry, I'm in a hurry.

Più cortese

Could you clear the table, please?
Yes, of course./No, sorry, I'm busy.

> ✏ **WB pp.232–233**

---

 lend or borrow?
lend = *prestare*   He lent me his book.
borrow = *prendere in prestito*   I borrowed his book.

Grammar check

3 Write sentences asking for permission or making requests. Sometimes there is more than one possibility.

1 It's very hot in your classroom. (you to your teacher)
   Could I open the window, please?
2 You haven't got any money. The bus ticket is €5. (you to your best friend)
3 After dinner there are lots of dirty dishes in the kitchen. (your mum to you)
4 You're at the cinema. The woman next to you receives lots of phone calls. (you to the woman)
5 There's a concert this evening. (you to your dad)
6 You've got a dentist's appointment during school. (you to your teacher)
7 Your cat is hungry. You're late for school. (you to your brother)
8 You haven't got a dictionary. You don't understand a word. (you to your friend)

Speaking • Asking for permission

4 Match the verbs (1–6) to the phrases (a–f).

1	_e_ share	a	a pencil
2	___ open	b	to the toilet
3	___ move	c	with Alessandra
4	___ work	d	the window
5	___ borrow	e	Marco's book
6	___ go	f	closer to the blackboard

In pairs.
A: you're the student. Ask permission to do the things you matched (1–6).
B: you're the teacher. Give or refuse permission. Give a reason if you refuse.

Example:
A Could I go to the toilet, please?
B Yes, of course you can.

When you finish, change roles.

Word recall Housework

5 Write the housework jobs in the spaces.

1 _____

2 _____

3 _____

4 _____

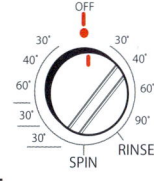
5 _____

6 _____

7 _____

8 _____

9 _____

Can you think of any more types of housework?

Speaking • Making requests

6 🔊 **4.22** Listen to the 4 conversations and write the requests you hear.

1 _____
2 _____
3 _____
4 _____

Listen again. What excuses do they make?

In pairs.
A: make requests using the housework list in Ex.5.
B: refuse and invent some good excuses. Change roles after each request.

Example:
A Can you make your bed, please?
B Sorry, but I've got a dentist's appointment in ten minutes.

Fast finishers!

Write the requests and excuses that you made in Ex.6.

Speaking

1 In pairs. Ask and answer the questions. **P T**

1 How do you get your money?
2 Do your parents ever pay you to do jobs in the house?
3 How much money do you spend a week?
4 What do you spend your money on?
5 Do you save any money?

Listening

Ella

Thomas

2 **◄)) 4.23** Read the questions. Listen to Ella and Thomas talking about money. Who does the interviewer ask each time? Write E, T or E+T (both) in the spaces.

1 ___ Do you get any pocket money from your parents?
2 ___ What do you do?
3 ___ What do you do specifically?
4 ___ How much do you earn every week?
5 ___ Do you save any money?
6 ___ What do you spend your money on?
7 ___ How do you get your money?
8 ___ How much do you earn every month?

Listen again. Write down Ella and Thomas's answers to the questions above.

In pairs. Compare your answers.

MAKING MONEY ONLINE

Going out in the evening, buying clothes, going on holiday, topping up your mobile… all these cost money. But where do you get it from? From your parents? From
5 your grandparents? Or do you work for it? *Network* spoke to two British teenagers who make their money online.

SOPHIE

My parents don't give me any pocket
10 money because my dad's unemployed at the moment and they haven't got much money. I found a really good way of making money last year. I take part in Internet surveys online.
15 It works like this: big companies which produce things for teenagers like mobiles, clothes and magazines, need to know what teenagers like and don't like. They pay agencies to collect this information for them. The agencies pay young
20 people to do the surveys online. Simple, eh? In practice, you don't get much for each survey, between 50p and £2 and they don't send you hundreds of surveys, but you can make enough pocket money if you do twenty surveys a week, like
25 me. Some of the surveys are quite interesting, too.

JAMES

I get about £10 a week pocket money and I do a few jobs around the house, so my parents give me a bit more, but it's not enough. I mean, when you go out with your mates it costs about £15 to get into a club!

30 So I've found a way to make more money. I'm really into computers, so I work online. I make quite a lot of money selling things on online auctions. It isn't hard. For example, when people buy an MP3 player at their local hypermarket, they sometimes

35 return it because they don't like it or because they find a better one somewhere else. I go to one of the big local supermarkets and buy a big box of stuff that people return to the shop. I pay a fixed price and I don't usually know what I'm buying exactly.

40 They're usually electrical goods like hairdryers, MP3 players and computer accessories. First I check that everything works and throw away the broken stuff, then I put the things on sale for auction on the web. I make about £150 a month and I reinvest most of the

45 money to buy more stuff to sell, but I spend quite a lot too.

Other ideas for making money online include translating documents, testing computer games by playing them, and

50 sponsored blogging, where they pay you for putting advertisements on your blog. So, don't sit around complaining about having no money. Use your imagination and get online!

Reading

3 **Before you read • In pairs. Ask and answer the questions.** 🅣

1 What do you use the Internet for?
2 Do you ever buy or sell things on the Internet?
3 How do you think people can make money using the Internet?

4 🔊 **4.24** **While you read • Read the article. Match the names to the online activities.**

	___ translating
Sophie	___ taking photos
James	___ selling things at auctions
	___ blogging
	___ playing computer games
	___ answering survey questions

5 **Vocabulary • Underline 6 words in the article that you don't know.**

1 Guess the meaning from the context and write a translation.
2 Check your answers in the glossary.

6 **Comprehension check • True or false? Write T or F. Correct the false sentences.** 🅟

1 ___ Sophie's family have got money problems.
2 ___ Big companies pay Sophie to do online surveys.
3 ___ Sophie does about twenty surveys a week.
4 ___ James repairs the electrical goods before he sells them.
5 ___ James makes about £400 a month.
6 ___ James spends all the money he earns.

Writing

7 **Write a short text (80–100 words) about where your money comes from and how you spend it. Use your answers to the questions in Ex.1 and Ex.2 to help you.** 🅣

I haven't got much money. My parents give me €10 pocket money a week and...

Whose...?

1 Read the questions and complete rules 1–2.

Whose pen is that?
Whose pencils are those?
Whose is that pen?
Whose are those pencils?

> Le domande con *Whose* si possono formare in due modi:
> 1 *Whose* + _____ + _____ + *this/that/these/those* + ?
> 2 *Whose* + _____ + *this/that/these/those* + _____ + ?

2 Write 2 questions with *whose + this/that/these/those* for these answers.

1 That's Martin's bike.
   Whose bike is that?/Whose is that bike?
2 These are James's DVDs.
3 That's my laptop.
4 This is Sue's watch.
5 Those are Sal and Peter's chocolates.
6 These are our books.
7 That is Vincent's T-shirt.
8 These are your socks.

Pronomi possessivi

3 Complete the table.

Aggettivi possessivi	Pronomi possessivi
my	4
1	yours
his	5
2	hers
our	6
3	theirs

4 Write answers to the questions in Ex.2 using possessive pronouns.

1 Whose bike is that? *It's his.*

Verbi modali • *can, could* e *may*

5 Read the sentences and answer questions 1–6.

Can I go to the party this evening?
Could I use your mobile, please?
May I look at your newspaper?
Can you make your bed, please?
Could you do the shopping, please?

> Quale verbo modale si usa per:
> 1 chiedere un permesso in modo informale?
>   _____
> 2 chiedere un permesso in modo cortese?
>   _____
> 3 chiedere un permesso in modo molto formale?
>   _____
> 4 fare una richiesta in modo informale? _____
> 5 fare una richiesta in modo cortese? _____
> 6 Quale forma del verbo segue *can, could* e *may*?
>   _____

6 Make a request or ask permission for each situation.

1 It's cold in your classroom. The window's open.
   _____
2 You don't know a word in an English lesson. You haven't got a dictionary.
   _____
3 It's Saturday and all your friends are going out.
   _____
4 You need €10 for your train ticket. You're with a friend.
   _____
5 You miss the last bus home from the station. You see your friend's father.
   _____
6 You're at your friend's house and you would like a glass of water.
   _____

Esercizi sommativi

7 Complete the dialogue with questions in the box.

> What time is it?   Can you meet me there?
> What's the dentist's address?
> What's your mobile number?
> Could I borrow it?   Whose is that bike?
> Where are you going now?   Can you phone me

Gerry ¹_____
Tom It's half past three.
Gerry Oh no! ²_____
Tom It's mine.
Gerry ³_____
Tom Yes, of course. Why?
Gerry I'm seeing the dentist at 4.00 and I'm late.
Tom ⁴_____
Gerry It's 14 Carlton Road.
Tom ⁵_____ when you leave there?
Gerry OK. ⁶_____
Tom It's 237525175.
Gerry ⁷_____
Tom I'm going to the library. ⁸_____
Gerry OK. See you later at the library.

8 Translation • Translate the sentences into English.

1 Di chi sono quelle matite? Sono di Marco.
2 Potresti prestarmi il tuo cellulare?
3 Posso spegnere il televisore per favore? Sì.
4 Di chi è quella giacca? È la mia.
5 Potresti sparecchiare per favore?
6 Puoi dare da mangiare al coniglio, per favore?
7 Di chi sono queste borse? Sono le loro!

Shopping for clothes

Dialogue 🎥 VIDEO

1 🔊 4.25 Rick goes into a clothes shop. He wants to buy a new shirt. Complete the dialogue with the questions in the box.

Have you got a smaller one?	How much is it?
Do you accept credit cards?	What colour is it?
What size are you?	Can I help you?

Woman	Hi there! 1 _____
Rick	Hello. Yes, I saw a really cool shirt in the window.
Woman	2 _____
Rick	It's blue.
Woman	One moment, please. ... Here it is. 3 _____
Rick	Large, I think.
Woman	Large? Here you are. Try this on.
Rick	It's a bit big. 4 _____
Woman	Yes, this one's a medium.
Rick	Ah, that's better.
Woman	Yes, it really suits you.
Rick	5 _____
Woman	It's £39.99.
Rick	OK. I'll take it. 6 _____
Woman	Yes, we do. You can pay over there at the cash desk.
Rick	Thanks.

🔊 4.26 Listen and check.

Say it right!

2 🔊 4.27 Listen. Then listen and repeat the sentences with the correct rhythm.

Woman	Can I help you?
Glen	Yes, I'd like to try on those <u>red trousers</u>, please.
Woman	Certainly. What size are you?
Glen	I'm a <u>medium</u>.
Woman	Here you are.
Glen	How much are they?
Woman	They're <u>£30</u>.
Glen	I'll take them.
Woman	Fine. Can you pay at the cash desk, please?

In pairs. Practise the dialogue. When you finish, change roles.

Now close your books. Can you say the dialogue from memory?

Speaking

3 In pairs. Use the photos to change the information underlined in the dialogue in Ex.2. Act out the dialogue. When you finish, change roles.

£79.99

£68

£28.50

£130

School uniforms in the UK

1 🔊 4.28 Read the text. Then answer the questions below.

Have your say: school uniform

In the UK most students wear a school uniform, but teachers, parents and students often disagree about whether uniforms are a good idea or not. Read what two students at a London comprehensive school say about their uniforms.

KATIE

'I don't really like wearing a school uniform. It's boring to wear the same clothes every day. Our uniform is a white shirt or T-shirt, and a V-neck, dark blue sleeveless jumper, and a dark blue blazer. The blazer's got the school badge on the pocket. We can wear either a dark blue and green tartan skirt or trousers. I wear blue shoes (not trainers) and blue socks. I'm seventeen and I'm in the sixth form, so I don't wear a school tie. When you're seventeen, you want to be creative with your clothes and express your individuality. Uniforms limit your freedom and they're also quite expensive. They're awful!'

TOM

'My uniform's similar to Katie's: a white shirt, a blue V-neck jumper and a blue blazer. Black trousers, black shoes or black trainers and grey socks. I'm sixteen, so I wear a school tie. Do I like it? Yes, I do, actually. I hate deciding what to wear in the morning, so a uniform's really handy! And of course the fact that you can't wear designer clothes means that you don't know who's rich and who's poor at school. That's a good thing. I think I'm a better student because of my uniform. It's like wearing special clothes to go to work – you take everything more seriously.'

So, what do you think? Are you for or against school uniforms?

1 Where do Katie and Tom go to school?
2 Why doesn't Katie like her school uniform?
3 Why does Tom like his school uniform?
4 What differences are there between girls' and boys' uniforms?
5 Why doesn't Katie wear a school tie?

Speaking

2 In pairs. Ask and answer the questions. **P T**

1 What do you usually wear to school?
2 How long do you spend choosing your clothes in the morning?
3 Are you for or against school uniforms?

🎥 **VIDEO** Now watch the Network video!

Did you know?

In the UK 'public schools' are, in fact, private. *Eton* and *Harrow* are probably the most famous public schools.

Word builder

London, England 8°C

Sydney, Australia 27°C

Quebec, Canada -10°C

Chicago, USA 10°C

Cork, Ireland 12°C **FOG**

Darwin, Australia 32.5°C

The weather

1 What's the weather like in these cities today? Match the sentences (1–6) to the photos (a–f).

1 ___ It's boiling hot and there's thunder and lightning.
2 ___ It's windy and it's quite cold.
3 ___ It's freezing and it's snowing.
4 ___ It's not very warm and it's wet and foggy.
5 ___ It's cloudy and it's raining.
6 ___ It's hot, sunny and dry.

🔊 **4.29** Listen and repeat. Then translate the sentences in your exercise book.

Speaking • What's the weather like?

2 Look at the photos again and try to remember the weather for each city. In pairs. B: cover the photos. A: ask questions.

Example:

A What's the temperature in Chicago?
B It's ten degrees.
A Is it raining?
B No, it isn't, but it's quite cold and windy.

When you finish, change roles.

Speaking • Talking about the weather

3 In pairs. Ask and answer questions about what you did the last time... **T**

1 it snowed.
2 it rained.
3 it was freezing.
4 it was foggy.
5 it was boiling hot.
6 there was thunder and lightning.

A What did you do the last time it snowed?
B I made a snowman and I went skiing. What did you do?

Dictation

4 🔊 **4.30** Some words are missing from these sentences. Listen and write the complete sentences.

1 It's cold today and it's raining.
_____

2 It's hot this morning.
_____

3 It's wet today and it's twelve degrees.
_____

4 It's cold and it's snowing here in Geneva today.
_____

WB p.243 Complete *The weather* in the Word store.   117

I'm going to work in Rome

1 🔊 **4.31** It's Wednesday and Sam and his sister, Fiona, are shopping in Edinburgh after school. Why do they have an argument? Listen and read.

Fiona Brrr! Are you going to play football this afternoon?

Sam No, I'm not. It's raining. This weather's really getting me down!

Fiona Yes, me too.

Sam I can't wait to go to Rome. At least it's always sunny there.

Fiona Rome? What do you mean?

Sam I'm going to Rome this summer.

Fiona What are you going to do there?

Sam I'm going to work in a café.

Fiona Huh! What do Mum and Dad think about it?

Sam I discussed it with them last night. They're not very happy about it, but they aren't going to stop me.

Fiona That's not fair! When I asked to work in Glasgow last summer, they said no!

Sam Yes, but you're a girl.

Fiona 'You're a girl?' What difference does that make? I don't believe it!

Sam I'm sorry. Let's not argue. Listen, Kali's going to buy tickets for the Glasvegas concert on Saturday. Do you want to come?

Fiona Yes, OK. But you can pay for me.

Sam Are you sure you want to come?

Fiona Sam!

Sam Only joking...

Real talk

is... really getting me down!	...mi sta buttando giù di morale!
I can't wait...	Non vedo l'ora...
That's not fair!	Non è giusto!

Comprehension check

2 True or false? Write T or F. Correct the false sentences. P

1 ___ Sam isn't going to play football because of the weather.
2 ___ Sam's going to work in Rome in the summer.
3 ___ Sam's parents don't want him to go to Rome.
4 ___ Fiona worked in Glasgow last summer.
5 ___ Sam's going to buy tickets for a concert.

What do you think?

1 Do you think Sam and Fiona's parents treated Fiona unfairly?
2 Do Italian parents treat boys and girls differently?
3 Do you like the idea of working in a different town in the summer?

Grammar

be going to (1) • Intenzioni

Forma affermativa
Kali**'s going to** buy tickets for a concert.

Forma negativa
I**'m not going to** have a birthday party.

Forma interrogativa e risposte brevi
Are they **going to** play football today?
Yes, they **are**./No, they **aren't**.
What**'s** he **going to** do there?

Si usa *be going to* per esprimere un'intenzione.

 **WB p.242**

Grammar check

3 Write sentences with the correct form of *be going to*.

1 I/not/spend next weekend at home
2 Robert/leave school at the end of the year
3 they/come to your party on Saturday night?
4 we/not/study German next year
5 you/meet me outside school?
6 I/send you my email address later
7 she/lend me her bicycle for the holidays
8 they/not play volleyball this evening
9 he/buy/new sunglasses
10 Dad/hoover the living room?
11 the students/not/wear a uniform
12 I/not/see Sally tomorrow

Grammar note

Ci sono vari modi di esprimere il futuro in inglese.
• Si usa il *Present simple* per parlare di orari.
• Si usa il *Present continuous* quando l'azione è gia programmata e chi parla è sicuro che succederà.
• Si usa *be going to* quando si tratta di un'intenzione.
Anna**'s having** a party on Saturday night after the concert. The concert **ends** at 11. I**'m going to** invite Joe.

Spesso, nella lingua parlata, con i verbi *go* e *come*, invece di *be going to* + *go/come*, si usa semplicemente il *Present continuous*.
I'm going to Joe's house. = I'm going to go to Joe's house.

 **WB p.243**

4 🔊 **4.32** Listen to 2 teenagers talking about what they are going to do next summer. Complete the first column in the table.

	is going to...	isn't going to...
Rebecca		
Dan		

Listen again and complete the second column.

In pairs. Ask and answer questions to check your answers.

Example:
A What's Rebecca going to do next summer?
B She's going to..., but she isn't going to...

Pronunciation • Weak *to*

5a 🔊 **4.33** Listen to the schwa /ə/ pronunciation of *to*.

He's going **to** /tə/ leave now.
I'm going **to** /tə/ Rome.

5b 🔊 **4.34** Listen to these sentences.

1 They're going **to** do the housework.
2 He's going **to** buy a phone.
3 She's going **to** have a party.
4 We're going **to** land at Gatwick.

🔊 **4.35** Listen and repeat.

Speaking • Next summer

6 What are you going to do next summer?
In pairs. Ask and answer the questions. 🅣

Example:
A What are you going to do next summer?
B I'm going to the USA.
A Great! Which cities are you going to visit?
B I'm going to visit Los Angeles and San Francisco.
A Lucky you! And who are you going with?

Fast finishers!

Write 6 sentences about your intentions for next summer. Write 3 things you're going to do and 3 things you aren't going to do.

We're going to be late!

1 🔊 **4.36** It's Saturday night. Sam, Fiona, Kali and Molly are at the stadium to see Glasvegas. Why is Sam a bit worried? Listen and read.

Get a move on, Sam!

Yeah! It's ten to nine. We're going to be late!

Wow! It's really full. Where shall we go?

Let's go to the back.

Yes, you can see more from there.

Hang on. I just want to get something to drink.

DRINKS

Great! We're just in time.

Yeah. Hey, the band's coming on stage. The concert's going to start now.

Oh no! Look at the sky! It's going to rain.

Who cares? What's a drop of rain? This is brilliant!

Here they are.

Listen to that guitar. He's going to sing Geraldine.

Cool! That's my favourite song!

Real talk

Get a move on!	Sbrigati!
It's really full	È veramente pieno

Comprehension check

2 Answer the questions.

1 Why's Fiona in a hurry?
2 Why do they go to the back?
3 What's the weather like?
4 What's the name of the band's first song?
5 Why's Molly pleased?

What do you think?

1 Do you think sitting at the back was a good decision?
2 Do you like going to concerts?
3 What was the last concert you went to?

Grammar

be going to (2) • Previsioni

It's ten to nine. We**'re going to** be late!
Here's the band. The concert**'s going to** start now.
Just look at those clouds! It**'s going to** rain.

Si usa *be going to* anche per fare delle previsioni basate sui dati oggettivi.

Si può anche usare *be about to* per parlare di un avvenimento o un'azione imminente.
It's about to rain. = It's going to rain.

✏️ WB pp.242–243

Grammar check

3 Read the sentences and write a prediction with *be going to* using the words in the box.

be late for work	cry	fall off
win the race	score	crash
miss the plane	be rich	

1 It's a quarter past eight and the bus is late. They start work at half past eight.
2 He's got the ball and he's near the goal.
3 We aren't at the airport. The plane leaves in an hour.
4 He's riding his bicycle and eating a sandwich.
5 The winning lottery ticket is number 46. You've got ticket number 46!
6 Hooray! I'm in first place and I've got 100 metres to go.
7 The road's icy and the car in front of the bus stops suddenly.
8 Her dad bought her an ice-cream, but she fell over and dropped it.

Word recall — The weather

4 🔊 4.37 Listen to the 6 sounds. What's the weather like?

1 *It's foggy.*
2 _____
3 _____
4 _____
5 _____
6 _____

Now write the words in the correct column. Add other weather words you know. In pairs. Compare lists.

Good weather	Bad weather

Speaking • Predicting the weather

5 Look at the international weather table for 15ᵗʰ August. What's the weather going to be like in the cities listed? **T**

Athens	35°C	☀️	Chicago	26°C ⛈️
Beijing	30°C	⛈️	Denver	0°C ❄️
Buenos Aires	16°C	☁️	Melbourne	10°C FOG
Cape Town	18°C	☁️	Washington	29°C ⛅

In pairs. Ask and answer questions.

Example:
A What's the weather going to be like in Athens?
B It's going to be boiling hot and sunny.

Predictions

6 Look at the pictures. What's going to happen? **P**
In pairs. Write as many sentences for each picture as possible.

1 *He's going to catch a plane. He's going to meet someone.*

Reading

1 Before you read • Look at the photos (a–c) and match them to the types of extreme weather (1–3).

1 ___ hailstorm
2 ___ tornado
3 ___ thunderstorm

2 🔊 4.38 While you read • Read the article. What is causing an increase in extreme weather events?

3 Vocabulary • Look at the words in bold in the article. Match them to their Italian translations.

1 ___ size   **a** alluvioni
2 ___ hailstones   **b** dimensioni
3 ___ flooding   **c** alzarsi
4 ___ burns   **d** chicchi di grandine
5 ___ heartbeat   **e** ustioni
6 ___ rise   **f** battito cardiaco

4 Comprehension check • Write information from the article next to the sentences.

1 _____ The electrical power of a lightning bolt.
2 _____ The date of the hailstorm in the village in Devon.
3 _____ The fastest wind speed of a tornado.
4 _____ The number of times lightning struck Mr Sullivan.
5 ____/_____ The number of tornadoes every year in the USA and England.
6 _____ The probability of lightning striking you.

WILD WEATHER!

Tornadoes, hailstorms and thunder and lightning are all examples of the wild weather we usually associate with the USA or countries in the tropics. Amazingly,
5 they are very common in the British Isles, too. So what phenomena are we talking about? *Network* journalist Martha Graham investigates the natural phenomena that devastate towns, regions and even whole
10 countries on our planet.

The USA has the most tornadoes and above all the most violent ones, with winds of 400 km/h. The fastest recorded wind speed of a tornado was 600 km/h in Oklahoma City in 1999. They have
15 over 1,000 tornadoes a year, but did you know that England actually has the most tornadoes in the world in relation to its **size**? It has more than 100 tornadoes every year, although they are smaller than American tornadoes and only last about ten
20 minutes.

Tornadoes aren't the only extreme weather that happens in the UK. In October 2008, a village in Devon experienced extraordinary weather. Nearly 2 metres of hailstones fell in one night.
25 The **hailstones** solidified into one huge piece of ice and everything in the streets was frozen solid. People couldn't move their cars or even open their doors. When it thawed, there was severe **flooding**. Many families abandoned
30 their homes. Nobody was killed, but hundreds of sheep died.

Listening

5 Match the seasons (1–4) to the photos (a–d).

1 ___ spring ☐   3 ___ autumn ☐
2 ___ summer ☐   4 ___ winter ☐

6 🔊 **4.39** Now listen to Amberly and Jake discussing their favourite season. Write A (Amberly) or J (Jake) next to the name of their favourite season in Ex.5. Then listen again and match the people (A or J) to the sentences (1–7).

1 ___ I quite like winter.
2 ___ I like going for walks in winter when it's sunny.
3 ___ I don't like winter here in England because it's so grey.
4 ___ There's a lot of variety in the weather.
5 ___ The days are longer so it's nice to go out in the evening.
6 ___ Autumn in England's awful – it's always cloudy and it rains.
7 ___ The weather's quite nice, but it's not too hot.

Speaking

7 In pairs. Ask and answer the questions. 🅣

1 What's your favourite season? Why?
2 What do you like doing during your favourite season?
3 Which seasons don't you like? Why?

Writing

8 Write a short text (100 words) about the seasons and what you like and don't like about them. 🅣

I like winter, spring and summer.
I like winter because...

9 Read the Study skills and check your text from Ex.8.

One very scary type of weather which is becoming more frequent is thunder and lightning. In June 2009 Sophie Frost, a 14-year-old, was under a
35 tree waiting for a storm to pass (not a good idea!) when lightning struck her. Luckily, the 300,000 volt bolt hit her MP3 player, and this fact saved her life. However, she received serious **burns**. Another
40 lucky victim was Roy Cleveland Sullivan, a US forest ranger. He was hit by lightning seven times and survived! But don't worry – you've only got a 1 in
45 600,000 chance of being struck by lightning.

Incredibly, a lightning strike can sometimes save a person's life. In July 2009, lightning struck a Serbian woman
50 called Nada Acimovich and it cured her irregular **heartbeat**!

What's causing this increase in extreme weather events? According to scientists from the US Climate Science Change Program, greenhouse
55 gases produced by factories, power stations, cars, lorries and planes are causing the Earth's temperature to **rise**. This causes extreme weather events. So we need to get our governments to introduce measures which reduce greenhouse gas
60 emissions and with a bit of luck, maybe we can stop the storms!

Study skills

Checking your work

Prima di consegnare all'insegnante un testo che hai scritto in inglese, controlla:

La punteggiatura
- Hai terminato ogni frase con un punto?
- Hai messo un punto interrogativo alla fine delle domande?
- Hai usato le lettere maiuscole dove servono? Attenzione, alcune parole che iniziano con la minuscola in italiano iniziano con la maiuscola in inglese, e.s. *Monday* = lunedì, *I* = io.

L'ortografia
- Molte parole inglesi contengono delle lettere che non si sentono, e.s. *Wednesday, flight*.

La grammatica
- Stai attento agli errori tipici, ad esempio non dimenticare la -s alla terza persona singolare del *Present simple*.

be going to (1) • Intenzioni

1 Read the sentences and complete rules 1–2.

I'm going to spend the summer in the USA.
They aren't going to move house next year.

> 1 Per esprimere un'intenzione si usa:
> soggetto + _____ + *going to* + _____
> 2 Per ottenere la forma negativa e
> _____ si seguono le regole per
> l'uso del verbo _____

2 Rewrite the sentences as questions.

1 I'm going to buy a scooter in June.
_____

2 We're going to have a party when school ends.
_____

3 Jessica and Nathan are going to get married next year.
_____

4 He's going to get a job for the summer.
_____

5 I'm going to go to Paris after I finish my exams.
_____

6 They're going to leave school at the end of the year.
_____

7 Paul's going to join a football club next month.
_____

8 We're going to have pizza for dinner.
_____

9 You're going to watch TV this evening.
_____

10 She's going to sing my favourite song.
_____

Now write the sentences in the negative.

be going to (2) • Previsioni

3 Read the sentences and answer questions 1–4.

a He's going to have a bath when he gets home.
b He's late for work and he's going to miss the train.
c Look at those clouds. I think it's going to rain.
d I'm going to leave home next year.
e Oh look! That scooter is about to hit that car.

> 1 Quali frasi esprimono intenzioni? _____
> 2 Quali frasi esprimono previsioni basate su dati oggettivi? _____
> 3 C'è una differenza grammaticale nella costruzione dei due tipi di frase? _____
> 4 Quale frase descrive un avvenimento imminente?
> _____
> Come si traduce in italiano? _____

4 Read the sentences and decide if they are intentions (I) or predictions (P).

1 ____ That cat's going to eat that bird.

2 ____ They're going to win the match.
3 ____ Mark's going to study Maths at university.
4 ____ I'm going to watch a film on TV this evening.
5 ____ We're going to go to the USA as soon as we have enough money.
6 ____ That dog's walking right on the edge of the path. He's going to fall in the river.

be going to, Present simple o Present continuous per il futuro?

5 Read the sentences and complete rules 1–2 with *Present simple* or *Present continuous*.

Our flight leaves at midday tomorrow.
I'm playing tennis at 6 o'clock.

> 1 Per parlare di programmi prestabiliti si usa _____.
> 2 Per parlare di orari al futuro si usa _____.

6 Complete the sentences with the correct form of the verbs in brackets.

1 That man _____ (crash) his car.
2 I _____ (see) the dentist at 4 o'clock today.
3 We _____ (meet) our friends outside the club at half past nine.
4 She _____ (work) in a shop when she leaves school.
5 The film _____ (start) at 6pm.
6 It's very cold. I think it _____ (snow).
7 The supermarket _____ (close) at 8pm.

Esercizi sommativi

7 Read the text and choose the correct alternative.

My friends and I ¹go/are going to an open-air concert in London tomorrow. It ²starts/'s starting at ten o'clock in the morning. We ³travel/'re travelling to London by bus. We ⁴'re taking/take something to eat and drink because it ⁵is/is going to be quite expensive to buy food and drink. We ⁶'re going to see/see some of my favourite bands. My dad says it ⁷'s raining/'s going to rain, but there aren't any clouds in the sky this evening, so I think it ⁸'s going to be/'s sunny.

8 Translation • Translate the sentences into English.

1 La tua mamma sta per partire?
2 Guarda il cielo – sta per nevicare.
3 C'era molto vento ieri.
4 Parto alle sette domani mattina.
5 Hai intenzione di uscire stasera?
6 Si congelava stamattina.
7 Guarda quelle due macchine! Stanno per fare un incidente.
8 Fa molto freddo a Edimburgo a dicembre.

Word builder

1 happy
2 upset
3 disappointed
4 embarrassed

5 angry
6 shocked

7 sad
8 surprised
9 bored

10 nervous
11 excited
12 scared
13 relieved
EXIT
ENTRANCE

Emotions adjectives

1 🔊 4.40 Look at the pictures. Listen and repeat the adjectives.

Now translate the adjectives into Italian.

1 _____	6 _____	11 _____
2 _____	7 _____	12 _____
3 _____	8 _____	13 _____
4 _____	9 _____	
5 _____	10 _____	

 Attenzione a questo *false friend:*
annoyed = *irritato*   *annoiato* = bored

Speaking • How do you feel?

2 How do you feel in these situations? In pairs. Ask and answer questions. **T**

How do you feel...
1 when you go into class just before a class test?
2 when you get a bad mark for some homework?
3 before you go to a party?
4 when you argue with a friend?
5 when someone is nasty to you?
6 when you go to the dentist's?
7 on the last day of school?

Word note

Gli aggettivi che terminano in *-ed* descrivono il sentimento di una persona, mentre gli aggettivi che terminano in *-ing* descrivono un avvenimento o una situazione:
Simon was very embarrass**ed** when he saw the surprise party.

The surprise party was very embarrass**ing** (for Simon).

Quasi tutti gli aggettivi in Ex.1 hanno entrambe le forme: annoyed, annoying; bored, boring, ecc.

Eccezioni: *scared, scary – relieved, a relief*
I was really scared when I had the accident. It was a scary experience.

When I passed the exam, I was relieved. Passing the exam was a relief.

Dictation

3 🔊 4.41 Listen and complete the sentences.

1 When he fell off his scooter, _____.
2 My teacher was _____.
3 Before the exam I _____.
4 After the exam _____.
5 I felt very _____.

WB p.249 Complete *Emotions adjectives* in the Word store.

Have you ever worked as a waiter?

1 🔊 **4.42** Sam meets Kali in the centre of Edinburgh. Why does Sam want to go to Rome? Listen and read.

Sam	Hi Kali. What are you doing here?
Kali	I'm meeting Molly in half an hour. **You look a bit upset.** What's wrong?
Sam	No, I'm OK. It's just that I've decided to go away for the summer.
Kali	Have you found a summer job, then?
Sam	Yeah, that's right.
Kali	What sort of job?
Sam	I found an advert on the Internet for a waiter in Rome.
Kali	Rome?
Sam	Yeah. I've been to Italy on holiday with my parents and I really liked it, but I've never been to Rome.
Kali	Have you ever worked as a waiter?
Sam	No, I haven't. But I worked in the kitchen of a café last summer.
Kali	And have you ever been away without your parents?
Sam	No, I haven't. What about you?
Kali	Yes, I have. I've still got loads of relatives in Indonesia, so I visit them once a year. I sometimes go **on my own.**
Sam	Cool! Anyway, I'm really excited. The only problem is that my sister's really angry about it.
Kali	Why? What's it got to do with her?
Sam	Well, she wanted to go away last year, but my parents said no.
Kali	Has she ever been away on her own?
Sam	No, she hasn't.
Kali	Well, I'm not surprised that she's angry, then! Hey, has she ever been to Rome?
Sam	No, she hasn't.
Kali	Why don't you ask her to go with you?
Sam	Kali! Please! **You can't be serious!**
Kali	No, **just joking.** Tell me all about this job…

Comprehension check

2 Complete the sentences with the correct names.

1 _____'s in town to meet a friend.
2 _____ has never been on holiday without his parents.
3 _____ visits his family abroad every year.
4 _____'s worried that his sister's angry.
5 _____ didn't let Fiona go away last year.

Real talk

You look a bit upset	Sembri un po' giù
on my own	da solo
You can't be serious!	Non parli mica sul serio?
Just joking	Stavo solo scherzando

What do you think?

1 How does Sam feel about the idea of taking his sister to Rome? Why?
2 Do you like the idea of making a long plane journey on your own?
3 What are the good and bad things about working in another country?

Grammar

Present perfect (1) • *ever*

Forma interrogativa e risposte brevi

Have you/I/we/they **ever worked** as a barman?
Yes, I/you/we/they **have**.
No, I/you/we/they **haven't**.

Has he/she/it **ever been** to Rome?
Yes, she/he/it **has**.
No, she/he/it **hasn't**.

La forma interrogativa del *Present perfect* si costruisce con:

verbo *have* + soggetto + participio passato

Il participio passato dei verbi regolari si forma aggiungendo *-ed/-d* alla forma base del verbo come per il *Past simple*.

I verbi irregolari, invece, hanno participi passati che vanno imparati a memoria (vedi pp.286–287).

 **WB p.248**

Grammar check

3 Write the past participles.

base form	past participle
be	_____
stay	_____
study	_____
play	_____
eat	_____
speak	_____
meet	_____
ride	_____

Then write questions using the verbs above and *ever*.

1 tennis?
   Have you ever played tennis?
2 Japanese food?
3 a famous person?
4 a motorbike?
5 English with an English person?
6 Latin?
7 youth hostel?
8 camping holiday?

Now answer the questions.

1 *Yes, I have./No, I haven't.*

Grammar note

Si usa il *Present perfect* con *ever* per fare domande su esperienze fatte nella vita. Non ha importanza quando queste esperienze sono accadute.

Have you ever seen Elbow in concert? **Yes, I have.**

Se la risposta è affermativa e si vuole sapere di più, nella domanda si usa il *Past simple* perchè si tratta di un'azione iniziata e conclusa in un momento specifico del passato.

A When **did you see** Elbow?
B **I saw** them last month.

 **WB p.248**

Word builder + Holidays (2)

4 Write an Italian translation of the phrases.

Accommodation
1 stay in a youth hostel _____
2 stay in a holiday village _____
Transport
3 go by scooter _____
4 go by bike _____
Activities
5 go windsurfing _____
6 go diving _____

WB p.249 Complete *Holidays (2)* in the Word store.

Speaking • Holiday experiences

5 Complete the *Network* Holiday Survey for your partner. In pairs. Ask and answer the questions. **P T**

Example:
A Have you ever stayed on a campsite?
B Yes, I have.
A When did you stay on a campsite?
B I went camping last year. I went to Turkey.
A What was it like?
B It was very exciting.

Network Holiday Survey

Have you ever…   yes   no

1 stayed in a hotel/a youth hostel?   ○   ○
2 stayed on a campsite?   ○   ○
3 stayed in a self-catering flat?   ○   ○
4 been on holiday in a camper van?   ○   ○
5 been on a plane?   ○   ○
6 been on holiday by car/motorbike?   ○   ○
7 had a holiday by the sea/in the mountains?   ○   ○
8 had a skiing holiday?   ○   ○
9 been on an English language course in the UK?   ○   ○
10 been on holiday without your parents?   ○   ○

I've never been to an adventure park

1 🔊 **4.43** Sam and Kali are deciding what to do on Bank Holiday Monday. Where do they decide to go? Listen and read.

Sam Where's Molly today?

Kali She's gone to Glasgow for the day with her parents. What are you doing on Monday?

Sam I don't know. The weather's been really awful recently. What's the forecast like?

Kali Hot and sunny.

Sam Great! Let's do something we've never done before.

Kali Right! But like what?

Sam Well, I'd like to do something a bit scary and exciting. I've never been to an adventure park.

Kali You mean those places where you climb rope ladders and cross bridges between trees?

Sam Yeah, that's right.

Kali Sounds like a good laugh. Molly's never been to an adventure park either. Let's invite her, too.

It's 6pm on Bank Holiday Monday...

Sam That was fantastic! It was really exciting!

Molly Yes, I've had a brilliant day. What about you, Kali?

Kali Yes, it was great. But I was a bit scared when we were in those high trees.

Fiona But that's the whole idea, Kali!

Real talk

Right! But like what?	Sì, ma che cosa?
Sounds like...	Sembra...
That's the whole idea	È proprio questo lo scopo

Comprehension check

2 Answer the questions.

1 Why doesn't Molly help plan the day out?
2 Why are Sam and Kali free on Monday?
3 Why does Sam want to go to an adventure park?
4 Who enjoyed the day a bit less than the others? Why?

What do you think?

1 Did they have a good time at the park?
2 Have you ever been to an adventure park?
3 Do you like doing scary things?

Grammar

Present perfect (2) • *never*

Forma affermativa
I/You/We/They**'ve had** a brilliant day.
He/She/It**'s eaten** Chinese food.

Forma negativa
I/You/We/They **haven't been** to an adventure park.
He/She/It **hasn't travelled** by plane.

Nota la differenza tra *ever* e *never*:
ever = mai (nelle domande)
never = non... mai (nelle affermazioni)
Has she **ever** been to an adventure park?
No, she's **never** been to an adventure park.

Si possono anche usare avverbi come *recently*
(recentemente) nelle frasi al *Present perfect*.
The weather's been really awful **recently**.

 **WB p.249**

 Nota la differenza tra *been* e *gone*:
She's **been** to Glasgow. (*È andata ed è tornata.*)
She's **gone** to Glasgow. (*È andata ed è ancora lì.*)

Grammar check

3 Use the words to write sentences in the Present perfect.

1 I/never/be/to Scotland
   I've never been to Scotland.
2 they/see/a play by Shakespeare
3 you/not dance/the tango
4 I/be/skiing recently
5 we/never/eat/Greek food
6 she/not play/tennis
7 my mum and dad/never/live/abroad
8 Nathan/go/to the supermarket

Pronunciation • *h-*

4a 🔊 **4.44** In English we usually pronounce *h-* at the beginning of words, but there are a few words where the *h-* is silent. Listen.

happy	**h**ave	**h**oliday
honest	**h**our	**h**onour

4b 🔊 **4.45** Listen and underline the silent *h-*.

1 Have you heard about Harry's homework?
2 He stayed here for an hour.
3 I hope you've had an interesting holiday.
4 Hannah is very honest and hard-working.

🔊 **4.46** Listen and check. Listen and repeat.

---

5 🔊 **4.47** How is the person feeling? Listen and write an adjective from the box.

shocked	happy	surprised
excited	angry	embarrassed

1 _____   4 _____
2 _____   5 _____
3 _____   6 _____

In pairs.
A: choose an emotion from 1–6 above. Say 'I've finished my homework.' expressing that emotion.
B: guess the emotion.

Speaking • Experiences

6 Look at the list of experiences. What do you think your partner has and hasn't done? Write 3 affirmative and 3 negative sentences.

You've met a famous person.
You've never watched a 3D film.

win a competition
travel by plane
meet a famous person
break something
sell something on the Internet
eat Chinese food
watch a 3D film
ride a horse
swim with dolphins
play tennis
sleep at a friend's house
lose some money
make lasagne
forget a birthday

In pairs.
A: read your sentences to your partner. Then ask questions to find out more.
B: say if A's guess is right. Then answer his/her questions. **T**

Example:
A You've met a famous person.
B Yes, you're right.
A Who did you meet?
B Last February I met Jovanotti on a plane.
A How did you feel?
B I was a bit embarrassed, but it was very exciting!

Fast finishers!

Write 3 affirmative and 3 negative sentences about the experiences you discussed in Ex.6.

Reading

1 Before you read • In pairs. Describe the pictures (a–c). **P**

What has happened? What's happening?
What do you think is going to happen?

2 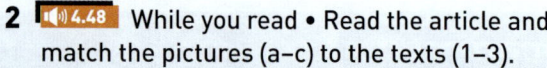 4.48 While you read • Read the article and match the pictures (a–c) to the texts (1–3).

3 Vocabulary • Look at the words in bold in the article. Match them to their Italian translations.

1 spazio _____
2 scivolai/sono scivolata _____
3 il conto _____
4 taglio di capelli _____
5 vassoio _____
6 pasticcio/disastro/lo sporco _____

It was SO embarrassing!

I've had lots of really embarrassing experiences when I've been on holiday with my parents. But I want to forget them – let's look at some of yours instead!

Jason, *Webtime* editor

1 ____

Callum, 16, *Padstow*

Sometimes my dad can be very
5 embarrassing. The most embarrassing
moment I've ever had was last year
when we went to Italy on holiday. My
dad likes learning foreign languages,
but he's absolutely terrible at them!
10 He studied Italian before we went to Rome. We
stayed in a nice hotel, visited the city and ate in
some amazing restaurants. Everything went OK
until the last day. We were at the hotel reception
and Dad wanted to pay **the bill**. He said to the man
15 on reception: 'Accettate la carta igienica?' instead
of 'Accettate la carta di credito?' The man said 'No,
mi dispiace, non accettiamo la carta igienica, ma
accettiamo la carta di credito' and started laughing
– he couldn't stop. We were all really embarrassed.

2 ____

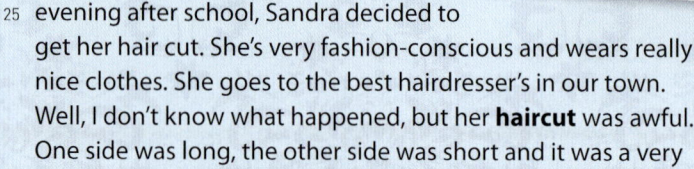

Amy, 17, *Manchester*

20 My most embarrassing moment was a few
weeks ago when I was at school. I've got
lots of good friends in my class, but my
two best friends are Sandra and Sarah. Or
at least, they were my best friends! One
25 evening after school, Sandra decided to
get her hair cut. She's very fashion-conscious and wears really
nice clothes. She goes to the best hairdresser's in our town.
Well, I don't know what happened, but her **haircut** was awful.
One side was long, the other side was short and it was a very
30 strange colour – orange with blue bits. Just awful! I didn't say
anything when I saw her at school, but I sent a text message
to Sarah saying, 'Have you seen Sandra's haircut? It's awful!'
Unfortunately, Sandra and Sarah's names are next to each
other on my contacts list and I sent the message to Sandra
35 instead of Sarah. Sandra was really angry and she hasn't
spoken to me since then.

4 Comprehension check • Answer the questions.

1 What did Callum do while he was in Rome?
2 Did the receptionist know what the boy's father really meant?
3 Which of Amy's friends decided to have her hair cut?
4 Why did Amy send the message to the wrong person?
5 Is Sandra Amy's friend now?
6 Why did Emma first drop the tray?
7 Why did she drop the tray the second time?
8 Who paid for the man's dinner?

Speaking

5 Read the questions and choose 3 you want to answer. **T**

1 What's the most embarrassing experience you've ever had?
2 What's the best thing that's ever happened to you?
3 What's the most beautiful place you've ever visited? Describe it.
4 What's the best film you've ever seen? Why?
5 What's the most interesting book you've ever read? Why?

In pairs. Ask and answer the questions. Give as much information as possible.

3

Emma, 18, *Leeds*

Last summer I had a
Saturday job as a waitress in
a restaurant. It was always
40 very busy and there wasn't
much **room** between the
tables. One day I had a **tray** with two plates of
roast beef, mashed potatoes and peas to take
to a table near the window. Unfortunately, I lost
45 my balance and the plates fell onto the floor.
The food landed on a man and covered his shirt
with mashed potato. I was so embarrassed! The
man was angry, so the manager came over and
apologized. I cleaned up the **mess** then started
50 work again. About twenty minutes later I took a
tray of desserts to the same table. I **slipped** on
the wet floor and dropped the tray of desserts
over the same man's shirt. Everybody in the
restaurant started laughing – even the man
55 at the table. I apologized again. The manager
came over and offered to pay for the man's
meal. (He deducted the cost from my wages, so
that wasn't so funny).

Listening

6 🔊 **4.49** Listen to Lia talking to a *Network* reporter about her best experience ever. Tick (✓) the correct photo.

Listen again and choose the correct alternative.

1 The competition took place in September/November last year.
2 Lia was in the **south-west/south-east** England team.
3 The competition took place in **Newcastle under Lyme/Newcastle-Upon-Tyne**.
4 Lia's winning time was 24.06 **minutes/seconds**.
5 Before the final Lia was very **nervous/excited**.
6 Lia and her friends celebrated in a **Chinese/Italian** restaurant.

Writing

7 Write a short text (100 words) about an experience you've had. **T**

Choose from:

- the most embarrassing
- the most boring
- the most exciting
- the scariest

Use the answers to these questions as a guide for your text:

- When did it happen?
- Who were you with?
- Where did it happen?
- What happened as a result?

Present perfect (1) • *ever*

1 Read the sentences. Complete rules 1–2 and answer questions 3–4.

Have you ever been to London? Yes, I have.
Has he ever eaten Indonesian food? No, he hasn't.
I've seen lots of horror films. I saw one last night.

> **1** La forma interrogativa del *Present perfect* si costruisce con:
> il presente del verbo _____ + soggetto + _____ + ?
> **2** Le risposte brevi si costruiscono con:
> *Yes/No*, + _____ + _____.
> **3** Si usa il *Present perfect* per parlare di un'azione passata in un tempo indeterminato o tempo determinato? _____
> **4** Quale tempo del verbo si usa per parlare di un'azione iniziata e conclusa in un momento specifico del passato? _____

2 Complete the table and answer questions 1–2.

forma base	participio passato
decide	1 _____
play	2 _____
visit	3 _____
be	4 _____
go	5 _____
eat	6 _____

1 Come si forma il participio passato dei verbi regolari? _____
2 C'è una regola per la formazione del participio passato dei verbi irregolari? _____

3 Write questions for these answers.

1 Yes, it has. It snowed in June last year.
 Has it ever snowed in June?
2 Yes, it has. Our car broke down a week ago.
3 Yes, they have. They went to New York at Christmas.
4 No, I haven't. I don't believe in ghosts!
5 Yes, she has. She stayed in a youth hostel in May.
6 Yes, we have. We went to Milan Cathedral on a school trip 2 weeks ago.

Present perfect (2) • *never*

4 Read the sentences and answer the question.

She's never been on holiday on her own.
They've never been to a rock concert.

> **1** Si usa *not* nelle frasi con *never*? _____

5 Reorder the words to make sentences.

1 good we've to some been concerts
2 played squash you ever have?
3 have German never they studied
4 different I've three lived countries in
5 J.K.Rowling has she read by books never any
6 your done you haven't homework
7 tried never windsurfing I've
8 a have new they ever bought car?

6 Complete the sentences with *been* or *gone*.

1 I've never _____ to Canada.
2 Joe's _____ to the shops. He went 5 minutes ago.
3 We've _____ to the new shopping centre twice.
4 I've _____ ice skating, but I've never _____ snowboarding.
5 Where have they _____? To the cinema, I think.
6 She's _____ to work in France for 3 months. She's very happy there.

Esercizi sommativi

7 Follow the instructions and write the dialogue in your exercise book.

Tom	[1]Ti chiede se sei mai stato ad un concerto rock.
You	[2]Rispondi di sì. Di' che sei stato ad un concerto reggae sabato scorso.
Tom	[3]Ti chiede se ti è piaciuto.
You	[4]Rispondi di no. Di' che non ti piace il reggae. È stato un po' noioso.
Tom	[5]Ti chiede se sei mai stato al *Windrush Club* a Newcastle.
You	[6]Digli di no. Digli che non sei mai stato a Newcastle.
Tom	[7]Dice che è un posto davvero elettrizzante. Ti chiede se vuoi andare con lui.
You	[8]Accetta.
Tom	[9]Ti propone di incontrarvi alle otto davanti al municipio.
You	[10]Di' che sei d'accordo. Salutalo.
Tom	[11]Ti saluta.

8 Translation • Translate the sentences into English.

1 Hai mai conosciuto una persona famosa?
2 Lucia non è mai stata a casa mia.
3 Mio padre è andato a Londra e ritorna lunedì.
4 È tardi e non abbiamo mangiato.
5 Ho visto Harry al centro sportivo un'ora fa.
6 Hai visto Katie recentemente? No.
7 Mio padre è stato a Reykyavik tre volte.
8 Hai visto la partita in TV ieri sera?

Talking on the phone

Dialogue 📹 VIDEO

1 🔊 **4.50** Rick phones his friend Amy. Listen and answer the questions.

1 Who answers the phone the first time Rick phones Amy?

_____

2 Is Amy at home?

_____

3 What does Rick decide to do?

_____

4 Who answers the phone when Rick calls again?

_____

5 What time are Rick and Amy going to meet?

_____

Word note

Nota questi modi di dire che si usano nelle telefonate:

Hello.	*Pronto?*
It's Rick.	*Sono Rick.*
Is Amy in?	*C'è Amy?*
Is that Amy?	*Sei Amy?*
It's me.	*Sono io.*
Hang on a minute, please.	*Aspetti/a un attimo, per favore.*

Say it right!

2 🔊 **4.51** Listen. Then listen and repeat the sentences with the correct rhythm.

Woman	Hello.
Daniel	Hello. This is Daniel. Is that Lily?
Woman	Hang on a minute, please. I'll go and get her.
Lily	Hello?
Daniel	Hi, Lily. It's me.
Lily	Hi, Daniel!
Daniel	Do you want to come round for dinner tonight?
Lily	Yes, I'd love to. What time shall I come?
Daniel	How about seven o'clock?
Lily	OK. I'll bring some ice-cream.
Daniel	Great! I'll see you at seven, then. Bye!
Lily	See you later.

In pairs. Practise the dialogue. When you finish, change roles.

Now close your books. Can you say the dialogue from memory?

Speaking

3 In pairs. Write the dialogue below.

A ¹Telefona al suo amico. Saluta e chiede se c'è.
B ²Il padre dell'amico risponde. Dice di aspettare.
C ³Il suo amico viene al telefono e saluta.
A ⁴Chiede al suo amico se vuole uscire a mangiare una pizza.
C ⁵Accetta l'invito. Chiede a che ora si devono trovare.
A ⁶Propone un'ora e offre di venire a casa di C.
C ⁷Dice che va bene. Saluta.
A ⁸Saluta e chiude.

A ¹ _____

B ² _____

C ³ _____

A ⁴ _____

C ⁵ _____

A ⁶ _____

C ⁷ _____

A ⁸ _____

Practise the dialogue. When you finish, change roles.

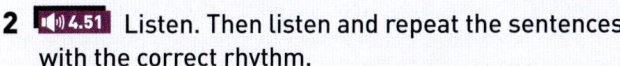

WB p.257   133

What's Scotland *really* like?

1 What do you associate with Scotland? Write 6 things.

1 _____   3 _____   5 _____
2 _____   4 _____   6 _____

In pairs. Compare lists. Have you got the same things?

2 🔊 **4.52** Read the post that Rory wrote for some Italian exchange students on his school website. Are any of the things you listed in Ex.1 in the text?

Did you know?
There are 787 islands in Scotland, but only about 97 are inhabited.

SCOTLAND
Myth and Reality

There's a red-haired man with a beard, wearing a kilt and playing the bagpipes. He's standing on a hill in front of a castle with the
5 wind blowing around him. Later, at home, he eats a plate of <u>haggis</u>, drinks a glass of whisky, and goes out Scottish dancing. For breakfast the next morning
10 he eats <u>porridge</u>. He speaks English with an accent that only other Scots can understand and firmly believes that there's a monster in Loch Ness. He's a bit
15 mean, he doesn't like the English and he's fanatical about football.

Is this your idea of Scottish people? Many people have this impression, but it's simply a stereotype. Scottish people aren't like that at all. Well, OK, they are a bit fanatical about
20 football...
Some Scottish people have got red hair, but most of them haven't. And they aren't especially mean. A lot of Scots are very friendly and they've certainly all got a great sense of humour. And what about the kilt? Well, Scotsmen are proud of their
25 past, and the kilt is a symbol of this past. It's made of a cloth called 'tartan'. Historically, every group of families, or 'clan', had its own tartan. These days, men wear their kilts on special occasions, such as weddings or New Year's Eve, but they don't wear a kilt every day! Many Scottish traditions disappeared
30 after the famous Battle of Culloden against the English in 1746. Many Scots have never forgotten this battle...
As for the accent, a lot of foreigners find the Scottish accent easier to understand than many English accents. In fact, a lot of great poets and orators come from Scotland.
35 Scotland's scenery is stunning and also varied: there are islands, <u>moors</u>, lakes and mountains. And what about the monster? Of course, most Scottish adults don't really believe that there's a monster in Loch Ness, but nobody minds the fact that the myth encourages thousands of tourists to come and
40 see the Scottish countryside!
OK, it's true that Scottish people make and drink excellent whisky, and they're mad about football, but that's because they have some of the best footballers in the world. Honest!

haggis *piatto fatto di stomaco di pecora ripieno di frattaglie*
porridge *fiocchi di avena con latte*
moors *brughiera*

3 Answer the questions.

1 Which of the stereotypes does Rory think are true?
2 What are Scottish people really like, according to Rory?
3 Why is the kilt important to Scotsmen?
4 When did lots of traditions start disappearing?
5 Why do lots of people decide to visit Scotland?

Speaking

4 In pairs. Ask and answer the questions. 🇹

1 Which of the stereotypes did you believe before reading the text?
2 Do you have a different view of Scottish people now?
3 Would you like to visit Scotland? Why?

🎥 **VIDEO** Now watch the Network video!

Word builder

Transport and places

1 Match the words (1–6) to the pictures (a–f).

1 ___ helicopter   3 ___ motorbike   5 ___ bike
2 ___ plane   4 ___ ship   6 ___ ferry

🔊 **5.02** Listen and repeat.

2 Complete the mind map with the words in the box.

car	helicopter	tram	bicycle (bike)
bus station	train	scooter	airport
skateboard	train station	boat	motorbike
ship	plane	taxi	ferry
coach	bus	port	coach station

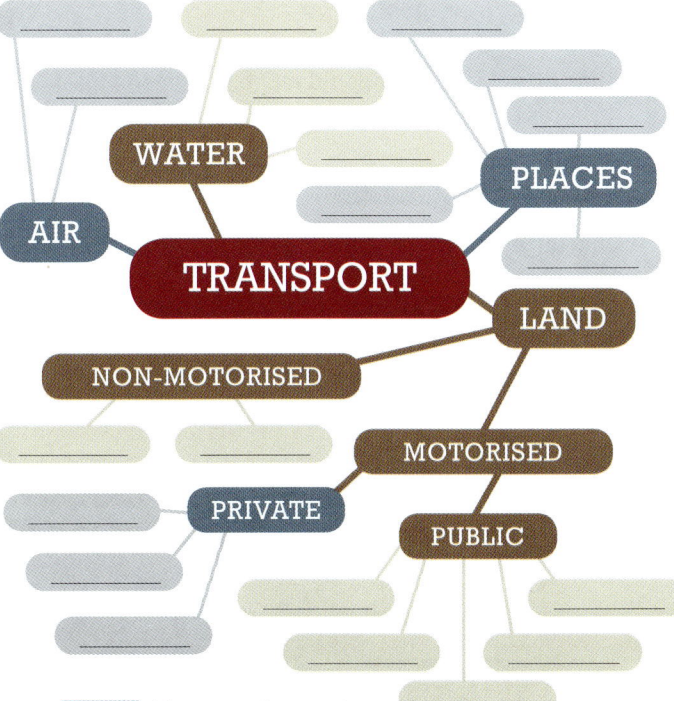

WATER
AIR
PLACES
TRANSPORT
LAND
NON-MOTORISED
MOTORISED
PRIVATE
PUBLIC

🔊 **5.03** Listen and repeat.

3 In pairs. Which vehicles do you use with these verbs? Write them down.

1 take/get _____
2 get on _____
3 get off _____
4 get into _____
5 get out of _____

> ⚠ go **by** car/train/plane/coach/bus/taxi
> go **on** foot (~~by foot~~)
> cycle/walk to school

Speaking • My journey

4 Think of a journey you often make, e.g. from home to the town centre or from school to a friend's house. 🅣 In pairs. Ask and answer the questions.

1 Where do you go?   3 How long does it take?
2 How do you get there?   4 How much does it cost?

Dictation

5 🔊 **5.04** Listen and complete the sentences.

1 We _____ to school _____ or
_____.
2 Where's the _____? It's _____
the _____.
3 Our _____ from the _____
in Dover at _____.
4 We _____ the _____ and _____
the _____ to the town centre.
5 _____ your _____ on the _____
or _____ it at the _____.

I've just fallen off my scooter

1 🔊 **5.05** Sam had an accident on his way home from school yesterday. Whose fault was the accident? Listen and read.

Charlotte	Hey, Sam! What's the matter?
Sam	Oh, ...Charlotte! I've just fallen off my scooter.
Charlotte	Are you all right?
Sam	I'm **a bit shaken up**, but look at my scooter! I've already had two accidents and I haven't finished paying for it yet.
Charlotte	So what happened?
Sam	**That stupid dog** ran out in front of me.
Charlotte	Oh!
Sam	What's wrong?
Charlotte	That's my dog! I let go of the lead for a second and he ran away. I'm so sorry, Sam.

Charlotte	Have you called your parents about the accident yet?
Sam	No, I haven't. And I'm not looking forward to telling them either.
Charlotte	I think you need to sit down for a moment. Let's go to that café over there.
Sam	OK.

Comprehension check

2 True or false? Write T or F. Correct the false sentences. 🅿

1 ___ This is the first time Sam's met Charlotte.
2 ___ This isn't Sam's first accident.
3 ___ Charlotte's embarrassed about what's happened.
4 ___ Sam's phoned his parents about the accident.
5 ___ Sam's worried about his parents' reaction.

Real talk

a bit shaken up	un po' scosso
That stupid dog	Quello stupido di un cane

What do you think?

1 In your opinion, is Sam very angry with Charlotte?
2 Have you ever ridden a motorbike or scooter?
3 Do you think they're dangerous?

Grammar

Present perfect (3) • *just, already, yet, still*

I've **just** fallen off my scooter. (= *appena*)

I've **already** had two accidents.
(= *già* in frasi affermative)

Have you called your parents **yet**?
(= *già* in frasi interrogative)

I have**n't** finished paying for it **yet**.
(= *non... ancora* in frasi negative)

Con il *Present perfect* si può usare *still* al posto di *yet*, ma solo nelle frasi negative.

I **still** haven't finished my homework. =
I haven't finished my homework **yet**.

WB p.258

Grammar check

3 Rewrite the sentences inserting *just*, *already* or *yet*.

1 She's had four cups of tea. That's too many.
2 Have you had dinner? No, I'm waiting for Mum.
3 We haven't had our exam results.
4 They've come back from their holidays. They're very suntanned.
5 I've seen the latest 3D film. I saw it last month.
6 Has she invited you to the party? No, she hasn't.
7 Have you finished your homework? I hope so, because it's time to go to school.
8 I've seen Robert Pattinson! He was in the shopping centre five minutes ago!

Rewrite the sentences using *still* where possible.

Pronunciation • *been*

4a 🔊 **5.06** Listen to the pronunciation of *been*.

Have you **been** /bɪn/ to the cinema recently?

4b 🔊 **5.07** Listen to these sentences.

1 I haven't **been** to his new house yet.
2 Have they **been** on holiday yet?
3 She's just **been** to Scotland.
4 We've never **been** to New York.

🔊 **5.08** Listen and repeat.

Word recall Transport

5 Write transport words in your exercise books under the headings *Land, Water, Air, Places.*
In pairs. Compare your lists.

Getting ready

6 🔊 **5.09** Sam's getting ready to go to Rome. Listen and tick (✓) the things Sam's already done and cross (✗) the things he hasn't done yet.

1 pack my bag ___
2 top up my phone ___
3 print out my plane ticket ___
4 buy my coach ticket ___
5 go to the bank ___
6 find my passport ___

In pairs. Ask and answer to check your answers.
A Has Sam packed his suitcase yet?
B Yes, he has. He's already packed it.

Speaking • Have you done it yet?

7 What have you already done today? Put a tick (✓) or cross (✗) in the spaces.

1 ___ have lunch
2 ___ see your parents
3 ___ brush your teeth
4 ___ do your homework
5 ___ have a Maths lesson
6 ___ read a magazine
7 ___ do any sport
8 ___ eat some fruit
9 ___ see your friends
10 ___ use your mobile

In pairs. Ask and answer questions.

Example:
A Have you had lunch yet?
B Yes, I have. I've already had lunch.
A What did you eat?
B I ate some pasta.

Speaking • What's just happened?

8 Look at the pictures. What have these people just done? In pairs. Ask and answer questions. 🔳

Where are you staying in Rome?

1  Kali's come to say goodbye to Sam. They're waiting for the airport coach. Why isn't Sam completely happy about going to Rome? Listen and read.

Kali	When does the plane leave?
Sam	At half past ten.
Kali	Don't worry, Sam. **You've got ages**. Have you got your ticket?
Sam	I'm looking for it now. Yes, I have. It's in my pocket.
Kali	And did you remember to pack your laptop?
Sam	Yes, Kali. Honestly! You're worse than my mother.
Kali	Sorry! Where are you staying in Rome?
Sam	I'm staying with the family that own the café.
Kali	Are they meeting you at the airport?
Sam	No, but I've got a map of the city.
Kali	You don't look very happy. What's the matter? Have you argued with Fiona again?
Sam	No, I haven't. We're friends now.
Kali	Well, **what is it**, then?
Sam	Well, do you know Charlotte Mason?
Kali	Yes, I do. She's really nice.
Sam	Well, we went out last night.
Kali	Really?
Sam	Yes, and she's fantastic!
Kali	Pity you're going to Rome, then.
Sam	Yes, it is. But she says she's going to come and visit me.
Kali	Great! But what about all those Italian girls?
Sam	Kali!

Comprehension check

2 Choose the correct alternative.

1 Kali says that Sam's **late/on time** for his plane.
2 Sam's going to live in a **hostel/with a family** in Rome.
3 Sam's sister **is still/isn't** angry with him.
4 Sam went out with **Kali/Charlotte** the previous evening.
5 **Kali/Charlotte** says **he's/she's** going to visit Sam.

Real talk

You've got ages	Hai un sacco di tempo
What is it?	Che c'è che non va?

What do you think?

1 Why do you think Sam isn't very happy?
2 Do you think Sam's going to see Charlotte again?
3 Do you believe in love at first sight?

Grammar

Ripasso dei tempi verbali

Trova le seguenti forme verbali nel dialogo dell'Esercizio 1 e scrivi le frasi.

1 Present simple verbo *be*

_____

2 Present simple

_____

3 Past simple

_____

4 Present continuous

_____

5 Present continuous – uso futuro

_____

6 Futuro – *be going to*

_____

7 Present simple – uso futuro

_____

8 Present perfect

_____

✏ **WB pp.258–259**

Grammar check

3 Complete the sentences with the correct tense of the verb in brackets.

1 We _____ (have) lunch at the café later.
2 They _____ (never, be) to Greece on holiday.
3 She always _____ (play) volleyball on Tuesday evenings.
4 _____ (you, buy) her a birthday present tomorrow?
5 I _____ (clear) the table at the moment.
6 What _____ (be) she like? Very nice, actually.
7 I _____ (buy) a new bike yesterday.
8 The bus _____ (arrive) at 6 o'clock tomorrow.

Speaking • Verb tense game

4 In pairs or small groups.

1 One person chooses a number from 1–8 and says a person's name.
2 The person has to say a sentence using the tense which corresponds to that number (see the *Grammar* box above).
3 He/She then chooses a number and a different person.

You score 1 point for a correct sentence. The student with the most points wins the game.

Example:
A Three, Carla.
B I played basketball last Sunday.
Teacher Correct! 1 point for Carla.
B Eight, Pietro.
C I have never been to Scotland.

Speaking • Questionnaire

5 In pairs. Ask and answer the questions. P

NETWORK QUESTIONNAIRE

How am I?

1 Are you happy at the moment? Why?

2 What do you do in your free time?

3 What are your friends like?

4 What book are you reading at the moment?

5 Have you had an interesting experience recently? (If so, describe it.)

6 Where are you going on holiday next summer?

7 What are you going to do when you leave school?

8 What did you do last weekend?

9 Have you ever been abroad?

10 Which is better, going out with your friends or going out with your girl/boyfriend?

Fast finishers!

Write 4 short paragraphs about your life. Use your answers from the quiz to help you. Include information about:

- home and school
- things you've done recently
- things you're going to do
- your feelings

SKATING

Reading

1 Read the Study skills. Then do Ex.2.

Study skills

Describing photos

Quando devi descrivere una foto, segui queste indicazioni:

1 Osserva accuratamente la foto per qualche minuto prima di descriverla.

2 Fatti delle domande sul contenuto della foto (che cosa vedi nella foto? Che tipo di posto è? Che cosa stanno facendo le persone e come si sentono?) e basa la descrizione sulle risposte.

3 Usa il *Present continuous* per descrivere quello che sta succedendo.

4 Usa espressioni come:
I think... because...
In the foreground/background... there is/are...
The person on the left/right is...

2 Before you read • In pairs. Describe the photo below. 🅿
Use these questions to help you:

1 What does the boy look like?
2 What's he doing?
3 Where is he?
4 What's the weather like?
5 Where do you think the boy's going?
6 How do you think he's feeling?

In 1871 the brothers John and Robert Naylor were the first people to walk 1,580km from John O'Groats, the most northern
5 point of mainland Britain, to Land's End, the most southern point. Over the last 150 years, people have walked, cycled, ridden a tandem, ridden
10 a motorbike (without stopping), flown a Harrier jet, pushed a wheelchair, and driven all sorts of cars between the two places. They have often done this to raise money
15 for charity.

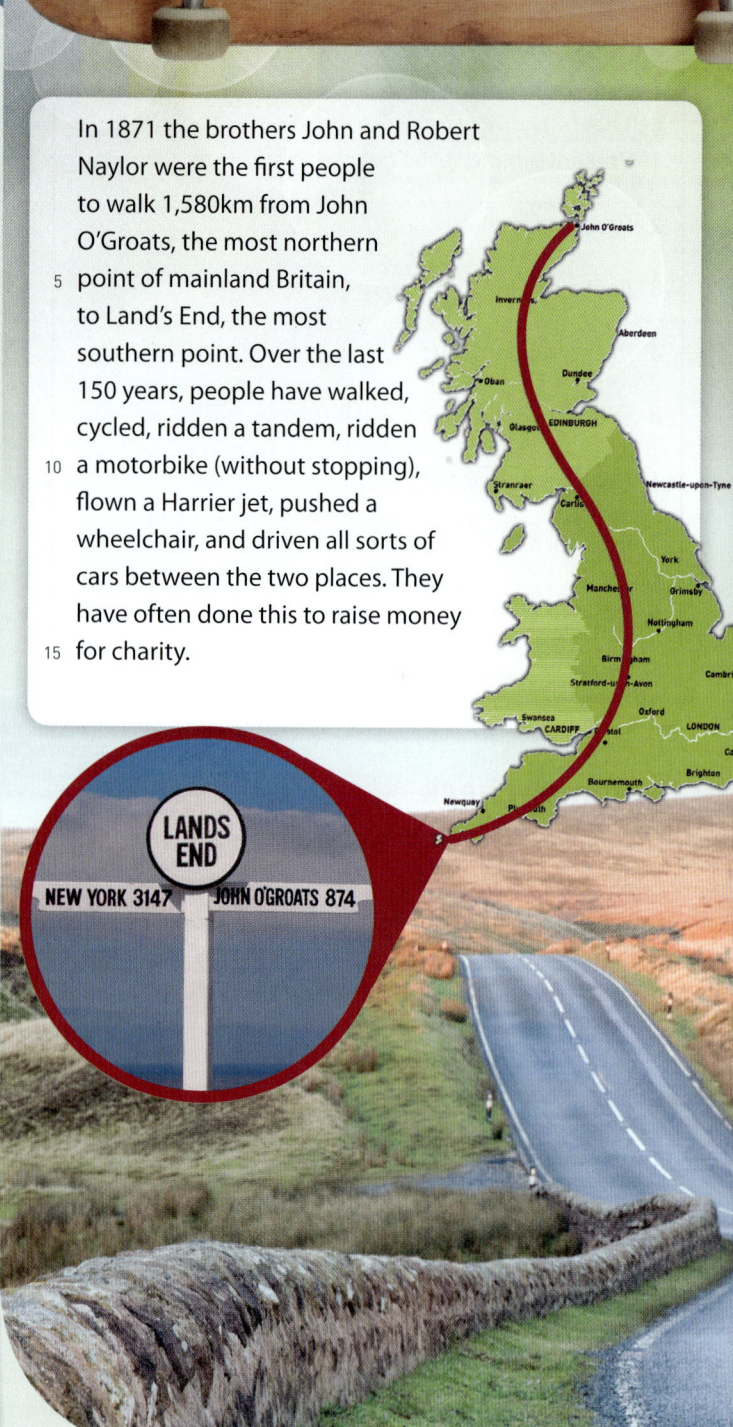

3 🔊 **5.11** While you read • Read the article and answer questions 2, 3 and 5 in Ex.2 again.

4 Vocabulary • Underline 6 words in the article that you don't know.

1 Guess the meaning from the context and write a translation.
2 Check your answers in the glossary.

FOR CHARITY

So what was different about Ben Stiff's journey? Well, Ben, 18, of Ipswich, made the journey in just 28 days – by skateboard! He did it to raise money for a charity that works to prevent heart disease and strokes,
20   called CORDA.

Ben decided to make his trip to raise awareness of the danger of strokes among young people. His close friend, Sophie, nearly died from a stroke at the age of 15 in 2007. 'The fact that someone younger than me
25   had a stroke was pretty shocking. We thought strokes were something that happened to people in their 60s and above,' said Ben.

Ben's journey was really hard. How far have you ever ridden your skateboard? Probably not more than a
30   couple of kilometres. Imagine doing it for 1,580km, up and down the hills of the Scottish Highlands and the English Lake District! Ben experienced all kinds of extreme weather, from hot sun to torrential rain to high winds. He travelled about 50km a day, so the
35   journey was physically very tough. Apart from aches and pains, Ben had a lot of trouble with verrucas and blisters on his feet.

Ben's journey was a great success and he made almost £4,000 for CORDA. His family and friends were
40   at Land's End to congratulate him on reaching the end of his 1,580km ride. Here's what Ben wrote in his blog about the moment he broke the ribbon at the finishing line at the end of his epic journey:

45   ❝ I closed my eyes, opened my arms and felt the soft kiss of ribbon on my chest, and at that moment I made my peace with the road. ❞

5   **Comprehension check • True or false? Write T or F. Correct the false sentences.** 🅟

1 ___ People only make the journey from Land's End to John O'Groats on foot.
2 ___ Ben made the journey because he wanted an adventure.
3 ___ One of Ben's friends died of a stroke when she was fifteen.
4 ___ Ben experienced a great variety of weather conditions during the journey.
5 ___ Ben was seriously ill during the journey.
6 ___ Ben wrote about his journey on the Internet.

Listening

6   🔊 **5.12**   Listen to the *Network* interview with Holly, who travelled round Europe by InterRail last summer. Tick (✓) the questions you hear.

1 ___ What is InterRail?
2 ___ How much did it cost?
3 ___ How much did you spend a day while you were travelling?
4 ___ Have you ever been away on your own?
5 ___ Who did you go with?
6 ___ Did you ever argue?
7 ___ Where did you stay?
8 ___ Which countries did you visit?
9 ___ Which country has the best trains?
10 ___ And the worst trains?
11 ___ Who did you meet?
12 ___ What were the best moments?
13 ___ And the worst moments?
14 ___ Do you want to go again?
15 ___ What's your advice to people thinking of doing InterRail?

Listen again and make notes of Holly's answers to the questions in your exercise book.

Speaking

7   In pairs. Plan an InterRail trip.

Discuss these points:

1 When?
2 Who with?
3 For how long?
4 Which countries?
5 Which cities/sights?
6 What accommodation?

When you finish, tell the class about your trip.

Writing

8   Imagine you're on the trip you planned in Ex.7. Use the answers to these questions to write an email (100 words) to your family. 🆃

- What's the weather like?
- Where have you been so far?
- What are you doing now?
- Where are you going next?
- What have been the best moments?
- What have been the worst moments?
- How are you getting on with your friend?

Present perfect (3) • *just, already, yet, still*

1 Match the sentences (1–5) to their Italian translations (a–e).

1 ___ He's just left.
2 ___ He's already left.
3 ___ He hasn't left yet.
4 ___ Has he left yet?
5 ___ He still hasn't left.

a È già partito?
b Non è ancora partito.
c Non è ancora partito.
d È già partito.
e È appena partito.

Now complete rules 1–4.

> 1 Si usano _____ e _____ nelle frasi affermative.
> 2 Si usa _____ nelle frasi interrogative e negative.
> 3 Si mettono _____ e _____ tra il soggetto e il verbo, mentre si mette _____ sempre alla fine della frase.
> 4 _____ ha lo stesso significato di *(not) yet*, ma si mette prima del verbo.

2 Write complete sentences.

1 he/leave for school/already
   He's already left for school.
2 you/not have dinner/yet

3 we/receive the letter/already

4 I/speak to Nathan/still

5 you/pass your test/yet?

6 she/get her exam results/just

3 Choose the correct alternative.

1 My dad hasn't found a new job still/yet/just/already.
2 I've still/yet/just got a letter from Jake. It arrived two minutes ago.
3 We're in Rome. We haven't visited the Vatican still/yet/just/already.
4 Rachel still/yet/just/already hasn't had an answer about her job.
5 He's still/yet/already been on holiday but he's very tired.
6 We've still/yet/just been to a concert in Hyde Park. It was great!

Ripasso dei tempi verbali

4 Write the name of the verb tense next to each sentence.

1 _____ He's never eaten Chinese food.
2 _____ I always spend the summer at the seaside.
3 _____ Did you see that film last night? No, I didn't.
4 _____ Is she having a bath? Yes, she is.
5 _____ I'm meeting Jessica outside school at four o'clock.
6 _____ They're going to have a party next month.
7 _____ Hurry up! The train leaves at 6pm.

Now match the verb tenses (1–7) to their uses (a–g). Write a number in the space.

> a ___ Per parlare di intenzioni nel futuro.
> b ___ Per parlare di un avvenimento al passato quando non è specificato il momento in cui è successo.
> c ___ Per parlare di appuntamenti al futuro.
> d ___ Per parlare di abitudini.
> e ___ Per parlare di azioni concluse in un momento preciso del passato.
> f ___ Per parlare di orari ufficiali al futuro.
> g ___ Per parlare di azioni in corso nel momento in cui si parla.

Esercizi sommativi

5 Complete the text with the correct tense of the verb in brackets. In some cases more than one answer is possible.

Tim Spencer [1]_____ (be) really lucky! He [2]_____ (just/win) a plane ticket to America in a competition. He [3]_____ (enter) the competition two months ago. He [4]_____ (start) his journey in New York next July, then he [5]_____ (travel) to San Francisco because he [6]_____ (have got) some friends there. At the moment he [7]_____ (finish) his exams at school and he [8]_____ (study) very hard. He [9]_____ (get) up at six o'clock every day and [10]_____ (study) for two hours before he goes to school. It's hard, but it's OK because he [11]_____ (look) forward to going away.

6 Translation • Translate the sentences into English.

1 Richard ha appena visto un film in televisione.
2 Hai già fatto la doccia? No.
3 Che cosa hai intenzione di fare l'estate prossima?
4 Abbiamo già ricevuto un invito alla festa.
5 Lei non ha mai giocato a tennis.
6 Non ho ancora visto i risultati dell'esame.

WB pp.258–267

Using public transport

Dialogue 🎬 VIDEO

1 🔊 **5.13** Charlotte's visiting friends in Brighton for the weekend. She's at the ticket office. Listen and complete the conversation with the sentences in the box.

> I'll get the coach
> The off-peak return fare
> And when are you coming back?
> Single or return?
> What time's the next train to Brighton, please?
> Have you got a Railcard?

Charlotte	1 _____
Man	It's at half past six.
Charlotte	OK. A ticket to Brighton, please.
Man	2 _____
Charlotte	Return, please.
Man	3 _____
Charlotte	No, I haven't.
Man	4 _____
Charlotte	On Sunday evening.
Man	5 _____
	is £27.60.
Charlotte	£27.60! That's very expensive!
Man	Well, the coach is a bit cheaper.
Charlotte	Thanks.
	6 _____

2 🔊 **5.14** Charlotte decides to go to Brighton by coach. Listen and write her journey details below.

1 Departure time: _____
2 Return time: _____
3 Cost of ticket: _____

Say it right!

3 🔊 **5.15** Listen. Then listen and repeat the sentences with the correct rhythm.

Man	A ticket to Liverpool, please.
Woman	Single or return?
Man	A return, please.
Woman	When are you leaving?
Man	This morning at ten past eleven.
Woman	And when are you coming back?
Man	On Sunday evening at quarter past seven.
Woman	The return fare is £66.20.
Man	OK. Here you are...

In pairs. Practise the dialogue. Now close your books. Can you say the dialogue from memory?

Speaking

4 In pairs. Choose one of the journeys below (A, B or C) and act out the dialogue at the ticket office.

	A	B	C
Destination	Exeter	Birmingham	Edinburgh
Transport	train	coach	train
Departure time	Monday 12.00	Sunday 15.00	Tuesday 09.12
Return time		Saturday 8.05	Thursday 17.40
Ticket type	Single: £14.70	Off-peak return ticket: £18.50	Peak-time return ticket: £108.30

When you finish, choose another journey and change roles.

WB p.267

On the Tube

1 Is there an underground where you live? What are the good and bad things about it?

2 🔊 5.16 Read this guide to the London Underground. What advantages and disadvantages of travelling by Tube are mentioned?

GOING TO LONDON?

Save time and money! Read the *Network Magazine* guide to the Tube.

BACKGROUND

The London Underground (also called *the Tube*) opened in 1863. It was the first underground railway system in the world. It introduced the world's first electric trains in 1890. The oldest line
5 is the Metropolitan. It opened on 10th January 1863. It was 6km long and soon carried 26,000 people every day. Now, believe it or not, there are 270 stations and 400km of track! Only the Shanghai Metro is bigger.

GOOD AND BAD!

10 The Tube is the fastest way to get around London because you avoid the traffic congestion on the roads. However, it's quite expensive, it can be very hot and uncomfortable in summer and there are often delays. The quality of the air is not very good
15 either. In fact, a 40-minute journey on the Tube is the same as smoking 2 cigarettes because of the dust in the air!

THE UNDERGROUND LINES

A man called Harry Beck designed the award-winning, elaborate Tube map in 1933 and was paid
20 5 guineas (about 6 euros) for the work. There are 11 Underground lines and each line has a different colour on the map. The longest is the red Central line, which is 74km long and has 49 stations! The shortest line is the Waterloo and City
25 – it's 2.4km long.

LONDON UNDERGROUND ZONES

The cost of an Underground ticket depends on which zone you are travelling from and to. There are six concentric zones. Zone 1 is the centre of London and Zone 6 is in the suburbs of London and includes London's most important airport, Heathrow.

TICKETS

30 You can buy tickets from machines and ticket offices at all stations. Single tickets are quite expensive, starting at £4.00 for one zone. The best thing a tourist can do to save money is to buy an off-peak Travelcard for zones 1 and 2. You can't use it before 9.30am, but it's worth it! You can get one-day and one-
35 week Travelcards.

OYSTERCARD

The cheapest way to travel on the Undergound is to use an Oystercard. You can buy a 'Visitor Oystercard' in advance online. Oystercards are smartcards that you put on a sensor at the ticket barriers and the cost of the ticket is deducted from your total
40 credit. You can top up online or at a ticket office.

> **Did you know?**
> Although they call it the Underground, 55% of the network is above ground.

3 Answer the questions.

1 What's special about the London Underground?
2 How many lines are there?
3 Which line is the longest?
4 How many zones are there on the network?
5 What's the least expensive way to travel on the Tube?

Speaking

4 In pairs. Ask and answer the questions. 🅿 🆃

1 When was the last time you visited a big city?
2 How did you travel around?
3 Have you ever been to London? Did you go on the Underground? What did you think of it?
4 What's the best way to travel around a big city? Why?

📹 **VIDEO** Now watch the Network video!

WORKBOOK

Contents

Grammar network

A Verbo *be*

Forma affermativa		Forma negativa		Forma interrogativa	Risposte brevi	
estesa	contratta	estesa	contratta		affermative	negative
I am	I'm	I am not	I'm not	Am I?	Yes, I am.	No, I'm not.
you are	you're	you are not	you aren't	Are you?	Yes, you are.	No, you aren't.
he/she/it is	he/she/it's	he/she/it is not	he/she/it isn't	Is he/she/it?	Yes, he/she/it is.	No, he/she/it isn't.
we are	we're	we are not	we aren't	Are we?	Yes, we are.	No, we aren't.
you are	you're	you are not	you aren't	Are you?	Yes, you are.	No, you aren't.
they are	they're	they are not	they aren't	Are they?	Yes, they are.	No, they aren't.

1 Nella lingua parlata e informale, quando il verbo segue il pronome soggetto (*I*, *You*, *He*, ecc.) nelle frasi affermative di solito si usa la forma contratta (*'m/'s/'re*):
She's a student.   *È una studentessa.*

 A differenza dell'italiano, in inglese il soggetto della frase deve sempre essere espresso:
We're English. (~~Are English.~~)   *Siamo inglesi.*

2 La forma contratta *'s* si può usare anche con i sostantivi e i nomi propri, ma non con quelli che terminano in *-s*:
My mum's a dentist.
ma:
Chris is my brother. (~~Chris's my brother.~~)

3 La forma contratta *'re* si può usare solo dopo i pronomi soggetto *You*, *We* e *They*. Non si può usare dopo i sostantivi o i nomi propri:
You're messy!
ma:
My brothers are messy! (~~My brothers're messy!~~)

4 Anche nel caso delle frasi negative, la forma contratta è molto più comune di quella estesa. Si può usare con tutti i pronomi, i sostantivi e i nomi propri:
I'm not tall.   *Non sono alto.*
My teacher isn't Mr Wright.
Il mio insegnante non è Mr Wright.
Luca and Teresa aren't my friends.
Luca e Teresa non sono i miei amici.

5 Nelle domande, le parole interrogative vanno prima del verbo *be*:
Where are you?   *Dove sei?*

6 Nelle risposte brevi affermative si usa sempre la forma intera di *be*, mentre nelle risposte brevi negative di solito si usa la forma contratta:
Are you cousins?   *Siete cugini?*
Yes, we are. (~~Yes, we're.~~)   *Sì.*
No, we aren't.   *No.*

7 Il verbo *be* corrisponde in italiano ai verbi 'essere' e 'stare' e si usa per:
- dare informazioni personali (nazionalità, età, occupazione):
I'm sixteen.   *Ho sedici anni.*
Oliver isn't Italian.   *Oliver non è italiano.*
- dire dove si trovano persone e cose:
Are they at home?   *Sono a casa?*

B Preposizioni di luogo (1)

1 Le preposizioni seguenti si usano per descrivere dove si trovano cose e persone:

in = *in*	under = *sotto*
on = *su, sopra*	behind = *dietro*

C Genitivo sassone

1 Il genitivo sassone si usa per indicare possesso o il rapporto esistente tra persone. Si forma così:

sostantivo singolare + *'s* + cosa posseduta

Deborah's bag   *la borsa di Deborah*

sostantivo plurale regolare + *'* + cosa posseduta

the students' books   *i libri degli studenti*

sostantivo plurale irregolare + *'s* + cosa posseduta
(*men*, *women*, *children*, ecc.)

the children's bikes   *le bici dei bambini*

più di un possessore + *'s* dopo il nome dell'ultimo possessore

Tim and Alice's house   *la casa di Tim e Alice*

2 L'articolo prima della cosa posseduta viene sempre omesso:
Luca's room (~~the Luca's room~~)   *la stanza di Luca*

3 Tuttavia, non sempre si usa il genitivo sassone per indicare possesso. Quando si parla di cose invece che di persone, si usa spesso una struttura simile a quella dell'italiano:
the date of the party (~~the party's date~~)   *la data della festa*

D Verbo *have got*

Forma affermativa		Forma negativa		Forma interrogativa	Risposte brevi	
estesa	contratta	estesa	contratta		affermative	negative
I have got	I've got	I have not got	I haven't got	Have I got?	Yes, I have.	No, I haven't.
you have got	you've got	you have not got	you haven't got	Have you got?	Yes, you have.	No, you haven't.
he/she/it has got	he/she/it's got	he/she/it has not got	he/she/it hasn't got	Has he/she/it got?	Yes, he/she/it has.	No, he/she/it hasn't.
we have got	we've got	we have not got	we haven't got	Have we got?	Yes, we have.	No, we haven't.
you have got	you've got	you have not got	you haven't got	Have you got?	Yes, you have.	No, you haven't.
they have got	they've got	they have not got	they haven't got	Have they got?	Yes, they have.	No, they haven't.

1 Nella lingua parlata informale di solito si usa la forma contratta (*'ve got/'s got*):
He's got a brother. *Ha un fratello.*
They haven't got a dog. *Non hanno un cane.*

2 Nelle domande, le parole interrogative vanno prima del verbo *have/has got*:
What have you got in that bag?
Che cos'hai in quella borsa?

3 Nelle risposte brevi si omette *got*. In quelle affermative si usa sempre la forma intera di *have*, mentre in quelle negative di solito si usa la forma contratta:
Have they got a daughter? *Hanno una figlia?*
Yes, they have. (Yes, they have got.) *Sì.*
No, they haven't. *No.*

4 Il verbo *have got* corrisponde in italiano al verbo 'avere' e si usa per:
• parlare di possesso:
We've got a car. *Abbiamo una macchina.*
• parlare di rapporti familiari e interpersonali:
She's got three brothers. *Ha tre fratelli.*
• descrivere alcune caratteristiche fisiche:
I've got long hair. *Ho i capelli lunghi.*

E *a/an, any, How many...?*

1 *a* e *an* sono articoli indeterminativi. Corrispondono a 'un', 'uno', 'una' (vedi Starter Book p.20):
• *a* si usa con sostantivi numerabili singolari che iniziano con consonante o suono consonantico:
a dog *un cane*
a university *un'università.*
• *an* si usa con sostantivi numerabili singolari che iniziano con vocale, suono vocalico o *h* muta:
an hour *un'ora*
an MP3 player *un lettore MP3.*

2 L'aggettivo indefinito *any* equivale all'italiano 'del', 'della', ecc. *Any* si usa con i sostantivi plurali nelle frasi negative e interrogative:
They haven't got any cousins.
Non hanno cugini.
Have you got any brothers?
Hai dei fratelli?

3 *How many...?* equivale all'italiano 'Quanti...?'/'Quante...?'. Si usa con i sostantivi plurali nelle frasi interrogative:
How many sisters have you got?
Quante sorelle hai?

Word store

Family — *La famiglia*

aunt (auntie) _____
brother _____
brother-in-law _____
cousin _____
daughter _____
father (dad) _____
father-in-law _____
grandfather (grandad) _____
grandmother (grandma) _____
husband _____
mother (mum) _____
mother-in-law _____
nephew _____
niece _____
parents _____
sister _____
sister-in-law _____
son _____

stepbrother _____
stepfather (stepdad) _____
stepmother (stepmum) _____
stepsister _____
uncle _____
wife _____

Real talk

Completa le espressioni dai dialoghi dello *Student's Book*.

_____ usual — *Come al solito*
You're so _____! — *Sei così disordinato!*
You're _____ — *Sei noioso*
_____ them a ring — *Chiamali*
_____ cares! — *Che importa!*
_____ a drink? — *Ti va qualcosa da bere?*
an _____ child — *Figlio unico*
_____ you! — *Beata te!*

Vocabulary

Family

1 Osserva l'albero genealogico e trova Martha. Scrivi che legame di parentela ha ogni persona con Martha sotto la figura corrispondente.

 Harry

 Margaret

1 _____

2 _____

 Daniel

 Lucy

 Adam

 Sarah

3 _____

4 _____

5 _____

6 _____

 Martha   Edward

 Rebecca

7 _____

8 _____

2 Osserva di nuovo l'albero genealogico e completa le frasi con la parola corretta.

1 Adam and Sarah are Rebecca's _____.
2 Edward is Lucy's _____.
3 Martha is Daniel's _____.
4 Lucy is Adam's _____.
5 Adam is Sarah's _____.
6 Lucy is Daniel's _____.
7 Rebecca is Lucy's _____.
8 Edward is Adam's _____.

3 Rispondi alle domande con i nomi dall'albero genealogico.

1 Who is Sarah's father-in-law?
_____
2 Who is Daniel's mother-in-law?
_____
3 Who is Sarah's sister-in-law?
_____
4 Who is Daniel's brother-in-law?
_____

4 Scrivi la parola corretta per ogni descrizione.

1 She's your father's wife, but she isn't your mother.
= _____
2 He's your mother's husband, but he isn't your father. = _____
3 His father is married to your mother.
= _____
4 Her mother is married to your father.
= _____

5 Rispondi alle domande in maniera personale.

1 What's your mum's name?
_____
2 What are your grandfathers' names?
_____
3 What are your brother and sister's names?
_____
4 How many uncles and aunties have you got?
_____
5 How many cousins have you got?
_____

Grammar

Verbo *be*

1 Scrivi frasi complete con *be*. Usa la forma contratta dove è possibile.

1 Chris/not be/my cousin

_____

2 Mum and Dad/be/at home

_____

3 I/not be/happy

_____

4 Thomas/be/a student

_____

5 you/not be/late

_____

6 we/be/in the same class

_____

7 my friends/not be/at school today

_____

8 your brother/be/a good swimmer

_____

2 Scrivi mini-dialoghi usando le parole date, la forma interrogativa di *be* e le risposte brevi.

1 you/be/English? (No)

_____

_____

2 Oliver/be/at the pool? (Yes)

_____

_____

3 you and your friend/be/from the USA? (Yes)

_____

_____

4 that girl/be/your cousin? (No)

_____

_____

5 your house/be/in Queen Street? (No)

_____

_____

6 Oliver and his family/from London? (Yes)

_____

_____

3 Scrivi il dialogo con *be* usando le parole date. Usa la forma contratta dove è possibile.

Mum　Who/your new teacher this year?
　　　　 ¹_____

Max　It/Mr Fletcher.
　　　　 ²_____

Mum　he/nice?
　　　　 ³_____

Max　Yes, ⁴_____. He/friendly.
　　　　 ⁵_____

Mum　the other students/nice?
　　　　 ⁶_____

Max　They/OK. ⁷_____

Preposizioni di luogo (1)

4 Abbina le preposizioni alle figure (1–4).

> behind　in　on　under

1 _____　2 _____　3 _____　4 _____

5 Scrivi mini-dialoghi sulla posizione degli oggetti nella figura. Usa le parole date, *Where*, *be* (alla forma contratta dove è possibile) e le preposizioni dell'Esercizio 4.

1 the DVDs?
　Where are the DVDs?
　They're under the bed.

2 the laptop?

_____

_____

3 the camera?

_____

_____

4 the chair?

_____

_____

5 the books?

_____

_____

Genitivo sassone

6 Riscrivi le frasi indicando i nomi dei possessori.

1 His father is my football coach. (Dan)
Dan's father is my football coach.

2 Their school is near my house. (My cousins)

3 His best friend is Sam. (Chris)

4 Their English teacher's from Liverpool. (Her children)

5 Her eyes are green. (My mum)

6 Their party is on Saturday night. (Her friends)

7 Their bikes are in the garden. (Nathan and Joseph)

8 Her grandmother lives in Twickenham. (Zoe)

7 C'è un errore in tre di queste frasi. Identifica gli errori e riscrivi le tre frasi correttamente.

1 This is Sandys phone.

2 My parents' car is a Vauxhall Astra.

3 James's eyes are blue.

4 Toms' teacher is very tall.

5 The childrens' dog is old.

6 Alice's sisters are 13 and 11.

Verbo *have got*

8 Completa il paragrafo con la forma corretta di *have got*.

I ¹_____ a very big family!
I ²_____ two brothers and a sister.
My dad ³_____ two brothers. My mum
⁴_____ a brother and sister. My uncles
and aunts are all married. They ⁵_____
children so I ⁶_____ eight cousins.
We ⁷_____ four grandparents too. My
brother's also married and he ⁸_____
two daughters so I'm an uncle too.

9 Scrivi un paragrafo (50–60 parole) sulla tua famiglia.

10 Scrivi mini-dialoghi con *have got*.

1 Ella and Joe/cousins in Australia? (Yes)

2 Mike/a messy bedroom? (Yes)

3 your rabbit/a name? (No)

4 Lisa/a new phone? (Yes)

5 you/a Lunapop CD? (No)

6 they/an MP3 Player? (No)

11 Rispondi alle domande in maniera personale e dai più informazioni possibili.

1 Have you got any DVDs?
Yes, I have. I've got about thirty. My favourite's...
oppure:
No, I haven't.

1 Have you got any DVDs?

2 Have you got any good books?

3 Have you got a mobile?

4 Have you got a scooter?

5 Have you got any pets?

6 Have you got an MP3 player?

a/an, any

12 Completa le frasi con *a*, *an* o *any*.

1 I haven't got _____ new mobile.
2 Has she got _____ brothers and sisters?
3 My aunt hasn't got _____ children.
4 Have they got _____ house in Sardinia?
5 Has your dad got _____ interesting job?
6 Nico hasn't got _____ pets.
7 I haven't got _____ MP3 player.
8 Have his parents got _____ Fiat 500?

Esercizi sommativi

13 In ogni frase, decidi se *'s* è l'abbreviazione di *is*, *has* o se è il genitivo sassone (*GS*).

1 Mum's got a new car. _____
2 He's a good friend. _____
3 Is this your aunt's house? _____
4 Oliver's school is in London. _____
5 Where's my bag? _____
6 My mobile's got the Internet. _____

14 Completa il paragrafo con le parole mancanti.

Jessica ¹_____ fifteen. She ²_____ from the UK, but she ³_____ English. She ⁴_____ from Scotland. She's ⁵_____ two brothers – Luke and Harry. They ⁶_____ seventeen and twelve. Jessica's ⁷_____ two uncles and an aunt, but she ⁸_____ got any cousins. Her Uncle Dave and Aunt Sue haven't got ⁹_____ children. Her Uncle Paul ¹⁰_____ got ¹¹_____ girlfriend, Donna, but they ¹²_____ married.

15 Scrivi il dialogo seguendo la traccia.

Kelly Chiedi a papà dov'è il tuo telefono.
1 _____

Dad Di' che è sul tavolo in cucina.
2 _____

Kelly Di' di no. Spiega che è il telefono della mamma.
3 _____

Dad Chiedi a Kelly se è nella sua camera.
4 _____

Kelly Di' di no. Non è sulla scrivania, non è sul pavimento, non è sotto il letto... Chiedi a Robert se ha il tuo (=di Kelly) telefono.
5 _____

Robert Di' di no. Di' che il suo telefono è vecchio. Di' che hai un bel telefono nuovo. Chiedi a Kelly se è nella sua borsa.
6 _____

Kelly Di' di sì!
7 _____

Chiedi dov'è la tua borsa.
8 _____

Dad Di' che non ce l'avete.
9 _____

16 Translation • Traduci il paragrafo in inglese sul tuo quaderno.

La mia camera è al piano di sopra. È molto disordinata! Ho un letto, una scrivania e un computer. Non ho libri nella mia camera. Sono in una stanza diversa. Ho molti DVD e videogiochi per il computer sulla mia scrivania. I miei libri scolastici sono sul pavimento. Il mio skateboard è sotto il letto e lo skateboard del mio amico è dietro la scrivania. Ho due fratelli. Hanno undici e dodici anni. Hanno una camera molto grande. La camera dei miei fratelli è molto ordinata!

Translation note

Ricorda che, a differenza dell'italiano, in inglese di solito si deve usare usa l'aggettivo indefinito *any* nelle frasi negative con sostantivi plurali:

Non ho cugini.
I haven't got any cousins. (~~I haven't got cousins.~~)

Grammar network

A Present simple (1)

Forma affermativa	Forma negativa		Forma interrogativa	Risposte brevi	
	estesa	contratta		affermative	negative
I play	I do not play	I don't play	Do I play?	Yes, I do.	No, I don't.
you play	you do not play	you don't play	Do you play?	Yes, you do.	No, you don't.
he/she/it plays	he/she/it does not play	he/she/it doesn't play	Does he/she/it play?	Yes, he/she/it does.	No, he/she/it doesn't.
we play	we do not play	we don't play	Do we play?	Yes, we do.	No, we don't.
you play	you do not play	you don't play	Do you play?	Yes, you do.	No, you don't.
they play	they do not play	they don't play	Do they play?	Yes, they do.	No, they don't.

1 La forma affermativa del *Present simple* con *I, You, We* consiste nella forma base del verbo.
I play football. *Gioco a calcio.*

2 Alla terza persona singolare, la forma affermativa del *Present simple* si ottiene aggiungendo *-s* alla forma base del verbo.
He plays football. *Gioca a calcio.*

3 Fai attenzione alle seguenti variazioni ortografiche quando aggiungi la *-s* della terza persona singolare alla forma base del verbo:
- se il verbo termina in *-s, -ch, -sh, -o, -x, -z*, si aggiunge *-es*:
  watch – watches, go – goes
- se il verbo termina in consonante + *-y, -y* diventa *-i* e si aggiunge *-es*:
  study – studies
  ma: **play – plays**

4 La forma negativa del *Present simple* si ottiene così:

> soggetto + *don't/doesn't* + forma base del verbo

I don't like sweets. *Non mi piacciono i dolci.*
He doesn't play football. *Non gioca a calcio.*

5 La forma interrogativa del *Present simple* si ottiene così:

> *Do/Does* + soggetto + forma base del verbo + ?

Does she play tennis? *Gioca a tennis?*
Do they use the Internet? *Usano internet?*

6 Le risposte brevi si formano così:

> *Yes*, + soggetto + *do/does*.
> *No*, + soggetto + *don't/doesn't*.

7 Il *Present simple* si usa per parlare di:
- dati di fatto:
  They don't eat meat. *Non mangiano la carne.*
- azioni abituali e routine:
  She wakes up early. *Si sveglia presto.*
- situazioni permanenti:
  They live in Rome. *Vivono a Roma.*
- orari (scolastici, dei treni, ecc.):
  School finishes at 3pm. *La scuola finisce alle 3:00.*

B Verbi + *-ing*

1 Quando i verbi di opinione (*like, love, hate, enjoy, can't stand*) sono seguiti da un altro verbo, di solito quest'ultimo è alla forma in *-ing*:
We love going to concerts. *Adoriamo andare ai concerti.*
I don't like eating fish. *Non mi piace mangiare il pesce.*
She hates dancing. *Odia ballare.*
Joe can't stand jazz. *Joe non sopporta il jazz.*
NB: *can't stand* è un verbo modale e quindi è invariabile per tutte le persone e non è mai usato con gli ausiliari (*do/does*).

2 La forma in *-ing* del verbo si ottiene aggiungendo *-ing* alla forma base del verbo.

3 Fai attenzione alle seguenti variazioni ortografiche quando aggiungi *-ing* alla forma base del verbo:
- se il verbo termina in consonante + *-e* (eccezione *be-being*), la *-e* cade:
  hide – hiding, arrive – arriving
- se il verbo termina in *-ie, -ie* diventa *-y*:
  die – dying, lie – lying
- se la sillaba finale del verbo è accentata e termina in consonante + vocale + consonante, la consonante finale raddoppia:
  re*fer* – referring
  NB: questa regola non vale se la sillaba non è accentata:
  o*ffer* – offering (~~offerring~~)
- se un verbo monosillabico termina in consonante + vocale + consonante, la consonante finale raddoppia:
  stop – stopping, swim – swimming

 Non si raddoppiano mai *-y* o *-w* alla fine del verbo:
pay – paying (~~payying~~)

Si raddoppia sempre la *-l* finale, anche quando la sillaba non è accentata:
travel – travelling
NB: in inglese americano si scrive *traveling*

4 Si possono usare gli avverbi *really* o *quite* prima dei verbi di opinione per modificarne il significato. *quite* si usa solo con i verbi *like* e *enjoy*:

I really hate studying in the evening.
Detesto davvero studiare di sera.
They quite like playing basketball.
A loro piace abbastanza giocare a basket.

 A differenza dell'italiano, in inglese le espressioni *very much* e *a lot* ('molto', 'tanto') vengono dopo il complemento oggetto e non subito dopo il verbo principale:
I like singing very much. *Mi piace molto cantare.*
NB: il verbo alla forma in *-ing* può fungere da sostantivo e può essere usato sia come soggetto che come complemento oggetto: **Skiing is exciting.**

C Pronomi personali complemento

I – me	it – it
you – you	we – us
he – him	you – you
she – her	they – them

1 I pronomi personali complemento possono essere usati al posto di un nome proprio o di un sostantivo quando sono il complemento oggetto o indiretto di una frase:
He phones his friends. – He phones them.
Telefona ai suoi amici. – Telefona loro.

Oliver hates pasta. – He hates it.
Oliver detesta la pasta. – La detesta.

 Mentre in italiano i pronomi complemento possono precedere il verbo, in inglese lo seguono sempre:
I want it. *Lo voglio.*

D *play, go e do*

1 *play, go* e *do* si usano così:
- *play* + uno sport di squadra in cui si usa la palla:
  play football *giocare a calcio*
- *go* + uno sport o un'attività alla forma in *-ing*:
  go swimming *andare a nuoto*
- *do* + uno sport individuale in cui non si usa la palla:
  do judo/karate *fare judo/karate*

NB: fanno eccezione *do fencing* (fare scherma), *do boxing* (fare box) e *do weight lifting* (fare sollevamento pesi).

Functions on film

E *So do I/Neither do I*

1 Per esprimere accordo con un'affermazione al *Present simple*, si possono usare le seguenti strutture:
- per esprimere accordo con una frase affermativa:
  A I love dancing. *Adoro ballare.*
  B So do I. *Anch'io.*
- per esprimere accordo con una frase negativa:
  A I don't like rugby. *Non mi piace il rugby.*
  B Neither do I. *Neanche a me.*

2 Per esprimere disaccordo con un'affermazione al *Present simple*, si possono usare le seguenti strutture:
- per esprimere disaccordo con una frase affermativa:
  A I love dancing. *Adoro ballare.*
  B Oh, I don't. *Io (invece) no.*
- per esprimere disaccordo con una frase negativa:
  A I don't like rugby. *Non mi piace il rugby.*
  B Oh, I do. *A me (invece) sì.*

Word store

Sports — *Sport*

do fencing _____
go mountain biking _____
go rollerblading _____
go snowboarding _____
go swimming _____
play basketball _____
play football _____
play volleyball _____

Free-time activities (1) — *Attività del tempo libero*

go out with friends _____
go shopping _____
listen to music _____
play computer games _____
play the guitar/the piano/
the drums _____
text/phone friends _____
use the Internet _____
watch TV/DVDs _____

Real talk

Completa le espressioni dai dialoghi dello *Student's Book*.

I'll _____ you	*Te li presento*
_____, you guys!	*Ciao, ragazzi!*
_____ him!	*Non dargli retta!*
He's obsessed _____	*È fissato con...*
_____ to gigs	*andare ai concerti*
I've _____ to go	*Devo andare*
By the _____	*A proposito*

Extra vocabulary • Skills and culture

brilliant	*fantastico*
cool	*forte, fantastico*
dangerous	*pericoloso*
difficult	*difficile*
fast	*veloce*
it's satisfying	*dà soddisfazione*
it's scary	*fa paura*
original	*originale*
to be passionate about	*essere appassionato di*
worried	*preoccupato*

Vocabulary

Sports & Free-time activities (1)

1 Osserva le figure e completa i nomi degli sport.

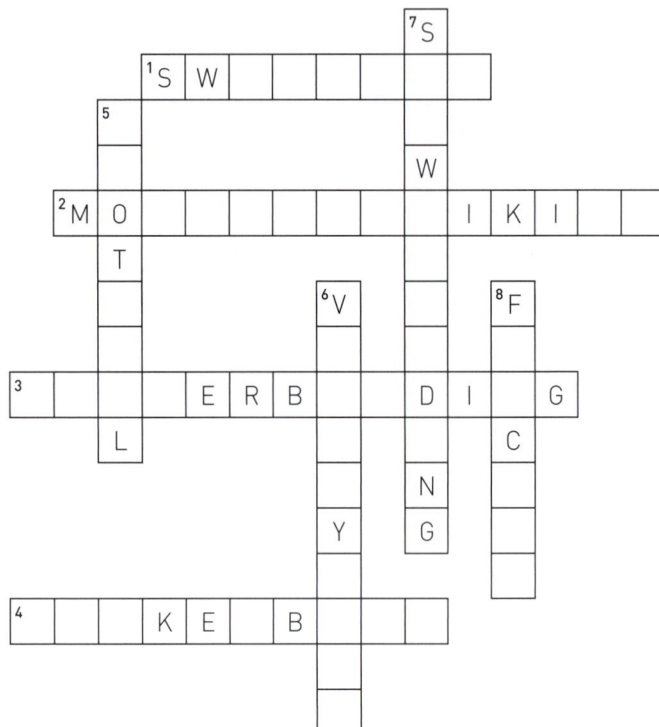

2 Riscrivi i nomi degli sport dell'Esercizio 1 aggiungendo il verbo adatto. Scegli fra *do*, *go* e *play*.

1 _____   5 _____
2 _____   6 _____
3 _____   7 _____
4 _____   8 _____

3 Abbina i verbi (1–8) ai sostantivi (a–h) per trovare le attività del tempo libero.

1 ___ go out   a computer games
2 ___ go   b the Internet
3 ___ listen to   c with friends
4 ___ play   d shopping
5 ___ play   e DVDs
6 ___ text   f music
7 ___ use   g the drums
8 ___ watch   h friends

Word skills

Prendere nota dei vocaboli (1)

È una buona abitudine prendere nota di vocaboli nuovi in inglese man mano che li impari. Usa uno dei seguenti metodi per annotare i vocaboli nuovi:

- Dedica ad ogni lettera dell'alfabeto almeno una pagina intera del quaderno. Scrivi la lettera dell'alfabeto in cima alla pagina corrispondente. Ricorda che l'alfabeto inglese ha più lettere di quello italiano! Puoi lasciare meno spazio per le lettere meno comuni (*x*, *z*, ecc.). Dividi la pagina in due colonne e scrivi la parola inglese in una colonna e la sua traduzione in un'altra colonna. Ogni volta che impari un nuovo vocabolo, scrivilo nella pagina giusta e scrivi anche la traduzione in italiano.

4 Scrivi le parole seguenti in ordine alfabetico.

> January   dance   zoo   evening   quick   hot
> train   big   Wednesday   intelligent

- Un altro metodo per annotare i vocaboli consiste nel dividere il quaderno in sezioni tematiche. Per esempio, potresti creare una sezione intitolata *Sports*, un'altra intitolata *Food*, un'altra *Personality adjectives*, ecc. In questo modo compilerai gradualmente diverse liste di vocaboli in inglese tradotti in italiano, divise per argomento.

5 Scrivi le parole seguenti in una delle tre categorie elencate nel paragrafo 2 qui sopra.

> strawberries   golf   generous   bread
> chocolate   funny   skiing   tennis   friendly

In entrambi i casi, è una buona idea scrivere una frase d'esempio per ogni vocabolo nuovo, che ti aiuterà a ricordare come puoi usarlo, per esempio:

> John's very <u>generous</u>. He always gives all his friends a birthday present.

- Se preferisci, puoi usare il computer per preparare una lista di vocaboli. In questo modo potrai aggiornare l'ordine alfabetico della lista ogni volta che aggiungi un vocabolo.

Grammar

Present simple (1)

1 Completa le frasi con la forma corretta dei verbi fra parentesi. Usa il *Present simple*. Fai attenzione alle variazioni ortografiche della terza persona singolare.

1 My sister _____ (buy) new clothes every Saturday.
2 My dad _____ (come) home at half past six.
3 Jack _____ (go) to judo class on Thursdays.
4 Sam always _____ (pass) all his exams.
5 Mum always _____ (cry) when she _____ (watch) a sad film.
6 Luca _____ (wash) his scooter every week.
7 Emma _____ (tidy) her room at the weekends.
8 My friend _____ (want) to go out on Friday.

2 Completa il paragrafo con la forma corretta dei verbi fra parentesi. Usa il *Present simple*.

Gemma and Jonathan [1]_____ (be) brother and sister. They [2]_____ (live) in Manchester and they [3]_____ (go) to the same school. Gemma [4]_____ (get up) early every day. She [5]_____ (have) a shower and then she [6]_____ (make) her breakfast. She [7]_____ (be) always ready for school at half past eight. Jonathan [8]_____ (sleep) until eight o'clock. Then he [9]_____ (run) around in a panic! They [10]_____ (take) the bus to school. Gemma [11]_____ (wait) for Jonathan at the bus stop, but on some days he [12]_____ (miss) the bus.

3 Scrivi frasi che sono vere per te al *Present simple*. Usa sia la forma affermativa che quella negativa.

1 I/live/in Verona
_____
2 the students in my class/wear/a school uniform
_____
3 my friends and I/like/football
_____
4 my favourite singer/come/from the USA
_____
5 my mum/speak/English
_____
6 I/use/a computer every evening
_____

4 Riscrivi le frasi affermative alla forma negativa e quelle negative alla forma affermativa.

1 You don't swim well.
_____
2 Georgia doesn't play the guitar.
_____
3 I go out with my friends on Saturdays.
_____
4 My brother plays volleyball.
_____
5 Lisa and Tom go to the cinema every weekend.
_____
6 His grandma doesn't use the Internet.
_____
7 I don't want to go.
_____
8 Mum doesn't work at the weekends.
_____

5 Scrivi 8 frasi facendo dei paragoni fra te e un tuo amico o un tuo famigliare. Pensa ai loro hobby, alle loro routine, e a quello che piace e non piace loro. Usa i verbi nel riquadro al *Present simple* come aiuto.

| eat | get up | go | like | listen to | live | play | study |

My cousin Lorenzo lives in Naples, but I live in Rome. We both go to school, but I go to a liceo and he goes to a scuola media. He doesn't like...

_____
_____
_____
_____
_____
_____
_____
_____
_____
_____
_____

6 Scrivi domande e risposte al *Present simple* usando le parole date.

1 you/like/rap music? (Yes)

_____

2 Sara/play/tennis? (No)

_____

3 the students/go/to school on Saturdays? (No)

_____

4 the train/arrive/at five o'clock? (Yes)

_____

5 your dad/work/in London? (No)

_____

6 those girls/come/from Australia? (Yes)

_____
_____

7 Completa il dialogo con la forma corretta dei verbi fra parentesi. Usa il *Present simple*.

Lydia Who ¹_____ (be) that boy in the photo with you, Harry?

Harry That ²_____ (be) my friend, Dean.

Lydia ³_____ (he/go) to our school?

Harry No, ⁴_____. He ⁵_____ (not go) to school now. He ⁶_____ (go) to university.

Lydia Really? How old ⁷_____ (he/be)?

Harry He ⁸_____ (be) 18. He ⁹_____ (study) Biology at York University.

Lydia ¹⁰_____ (his parents/live) here?

Harry Yes, ¹¹_____. They ¹²_____ (live) near my house. Why ¹³_____ (you/be) so interested?

Lydia Oh, no reason. ¹⁴_____ (he/come home) in the holidays?

Harry Yes, ¹⁵_____. He's got a girlfriend here!

Verbi + *-ing*

8 Completa le frasi con la forma in *-ing* dei verbi fra parentesi.

1 My mum hates _____ (wash) the car.
2 We like _____ (study) other languages.
3 I prefer _____ (cycle) to _____ (walk).
4 They can't stand _____ (shop) for clothes.
5 My friend loves _____ (control) the situation.
6 I like _____ (play) computer games.
7 She doesn't like _____ (lie) in the sun all day.
8 I hate _____ (arrive) late.

9 Osserva le informazioni nella tabella. Scrivi domande complete usando la forma corretta dei verbi. Poi scrivi le risposte brevi.

	shop	ski	watch horror films	eat curry
Kate	☹	☺ ☺	☹	☹ ☹
Edward	☺ ☺	☹	☺ ☺	☺
Sally & Mark	☹ ☹	☹	☹ ☹	☺ ☺
you	?	?	?	?

1 Kate/like/shop?

_____

2 Edward/like/eat curry?

_____

3 Sally and Mark/like/ski?

_____

4 Sally and Mark/like/eat curry?

_____

5 you/like/watch horror films?

_____

6 you/like/ski?

_____

10 Osserva di nuovo la tabella dell'Esercizio 9. Scrivi frasi su quello che piace e non piace alle persone usando i verbi nel riquadro.

hate   not like   like   love

1 Kate – ski

_____

2 Edward – eat curry

_____

3 Sally and Mark – watch horror films

_____

4 Kate – shop

_____

5 Sally and Mark – ski

_____

6 I – eat curry

_____

Pronomi personali complemento

11 Abbina le frasi al pronome personale complemento corretto.

1 History is my favourite subject. I love _____.

2 I walk to school. My sister comes with _____.

3 Who are those boys? I don't know _____.

4 My cousin's name is Annabel Blake. Do you know _____?

5 Our mum takes _____ to our swimming lessons.

6 Do you know Mr Weston? Does he teach _____?

7 Thomas is really funny. I like _____.

8 This is my new scooter. What do you think of _____?

you
us
him
it
them
her
me
it

12 Metti le parole seguenti nell'ordine corretto per scrivere delle frasi. Poi traducile in italiano.

1 loves   her   he

_____

_____

2 them   like   I

_____

_____

3 it   can't   we   stand

_____

_____

4 doesn't like   he   me

_____

_____

5 she   us   teaches

_____

_____

6 know   they   you

_____

_____

Esercizi sommativi

13 Rispondi alle domande usando le informazioni fra parentesi. Usa le risposte brevi e i pronomi personali complemento.

1 Does Donna like romantic songs? (✓ – love)
   Yes, she does. She loves them.

2 Do you like basketball? (✗ – hate)

_____

3 Does Tony like Lady Gaga? (✗ – can't stand)

_____

4 Do your parents like your boyfriend? (✓ – love)

_____

5 Does Rebecca like dogs? (✗ – can't stand)

_____

6 Do your friends like working at the weekend? (✗ – hate)

_____

14 Scrivi il dialogo seguendo la traccia.

Jake Domanda a Sara se le piace la musica rap.
1 _____

Sara Di' di sì. Chiedigli perché.
2 _____

Jake Di' che sabato c'è un concerto. Chiedile se vuole venire.
3 _____

Sara Di' che non sei sicura. Adori ascoltare la musica rap, ma non ti piace andare ai concerti.
4 _____

Jake Chiedile perché no.
5 _____

Sara Di' che ti piace stare seduta e comoda!
6 _____

Jake Di' che non le credi.
7 _____

Sara Di' che è vero. I tuoi amici vanno a molti concerti, ma non vai con loro.
8 _____

Jake Dille di telefonarti domani.
9 _____

15 Translation • Traduci il paragrafo in inglese sul tuo quaderno.

Io e la mia ragazza siamo molto diversi. Io adoro il calcio, il basket e il tennis, ma a lei non piace fare sport. A lei piace ascoltare musica rock, ma io non la sopporto. Io detesto i film romantici, ma lei li adora. Non ascoltiamo musica e non guardiamo DVD. Che cosa facciamo? Usciamo con gli amici, ma non ci piace fare le stesse cose. A lei piace davvero andare a far spese, ma io non lo sopporto. Che importa? Lei piace a me e io piaccio a lei.

Translation note

Ricorda che, a differenza dell'italiano, in inglese il verbo *like* ha una costruzione personale. *Like* quindi concorda con il soggetto, non con il complemento:

Le piacciono i bambini.
She likes children.
(~~She like children./Children like her.~~)

Sporting families

The world of international sport is full of people with the same surname – and the same passions. In many sports, family members
5 **play or race against their brothers, sisters or cousins.**

The most famous example of competitive <u>siblings</u> is probably the Williams sisters – Venus and Serena. These sisters from Los Angeles, USA, are tennis
10 <u>champions</u>. Together, they have got 18 international <u>titles</u>. The German racing drivers, Michael and Ralf Schumacher, are both stars of Formula One, and the Italian brothers, Francesco and Edoardo Molinari, from Turin, are now world champions at golf. Their
15 success is unusual because golf is not a traditional or a very popular sport in Italy.

Peyton and Eli Manning are famous brothers in the USA. They play American football and are captains of the Indianapolis Colts and the New York Giants. The
20 two teams sometimes compete together.

There are lots of brothers in international football. People in England always remember Jack and Bobby Charlton, both members of England's winning World Cup team in 1966. Famous English footballers Rio,
25 Les and Anton Ferdinand are all from the same family, but Les is Rio and Anton's cousin, not their brother. But the most extreme sporting family is probably the Tuilagi brothers in the UK. The seven Tuilagis are originally from Samoa, but six of them now play for
30 different British rugby teams!

Glossary

<u>siblings</u>	fratelli
<u>champions</u>	campionesse
<u>titles</u>	titoli

Reading comprehension

*

1 🔊 **S.071** Leggi il testo e abbina i personaggi dello sport allo sport che praticano e alla loro nazionalità.

	name	sport	nationality
1	the Williams	golf	American
2	the Schumachers	football	American
3	the Molinaris	rugby	German
4	the Mannings	tennis	Italian
5	the Ferdinands	American football	Samoan
6	the Tuilagis	Formula One	British

**

2 Scegli l'alternativa corretta.

1 The first names of the Williams sisters are
   a Venus and Serena.   b Tracey and Rio.
2 The Schumachers are
   a racing drivers.   b team captains.
3 Golf isn't very popular in
   a the USA.   b Italy.
4 American footballers Peyton and Eli Manning play for
   a the same team.   b different teams.
5 Rio and Anton are Les Ferdinand's
   a brothers.   b cousins.
6 The Tuilagi brothers live in
   a the UK.   b Samoa.

***

3 Rispondi alle domande.

1 Which city do the Williams sisters come from?

_____

2 How many international titles have they got?

_____

3 Which sport has famous brothers who are both team captains?

_____

4 Who are Jack and Bobby Charlton?

_____

5 What sport do the Ferdinands play?

_____

6 How many of the Tuilagi brothers play for British rugby teams?

Culture note

Nel 1966 l'Inghilterra ha ospitato i campionati mondiali di calcio nel famoso *Wembley Stadium* a Londra e ha vinto – battendo la Germania Ovest 4–2. Il calciatore brasiliano Pelé chiamò Wembley 'la cattedrale del calcio'.
Wembley Stadium fu costruito nel 1923 ma fu demolito nel 2003 e rimpiazzato da uno stadio completamente nuovo che ha aperto nel 2007.

Listening comprehension

4 🔊 **S.072** Eva e la sua famiglia fanno la stessa attività nel tempo libero. Ascolta e abbina le parti iniziali delle frasi (1–5) alle loro conclusioni (a–e). *

1 ___ Eva and her family   **a** on Saturdays.
2 ___ Eva's parents have got   **b** two brothers.
3 ___ Eva's parents are   **c** a martial arts school.
4 ___ Eva's got   **d** love judo.
5 ___ Eva helps at the school   **e** judo instructors.

5 🔊 **S.072** Riascolta e completa le frasi. **

1 The most _____ sports at the school are judo, karate and tae kwon do.
2 Eva's _____ is one of the karate instructors.
3 Eva's _____ do competitions all over the UK.
4 Eva doesn't like _____ _____.
5 Eva hasn't got any _____ _____.
6 When she hasn't got a judo class, Eva does her _____.

6 🔊 **S.072** Riascolta e rispondi alle domande. ***

1 When do students go to Eva's parents' school?
_____
2 How old are Eva's brothers?
_____
3 Where do William and Alex do judo competitions?
_____
4 Who teaches Eva judo?
_____
5 When does Eva have judo classes?
_____
6 What other things does Eva do in her free time?
_____

Dictation

7 🔊 **S.073** Ascolta e scrivi le frasi che senti.

1 _____
2 _____
3 _____
4 _____
5 _____
6 _____

Writing

Writing skills

Pronomi e aggettivi possessivi

8 Leggi le informazioni e completa gli esempi con il pronome o l'aggettivo possessivo corretto (*we*, *him*, *my*, ecc.).

- I pronomi si usano al posto dei sostantivi o dei nomi propri. Ci sono pronomi soggetto:

  ~~Mrs Bellamy~~ is our Maths teacher.→
  ¹_____ is our Maths teacher.

  ~~My cousins~~ live in Scotland. →
  ²_____ live in Scotland.

- e pronomi complemento:

  I love ~~swimming~~. → I love ³_____.

  We meet ~~our friends~~ after school.→
  We meet ⁴_____ after school.

- Gli aggettivi possessivi si usano per indicare possesso. Si possono usare al posto del genitivo sassone:

  ~~John's~~ computer is very old. →
  ⁵_____ computer is very old.

  ~~The students'~~ homework is difficult. →
  ⁶_____ homework is difficult.

- Ricorda che *his* si usa quando il possessore è maschile, e *her* quando il possessore è femminile:

  ~~Sara's~~ brother is at university.→
  ⁷_____ brother is at university.

  ~~My uncle's~~ wife is Spanish. →
  ⁸_____ wife is Spanish.

- L'uso dei pronomi e degli aggettivi possessivi permette di evitare ripetizioni e rende la lingua più scorrevole.

  Ora fai l'Esercizio 9 tenendo presente le regole sui pronomi e gli aggettivi possessivi.

9 Scrivi un breve testo (75–100 parole) su un tuo amico o famigliare. Includi le risposte alle seguenti domande: 🇹

- What's his/her name?
- How old is he/she?
- Where does he/she live?
- Who does he/she live with? Describe his/her family.
- What does he/she do (study, work, etc)? Does he/she like it?
- What does he/she like doing in his/her free time? What doesn't he/she like?

Inizia così:

My ...'s name is...

Functions on film

Agreeing and disagreeing

A Completa i 4 mini-dialoghi con una o più parole nel riquadro.

> do   don't   neither   so

1 A Do you like Jessie J?
  B No, I ¹_____.
  C ²_____ ³_____ I. I can't stand her.
2 A Do you like our French lessons?
  B Yes, I ⁴_____.
  C Oh, I ⁵_____. They're boring.
3 A Do you like coffee?
  B No, I ⁶_____.
  C Oh, I ⁷_____. I love it.
4 A Do you like our new teacher?
  B Yes, I ⁸_____.
  C ⁹_____ ¹⁰_____ I. He's really funny.

B Scrivi il dialogo seguendo la traccia.

Megan Chiedi a Leo qual è il suo programma televisivo preferito.
1 _____

Leo Di' che è *Top Gear*. Di' che ti piacciono i programmi sulle macchine.
2 _____
_____

Megan Di' che a te non piacciono. Pensi che siano noiosi. Ti piace guardare film alla televisione.
3 _____

Leo Esprimi accordo. Ma di' che non ti piacciono i film romantici.
4 _____

Megan Esprimi accordo.
5 _____

Grammar network

A Present simple (2) • Avverbi di frequenza

0%	She **never** eats meat. Non mangia *mai* la carne.
10%	They **hardly ever** watch TV. Non guardano *quasi mai* la televisione.
40%	I **sometimes** listen to the radio. *Qualche volta* ascolto la radio.
60%	We **often** go shopping. *Spesso* andiamo a far spese.
90%	You **usually** get up early. *Di solito* ti alzi presto.
100%	He **always** does his homework. Fa *sempre* i compiti.

1 Gli avverbi di frequenza si usano con il *Present simple* e generalmente, in frasi affermative, precedono il verbo principale, ma seguono il verbo *be*:
We never go to the cinema. *Non andiamo mai al cinema.*
He is often tired. *È spesso stanco.*

2 Con il verbo *have got*, gli avverbi di frequenza si mettono tra *have* e *got*:
I have always got my MP3 player in my bag.
Ho sempre il mio lettore MP3 in borsa.

3 Nelle frasi negative, gli avverbi di frequenza di solito precedono il verbo principale, ma seguono il verbo *be*:
She doesn't always finish her homework.
Non sempre finisce i compiti.
I'm not usually late for lessons.
Di solito non arrivo in ritardo alle lezioni.
I haven't usually got my school diary at home.
Di solito non ho il mio diario a casa.

4 Nelle frasi interrogative, gli avverbi di frequenza seguono il soggetto:
Does Jack often walk to school?
Jack va spesso a scuola a piedi?
Are you always happy? *Sei sempre felice?*
Have they usually got homework on Fridays?
Di solito hanno compiti di venerdì?

! A differenza dell'italiano, in inglese la doppia negazione non è possibile, quindi *never, hardly ever* e altri avverbi di frequenza con un significato negativo si usano con un verbo alla forma affermativa:
I never do homework on Friday.
(~~I don't never do homework on Friday.~~)
Non faccio mai i compiti il venerdì.
He's hardly ever at home.
(~~He isn't hardly ever home.~~)
Non è quasi mai a casa.

5 Il *Present simple* con gli avverbi di frequenza si usa per parlare di ogni quanto si verifica un evento o della frequenza con la quale si compie un'azione.

B Espressioni di frequenza

1 Il *Present simple* può essere usato con le seguenti espressioni per parlare in modo più specifico della frequenza con cui si verifica un'azione:

> every… = *ogni…*
> every time = *ogni volta*
> once/twice a… = *una volta/due volte al…*
> three/four times a… = *tre/quattro volte al…*
> a couple of times a… = *un paio di volte al…*

I visit my grandparents every Sunday.
Vado a trovare i miei nonni ogni domenica.
I eat fruit twice a day.
Mangio della frutta due volte al giorno.
We have an English test four times a year.
Facciamo una verifica di inglese quattro volte all'anno.

2 Queste espressioni si mettono di solito alla fine delle frasi:
I study every evening. *Studio ogni sera.*
I don't study every evening. *Non studio ogni sera.*
Do you study every evening? *Studi ogni sera?*

 Le espressioni *one time* e *two times* non esistono in inglese. 'Una volta' e 'due volte' si traducono con *once* e *twice*.
I go to the gym once a week.
(~~I go to the gym one time a week.~~)
Vado in palestra una volta a settimana.

3 Per chiedere della frequenza di un evento o di un'azione si usa *How often…?*
How often do you eat pizza? I eat pizza once a week.
Quanto spesso mangi la pizza? Mangio la pizza una volta a settimana.

C *at, on, in* con espressioni di tempo

1 Le preposizioni *at*, *on* e *in* si usano spesso con espressioni di tempo in frasi al *Present simple*:

- *at* si usa con le ore, le festività, e con *weekend* e *night*:
  I get up at seven o'clock.
  Mi alzo alle sette.
  We go skiing at Christmas.
  Andiamo a sciare a Natale.
  My dad works at night.
  Il mio papà lavora di notte.

- *on* si usa con i giorni della settimana e le date:
  We do PE on Wednesdays.
  Facciamo educazione fisica il mercoledì.
  We always have a party on December 31st.
  Facciamo sempre una festa il 31 dicembre.

- *in* si usa con i mesi, le stagioni e le parti del giorno (eccetto *night*: vedi sopra):
  We usually go to the beach in August.
  Di solito andiamo alla spiaggia ad agosto.
  It doesn't always snow in the winter.
  Non nevica sempre in inverno.
  Do you like studying in the evening?
  Ti piace studiare di sera?

2 Queste espressioni di solito si mettono alla fine delle frasi.

D Espressioni con *have*

1 *have*, come *have got*, corrisponde al verbo 'avere' in italiano. Tuttavia, ci sono differenze importanti nella forma e nell'uso di *have* e *have got*.

2 Il verbo *have* si usa nelle seguenti espressioni con un sostantivo con il significato di fare o svolgere un'azione. A differenza del verbo *have got*, il verbo *have* si comporta come un verbo regolare e richiede gli ausiliari *do/does* alle forme negativa e interrogativa:

> have breakfast = *fare colazione*
> have lunch = *pranzare*
> have dinner = *cenare*
> have a snack = *fare uno spuntino*
> have a drink = *prendere qualcosa da bere*
> have something to eat = *prendere qualcosa da mangiare*
> have a bath = *farsi il bagno*
> have a shower = *farsi la doccia*
> have a wash = *lavarsi*
> have a party = *fare una festa*
> have fun/a good time = *divertirsi*
> have a rest = *riposarsi*
> have a break = *fare una pausa*

We don't have a break in the afternoon.
Non facciamo una pausa nel pomeriggio.
What do you have for breakfast?
Cosa mangi a colazione?

3 Il verbo *have* si può anche usare in alternativa a *have got* per esprimere possesso:
I have a lot of work to do.
Ho tanto lavoro da fare.

Word store

Daily routine — *Routine quotidiana*

brush (my) teeth	_____
do (my) homework	_____
finish school	_____
get dressed	_____
get home	_____
get up	_____
go to bed	_____
go to school	_____
have a bath	_____
have a break	_____
have a shower	_____
have a snack	_____
have a wash	_____
have breakfast	_____
have dinner	_____
have lunch	_____
start school	_____

Word builder +

Free-time activities (2) — *Attività del tempo libero*

go dancing	_____
go for a ride (on a scooter)	_____
go for a walk	_____
hang around with friends	_____
have a chat	_____
have a… lesson	_____
rent a DVD	_____

Real talk

Completa le espressioni dai dialoghi dello Student's Book.

I'm fed _____	*Sono stufa*
_____,…	*E comunque,…*
_____ on!	*Dai!*
It's got _____ to _____ with you	*Non ti riguarda*
It's _____ it.	*Ne vale la pena.*
_____ pressure	*sotto pressione*

Vocabulary

Daily routine

1 Osserva le figure. Scrivi frasi sugli orari in cui Matt svolge certe attività ogni giorno.

 7.15

 7.30

1 *He gets up at* _____

2 _____

 7.45

 8.20

3 _____

4 _____

 8.40

 15.30

5 _____

6 _____

 15.50

 17.00

7 _____

8 _____

 22.15

 22.30

9 _____

10 _____

2 Completa i nomi dei pasti con le lettere mancanti.

1 b_____   3 d_____

2 l_____   4 a sn_____

The time

3 Scrivi le ore in forma estesa.

1 8.30   *half past eight* _____

2 3.10   _____

3 7.50   _____

4 10.15   _____

5 1.55   _____

6 5.20   _____

7 2.45   _____

8 9.35   _____

Grammar

Present simple (2) • Avverbi di frequenza

1 Leggi le frasi. Poi scrivi i sei nomi nell'ordine corretto, iniziando dalla persona che si alza presto più frequentemente.

Elliot usually gets up early.
Harry hardly ever gets up early.
Kelly often gets up early.
Jessica never gets up early.
George always gets up early.
Yasmin sometimes gets up early.

1 _____
2 _____
3 _____
4 _____
5 _____
6 _____

2 Riscrivi le frasi inserendo al posto giusto l'avverbio di frequenza fra parentesi.

1 We watch TV in the mornings. (hardly ever)
_____
_____

2 English songs are difficult to understand. (sometimes)
_____
_____

3 The boys play football at school. (often)
_____
_____

4 Do you wear jeans? (usually)
_____
_____

5 I eat fish. (hardly ever)
_____
_____

6 Does she walk to school? (always)
_____
_____

7 Tom's late for lessons. (never)
_____
_____

8 Do they have lunch at home? (usually)
_____
_____

9 Anna's tired after school. (often)
_____
_____

10 I read a book in the evenings. (sometimes)
_____
_____

3 Ogni quanto fai queste attività? Scrivi frasi che sono vere per te con gli avverbi di frequenza.

1 play computer games after school?
_____

2 forget your homework?
_____

3 study on a Saturday?
_____

4 be tired on a Monday morning?
_____

5 go to bed after 11pm?
_____

6 sing in the shower?
_____

7 watch TV in the morning?
_____

8 be late for school?
_____

9 write long emails?
_____

10 see your grandparents?
_____

Altre espressioni di frequenza

4 Riscrivi le frasi sostituendo le espressioni di frequenza con gli avverbi nel riquadro.

> often   sometimes   hardly ever

1 They visit their grandparents every weekend.
_____

2 I walk to school twice a week.
_____

3 She tidies her room three times a year.
_____

4 My dad's in London every Tuesday.
_____

5 She comes out with us twice a month.
_____

6 We get homework twice a week.
_____

7 You go to the seaside in August every year.
_____

8 He goes snowboarding once a year.
_____

9 It is very warm in December once every ten years.
_____

10 They enjoy reading books every day.
_____

5 Osserva le agende di Emma e Cameron. Scrivi frasi con il *Present simple* e le espressioni ... *(times) a ...,* o *never.*

Emma	Cameron
Monday	gym	
Tuesday		football
Wednesday		
Thursday	gym	
Friday	judo	judo
Saturday	dance class	football
Sunday		football

1 Emma/go to the gym

_____

2 Cameron/go to the gym

_____

3 Cameron/play football

_____

4 Emma and Cameron/do judo

_____

5 Emma and Cameron/play tennis

_____

6 Emma/have a dance class

_____

6 Scrivi risposte personali alle domande usando il *Present simple* e le espressioni ... *(times) a ...,* o *every ....* Se non fai mai certe attività, usa *never.*

1 How often do you brush your teeth?

_____

2 How often does your mum go to a supermarket?

_____

3 How often do your friends have parties?

_____

4 How often do you eat pasta?

_____

5 How often do you and your family go on holiday?

_____

6 How often do you watch films on DVD?

_____

at, on, in con espressioni di tempo

7 Scrivi le espressioni di tempo nella colonna corretta.

Fridays   half past three   October   the autumn
June 21st   Monday   night   Christmas
November 17th   the evening   February   ten to nine

at	on	in
_____	_____	_____
_____	_____	_____
_____	_____	_____
_____	_____	_____

8 Scrivi frasi con il *Present simple*, aggiungendo la preposizione corretta: *at, on* o *in.*

1 I/have/a shower/the morning

_____

2 you/go shopping/the weekend?

_____

3 Max/play basketball/Wednesdays?

_____

4 I/have/a party with my friends/Hallowe'en

_____

5 the school year/start/September

_____

6 we/go/to the seaside/the summer

_____

7 my dad/get up/quarter past six

_____

8 my birthday/be/28th May

_____

9 Rispondi alle domande in maniera personale. Devi usare *at, on* o *in* in ogni risposta.

1 What time do you usually go to bed?

_____

2 When do you study English at school?

_____

3 When does your school year finish?

_____

4 When's your birthday?

_____

5 What time do you start your homework?

_____

6 When do you usually go on holiday?

_____

7 When do you go shopping?

_____

8 What time do you have dinner?

_____

Espressioni con *have*

10 Scegli l'alternativa corretta.

1 You **have/'ve got** my phone!
2 I **have/'ve got** a snack in the afternoon.
3 My dad **has/'s got** friends in the USA.
4 We **have/have got** breakfast in the kitchen every day.
5 She **has/has got** a bath every evening.
6 They **have/'ve got** a new car.

11 Scrivi frasi e domande complete usando le parole date e *have* o *have got*.

1 Tony/a computer at home?
_____

2 she/often/lunch at a café
_____

3 they/a party/at Christmas?
_____

4 the students/not/a break/at 10 o'clock
_____

5 we/not/any lessons this afternoon
_____

6 my mum/a new job in London
_____

> **Esercizi sommativi**

12 Rispondi alle domande. Prima di tutto specifica la frequenza e poi aggiungi dettagli su quando fai le attività.

1 How often do you do sport?
I do sport twice a week. I play tennis on Tuesday evenings, and I go to a gym every Saturday.
_____
_____

2 How often do you study Maths?
_____
_____

3 How often do you meet your friends?
_____
_____

4 How often do you use a computer?
_____
_____

13 Scegli l'alternativa corretta per completare il dialogo.

Amy I'm really hungry! **¹Do you have/Have you got** any chocolate?
James No, I **²don't/haven't**! And lunch is **³at/on** half past twelve.
Amy I know. But I don't want to wait!
James **⁴I never am/I'm never** hungry in the morning. **⁵I always have/I've always got** a big breakfast.
Amy **⁶I never have/I don't never have** breakfast.
James Why not?
Amy **⁷I get up always/I always get up** late! I'm not very good **⁸in/on** the morning.
James That's terrible! Do you have breakfast **⁹at/on** the weekend?
Amy No, I don't. I get up **¹⁰at/on** lunchtime!

14 Translation • Traduci il paragrafo in inglese sul tuo quaderno.

Tanya adora proprio nuotare, e spesso fa delle gare. Si alza sempre alle sei. Fa colazione e poi si lava, e di solito parte da casa alle sette. Non va a scuola alle sette – va a lezione di nuoto. Tanya fa lezioni di nuoto ogni giorno prima di scuola. Va anche a nuotare il fine settimana. Fa gare quattro o cinque volte all'anno. Non ha altri hobby perché non ha tempo libero!

> **Translation** note
>
> Ricorda che, a differenza dell'italiano, in inglese ci sono regole precise per la posizione degli avverbi di frequenza nella frase:
>
> *Faccio sempre i compiti./Faccio i compiti sempre.*
> I always do my homework.
> (~~Always I do my homework./I do my homework always.~~)

Grammar network

A Present continuous (1) e (2)

Forma affermativa		Forma negativa		Forma interrogativa	Risposte brevi	
estesa	contratta	estesa	contratta		affermative	negative
I am eating	I'm eating	I am not eating	I'm not eating	Am I eating?	Yes, I am.	No, I'm not.
you are eating	you're eating	you are not eating	you aren't eating	Are you eating?	Yes, you are.	No, you aren't.
he/she/it is eating	he/she/it's eating	he/she/it is not eating	he/she/it isn't eating	Is he/she/it eating?	Yes, he/she/it is.	No, he/she/it isn't.
we are eating	we're eating	we are not eating	we aren't eating	Are we eating?	Yes, we are.	No, we aren't.
you are eating	you're eating	you are not eating	you aren't eating	Are you eating?	Yes, you are.	No, you aren't.
they are eating	they're eating	they are not eating	they aren't eating	Are they eating?	Yes, they are.	No, they aren't.

1 Il *Present continuous* si ottiene con il soggetto + *am/is/are* + forma in *-ing* del verbo. Per la formazione dei verbi in *-ing*, vedi Unit 2 p.152.

2 Nelle risposte brevi affermative al *Present continuous* si usa sempre la forma intera, mentre nelle risposte brevi negative di solito si usa la forma contratta:
Are you getting off the bus?
Stai scendendo dall'autobus?
Yes, I am. (~~Yes, I'm.~~)   *Sì.*
No, I'm not.   *No.*

3 Il *Present continuous* si usa per:
- descrivere un'azione che è in corso di svolgimento nel momento in cui si parla:
I'm waiting for the bus at the moment.
Sto aspettando l'autobus in questo momento.

- descrivere un'azione o una situazione temporanea di una certa durata ma che non è necessariamente in corso di svolgimento nel momento in cui si parla:
He's learning to play basketball this year.
Sta imparando a giocare a basket quest'anno.
My mum's working in Milan this week.
Mia madre lavora a Milano questa settimana.

- parlare di cambiamenti che si svolgono gradualmente:
My shoes are getting old.
Le mie scarpe stanno diventando vecchie.
The cost of living is increasing.
Il costo della vita sta aumentando.

- descrivere le azioni che si vedono in una fotografia o un quadro:
In this picture we're dancing.
In questa foto stiamo ballando.

 A differenza dell'italiano, in inglese non si può usare il *Present simple* per descrivere un'azione in corso di svolgimento nel momento in cui si parla:
We're checking our homework.
Controlliamo/Stiamo controllando i nostri compiti.

B Present continuous o Present simple?

1 Il *Present continuous* si usa per parlare di azioni in corso di svolgimento e di azioni o situazioni temporanee:
The lesson's starting.
La lezione sta iniziando.

2 Il *Present simple* invece (vedi Unit 2 p.152) si usa per parlare di fatti, situazioni permanenti e abitudini o routine:
Lessons start at 8am.
Le lezioni iniziano alle 8:00.

3 Il *Present continuous* si usa spesso con le seguenti espressioni di tempo:

> (right) now = *(proprio) ora*
> at the moment = *in questo momento*
> today = *oggi*
> this afternoon/evening = *oggi pomeriggio/stasera*
> this week/month = *questa settimana/questo mese*
> these days = *in questi giorni*

She's having a shower at the moment.
Si sta facendo la doccia in questo momento.
We aren't going out much this month.
Non stiamo uscendo molto questo mese.

4 Il *Present simple* invece si usa spesso con le seguenti espressioni e avverbi di frequenza (vedi Unit 3 p.162 per l'elenco completo):

> on Fridays = *tutti i venerdì*
> at the weekends = *nei fine settimana*
> usually = *di solito*
> every day = *ogni giorno*
> never = *mai*

She goes to football training on Mondays and Wednesdays.
Va a fare allenamento di calcio tutti i lunedì e venerdì.
They usually go to the beach at the weekends.
Di solito vanno alla spiaggia nei fine settimana.

5 I verbi di stato non vengono di solito usati al *Present continuous*. Questi verbi spesso descrivono stato, possesso, sentimenti, opinioni e processi mentali. Alcuni verbi di stato comuni sono:

be = *essere*	own = *possedere*
believe = *credere*	prefer = *preferire*
belong = *appartenere*	promise = *promettere*
hate = *odiare*	remember = *ricordare*
have got = *avere (possedere)*	seem = *sembrare*
know = *conoscere, sapere*	think = *pensare*
like = *piacere*	understand = *capire*
love = *amare*	want = *volere*
mean = *significare*	wish = *desiderare*
need = *avere bisogno di*	

What does this word mean?
(*What's this word meaning?*)
Che cosa significa questa parola?

I don't understand this exercise.
(*I'm not understanding this exercise.*)
Non capisco questo esercizio.

 A volte lo stesso verbo può essere un verbo di stato o meno, a seconda del suo significato:
What do you think of that jacket?
Che te ne pare di quella giacca?
What are you thinking about?
A che cosa stai pensando?

6 Tuttavia, a volte si usano i verbi di stato al *Present continuous* per enfatizzare una situazione temporanea o per rendere più forte un sentimento:
Normally John is very nice, but today he's being really horrible.
John di solito è molto carino, ma oggi è davvero orribile.

Functions on film

C Let's..., Shall...?, How about...?/ Do you fancy...?

1 Quando si danno dei suggerimenti o quando si propone di fare qualcosa a qualcuno, si possono usare le seguenti strutture:

> *Let's* + forma base del verbo

Let's watch a DVD.   *Guardiamo un DVD.*

> *Shall we* + forma base del verbo + ?

Shall we watch a DVD?   *(Vuoi che) Guardiamo un DVD?*

> *How about/Do you fancy* + verbo alla forma in *-ing* + ?

How about/Do you fancy watching a DVD?
Che ne pensi di/Ti va di guardare un DVD?

2 Per accettare una proposta si può dire:
That sounds great!/That's a good idea!

3 Per rifiutare una proposta si può dire:
No thanks, I don't feel like it./No, sorry, I don't like...

Word store

School subjects   *Materie scolastiche*

Science   _____
Biology   _____
Chemistry   _____
IT (Information Technology)   _____
Maths   _____
Physics   _____
Humanities   _____
Citizenship   _____
Geography   _____
History   _____
Italian   _____
RE (Religious Education)   _____
Languages   _____
English   _____
French   _____
German   _____
Greek   _____
Latin   _____
Spanish   _____
PE (Physical Education)   _____
basketball   _____
football   _____
swimming   _____
volleyball   _____

Real talk

Completa le espressioni dai dialoghi dello *Student's Book*.

What's the _____?   *Che c'è?*
Come _____ it   *Smettila*
I'm sorry to _____ you   *Mi dispiace disturbarLa*
It's _____ that...   *È solo che...*
Is he getting _____ OK with...?   *Va d'accordo con...?*
I _____   *Ho capito*

Extra vocabulary • Skills and culture

another country	*un'altra nazione*
art gallery	*galleria d'arte*
castle	*castello*
museum	*museo*
nature reserve	*riserva naturale*
outdoor activity centre	*centro di attività sportive all'aperto*
theme park	*parco a tema*

Exercises

Vocabulary

School subjects

1 Guarda le foto e completa i nomi delle materie scolastiche.

1 G_____

2 M_____

3 H_____

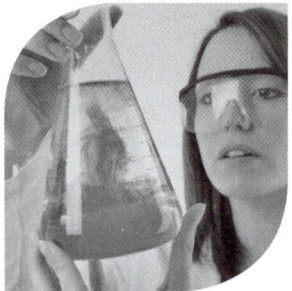

4 C_____

5 P_____

6 B_____

7 F_____

8 C_____

2 Leggi le definizioni e scrivi i nomi delle lingue.

1 They speak this language in Madrid. _____
2 They speak this language in Paris. _____
3 This is the ancient language of Rome. _____
4 They speak this language in Australia. _____
5 They speak this language in Berlin. _____
6 This language from Athens has an ancient and a modern form. _____

3 Qual è il significato di queste abbreviazioni inglesi relative alle materie scolastiche?

1 PE = _____
2 RE = _____
3 IT = _____

Word skills

Parole simili (*cognates* e *false friends*)

Molte parole, soprattutto quelle di origine greca o latina, sono simili in inglese e in italiano e quindi è facile indovinarne il significato.

Per esempio, *Geography* = geografia e *Technology* = tecnologia. Queste parole si chiamano *cognates*. Ci sono inoltre moltissime parole inglesi che vengono usate in italiano, per esempio *email* e *computer*.

4 Prova a indovinare il significato dei *cognates* in neretto in queste frasi.

1 My favourite subjects at school are **Music** and **Biology**. ¹_____ ²_____
2 Anna wants to be a **pharmacist**. She's doing a **course** at **university**. ³_____ ⁴_____ ⁵_____
3 You need lots of **qualifications** if you want to be a **dentist**. ⁶_____ ⁷_____

Tuttavia ci sono anche parole che sono simili in inglese e in italiano ma che hanno un significato diverso. Per esempio, *story* = favola/racconto (~~storia~~); *library* = biblioteca (~~libreria~~). Queste parole si chiamano *false friends*. Non ti devi far confondere dall'ortografia. Se hai dubbi, controlla il significato della parola inglese nel dizionario.

5 Scrivi la traduzione in italiano dei *false friends* in neretto in queste frasi. Poi controlla le risposte in un dizionario.

1 My **parents** are arriving now. = _____
2 He's a **sympathetic** person. = _____
3 Her **camera** is very modern. = _____
4 They work in a **factory**. = _____
5 This film is **annoying**! = _____
6 You're very **brave**! = _____

6 Ora scrivi la traduzione in inglese di queste parole italiane. Usa il dizionario se necessario.

1 parenti _____
2 simpatico _____
3 camera _____
4 fattoria _____
5 annoiare _____
6 bravo _____

Grammar

Present continuous (1) e (2)

1 Completa il testo con la forma corretta dei verbi nel riquadro. Usa il *Present continuous*.

> feel listen make do read start watch work

It's a normal evening in our house. I ¹_____ my homework and I ²_____ to music at the same time. My brothers ³_____ TV and my sister ⁴_____ a book. My mum ⁵_____ at the computer and my dad's in the kitchen. He ⁶_____ to cook dinner. I don't know what he ⁷_____ tonight, but we ⁸_____ all _____ hungry!

2 Descrivi le foto (1–3) usando il *Present continuous.* Di' dove si trovano le persone e gli animali e che cosa stanno facendo. Le parole nel riquadro possono esserti d'aiuto.

> the boy   the girl   the dog   some children   walk
> listen to   look at   play   sit   write

3 Scrivi 5 frasi al *Present continuous* sulle cose che non stanno succedendo in questo momento.

I'm not watching TV.

1 _____
2 _____
3 _____
4 _____
5 _____

4 Scrivi frasi affermative e negative al *Present continuous* usando le parole date, come nell'esempio.

1 We/study/Spanish/this year (not this afternoon – study/Maths)
   We're studying Spanish this year, but we aren't studying it this afternoon. We're studying Maths.

2 I/read/an interesting book/this week (not at the moment – watch/a DVD)
   _____
   _____
   _____

3 Jack/have/driving lessons/these days (not today – ride his bike)
   _____
   _____

4 The students/work on a History project/this term (not this morning – have/a school trip)
   _____
   _____
   _____

5 My mum and dad/paint/our kitchen/this week (not this morning – buy/some new chairs)
   _____
   _____
   _____

5 Completa il dialogo con la forma corretta del *Present continuous* e le parole fra parentesi o le risposte brevi.

Anna Hi, Sam. [1]_____? (Where/you/go)

Sam [2]_____ (I/go) to Alex's house.

Anna [3]_____ (What/you/use) that big bag for?

Sam [4]_____ (I/take) my school books with me. [5]_____ (We/study) for a Science test this week. It's terrible this year! [6]_____ (Our teachers/give) us tests all the time!

Anna Oh dear. [7]_____ (you/study) French this year?

Sam No, [8]_____. [9]_____ (I/not/do) any languages now.

Anna How's your sister? [10]_____ (she/enjoy) university?

Sam Yes, [11]_____.

Anna [12]_____? (What/she/study) I can't remember.

Sam [13]_____ (She/do) History, but [14]_____ (she/not study) a lot, if you ask me. [15]_____ (She/go) to parties all the time!

6 Rileggi il dialogo nell'Esercizio 5. Sottolinea 2 domande al *Present continuous* che si riferiscono a situazioni temporanee e cerchiane 2 che si riferiscono a qualcosa che sta succedendo in questo momento. Riscrivi le domande in basso.

_____
_____
_____
_____

Present continuous o Present simple?

7 Scrivi frasi al *Present continuous* o al *Present simple* usando le parole date.

1 Alice/stay/in London/this year.
_____

2 you/often/go/to the cinema?
_____

3 my sister/have/a piano lesson/once a week.
_____

4 I/not play/computer games/now.
_____

5 they/study/today?
_____

6 he/have/a PE lesson/on Tuesdays.
_____

7 Tom/not watch TV/every day.
_____

8 Dad/not work/this morning.
_____

8 Indica se ciascuna espressione di tempo viene di norma usata con il *Present continuous* o il *Present simple.* Scrivi *PC* o *PS*.

1 ___ usually
2 ___ at the moment
3 ___ twice a year
4 ___ sometimes
5 ___ on Fridays
6 ___ this term
7 ___ this morning
8 ___ every August

9 Completa il testo con il *Present continuous* o il *Present simple* dei verbi fra parentesi.

Katy Roberts [1]_____ (be) fifteen. She [2]_____ (play) football in a local girls' team. Girls' football [3]_____ (become) very popular in the UK these days. Lots of girls [4]_____ (regularly/play) football at school. Katy [5]_____ (train) with her team every Saturday morning, and they [6]_____ (usually/play) matches on Sundays. Katy [7]_____ (always/go) in goal. They [8]_____ (train) a lot this month because they [9]_____ (have got) some important matches. It [10]_____ (be) Saturday today. It [11]_____ (rain) a lot but Katy [12]_____ (practise) with the team.

10 Oggi è una giornata insolita per Eddie. Osserva le informazioni e scrivi un paragrafo sulla sua situazione. Usa il *Present simple* e il *Present continuous*.

usually	today
go out with friends	organize a party for his parents
jeans/T-shirt	party clothes
sandwiches for lunch	special food
modern music	music from the 1980s

Inizia così:
Eddie usually goes out with his friends on Saturdays, but this Saturday...

11 Scrivi le frasi al *Present continuous*, dove è possibile. Se la forma in *-ing* non è possibile, usa il *Present simple*.

1 We/enjoy/the party.
_____

2 Rob/know/all the answers to the test.
_____

3 I/not remember/his name.
_____

4 Sara/not feel/well today.
_____

5 you/believe/his explanation?
_____

6 What results/you/hope/for/in the exam?
_____

12 Completa il testo con il *Present continuous* o il *Present simple* dei verbi nel riquadro.

> be   do   have got   have   not like
> not understand   not work   study   think   worry

Today ¹_____ Wednesday. I ²_____ Wednesdays because we ³_____ a Latin lesson in the afternoon! This term we ⁴_____ some Latin poems and I ⁵_____ them! My teacher ⁶_____ that I ⁷_____ hard this year, but I ⁸_____ my best! We ⁹_____ a test today and I ¹⁰_____ about it a lot.

Esercizi sommativi

13 Scrivi lo scambio telefonico seguendo la traccia.

Laura Saluta Ben e chiedi che cosa sta facendo.
1 _____

Ben Di' che stai usando Internet.
2 _____

Laura Chiedi a Ben se sta facendo i compiti.
3 _____

Ben Di' di no. Spiega che stai guardando dei video di musica.
4 _____

Chiedi a Laura se le piace la musica rock.
5 _____

Laura Di' che l'ascolti qualche volta, ma che ami veramente la musica pop.
6 _____

Ben Di' che stai ascoltando un sacco di musica rock vecchia al momento.
7 _____

Chiedi a Laura che cosa sta facendo adesso.
8 _____

Laura Di' che stai facendo i compiti di francese e che ti serve aiuto.
9 _____

Pensi che siano davvero difficili.
10 _____

14 Ci sono 8 errori di ortografia o di uso dei tempi verbali in questo testo. Identificali e correggili.

Sophie is haveing some problems at school this year.
1 _____

She's in a different class to her friends and she feeling lonely.
2 _____

She isn't knowing the other students in her class and they're never including her in their conversations.
3 _____
4 _____

She's studying some new subjects and she isn't liking all of them.
5 _____

Her homework is difficult and she doesn't have a lot of time for her hobbies – dancing and runing.
6 _____

She's usually going to a dance class twice a week, but at the moment she misses a lot of those lessons.
7 _____
8 _____

15 Translation • Traduci l'email in inglese sul tuo quaderno.

Inbox

Ciao Tom,
Come stai? Che cosa stai facendo quest'estate? Io sto facendo molti compiti e ho anche un lavoro. Sto lavorando in un ristorante questo mese. Lavoro lì ogni venerdì e sabato sera. Inizio alle sei e finisco alle undici. Sono sempre stanca il fine settimana, ma mi sto divertendo quest'estate. Non sto uscendo con i miei amici, ma adesso ho un sacco di soldi.
E mi servono davvero i soldi! Spero che anche tu ti stia godendo le vacanze.
Emma

Translation note

Ricorda che il presente indicativo si può tradurre in inglese sia con il *Present simple* che con il *Present continuous* a seconda del contesto. Per scegliere il tempo verbale corretto in inglese, considera i seguenti punti:

• il verbo al presente indicativo da tradurre descrive un'abitudine, una routine o un'azione in corso di svolgimento?

• c'è un'espressione di tempo o un avverbio di frequenza che ti aiuta nella scelta del tempo?

• il verbo al presente indicativo da tradurre è un verbo di stato?

IT'S GOOD TO TALK!

Teenagers all over the world have problems with schoolwork, friends or families.

Unhappy students often have <u>behaviour</u> problems at school. They don't study or go to lessons. In the UK, schools sometimes suspend students
5 for bad behaviour: they ask them to stay away from school for a period of time. In serious cases, the head teacher excludes the student, and the student never returns to that school.

But schools can help teenagers with their problems. Jasmine (15) explains what happens in her school:
10 'At our school we have a school <u>council</u>. School councils are becoming popular in the UK. Students choose two people from their class to be on the council. I represent my class with another girl. All the council members meet regularly with a teacher. We discuss what is happening in the school, and we try to solve problems.'

15 But some problems are very personal. If a school thinks that a student is having difficulties, they sometimes ask a professional <u>counsellor</u> to come to the school. Some schools even have a permanent school counsellor. Students visit the counsellor and talk about their problems in private.

A few schools use mentoring with unhappy students. A mentor is a
20 person who becomes your friend, listens to you and helps you. Some schools choose students in the same school year to be mentors to students with problems. In other schools, students have an adult mentor who isn't part of their school. Carol (16) is a mentor at her school. 'A mentor's job is to be a good example to other
25 students and to help them with their problems,' she explains. 'At the moment I'm helping another student in my year. He's stressed because we've got important exams this year. I really want to help him.'

Glossary

behaviour	(di) comportamento
council	comitato, consiglio
counsellor	consulente

Reading comprehension

1 🔊 **S.074** Leggi il testo e abbina le parti iniziali delle frasi (1–4) alle loro conclusioni (a–d).

1 ___ Unhappy teenagers
2 ___ Head teachers
3 ___ School councils
4 ___ Counsellors

a are groups of students and teachers.
b help students with their personal problems.
c sometimes suspend or exclude students.
d sometimes have problems with schoolwork.

2 Scegli l'alternativa corretta.

1 Teenagers in the UK **sometimes/never** have problems at school.
2 In the UK, head teachers **can/can't** tell a bad student to leave the school.
3 School councils **decide which subjects students study/talk about events and problems** at school.
4 There is a permanent school counsellor at **all/some** British schools.
5 School mentors are **always/sometimes** adults.
6 Carol is a mentor to a student in **the same/a different** year at her school.

3 Rispondi alle domande.

1 What happens when a school in the UK suspends a student?
_____

2 What happens when a school excludes a student?
_____

3 How many students from each class are usually on a school council?
_____

4 What does a school counsellor do?
_____

5 What is the job of a school mentor?
_____

6 Carol is trying to help a student at her school. What is his problem?
_____

Culture note

La maggior parte degli studenti nel Regno Unito frequentano la scuola, dove devono rimanere fino all'età di 16 anni. Ma non hanno l'obbligo legale di andare a scuola. In alternativa i genitori hanno il diritto di educare i propri figli a casa. Circa 40,000 studenti nel Regno Unito ricevono un'istruzione parentale a casa.

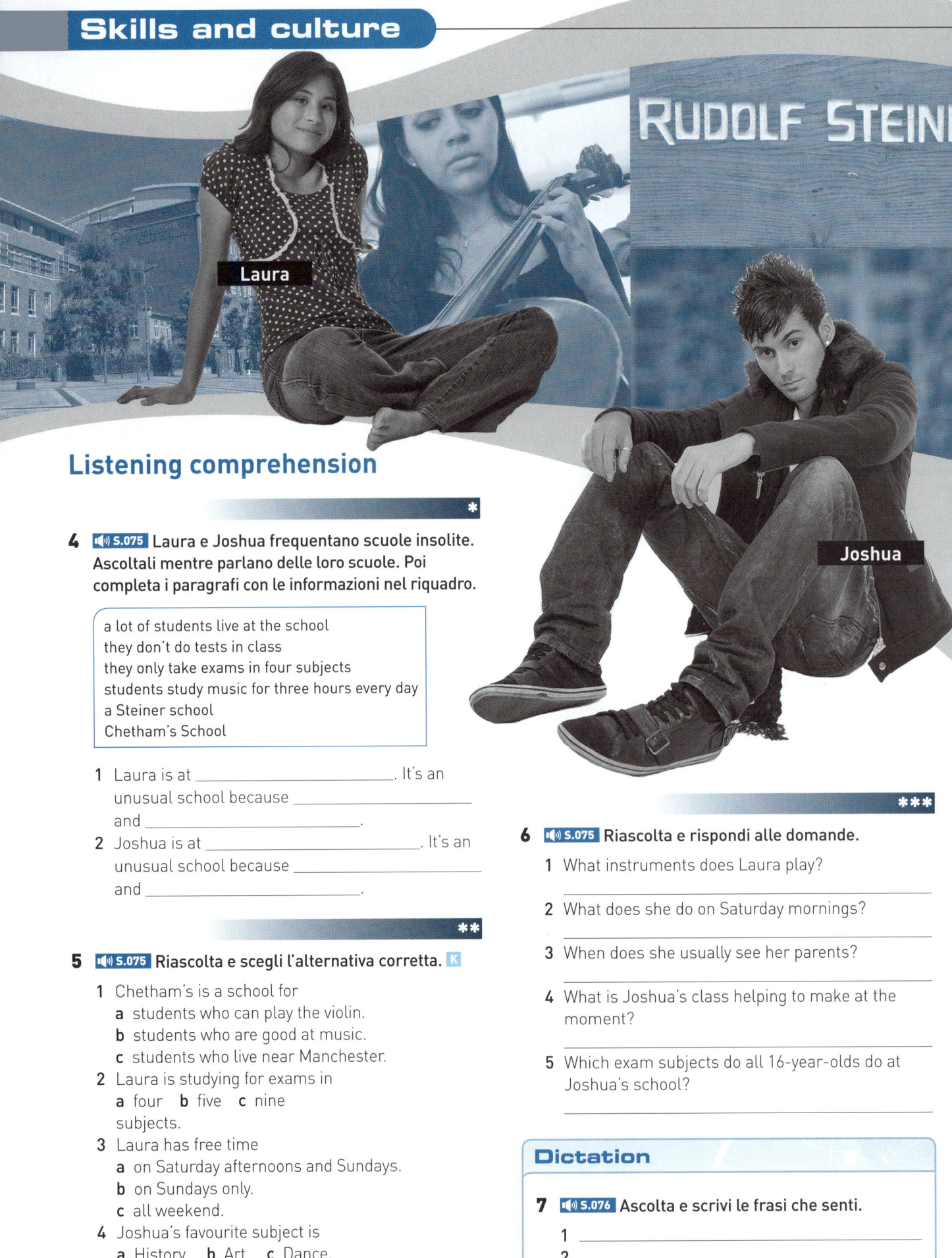

Laura

Joshua

RUDOLF STEINE

Listening comprehension

*

4 🔊 **S.075** Laura e Joshua frequentano scuole insolite. Ascoltali mentre parlano delle loro scuole. Poi completa i paragrafi con le informazioni nel riquadro.

> a lot of students live at the school
> they don't do tests in class
> they only take exams in four subjects
> students study music for three hours every day
> a Steiner school
> Chetham's School

1 Laura is at _____. It's an unusual school because _____ and _____.

2 Joshua is at _____. It's an unusual school because _____ and _____.

**

5 🔊 **S.075** Riascolta e scegli l'alternativa corretta. **K**

1 Chetham's is a school for
   a students who can play the violin.
   b students who are good at music.
   c students who live near Manchester.
2 Laura is studying for exams in
   a four   b five   c nine
   subjects.
3 Laura has free time
   a on Saturday afternoons and Sundays.
   b on Sundays only.
   c all weekend.
4 Joshua's favourite subject is
   a History.   b Art.   c Dance.
5 Students at Joshua's school
   a do some exams
   b don't do any exams
   c do Music exams
   when they are 16.

***

6 🔊 **S.075** Riascolta e rispondi alle domande.

1 What instruments does Laura play?
   _____
2 What does she do on Saturday mornings?
   _____
3 When does she usually see her parents?
   _____
4 What is Joshua's class helping to make at the moment?
   _____
5 Which exam subjects do all 16-year-olds do at Joshua's school?
   _____

Dictation

7 🔊 **S.076** Ascolta e scrivi le frasi che senti.

1 _____
2 _____
3 _____
4 _____
5 _____
6 _____

Writing

Writing skills

La punteggiatura

8 Leggi le seguenti regole sulla punteggiatura inglese. Completale con il segno corretto di punteggiatura nell'elenco.

> capital letters (ABC)   commas (,)
> apostrophes (')   full stops (.)

1 _____ vengono usate all'inizio di una frase:

There are about 500 students at my school.

e anche per la prima persona singolare del pronome soggetto, per nomi propri e di nazione, per le nazionalità e le materie scolastiche:

I like Mr Reed. He's Scottish. He teaches Maths and Science.

2 _____ vengono usati per denotare le lettere mancanti:

I'm 15. We don't do any important exams this year.

e anche per il genitivo sassone:

My friend's favourite subject is Music.

3 _____ vengono usate per separare le parti in una frase e i sostantivi in un elenco:

On Tuesdays we have French, History, Art and PE.

4 _____ vengono usati alla fine di una frase:

We often have tests.

Ora fai l'Esercizio 9 in basso tenendo presente le regole di punteggiatura.

9 Scrivi un breve testo (75–100 parole) sulla tua scuola e le materie che studi. Includi le risposte alle seguenti domande: **T**

- What's the name of your school and where is it?
- How many students are there in your class?
- What subjects do you study?
- What special topics are you studying this year/term?
- Are you studying for any tests or exams?
- How often do you study English?
- What are your favourite subjects?
- Which subjects don't you like?

Inizia così:

The name of my school is...

Functions on film

Making suggestions

A Completa i 4 mini-dialoghi con le parole nel riquadro.

> about   fancy   let's (x2)   feel
> shall (x2)   sorry   sounds   that's

1 A Do you ¹_____ having a pizza?
  B That ²_____ great!
2 A ³_____ we go swimming?
  B ⁴_____ a good idea! ⁵_____ meet at six o'clock.
3 A ⁶_____ go bowling!
  B No thanks, I don't ⁷_____ like it.
4 A What ⁸_____ we do tonight?
  B How ⁹_____ watching the new James Bond film?
  A No, ¹⁰_____. I don't like James Bond.

B Scrivi il dialogo seguendo la traccia.

Amy Chiedi a Tom quello che dovrebbero fare stasera.
1 _____

Tom Proponi di andare a pattinare.
2 _____

Amy Rifiuta la proposta di Tom e spiega che non te la senti.
3 _____

Tom Proponi di andare al cinema.
4 _____

Amy Accetta il suggerimento con entusiasmo.
5 _____

Tom Suggerisci di incontrarvi a casa tua alle 7.
6 _____

Amy Sei d'accordo.
7 _____

Grammar network

A *can* • Abilità

Forma affermativa	Forma negativa	Forma interrogativa	Risposte brevi	
			affermative	negative
I can	I can't	Can I?	Yes, I can.	No, I can't.
you can	you can't	Can you?	Yes, you can.	No, you can't.
he/she/it can	he/she/it can't	Can he/she/it?	Yes, he/she/it can.	No, he/she/it can't.
we can	we can't	Can we?	Yes, we can.	No, we can't.
you can	you can't	Can you?	Yes, you can.	No, you can't.
they can	they can't	Can they?	Yes, they can.	No, they can't.

1 *Can* è un verbo modale e dunque è invariabile per tutte le persone, non è mai usato con gli ausiliari ed è sempre seguito dalla forma base del verbo:
Can she play golf? (~~Does she can play golf?~~)
Sa giocare a golf?
We can ski. (~~We can to ski.~~)
Sappiamo sciare.

2 La forma affermativa si ottiene così:

> soggetto + *can* + forma base del verbo

Mary can speak French. *Mary sa parlare francese.*

3 La forma negativa si ottiene così:

> soggetto + *can't* + forma base del verbo

I can't swim. *Non so nuotare.*
NB: esiste anche la forma negativa estesa *cannot* ma si usa soltanto nell'inglese scritto e parlato formale.

4 La forma interrogativa si ottiene invertendo l'ordine del soggetto e di *can*:

> *Can* + soggetto + forma base del verbo + ?

Can he play the guitar? *Sa suonare la chitarra?*

5 Le risposte brevi si formano così:

> *Yes*, + soggetto + *can.*
> *No*, + soggetto + *can't.*

6 *Can* si usa per parlare di abilità o capacità in generale e può essere tradotto in italiano con 'sapere', 'essere capace di', 'essere in grado di', 'potere' e 'riuscire a':
My brother can understand a bit of Japanese
Mio fratello riesce a capire un po' di giapponese.

7 Le seguenti espressioni avverbiali possono essere usate in frasi affermative con *can* per indicare il grado di abilità. Si mettono sempre alla fine della frase:

> quite well = *abbastanza bene*
> well = *bene*
> very/really well = *molto/davvero bene*

I can ride a horse quite well.
So andare a cavallo abbastanza bene.

8 Le seguenti espressioni avverbiali possono essere usate in frasi negative con *can't* per indicare il grado di abilità. Si mettono sempre alla fine della frase:

> (not)... very well = (non)... molto bene
> (not)... at all = (non)... affatto, per niente

They can't sing very well.
Non sanno cantare molto bene.
She can't speak Italian at all.
Non sa parlare per niente italiano.

9 Per descrivere quanto una persona è brava a fare qualcosa si può anche usare la seguente struttura:

> | verbo *be* + | *brilliant*
quite/very/really good
(not) very good
hopeless/terrible | + *at* + | sostantivo/
verbo in *-ing* |

She's good at singing, but she's hopeless at dancing!
È brava a cantare ma è negata a ballare!

10 Si può usare *can* anche per fare richieste, per chiedere il permesso di fare qualcosa oppure per chiedere un favore a qualcuno:
Can I go to Jack's house tonight?
Posso andare a casa di Jack stasera?
Can you pass me my bag, please?
Puoi passarmi la mia borsa per favore?

11 Esiste anche la forma *be able to* + forma base del verbo per parlare di abilità:
I'm able to run 15 km without stopping.
Sono in grado di correre 15 km senza fermarmi.

Be able to è più usato al passato e al futuro; *can* è più usato al *Present simple*.

B Present continuous (3) • Il futuro

1 Oltre ad essere usato per parlare di azioni in corso di svolgimento (vedi Unit 4 p.168), il *Present continuous* si può anche usare per parlare di programmi precisi e accordi stabiliti per il futuro:

I'm travelling to Scotland next Thursday.
Vado in Scozia giovedì prossimo.
We aren't having a holiday this year.
Non andiamo in vacanza quest'anno.

2 Il *Present continuous* con valore di futuro è spesso accompagnato da un'espressione di tempo futuro:

> tomorrow morning/afternoon/evening
>   = *domani mattina/pomeriggio/sera*
> this evening/week/month/year
>   = *questa sera/settimana/questo mese/quest'anno*
> next weekend/year/Monday
>   = *il prossimo fine settimana/l'anno prossimo/lunedì prossimo*
> at 8 o'clock/the weekend/Christmas
>   = *alle otto/al fine settimana/a Natale*
> on Tuesday/June 17th = *martedì/il 17 giugno*
> in May/2019/a month's time
>   = *a maggio/nel 2019/tra un mese*
> tonight = *stasera*

C Present simple (3) • Il futuro

1 Oltre che per parlare di dati di fatto, azioni abituali e situazioni permanenti (vedi Unit 2 p.152) il *Present simple* si può anche usare per il futuro, quando si parla di programmi e di orari ufficiali. Si può tradurre in italiano con il presente indicativo oppure con il futuro:
The flight arrives at three.
Il volo arriva alle tre./Il volo arriverà alle tre.
The Italian course starts on September 12th.
Il corso di italiano inizia il 12 settembre./Il corso di italiano inizierà il 12 settembre.

2 Il *Present simple* con valore di futuro è spesso accompagnato da un'espressione di tempo futuro:
School finishes in a week's time.
La scuola finisce fra una settimana.
The film starts at six o'clock.
Il film inizia alle sei.

Word store

Ordinal numbers — *Numeri ordinali*

first (1st) _____
second (2nd) _____
third (3rd) _____
fourth (4th) _____
fifth (5th) _____
sixth (6th) _____
seventh (7th) _____
eighth (8th) _____
ninth (9th) _____
tenth (10th) _____
eleventh (11th) _____
twelfth (12th) _____
thirteenth (13th) _____
sixteenth (16th) _____
twentieth (20th) _____

Months — *Mesi*

January _____
February _____
March _____
April _____
May _____
June _____
July _____
August _____
September _____
October _____
November _____
December _____

Dates — *Date*

April the sixteenth _____
the fifth of October _____

Word builder +

Abilities — *Abilità*

play basketball _____
play tennis _____
play the piano _____
ride a horse _____
sing _____
ski _____
speak French _____
swim _____

Real talk

Completa le espressioni dai dialoghi dello *Student's Book*.

Don't be _____! — *Non fare il patetico!*
I'm _____! — *Me ne vado!*
_____,... — *A dire il vero,...*
That's _____ news! — *Che bella notizia!*
Hang _____ — *Aspetta un attimo*
See you _____! — *Ci vediamo dopo!*

Extra vocabulary • Festivals

April Fool's Day	*primo aprile*
Birthday	*compleanno*
Bonfire Night	*Notte dei falò*
Christmas Day	*Natale*
Hallowe'en	*Halloween*
May Day	*primo di maggio*
New Year's Eve	*ultimo dell'anno*
Valentine's Day	*San Valentino*

Vocabulary

Dates

1 Scrivi i numeri ordinali in forma estesa.

1 16 = *sixteenth*
2 29 = _____
3 20 = _____
4 2 = _____
5 11 = _____
6 31 = _____

7 4 = _____
8 12 = _____
9 23 = _____
10 25 = _____
11 8 = _____
12 13 = _____

2 Completa il cruciverba con i nomi dei 12 mesi. Inizia da dicembre e scrivi gli altri mesi dove si possono inserire le lettere corrispondenti.

3 Scrivi le date in forma estesa.

1 13/5   *the thirteenth of May*
2 30/8   _____
3 22/2   _____
4 4/12   _____
5 15/10   _____
6 10/1   _____
7 21/7   _____
8 8/4   _____
9 19/11   _____
10 27/9   _____

4 Rispondi alle domande con le date scritte in forma estesa.

1 What is the date today?
_____

2 When is your birthday?
_____

3 When is your mum's birthday?
_____

4 When is New Year's Day?
_____

5 When is Liberation Day in Italy?
_____

6 When is *Ferragosto*?
_____

Grammar

can • Abilità

1 Osserva la tabella. Completa la colonna *You*. Poi scrivi frasi complete su quello che Mark, Fiona e tu sapete e non sapete fare. Usa *can* e *can't*.

	MARK	FIONA	YOU
ride a horse	X	✓	○
play the guitar	✓	X	○
speak Spanish	X	X	○
cook	✓	✓	○

1 Mark/ride a horse

2 Mark /play the guitar

3 Fiona/play the guitar

4 Mark and Fiona/speak Spanish

5 Mark and Fiona/cook

6 I/play the guitar

2 Riordina le parole per formare domande complete, poi completa le risposte brevi.

1 your can sing dad ?

No, _____.

2 a you motorbike can ride ?

Yes, _____.

3 food cook Italian Angela can ?

Yes, _____.

4 friends speak English can your ?

No, _____.

5 you sister swim can and your ?

Yes, _____.

6 tennis Edward can play ?

No, _____.

3 Osserva di nuovo la tabella dell'Esercizio 1. Scrivi altre 6 domande e risposte con *can* su quello che le persone della tabella sanno e non sanno fare.

1 *Can Fiona ride a horse?*
  Yes, she can.

2 _____

3 _____

4 _____

5 _____

6 _____

7 _____

4 Completa le frasi indicando quanto sei bravo o no a fare queste cose. Usa *brilliant*, *quite/very/really good*, (*not*) *very good*, *hopeless* o *terrible*.

1 (sing) *I'm not very good at singing.*
2 (swim) _____
3 (play tennis) _____
4 (speak English) _____
5 (ski) _____
6 (dance) _____

5 Scrivi frasi spiegando il tuo livello di abilità. In ogni frase usa *can* o *can't* e una delle espressioni avverbiali dell'Esercizio 4.

1	sing
2	play rugby
3	understand French
4	do judo
5	swim
6	make pizza

Espressioni di tempo futuro

6 Scegli l'alternativa corretta.

1 The exam is **at/on** the fifteenth of June.
2 What are you doing **this/today** afternoon?
3 We're going to a party **this night/tonight**.
4 I'm leaving **next/tomorrow** morning.
5 They're arriving in two **days/days'** time.
6 Do you want to go to London **at the next/next** weekend?

7 Rispondi alle domande in maniera personale. Usa un'espressione di tempo futuro per ogni frase.

1 When is your next English lesson?

_____

2 When does school finish today?

_____

3 When do the summer holidays start?

_____

4 When is your 18th birthday?

_____

5 When can you watch your favourite TV programme again?

_____

Present continuous (3) • Il futuro

8 Osserva il calendario di Ruby e Jake. Scrivi frasi sulla settimana prossima con la forma corretta (affermativa o negativa) del *Present continuous*.

MON	_____
TUES	Jake: rugby match 6pm
WED	Grandad's birthday (Ruby and Jake to his house after school)
THURS	Ruby: dance class 4.30pm
FRI	Jake: Maths test
SAT	Helen and Dave's wedding (Brighton) 2pm
SUN	At home!

1 Jake/play in a rugby match/next Monday

_____

2 Ruby and Jake/go to their grandad's house/next Wednesday

_____

3 Ruby/have a dance class/on Thursday afternoon

_____

4 Ruby/have a Maths test/next Friday

_____

5 Helen and Dave/get married/next weekend

_____

6 they/get married/in London

_____

9 Scrivi domande sulle attività del calendario usando le parole date e il *Present continuous*. Poi rispondi alle domande.

1 what/Jake/do/next Tuesday evening?

_____

_____

2 where/Ruby and Jake/go/on Wednesday?

_____

3 who/have a Maths test/on Friday?

_____

4 where/Helen and Dave/get married?

_____

5 what time/Helen and Dave/get married?

_____

10 Leggi le informazioni sulla gita scolastica. Poi completa il dialogo con il *Present continuous* e le informazioni mancanti.

CLASS 11 C

**Trip to Chester
(Thursday, 8th May)
with Mrs Hurst and
Mr Meads**

Leave school by bus: 9am

Arrive back at school:
3.30pm

Please wear school uniform
and bring sandwiches.

Milly	¹(you/go) _____ on the school trip on Thursday, Rob?
Rob	Yes, ²_____. What time ³(we/leave) _____?
Milly	⁴_____
Rob	⁵(we/wear) _____ school uniform?
Milly	⁶_____ – unfortunately!
Rob	⁷(Mrs Evans/come) _____ with us?
Milly	⁸_____
Rob	⁹Which teachers/come? _____
Milly	¹⁰_____

Present simple (3) • Il futuro

11 Osserva l'annuncio e completa il paragrafo con i verbi nel riquadro alla forma corretta del *Present simple*.

> be   finish   perform   start (x2)   study

A new DJ skills course for teenagers **1**_____ in February at Redwall Community College. The classes **2**_____ on Monday nights. The course **3**_____ on 13th February and **4**_____ on 3rd April. Students **5**_____ with a professional DJ and they **6**_____ at a special club night at the end of the course.

12 Scrivi domande e risposte sul futuro.

1 What time/the concert/start? (8.30pm)

_____

2 that train/stop/at Newbury? (No)

_____

3 When/the library/open tomorrow? (10am)

_____

4 When/Rebecca/start/university? (next October)

_____

5 your swimming lessons/finish/in July? (Yes)

_____

6 What time/the plane/leave? (4.15pm)

_____

Esercizi sommativi

13 Completa il dialogo con la forma corretta del *Present simple* o del *Present continuous*.

Alex   **1**_____ (What/you/do) tonight, Libby?

Libby   I **2**_____ (go) to the cinema with Alice and Joe. **3**_____ (you/want) to come?

Alex   **4**_____? (What film/you/see)

Libby   *Urban Hero.*

Alex   **5**_____? (What time/it/start)

Libby   It **6**_____ (start) at 7.15, but we **7**_____ (meet) at 6.30.

Alex   And **8**_____? (what time/it/finish)

Libby   At 10 o'clock. We **9**_____ (take) a bus home after the film. It **10**_____ (leave) at 10.20.

14 Osserva la legenda. Scrivi frasi sul livello di abilità delle persone. Poi, usando le parole date, scrivi altre frasi sui loro piani futuri.

> **KEY**
> ✓✓✓ = really well   ✗ = not very well
> ✓✓ = well   ✗✗ = not at all
> ✓ = quite well

1 Daniel – play the guitar – ✓
play/in a concert/next week
his parents/come/to the concert

_____

_____

2 Kate – sing – ✗
have/a singing lesson after school tomorrow
the lesson/start/four o'clock

_____

_____

3 Thomas – speak Italian – ✗✗
go/to Italy/next year
start Italian classes/in September

_____

_____

4 Ella – ride a horse – ✓✓✓
ride/in a competition/at the weekend
the competition/be/near Oxford

_____

_____

15 Translation • Traduci il dialogo in inglese sul tuo quaderno.

Leo   ¹Che cosa fai sabato?
Nathan   ²Vado al mare con mio fratello. Vuoi venire?
Leo   ³Non lo so. Come ci andate?
Nathan   ⁴In treno. Parte alle nove meno dieci, e prendiamo l'autobus fino alla stazione.
Leo   ⁵Vi alzate presto?
Nathan   ⁶Sì. Ci alziamo alle sette e mezzo.
Leo   ⁷È molto presto! E ho un altro problema.
Nathan   ⁸Che cosa?
Leo   ⁹Non so nuotare.
Nathan   ¹⁰Davvero?
Leo   ¹¹Sì. Ma farò delle lezioni in estate.
Nathan   ¹²Vieni con noi la prossima volta, allora.

Translation note

Ricorda che, a differenza dell'italiano in inglese non si può sempre usare il *Present simple* per parlare di piani o programmi futuri. Quando un evento futuro deriva da una decisione personale, si deve invece usare il *Present continuous*:

Decisione personale	Orario ufficiale
Partiamo domani.	*Il treno parte domani alle 10.*
We're leaving tomorrow.	The train leaves tomorrow
(We leave tomorrow.)	at 10 o'clock.

Grammar network

A Preposizioni di luogo (2)

1 Le preposizioni seguenti si usano per descrivere la posizione delle persone o delle cose in relazione l'una all'altra (vedi anche Unit 1 p.146):

behind = *dietro a*	between = *fra*
in = *in*	in front of = *davanti a*
near = *vicino*	next to = *vicino a, accanto a*
on the corner of X and Y = *all'angolo di X e Y*	
on the left/right = *sulla sinistra/destra*	
opposite = *di fronte a*	

I usually sit next to Michele in class.
Di solito mi siedo accanto a Michele in classe.

The newsagent's is opposite the station.
L'edicola è fronte alla stazione.

B *there is/are*

1 *There is/there are* corrispondono a 'c'è/ci sono':
- *there is* si usa davanti a un sostantivo singolare o un elenco di vocaboli di cui il primo è singolare:
  There's a café next to the library.
  C'è un bar vicino alla biblioteca.
- *there are* si usa davanti a un sostantivo plurale o un elenco di vocaboli di cui il primo è plurale:
  There are twenty-one students in my class.
  Ci sono ventuno studenti nella mia classe.

2 La forma negativa si ottiene usando la forma negativa del verbo *be*:
There isn't a theatre in our town.
Non c'è un teatro nella nostra città.

3 La forma interrogativa si ottiene invertendo l'ordine di *there* e del verbo *be*:
Is there an Italian restaurant in this street?
C'è un ristorante italiano in questa strada?

4 Le risposte brevi si formano così:

> Yes, + there + is/are.
> No, + there + isn't/aren't.

5 Si usano *there is/there are* per chiedere o indicare dove si trovano edifici, oggetti o persone.
Is there a bank near here? Yes, there is – in Oxford Road.
C'è una banca qui vicino? Sì, in Oxford Road.

C *some/any*

1 *some* e *any* si usano per parlare di quantità non specificate. Corrispondono all'italiano 'dei', 'degli', 'delle':
- *some* si usa con i sostantivi plurali nelle frasi affermative:
  We've got some sandwiches for lunch.
  Abbiamo dei tramezzini per pranzo.
  There are some cafés in the shopping centre.
  Ci sono dei bar nel centro commerciale.

- *any* si usa con i sostantivi plurali nelle frasi negative e interrogative:
  There aren't any cafés in the shopping centre.
  Non ci sono dei bar nel centro commerciale.
  Are there any cafés in the shopping centre?
  Ci sono dei bar nel centro commerciale?
  We haven't got any sandwiches for lunch.
  Non abbiamo dei tramezzini per pranzo.
  Have we got any sandwiches for lunch?
  Abbiamo dei tramezzini per pranzo?

 A differenza dell'italiano, in inglese i partitivi *some* e *any* devono essere sempre usati:
I haven't got any sisters.
(I haven't got sisters.)
Non ho sorelle.

D L'imperativo

1 La forma affermativa dell'imperativo si ottiene con la forma base del verbo:
Cross the road.   *Attraversa la strada.*

2 La forma negativa si ottiene con l'ausiliare *Don't* davanti al verbo.
Don't turn left.   *Non girare a sinistra.*

 A differenza dell'italiano, in inglese esiste una sola forma dell'imperativo per tutte le persone.

3 L'imperativo si usa per dare indicazioni stradali, dare instruzioni o ordini, dare avvertimenti e offrire qualcosa. In inglese l'imperativo non si usa mai per fare richieste.

Go straight on.	Look out!
Vai dritto.	*Attento!*
Finish the test now, please.	Have a biscuit.
Finite il test ora, per favore.	*Prendi un biscotto.*
Be quiet!	
Fate silenzio!	

E Preposizioni e avverbi di moto

1 Si usano le preposizioni e gli avverbi di moto con i verbi di movimento (*go*, *come*, *turn*, *walk*, *drive*):

> across = *attraverso*
> down, along = *giù per, lungo*
> left = *a sinistra*
> over = *sopra*
> past = *oltre, davanti a*
> right = *a destra*
> straight on = *sempre diritto*
> through = *attraverso, per*
> under = *sotto*

Go across the park.
Attraversa il parco.

Go down/along Green Street.
Vai lungo Green Street.

Turn left/right at the bank.
Gira a sinistra/destra alla banca.

Drive over/under the bridge.
Passa (in macchina) sopra/sotto il ponte.

Don't go past the post office.
Non andare oltre l'ufficio postale.

Go straight on as far as the library.
Vai dritto fino alla biblioteca.

Go through the market and the station is opposite.
Attraversa il mercato e la stazione si trova di fronte.

Functions on film

F *Could...?*

1 Abbiamo già visto (vedi Unit 5 p.178) che *can* può essere usato per fare richieste. In situazioni più formali, si può anche usare *could* per:

- chiedere il permesso di fare qualcosa:
  Could I borrow your pen?
  Potrei prendere in prestito la tua penna?

- chiedere un favore a qualcuno in modo cortese:
  Could you bring me some water, please?
  Mi potresti portare dell'acqua, per favore?

Word store

Places in a town — *Posti in città*

bank	_____
bus station	_____
bus stop	_____
café	_____
car park	_____
chemist's	_____
church	_____
clothes shop	_____
coach station	_____
hospital	_____
leisure centre	_____
library	_____
market	_____
newsagent's	_____
park	
post office	_____
restaurant	_____
shoe shop	_____
shopping centre	_____
stadium	_____
(train) station	_____
supermarket	_____
takeaway	_____
tourist information centre	_____
town hall	_____

Word builder +

City adjectives — *Aggettivi per descrivere la città*

beautiful	_____
civilized	_____
different	_____
exciting	_____
expensive	_____
fantastic	_____
friendly	_____
interesting	_____
lively	_____
modern	_____
wonderful	_____

Real talk

Completa le espressioni dai dialoghi dello *Student's Book*.

Check _____	*Dai un'occhiata a*
Mind _____	*Però,.../Detto questo,...*
I _____	*Scommetto che*
I'm dying _____	*Non vedo l'ora di*
_____ you!	*vederti!*
_____ far as	*fino a*
You can't _____ it	*Non può sbagliarsi*
I think I've _____ that	*Credo di aver capito*

Extra vocabulary • Directions

Go down/along (Oxford Road)	*Percorri (Oxford Road)*
Turn left (at)/Turn right (at)	*Gira a sinistra (a)/Gira a destra (a)*
Go straight on as far as)	*Vai dritto (fino a)*
Go across (the road)	*Attraversa (la strada)*
Go through (the park)	*Attraversa (il parco)*
Go past (the café)	*Vai oltre (il bar)*
Go under/over (the bridge)	*Passa sotto/sopra (il ponte)*
It's on the left./It's on the right.	*Si trova sulla sinistra./ Si trova sulla destra.*
Take the first turning on the left/right.	*Prendi la prima strada a sinistra/a destra.*
Cross (Park Street).	*Attraversa (Park Street).*

Vocabulary

Places in a town

1 Traduci i nomi dei dieci negozi e posti in città. Scrivili nel cruciverba e scopri il posto misterioso (?).

> 1 banca   2 chiesa   3 negozio di scarpe   4 ospedale
> 5 ufficio postale   6 mercato   7 ristorante
> 8 farmacia   9 fermata dell'autobus   10 municipio

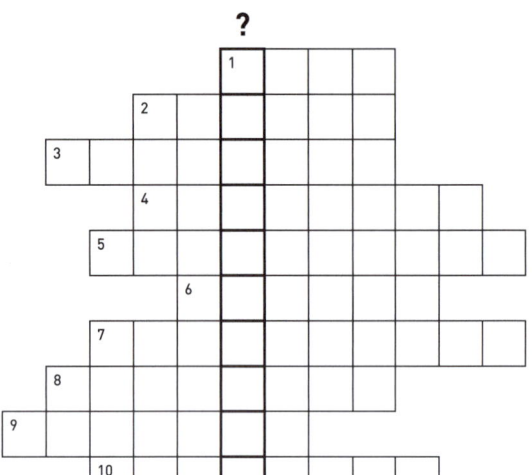

2 Leggi le definizioni e completa i nomi dei posti e dei negozi.

1 You buy hot food from here and take it home to eat = t_____
2 You buy newspapers and magazines here = n_____
3 You do sports here = l_____ c_____
4 You get information from here about things to visit in a town = t_____ i_____ c_____
5 You travel by train from here = s_____
6 You leave your car here = c_____ p_____
7 You get books from here and take them home for short periods = l_____
8 You watch football matches and big sports events here = s_____

Preposizioni di luogo (2)

3 Osserva le piantine (1–5) e completa le frasi con le preposizioni mancanti.

1 The park is _____ Queen Street.
2 The tourist information centre is _____ the café.
3 The shopping centre is _____ the bus station.
4 The car park is _____ the library.
5 The bus stop is _____ the supermarket.

Word skills

Prendere nota dei vocaboli (2)

Come già visto in Unit 2, un altro metodo per prendere nota di vocaboli nuovi (oltre a scriverli in ordine alfabetico o in liste divise per argomento) è quello di usare le mappe concettuali o *mind maps*. La mappa concettuale permette di suddividere i vocaboli in categorie all'interno di un argomento più ampio. Qui sotto puoi vedere un esempio di una mappa concettuale relativa all'argomento *Places in a town*.

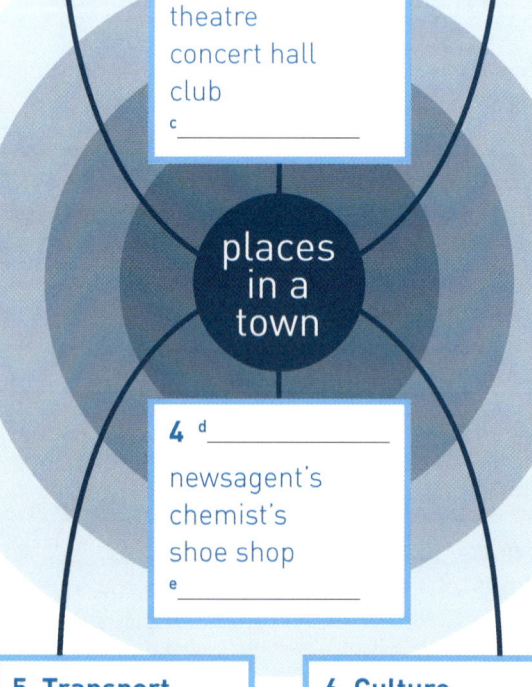

1 Eating
restaurant
takeaway
a _____

2 b _____
leisure centre
swimming pool
stadium

3 Entertainment
theatre
concert hall
club
c _____

4 d _____
newsagent's
chemist's
shoe shop
e _____

places in a town

5 Transport
train station
f _____
bus stop
coach station

6 Culture
museum
art gallery
library

A Osserva la mappa concettuale. Scrivi i titoli mancanti in 2 e 4.

B Aggiungi altri vocaboli in 1, 3, 4 e 5.

C Crea una mappa concettuale per gli argomenti *Sports* e *Free-time activities* (vedi Unit 2).

Grammar

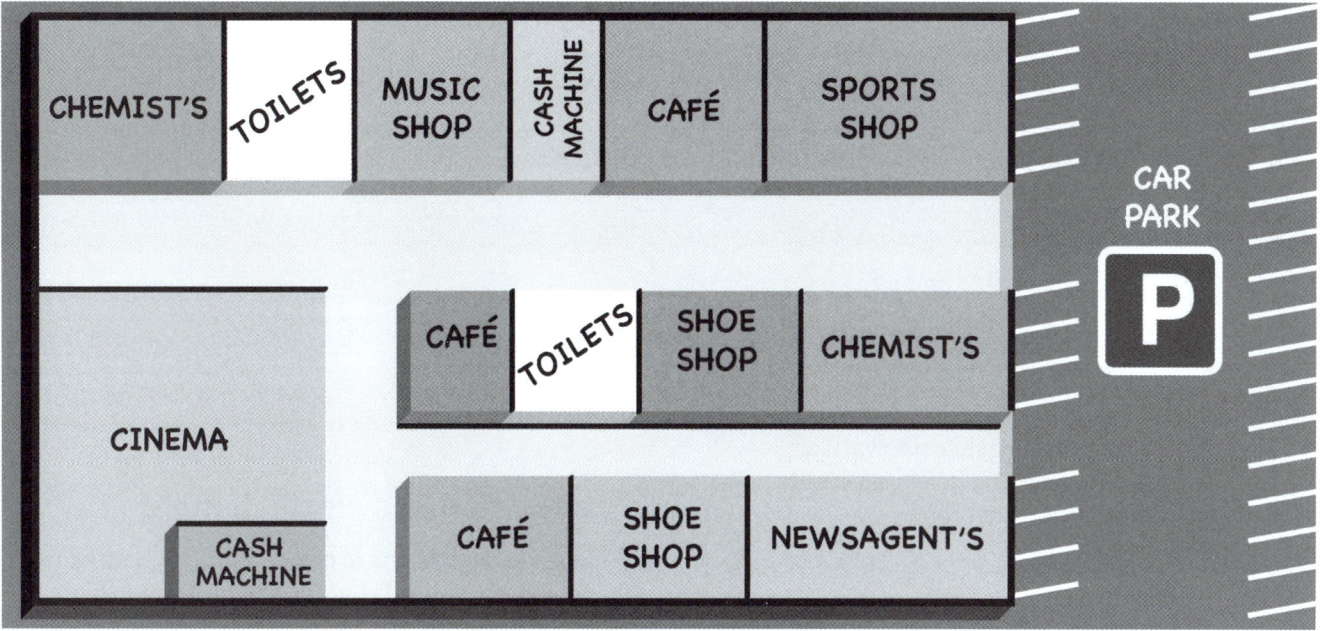

there is/are

1 Osserva la piantina del centro commerciale qui sopra. Scrivi frasi sui negozi e i servizi che vedi. Usa *there is/are + a/an/two/three*, ecc.

1 music shop

_____

2 shoe shop

_____

3 cinema

_____

4 café

_____

5 car park

_____

6 chemist's

_____

2 Usa le parole date per scrivere domande complete sul centro commerciale. Usa *there is/are*. Poi scrivi le risposte brevi.

1 three cafés?

_____

_____

2 a newsagent's?

_____

_____

3 a sports shop?

_____

_____

4 two music shops?

_____

_____

5 a supermarket?

_____

_____

some/any

3 Completa le frasi sul centro commerciale con *some* o *any*.

1 There aren't _____ bookshops.
2 It's got _____ friendly cafés.
3 There are _____ modern toilets.
4 It's got _____ cash machines.
5 It hasn't got _____ interesting computer shops.
6 It hasn't got _____ food shops.

4 Completa il dialogo con *some*, *any* o *a*.

Ed What do you think of the new shopping centre?

Joe It's OK. They've got [1]_____ good shops there. There's [2]_____ really fantastic sports shop.

Ed Are there [3]_____ games shops there? I want to buy [4]_____ new computer games.

Joe No, there aren't. And there isn't [5]_____ computer shop.

Ed Are there [6]_____ music shops?

Joe Yes. There's [7]_____ great music shop.

Ed Maybe they've got [8]_____ games there.

5 Rispondi alle domande in maniera personale. Usa le preposizioni di luogo dove è necessario.

1 Where is your house?

_____

2 How many bedrooms are there in your house?

_____

3 Is there a café near your school?

_____

4 How many students are there in your class?

_____

5 Where do you usually sit in an English lesson?

_____

L'imperativo

6 Osserva la piantina. Immagina di trovarti al bar. Completa il dialogo con la forma corretta dell'imperativo dei verbi nel riquadro.

> cross   go   turn

Woman Excuse me. How do I get to the post office, please?

You OK, well this is Chester Street. ¹_____ down this street. ²_____ under the bridge but ³_____ past the bank. ⁴_____ the street at the bank and then ⁵_____ right into Kingston Road. ⁶_____ down Kingston Road and ⁷_____ right. That's Broadgate. ⁸_____ straight on – ⁹_____ right again immediately. The post office is on the left.

7 Immagina di trovarti al municipio. Scrivi le indicazioni stradali dal municipio alla banca.

_____

_____

_____

_____

_____

_____

_____

_____

_____

_____

_____

Preposizioni e avverbi di moto

8 Leggi la descrizione di come Charlie va a scuola ogni giorno. Scegli la preposizione o l'avverbio corretto per completare la descrizione.

'I get the bus to school every morning. It goes ¹**down/left** Aston Road and ²**straight on/under** the railway bridge. Then it turns ³**past/right** and we go ⁴**down/through** the town centre. Finally, we go ⁵**over/through** the river and ⁶**left/past** the shopping centre. My school's in Sandford Way, near the shopping centre.'

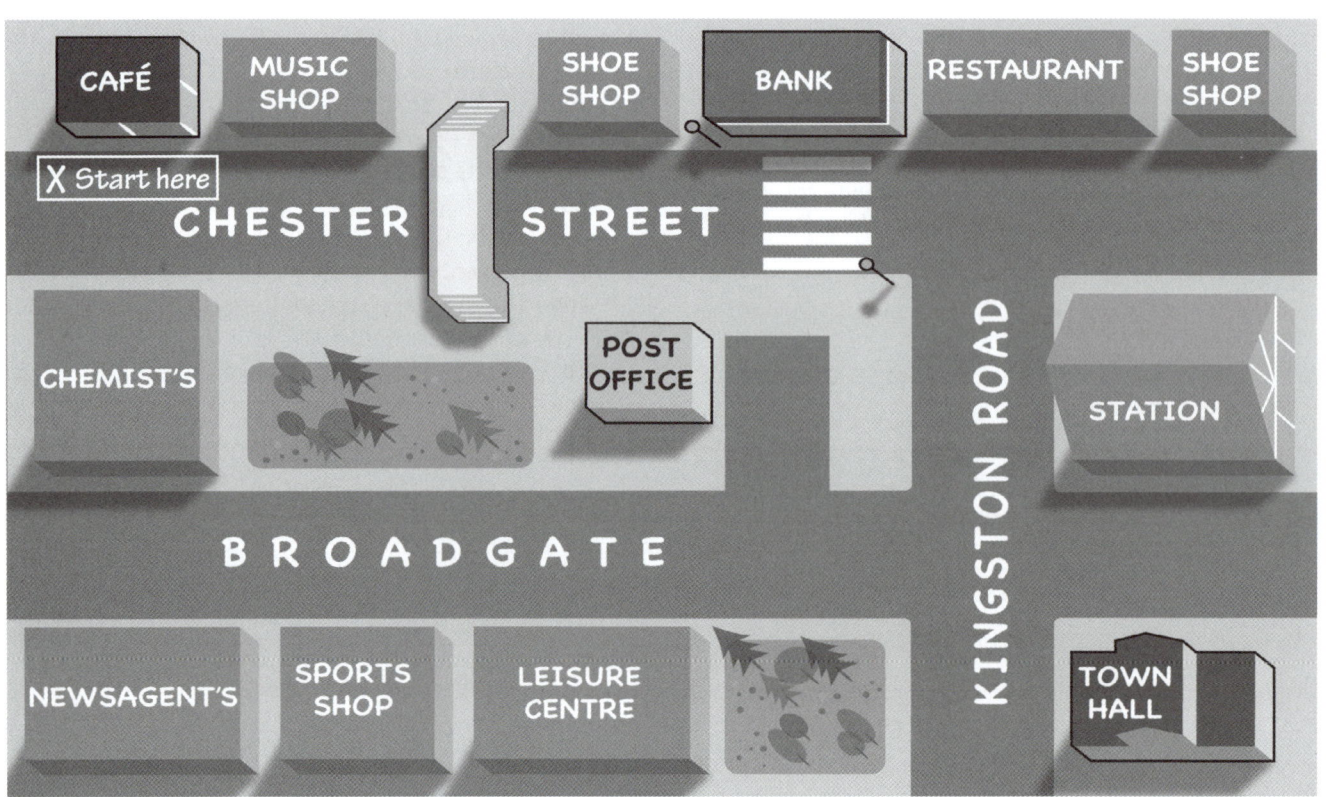

Esercizi sommativi

| JOE'S CAFÉ | BANK | WEST STREET CAFÉ | | NEWSAGENT'S |

WEST STREET

NORTH STREET

SUPERMARKET	LIBRARY	POST OFFICE	TOWN HALL
		CLOTHES SHOP	LEISURE CENTRE
		CHEMIST'S	BOOKSHOP
			RESTAURANT

BUS BUS BUS

---

9 Osserva la piantina e completa le frasi sui posti e i negozi con la forma corretta di *there is/are* e *a*, *an*, *some* o *any*.

1 _____ restaurant in North Street.
2 _____ hospital in North Street.
3 _____ bank in West Street.
4 _____ shoe shops in West Street.
5 _____ bus stops in North Street.
6 _____ cafés in West Street.

10 Osserva la piantina qui sopra. Scrivi domande complete usando le parole date. Poi scrivi le risposte.

1 there/be/a chemist's/in North Street?
_____
_____

2 where/be/it?
_____
_____

3 there/be/shops/in North Street?
_____
_____

4 there/be/a library?
_____
_____

5 where/be/it?
_____
_____

6 there/be/a bus stop/in West Street?
_____
_____

7 where/be/it?
_____
_____

8 there/be/takeaways/in North Street or West Street?
_____
_____

11 Immagina di trovarti al Joe's café. Qualcuno ti chiede come arrivare al negozio di abbigliamento. Completa le indicazioni stradali.

Go down West Street. Go [1]_____ the library. The post office is on the [2]_____ of West Street and [3]_____ [4]_____. [5]_____ right. Go [6]_____ North Street. The clothes shop is [7]_____ the bookshop, next to the [8]_____.

12 Translation • Traduci il dialogo in inglese sul tuo quaderno.

Man [1]*Come arrivo al centro di informazioni turistiche?*

Ollie [2]*Vada dritto, oltre il municipio. Poi giri a destra alla biblioteca. Poi vada lungo Hanover Street e attraversi il fiume. Il centro di informazioni turistiche è nel parcheggio, accanto al supermercato.*

Man [3]*Grazie.*

Ollie [4]*Non c'è di che. Non può sbagliarsi.*

Translation note

Ricorda di fare attenzione a come traduci il presente indicativo e l'imperativo. In inglese, il presente richiede sempre l'uso del soggetto, mentre l'imperativo non lo richiede mai:

Cantate bene. (presente)	You sing well.
Cantate bene! (imperativo)	Sing well!
You speak quietly. (presente)	*Parli a voce bassa.*
Speak quietly! (imperativo)	*Parla a voce bassa!*

MANCHESTER
MY CITY

Manchester is famous all over the world for one of its football teams – Manchester United. But do you know any other facts about the city?

Manchester is in the north-west of England. The population of Manchester and its suburbs is over 2 million. The city is famous for its historic buildings from the
5 Industrial Revolution. But there are lots of modern attractions in Manchester too.

The Trafford Centre is an enormous shopping centre with hundreds of shops and around sixty restaurants, but my favourite part of the city is Salford Quays. It's an area of modern shops, cafés and museums on the old Manchester Ship Canal. There's a big arts centre there called the Lowry. It's got theatres and an art gallery.

10 Another interesting area is Chinatown. There are lots of Chinese shops and restaurants, and some restaurants from other Asian countries like Thailand and Malaysia. The area is very busy on Sunday mornings.

Manchester is great for nightclubs and music. There are lots of famous English bands and pop singers from Manchester, including Oasis and Take That. The
15 nightlife is very good and the city is very lively at night. The Warehouse Project is a club in an enormous space under one of Manchester's train stations. It can hold nearly 2,000 people.

And if you want to know more about Manchester United, go and visit the team's stadium, Old Trafford. It's the UK's second biggest football stadium – there
20 are places for 76,000 fans. Take a tour of the stadium and visit the Manchester United museum. It's a really interesting place to visit – but don't tell my brother. He's a Manchester City fan!

Salford Quays

Glossary	
suburbs	periferia
Industrial Revolution	Rivoluzione Industriale
hold	contenere
biggest	il più grande

The Lowry

Reading comprehension

*

1 🔊 **S.077** Leggi il testo su Manchester. Abbina i nomi dei luoghi (1–5) alle loro descrizioni (a–e).

1 ___ Old Trafford		a	a nightclub
2 ___ Chinatown		b	a shopping centre
3 ___ The Lowry		c	a football stadium
4 ___ The Trafford Centre		d	an area of shops and restaurants
5 ___ The Warehouse Project		e	an arts centre

**

2 Scrivi *T* (*true*), *F* (*false*) o *DS* (*doesn't say*, se l'informazione non si trova nel testo) accanto alle affermazioni. 🅿

1 ___ The population of Manchester and its suburbs is 2.3 million.
2 ___ There is a canal at Salford Quays.
3 ___ There are only Chinese restaurants in Chinatown.
4 ___ The Warehouse Project is a club in a train station.
5 ___ The Manchester City football team play at Old Trafford.
6 ___ The tour of Old Trafford is very expensive.

***

3 Rispondi alle domande.

1 Where in the UK is Manchester?

_____

2 What is there at the Lowry?

_____

3 When is a good time to go to Chinatown?

_____

4 What are the names of two famous pop bands from Manchester?

_____

5 How many people can visit the Warehouse Project every night?

_____

6 How many people can watch a match at Old Trafford?

_____

Culture note

Manchester era una volta una città romana e si chiamava *Mamcunian*. Oggi gli abitanti di Manchester sono ancora chiamati *Mancunians*. Ma fu tra il XVIII e il XIX secolo, durante la Rivoluzione Industriale, che Manchester ebbe un ruolo significativo e diventò uno dei centri più importanti del mondo per la produzione tessile. Ma questa cominciò a declinare negli anni sessanta.

Listening comprehension

4 🔊 **S.078** Ascolta il tour in autobus di Cardiff. Scrivi i nomi dei luoghi sotto la foto corrispondente. *

> Cardiff Bay   Cardiff Castle
> Wales Millennium Centre   Millennium Stadium

1 _____

2 _____

3 _____

4 _____

5 🔊 **S.078** Tutte queste frasi sono false. Ascolta e scrivi la versione corretta delle frasi. **

1 Cardiff is the capital city of Scotland.
_____

2 The Millennium Stadium is an old building.
_____

3 The top sport in Wales is football.
_____

4 The Wales Millennium Centre is a shopping centre.
_____

5 There are three theatres at the Wales Millennium Centre.
_____

6 There aren't any guided tours of Cardiff Castle.
_____

6 🔊 **S.078** Riascolta e rispondi alle domande. ***

1 How old is Cardiff Castle?
_____

2 How many people can watch a match at the Millennium Stadium?
_____

3 What other events can you see at the Millennium Stadium?
_____

4 When is it not possible to have a tour of the Millennium Stadium?
_____

5 Which area of Cardiff has lots of bars and cafés near the water?
_____

6 What is on the front of the Wales Millennium Centre?
_____

> ### Dictation
>
> **7** 🔊 **S.079** Ascolta e scrivi le frasi che senti.
>
> 1 _____
> 2 _____
> 3 _____
> 4 _____
> 5 _____
> 6 _____

Writing

Writing skills

Scrivere i numeri e le date

8 Ci sono delle differenze fra l'inglese e l'italiano nell'uso delle date e dei numeri. Osserva i seguenti esempi e scegli l'alternativa corretta per completare le regole.

There are two thousand three hundred and seventy-eight students at the university. → There are 2,378 students at the university.

- in inglese, quando si scrivono numeri superiori al mille, di solito si separano le migliaia dagli altri numeri con [1]un punto/una virgola.

He can run a kilometre in 4.5 minutes.

- quando si scrivono numeri decimali, si separano i numeri superiori a uno dai decimali con [2]un punto/una virgola.

I've got eleven pounds forty-five. → I've got £11.45.

- quando si scrivono i prezzi, si separano le sterline dai *pence* con [3]un punto/una virgola.

~~the twenty-seventh of January, 2004~~ → 27th January, 2004
January 27th, 2004
27.1.04
27/1/04

- ci sono modi diversi per scrivere le date.

Ora fai gli Esercizi 9 e 10 tenendo presente le regole sui numeri e sulle date.

9 Rispondi alle domande usando numeri, non parole.

1 Write today's date. Include the year.

2 Write your date of birth. Include the year.

3 What is 500 x 10?

4 If one euro = 85 pence, how much is ten euros?

5 What is 6.4 – 3.1?

6 What is 999 + 5?

10 Scrivi un breve testo (75–100 parole) su una città o un paese che conosci bene. Includi le risposte alle seguenti domande: **T**

- Where is the town or village?
- How many people live there?
- What important places are there?
- Are there any interesting statistics about the town?

Functions on film

At the Tourist Information Centre

A Abbina le parti iniziali delle richieste (1–4) alle loro conclusioni (a–d).

1 Are there any
2 Can I have
3 Could you recommend
4 How much

a a good place to eat?
b is a room?
c two tickets for the bus tour, please?
d hotels near the station?

1 ___ 2 ___ 3 ___ 4 ___

B Bella si trova in un ufficio di informazioni turistiche. Completa il dialogo.

Man Hello.
Bella Hello. Are [1]_____ _____ youth hostels near here?
Man Yes, [2]_____ a youth hostel on Union Street.
Bella Thanks. [3]_____ _____ _____ it?
Man [4]_____ £12.50 a night.
Bella [5]_____ you [6]_____ a cheap place to eat near here?
Man Yes, there's the Corner Café on Hendon Street.
Bella Thank you. [7]_____ _____ _____ a map of the city, please?
Man Certainly. [8]_____ you are.
Bella Thanks for your [9]_____.
Man [10]_____ welcome.

C Immagina di trovarti all'ufficio di informazioni turistiche di Bath. Completa la tua parte del dialogo.

Woman Good morning.
You [1]_____
Woman Yes, there's a youth hostel on Bathwick Hill.
You [2]_____
Woman It's £14 a night.
You [3]_____
Woman Yes, there's a fish and chip shop or a pizza restaurant in Kingsmead Square.
You [4]_____
Woman You're welcome.

At any time

Tourist information

Grammar network

A Sostantivi numerabili e non numerabili

1 I sostantivi numerabili (*countable nouns*) si riferiscono a cose che si possono contare e quindi possono essere sia singolari che plurali: **one car – two cars**

2 Con i sostantivi numerabili si può usare sia l'articolo indeterminativo (*a/an*) che l'articolo determinativo (*the*): **a computer – the computer – the computers**

3 I sostantivi non numerabili (*uncountable nouns*) si riferiscono a cose che non si possono contare e quindi si usano solo al singolare: **bread** (~~breads~~)

4 Con i sostantivi non numerabili non si usa mai l'articolo indeterminativo (a/an):
She's got the water. (~~She's got a water.~~)   *Ha l'acqua.*

5 I sostantivi non numerabili sono sempre accompagnati da un verbo alla forma singolare:
That wine comes from South Africa.
Quel vino viene dal Sud Africa.

6 A volte lo stesso sostantivo può essere usato sia come sostantivo numerabile che come sostantivo non numerabile, con un leggero cambiamento di significato:
Please buy some coffee.   *Per favore compra del caffè.*
Can we have three coffees, please?
Prendiamo tre caffè, per favore.

> ⚠️ Alcuni sostantivi che sono numerabili in italiano non lo sono in inglese e dunque, in inglese, prendono il verbo alla terza persona singolare:
>
> advice = *consigli*   information = *informazioni*
> furniture = *mobili*   news = *notizie*
> homework = *compiti*   money = *soldi*

B some/any

1 Come abbiamo visto (vedi Unit 6 p.184), *some* e *any* si possono usare con i sostantivi numerabili plurali per parlare di quantità indefinite. Si possono anche usare con i sostantivi non numerabili:
We've got some butter, but we haven't got any milk.
Abbiamo del burro, ma non abbiamo latte.

C much/many, a lot of/lots of

1 Per fare domande sulla quantità, in inglese si usano:
- *How much... ?* ('Quanto...?', 'Quanta...?') con i sostantivi non numerabili:
  How much sugar do we need?
  Di quanto zucchero abbiamo bisogno?
- *How many... ?* ('Quanti...?', 'Quante...?') con i sostantivi numerabili:
  How many apples have you got?
  Quante mele hai?

2 'Molto', 'molta', 'molti' e 'molte' si traducono in diversi modi in inglese, a seconda del tipo di frase:
- *much* si usa nelle frasi negative e interrogative con i sostantivi non numerabili:
  I haven't got much money.   *Non ho molti soldi.*
  Is there much traffic today?   *C'è molto traffico oggi?*
- *many* si usa nelle frasi negative e interrogative con i sostantivi numerabili plurali:
  I don't want many beans.
  Non voglio molti fagioli.
  Are there many pears on the table?
  Ci sono molte pere sul tavolo?
- *a lot of/lots of* si usano nelle frasi affermative sia con i sostantivi non numerabili che con i sostantivi numerabili plurali:
  We need a lot of sugar./We need lots of sugar.
  Abbiamo bisogno di molto zucchero.
  We need a lot of potatoes./We need lots of potatoes.
  Abbiamo bisogno di molte patate.

D (a) little (bit of)/(a) few

1 'Un po' di', 'alcuni', 'qualche' ecc. si traducono in diversi modi in inglese, a seconda del tipo di sostantivi a cui si riferiscono:
- *a little/a little (bit of)* si usano con i sostantivi non numerabili:
  I've got a little bit of chocolate.
  Ho un po' di cioccolata.
- *a few* si usa con i sostantivi numerabili plurali:
  Have you got a few minutes?
  Hai qualche minuto?

2 Quando *little* e *few* si usano senza l'articolo indeterminativo (*a*), hanno un significato negativo, equivalente all'italiano 'poco', 'poca', 'pochi', 'poche'. Spesso vengono preceduti do *very*:
He's got (very) few friends.
Ha (davvero) pochi amici.

3 L'uso di *little* e *few* è formale. Nella lingua informale si possono usare al loro posto *not much/not many*:
They haven't got much free time.
Non hanno molto tempo libero.
He hasn't got many friends.
Non ha molti amici.

4 Nelle frasi affermative si può anche usare l'espressione *hardly any* per enfatizzare il concetto di 'veramente poco':
They've got hardly any free time/friends.
Hanno veramente poco tempo libero/pochi amici.

E too much/many, (not) enough

1 *too much/many* corrispondono a 'troppo', 'troppa', 'troppi', 'troppe':
- *too much* si usa con i sostantivi non numerabili:
  Don't drink too much coffee!   *Non bere troppo caffè!*

- *too many* si usa con i sostantivi numerabili plurali:
  There are too many cars here.
  Ci sono troppe macchine qui.

2 (not) *enough* corrisponde a '(non) abbastanza, (non) a sufficienza'. Si usa sia con i sostantivi non numerabili che con i sostantivi numerabili plurali:
  We've got enough eggs.   *Abbiamo abbastanza uova.*
  Have you got enough money?   *Hai soldi a sufficienza?*
  There aren't enough people for a game of football.
  Non ci sono abbastanza persone per una partita di calcio.
  She hasn't got enough time to help us.
  Non ha abbastanza tempo per aiutarci.

⚠ Ricorda che tutte queste espressioni di quantità (*some, any, not much, not many, a lot of, lots of, (a) little, (a) few, too much, too many, (not) enough, hardly any*) si possono usare come pronomi quando le cose a cui si riferiscono sono già state menzionate. Quando si usano *a lot* e *lots* come pronomi, si deve omettere *of*:

A Are there any CDs in the car?
B Yes, there are – but not many. (= not many CDs)

A Do you need another egg?
B No, thanks. I've got enough. (= enough eggs)

A How much coffee have we got?
B We've got lots. (= lots of coffee)

Word store

Food and drink   *Cibi e bevande*

meat _____
beef _____
chicken _____
lamb _____
pork _____
veal _____
fish _____
salmon _____
seafood _____
fruit and vegetables _____
apples _____
carrots _____
courgettes _____
green beans _____
lettuce _____
oranges _____
pears _____
peas _____
potatoes _____
tomatoes _____
dairy products _____
butter _____
cheese _____
eggs _____
milk _____
basics _____
bread _____
pasta _____
rice _____
sweet things _____
biscuits _____
cakes _____
drinks _____
beer _____
coke _____
mineral water _____
orange juice _____
wine _____

condiments _____
oil _____
pepper _____
salt _____
vinegar _____

Word builder +

Food quantities and containers   *Quantità e contenitori di cibo*

bottle _____
box _____
can _____
carton _____
loaf _____
packet _____
pot _____
tin _____

Word builder +

Shops   *Negozi*

baker's _____
bookshop _____
electrical goods shop _____
greengrocer's _____
hairdresser's _____
service station _____

Real talk

Completa le espressioni dai dialoghi dello *Student's Book*.

What do you _____?   *Che cosa ti va?*
I'm _____   *Sto morendo di fame*
One more _____   *Un'ultima cosa*
_____ about the _____   *Peccato per il tempo*
What's _____ with it?   *Che cosa ha che non va?*
_____ _____ there   *Hai proprio ragione*
Good _____   *É vero*

Vocabulary

Food and drink

1 Completa le parole con le lettere mancanti.

 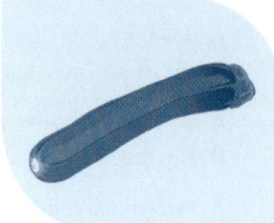

1 _ _ _ le   2 c _ _ r _ e _ _ e

3 _ _ _ _ _ b _ _ _ s   4 _ e _ r

5 _ _ _ s   6 _ o t _ _ _ _ s

 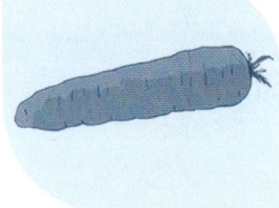

7 t _ _ _ t _   8 _ _ _ r _ _

2 Riordina le lettere per trovare i nomi dei 6 tipi di carne e pesce.

1 bmal   _____
2 krop   _____
3 mansol   _____
4 febe   _____
5 leva   _____
6 nicchek   _____

3 Raggruppa i cibi e le bevande nel riquadro in 5 categorie. Poi scrivi 5 frasi complete.

> beer   biscuits   butter   cakes   cheese   oranges
> ~~pasta~~   pepper   pears   ~~rice~~   salt   wine

1 *Pasta and rice are basic foods.*
2 _____
3 _____
4 _____
5 _____
6 _____

4 Abbina le parole (1–8) ai cibi e alle bevande (a–h).

1 ___ a can of   a tomatoes
2 ___ a box of   b yoghurt
3 ___ a carton of   c coke
4 ___ a tin of   d rice
5 ___ a loaf of   e orange juice
6 ___ a packet of   f bread
7 ___ a pot of   g milk
8 ___ a bottle of   h chocolates

5 Ora scrivi le espressioni complete dell'Esercizio 4 sotto le figure.

1 _____   2 _____

3 _____   4 _____

5 _____   6 _____

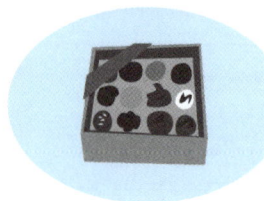 

7 _____   8 _____

Grammar

Sostantivi numerabili e non numerabili

1 Scrivi le parole del riquadro nella colonna corretta.

> banana bread car girl house idea intelligence meat money paper potato water

Countable	**Uncountable**
_____	_____
_____	_____
_____	_____
_____	_____
_____	_____
_____	_____

2 Completa le frasi con la forma affermativa (✓) o negativa (✗). Usa la forma corretta di *be* + *some* o *any*.

1 There _____ _____ people in the street. (✓)
2 _____ there _____ milk in the fridge?
  No, there _____.
3 There _____ _____ bread in that shop. (✗)
4 There _____ _____ chocolate in my bag. (✓)
5 _____ there _____ games on your phone?
  Yes, there _____.
6 There _____ _____ rice in the packet. (✓)
7 There _____ _____ students in the classroom. (✗)
8 _____ there _____ salt on these potatoes?
  No, there _____.

much/many, a lot of/lots of

3 Completa le domande con le espressioni nel riquadro.

> How much   How many   is there   are there

1 _____ _____ biscuits _____ _____ in the tin?
  Only six.
2 _____ _____ pasta _____ _____?
  Two packets.
3 _____ _____ fruit _____ _____ in your lunchbox?
  One orange and one banana.
4 _____ _____ people _____ _____ in your family?
  Five.
5 _____ _____ time _____ _____ before the lesson?
  Only five minutes.

4 Scegli l'alternativa corretta.

Alice Hi James. What are you doing tonight?
James I'm working – unfortunately! I've got ¹a lot of/much work to do. Have you got ²much/many homework this week?
Alice No, not really. I've got an Art project. That's taking ³a lot of/much time, but I'm enjoying it. Are you going to Jake's party on Saturday? ⁴A lot of/Many people from our class are going.
James No, I'm not. I've got too much work! I don't go to ⁵many/much parties these days!
Alice That's a pity. I haven't got ⁶many/much free time in the week, but I always go out at the weekends.

5 Descrivi la quantità dei cibi nelle figure. Usa la forma corretta di *there is/are (not)* con *a lot of/much/many*.

1 _____
  _____

2 _____
  _____

3 _____
  _____

4 _____
  _____

5 _____
  _____

6 _____
  _____

6 Completa le domande con *How much... ?* o *How many... ?*. Poi osserva le quantità indicate fra parentesi e rispondi alle domande con *(not) much*, *(not) many* o *a lot*.

<u>*How much*</u> cheese have we got? (50g)
<u>*We haven't got much.*</u>

1 _____ _____ potatoes have we got? (4)

2 _____ _____ money have we got? (£2.50)

3 _____ _____ bananas have we got? (9)

4 _____ _____ coke have we got? (6 bottles)

5 _____ _____ tomatoes have we got? (3)

(a) little (bit of)/(a) few

7 Scegli l'alternativa corretta.

1 Do you want **a few/a little** biscuits with your drink?
2 There's **a few/a little bit of** orange juice in this carton.
3 Have you got **a few/a little** free time this afternoon?
4 We need **a few/a little bit of** apples for this cake.
5 We know **a few/a little** people in the UK.
6 I like **a few/a little bit of** milk in my tea.

8 Osserva la lista di ingredienti nella ricetta. Riscrivi la lista con *a little*, *a few* o *a lot of* al posto delle quantità precise.

web browser

Luxury Chocolate Cake
INGREDIENTS

• 2 packets of biscuits
• 40g of butter
• 500g of chocolate
• 2 large eggs/3 small eggs
• 1 litre of cream
• 2 or 3 strawberries

For this recipe you need:

_____
_____
_____
_____
_____

9 Metti un *tick* (✓) sotto ☺ se la frase ha un significato positivo, o sotto ☹ se la frase ha un significato negativo.

	☺	☹
1 I go to a few concerts every year.		
2 I go to few concerts every year.		
3 I've got a little free time this weekend.		
4 I've got little free time this weekend.		
5 I've got few friends.		
6 I've got a few friends.		
7 I've got little money.		
8 I've got a little money.		

10 Riscrivi le frasi con *much* o *many*, mantenendo lo stesso significato.

1 I've got few computer games.

_____

2 We eat little meat in our family.

_____

3 There's little food in the house.

_____

4 There are few people in town today.

_____

5 I know few students at this school.

_____

6 They've got little imagination.

_____

too much/many, (not) enough

11 Completa il paragrafo con *much*, *many* o *enough*.

This is a terrible party! The music is boring. They're playing too ¹_____ old songs. There are too ²_____ people and there isn't ³_____ space for dancing. There aren't ⁴_____ interesting people to talk to and there isn't ⁵_____ drink. They've got ⁶_____ food, but it's really disgusting. There are some pizzas, but there's too ⁷_____ tomato sauce on them and not ⁸_____ cheese. I'm going home!

12 Scrivi frasi complete usando le parole date e *too much*, *too many* o *(not) enough*.

1 We/have got/information. (not enough)

_____

2 There/be/people/in that shop. (too...)

_____

3 Some people/have got/money! (too...)

_____

4 you/have got/bread? (enough)

_____

5 I/buy/clothes! (too...)

_____

6 There/be/salt/in this food. (too...)

_____

Esercizi sommativi

13 Completa il dialogo con le parole nel riquadro.

enough (x2)   few   little (x2)   many
lots   much (x2)   too much   some

Gemma I'm going shopping. Do you want anything?

Dad I'm not sure. I'm cooking risotto tonight – here's the recipe. Well, I need some rice, obviously. How ¹_____ have we got?

Gemma Hmmm – there isn't ²_____ for all of us. There's only a ³_____ rice in the packet. Are you putting any vegetables in the risotto?

Dad Yes, I am. We don't eat ⁴_____ vegetables, in my opinion! I need ⁵_____ peas...

Gemma That's OK. There are ⁶_____ of peas in the freezer.

Dad And... how ⁷_____ courgettes do I need? Oh – just two.

Gemma We haven't got any courgettes. I can buy a ⁸_____ at the supermarket.

Dad And we haven't got ⁹_____ wine. I always put a ¹⁰_____ white wine into risotto.

Gemma OK. Rice, courgettes and white wine.

Dad Oh – and don't spend ¹¹_____ money!

14 Completa le domande del questionario sulla salute. Poi rispondi in maniera personale.

Health questionnaire

1 _____ _____ portions of fruit or vegetables do you eat every day? _____

2 _____ _____ water do you drink every day? _____

3 _____ _____ times every week do you do sport or exercise? _____

4 Do you eat _____ cakes and biscuits? _____

5 Do you drink _____ tea or coffee? _____

6 How _____ sleep do you have every night? _____

15 Ora guarda le risposte che hai dato nell'Esercizio 14. Scrivi una frase completa per ogni risposta. Usa alcune o tutte le espressioni nel riquadro.

too much   too many   enough
not enough   not much   not many

I eat enough fruit and vegetables every day.

1 _____

2 _____

3 _____

4 _____

5 _____

6 _____

16 Translation • Traduci il dialogo in inglese sul tuo quaderno.

Girl ¹Mi scusi. Lavoro al centro sportivo. Può rispondere a delle domande oggi?

Man ²Oh – OK. Ma non ho molto tempo!

Girl ³Va bene. Non mi serve molto tempo. Prima domanda – quante volte alla settimana usa il centro sportivo?

Man ⁴Due o tre volte alla settimana.

Girl ⁵OK. Seconda domanda – offriamo abbastanza sport in questo centro sportivo?

Man ⁶Sì. Ci sono molti sport diversi qui.

Girl ⁷Terza domanda – può dirmi che cosa non le piace del centro sportivo?

Man ⁸Dunque, c'è sempre troppa gente nella piscina. Penso che la piscina non sia aperta per abbastanza ore ogni giorno...

Translation note

Considera i seguenti punti prima di decidere 'un po' di', 'molto' o 'troppo' come tradurre in inglese:

• il sostantivo è numerabile o non numerabile?

• la frase è affermativa, negativa o interrogativa?

Ho molti amici.	I've got a lot of friends.
Non ho molti amici.	I haven't got many friends.
Hai molto lavoro oggi?	Have you got much work today?

Grammar network

A Past simple • Verbo *be*

| Forma affermativa | Forma negativa | | Forma interrogativa | Risposte brevi | |
	estesa	contratta		affermative	negative
I was	I was not	I wasn't	Was I?	Yes, I was.	No, I wasn't.
you were	you were not	you weren't	Were you?	Yes, you were.	No, you weren't.
he/she/it was	he/she/it was not	he/she/it wasn't	Was he/she/it?	Yes, he/she/it was.	No, he/she/it wasn't.
we were	we were not	we weren't	Were we?	Yes, we were.	No, we weren't.
you were	you were not	you weren't	Were you?	Yes, you were.	No, you weren't.
they were	they were not	they weren't	Were they?	Yes, they were.	No, they weren't.

1 Nella lingua parlata e informale, nelle frasi negative, di solito si usa la forma contratta.

2 Il *Past simple* si usa per parlare di situazioni o azioni concluse nel passato. Si può tradurre in italiano con l'imperfetto, il passato prossimo o il passato remoto *wasn't/weren't*:
I was at home yesterday.   *Ero a casa ieri.*
He was ill yesterday.   *È stato malato ieri.*
The stadium was built in 1923.
Lo stadio fu costruito nel 1923.

B Espressioni di tempo passato

1 Le espressioni seguenti si usano spesso con il *Past simple* per specificare quando un'azione è avvenuta:

> an hour/a week/a month ago = *un' ora/una settimana/un mese fa*
> last week/month/year/Wednesday = *la settimana scorsa/ il mese scorso/l'anno scorso/mercoledì scorso*
> last night = *ieri sera/ieri notte*
> yesterday morning = *ieri mattina*

C Preposizioni di luogo (3) • *in, at*

1 La preposizione *in* si usa per indicare la posizione in uno spazio tridimensionale:
Dad's in the kitchen.   *Papà è in cucina.*
We're in the car.   *Siamo in macchina.*
I was in bed at eleven o'clock.   *Ero a letto alle undici.*

2 La preposizione *at* si usa quando si parla di luoghi in generale, per esempio *at the shops, at the beach,* ecc.

3 *at* si usa anche quando ci si riferisce a istituzioni in senso astratto, per esempio *at school, at work, at church, at university,* ecc. In questo caso non si usa l'articolo determinativo dopo *at*:
We were at church earlier.   *Eravamo in chiesa prima.*

4 *at* si usa con l'articolo determinativo quando ci si riferisce all'edificio piuttosto che all'istituzione:
There is a wedding at the church today.
C'è un matrimonio in/nella chiesa oggi.

D *be born*

1 Per dire quando/dove si è nati, si usa il *Past simple* del verbo *be born*:
They were born in 1993.   *Sono nati nel 1993.*
He was born in Scotland.   *È nato in Scozia.*

E Past simple • Verbi regolari

| Forma affermativa | Forma negativa | |
	estesa	contratta
I walked	I did not walk	I didn't walk
you walked	you did not walk	you didn't walk
he/she/it walked	he/she/it did not walk	he/she/it didn't walk
we walked	we did not walk	we didn't walk
you walked	you did not walk	you didn't walk
they walked	they did not walk	they didn't walk

1 Il *Past simple* dei verbi regolari è invariabile per tutte le persone e si ottiene aggiungendo *-ed* alla forma base del verbo.

2 Fai attenzione alle seguenti variazioni ortografiche quando aggiungi *-ed* alla forma base del verbo:
• se il verbo termina in *-e*, si aggiunge *-d*:
live – lived, arrive – arrived
• se il verbo termina in consonante + *-y*, *-y* diventa *-i* e si aggiunge *-ed*:
study – studied, marry – married   ma: stay – stayed
• se la sillaba finale del verbo è accentata e termina in consonante + vocale + consonante, la consonante finale raddoppia:
prefer – preferred
NB: questa regola non vale se la sillaba non è accentata:
offer – offered (~~offerred~~)
• se un verbo monosillabico termina in consonante + vocale + consonante, la consonante finale raddoppia:
stop – stopped

 Non si raddoppiano mai -*y* o -*w* alla fine del verbo: delay – delayed (~~delayyed~~)

Si raddoppia sempre -*l* finale, anche quando la sillaba non è accentata: cancel – cancelled

3 La forma negativa del *Past simple* si ottiene con l'ausiliare *didn't* seguito dalla forma base del verbo:
We didn't watch the match last Saturday.
Non abbiamo visto la partita sabato scorso.

4 La forma interrogativa del *Past simple* si ottiene così:

> *Did* + soggetto + forma base del verbo + ?

Where did she go yesterday?   *Dove è andata ieri?*

F Past simple • Verbi irregolari

1 La forma affermativa del *Past simple* dei verbi irregolari non segue regole precise e va quindi imparata a memoria. Vedi la lista alle pagine 286–287. Come nel caso dei verbi regolari, il *Past simple* dei verbi irregolari è invariabile per tutte le persone.
make – made
I made a cake yesterday.
Ho fatto una torta ieri.

eat – ate
We ate too much food at Christmas.
Abbiamo mangiato troppo a Natale.

2 Le forme negativa e interrogative dei verbi irregolari si ottengono come quelle dei verbi regolari, con gli ausiliari *didn't/did* seguiti dalla forma base del verbo:
I didn't see Carla yesterday.
Ieri non ho visto Carla.

What time did you get up this morning?
A che ora ti sei alzato stamattina?

Functions on film

G *will e would like*

1 *will* e *would* sono verbi modali e dunque sono invariabili per tutte le persone, e non sono mai usati con i verbi ausiliari. Sono dunque seguiti dalla forma base del verbo.

2 Nella lingua parlata e informale, quando il verbo segue il pronome soggetto, nelle frasi affermative di solito si usa la forma contratta (*'ll, 'd*).

3 *will* può essere usato quando si prendono delle decisioni spontanee:
I'll have the pasta, please.   *Prendo la pasta, per favore.*
I'll phone her now.   *Adesso le telefono.*

4 *would like* si usa per:
- chiedere qualcosa, per esempio ordinare del cibo al ristorante:
  What would you like?   I'd like some apple pie, please.
  Che cosa desidera?   Vorrei della torta di mele, per favore.
- offrire qualcosa a qualcuno:
  Would you like some water?
  Vuole dell'acqua?
- esprimere una preferenza:
  I'd like to see this play.
  Vorrei/Mi piacerebbe vedere questo spettacolo.
- fare una richiesta cortese:
  We'd like two coffees, please.
  Vorremmo due caffè, per favore.

NB: in inglese, quando si fa una richiesta o si ordina in un ristorante o in un bar, non si usa *Give me/us*.

Word store

Holidays (1)   *Vacanze*

Types of holiday _____
go on an adventure holiday _____
go to the Alps/Dolomites _____
go to the seaside _____
Accommodation _____
stay in a B&B _____
stay in a hotel _____
stay on a campsite _____
Transport _____
go by car _____
go by coach _____
go by ferry _____
go by plane _____
go by train _____
Activities _____
do water sports _____
eat out _____
go sightseeing _____
go to clubs _____
go to the beach _____

Opinion adjectives _____
boring _____
clean _____
delicious _____
dirty _____
disgusting _____
exciting _____
relaxing _____
tiring _____

Real talk

Completa le espressioni dai dialoghi dello *Student's Book*.

Poor _____   *Poverino*
_____ he comes   *Eccolo*
I'll _____...   *Prendo...*
How did you _____ on...?   *Come è andata...?*
What _____ Luca _____?   *Com'era Luca?*

Vocabulary

Holidays (1)

1 Osserva le figure e completa i nomi dei mezzi di trasporto.

1 p _ _ _ _

2 _ _ _ _ y

3 c _ _ _ _

4 _ _ r

5 _ _ _ _ n

2 Completa le descrizioni di dove queste persone sono state durante le vacanze.

1 My last holiday was in a h_ _ _ _l in the A_ _s.

2 We stayed in a _&_ in London.

3 We were at a c_mp_ _ _ _ _ at the s_ _s_ _ _ .

3 Abbina i verbi (1–5) alle parole (a–e) per trovare delle attività che si fanno in vacanza.

1 ___ do   **a** clubs
2 ___ eat   **b** sightseeing
3 ___ go   **c** water sports
4 ___ go to   **d** out
5 ___ go to   **e** the beach

4 Scrivi gli aggettivi del riquadro nella colonna corretta – positivi ☺ o negativi ☹.

> boring   dirty   clean   delicious
> exciting   disgusting   tiring   relaxing

☺	☹
_____	_____
_____	_____
_____	_____
_____	_____

Word skills

I suffissi degli aggettivi

Gli aggettivi si formano spesso con sostantivo + suffisso. Il suffisso può darti indizi utili sul significato dell'aggettivo. Per esempio: *tiring* – affaticante, *tired* – stanco

5 Dividi in gruppi gli aggettivi dati a seconda del suffisso. Guarda nel dizionario le parole che non conosci e scrivile nel quaderno dei vocaboli.

> automatic   bored   careless   crazy   excited
> fantastic   freezing   funny   helpful   hopeless
> interesting   romantic   shocking   skilful   sunny
> thoughtless   tired   useful

6 Che differenza c'è fra queste coppie di aggettivi? Annotane il significato nel quaderno dei vocaboli.

1 tasty/tasteless
2 useful/useless
3 boring/bored
4 exciting/excited

7 Trova un aggettivo adatto per descrivere:

1 ... a thing with a lot of beauty _____
2 ... a person without a home _____
3 ... a place with a lot of noise _____
4 ... a thing that frightens you _____

Grammar

Past simple • Verbo *be*

1 Completa le frasi su quello che è successo ieri in maniera personale. Usa *was*, *wasn't*, *were* o *weren't*.

Yesterday...
1 I _____ ill.
2 my mum _____ at work.
3 the students in my class _____ at school.
4 I _____ tired all day.
5 we _____ on holiday.
6 my favourite singers _____ on TV.
7 my friends _____ at a party.
8 I _____ in bed at 9pm.

2 Scrivi domande e risposte con le parole date e la forma corretta del *Past simple* del verbo *be*.

1 you/be/at home/last weekend? (No)
_____
_____

2 your parents/be/at work/yesterday? (No)
_____
_____

3 Barbara/be/at university/last year? (Yes)
_____
_____

4 David/be/ill/yesterday? (No)
_____
_____

5 you and your family/be/on holiday/last week? (Yes)
_____
_____

6 the bus/be/late/this morning? (Yes)
_____
_____

3 Completa il dialogo con la forma corretta del *Past simple* del verbo *be*.

Joe Hi, Hannah. ¹_____ (you/be) at Kelly's party on Friday?
Hannah Yes, ²_____.
Joe ³_____ (it/be) good?
Hannah Yes, ⁴_____. There ⁵_____ (be) a lot of people there. Why ⁶_____ (you/not/be) there?
Joe We ⁷_____ (be) in London. ⁸_____ (Sophie and Matt/be) at the party?
Hannah Sophie ⁹_____ (be) there but Matt ¹⁰_____ (not be).
Joe That's interesting. ¹¹Why _____ (Sophie/be) there without Matt?
Hannah I don't know! Maybe Matt ¹²_____ (be) ill!

Espressioni di tempo passato

4 Immagina che sia venerdì 23 agosto. Abbina le date (1–6) alle espressioni di tempo passato (a–f).

1 Friday, 16ᵗʰ August
2 July
3 March
4 Monday 19ᵗʰ August
5 Saturday 17ᵗʰ + Sunday 18ᵗʰ August
6 Thursday, 22ⁿᵈ August

a yesterday
b last weekend
c a week ago
d five months ago
e four days ago
f last month

1 ___ 2 ___ 3 ___ 4 ___ 5 ___ 6 ___

5 Scrivi frasi vere su dove tu, la tua famiglia e i tuoi amici eravate in questi momenti passati. Scegli il soggetto delle frasi e usa il *Past simple* affermativo o negativo.

1 (last night)
My parents weren't at home last night.
2 (last summer)
_____
3 (at 7 o'clock this morning)
_____
4 (three days ago)
_____
5 (last weekend)
_____
6 (yesterday afternoon)
_____

Preposizioni di luogo (3): *in, at*

6 Completa le frasi con *in* o *at*.

1 My sister's _____ university _____ Edinburgh.
2 Mum's _____ the supermarket this morning.
3 We were _____ the beach yesterday afternoon.
4 I'm _____ the bath.
5 John was _____ the leisure centre this morning.
6 Do you live _____ Italy?
7 Linda is _____ bed because she's ill.
8 I was _____ home last weekend.

be born

7 Scrivi frasi complete usando le parole date e la forma corretta di *be born*.

1 my mum/be born/in 1975
_____

2 Sam/be born/in August?
_____

3 the girls/be born/in South Africa
_____

4 Where/you/be born?
_____

5 I/be born/in Liverpool
_____

6 we/be born/in Ireland
_____

Past simple • Verbi regolari e irregolari

8 Scrivi il *Past simple* di questi verbi regolari, facendo attenzione alle variazioni ortografiche.

1 decide _____
2 try _____
3 cook _____
4 copy _____
5 drop _____
6 enjoy _____
7 play _____
8 remember _____
9 watch _____
10 invite _____
11 close _____
12 control _____
13 refer _____
14 wait _____

9 Completa la tabella con il verbo alla forma base o al *Past simple*. Tutti i verbi elencati sono irregolari.

Forma base	Past simple
1 _____	spoke
write	7 _____
2 _____	went
eat	8 _____
3 _____	saw
drink	9 _____
4 _____	came
do	10 _____
5 _____	took
read	11 _____
6 _____	found

10 Completa il paragrafo con la forma corretta dei verbi regolari e irregolari fra parentesi. Usa il *Past simple*.

My parents [1]_____ (meet) when they [2]_____ (be) students at Bristol University. They [3]_____ (study) there in the 1980s. They [4]_____ (leave) university in 1988 and they [5]_____ (marry) in 1990. They [6]_____ (move) to Scotland in the 1990s. I [7]_____ (be born) in 1995 and my sister [8]_____ (be born) in 1997. We [9]_____ (like) living in Scotland, but two years ago we [10]_____ (come) back to England because my dad [11]_____ (get) a job in Manchester. My sister and I [12]_____ (change) schools, but our new school is OK.

11 Correggi questi fatti storici seguendo l'esempio come modello. Le informazioni corrette sono fra parentesi.

1 The Second World War started in 1949. (1939)
The Second World War didn't start in 1949. It started in 1939.

2 Manzoni wrote *Romeo and Juliet*. (Shakespeare)
_____

3 Zucchero sang *Ora*. (Jovanotti)
_____

4 Michelangelo painted *La Gioconda*. (Leonardo)
_____

5 Nelson Mandela was born in 1920. (1918)
_____

6 Steven Spielberg made the film *Avatar*. (James Cameron)
_____

7 The Greeks built the Coliseum. (the Romans)
_____

8 The *Risorgimento* happened in the 1900s. (1800s)
_____

12 Scrivi domande al *Past simple* per queste risposte.

1 _____?
I put it on the kitchen table.

2 _____?
We left at half past ten.

3 _____?
Because I was ill.

4 _____?
They went to the swimming pool.

5 _____?
I met Kelly and Matt.

6 _____?
I had a sandwich and some fruit.

13 Completa il dialogo con le parole fra parentesi. Usa la forma corretta del *Past simple*.

Megan ¹_____ (What/you/do) at the weekend, Jack?

Jack I ²_____ (not do) much, really. I ³_____ (play) football on Saturday morning and my cousins ⁴_____ (come) to visit in the afternoon. I just ⁵_____ (relax) on Sunday. What about you?

Megan We ⁶_____ (go) to London on Sunday.

Jack Great! ⁷_____ (How/you/get) there?

Megan Mum ⁸_____ (take) us in the car.

Jack ⁹_____ (How long/you/stay) there? ¹⁰_____ (What/you/see)?

Megan Well, we ¹¹_____ (not see) any of the famous sights. In fact, it ¹²_____ (be) a disaster. Mum ¹³_____ (lose) her bag and we ¹⁴_____ (spend) all afternoon at the police station!

Esercizi sommativi

14 Ci sono 8 errori grammaticali in questo paragrafo. Identificali e correggili.

We had a fantastic holiday in Spain the last August. Our hotel was near the beach.

1 _____

It had a big swimming pool too. We useded the swimming pool every morning.

2 _____

We goed to the beach in the afternoon. We ate a lot of Spanish food. It were delicious!

3 _____

4 _____

There were lots of good clubs and restaurants at the town,

5 _____

but we didn't went out every night. Some evenings we staied in the hotel.

6 _____

7 _____

We did really enjoyed the holiday and we didn't want to come home!

8 _____

15 Completa il paragrafo con il *Present simple*, *Present continuous* o *Past simple* dei verbi fra parentesi.

My name ¹_____ (be) Darren. I ²_____ (be) 16 and I ³_____ (go) to St Peter's School in Bedford. At the moment I ⁴_____ (study) for my GCSE exams. These exams ⁵_____ (be) very important. All the teenagers in the UK ⁶_____ (do) GCSEs when they ⁷_____ (be) 16. I ⁸_____ (do) the exams in June next year. After the exams my parents ⁹_____ (take) me and my sister on a big holiday. We ¹⁰_____ (go) to the USA! We ¹¹_____ (not have) a holiday last year because my parents ¹²_____ (have) too much work. Mum and Dad ¹³_____ (go) to the USA before they ¹⁴_____ (get married), and they really ¹⁵_____ (enjoy) it!

16 Translation • Traduci il dialogo in inglese sul tuo quaderno.

Lee ¹Che cosa farete durante le vacanze estive?

Emily ²Andremo a casa di mia zia per una settimana.

Lee ³Dove vive?

Emily ⁴In Galles. Si è trasferita tre anni fa.

Lee ⁵Siamo andati in Galles l'estate scorsa. Il tempo non era molto bello, ma abbiamo fatto una vacanza meravigliosa.

Emily ⁶Che cosa avete fatto?

Lee ⁷Siamo andati in spiaggia, abbiamo fatto degli sport d'acqua e abbiamo visitato Cardiff.

Emily ⁸Andate in vacanza quest'anno?

Lee ⁹Sì. Andiamo sempre via in agosto. Quest'anno andremo in Francia.

Translation note

Per scegliere il tempo verbale corretto in inglese, considera attentamente il contesto e le espressioni di tempo usate nelle frasi in italiano. Per esempio:

Di solito non bevo caffè.
= *Present simple* (usually):
I don't usually drink coffee.

Non studio in questo periodo.
= *Present continuous* (at the moment):
I'm not studying at the moment.

Andiamo al mare venerdì prossimo.
= *Present continuous* (next Friday):
We're going to the seaside next Friday.

Sono partiti tre giorni fa.
= *Past simple* (ago):
They left three days ago.

Italian FOOD COMES TO THE UK

ITALIAN FOOD is very popular in the UK, but how did the British taste for Italian food begin? Over 100 years ago, thousands of Italians decided to leave Italy because conditions there were very difficult. A lot of
5 them came to London, but many more travelled to Liverpool and Glasgow, on the west coast of Britain, because they wanted to travel to America. Some of them changed their plans and stayed in these British cities instead. At that time, British people weren't
10 very interested in food from different countries, but some of the Italian immigrants started businesses selling Britain's favourite meal – fish and chips. They soon added Italian ice-cream to the menu, and Italian ice-cream shops became a popular tradition
15 in Scotland and the north of England.

In the 1970s, British people started to go on cheap holidays to different countries. When they came home, a lot of them wanted to eat the food that they tried on holiday. Pizza and pasta restaurants became
20 popular places to eat out. But there are lots of differences between authentic Italian food and some 'Italian' food in the UK. British people like a large variety of things on their pizzas. There are some unusual ingredients, like <u>pineapple</u> or chicken curry!
25 And don't forget a little <u>garlic</u> bread with your pizza – a long loaf of bread cooked with butter and garlic. Italian desserts are popular too, especially tiramisù and panna cotta. But British people in an Italian restaurant sometimes order a cappuccino at the end
30 of a meal.

These days British people drink all types of Italian coffee. Cappuccinos and espressos are common in cafés, and a 'latte' is a very <u>milky</u> coffee. But many coffee shops offer extra additions that you don't
35 usually find in Italy: special flavours for your coffee like <u>hazelnut</u> or <u>toffee</u>.

Glossary

pineapple	ananas
garlic	aglio
milky	al latte
hazelnut	nocciola
toffee	mou

Reading comprehension

*

1 🔊 **S.080** Leggi il testo e abbina le parti iniziali delle frasi (1–6) alle loro conclusioni (a–f).

1	Fish and chips	**a**	is a type of coffee in the UK.
2	Pizza	**b**	is an addition to coffee in the UK.
3	Pineapple	**c**	became popular in the 1970s.
4	Garlic bread	**d**	was a popular meal 100 years ago.
5	A latte	**e**	can go on a pizza in the UK.
6	Hazelnut	**f**	often comes with pizza in the UK.

1 ___ 2 ___ 3 ___ 4 ___ 5 ___ 6 ___

**

2 Tutte queste frasi sono false. Scrivi la versione corretta delle frasi.

1 A hundred years ago, British people ate a lot of food from different countries.

2 The first Italian businesses in Scotland were pizza restaurants.

3 American people brought ice-cream to the UK.

4 British people started to go on holiday to other countries in the 1800s.

5 British people sometimes put pineapple on pasta.

6 The ingredients for garlic bread are bread, oil and garlic.

***

3 Rispondi alle domande.

1 Why did a lot of Italians leave Italy around 1900?

2 Why did thousands of them come to Liverpool and Glasgow?

3 What did a lot of Italians do instead of leaving Britain?

4 When did pizza and pasta restaurants start to become popular in the UK?

5 What is 'a latte' in the UK?

6 What can you put in coffee in the UK that you don't find in Italy?

7 Which Italian desserts are common in the UK?

8 What do British people sometimes drink at the end of an Italian meal?

Culture note

Il caffè è la bevanda più diffusa nel mondo: beviamo più di 400 miliardi di tazze di caffè all'anno. Con la maggiore diffusione del caffè e dei bar nel Regno Unito negli ultimi anni, gli inglesi sono arrivati a bere circa 70 milioni di tazze di caffè al giorno, e nel 2010 hanno speso £730 milioni in caffè. Il caffè espresso è il più comune nel sud-est dell'Inghilterra.

Tuttavia, il thè rimane la bevanda preferita del Regno Unito. I britannici bevono 165 milioni di tazze di thè al giorno – 60.2 miliardi di tazze di thè all'anno!

Listening comprehension

*

4 🔊 **S.081** Ascolta le quattro persone che parlano dell'ultima volta in cui hanno mangiato cibo italiano. Metti un *tick* (✓) accanto ai cibi che senti nominare.

pizza ☐ garlic bread ☐ butter ☐ salad ☐
ice-cream ☐ apple pie ☐ latte ☐
cappuccino ☐ pasta ☐ beer ☐ wine ☐
tiramisù ☐ lasagne ☐ spaghetti bolognese ☐
cannelloni ☐ macaroni ☐

**

5 🔊 **S.081** Riascolta e scegli l'alternativa corretta.

1 Sally had **beef/chicken** on her pizza.
2 Sally had **a little/a lot of** salad.
3 Tom **eats a lot of/doesn't eat much** Italian food.
4 Tom had **an espresso/a cappuccino** yesterday.
5 Vicky had pasta with **seafood/tomatoes**.
6 Vicky had some **red/white** wine.
7 Vicky's friend ate **ice-cream/tiramisù** for dessert.
8 Alex **liked/didn't like** the lasagne at school yesterday.

***

6 🔊 **S.081** Riascolta e rispondi alle domande.

1 When did Sally go to Pizza Palace?
2 What did she have with her pizza?
3 What did she have for dessert?
4 What did Tom have with his coffee?
5 What did Vicky's friend eat in the restaurant?
6 What did they have after their dessert?
7 Why didn't Alex like the lasagne?
8 What other Italian foods do they get for lunch at his school?

Dictation

7 🔊 **S.082** Ascolta e scrivi le frasi che senti.

1
2
3
4
5
6
7
8

Writing

Writing skills

Descrivere un evento passato

8 Quando descrivi un evento passato, quello che scrivi risulterà più scorrevole se le informazioni che presenti seguono un ordine preciso.

- è buona abitudine iniziare il paragrafo con una frase di apertura che riassuma le informazioni che stai per dare. ¹Quale di queste frasi secondo te è la più adatta per iniziare un paragrafo intitolato *My Last Holiday*?

  a I had a fantastic holiday last year.

  b We arrived at our hotel in the afternoon.

  c The campsite had a good swimming pool.

  d Our holiday in Spain last August was a disaster!

- quando descrivi una sequenza di eventi, usa espressioni di sequenza temporale (*first, next* ecc.) per suddividere le informazioni e mettere in ordine i vari eventi.

  Per descrivere gli eventi iniziali: *First, At the start*

  Per mettere in ordine gli eventi successivi: *Next, Then, After that, Afterwards*

  Per descrivere gli eventi finali: *Finally, At the end*

- concludi il paragrafo con una frase che riassuma di nuovo le informazioni contenute nel paragrafo, oppure con una frase che esprima un'opinione personale. ²Quale di queste frasi è la più adatta per concludere il paragrafo sulle vacanze?

  a We arrived home on Saturday 19ᵗʰ July.

  b It was a terrible holiday from start to finish!

  c The hotel was fantastic!

  Ora fai l'Esercizio 9 tenendo presente le regole su come presentare una sequenza di informazioni.

9 Scrivi un breve testo (75–100 parole) sulla vacanza più recente che hai fatto. Includi le risposte alle seguenti domande: **T**

- Where did you go?
- Was it good?
- Who did you go with?
- Where did you stay?
- What did you do?

Non dimenticare una frase di apertura e una di chiusura.

Functions on film

Eating out

A Indica se le frasi (1–5) vengono dette dal cliente (*C*) o dal cameriere (*W*).

1 I'll have spaghetti, please. ____
2 What would you like? ____
3 Are you ready to order? ____
4 I'd like chocolate ice-cream, please. ____
5 Could I have the bill, please? ____

B Completa il dialogo.

Waitress Hello. Are you ready to ¹_____?
Customer Yes, I'll ²_____ tomato salad for my starter, please.
Waitress Certainly. What would you ³_____ for your main ⁴_____?
Customer ⁵_____ like lasagne, please.
Waitress And what ⁶_____ you like ⁷_____ drink?
Customer Pineapple juice, ⁸_____.

After 30 minutes...

Customer Could I have the ⁹_____, please?
Waitress Yes, of ¹⁰_____.

C Osserva il menu e completa il dialogo. Scegli quello che preferisci dal menu.

menu

starters
Tomato soup
Garlic bread
Seafood pasta

main courses
Vegetarian lasagne
Chicken
Hamburger
(All served with chips or salad)

drinks
Mineral water
Apple juice
Orange juice

Waiter Hello. Are you ready to order?
You ¹_____
Waiter What would you like for your starter?
You ²_____
Waiter And for your main course?
You ³_____
Waiter What would you like to drink?
You ⁴_____
At the end of the meal
You ⁵_____
Waiter Yes, certainly.

Grammar network

A Past simple • Forma interrogativa e risposte brevi

Forma interrogativa	Risposte brevi	
	affermative	negative
Did I walk/go?	Yes, I did.	No, I didn't.
Did you walk/go?	Yes, you did.	No, you didn't.
Did he/she/it walk/go?	Yes, he/she/it did.	No, he/she/it didn't.
Did we walk/go?	Yes, we did.	No, we didn't.
Did you walk/go?	Yes, you did.	No, you didn't.
Did they walk/go?	Yes, they did.	No, they didn't.

1 Come abbiamo visto (Unit 8 p.201), la forma interrogativa del *Past simple* si ottiene così:

> *Did* + soggetto + forma base del verbo + ?

Did the children enjoy the trip?
È piaciuta la gita ai bambini?

2 Le risposte brevi si formano così:

> *Yes*, + soggetto + *did*.
> *No*, + soggetto + *didn't*.

3 Le regole per la forma interrogativa e le risposte brevi sono le stesse sia per i verbi regolari che per i verbi irregolari:
Did he stay for a long time?
È rimasto a lungo?
Did he eat dinner with you?
Ha cenato con te?

 Ricorda che l'ausiliare *did* non si usa con il verbo *be*:
Was he at school yesterday?
(~~Did he be at school yesterday?~~)
Era a scuola ieri?

B *could* • Abilità e possibilità

Forma affermativa	Forma negativa		Forma interrogativa	Risposte brevi	
	estesa	contratta		affermative	negative
I could	I could not	I couldn't	Could I?	Yes, I could.	No, I couldn't.
you could	you could not	you couldn't	Could you?	Yes, you could.	No, you couldn't.
he/she/it could	he/she/it could not	he/she/it couldn't	Could he/she/it?	Yes, he/she/it could.	No, he/she/it couldn't.
we could	we could not	we couldn't	Could we?	Yes, we could.	No, we couldn't.
you could	you could not	you couldn't	Could you?	Yes, you could.	No, you couldn't.
they could	they could not	they couldn't	Could they?	Yes, they could.	No, they couldn't.

1 Come abbiamo già visto (Unit 5 p.178) il verbo modale *can* si usa per parlare di abilità:
I can play the piano and the guitar.
So suonare il piano e la chitarra.

2 *Can* può essere anche usato per indicare che è possibile (c'è la possibilità di) fare qualcosa. In questo caso corrisponde al verbo italiano 'potere':
You can see all the new films in that cinema.
Si possono vedere tutti i film nuovi in quel cinema.

3 La forma passata di *can* è *could*. Come *can*, *could* è un verbo modale ed è quindi invariabile per tutte le persone, non si usa mai con i verbi ausiliari ed è sempre seguito dalla forma base del verbo:
We could use the gym in the hotel.
(~~We could to use the gym in the hotel.~~)
Potevamo usare la palestra nell'albergo.

4 La forma affermativa di *could* si ottiene così:

> soggetto + *could* + forma base del verbo

My dad could play rugby very well when he was younger.
Mio padre sapeva giocare a rugby molto bene quando era giovane.

5 La forma negativa di *could* si ottiene così:

> soggetto + *couldn't* + forma base del verbo

We couldn't decide what to eat.
Non siamo riusciti a decidere che cosa mangiare.

6 La forma interrogativa si ottiene invertendo il soggetto e *could*:

> *Could* + soggetto + forma base del verbo + ?

Could you speak English then?
Sapevi parlare l'inglese allora?

7 Le risposte brevi si formano così:

> *Yes*, + soggetto + *could*.
> *No*, + soggetto + *couldn't*.

Could you talk when you were one? No, I couldn't?
Saperi parlare quando avevi un anno? No.

 Anche *could*, come *can*, può essere accompagnato dalle espressioni *quite/very/really well*, ecc.

I couldn't ski very well two years ago.
Non sapevo sciare molto bene due anni fa.

8 Le frasi con *could* possono esprimere:

- abilità nel passato:
  He could swim when he was five.
  Sapeva nuotare quando aveva cinque anni.

- possibilità o impossibilità nel passato:
  When we lived in Cornwall, we could go to the beach every day.
  Quando vivevamo in Cornovaglia, potevamo andare in spiaggia ogni giorno.
  We couldn't get tickets for the concert.
  Non siamo riusciti a prendere i biglietti per il concerto.

C Verbi + preposizioni nelle domande

1 Quando il verbo principale di una domanda richiede una preposizione, questa si mette dopo il verbo (+ complemento oggetto) oppure alla fine della frase, ma mai all'inizio:
Where did you get those jeans <u>from</u>?
(~~From where did you get those jeans?~~)
Dove hai preso quei jeans?
What did you open the box <u>with</u>?
(~~With what did you open the box?~~)
Con che cosa hai aperto la scatola?
Who did you see the film <u>with</u> last night?
Con chi hai visito il film ieri sera?

Ricorda che alcuni verbi usati comunemente in inglese sono accompagnati da una preposizione:
look <u>at</u> = *guardare*
wait <u>for</u> = *aspettare*
listen <u>to</u> = *ascoltare*
look <u>for</u> = *cercare*
Queste preposizioni non si possono mai omettere se la frase ha un complemento:
What are you looking <u>at</u>?   *Che cosa stai guardando?*
Who are you waiting <u>for</u>?   *Chi stai aspettando?*
What are you listening <u>to</u>?   *Che cosa stai ascoltando?*
What are you looking <u>for</u>?   *Che cosa stai cercando?*

Word store

The media	*I mezzi di comunicazione*
TV	_____
advert	_____
cartoon	_____
chat show	_____
documentary	_____
film	_____
quiz show	_____
reality show	_____
sitcom	_____
soap	_____
sports programme	_____
talent show	_____
the news	_____
Printed media	_____
book	_____
comic	_____
magazine	_____
newspaper	_____

the Internet	_____
blog	_____
email	_____
social network site	_____
wiki	_____

Real talk

Completa le espressioni dai dialoghi dello *Student's Book*.

definitely the _____	*decisamente il migliore*
I didn't _____ around	*Non sono rimasta*
_____ so _____	*Sei così fortunato*
It _____ _____	*È stato difficile*
Not _____ at _____!	*Mica male!*

Vocabulary

The media

1 Leggi le descrizioni dei programmi televisivi. Scrivi i nomi dei tipi di programmi usando le parole del riquadro.

> film   reality show   chat show   documentary   news
> talent show   soap   sports programme   quiz show   sitcom

Channel 1

7PM ELEPHANT SAFARI
A real-life look at these animals in their South African home.
1 _____

8PM TEACHER FOR A WEEK
Three ordinary teenagers work as teachers for a week. Are they successful?
2 _____

9PM NATIONAL AND LOCAL 3 _____
All the important stories of the day from around the country and from your area.

9.45PM SANDRA AND FRIENDS
Sandra Smith talks to this week's celebrities.
4 _____

10.30PM THE LATE 5 _____
Terminator 2 with Arnold Schwarzenegger

Channel 2

6.30PM TRUE OR FALSE?
Who wins the £5,000 prize tonight?
6 _____

7.00PM RUTLAND STREET
What's happening with your favourite characters in Rutland Street this week?
7 _____

7.30PM OUR HOUSE
Gemma and Mark are embarrassed by their Dad. He wants to go to a club with them!
8 _____

8.00PM THE WOW-FACTOR
There are only six young singers in the competition now.
9 _____

9.00PM GOAL!
Today's football matches
10 _____

2 Leggi le prime pagine e i titoli. Completa i nomi dei tipi di mezzi di comunicazione a stampa.

 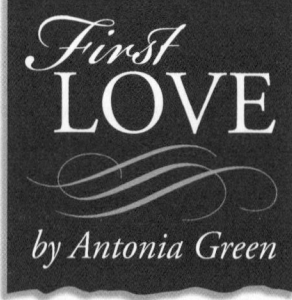  

1 m_____   2 b_____   3 n_____   4 c_____

3 Scrivi che tipi di siti web sono quelli elencati qui di seguito.

1 www.connectwithfriends.co.uk

_____

2 www.myteenageweek.co.uk

_____

3 www.netmailforyou.com

_____

Grammar

Past simple • Forma interrogativa e risposte brevi

1 Trasforma le frasi da affermative a interrogative. Inizia ogni domanda con *Did*.

1 George took his lunch to school.

2 Mum made this cake.

3 Our team won the match.

4 The students passed the exam.

5 Laura left her bag at the gym.

6 Jake saw the film yesterday.

7 They went to the concert last night.

8 The boys missed a lesson this morning.

2 Scrivi domande complete al *Past simple*. Poi scrivi le risposte brevi dal riquadro.

> Yes, they did.   Yes, he did.   Yes, it did.
> No, we didn't.   No, she didn't.   No, I didn't.

1 you and Emma/go/to Anna's party?

2 your parents/buy/that phone for you?

3 Dave/get/my email?

4 Fiona/phone/last night?

5 you/watch/the news last night?

6 the bus/arrive late?

3 Scrivi le risposte brevi come indicato.

1 A Did the lesson start at 9 o'clock?
B ✗ _____

2 A Did you have any breakfast today?
B ✓ _____

3 A Did your brother go on the school trip?
B ✗ _____

4 A Did Sara work last summer?
B ✗ _____

5 A Did Tom remember your birthday?
B ✓ _____

6 A Did your friends enjoy the film?
B ✓ _____

4 Scrivi domande per le risposte sottolineate.

1 A _____ last night?
B We went to a French restaurant.

2 A _____ yesterday?
B I met my cousins.

3 A _____?
B I found it in the street.

4 A _____?
B I phoned her because it was her birthday.

5 A _____?
B We travelled there by train.

6 A _____?
B I had a cheese sandwich and some fruit for lunch.

5 Leggi l'articolo di giornale. Poi scrivi le 6 domande che l'intervistatore ha fatto per ottenere le informazioni sottolineate.

Alexa Vine

Pop star Alexa Vine arrived in London last Thursday. She spent the weekend at a film studio. She made a new video there. It was very tiring. Yesterday she went to Camden Market. She liked it.

1 _____?
2 _____?
3 _____?
4 _____?
5 _____?
6 _____?

could • Abilità e possibilità

6 Osserva le seguenti frasi con *could/couldn't*. Scrivi *A* se la frase denota abilità o *P* se denota possibilità.

1 ___ I could ride a bike when I was 6.
2 ___ My mum could speak Russian when she was a student.
3 ___ It rained yesterday so we couldn't go to the park.
4 ___ I couldn't understand people when we went to France!
5 ___ The hotel wasn't near the sea, but you could swim in the swimming pool.
6 ___ I couldn't buy any food because the shops were closed.

7 Scrivi frasi complete al passato con la forma corretta dei verbi fra parentesi.

1 There (be) a lot of snow last winter. We (can) go skiing every weekend.
_____

2 I (can ✗) do my homework because I (leave) my books at school.
_____

3 We (go) to the new leisure centre, but it (not be) very good. You (can ✗) play basketball there.
_____

4 When I (be) small, I (can) see the sea from my bedroom window.
_____

5 We (take) Dad's car to the garage, but they (can ✗) repair it.
_____

6 We (go) to a great pizzeria. You (can) make your own pizzas there!
_____

8 Scrivi domande e risposte al passato usando le parole date.

1 (you/can) read when you (be) 5? (Yes)
_____
_____

2 (they/can) go swimming when they (be) on holiday? (Yes)
_____
_____

3 (Samantha/can) drive when she (be) at university? (No)
_____
_____

4 (Dad/can) cook when he (meet) Mum? (No)
_____
_____

5 (you/can) communicate with people when you (be) in Italy? (Yes)
_____
_____

9 Osserva la tabella. Poi completa le frasi su quello che Dean sa fare adesso e quello che sapeva fare 10 anni fa. Usa *can*, *can't*, *could* e *couldn't*.

	10 years ago	Now
1 drive a car	✗	✓
2 swim	✓	✓
3 skateboard	✓	✗
4 speak French	✗	✓
5 play an instrument	✗	✗

1 10 years ago Dean _____ drive a car, but now he _____.
2 Dean _____ swim 10 years ago, and he _____ swim now.
3 10 years ago Dean _____ skateboard, but he _____ do it now.
4 Dean _____ speak French now, but he _____ 10 years ago.
5 Dean _____ play an instrument 10 years ago, and he _____ play one now!

Verbi + preposizioni nelle domande

10 Scrivi le traduzioni in inglese di questi verbi italiani. Ogni verbo in inglese ha una preposizione.

1 ascoltare _____
2 aspettare _____
3 cercare _____
4 guardare _____
5 chiedere qualcosa _____

11 Scrivi le domande per queste frasi.

1 _____?
   That girl comes <u>from France</u>.
2 _____?
   I wrote about <u>the 1940s</u> for my History project.
3 _____?
   Johnny went on holiday with <u>his girlfriend</u>.
4 _____?
   We talked about <u>last week's party</u>.
5 _____?
   Anna worked for <u>her dad</u> last summer.
6 _____?
   I want to talk to <u>my teacher</u> after the lesson.

12 Traduci le domande in inglese, facendo attenzione alla posizione delle preposizioni.

1 Con chi sei andata alla festa?

_____

2 Che cosa state cercando?

_____

3 A chi stai parlando?

_____

4 Da dove viene quella gente?

_____

5 Di che cosa avete parlato?

_____

6 Per chi hai comprato quei fiori?

_____

7 Che tipo di tramezzino hai chiesto?

_____

8 Chi stai aspettando?

_____

Esercizi sommativi

13 Completa il dialogo.

Natasha	What ¹_____ you do at the weekend?
William	Nothing. I had a lot of homework so I ²_____ go out. What about you?
Natasha	I went to a music festival.
William	Really? ³_____ did you go ⁴_____?
Natasha	I went with my dad. He often goes to festivals.
William	⁵_____ type of music does he listen ⁶_____?
Natasha	Rock music. He played the guitar with a rock group in the 1980s.
William	Really? ⁷_____ ⁸_____ play with a famous group?
Natasha	No, ⁹_____ ¹⁰_____. But he ¹¹_____ play really well. We've got some old videos of him. There was just one problem with his band.
William	What was that?
Natasha	The singer ¹²_____ sing at all!

14 Completa il dialogo con la forma corretta del passato dei verbi fra parentesi.

Sophie	¹_____ (you/watch) *Dancing on Ice* on Saturday?
Eve	No, ²_____. I ³_____ (not watch) much at the weekend. ⁴_____ (it/be) good?
Sophie	Yes, ⁵_____. That boy from *Hollyoaks* ⁶_____ (be) on it.
Eve	⁷_____ (he/can) skate?
Sophie	No, ⁸_____! He ⁹_____ (not can) skate at all!
Eve	¹⁰_____ (who/he/skate with)?
Sophie	A professional ice skater. She ¹¹_____ (can) skate really well but she ¹²_____ (not can) control him!
Eve	¹³_____ (they/lose)?
Sophie	No, ¹⁴_____! People ¹⁵_____ (vote) for them because they ¹⁶_____ (think) they ¹⁷_____ (be) funny.

15 Translation • Traduci il dialogo in inglese sul tuo quaderno.

Jason	¹Hai guardato la partita di calcio ieri sera?
Steve	²Di che partita stai parlando?
Jason	³La partita fra il Barcellona e il Chelsea.
Steve	⁴No. Ha vinto il Chelsea?
Jason	⁵No. Hanno giocato malissimo. Ci siamo proprio annoiati.
Steve	⁶Con chi hai guardato la partita?
Jason	⁷Con Adam. Non poteva guardarla a casa perché sua mamma non sopporta il calcio!

Translation note

Ricorda che, a differenza dell'italiano, in inglese è considerato molto brusco rispondere solo con *Yes* o *No*. È molto più naturale e cortese usare le risposte brevi:

Hai visto Donna ieri? No.
Did you see Donna yesterday? No, I didn't. (~~No.~~)

Sono partiti presto? Sì.
Did they leave early? Yes, they did. (~~Yes.~~)

Grammar network

A Subject and object questions

Soggetto	Complemento
Who took you to the concert? *Chi ti ha portato al concerto?*	**Who** did you see in town? *Chi hai visto in centro?*
What made that noise? *Che cosa ha causato quel rumore?*	**What** do you do on Sundays? *Che cosa fai di domenica?*
Which family lives here? *Quale famiglia vive qui?*	**Which** teacher did you speak to? *Con quale insegnante hai parlato?*
How many students use this classroom? *Quanti studenti usano quest'aula?*	**How many** DVDs did you buy? *Quanti DVD hai comprato?*

1 Le parole interrogative elencate sopra (*Who, What, Which, How many*) si possono usare nelle domande sia come soggetto che come complemento.

2 Al *Present simple*, quando la parola interrogativa si riferisce al soggetto, la domanda non prende l'ausiliare e si forma così:

> Pronome interrogativo + verbo al *Present simple* + complemento + ?

<u>Who</u> teaches Maths at your school? <u>Mr Smith</u> teaches Maths at my school.
Chi insegna matematica nella tua scuola? Mr Smith insegna matematica nella mia scuola.

3 Al *Present simple*, quando la parola interrogativa si riferisce al complemento, la domanda si forma con l'ausiliare così:

> Pronome interrogativo + *do/does* + soggetto + forma base del verbo + complemento + ?

<u>Who</u> do you go to school with? I go to school <u>with Joe</u>.
Con chi vai a scuola? Vado a scuola con Joe.

4 Al *Past simple*, quando la parola interrogativa si riferisce al soggetto, la domanda non prende l'ausiliare e si forma così:

> Pronome interrogativo + verbo al *Past simple* + complemento + ?

<u>Who</u> broke the window? <u>Mark</u> broke the window.
Chi ha rotto la finestra? Mark ha rotto le finestra.

5 Al *Past simple*, quando la parola interrogativa si riferisce al complemento, la domanda si forma con l'ausiliare così:

> Pronome interrogativo + *did* + soggetto + forma base del verbo + complemento + ?

<u>Who</u> did you invite to the party? We invited <u>all our friends</u>.
Chi avete invitato alla festa? Abbiamo invitato tutti i nostri amici.

 Nelle domande con l'ausiliare (*do/does/did*) in cui il verbo principale è accompagnato da una preposizione, quest'ultima si mette alla fine della domanda oppure dopo il verbo (+ complemento oggetto). Vedi Unit 9 p.211:

Who do you go to school **with**? *Con chi vai a scuola?*

Tuttavia, nelle domande con un pronome interrogativo come soggetto, la preposizione occupa la posizione usuale:

Who walks to school **with** you?
Chi va a scuola con te?

B be like vs. look like vs. like

1 Per chiedere che carattere ha qualcuno si usa questa struttura:

> *What* + *is/are* + soggetto + *like* + ?

What is your mum like? She's cheerful and energetic.
Com'è tua madre? È allegra ed energica!

2 Per chiedere che aspetto fisico ha qualcuno si usa questa struttura:

> *What* + *do/does* + soggetto + *look like* + ?

What does your dad look like?
He's tall and he's got short, black hair.
Com'è/Che aspetto ha il tuo papà?
È alto e ha i capelli corti e neri.

3 Per chiedere che cosa piace o non piace (fare) a qualcuno si usa la seguente struttura:

> *What* + *do/does* + soggetto + *like* (+ forma in *-ing*) + ?

What do the boys like doing? They like playing rugby.
Che cosa piace fare ai ragazzi? A loro piace giocare a rugby.

What films do you like? I like science fiction films.
Che film ti piacciono? Mi piacciono i film di fantascienza.

C Ordine degli aggettivi

> He's got short, straight, black hair.
> *Ha i capelli corti, dritti e neri.*
>
> I've got a trendy, new, pink phone.
> *Ho un telefono alla moda, nuovo e rosa.*

1 In inglese, gli aggettivi qualificativi sono invariabili in genere e numero e precedono sempre il sostantivo a cui si riferiscono.

2 Quando si usano due o più aggettivi per descrivere un sostantivo, è necessario separarli con una virgola. Non si usa mai la congiunzione *and*:

I found a wonderful, new, Italian restaurant yesterday. (~~I found a wonderful and new Italian restaurant yesterday.~~)
Ieri ho scoperto un meraviglioso ristorante italiano nuovo.

3 Di solito l'ordine degli aggettivi prima di un sostantivo è il seguente:

opinione + grandezza + età + colore + nazionalità

an interesting little old red British car

⚠ La regola appena descritta è utile per decidere in che ordine mettere gli aggettivi. Tuttavia, in inglese è raro usare più di tre aggettivi per descrivere un sostantivo.

4 Quando si descrivono i capelli, la lunghezza viene sempre per prima nelle descrizioni. Il tipo e il colore seguono la lunghezza nell'ordine che si preferisce:

She's got short, curly, red hair. / She's got short, red, curly hair.

Ha i capelli corti, ricci e rossi. / Ha i capelli corti, rossi e ricci.

Word store

Personality adjectives (1)
Aggettivi che descrivono la personalità

boring	_____
cautious	_____
cheerful	_____
clever	_____
confident	_____
decisive	_____
easy-going	_____
energetic	_____
generous	_____
grumpy	_____
impulsive	_____
indecisive	_____
insecure	_____
interesting	_____
lazy	_____
outgoing	_____
selfish	_____
sensible	_____
sensitive	_____
shy	_____
silly	_____
stupid	_____
thick-skinned	_____
uptight	_____

Real talk

Completa le espressioni dai dialoghi dello *Student's Book*.

_____ of people	*un sacco di gente*
I'm _____!	*Sono distrutta!*
_____ _____ with him?	*Che cos'ha?*
He's a good _____	*È divertente*
I _____	*voglio dire*
Oh, _____ he _____!	*Sì che lo è.*
What _____ you _____ that?	*Cosa te lo fa pensare?*

Vocabulary

Personality adjectives (1)

1 Leggi le descrizioni delle persone e completa gli aggettivi di personalità.

1 Melanie is emotional and she often cries at sad situations. She's sen_____.

2 Tom doesn't like meeting new people or doing things in front of the class. He's s_____.

3 Katy doesn't like doing sport or getting up early. She's l_____.

4 Harry doesn't plan his actions, or think about them before he does them. He's im_____.

5 Emily can never make a decision. She's in_____.

6 George is relaxed and it's very difficult to offend him. He's e_____-g_____.

2 Abbina i seguenti aggettivi ai loro contrari dell'Esercizio 1. Scrivi 1–6 negli spazi

cautious ___   decisive ___   energetic ___
outgoing ___   thick-skinned ___   uptight ___

3 Scrivi gli aggettivi del riquadro con un significato positivo nella colonna ☺. Poi scrivi i loro contrari nella colonna ☹.

> boring   cheerful   clever   confident   generous
> grumpy   insecure   interesting   selfish
> sensible   silly   stupid

_____	_____
_____	_____
_____	_____
_____	_____
_____	_____
_____	_____

4 Abbina i *false friends* (1–6) alle loro traduzioni (a–f).

1 ___ sensible	**a** ansioso
2 ___ sensitive	**b** assennato
3 ___ sympathetic	**c** nervoso
4 ___ nice	**d** sensibile
5 ___ irritable	**e** comprensivo
6 ___ nervous	**f** simpatico

Word skills

Indovinare il significato dei vocaboli dal contesto

A volte, il contesto in cui compare un vocabolo che non conosci può aiutarti a il significato indovinarne. Prima di tutto è utile identificare che parte del discorso è il vocabolo che non conosci (sostantivo, verbo ecc.).

5 Osserva le 3 parole evidenziate in neretto nel testo. Qual è a) un sostantivo   b) un verbo c) un aggettivo?

Max and his brother Robert are very different. Max is outgoing and cheerful. He's got a lot of friends and he likes meeting new people. But Robert can be **moody**. One minute he's happy and easy-going, the next minute he's grumpy or sad. Last week the boys went to a party for their grandparents' **anniversary**. Their grandparents got married 50 years ago. Robert was cheerful when he arrived, but then he thought it was boring. He **sulked** all evening. He sat alone in a corner and he refused to talk to other people.

6 Sottolinea le frasi del testo che:

a) descrivono il carattere di Robert
b) descrivono il motivo della festa
c) descrivono il comportamento di Robert alla festa

Come tradurresti le parole evidenziate in neretto nel brano?

7 Ora controlla i vocaboli *moody*, *anniversary* e *sulk* in un dizionario bilingue. Le definizioni in italiano corrispondono alle tue traduzioni?

Grammar
Subject and object questions

1 Indica se le parole interrogative evidenziate in neretto si riferiscono al soggetto (*S*) o al complemento (*C*).

1 ___ **What** do you have for breakfast?
2 ___ **Who** left this bag here?
3 ___ **How many cups of coffee** do you drink every day?
4 ___ **Which teachers** give a lot of homework?
5 ___ **Who** did you speak to?
6 ___ **How many people** play in that band?
7 ___ **What** makes you upset?
8 ___ **Which sports** do you play?
9 ___ **What kind of music** do you like?
10 ___ **What** happened yesterday?

2 Abbina le domande (1–6) alle risposte (a–f).

1 ___ Who invited you to the party?
2 ___ Who did you invite to the party?
3 ___ How many people phoned you this morning?
4 ___ How many people did you phone this morning?
5 ___ Which girl do you like?
6 ___ Which girl likes you?

a Amanda likes me.
b Four people phoned me.
c Peter invited me.
d I like Sarah.
e I invited all my friends.
f I phoned three people.

3 Completa le domande per le risposte sottolineate.

1 Who _____?
  Jack won the competition.
2 Who _____?
  I texted my friend Rebecca.
3 Who _____?
  Alice cooked the meal.
4 Who _____?
  Dad told me the news.
5 Who _____?
  They took their grandma to the station.
6 Who _____?
  We played tennis with our cousins.
7 Who _____?
  Grandma made that cake.
8 Who _____?
  I saw all my classmates at the party.
9 Who _____?
  Manzoni wrote I Promessi Sposi.
10 Who _____?
  Sam and Tom played football yesterday.

4 Un detective sta facendo delle indagini su un omicidio. Osserva i suoi appunti e completa le 6 domande che ha fatto per ottenere le informazioni contenute negli appunti.

> Who killed Lord Harford?
> 1 Ten people work at Harford Hall
> 2 Four people worked on 11th March (including Fred Turner)
> 3 Fred Turner hated Lord Harford
> 4 At 9.30 Mary Jones saw Fred Turner with a pistol
> 5 At 10.30am Lord Harford's wife heard a loud noise
> 6 Mary Jones found Lord Harford's dead body in the library

1 How many _____?
2 How many _____?
3 Who did _____?
4 Who saw _____?
5 Who _____?
6 What did _____?

be like vs. *look like* vs. *like*

5 Scrivi domande per queste risposte. Usa *be like* al *Present simple* o al *Past simple*.

1 (your brother)
  _____?
  He's outgoing and friendly.
2 (the film)
  _____?
  It was exciting.
3 (the people at the party)
  _____?
  They were really boring.
4 (their new song)
  _____?
  It's fantastic.
5 (the pizzas in that restaurant)
  _____?
  They aren't very nice.
6 (the French test)
  _____?
  It was really difficult.

6 Scrivi domande con *look like*. Poi rispondi in maniera personale.

1 (your best friend)

_____?

_____

2 (you)

_____?

_____

3 (your English teacher)

_____?

_____

4 (your family's car)

_____?

_____

5 (your favourite singer)

_____?

_____

7 Osserva la tabella e scrivi frasi complete su quello che piace e non piace fare a Sandy, Paula e Dan.

	play tennis	swim	dance
Sandy	☺	☺	☹
Paula	☹	☺	☺
Dan	☹	☹	☺

1 Sandy/play tennis

_____

2 Paula and Dan/dance

_____

3 Dan/swim

_____

4 Sandy/dance

_____

5 Paula and Dan/play tennis

_____

6 Sandy and Paula/swim

_____

8 Scegli l'alternativa corretta.

Ellen Hi, Louise. What are you doing here?

Louise I'm meeting my friend Rachel. She's very late!

Ellen [1]How/What does she [2]look/looks like?

Louise She's tall and she's got blue hair. You can't miss her!

Ellen Blue hair! Hmm... I can't see her. What about clothes? What [3]does/is she like [4]wear/wearing?

Louise She [5]like/likes [6]wear/wearing really colourful clothes.

Ellen She sounds interesting. What [7]is/does she like?

Louise [8]She's/She's like very confident and outgoing. Stay and meet her!

9 Scrivi domande per queste risposte usando le parole fra parentesi e la forma corretta di *be like*, *look like* o *like doing*.

1 (your Maths teacher)

_____?

He's tall and he's got short, brown hair.

2 (Victoria)

_____?

She isn't very nice. She's selfish and lazy.

3 (your parents)

_____?

They're very easy-going.

4 (John)

_____?

He likes reading and playing the guitar.

5 (your brother)

_____?

He's quite tall and he's got short, blond hair.

6 (the children)

_____?

They like playing computer games.

Ordine degli aggettivi

10 Inserisci gli aggettivi nell'ordine corretto in queste frasi. A volte più di un'alternativa è possibile.

1 My mum's got _____ hair.
(brown   short)

2 I've got _____ hair.
(black   long   wavy)

3 Grandma's got _____ hair.
(curly   grey   short)

4 Tessa's got _____ hair.
(blond   long)

5 Thomas has got _____ hair.
(red   short   straight)

11 Riscrivi le frasi, inserendo al posto giusto l'aggettivo fra parentesi.

1 He got a fantastic, new scooter for his birthday. (blue)

_____

2 Who's that tall, young man? (Spanish)

_____

3 I like your new, black bag. (big)

_____

4 I hate this grey, English weather! (horrible)

_____

5 We watched a boring, French film. (old)

_____

12 Scrivi frasi complete inserendo nell'ordine corretto gli aggettivi fra parentesi.

1 What's that building? (old strange)

_____

2 We live in a flat. (**big** modern _nice_)

_____

3 Dad's got a car. (**BLUE JAPANESE new**)

_____

4 I love Helen's hair. (long **RED**)

_____

5 We stayed in a hotel. (_beautiful_ **French** little)

_____

> **Esercizi sommativi**

13 Completa il dialogo con le parole nel riquadro.

> What   What's   Who   look   won
> did   short   new   nice   blond

Mum   How was school today?
Connor It was OK. We had a big football match this afternoon.
Mum   Who [1]_____ you play against?
Connor St Andrew's School.
Mum   [2]_____ [3]_____?
Connor Our team! Oh, and there's a [4]_____ [5]_____ girl in our class.
Mum   [6]_____ she like?
Connor She's shy but she's friendly. Her name's Megan Smith.
Mum   Oh – I think I know her. [7]_____ does she [8]_____ like?
Connor She's got [9]_____, [10]_____ hair and green eyes.
Mum   You fancy her!
Connor Mum!!

14 Scrivi il dialogo seguendo la traccia.

Kelly Chiedi ad Emma chi era al telefono.
1 _____

Emma   Di' che era Daniel Clark. Chiedi a Kelly se lo conosce.
2 _____

Kelly Chiedi che aspetto ha.
3 _____

Emma   Di' che ha i capelli corti e rossi.
4 _____

Kelly Chiedi ad Emma se è il suo ragazzo.
5 _____

Emma   Di' di no. È un amico e vi piace fare le stesse cose.
6 _____

Kelly Chiedi com'è di carattere.
7 _____

Emma   Di' che è intelligente e sensibile.
8 _____

Kelly Di' che pensi di conoscerlo. Di' che ha la ragazza all'università.
9 _____

Emma   Chiedi a Kelly chi gliel'ha detto.
10 _____

15 Translation • Traduci il dialogo in inglese.

Dad   [1]Com'era la tua lezione di danza?
Alice [2]Non mi è piaciuta. Abbiamo un'insegnante nuova, Miss Proctor.
Dad   [3]Che carattere ha?
Alice [4]È molto permalosa. La lezione è stata bruttissima.
Dad   [5]Chi era la tua insegnante l'anno scorso?
Alice [6]Era Miss Davis.
Dad   [7]Che cosa le è successo?
Alice [8]Si è trasferita a Londra.
Dad   [9]Non riesco a ricordarmela. Che aspetto ha?
Alice [10]È snella e carina. Ha dei bei capelli lunghi e biondi.
Dad   [11]Ah, sì. Adesso me la ricordo!

> ### Translation note
>
> Ricorda che 'Come' si può tradurre in vari modi in inglese. Pensa attentamente al tipo di domanda e non tradurre 'Come' automaticamente con _How_:
>
> _Come vai in palestra?_ How do you get to the gym?
>
> _Come stai oggi?_   How are you today?
>
> ma:
>
> _Com'è il nuovo insegnante?_
> What's the new teacher like?
> (~~How's the new teacher?~~)
>
> _Com'è tua cugina fisicamente?_
> What does your cousin look like?
> (~~How's your cousin physically?~~)

SOAP OPERAS FAQS

Soap operas (or soaps) are the world's favourite TV programmes. Here are some FAQs (frequently asked questions) about the world of soaps.

Where does the expression 'soap opera' come from?

5 The first soap operas were radio programmes. In the 1930s, radio <u>audiences</u> could listen to exciting drama <u>serials</u> about the lives of ordinary people for the first time. The sponsors of these programmes were often the makers of <u>cleaning products</u>. The stories were very emotional and dramatic, like an opera. So the term 'soap opera' was born.

Did TV soap operas first appear in the USA?

10 Yes, they did. A serial called *Faraway Hill* appeared on American TV in 1946. The main character was a woman from New York. Her husband died and she moved to the country and fell in love with a new man.

What are the characters in soap operas like?

15 There are some types of characters that appear in most soap operas all over the world: for example, strong grandmothers, impulsive young lovers and selfish 'bad boys'. The women characters in soaps are usually strong and confident, but also sensitive. Characters in American soaps are often rich and <u>glamorous</u>, but UK soaps concentrate on ordinary working people. The top
20 TV programme in the UK is *EastEnders*, a soap <u>set</u> in a poor area of London. Another popular British programme is *Hollyoaks*, a soap all about teenagers in Chester, in the north-west of England.

How many people watch soap operas?

In the UK, the usual audience for *EastEnders* is around 9 million people. But
25 the world's favourite soap is *The Bold and the Beautiful*, an American serial set in a Los Angeles fashion business. It has an audience of 35 million around the world. A lot of these people live in South America, where soaps are incredibly popular. The South American version of a soap is called a *telenovela*. A *telenovela* is different from a soap because it has a beginning,
30 a middle and an end. Popular soaps usually continue forever!

Glossary

audiences	ascoltatori, spettatori
serials	fiction a puntate
cleaning products	prodotti per le pulizie
glamorous	affascinanti
set	ambientata

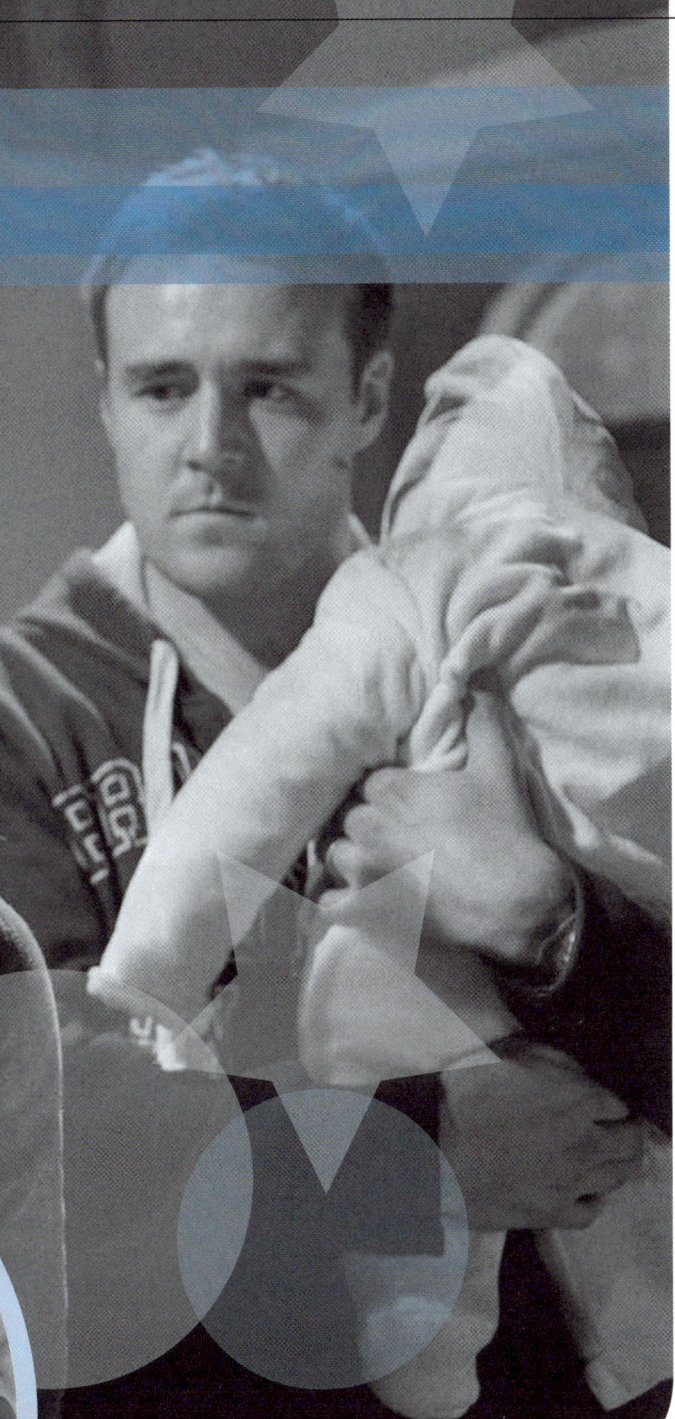

2 Vero o falso? Scrivi *T* (*true*) o *F* (*false*). Correggi le frasi false. 🄿

**

1 ___ The first soap operas were TV programmes.
_____

2 ___ Businesses who made cleaning products were the sponsors of the first soap operas.
_____

3 ___ The main character in *Faraway Hill* was a woman.
_____

4 ___ Young people in love appear in most soap operas.
_____

5 ___ UK soap characters are usually rich and glamorous.
_____

6 ___ *Hollyoaks* is an American soap.
_____

7 ___ *The Bold and the Beautiful* is set in South America.
_____

8 ___ A *telenovela* is a soap from South America.
_____

***

3 Rispondi alle domande.

1 When did radio soap operas first begin?
_____

2 What was the name of the first TV soap?
_____

3 What are the women characters in soaps usually like?
_____

4 What is the UK's favourite soap?
_____

5 How big is its normal audience?
_____

6 What is the world's favourite soap?
_____

7 How big is its global audience?
_____

8 How is a *telenovela* different from a soap?
_____

Reading comprehension

*

1 🔊 **S.083** Leggi il testo. Poi leggi le informazioni sui personaggi 1–4. A quali delle *soap operas* menzionate nel testo pensi che potrebbero appartenere? Scrivi i nomi delle *soap operas*.

1 Hamid is a London taxi driver.
_____

2 Tamsin is a student at Chester University.
_____

3 Lex works on an American ranch.
_____

4 Shelley is an American fashion designer.
_____

Culture note

EastEnders è andata in onda per la prima volta in Gran Bretagna nel 1985, ma la *soap opera* di più vecchia data della TV britannica è *Coronation Street*. È ambientata a Manchester e viene trasmessa dal 1960. *The Archers*, una *soap opera* radiofonica della BBC, ambientata in un paese immaginario della campagna inglese, viene trasmessa dal 1950 ed è la più vecchia serie a puntate del mondo.

Listening comprehension

*

4 🔊 S.084 Ascolta Kate e sua madre mentre parlano di una *soap opera* intitolata *Together Forever*. Scegli l'alternativa corretta.

1 Daniel asked Charlotte to **leave with him/be his wife.**
2 Charlotte said **yes/no.**
3 George is Daniel's **brother/father.**
4 Mr Fletcher **knows/doesn't know** Charlotte's secret.
5 Arabella is **a new/an old** character in the soap.

**

5 🔊 S.084 Riascolta e completa con le parole mancanti il riassunto della puntata di ieri di *Together Forever*.

Last night's *Together Forever* was exciting. Charlotte couldn't say yes to Daniel's offer, because she secretly ¹_____ another man – Daniel's ²_____. Mr Fletcher found a ³_____ from him, and Charlotte ⁴_____ invent a story about it, so he knows the ⁵_____ too. Daniel got angry and left in a ⁶_____. On *Together Forever*, that usually means that a character ⁷_____ ⁸_____ back again. A new character appeared. She's pretty, with ⁹_____, ¹⁰_____, wavy hair.

***

6 🔊 S.084 Riascolta e rispondi alle domande.

1 Who missed *Together Forever* last night?

_____

2 Who does Charlotte love?

_____

3 Who knows about the secret?

_____

4 Who told him?

_____

5 How does Charlotte feel now?

_____

6 Where did Kate see a photo of Arabella?

_____

7 Who is beautiful, but lazy and selfish?

_____

8 Which type of characters in the soap does Kate like?

_____

British soap: *Emmerdale*

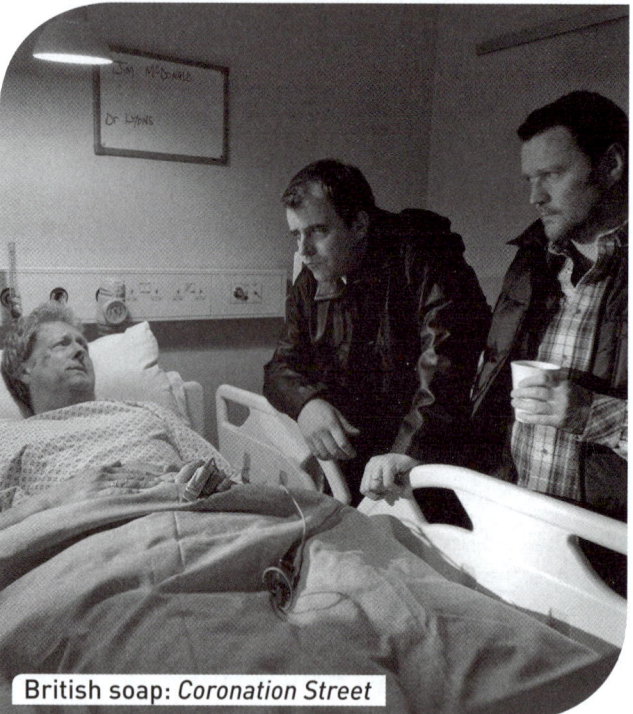

British soap: *Coronation Street*

Dictation

7 🔊 S.085 Ascolta e scrivi le frasi che senti.

1 _____
2 _____
3 _____
4 _____
5 _____
6 _____
7 _____
8 _____

Writing

Writing skills

Scrivere un'email

8 Osserva l'email e sottolinea le seguenti informazioni:

1 l'indirizzo email del destinatario
2 l'indirizzo email del mittente
3 la data e l'ora in cui è stata mandata
4 l'argomento del messaggio

Inbox — □ X

From: simon.foster@worldnet.com
Subject: meeting my cousin
Date: 13 March 10:58:32
To: zoe153@telemail.co.uk

Hi Zoe!
Can you do a favour for me next Saturday afternoon? My cousin Tara's arriving at the train station, but I can't meet her. Are you free then? Can you go and meet her? Her train arrives at 3.25 from Southampton. Let me know. Thanks! You can come to Joe's Café after you meet her.
Love,
Simon

- le email fra amici di solito hanno un linguaggio molto informale:
  [5]Sottolinea l'espressione che Simon usa per salutare Zoe.
  [6]Sottolinea come Simon conclude l'email.
  [7]Va a capo fra un elemento e l'altro dell'email? ___
  [8]Inizia la prima frase con la lettera minuscola o maiuscola? ___

  Ora fai l'Esercizio 9 tenendo presente in che posizione vanno i vari elementi di un'email.

9 Immagina di essere Zoe. Scrivi un email (75–100 parole) per rispondere a quella di Simon. Includi queste informazioni: P T

- say that you can meet his cousin at the station next Saturday
- say that you can be there at 3.15
- ask what Tara looks like
- ask what she likes wearing

Functions on film

At the Lost Property Office

A Completa il dialogo con le frasi nel riquadro.

> I was on the number 52 bus at about half past ten.
> Certainly. That's fantastic!
> It's small and quite old. It's a Rokio 300.
> Yes. I left my phone on the bus this morning.

Woman Good afternoon. Can I help you?
Girl [1] _____
Woman Oh dear. Which bus were you on?
Girl [2] _____
Woman And what does it look like?
Girl [3] _____
Woman Just a minute. I'll have a look for you.

Two minutes later...

Woman Yes, here it is. Can you sign this form, please?
Girl [4] _____

B Scrivi il dialogo seguendo la traccia.

Woman Saluta la ragazza. Chiedile se puoi essere d'aiuto.
[1] _____

Girl Di' che eri su un treno alle quattro e mezzo ieri. Pensi di aver lasciato la tua giacca sul treno.
[2] _____

Woman Chiedi che treno era.
[3] _____

Girl Di' che era il treno delle 2.35 da Euston.
[4] _____

Woman Chiedi com'è la giacca.
[5] _____

Girl Di' che è blu e grigia.
[6] _____

Woman Offriti di dare un'occhiata.
[7] _____

Two minutes later...

Woman Di' che ti dispiace ma non è lì. Chiedi alla ragazza di riempire un modulo.
[8] _____

Girl Esprimi accordo.
[9] _____

Woman Di' che la contatterai.
[10] _____

225

Grammar network

A Comparativo di maggioranza

Aggettivi monosillabi	Aggettivo	Comparativo di maggioranza
la maggior parte degli aggettivi monosillabi	short tall	short**er** tall**er**
aggettivi che terminano in **-e**	nice safe	nice**r** safe**r**
aggettivi che terminano in vocale + consonante	big hot	big**ger** hot**ter**
Aggettivi di 2 o più sillabe	**Aggettivo**	**Comparativo di maggioranza**
la maggior parte degli aggettivi	modern comfortable	**more** modern **more** comfortable
aggettivi bisillabi che terminano in **-er**, **-ow**, **-le**	clever narrow simple	clever**er** narrow**er** simpl**er**
aggettivi bisillabi che terminano in consonante + **-y**	trendy easy	trend**ier** eas**ier**

1 Nelle frasi al comparativo, il secondo termine di paragone è preceduto da *than*:
James is taller than his brother.
James è più alto di suo fratello.

2 I seguenti aggettivi hanno una forma irregolare del comparativo di maggioranza:
good – better   *buono – migliore*
Casual clothes are better than smart clothes.
I vestiti sportivi sono migliori di quelli eleganti.
bad – worse   *cattivo, scadente – peggiore*
The weather is worse today than yesterday!
Oggi il tempo è peggiore di ieri!
far – farther/further   *lontano – più lontano*
My house is farther from school than your house.
La mia casa è più lontana da scuola della tua casa.

 Quando si confrontano due cose, si usa spesso *the* + aggettivo + *one* per evitare la ripetizione. Corrisponde all'italiano 'quello', (ecc.) + aggettivo:
The red T-shirt is nicer than the blue one.
La maglietta rossa è più bella di quella azzurra.

3 Si usa il comparativo di maggioranza per confrontare due luoghi, cose o persone.
London's bigger than Glasgow.
Londra è più grande di Glasgow.

4 Per paragonare due verbi o attività, in inglese si usa la forma dei verbi in *-ing*, non l'infinito come in italiano:
Going out is better than staying at home.
Uscire è meglio che stare a casa.

B Comparativo di uguaglianza e di minoranza

1 Il comparativo di uguaglianza indica che due luoghi, cose o persone sono simili. Si ottiene allo stesso modo per tutti gli aggettivi:

as + aggettivo + *as*

The white trousers are as cheap as the red ones.
I pantaloni bianchi sono economici quanto quelli rossi.

2 Si usa la forma negativa per indicare che due luoghi, cose o persone sono diversi in qualche modo:

not as + aggettivo + *as*

I'm not as tall as you.   *Non sono alto quanto te.*

3 Il comparativo di minoranza si ottiene allo stesso modo per tutti gli aggettivi:

less + aggettivo + *than*

My jacket is less trendy than your jacket.
La mia giacca è meno alla moda della tua.

4 Nelle frasi al comparativo di minoranza il secondo termine di paragone è preceduto da *than*.

5 *less ... than* ha un significato simile a *not as ... as*, ma *not as ...as* è più comunemente usato.

6 Per intensificare il significato del paragone si possono usare le espressioni *a bit*, *a little*, *much* e *a lot* davanti al comparativo di maggioranza o di minoranza:
Sophie's a bit/a little taller than me.
Sophie è un po' più alto di me.

C Superlativo relativo

Aggettivi monosillabi	Aggettivo	Superlativo relativo
la maggior parte degli aggettivi monosillabi	short tall	**the** short**est** **the** tall**est**
aggettivi che terminano in **-e**	nice safe	**the** nice**st** **the** safe**st**
aggettivi che terminano in vocale + consonante	big hot	**the** big**gest** **the** hot**test**
Aggettivi di 2 o più sillabe	**Aggettivo**	**Superlativo relativo**
la maggior parte degli aggettivi	modern comfortable	**the most** modern **the most** comfortable
aggettivi bisillabi che terminano in **-er**, **-ow**, **-le**	clever narrow simple	**the** clever**est** **the** narrow**est** **the** simpl**est**
aggettivi bisillabi che terminano in consonante + **-y**	trendy easy	**the** trend**iest** **the** eas**iest**

1 Gli aggettivi superlativi sono preceduti dall'articolo determinativo *the*, a meno che non si usa un aggettivo possessivo:

Jenny is the cleverest student.
Jenny è la più interlligente studente.
These are my nicest shoes. (~~These are the my nicest shoes.~~)
Queste sono le mie scarpe più belle.

2 I seguenti aggettivi hanno una forma irregolare del superlativo:

good – the best   *buono – il migliore*
History is the best school subject.
Storia è la materia scolastica migliore.

bad – the worst   *cattivo, scadente – il peggiore*
You're the worst singer I know!
Sei il peggior cantante che conosca!

far – the farthest /the furthest   *lontano – il più lontano*
Which town is the furthest from London?
Quale città è la più lontana da Londra?

3 Il superlativo relativo di minoranza di tutti gli aggettivi si ottiene mettendo *the least* davanti all'aggettivo:

Sarah is the least confident person I know.
Sarah è la persona meno sicura di sé che conosca.

 A differenza dell'italiano, in inglese quando un superlativo si riferisce a un gruppo di luoghi, cose o persone, di solito si usa la preposizione *in*, not *of*:

He's the funniest student in the class.
È lo studente più divertente della classe.
New York is the most exciting city in the world.
New York è la città più emozionante del mondo.

4 Si usa il superlativo relativo per indicare che un luogo, una cosa o una persona ha più di una qualità rispetto agli altri di quel gruppo:

He's the best candidate for the job.
È il miglior cadidato per il lavoro.

Word store

Clothes — *Vestiti*

Items of clothing _____
anorak _____
a pair of... _____
boots _____
cardigan _____
coat _____
dress _____
gloves _____
hat _____
jacket _____
jeans _____
jumper _____
sandals _____
scarf _____
shirt _____
shoes _____
shorts _____
skirt _____
socks _____
sweatshirt _____
swimming costume _____
tights _____
tracksuit _____
trainers _____
trousers _____
T-shirt _____
Adjectives for clothes _____
boring _____
casual _____
cheap _____
comfortable _____

expensive _____
nice _____
old-fashioned _____
smart _____
trendy _____

Word builder +

Personality adjectives (2) — *Aggettivi che descrivono la personalità*

charismatic _____
funny _____
old _____
talented _____
ugly _____
young _____

Real talk

Completa le espressioni dai dialoghi dello *Student's Book*.

I can't _____ my   *Non riesco a*
_____ up   *decidermi*
_____ you _____   *Ecco qua*
_____ honest   *Dimmi la verità*
It's a _____-off   *Costa di più di quanto vale*
_____ as...   *Visto che...*
You haven't _____   *Non hai la più pallida*
a _____ about...   *idea di...*
a _____ welcome   *un benvenuto caloroso*

Vocabulary

Clothes

1 Scrivi i nomi dei capi di abbigliamento accanto alla parte del corpo corrispondente.

> boots gloves hat jacket jeans jumper
> sandals scarf shirt shoes shorts
> skirt socks sweatshirt T-shirt
> tights trainers trousers

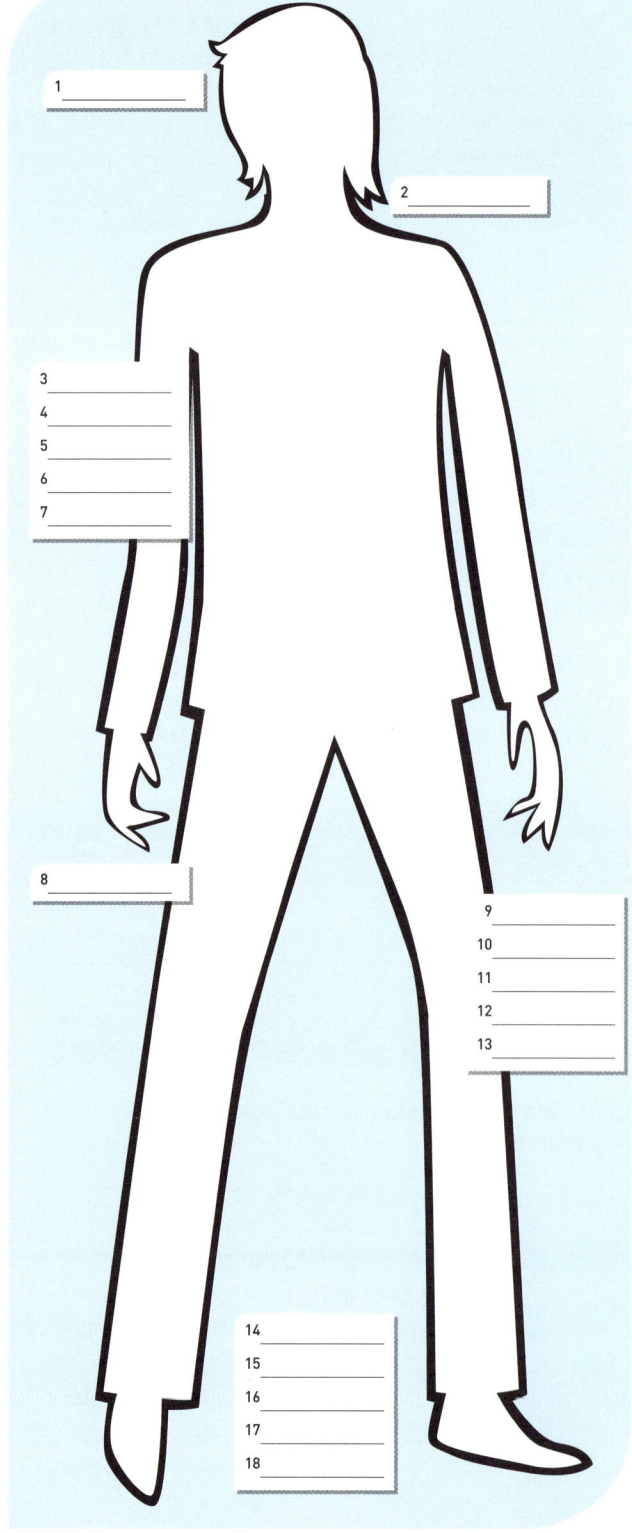

1 _____

2 _____

3 _____
4 _____
5 _____
6 _____
7 _____

8 _____

9 _____
10 _____
11 _____
12 _____
13 _____

14 _____
15 _____
16 _____
17 _____
18 _____

2 Completa i nomi di questi capi di abbigliamento.

1 c_____n

2 d_____s

3 s_____g
  c_____e

4 c_____t

5 t_____t

6 a_____k

Adjectives for clothes

3 Trova i contrari degli aggettivi (1–6) nel riquadro.

> beautiful boring casual expensive old trendy

1 interesting   _____
2 smart   _____
3 cheap   _____
4 ugly   _____
5 young   _____
6 old-fashioned   _____

Grammar
Comparativo di maggioranza

1 Scrivi il comparativo di questi aggettivi.

Adjective	Comparative
1 fat	_____
2 slow	_____
3 silly	_____
4 large	_____
5 thin	_____
6 small	_____
7 sad	_____
8 angry	_____
9 fast	_____
10 clever	_____

2 Completa il paragrafo con i comparativi degli aggettivi fra parentesi.

My sister Hannah is only two years [1]_____ (old) than me, but we're very different. She looks very different to me. Her hair is [2]_____ (dark) and [3]_____ (long) than my hair, and she's [4]_____ (slim) than me. In fact, I suppose she's [5]_____ (pretty) than me! Our personalities are different, too. I'm [6]_____ (confident) and [7]_____ (outgoing), but I suppose that I'm [8]_____ (lazy) too. Hannah is [9]_____ (serious) than me. She's [10]_____ (intelligent) and she's [11]_____ (good) at studying. Well – my grades at school are always [12]_____ (bad) than her grades!

3 Scrivi 6 frasi usando le parole date. Paragona le cose o persone usando il comparativo degli aggettivi nel riquadro.

> boring   cool   exciting   good   ~~interesting~~   talented   trendy

Geography/Science
Science is more interesting than Geography. _____

1 Maths/English

_____

2 swimming/dancing

_____

3 computer games/reading

_____

4 Juventus/Lazio

_____

5 you/your best friend

_____

6 my clothes/my friend's clothes

_____

Comparativo di uguaglianza e di minoranza

4 Riscrivi le frasi dell'Esercizio 3 con *not as... as*, mantenendo lo stesso significato.

1 _____
  _____
2 _____
  _____
3 _____
  _____
4 _____
  _____
5 _____
  _____
6 _____
  _____

5 Unisci le due frasi con *not as... as* per indicare la differenza fra le due persone o cose.

1 Arthur is 77 years old. George is 81 years old.

_____

2 Jane is 1m 70cm. Alice is 1m 65cm.

_____

3 Ben's car can go at 170km an hour. Rob's car can go at 190km an hour.

_____

4 The brown boots are £70. The black boots are £80.

_____

5 The first book in the series has got 524 pages. The second book in the series has got 430 pages.

_____

6 The blue suitcase is 10kg. The grey suitcase is 8kg.

_____

6 Completa le frasi mantenendo lo stesso significato di quelle originali. Usa *less* + aggettivo + *than*. A volte dovrai usare lo stesso aggettivo della frase originale, altre volte il suo contrario.

1 The white T-shirt is cheaper than the red T-shirt.
The white T-shirt _____

2 These sandals aren't as trendy as those trainers.
These sandals _____

3 Today isn't as hot as yesterday.
Today _____

4 Doing homework is more boring than playing football.
Doing homework _____

5 Rachel is more outgoing than her sister.
Rachel _____

6 Jeans aren't as comfortable as tracksuits.
Jeans _____

7 Osserva le foto. Scrivi 8 frasi complete facendo paragoni fra i due ragazzi. Usa alcune delle parole nel riquadro e *much* o *a bit* dove necessario.

David

Greg

nouns:	hair eyes face clothes jacket
adjectives:	tall slim young trendy smart old-fashioned large short long curly dark

1 _____
2 _____
3 _____
4 _____
5 _____
6 _____
7 _____
8 _____

Superlativo relativo

8 Scrivi il superlativo di questi aggettivi.

Adjective	Superlative
1 noisy	the _____
2 slim	the _____
3 dark	the _____
4 late	the _____
5 hot	the _____
6 lazy	the _____
7 sweet	the _____
8 nice	the _____
9 wet	the _____
10 tall	the _____

9 Completa le domande con il superlativo degli aggettivi fra parentesi. Poi rispondi in maniera personale.

Of all the people you know, who...

1 is _____ (intelligent)?
_____

2 is _____ (good) at English?
_____

3 has got _____ (long) hair?
_____

4 has got _____ (interesting) hobby?
_____

5 has got _____ (cool) car?
_____

6 wears _____ (trendy) clothes?
_____

7 is _____ (bad) dancer?
_____

8 is _____ (cheerful)?
_____

10 Completa le frasi sull'Italia con il superlativo degli aggettivi nel riquadro.

famous high large long old populated

1 Mont Blanc is _____ mountain.
2 Lake Garda _____ lake.
3 The Po is _____ river.
4 Bologna has got _____ university.
5 The Coliseum is probably _____ monument.
6 Rome is _____ city.

11 Riscrivi le frasi con *the least* mantenendo lo stesso significato. Ricordati di usare il contrario dell'aggettivo originale in ogni frase.

1 This is the most boring book in the world!

_____

2 These sunglasses are the cheapest.

_____

3 He's the most confident person I know.

_____

4 Emily is the silliest child in the class.

_____

5 Part Two of the test is the easiest part.

_____

6 I wore my smartest clothes to the party.

_____

Esercizi sommativi

12 C'è un errore in ogni frase. Identificalo e riscrivi la frase corretta.

1 I think that Formula One is the dangerousest sport.

_____

2 Your school work is gooder than last year.

_____

3 My mum is least impulsive person in our family.

_____

4 Sam is the most tall boy in the class.

_____

5 A car is noisyer than a bike.

_____

6 I'm not outgoing as my brother.

_____

7 I hate eating cheese, but eating fish is more worse!

_____

8 Skiing is much exciting than skateboarding.

_____

9 Everest is the highest mountain of the world.

_____

10 You're bit taller than me.

_____

13 Scrivi 8 frasi facendo paragoni fra te e due dei tuoi amici. Usa aggettivi di tua scelta e le parole del riquadro.

-er than   more… than   not as… as   a bit
much   the… -est   the most…   the least…

1 _____
2 _____
3 _____
4 _____
5 _____
6 _____

7 _____
8 _____

14 Translation • Traduci il paragrafo in inglese sul tuo quaderno.

Londra è la città più popolare del Regno Unito fra i turisti. Ma la seconda città nella lista è Edimburgo, la capitale della Scozia. Edimburgo non è la città più grande della Scozia. Glasgow è più grande, ma Edimburgo è più popolare fra i turisti perché i suoi edifici sono più antichi e più belli. L'edificio più famoso è il castello di Edimburgo. Ma molte persone dicono che Edimburgo non è tanto interessante quanto Glasgow. Glasgow è una città più chiassosa e più elettrizzante. Ha negozi e discoteche migliori, e un'architettura fra le più moderne del Regno Unito.

Translation note

Ci sono molte differenze sottili fra il comparativo e il superlativo in inglese e in italiano. Cerca di non tradurre parola per parola dall'italiano. Ricorda le seguenti differenze:

- mentre in italiano per formare il comparativo di maggioranza degli aggettivi si usa 'più', in inglese si usa *more* solo con gli aggettivi plurisillabi:
  Sono più vecchio di mio fratello.
  I'm older than my brother.
  (I'm more old than my brother.)

  Casa mia è più moderna della tua.
  My house is more modern than yours.

- quando traduci un comparativo di uguaglianza in inglese, ricorda di usare *as* sia prima che dopo l'aggettivo:
  Sono intelligente quanto te.
  I'm as clever as you.
  (I'm clever as you.)

  Non siamo tanto ricchi quanto loro.
  We aren't as rich as them.
  (We aren't rich as them.)

- mentre in italiano per formare il superlativo degli aggettivi si usa 'il più', in inglese si usa *the most* solo con gli aggettivi plurisillabi:
  Qual è la maglietta più carina?
  Which is the nicest T-shirt?
  (Which is the most nice T-shirt?)

  Storia è la materia più interessante.
  History is the most interesting subject.

- quando in una frase al superlativo compare l'espressione 'del mondo', ricorda che in inglese devi usare la preposizione *in*, non *of*:
  Questa è la macchina più veloce del mondo.
  This is the fastest car in the world.
  (This is the fastest car of the world.)

Grammar network

A *Whose...?*

1 Il pronome e aggettivo interrogativo *Whose...?* si usa per chiedere a chi appartiene qualcosa e corrisponde a 'Di chi...?' in italiano.

2 Se *Whose...?* è usato come pronome ha una costruzione simile all'italiano:

> *Whose* + *is/are* + *the/this* (ecc.) + sostantivo +?

Whose are those trainers?
Di chi sono quelle scarpe da ginnastica?

3 Se *Whose...?* è usato come aggettivo, è seguito da un sostantivo:

> *Whose* + sostantivo + *is/are* + *this* (ecc.) +?

Whose trainers are those?
Di chi sono quelle scarpe da ginnastica?

4 *Whose... ?* si può usare con i pronomi soggetto al posto dei sostantivi:
Whose is it?   *Di chi è?*
Whose are they?   *Di chi sono?*

 Stai attento a non confonderti fra *Whose* e *Who's* (*Who is*):
  Whose child is that?   *Di chi è quel bambino?*
  Who's that child?   *Chi è quel bambino?*

B Pronomi possessivi

my – mine	our – ours
your – yours	your – yours
his – his	their – theirs
her – hers	

1 Per rispondere alle domande con *Whose...?*, si possono usare i pronomi possessivi. Si usano per evitare di ripetere un sostantivo che è già stato menzionato ed equivalgono ai pronomi italiani 'il mio, 'le mie', ecc.:
Whose jacket is this? It's mine. (= It's my jacket.)
Di che è questa giacca? È mia. (= È la mia giacca.)

2 A differenza dell'italiano, c'è solo una forma del pronome possessivo per ogni persona. Si forma aggiungendo *-s* all'aggettivo possessivo, eccetto nel caso di *my* e *his*.
That's mine and this is his.
Quello è il mio e questo è il suo (= di lui).

 Non esiste il pronome possessivo per l'aggettivo possessivo *its*.
  Whose bed is that? It's the dog's. (~~It's its.~~)
  Di chi è quella cuccia? È del cane.

3 Si può usare il genitivo sassone (possessore + *'s*) al posto dei pronomi possessivi per rispondere a una domanda con *Whose...?* (vedi Unit 1 p.146):
Whose are these CDs? They're Paul's.
Di chi sono questi CD? Sono di Paul.

Whose car is this? It's our English teacher's.
Di chi è questa macchina? È della nostra insegnante di inglese.

C Verbi modali • *can, could* e *may* (permesso e richieste)

1 Abbiamo già visto (vedi pagine 178 e185) come *can* e *could* possono essere usati per chiedere il permesso di fare qualcosa o per fare una richiesta a qualcuno. *Could* è più cortese di *can*.

2 Per chiedere il permesso di fare qualcosa o per fare una richiesta, si usa la seguente struttura:

> *Can/Could* + *I/we* + verbo + ?

• **permesso:**
Can I go out tonight?
Posso uscire stasera?

• **richieste:**
Can I have a map of Oxford, please?
Posso prendere una piantina di Oxford, per favore?
Could we borrow your camera?
Potremmo prendere in prestito la tua macchina fotografica?

3 Per chiedere a qualcuno di fare qualcosa, si usa la seguente struttura:

> *Can/Could* + *you* + verbo + ?

Can you drive me to the party?
Puoi portarmi in macchina alla festa?
Could you close the window, please?
Potresti chiudere la finestra, per favore?
Could you recommend places to eat near the hostel?
Potresti raccomandarci dei posti dove mangiare vicino all'ostello?

4 Nelle richieste si usano spesso i verbi *lend* (prestare) e *borrow* (prendere in prestito):
• si usa *Can/Could* + *I/we* + *borrow...?* per chiedere in prestito qualcosa:
Can I borrow your newspaper, please?
Posso prendere in prestito il tuo giornale, per favore?
• si usa *Can/Could* + *you* + *lend* + *me/us...?* per chiedere a qualcuno di prestare qualcosa:
Could you lend me your newspaper, please?
Potresti prestarmi il tuo giornale, per favore?

5 Si può anche usare *May I/we...?* per chiedere il permesso di fare qualcosa o fare una richiesta. Non si può usare *May you...?*. *May* è molto più formale di *can* e *could* e questo uso di *May* sta diventando sempre meno comune nell'inglese parlato:

May I see your passport?
Posso vedere il Suo passaporto?

Could you help me, please? (~~May you help me, please?~~)
Mi potresti aiutare, per favore?

6 Ricorda che *can*, *could* e *may* sono verbi modali e come tali:

- sono invariabili per tutte le persone:
 Can Gemma/you/they stay at our house tonight?
 Gemma può/Puoi/Possono restare a casa nostra stasera?
- non si usano mai con il verbo ausiliare:
 Could you close the door, please?
 (~~Do you could close the door, please?~~)
 Potresti chiudere la porta, per favore?

- sono sempre seguiti dalla forma base del verbo:
 May I use your phone?
 (~~May I to use your phone?~~)
 Posso usare il Suo telefono?

7 Quando si risponde a delle richieste di permesso, si usano spesso le risposte brevi con *can* o *may*:

Can I use your computer? Yes, you can.
Posso usare il tuo computer? Sì.

Can you lend me £5? No, I can't, sorry.
Puoi prestarmi £5? No, scusa, non posso.

May I use your computer? Yes, you may.
Posso usare il Suo computer? Sì

8 Di solito non si usano le riposte brevi con *could*. Si preferisce rispondere con l'espressione *Yes, of course* o *No, sorry.*

Could I use your computer? Yes, of course.
(~~Yes, you could.~~)
Posso usare il tuo computer? Sì, certo.

Word store

Rooms and furniture	*Stanze e mobili*
Rooms	_____
bathroom	_____
bedroom	_____
dining room	_____
garage	_____
garden	_____
kitchen	_____
living room	_____
study	_____
Furniture	_____
armchair	_____
bed	_____
bookcase	_____
chair	_____
desk	_____
fridge	_____
sofa	_____
table	_____
wardrobe	_____
washing machine	_____

Housework	*Lavori di casa*
clear the table	_____
cut the grass	_____
do the ironing	_____
do the shopping	_____
do the washing	_____
do the washing-up	_____
feed a pet	_____

hoover (a room)	_____
make (my) bed	_____
take out the rubbish	_____
tidy (my) bedroom	_____

Real talk

Completa le espressioni dai dialoghi dello *Student's Book*.

Get _____!	*Giù le mani!/Vai via!*
_____ going _____?	*Che cosa sta succedendo?*
_____ we go	*Ci risiamo*
Where on _____...?	*Dove diavolo...?*
_____ _____ for?	*Per cosa sono?*

Extra vocabulary • Skills and culture

online auctions	*aste online*
pocket money	*paghetta*
top up (your) mobile	*ricaricare il cellulare*
sponsored blogging	*tenere un blog sponsorizzato*
be (really) into (something)	*essere (davvero) interessato in (qualcosa)*
be unemployed	*essere disoccupato*
collect information	*raccogliere informazioni*
make (more) money	*guadagnare/fare (più) soldi*
pay a fixed price	*pagare un prezzo fisso*
reinvest (money)	*rinvestire (soldi)*
take part in surveys	*partecipare a indagini*

Vocabulary

Rooms and furniture

1 Completa i nomi delle stanze in cui si trovano questi mobili.

1 bath and shower = b_____
2 bed and wardrobe = b_____
3 sofa and armchair = l_____ r_____
4 large table and chairs = d_____ r_____
5 fridge and washing machine = k_____
6 desk, chair and bookcase = s_____

2 Rispondi alle domande sulla tua casa.

1 How many bedrooms are there?
_____

2 Have you got a garage?
_____

3 Is there a garden?
_____

4 Which rooms have got a TV?
_____

5 Where do you eat breakfast?
_____

6 What furniture is there in your bedroom?
_____
_____
_____

Housework

3 Abbina i verbi (1–6) ai sostantivi (a–f).

1 ___ cut		**a** a room
2 ___ do		**b** the washing
3 ___ feed		**c** a bed
4 ___ hoover		**d** the rubbish
5 ___ make		**e** a pet
6 ___ take out		**f** the grass

4 Scrivi frasi con gli avverbi di frequenza spiegando ogni quanto fai questi lavori di casa.

1 _____ clear the table.
2 _____ do the ironing.
3 _____ do the shopping.
4 _____ do the washing-up.
5 _____ tidy my bedroom.

Usare il dizionario bilingue italiano/inglese (2)

Quando cerchi un vocabolo inglese nel dizionario, ricorda che lo troverai elencato in ordine alfabetico alla forma base. Per esempio, i sostantivi sono elencati al singolare, non al plurale.

5 Completa queste regole sulla formazione del plurale dei sostantivi:

- con la maggior parte dei sostantivi: si aggiunge -s alla forma singolare
- con i sostantivi che terminano in -s, -sh, -ch, -x, -o o -z: si aggiungono [1]_____
- con i sostantivi che terminano in consonante + -y: -y diventa [2]_____, e si aggiunge [3]_____
- con alcuni sostantivi che terminano in -f: -f diventa -v e si aggiunge -es
- alcuni sostantivi di uso comune hanno il plurale irregolare, per esempio man – men, woman – [4]_____, child – [5]_____

6 Adesso scrivi il singolare di questi sostantivi plurali.

> cities   windows   boxes   policemen   halves

Ricorda che i verbi sono elencati nel dizionario alla forma base, senza la -s del *Present simple* o qualsiasi altro suffisso (per esempio -ing o -ed). Tuttavia, le forme irregolari del *Past simple* sono di solito elencate separatamente.

7 Scrivi la forma base di questi verbi.

> kisses   putting   ignored   trying   robbed

Anche gli aggettivi sono elencati nel dizionario alla forma base, mai al grado comparativo o superlativo.

8 Scrivi la forma base di questi aggettivi.

> wider   heavier   hardest   brightest

9 Usa un dizionario per controllare i vocaboli evidenziati in neretto in questo paragrafo. Ricorda che devi cercare la forma base di ogni vocabolo.

My bedroom is quite large. There's a big bed, a desk, some **shelves** and a lot of **posters**. When I was younger I **shared** a bedroom with my little sister. She's got a bedroom next to mine now. My room's a lot **neater** than hers. She **collects teddies**, and her room is full of them!

Grammar

Whose...?

1 Scrivi due domande possibili con *Whose* per ognuna di queste cose.

those bikes
Whose are those bikes?
Whose bikes are those?

1 this drink
_____
_____
_____
_____

2 this book
_____
_____
_____
_____

3 those shoes
_____
_____
_____
_____

4 that car
_____
_____
_____
_____

5 these glasses
_____
_____
_____
_____

2 Traduci queste frasi in italiano.

1 Whose is that cat?
_____

2 Whose children are they?
_____

3 Who's your English teacher?
_____

4 Who's this in the photo?
_____

5 Whose house is that?
_____

6 Who's that girl?
_____

3 Completa le domande con *Who*, *Who's* o *Whose*.

Who WHO'S Who Whose

1 _____ are those bags?
2 _____ are you talking to?
3 _____ is this desk?
4 _____ teaches Maths at your school?
5 _____ your favourite singer?
6 _____ wants to come with me?
7 _____ clothes are these?
8 _____ in the bathroom?

Pronomi possessivi

4 Riscrivi le frasi sostituendo le parole in neretto con il pronome possessivo corrispondente.

1 This isn't mum and dad's car. **Their car** is blue.
_____

2 Your food's ready, but **our food** isn't.
_____

3 Her clothes are trendy, but I don't like **his clothes**.
_____

4 Your life is more exciting than **my life**!
_____

5 I've got my coat. Have you got **your coat**?
_____

6 Which house is **her house**?
_____

5 Sostituisci le parole in neretto con il pronome possessivo corrispondente.

Mum	Ben – whose jacket is this? Is it **your jacket** [1]_____?
Ben	No, it isn't **my jacket** [2]_____. Is it Sarah's?
Mum	Of course it isn't **Sarah's** [3]_____! It's a boy's jacket.
Ben	Maybe it's Jamie's. He was here yesterday.
Mum	I don't think it's **Jamie's** [4]_____. It's too big. And can you move these computer games, please?
Ben	They aren't **our games** [5]_____. Sarah was at Nick and Rachel's house last night. Maybe they're **their games** [6]_____.
Mum	I don't care whose they are! Just move them!

6 Scrivi domande con *Whose*, mantenendo le parole nell'ordine in cui si trovano nella traccia. Poi rispondi con il pronome possessivo corrispondente.

1 Whose/skateboard/that?
(his skateboard)

_____?
_____

2 Whose/these/photos?
(our photos)

_____?
_____

3 Whose/this/sandwich?
(your sandwich)

_____?
_____

4 Whose/computer/that?
(her computer)

_____?
_____

5 Whose/books/those?
(my books)

_____?
_____

7 Scrivi le risposte a queste domande. Usa il genitivo sassone.

1 **Whose are these gloves?**
(Holly)
_____

2 **Whose homework is this?**
(Harry)
_____

3 **Whose games are these?**
(the children)
_____

4 **Whose is this sweatshirt?**
(my brother)
_____

5 **Whose are those bikes?**
(the boys)
_____

6 **Whose dog is that?**
(Mr Taylor)
_____

Verbi modali • *can*, *could* e *may* (permesso e richieste)

8 Scrivi richieste con *Can*, *Could* o *May* per queste situazioni. Fai attenzione al livello di formalità indicato fra parentesi.

1 You want to go to the bathroom. (informal)
_____?

2 You want to borrow a pen. (very formal)
_____?

3 You and a friend want to have some more bread. (informal)
_____?

4 You want to get a drink. (formal)
_____?

5 You and a friend want to take photographs. (very formal)
_____?

6 You want to leave your jacket here. (formal)
_____?

9 Scrivi richieste con *Can* o *Could* chiedendo a queste persone di fare le cose indicate fra parentesi. Fai attenzione al livello di formalità che devi usare in ogni situazione.

1 A woman on the bus (move her bag)
_____?

2 Your mum (take you to the leisure centre)
_____?

3 Your teacher (look at your homework)
_____?

4 Your friend (lend you a pen)
_____?

5 An English person in the street (repeat the question)
_____?

6 Your dad (give you some money)
_____?

10 Osserva le risposte date alle richieste. Metti un *tick* (✓) accanto a quelle che sono corrette. Metti una crocetta (✗) accanto a quelle che sono sbagliate e sostituiscile con *Yes, of course*.

1 A Can I look at your magazine?
B Yes, you can. ☐ _____

2 A May we sit here?
B Yes, you may. ☐ _____

3 A Could you open this door, please?
B Yes, I could. ☐ _____

4 A Can you take a photo of us, please?
B Yes, I can. ☐ _____

5 A Can we use mobile phones in here?
B Yes, you can. ☐ _____

6 A Could I have another sandwich, please?
B Yes, you could. ☐ _____

11 Scrivi il dialogo seguendo la traccia.

Jonathan	Chiedi se puoi uscire stasera.
Dad	Dai il permesso di uscire. Chiedi a Jonathan dove vuole andare.
Jonathan	Di' che vuoi andare al cinema. Chiedi al papà se ti può prestare £15.
Dad	Acconsenti.
Jonathan	Chiedi se puoi andare in un nightclub dopo il cinema.
Dad	Rifiuta. Digli di tornare a casa alle dieci e mezzo.
Jonathan	Di' che non ci sono autobus dopo le dieci. Chiedi al papà di incontrarti dopo il film.
Dad	Acconsenti.

Esercizi sommativi

12 Scrivi domande e risposte. Scrivi le domande con *Whose* e dai risposte usando un pronome possessivo o il genitivo sassone.

1 these jeans? (she)

_____
_____

2 that scooter? (my brother)

_____
_____

3 this phone? (I)

_____
_____

4 that guitar? (Kate)

_____
_____

5 those CDs? (we)

_____
_____

6 this jacket? (Mum)

_____
_____

7 this can of coke? (you)

_____
_____

8 these things? (my friends)

_____
_____

13 Completa il dialogo.

Mum	Jasmine – your room's a terrible mess. Can [1]_____ tidy it, please?
Jasmine	Oh, OK. Can [2]_____ go to Rebecca's house after that?
Mum	Yes, [3]_____ course.
Jasmine	Yuk! [4]_____ socks are these? [5]_____ aren't mine!
Mum	Put them in Robert's room. They're probably [6]_____.
Jasmine	And this cardigan?
Mum	Well, it isn't [7]_____! I've only got a red cardigan. I don't know [8]_____ that one is!
Jasmine	Mum – could [9]_____ take me to Rebecca's house later?
Mum	Sorry, [10]_____ busy. There's a bus at ten past eleven!

14 Translation • Traduci il dialogo in inglese sul tuo quaderno.

Dad	[1]Matthew, puoi portare fuori la spazzatura, per favore?
Matthew	[2]Oh, no! L'ho portata fuori ieri!
Dad	[3]Beh, portala fuori di nuovo, per favore!
Matthew	[4]Posso avere £10 per i lavori di casa?
Dad	[5]No, non puoi! Dunque – di chi sono tutte queste cose? Di chi è questo telefono? E di chi sono questi CD?
Matthew	[6]Il telefono è mio e i CD sono di William.
Dad	[7]Puoi metterli nella sua stanza, per favore?
Matthew	[8]OK. Posso guardare il tuo nuovo DVD più tardi?
Dad	[9]Sì, naturalmente.

Translation note

Quando traduci una richiesta dall'italiano all'inglese, per decidere che verbo modale usare (*can*, *could* o *may*), considera quanto formale è il tono della conversazione. Tieni presente il tipo di rapporto che esiste fra i due interlocutori e la situazione in cui si trovano. Come regola generale:

Posso...?/Puoi...? = Can...?
Potrei...?/Potresti...?/Potrebbe...? = Could...?
Potrei...? = May...?

Ricorda che *may* non si usa mai con *you*:

Please could you help me?
(~~Please may you help me?~~)

A passion for fashion

Shona Swift is 17. She goes to school, but she's also got a business. Shona told us how she makes money from her passion – fashion!

5 'I make money buying and selling vintage clothes. Vintage clothes are old, <u>second-hand</u> clothes, usually from between the 1950s and the 1980s. They're very popular at the moment. A lot of people think that vintage clothes are nicer than modern clothes and more <u>stylish</u>. They're often
10 stronger, too – they don't fall to pieces after a year!'

Shona lives in a town with a lot of charity shops. She looks in the shops for vintage clothes after school and on Saturdays.

'It's really surprising what people give to charity shops. For example, last week I found a fantastic long dress from the
15 1970s. It wasn't in good condition, but my aunt is good at <u>sewing</u>, and she often repairs clothes for me.'

Shona sells the clothes at <u>car boot sales</u> every Sunday. She attracts a lot of regular customers.

'The rarest clothes, and the ones that get the best prices,
20 are things from the 1950s and 60s. It's really exciting when I find something that is older than 1970. Clothes from the 1980s are becoming more popular these days – big, colourful jumpers, thin jeans. They aren't as hard to find as the older clothes, because my friends' parents sometimes give me
25 their old things. My best friend's dad gave me his punk jacket the other day! He isn't as slim as he was then!'

What future plans does Shona have for the business? At the moment she's creating a website.

'I only do car boot sales from March to October. I need a
30 website to make my business larger and easier to find.'

Glossary

second-hand	di seconda mano
stylish	eleganti
sewing	cucito
car boot sales	vendita all'aperto di oggetti usati

A passion for fashion

Reading comprehension

1 🔊 **S.086** Leggi il testo e abbina le parti iniziali (1–6) delle frasi alle loro conclusioni (a–f).

1 ___ Shona makes money   **a** charity shops.
2 ___ She sells them at   **b** they're elegant.
3 ___ People like vintage clothes because   **c** from vintage clothes.
4 ___ Shona gets the clothes from   **d** creating a website.
5 ___ She's got a lot of   **e** car boot sales.
6 ___ At the moment she's   **f** regular customers.

2 Scegli l'alternativa corretta.

1 Shona buys and sells   **a** old clothes.   **b** modern clothes.   **c** clothes that her aunt makes.
2 At the moment, vintage clothes are   **a** hard to find.   **b** popular.   **c** cheap.
3 Shona sells the clothes   **a** on Sundays.   **b** on Saturdays.   **c** after school.
4 The dress from the 1970s was   **a** in good condition.   **b** in perfect condition.   **c** in bad condition.
5 Clothes from the 1950s and 1960s are   **a** the most colourful.   **b** the rarest.   **c** the cheapest.
6 People are buying a lot of clothes from the   **a** 1970s.   **b** 1980s.   **c** 1990s.
7 She gets a lot of 1980s clothes from   **a** her customers.   **b** her aunt.   **c** her friends' parents.
8 Shona's best friend's dad gave her a   **a** pair of jeans.   **b** jumper.   **c** jacket.

3 Rispondi alle domande.

1 Why do some people prefer vintage clothes to modern clothes?

_____

2 When does Shona search for clothes to sell?

_____

3 What does her aunt do for her?

_____

4 Which clothes get the best prices?

_____

5 What did Shona find in a charity shop last week?

_____

6 Why did her friend's dad give her something to sell?

_____

7 In which months does Shona go to car boot sales?

_____

8 Why does she want a website?

_____

Culture note

I *charity shops* sono molto diffusi in Gran Bretagna. Questi negozi sono gestiti da organizzazioni a scopo benefico (per esempio *Oxfam*, *British Red Cross*, *Cancer Research UK*) e tutto il loro ricavato è devoluto in beneficenza. Le persone regalano vestiti, libri e oggetti domestici che non usano più, e i *charity shops* li rivendono al pubblico.

I *car boot sales* sono molto popolari nel Regno Unito. Si svolgono durante i fine settimana, specialmente in primavera e in estate. Le persone portano in macchina degli oggetti in un luogo pubblico (di solito un campo o un parcheggio), dove li espongono su bancarelle per alcune ore e li vendono.

Listening comprehension

*

4 🔊 **S.087** Ascolta Shona mentre parla con tre clienti della sua bancarella. Che cosa stanno cercando? Completa le frasi. Comprano qualcosa da Shona? Scegli l'alternativa corretta.

1 A man is looking for a man's _____ from the _____. He **buys/doesn't buy** one from Shona.
2 A woman is looking for a _____ to wear at a _____. She **buys/doesn't buy** one from Shona.
3 A girl is looking for a red _____ for a show at _____. She **buys/doesn't buy** one from Shona.

**

5 🔊 **S.087** Riascolta e scegli l'alternativa corretta.

1 Shona says that shirts from the 1970s are **hard/easy** to find.
2 She's **got/hasn't got** a shirt from the 1970s.
3 Shona's always got **new/the same** things to sell.
4 The woman likes a dress from the **1950s/1960s**.
5 The dress costs **£15/£50**.
6 Shona's got **one/more than one** dress.
7 She's got **a few/a lot of** hats.
8 The girl's friends **have got/haven't got** hats for the show.

***

6 🔊 **S.087** Riascolta e rispondi alle domande.

1 Why doesn't the man want the shirt?
_____
2 What did Shona have last week?
_____
3 Whose wedding is the woman going to?
_____
4 What is the oldest thing that Shona's got at the moment?
_____
5 What does the woman think about the price of the dress?
_____
6 Where did the girl go yesterday?
_____
7 What did she think of the clothes there?
_____
8 What does Shona offer to do?
_____

Dictation

7 🔊 **S.088** Ascolta e scrivi le frasi che senti.

1 _____
2 _____
3 _____
4 _____
5 _____
6 _____

Writing

Writing skills

Svolgere un testo descrittivo

8 Quando devi scrivere la descrizione di una persona, un luogo o una cosa, è fondamentale che la organizzi attentamente:

- prima di tutto, pensa a quali aspetti della persona, luogo o cosa vuoi includere nella tua descrizione. Immagina di dover descrivere una città. Aggiungi a questa lista altri tre o quattro punti che vuoi includere:
  where the town is _____
  _____
  _____
  _____
  _____

- in secondo luogo, decidi in che ordine vuoi presentare le informazioni. Numera i punti della lista sopra nell'ordine appropriato.

- ricorda che gli aggettivi sono molto importanti in un testo descrittivo perché aggiungono informazioni:
  London is a fascinating, cosmopolitan city.
  Puoi anche usare aggettivi al grado comparativo o superlativo:
  It isn't as beautiful as some capital cities, but I think it's the most exciting place in the world.

- scrivi una frase di apertura e una di chiusura, in cui riassumi il contenuto generale della descrizione. In un testo descrittivo, di solito è appropriato includere le tue opinioni e le tue emozioni o sensazioni:
  London is one of my favourite places to visit.
  London is a wonderful city, but I wouldn't like to live there!

  Ora fai l'Esercizio 9, tenendo presente i punti sopra su come preparare una descrizione.

9 Scrivi un breve testo (75–100 parole) su un paese o una città in Italia. Includi i punti a cui hai pensato sopra. Non dimenticarti di usare aggettivi e di includere una frase di apertura e una di chiusura. **T**

Functions on film

Shopping for clothes

A Completa le domande che faresti in queste situazioni:

1. Vuoi sapere il prezzo di un paio di scarpe da ginnastica bianche:
   _____ _____ _____ those white trainers?
2. Vuoi provare un paio di jeans:
   _____ _____ _____ _____ those jeans, please?
3. Vuoi sapere che taglia porta qualcuno:
   _____ _____ _____ you?
4. Il maglione che misuri è troppo piccolo:
   Have you got _____ _____ _____?
5. La giacca che misuri è troppo grande:
   Have you got _____ _____ _____?
6. Vuoi pagare con la carta di credito:
   _____ _____ accept _____ _____?

B Scrivi il dialogo seguendo la traccia.

Girl	[1]Saluta Chloe e chiedi se puoi essere d'aiuto.
Chloe	[2]Di' che stai cercando dei pantaloni neri.
Girl	[3]Chiedi che taglia porta.
Chloe	[4]Di' 'media'.
Girl	[5]Di' 'Eccoli qui' e chiedile di provare i pantaloni.
Chloe	[6]Di' che sono un po' piccoli. Chiedi se ne ha di più grandi.
Girl	[7]Di' di sì.
Chloe	[8]Di' che vanno meglio. Chiedi quanto costano.
Girl	[9]Di' '£18.99'.
Chloe	[10]Di' che li prendi.

Grammar network

A *be going to* (1) • Intenzioni

Forma affermativa		Forma negativa		Forma interrogativa	Risposte brevi	
estesa	contratta	estesa	contratta		affermative	negative
I am going to leave	I'm going to leave	I am not going to leave	I'm not going to leave	Am I going to leave?	Yes, I am.	No, I'm not.
you are going to leave	you're going to leave	you are not going to leave	you aren't going to leave	Are you going to leave?	Yes, you are.	No, you aren't.
he/she/it is going to leave	he/she/it's going to leave	he/she/it is not going to leave	he/she/it isn't going to leave	Is he/she/it going to leave?	Yes, he/she/ it is.	No, he/she/it isn't.
we are going to leave	we're going to leave	we are not going to leave	we aren't going to leave	Are we going to leave?	Yes, we are.	No, we aren't.
you are going to leave	you're going to leave	you are not going to leave	you aren't going to leave	Are you going to leave?	Yes, you are.	No, you aren't.
they are going to leave	they're going to leave	they are not going to leave	they aren't going to leave	Are they going to leave?	Yes, they are.	No, they aren't.

1 Per esprimere un'intenzione, in inglese si usa la seguente struttura:

> soggetto + *is/are* + *going to* + forma base del verbo

We're going to have a party next Friday.
Abbiamo intenzione di fare/Facciamo/Faremo una festa venerdì prossimo.

2 La forma negativa si ottiene così:

> soggetto + *isn't/aren't* + *going to* + forma base del verbo

He isn't going to do his homework tonight.
Non ha intenzione di fare/Non fa/Non farà i compiti stasera.

3 La forma interrogativa si ottiene invertendo il soggetto e il verbo *be*:
Are you going to have a party next Friday?
Avete intenzione di fare/Fate/Farete una festa venerdì prossimo?
Is he going to do his homework tonight?
Ha intenzione di fare/Fa/Farà i compiti stasera?

4 Le risposte brevi si formano così:

> *Yes*, + soggetto + *am/is/are.*
> *No*, + soggetto + *'m not/isn't/aren't.*

5 Si usa *be going to* per parlare di intenzioni e progetti, di qualcosa che si è deciso di fare in futuro. *Be going to* equivale al futuro semplice italiano, al presente indicativo usato con significato di futuro, e all'espressione 'avere intenzione di'. È spesso usato con espressioni di tempo futuro (vedi Unit 5 p.179):
Si sposeranno l'anno prossimo.
They're going to get married next year.
Andiamo al mare domani.
We're going to the seaside tomorrow.
Ho intenzione di vedere Ben sabato prossimo.
I'm going to see Ben next Saturday.

 Quando più di un verbo dipende da *be going to* nella stessa frase, non serve ripetere *be going to* ogni volta:
Tonight I'm going to stay in and watch TV.
Stasera rimango a casa e guardo la TV.

6 A differenza dell'italiano, in inglese quando si parla del futuro, si usa il *Present simple* dopo le congiunzioni temporali *when*, *as soon as*, *before* e *after*:
- **when** = *quando*
Are you going to look for a job when you leave school?
Cercherai un lavoro quando finirai la scuola?
- **as soon as** = *(non) appena*
As soon as I have some free time, I'm going to join a gym.
Appena avrò un po' di tempo libero mi iscriverò in palestra.
- **before** = *prima di*
Are you going to eat before you go out?
Mangerai prima di uscire di casa?
- **after** = *dopo (che)*
After she finishes her exams, Kim's going to go on holiday.
Dopo che avrà finito gli esami, Kim andrà in vacanza.

B *be going to* (2) • Previsioni

1 *be going to* si può anche usare per fare una previsione futura quando questa si basa su dati oggettivi:
It's raining and you haven't got an umbrella. You're going to get wet.
Sta piovendo e non hai un ombrello. Ti bagnerai.
He's driving too fast. He's going to crash.
Guida troppo veloce. Farà un incidente.

2 Questo uso di *be going to* equivale all'uso italiano del futuro semplice:
It's midnight and you're still studying. You're going to be tired tomorrow.
È mezzanotte e stai ancora studiando. Domani sarai stanco.

3 Si può fare riferimento a un avvenimento o un'azione imminente che si sta per compiere usando la seguente struttura:

> soggetto + *is/are* + *about to* + forma base del verbo

I'm about to go to bed.
Sto per andare a letto.

4 *be about to* equivale alle espressioni italiane 'stare per...' o 'essere sul punto di...':
He's about to leave for London.
Sta per andare a Londra.

 Ricorda che non si può usare *be about to* con espressioni di tempo futuro:

We're about to have dinner.
(~~We're about to have dinner in ten minutes' time.~~)
Stiamo per cenare.

C *be going to*, Present simple o Present continuous per il futuro?

be going to
We're going to leave soon.
They're getting their coats and bags. They're going to leave.

Present simple
The train leaves at ten o'clock tomorrow morning.

Present continuous
We're leaving on Tuesday.

1 In inglese per esprimere il futuro si usano strutture diverse a seconda del tipo di situazione a cui si fa riferimento:

- si usa il *Present simple* per parlare di eventi nel futuro che fanno parte di programmi o orari ufficiali:
  School begins again on 6th September.
  La scuola riprende il 6 settembre.
  The flight arrives at seven o'clock tomorrow morning.
  Il volo arriva domani mattina alle sette.

- si usa il *Present continuous* per parlare di un'azione già programmata o un appuntamento prestabilito, spesso con un riferimento temporale preciso. È difficile che il programma o appuntamento verranno cambiati:
  I'm starting a Spanish course in October.
  Inizierò un corso di spagnolo in ottobre.
  They're moving to Australia next year.
  Si trasferiscono in Australia l'anno prossimo.

- si usa *be going to* per esprimere un'intenzione su qualcosa che si è deciso di fare. Si usa anche per fare una previsione basata su dati oggettivi:
  We're going to buy some new clothes next Saturday.
  Compreremo dei vestiti nuovi sabato prossimo.
  It's 8 o'clock in the morning and it's already 20 degrees. It's going to be a hot day.
  Sono le 8 di mattina e ci sono già 20 gradi. Sarà una giornata calda.

Word store

The weather *Il tempo atmosferico*

boiling hot	_____
cloudy	_____
cold	_____
degrees	_____
dry	_____
foggy	_____
freezing	_____
hot	_____
lightning	_____
rain (v)	_____
snow (v)	_____
sunny	_____
temperature	_____
thunder	_____
warm	_____
wet	_____
windy	_____

Real talk

Completa le espressioni dai dialoghi dello *Student's Book*.

... is really getting _____ _____!	*... mi sta buttando giù di morale!*
I _____ wait...	*Non vedo l'ora...*
That's not _____!	*Non è giusto!*
Get a _____ on!	*Sbrigati!*
It's _____ full	*È veramente pieno*

Extra vocabulary • Skills and culture

flooding	*inondazione*
hailstones	*grandine*
lightning bolt	*saetta*
storm	*tempesta*
tornado	*tornado, tromba d'aria*

Vocabulary

The weather

1 Scrivi in ordine gli aggettivi nel termometro, mettendo in cima quello più caldo.

> cold   hot   warm   boiling hot   freezing

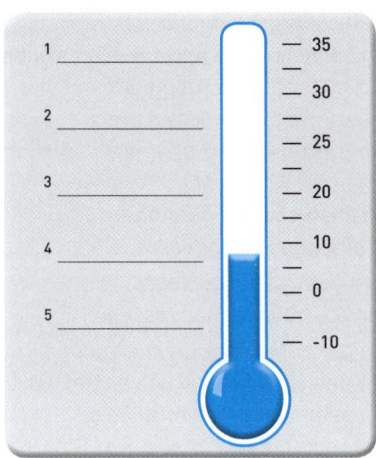

1 _____
2 _____
3 _____
4 _____
5 _____

— 35
— 30
— 25
— 20
— 10
— 0
— -10

2 Completa le parole per descrivere il tempo atmosferico.

1 r_____n

2 c_____y

3 w_____y

4 s_____w

5 t_____r and
   l_____g

6 s_____y

7 f_____y

3 Leggi le definizioni e riordina le parole.

1 An adjective to describe a rainy day
   twe = _____
2 An adjective to describe a sunny day
   rdy = _____
3 A measurement of temperature
   edereg = _____

Parti del discorso

4 Abbina queste parole alla parte del discorso corrispondente.

silly   she   ask   under   often   door

**noun   verb   adjective   adverb
pronoun   preposition**

Mentre in italiano la forma base dei verbi ha dei suffissi specifici per identificarli (*-are, -ere, -ire*), e quasi tutti gli aggettivi terminano in *-o, -a* o *-e*, in inglese è difficile identificare a che parte del discorso appartiene un vocabolo dalla sua struttura.

Solo alcune parti del discorso hanno dei suffissi riconoscibili in inglese: gli aggettivi (vedi Unit 8 p.202: *Word skills*) e gli avverbi. Spesso è difficile capire se un vocabolo nuovo è, per esempio, un sostantivo o un verbo. Tuttavia, si può cercare di indovinare che parte del discorso è un vocabolo nuovo dalla sua posizione nella frase o dalle parole che lo precedono o lo seguono.

5 Indovina quale parola evidenziata in neretto in questo paragrafo è un sostantivo, quale è un verbo, quale è un aggettivo e quale è una preposizione. Da che cosa sei riuscito a dedurlo?

> The UK's **climate** is called temperate. That means that it has wet, **mild** winters and warm summers. The sea **around** the UK can **affect** its weather.

Se non riesci a indovinare puoi usare il dizionario.

6 Osserva questo lemma preso da un dizionario. Che parte del discorso è *storm*? Da cosa si capisce?

> **storm** [stɔːm] *n.* very bad weather with strong winds and rain

7 Cerca queste parole in un dizionario. Scopri che parte del discorso sono e che cosa significano.

> misty   shine   frost   overcast

Alcuni vocaboli inglesi come *snow* e *rain* possono essere parti diverse del discorso, a volte con una traduzione piuttosto diversa. Ricorda di scegliere la definizione adatta all'uso che ne devi fare.

8 Cerca queste parole in un dizionario e trovane il significato come verbo e come sostantivo.

flood _____/_____
blow _____/_____
ice _____/_____

Grammar
be going to (1) • Intenzioni

1 Scrivi frasi complete con la forma corretta di *be going to* usando le parole date.

1 Daniel/buy some new trainers/on Saturday

_____

2 we/not have/a holiday/this summer

_____

3 our teacher/give us a test/next week

_____

4 I/not wait here/all night!

_____

5 my parents/get a new car/next month

_____

6 Hannah/not come out/this evening

_____

2 Rispondi in maniera personale a queste domande.

1 What are you going to do after school tomorrow?

2 What are you going to watch on TV at the weekend?

3 What time are you going to go to bed tonight?

4 Where are you going to be next Monday morning?

5 What are you going to do when you're 16?

6 Who are you going to spend time with in the next holidays?

3 Riordina le parole per formare domande. Poi scrivi la risposta breve corretta dal riquadro.

> No, it isn't.   No, she isn't.   No, we aren't.
> Yes, he is.   Yes, they are.

1 make dinner Dad going is tonight to?

_____

_____

2 going to DVD you that watch are?

_____

_____

3 is going eat to food its dog the?

_____

_____

4 to school students at the are stay late going?

_____

_____

5 invite to party me going is her to Jessica?

_____

_____

4 Completa questa intervista con un calciatore famoso usando le parole date e *be going to*. Poi scrivi le riposte brevi.

Interviewer Roberto, that was a great match.
¹_____ (you/celebrate) with the other players tonight?

Roberto No, ²_____.
I ³_____ (have) a quiet night at home. I don't like parties very much.

Interviewer You're having a great season with Liverpool. ⁴_____ (you/stay) with the team next year?

Roberto Yes, ⁵_____. I haven't got any plans to move.

Interviewer Great. So ⁶_____ (you/buy) a house here in Liverpool?

Roberto No, ⁷_____.
I ⁸_____ (buy) a house in the country.

Interviewer And ⁹_____ (your wife and children/move) to England?

Roberto Yes, ¹⁰_____. They ¹¹_____ (stay) in Portugal until the summer, and then they ¹²_____ (come) here in July.

5 Scrivi frasi complete usando *be going to* e le parole date.

1 I/look for a flat/as soon as/I/get a job

_____

2 you/see/Mark/before/you/go/on holiday?

_____

3 after/they/see/the film/they/go/for a pizza

_____

4 Sue/finish/with her boyfriend/when/she/see/ him tonight

_____

5 I watch/TV/after/I/finish/this exercise

_____

be going to (2) • Previsioni

6 Osserva le previsioni del tempo per queste città. Scrivi frasi complete con la forma corretta (affermativa o negativa) di *be going to*.

Sydney	Rome	London	Oslo
35º	20º	7º	-2º

1 it/be/sunny in Sydney

_____

2 it/be/warm in Rome

_____

3 the weather in London/be/hot

_____

4 Oslo/have/warm temperatures

_____

5 it/rain/in Sydney

_____

6 people in London/need/umbrellas

_____

7 it/be cloudy/in Rome

_____

8 people in Oslo/be/cold

_____

7 Leggi le frasi che descrivono alcune situazioni e scrivi delle previsioni con *be going to*.

1 John's homework is four days late. He left it at home again this morning. He's telling the teacher now.

_____

2 Samantha was too busy to eat breakfast and she only had some fruit for lunch. Dinner in her house is at 7 o'clock.

_____

3 Isabelle is a vegetarian. She's at a friend's house for lunch. Her friend's mum is making a ham salad.

_____

4 Paul wants a new computer for his birthday. He knows that his parents went to a computer shop last week.

_____

5 Oliver and Mark hate heavy metal music and they haven't got much money. Yesterday their friends asked them to go to a heavy metal festival with them in the summer.

_____

8 Scrivi frasi complete su quello che stanno per fare le persone. Usa le parole date e la forma corretta di *be about to*.

1 Lisa/go out

_____

2 the boys/get on the bus

_____

3 we/have breakfast

_____

4 I/do my homework

_____

5 you/take my bag!

_____

6 Peter/phone his mum

_____

9 Leggi le frasi e scrivi che cosa sta per succedere usando *be about to*.

1 Katy's getting her MP3 player out of her bag.

_____

2 The passengers are all on the bus and the driver is starting the engine.

_____

3 The children are putting on their pyjamas.

_____

4 The match finishes at 4pm. It's 3.57 now.

_____

5 The students are sitting at their desks with exam papers. The exam starts in five minutes.

_____

6 Tom is wearing his coat and he's opening the front door.

_____

be going to, Present simple o Present continuous?

10 Completa il testo con la forma corretta del futuro: *be going to* o il *Present simple*.

Fiona ¹_____ (have got) a music exam next Saturday in a different town. The exam ²_____ (start) at 2pm and it ³_____ (finish) at 3.15. Fiona's parents ⁴_____ (be) at a party in the afternoon, so Fiona ⁵_____ (travel) by bus to her exam. The best bus ⁶_____ (leave) at 1.20 and it ⁷_____ (arrive) at 1.40. It ⁸_____ (not stop) at lots of different bus stops. Fiona ⁹_____ (be) very nervous, but she thinks she ¹⁰_____ (pass) the exam.

11 Completa le frasi con la forma corretta del futuro: *be going to* o il *Present continuous*.

1 I _____ (see) the doctor tomorrow at 3.45.

2 We _____ (fly) to Barbados on Saturday 4th May.

3 It _____ (be) cold and cloudy tomorrow.

4 Harry _____ (go) to the Alps at Christmas.

5 The girls _____ (start) at a new school in September.

6 I'm bored. I _____ (phone) my friends.

7 You're drinking too much coffee. You _____ (not sleep) well tonight.

8 They've got five goals and we've got one. We _____ (lose).

Esercizi sommativi

12 Scegli l'alternativa corretta.

My name's Sasha. I'm 18 and I got my exam results last week. They were really good, so I **[1]have/'m going to have** a party with my friends this weekend! **[2]I/I'm about to** phone them now to organize it. I've got a place at university. **[3]I'm going to/I going to go** to Cardiff University next October. **[4]I'm studying/I'm going to study** Modern Languages there for three years. The course **[5]starts/is going to start** on October 15th so on October 12th **[6]I move/I'm moving** to a student flat in Cardiff centre. **[7]It's being/It's going to be** really exciting! The course **[8]finishes/is finishing** on December 12th for the Christmas holidays. **[9]I don't come/I'm not going to come** home before then! **[10]I'm staying/I'm going to stay** in Cardiff every weekend to have some fun!

13 Osserva le informazioni sul volo per Beijing. Poi completa il dialogo usando la forma corretta del futuro dei verbi fra parentesi. Scrivi le risposte mancanti dove necessario.

Name:	Mr H. Prescott
Destination:	Beijing
Flight number:	BrA532 (Brit Air)
Leave:	Thursday 17th February 13.30
Arrive:	Friday 18th February 09.30
One stop:	Amsterdam

Joe [1]_____ (when/you fly) to Beijing?

Dad [2]_____

Joe [3]_____ (what time/your flight/leave)?

Dad [4]_____

Joe [5]_____ (when/it arrive) in Beijing?

Dad [6]_____

Joe That's a long flight! [7]_____ (the plane/stop) on the journey?

Dad [8]_____

Joe [9]_____ (you/fly) with Brit Air?

Dad [10]_____

Joe [11]_____ (you/have) any free time in Beijing?

Dad I don't know. But I [12]_____ (try) to see the famous sights.

14 Translation • Traduci il paragrafo in inglese sul tuo quaderno.

Ieri io e i miei amici abbiamo deciso di andare al cinema. Vogliamo vedere il nuovo film con Johnny Depp. Il film inizia alle 8.40. Ci incontriamo a The Pizza Factory alle 6.30 stasera e mangiamo lì. Poi prendiamo l'autobus delle otto per il cinema. Il film finisce alle 10.30. Sarà bellissimo! Spero che la sorellina di Donna non venga con noi. Sto per mandare a un SMS a Donna.

Translation note

In italiano si usa comunemente il presente indicativo per esprimere un'intenzione o una cosa programmata. Il presente indicativo è spesso intercambiabile con il futuro:

Il mese prossimo andiamo/andremo a Londra.

Quando si traduce una frase italiana al presente indicativo non si può sempre presumere che la frase corrispondente in inglese sia al *Present simple*:

- se la frase si riferisce a un evento o orario ufficiale si usa il *Present simple*:
Il concerto inizia alle otto stasera.
The concert starts at eight o'clock tonight.

- se la frase si riferisce a programmi o appuntamenti prestabiliti si usa il *Present continuous*:
Mi vedo con Jon stasera.
I'm seeing Jon this evening.

- se la frase si riferisce a un'intenzione si usa *be going to*:
Faccio i compiti domani.
I'm going to do my homework tomorrow.

Grammar network

A Present perfect (1) • *ever*

| Forma affermativa | | Forma negativa | | Forma interrogativa | Risposte brevi | |
estesa	contratta	estesa	contratta		affermative	negative
I have seen	I've seen	I have not seen	I haven't seen	Have I seen?	Yes, I have.	No, I haven't.
you have seen	you've seen	you have not seen	you haven't seen	Have you seen?	Yes, you have.	No, you haven't.
he/she/it has seen	he/she/it's seen	he/she/it has not seen	he/she/it hasn't seen	Has he/she/it seen?	Yes, he/she/it has.	No, he/she/it hasn't.
we have seen	we've seen	we have not seen	we haven't seen	Have we seen?	Yes, we have.	No, we haven't.
you have seen	you've seen	you have not seen	you haven't seen	Have you seen?	Yes, you have.	No, you haven't.
they have seen	they've seen	they have not seen	they haven't seen	Have they seen?	Yes, they have.	No, they haven't.

1 Il *Present perfect* si ottiene con *have/has* e il participio passato del verbo principale.

2 Il participio passato dei verbi regolari è uguale al *Past simple* (vedi Unit 8 p.200): **listen – listened – listened**

3 Il participio passato dei verbi irregolari non segue regole precise e va quindi imparato a memoria. Vedi la lista alle pagine 286–287: **eat – ate – eaten**

4 Il *Present perfect* si usa per:
- parlare o chiedere delle esperienze o degli avvenimenti che sono successi durante la vita ma senza riferimento a un momento specifico:
  My mum's lived abroad.
  La mia mamma ha vissuto all'estero.
- parlare di azioni in un periodo iniziato nel passato che non si è ancora concluso, per esempio *today*, *this morning/evening*, *this week/month/year*:
  Have you seen Julia this morning?
  Hai visto Julia stamattina?
  (È ancora mattina quando viene fatta la domanda.)

5 Per chiedere se si è mai fatta una certa esperienza nella vita, si usa *ever*. *Ever* precede sempre il participio passato:
Have you ever met a famous person? Yes, I have.
Hai mai incontrato una persona famosa? Sì.

B Present perfect o Past simple?

1 Il *Present perfect* si usa per parlare di esperienze fatte nella vita oppure in un periodo di tempo che non è ancora concluso. L'enfasi è sul fatto piuttosto che sul momento preciso in cui questo è avvenuto. Per questo motivo, il *Present perfect* non si usa mai con espressioni di tempo passato:
Jack's flown a plane. (Jack's flown a plane last week.)
Jack ha pilotato un aereo.

I've had three holidays this year.
Ho fatto tre vacanze quest'anno.

2 Il *Past simple* si usa per specificare esattamente quando è stata compiuta un'azione o si è verificato un avvenimento. Le frasi al *Past simple* si riferiscono a un'azione conclusa in un periodo di tempo concluso e di solito si usano con espressioni di tempo passato:
Jack flew a plane two years ago.
Jack ha pilotato un aereo due anni fa.
I had three holidays last year.
Ho fatto tre vacanze l'anno scorso.

3 Quando si racconta di esperienze fatte o si danno notizie, di solito si comincia con il *Present perfect* e poi si usa il *Past simple* per dare dettagli più precisi sull'avvenimento (dove, quando, ecc.):
I've ridden a horse. I rode last summer, when we were on holiday in France.
Ho fatto equitazione. Ho fatto equitazione l'estate scorsa, quando eravamo in vacanza in Francia.
Guess what? Mel's passed all her exams! She got her results yesterday.
Indovina? Mel ha superato tutti i suoi esami! Ha avuto i risultati ieri.

4 Quando si chiede a qualcuno delle esperienze che ha fatto, di solito si comincia la conversazione con la domanda *Have you ever…?* Se la risposta è affermativa, si usa il *Past simple* per fare domande più dettagliate:
A **Have you ever eaten Thai food?**
B **Yes, I have.**
A **What was it like?**
B **It was delicious. I ate lots.**
A **When did you try it?**
B **About two months ago.**
A *Hai mai mangiato il cibo tailandese?*
B *Sì.*

A *Com'era?*
B *Era delizioso. Ne ho mangiato tanto!*
A *Quando l'hai provato?*
B *Circa due mesi fa.*

C Present perfect (2) • *never*

1 Per dire che non si è mai fatta una certa esperienza nella vita, il *Present perfect* è spesso accompagnato da *never*.

Never si usa nelle affermazioni con significato negativo e precede sempre il participio passato:
I've never played golf.   *Non ho mai giocato a golf.*
Jess has never stayed in a luxury hotel.
Jess non è mai stata in un albergo di lusso.

 Ricorda che in inglese la doppia negazione non è possibile, quindi le frasi con *never* hanno sempre il verbo alla forma affermativa:

He's never seen a *Star Wars* film.
(He hasn't never seen a *Star Wars* film.)
Non hai mai visto nessun film di Guerre Stellari.

D Present perfect • Altri avverbi di tempo

1 Per parlare di azioni recenti che sono successe in un momento imprecisato, il *Present perfect* può essere accompagnato da avverbi come *recently* e *lately*:

He's been very tired recently.
È molto stanco recentemente.
We haven't seen Rachel lately.
Non abbiamo visto Rachel ultimamente.

2 Si usa spesso l'avverbio *before* con il *Present perfect* quando si chiede o si parla di esperienze fatte o non fatte:
I've seen that boy before somewhere.
Ho già visto quel ragazzo da qualche parte.

He's never eaten octopus before. This is the first time.
Non ha mai mangiato il polpo prima. Questa è la prima volta.

Have you been to this pizzeria before?
Sei stato in questa pizzeria prima d'ora?

E *been* o *gone*?

1 Il verbo *go* ha due forme del participio passato:
- *been* si usa per parlare di qualcuno che è andato in un posto ed è tornato:
  Alice and Charlie have been to London.
  Alice e Charlie sono stati a Londra.
- *gone* si usa per parlare di qualcuno che è andato da qualche parte e non è ancora tornato:
  Alice and Charlie have gone to London.
  Alice e Charlie sono andati a Londra.

NB: *been* è anche il participio passato del verbo *be*:
I've been at home all day.
Sono stato a casa tutto il giorno.

Word store

Emotions adjectives — *Aggettivi per descrivere emozioni*

angry	_____
annoyed	_____
annoying	_____
bored	_____
boring	_____
disappointed	_____
disappointing	_____
embarrassed	_____
embarrassing	_____
excited	_____
exciting	_____
happy	_____
nervous	_____
relieved	_____
sad	_____
scared	_____
scary	_____
shocked	_____
shocking	_____
surprised	_____
surprising	_____
upset	_____

Word builder +

Holidays (2) — *Vacanze*

Accommodation	_____
stay in a holiday village	_____
stay in a youth hostel	_____
Transport	_____
go by bike	_____
go by scooter	_____
Activities	_____
go diving	_____
go windsurfing	_____

Real talk

Completa le espressioni dai dialoghi dello *Student's Book*.

You _____ a _____ upset	*Sembri un po' giù*
on my _____	*da solo*
You _____ be serious!	*Non parli mica sul serio?*
Just _____	*Stavo solo scherzando*
Right! But like _____?	*Sì, ma che cosa?*
Sounds _____...	*Sembra...*
_____ the _____ idea	*È proprio questo lo scopo*

Vocabulary

Emotions adjectives

1 Scrivi gli aggettivi del riquadro nella colonna corretta.

> angry   bored   excited   exciting   happy
> nervous   relieved   upset

Positive ☺	Negative ☹
_____	_____
_____	_____
_____	_____
_____	_____

2 Scrivi due aggettivi diversi che si possono formare usando questi verbi.

1 shock _____
_____

2 embarrass _____
_____

3 surprise _____
_____

4 annoy _____
_____

5 disappoint _____
_____

6 scare _____
_____

3 Leggi le frasi e completale con aggettivi che descrivono le emozioni.

1 Richard loves sports and he really wants to go windsurfing. His uncle is taking him windsurfing tomorrow. Richard's _____ .

2 Emily saw her friend steal some make-up from a shop. She thinks this is really _____ .

3 Mark wants to go to a concert by his favourite band. He phones for tickets, but he can't get any. He feels _____ .

4 Fiona hates Geography and never understands the lessons. This Geography lesson is 50 minutes long and the teacher is talking non-stop. Fiona feels _____ .

5 Misha is trying to do her homework but her little brother is making a lot of noise and never stops. She thinks that he's _____ .

6 Zoe is late and she's running for the school bus. It's 8.15 and the bus usually leaves at 8.10. She arrives at the bus stop and the bus is still there. Zoe feels _____ .

Word skills

Word families

Molti vocaboli derivano da altri vocaboli (spesso altre parti del discorso). Per esempio, dal verbo *excite* derivano sia gli aggettivi *exciting* e *excited* che il sostantivo *excitement*.

4 Questi aggettivi derivano da verbi. Quali sono i verbi originali?

> creative   closed   sleepy

5 Questi aggettivi derivano da sostantivi. Quali sono i sostantivi originali?

> foggy   careful   hopeless

6 Questi sostantivi derivano da verbi. Quali sono i verbi originali?

> teacher   actress   builder

Quando prendi nota di un vocabolo, ti potrà essere utile elencarlo in una lista con gli altri vocaboli che appartengono alla stessa famiglia. Puoi annotarli usando una mappa concettuale (*mind map*), mettendo la parola da cui derivano nel mezzo. Le famiglie di parole possono essere aggiunte man mano che impari nuovi vocaboli.

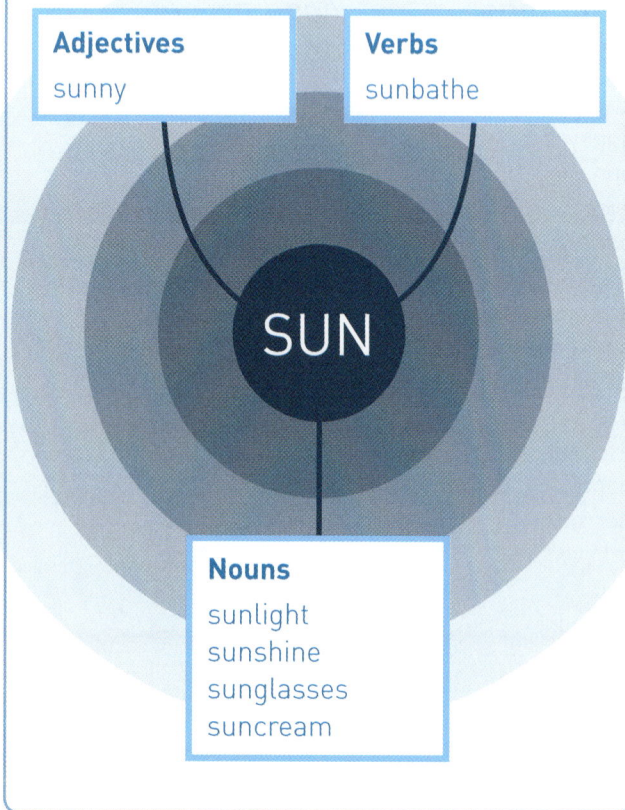

Adjectives
sunny

Verbs
sunbathe

SUN

Nouns
sunlight
sunshine
sunglasses
suncream

Grammar

Present perfect (1) • *ever*

1 Scrivi il participio passato di questi verbi. Alcuni sono regolari, altri sono irregolari.

1 take _____
2 watch _____
3 come _____
4 decide _____
5 teach _____
6 ask _____
7 see _____
8 speak _____
9 swim _____
10 start _____
11 dance _____
12 bring _____

2 Scrivi frasi complete al *Present perfect* usando le parole date.

1 Alison/try/snowboarding
_____

2 I/not read/any books in English
_____

3 we/travel/around Australia
_____

4 Grandma/not use/the Internet
_____

5 you/not meet/my brother
_____

6 Justin and Steve/be/on TV
_____

3 Scrivi domande complete con *ever...?* usando le parole date. Poi rispondi in maniera personale usando le risposte brevi.

1 you/stay in hospital?
_____

2 your mum/buy you a computer?
_____

3 you/make a pizza?
_____
_____

4 your favourite band/play in Italy?
_____
_____

5 you/meet a British person?
_____
_____

6 your favourite singer/record a bad song?
_____
_____

Present perfect o Past simple?

4 Scrivi frasi e domande complete usando le parole date e il *Present perfect* o *Past simple*.

1 Robert/not/live abroad
_____

2 Mary/finish her homework/an hour ago
_____

3 I/not see/Jess/this week
_____

4 your parents/ever/meet your English teacher?
_____

5 you/stay at home/yesterday?
_____

6 we/not go out/last night
_____

5 Leggi le battute e scrivi i 3 dialoghi usando le parole date e il *Present perfect* o *Past simple*.

1 A you/ever/learn to play a musical instrument?
   B ✓
   A What/you/learn?
   B I/have/piano lessons when I/be/at primary school. But I/stop/when I/be/11.
   A _____
   B _____
   A _____
   B _____

2 A you/ever/meet a famous person?

   B ✓

   A Who/you/meet?

   B I/meet/Mollie from The Saturdays. She/be/at the music shop/last year. They/invite her for the afternoon.

   A _____

   B _____

   A _____

   B _____

3 A you/ever/win a competition?

   B ✓

   A What/you/win?

   B I/win/a judo competition about three years ago. My photo/be/in the newspaper!

   A _____

   B _____

   A _____

   B _____

6 Completa il dialogo con le parole fra parentesi. Usa il *Present perfect* o *Past simple*.

Leo	Hi, Tanya. ¹_____ (you/see) Megan recently?
Tanya	No, ²_____. ³_____ (she/go) on holiday?
Leo	I don't know. I ⁴_____ (see) her last week, at Kim and Georgia's party.
Tanya	Oh, yes. What ⁵_____ (the party/ be) like?
Leo	Great! They ⁶_____ (have) some Spanish food there – tapas. ⁷_____ (you/ever/try) it?
Tanya	Yes, ⁸_____. I ⁹_____ (go) to Spain on holiday last year. I ¹⁰_____ (eat) a lot of Spanish food. ¹¹_____ (you/ever/go) there?
Leo	No, ¹²_____.

Present perfect (2) • *never*

7 Scrivi frasi in maniera personale usando la forma affermativa del *Present perfect* e *never* dove è necessario.

  1 I/study French

    _____

  2 I/have a holiday in the USA

    _____

  3 I/see a UFO

    _____

  4 I/write a poem

    _____

  5 I/ride a horse

    _____

  6 I/watch a football match in a stadium

    _____

8 Scrivi domande e frasi al *Present perfect* usando le parole date e i verbi nel riquadro. Aggiungi *ever* o *never*.

> eat   forget   listen to   make   play   read   ride   win

  1 Paula/volleyball?

    _____

  2 I/a *Twilight* book

    _____

  3 Chris/a scooter?

    _____

  4 we/Japanese food

    _____

  5 you/your homework?

    _____

  6 their team/a match

    _____

  7 my mum/a cake

    _____

  8 your parents/one of your CDs?

    _____

Present perfect • **Altri avverbi di tempo**

9 Rispondi alle domande con frasi complete, dando più informazioni possibili.

  1 Have you seen any good films recently?

    _____

  2 Have you done much exercise lately?

    _____

  3 Have you been out with your friends much recently?

    _____

  4 What have you done at school recently?

    _____

    _____

  5 What's the weather been like recently?

    _____

    _____

been o gone?

10 Completa il dialogo con *been* o *gone*.

Laura Why wasn't William at school yesterday?

Joe He's ¹_____ on holiday with his family. They left on Saturday.

Laura Oh! Where have they ²_____?

Joe To Canada. They've got family there.

Laura Lucky him! I've never ³_____ outside Europe. Have you ever ⁴_____ to Canada?

Joe No, I haven't. But I've ⁵_____ to the USA.

Laura What's the weather like in Canada at the moment?

Joe It's ⁶_____ very cold so they've had snow.

Laura Has his brother ⁷_____ with them?

Joe Yes, he has. They've all ⁸_____ together.

Esercizi sommativi

11 Completa il paragrafo con i verbi fra parentesi al *Present simple*, *Present continuous*, *Present perfect* o *Past simple*.

Leanne ¹_____ (be) excited because next week her class ²_____ (go) on a school trip. They ³_____ (spend) a week at an adventure centre in Scotland. Leanne ⁴_____ (never/go) to Scotland. She ⁵_____ (be) a bit nervous because she ⁶_____ (not do) many sports before. The students ⁷_____ (have) lessons in skiing and canoeing. Leanne ⁸_____ (try) skiing two years ago, when she ⁹_____ (go) to the Alps with her family, but she ¹⁰_____ (not have) much success!

12 Completa il dialogo con le parole fra parentesi. Usa il *Present simple*, *Present continuous*, *Present perfect* o *Past simple*.

Ellen ¹_____ (you/ever/go) to the South of France, Mum?

Mum Yes, ²_____. I ³_____ (go) to Cannes about 15 years ago. Why?

Ellen There ⁴_____ (be) an advert in this newspaper. They ⁵_____ (look for) young people to work at a summer camp there.

Mum ⁶_____ (you/think about) trying to get a job?

Ellen I ⁷_____ (not know). I ⁸_____ (never have) a summer job before.

Mum And you ⁹_____ (never go) abroad alone before!

Ellen I ¹⁰_____ (tell) Kelly about it this morning. She ¹¹_____ (think about) it too.

Mum When ¹²_____ (the job/start)?

Ellen On the 15ᵗʰ July. And it ¹³_____ (finish) on 9ᵗʰ September.

13 Translation • Traduci il paragrafo in inglese sul tuo quaderno.

La settimana scorsa il mio amico mi ha dato un biglietto per un concerto rock. Ci andiamo il mese prossimo. Sono davvero elettrizzato perché adoro il gruppo! Ho comprato tutti i loro CD e ho visto tutti i loro video, ma non sono mai stato a uno dei loro concerti. Sarà bellissimo! Sono già stato a un concerto rock. Ci sono andato con mio fratello l'anno scorso, ma non mi è piaciuto molto. Era davvero costoso e non siamo riusciti a vedere il gruppo!

Translation note

Ricorda che il passato prossimo ('ho mangiato') sebbene abbia una struttura simile a quella del *Present perfect* (*I have eaten*), si può tradurre in inglese sia con il *Past simple* che con il *Present perfect*. Per scegliere il tempo verbale corretto in inglese, considera attentamente i seguenti punti:

• il verbo è accompagnato da un'espressione di tempo passato che si riferisce a un periodo già concluso? ('due ore fa', 'l'anno scorso', 'ieri', ecc.)? = *Past simple*:
Non ho fatto i compiti ieri sera.
I didn't do my homework last night.

• il verbo non è accompagnato da un'espressione di tempo passato e si riferisce a un'esperienza fatta in un momento non specifico del passato? = *Present perfect*:
Ha vissuto in molti paesi diversi.
He's lived in lots of different countries.

• il verbo è accompagnato dall'avverbio 'mai'? = *Present perfect*:
Sei mai stato a Roma?
Have you ever been to Rome?

Non abbiamo mai visto un film in 3D.
We've never seen a film in 3D.

• il verbo è accompagnato da un avverbio come 'ultimamente' che si riferisce a un periodo non ancora concluso? = *Present perfect*:
Hai parlato con Dave ultimamente?
Have you spoken to Dave recently?

MY SCOTLAND

11, South Street
Thurso, Caithness
Scotland
KW14 5TY

12th June

5

Dear Alessandro,

Thank you for your letter. I've never written to an Italian person before! Your life is very different from mine.

I live in a town called Thurso. It's in Caithness – the most <u>northern</u> region of
10 Scotland. Thurso is the largest town in this region. It's about 300km from Edinburgh and 1,000km from London. In fact, it's closer to Norway than to London! It even gets its name from Norway, because <u>Vikings</u> lived here hundreds of years ago.

The weather in Caithness is very different from the weather in England.
15 It's always colder than the rest of the UK. The summers here can be very sunny, but the temperatures are only around 13°C. The winters have been bad recently, with temperatures of around -15°C. And it's windy all year!

But the good news is the weather creates perfect conditions for surfing! There are some great surfing beaches here. The weather's good today, so I'm
20 going to practise my surfing technique this evening. It's a sunny day and we're going to have <u>daylight</u> until about 10pm. We get lots of daylight in the summer because we are so far north. I've been surfing lots of times, but I'm not an expert! My brother is really good at it. He's going to be a surfing champion one day!

I'm sending a map of Caithness and a photo of one of the beaches near here with this
25 letter. What are the summers and winters like in Italy? What do you usually do in the summer? Have you ever been surfing?

All the best,
Duncan

Glossary	
northern	settentrionale
Vikings	vichinghi
daylight	luce del sole

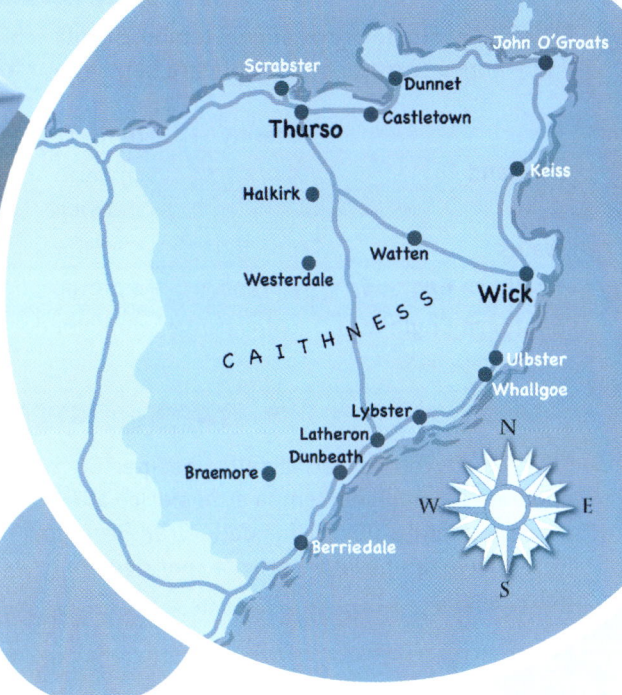

Reading comprehension

1 🔊 **S.089** Leggi la lettera di Duncan. Poi leggi il riassunto e scegli l'alternativa corretta.

Duncan lives in a town in the [1]centre/north of Scotland. Its name, Thurso, comes from [2]England/Norway because Vikings once lived there. The weather in the north of Scotland is [3]colder/warmer than the weather in England. There's a lot of [4]fog/wind all year, but it can be sunny too. The beaches near Thurso are good for [5]sunbathing/surfing. In the [6]summer/winter there is a lot of daylight. Duncan has been surfing [7]a few/lots of times. He [8]is better than/isn't as good as his brother.

2 Vero o falso? Scrivi *T* (*true*) o *F* (*false*). Correggi le frasi false. 🅿

1 ___ Duncan has written to an Italian person before.

2 ___ Caithness is a town in Scotland.

3 ___ Thurso is nearer to Norway than to London.

4 ___ Summers in Caithness are always cloudy.

5 ___ The winter weather in Caithness hasn't been good recently.

6 ___ Duncan wants to go surfing tonight.

7 ___ It's going to be dark at 9pm tonight.

8 ___ Duncan's brother can surf very well.

3 Rispondi alle domande.

1 Which region of Scotland is the furthest north?

2 Which is the largest town in this region?

3 How far is Thurso from London?

4 What is the normal summer temperature in Caithness?

5 How low have the winter temperatures been recently?

6 What's the weather like in Thurso today?

7 What prediction does Duncan make about his brother?

8 What two things does Duncan send with his letter?

Culture note

Il surf è diventato molto popolare nel Regno Unito negli ultimi anni. Molte spiagge del Regno Unito, insieme alle condizioni atmosferiche della Gran Bretagna, offrono le condizioni ideali per fare surf. I posti migliori per praticare questo sport sono il Devon, la Cornovaglia, la costa occidentale del Galles e la parte settentrionale della Scozia.

Listening comprehension

4 🔊 **S.090** Ascolta le previsioni del tempo. Scegli l'alternativa corretta per completare la tabella.

	recently	tomorrow
Scotland	cold/warm	colder/ warmer
Wales	sun/cloud	sun/cloud
Northern England	rain/snow	sun/rain
Southern England	cold/warm	sun/cloud

5 🔊 **S.090** Riascolta e traccia delle linee per abbinare i simboli del tempo atmosferico alle parti corrispondenti sulla cartina della Gran Bretagna. Poi scrivi le temperature previste per domani nella tabella.

6 🔊 **S.090** Riascolta e rispondi alle domande.

1 Which month of the year is it?
_____
2 What temperature has Scotland had recently?
_____
3 What sort of weather has Scotland had recently?
_____
4 What temperature has the south of England had recently?
_____
5 Is the snow going to continue in Scotland?
_____
6 Where is it going to be less warm tomorrow?
_____

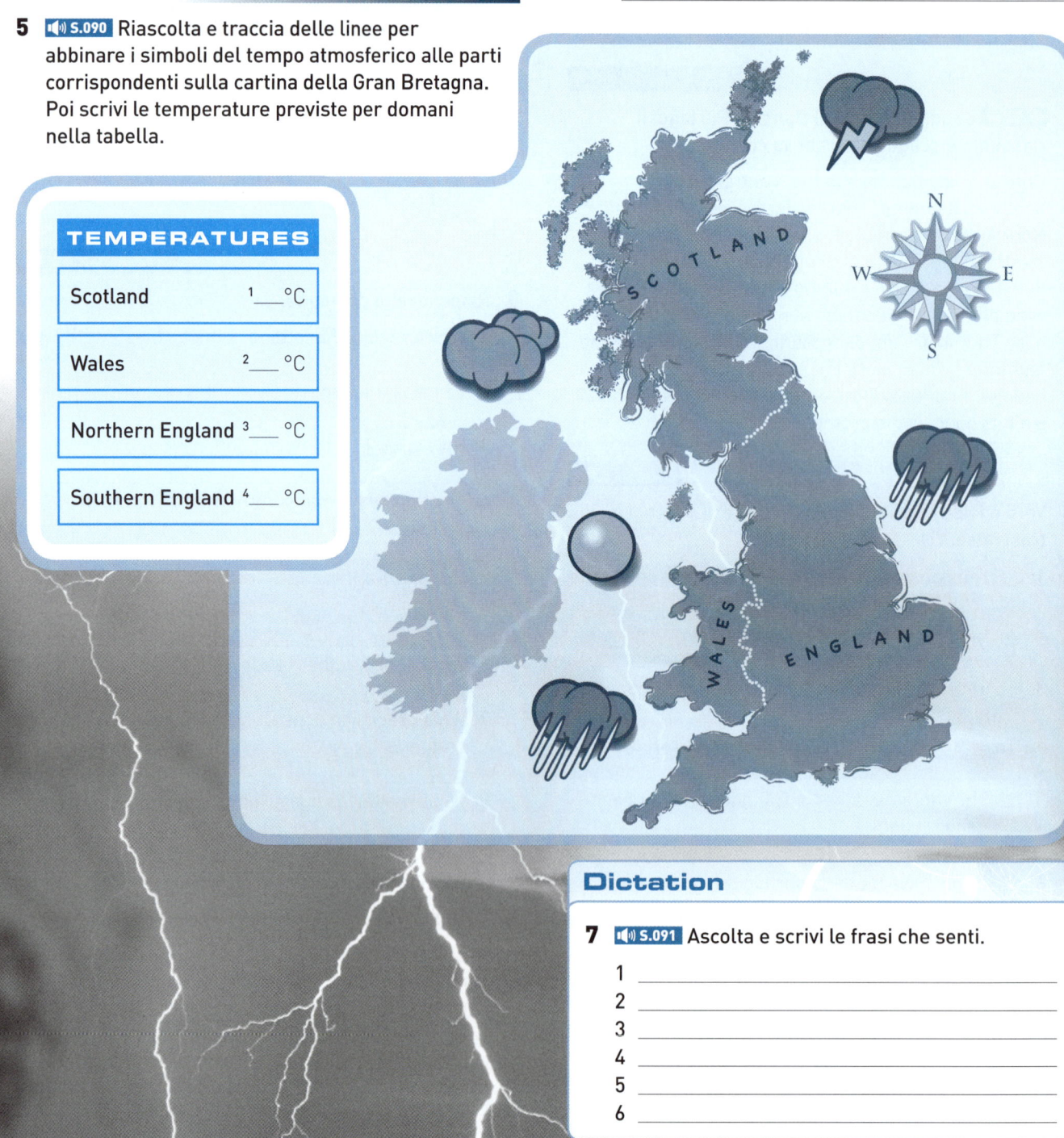

TEMPERATURES

Scotland	1 ___°C
Wales	2 ___°C
Northern England	3 ___°C
Southern England	4 ___°C

Dictation

7 🔊 **S.091** Ascolta e scrivi le frasi che senti.

1 _____
2 _____
3 _____
4 _____
5 _____
6 _____

Writing

Writing skills

Scrivere una lettera informale

8 Quando devi scrivere una lettera, è importante che tutte le sezioni che la compongono siano al posto giusto:

- osserva di nuovo la lettera di Duncan a p.254 e trova:

  1 la data della lettera: riga ___
  2 l'indirizzo di Duncan: righe ___
  3 il saluto di apertura: riga ___
  4 il saluto di chiusura e la sua firma: righe ___

La lettera deve essere chiaramente divisa in paragrafi, ciascuno con informazioni diverse.

> Osserva di nuovo la lettera. Ci sono 5 paragrafi nella parte principale. Numerali e decidi in quale paragrafo Duncan:
>
> 5 parla del tempo atmosferico del posto in cui vive ___
> 6 introduce la lettera ___
> 7 parla di surf ___
> 8 dice ad Alessandro che cosa spedisce con la lettera ___
> 9 descrive il posto in cui vive ___
>
> Trova le tre domande che Duncan fa ad Alessandro in cui gli chiede di dare delle risposte nella sua prossima lettera.
>
> Ora fai l'Esercizio 9.

9 Immagina di essere Alessandro. Scrivi la risposta alla lettera di Duncan (75–100 parole), usando la sua lettera come modello. Segui queste indicazioni: P T

- Write your address and the date in the correct places.
- Write an opening greeting.
- Write an opening paragraph. Say that you enjoyed reading Duncan's letter. Give your opinion of the place where he lives.
- Answer Duncan's three questions, starting a new paragraph for each one.
- Write a closing paragraph. Say that you're sending some information about your home town.

Functions on film

Talking on the phone

A Metti le battute del dialogo nell'ordine corretto (1–9).

___	Eve	Do you want to go to the cinema this evening?
___	Eve	Great! I'll see you at six, then. Bye!
___	Eve	Hi, Greg. It's Eve.
___	Eve	Let's meet at six o'clock at my house.
1	Greg	Hello.
___	Greg	Oh, hi, Eve.
___	Greg	OK. I'll come on my scooter.
___	Greg	See you then.
___	Greg	That's a great idea. What time shall we meet?

B Completa il dialogo.

Mrs Evans	Hello.
Jacob	Hello, Mrs Evans. Is Mark ¹_____?
Mrs Evans	Yes, he is. ²_____ _____ Jacob?
Jacob	Yes, it is.
Mrs Evans	³_____ on ⁴_____ minute, please.
Mark	Hello?
Jacob	Hi, Mark. ⁵_____ me.
Mark	Oh, hi.
Jacob	Do you want to go swimming later?
Mark	OK. What time ⁶_____ we meet?
Jacob	⁷_____ meet at three o'clock at the swimming pool.
Mark	Great. ⁸_____ you at 3.
Jacob	Bye.

C Scrivi il dialogo seguendo la traccia.

Mr Clark	¹Rispondi al telefono.
Debbie	²Rispondi. Di' chi sei e chiedi se Becky è in casa.
Mr Clark	³Chiedile di aspettare un minuto.
Becky	⁴Rispondi al telefono.
Debbie	⁵Salutala e di' chi sei. Chiedile se vuole venire a vedere dei DVD stasera.
Becky	⁶Accetta l'invito. Chiedi a che ora devi andare a casa di Debbie.
Debbie	⁷Suggerisci alle sette.
Becky	⁸Esprimi accordo. Di' che porterai il tuo nuovo DVD.
Debbie	⁹Saluta e termina la chiamata.

Grammar network

A Present perfect (3) • *just, already, yet, still*

1 Per descrivere un'azione avvenuta molto recentemente, si usa il *Present perfect* con l'avverbio *just* (appena). *Just* viene messo tra *have/has* e il participio passato:

> soggetto + *have/has* + *just* + participio passato

I've just seen your sister.   *Ho appena visto tua sorella.*

2 Per descrivere un'azione avvenuta prima del previsto, si usa il *Present perfect* alla forma affermativa con l'avverbio *already* (già). *Already* viene messo tra *have/has* e il participio passato:

> soggetto + *have/has* + *already* + participio passato

We've already done the housework.
Abbiamo già pulito la casa.

3 Per informarsi se un'azione è avvenuta, si usa il *Present perfect* alla forma interrogativa con l'avverbio *yet* (già):

> *Have/Has* + soggetto + participio passato + *yet* + ?

Have you had lunch yet?   *Hai già pranzato?*

4 Per descrivere un'azione che non è ancora avvenuta, si usa il *Present perfect* alla forma negativa con l'avverbio *yet* (non... ancora):

> soggetto + *haven't/hasn't* + participio passato + *yet*

The bus hasn't left yet.   *L'autobus non è ancora partito.*

NB: *yet* si mette sempre alla fine della frase o della domanda.

5 Si può usare anche l'avverbio *still* per descrivere un'azione che non è ancora avvenuta. *Still* può esprimere una sfumatura di sorpresa o irritazione per il fatto che l'azione non è stata completata:

> soggetto + *still* + *haven't/hasn't* + participio passato

The bus still hasn't left!   *L'autobus non è ancora partito!*

 Ricorda che l'uso di *already/yet* in inglese non coincide perfettamente con quello di 'già/non... ancora' in italiano. Gli avverbi italiani si traducono così:

- 'già' nelle frasi affermative = *already*:

Ha già fatto i compiti.
He's already done his homework.

- 'già' nelle domande = *yet*:

Ha già fatto i compiti?
Has he done his homework yet?

- 'non... ancora' nelle frasi negative = *yet*:

Non ha ancora fatto i compiti.
He hasn't done his homework yet.

B Ripasso dei tempi verbali

1 Present simple
We study Maths on Tuesdays and Fridays.

2 Past simple
My dad studied Chemistry in the 1980s.

3 Present continuous
My sister's studying in her room at the moment.

4 Present simple – uso futuro
The bus leaves at 6am tomorrow.

5 Present continuous – uso futuro
Next month we're studying English literature.

6 *be going to* – futuro
I'm going to study medicine when I'm older.

7 Present perfect
I've never studied Spanish.

1 Si usa il *Present simple* per parlare di abitudini e routine quotidiane. La forma affermativa si ottiene così:

> soggetto + forma base del verbo (+ *-s*)

I play the guitar.   *Suono la chitarra.*

Ricorda che la terza persona del *Present simple* si ottiene aggiungendo *-s* alla forma base del verbo:
He plays the guitar.   *Suona la chitarra.*

La forma negativa si ottiene così:

> soggetto + *don't/doesn't* + forma base del verbo

I don't play the guitar.   *Non suono la chitarra.*

La forma interrogativa si ottiene così:

> *Do/Does* + soggetto + forma base del verbo + ?

Does he play the guitar?   *Suona la chitarra?*

2 Si usa il *Past simple* per parlare di azioni concluse in un momento preciso del passato. La forma affermativa dei verbi regolari si ottiene così:

> soggetto + forma base del verbo + *-ed/-d*

I enjoyed the film.   *Il film mi è piaciuto.*

NB: i verbi irregolari hanno una forma del *Past simple* che va imparata a memoria (vedi pp.286–287).

La forma negativa di tutti i verbi si ottiene così:

> soggetto + *didn't* + forma base del verbo

I didn't enjoy the film.   *Il film non mi è piaciuto.*

La forma interrogativa di tutti i verbi si ottiene così:

> *Did* + soggetto + forma base del verbo + ?

Did Jack enjoy the film?   *Il film è piaciuto a Jack?*

3 Si usa il *Present continuous* per parlare di azioni in corso nel momento in cui si parla. La forma affermativa si ottiene così:

> soggetto + *is/are* + forma in *-ing* del verbo

I am working.   *Sto lavorando.*

La forma negativa si ottiene così:

> soggetto + *isn't/aren't* + forma in *-ing* del verbo

He isn't working.   *Non sta lavorando.*

La forma interrogativa si ottiene così:

> *Is/Are* + soggetto + forma in *-ing* del verbo + ?

Is she working?   *Sta lavorando?*

4 Si usa il *Present simple* anche per parlare di orari e programmi ufficiali al futuro:
The train leaves at 8.30 tomorrow morning.
Il treno parte alle 8:30 domani mattina.

5 Si usa il *Present continuous* anche per parlare di appuntamenti e programmi prestabiliti al futuro:
We're having a party next Friday.
Venerdì prossimo faremo una festa.

6 Si usa *be going to* per esprimere intenzioni o per fare previsioni basate su dati oggettivi. La forma affermativa si ottiene così:

> soggetto + *is/are* + *going to* + forma base del verbo

I'm going to buy some new clothes today.
Oggi comprerò dei vestiti nuovi.

It's freezing. It's going to snow.
Fa freddissimo. Nevicherà.

La forma negativa si ottiene così:

> soggetto + *isn't/aren't* + *going to* + forma base del verbo

I'm not going to buy any CDs.   *Non comprerò nuovi CD.*

La forma interrogativa si ottiene così:

> *Is/Are* + soggetto + *going to* + forma base del verbo + ?

Are you going to come with me?
Vieni/Verrai con me?

7 Si usa il *Present perfect* per parlare di un avvenimento al passato quando non è specificato il momento in cui è successo. Si usa anche per parlare di azioni in un periodo di tempo iniziato nel passato che non si è ancora concluso. La forma affermativa si ottiene così:

> soggetto + *have/has* + participio passato del verbo

They've been to Australia.   *Sono stati in Australia.*

La forma negativa si ottiene così:

> soggetto + *haven't/hasn't* + participio passato del verbo

We haven't been to Australia.
Non siamo stati in Australia.

La forma interrogativa si ottiene così:

> *Have/Has* + soggetto + participio passato del verbo + ?

Have you been to Australia?   *Sei stato in Australia?*

Word store

Transport — *Mezzi di trasporto*

bicycle (bike) _____
boat _____
bus _____
car _____
coach _____
ferry _____
helicopter _____
motorbike _____
plane _____
scooter _____
ship _____
skateboard _____
taxi _____
train _____
tram _____

Transport places — *Luoghi di trasporto*

airport _____
bus station _____
coach station _____
port _____
train station _____

Transport verbs — *Verbi relativi ai trasporti*

cycle _____
drive (a vehicle)
drive (somebody) _____
fly back _____
fly to _____
get into (the car) _____
get off (the bus/train/bike) _____
get on (the bus/train/bike) _____
get out of (the car) _____
take/get (the bus/train) _____
walk _____

Real talk

Completa le espressioni dai dialoghi dello *Student's Book*.

a bit _____ up   *un po' scosso*
That _____ dog   *Quello stupido di un cane*
You've got _____   *Hai un sacco di tempo*
_____ is it?   *Che c'è che non va?*

Vocabulary

Transport and places

1 Completa il cruciverba con i nomi dei veicoli.

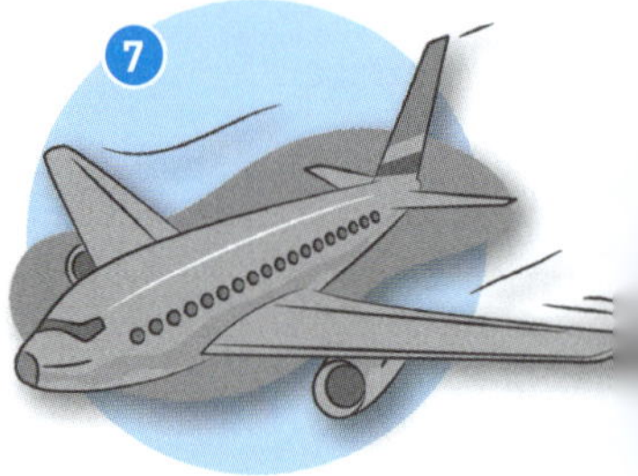

2 Rispondi alle domande.

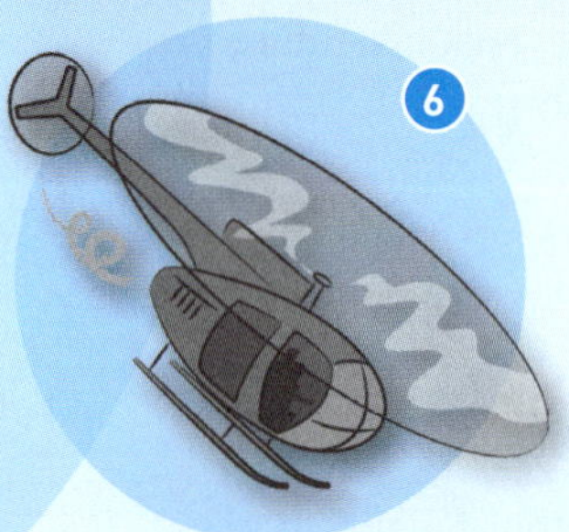

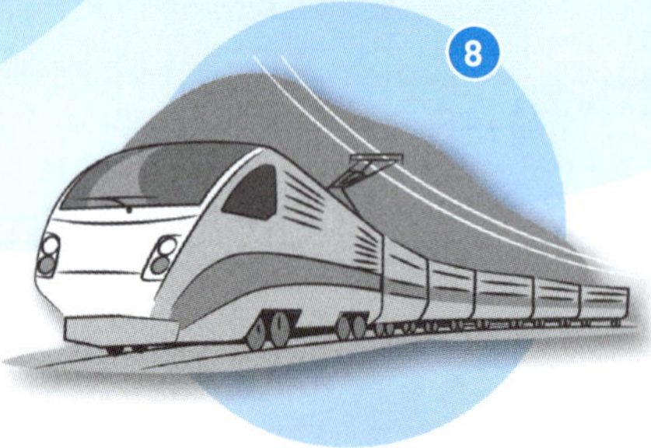

1 Which vehicle is a car that takes paying passengers?
_____
2 Which vehicle can take tourists on a sightseeing trip by road?
_____
3 Which vehicle can take paying passengers on a short journey by sea?
_____
4 What is the difference between a boat and a ship?
_____
5 What is the short name for a bicycle?
_____

3 Scrivi i nomi di:

1 an Italian airport
_____
2 a train station in Rome or Milan
_____
3 two Italian ports
_____

4 Completa le frasi con i verbi specifici per ogni mezzo di trasporto.

1 Emma's sitting on a plane. She's about to _____ to Brazil.
2 Kevin's in his car. He's about to _____ to work.
3 Connor's leaving his house. He doesn't need a vehicle. He's about to _____ to school.
4 Sarah's on her bicycle. She's about to _____ to the shops.
5 Dean's at the bus stop. He's about to _____ the bus to town.

5 Scegli le preposizioni corrette.

1 Get **into/on** the car now, please!
2 He got **out of/off** his motorbike.
3 Where do we get **into/on** the ferry?
4 Let's get **out of/off** the taxi here.

Grammar

Present perfect (3) • *just, already, yet, still*

1 Leggi le frasi e dai spiegazioni usando le parole date e il *Present perfect* con *just*.

1 Sophie's scared. (see a ghost)
She's just seen a ghost.

2 The children are happy. (open their presents)
_____

3 I'm sad. (watch a sad film)
_____

4 Oliver's disappointed. (receive his exam results)
_____

5 We're excited. (hear some good news)
_____

6 My parents are tired. (clean the house)
_____

2 Completa i mini-dialoghi fra Andy e la sua mamma. Andy ha già fatto tutte le cose che la sua mamma gli sta ordinando di fare. Scrivi le risposte di Andy usando il *Present simple* e *already*.

Mum	Tidy your room!	
Andy	*I've already tidied it!*	
1 Mum	Make your bed!	
Andy	_____	
2 Mum	Clean your shoes!	
Andy	_____	
3 Mum	Do your homework!	
Andy	_____	
4 Mum	Phone your grandma!	
Andy	_____	
5 Mum	Feed the cats!	
Andy	_____	

3 Riscrivi le frasi inserendo *already* o *yet*.

1 I haven't finished my school project.
_____

2 Have you sent that email?
_____

3 We've had lunch.
_____

4 Dad's left for work.
_____

5 Has your sister moved to London?
_____

6 Have Cathy and Sam arrived?
_____

7 We haven't paid for the meal.
_____

8 I've seen that film.
_____

4 Amy e Rob stanno organizzando una festa a casa di Amy. Completa le domande che Rob fa a Amy, usando il *Present perfect* e *yet*.

1 ask your parents?

_____ ?

Yes, I have.

2 buy the food?

_____ ?

No, I haven't.

3 text your friends?

_____ ?

Yes, I have.

4 organize the music?

_____ ?

Yes, I have.

5 tidy the living room?

_____ ?

No, I haven't.

6 choose your clothes?

_____ ?

No, I haven't.

5 Osserva le risposte di Amy nell'Esercizio 4. Per ogni cosa, scrivi se l'ha già fatta o se non l'ha ancora fatta. Usa il *Present perfect* con *already* o *still*.

1 She _____
2 She _____
3 She _____
4 She _____
5 She _____
6 She _____

Exercises

Ripasso dei tempi verbali

6 Leggi il testo e scegli l'alternativa corretta.

Edward ¹**has/is having** a long journey to school every day. Last year he ²**has been/was** at a different school. It ³**has been/was** near his house and he ⁴**can/could** walk there every day. But now Edward's dad ⁵**drives/drove** him to the bus station every morning. Next Edward ⁶**gets/ 's getting** a bus, then he ⁷**walks/has walked** another kilometre to school. Edward's mum can't take him to school because she ⁸**'s never learning/ 's never learned** how to drive. And at the moment she ⁹**works/'s working** at night in a hospital. So when Edward ¹⁰**leaves/left** the house every morning, she ¹¹**'s sleeping/'s slept** in bed. She ¹²**'s starting/'s started** driving lessons next month. Her first lesson ¹³**is/'s going to be** on May 22ⁿᵈ. She ¹⁴**'s going to be/was** nervous!

7 Completa il testo con la forma corretta dei verbi fra parentesi.

Kate ¹_____ (be) really excited, because tomorrow she ²_____ (fly) to the USA with her family. They ³_____ (stay) with their uncle and aunt near New York for two weeks. Kate ⁴_____ (already pack) her bags. She ⁵_____ (pack) most of her things two days ago. She ⁶_____ (be) in a panic yesterday because she ⁷_____ (not can) find her passport or her MP3 player. She ⁸_____ (find) her passport last night, but she ⁹_____ (still not find) her MP3 player. She ¹⁰_____ (be) a bit annoyed because she ¹¹_____ (love) listening to music. Kate ¹²_____ (go) to bed early tonight. Their flight ¹³_____ (leave) at 9am, so they ¹⁴_____ (leave) the house at 6am. They ¹⁵_____ (be) tired but excited in the morning.

U.S. IMMIGRATION
MAY 17 2011
ADMITTED
UNTIL

8 Completa il dialogo usando le parole fra parentesi. Usa il tempo verbale corretto.

Daniel ¹_____ (What/you/do) at the weekend, Jo?
Jo I ²_____ (not have got) any plans.
Daniel I ³_____ (go) to the new shopping centre with Matt on Saturday. ⁴_____ (you/want) to come?
Jo Oh, OK. I ⁵_____ (go) there last week with Donna. We really ⁶_____ (enjoy) it. But you ⁷_____ (not like) shopping!
Daniel I ⁸_____ (know)! But a famous person ⁹_____ (open) the music shop there at 11am.
Jo Oh, really? Who?
Daniel We ¹⁰_____ (not know). Matt ¹¹_____ (read) about it in the paper yesterday. But now he ¹²_____ (forgot) the person's name!
Jo Let's go anyway! I ¹³_____ (never see) a famous person.
Daniel I ¹⁴_____ hope we ¹⁵_____ (not be) disappointed!

Esercizi sommativi

9 Leggi il dialogo e scegli l'alternativa corretta.

Amanda Hi, Harry.
Harry Sorry I'm late. I was ¹**at/in** Jake's house and I missed the bus to town.
Rob We've ²**already/yet** ordered our food. What ³**do you want/you want**?
Harry ⁴**I've/I'm** really cold. ⁵**Has/Have** they got any soup?
Amanda Yes, they ⁶**has/have** – carrot soup.
Harry OK. Excuse me, could ⁷**I/you** have ⁸**any/some** carrot soup, please?
Waiter Oh, I'm sorry. ⁹**We/We've** just finished the carrot soup. But I think ¹⁰**there's/there are** some tomato soup.
Harry OK, ¹¹**I/I'll** have that, thanks. Hey, is that Susannah?
Rob ¹²**At who are you looking?/Who are you looking at?**
Harry That girl with the ¹³**short, blond/blond, short** hair. Oh, no. It isn't her. She's isn't ¹⁴**pretty as/as pretty as** Susannah, and she's ¹⁵**older/more old**.

10 Completa le frasi con la forma corretta delle parole fra parentesi.

1 That's Paula's book. Give it to _____, please. (she)
2 When I was five I _____ read very well. (can)
3 I love _____ basketball. (play)
4 China is _____ than Japan. (big)
5 We _____ lots of new clothes last week. (buy)
6 Is that your _____ car? (parents)
7 I think that doing sport is _____ than playing computer games. (good)
8 Don't talk to _____! (they)
9 Whose is this phone? Is it _____? (you)
10 Have you ever _____ to do your homework? (forget)
11 Milly is the _____ person in the class. (clever)
12 Those are the _____ games. (children)

11 Completa il paragrafo con una parola per ogni spazio vuoto.

Ben and [1]_____ sister Rebecca are going [2]_____ Italy [3]_____ the summer. They're very excited because they [4]_____ never [5]_____ there before. Rebecca can speak Italian quite well, but Ben [6]_____ speak it at [7]_____. He knows a [8]_____ Italian words for food and drink, so he's going [9]_____ try to order some meals. They're staying with [10]_____ Uncle Peter. He lives [11]_____ Bologna. He's [12]_____ English teacher there. [13]_____ wife, Sara, is Italian. They got married two years [14]_____. Ben and Rebecca haven't met Sara [15]_____, but they're sure that they [16]_____ going [17]_____ like [18]_____.

12 Translation • Traduci il paragrafo in inglese sul tuo quaderno.

John Woods ha sedici anni. È inglese ed è studente in una scuola a Birmingham. La sua materia preferita è il francese. Sa parlare bene il francese e prende sempre i voti migliori quando c'è una verifica. John è andato in Francia l'anno scorso. È stato con un ragazzo francese e la sua famiglia per due settimane. La scuola ha organizzato il viaggio. John non riusciva a capire sempre i suoi amici francesi, ma ha imparato molte cose sulla lingua e sulla gente. Adesso vuole visitare Parigi. Non c'è mai stato. C'è solo un problema – non ha abbastanza soldi! La settimana prossima incomincerà un lavoro in un bar. Ha intenzione di risparmiare tutti i soldi e di comprare un biglietto ferroviario per Parigi!

13 Translation • Traduci il dialogo in inglese sul tuo quaderno.

Mum [1]Alice – vieni qui e aiutami, per favore.
Alice [2]Ma sono al telefono!
Mum [3]Con chi stai parlando?
Alice [4]Con Yasmin. Le sto chiedendo dei compiti per casa.
Mum [5]Oh – OK. Ma non stare al telefono tutta la sera.

Dieci minuti dopo...

Alice [6]Sono pronta. Ho appena finito.
Mum [7]Grazie. Ho incontrato Yasmin? Che aspetto ha?
Alice [8]È abbastanza alta, con capelli lunghi e scuri.
Mum [9]No – non l'ho incontrata. Dunque, puoi aiutarmi a lavare i piatti, per favore.
Alice [10]OK.
Mum [11]E riordina questa stanza! Di chi sono queste scarpe?
Alice [12]Sono mie.
Mum [13]Chi le ha messe sul tavolo?
Alice [14]Non lo so!

Translation note

Per scegliere il tempo verbale corretto in inglese, considera attentamente gli avverbi e le espressioni di tempo usati nelle frasi in italiano. Per esempio:

- gli avverbi di frequenza con presente indicativo ('sempre', 'di solito', ecc.) richiedono l'uso del *Present simple* in inglese:

  Di solito non vado a scuola a piedi.
  I don't usually walk to school.

- le espressioni di tempo che si riferiscono a un periodo o a una situazione temporanea presente ('oggi', 'ora', 'in questo momento', ecc.) richiedono l'uso del *Present continuous* in inglese:

  Lavorano molto in questo periodo.
  They're working a lot at the moment.

- le espressioni di tempo che si riferiscono a un periodo già concluso ('ieri', 'sabato scorso', ecc.) richiedono l'uso del *Past simple* in inglese:

  L'anno scorso siamo andati in Francia.
  Last year we went to France.

- gli avverbi 'appena', 'già', 'non ancora' e '(non) mai' usati in una frase al passato prossimo, richiedono l'uso del *Present perfect* in inglese:

  Ho già fatto colazione.
  I've already had breakfast.

800 BRITISH ISLES

SHETLAND ISLANDS

ORKNEY ISLANDS

SARK

HEBRIDES

NORTH SEA

ABERDEEN

SCOTLAND

EDINBURGH

ISLE OF MAN

NORTH ATLANTIC OCEAN

BELFAST

ISLE OF MAN

IRELAND

DUBLIN

IRISH SEA

ENGLAND

WALES

CARDIFF

LONDON

ENGLISH CHANNEL

SCILLY ISLES

SEA

SCILLY ISLES

ISLE OF WIGHT

CHANNEL ISLANDS

CHANNEL ISLANDS

We often refer to Great Britain as 'an island'. But, of course, it isn't just one island – it's a collection of over 800 islands. Some are large and some are small. Some are <u>inhabited</u> and some are not. Scotland has the biggest number of islands, including groups of remote islands like the Hebrides, the Orkney Islands and the Shetland Islands. The Isle of Man in the Irish Sea has its own <u>Celtic</u> culture, and the islands near the south coast of England – the Scilly Isles, the Isle of Wight and the Channel Islands – have good weather and are very popular with tourists.

You can travel to the larger British islands by plane or by ferry from the <u>mainland</u>. For example, if you want to travel to the Shetlands, most people take a ferry from Aberdeen. The journey to Lerwick, the capital, is 12 hours. You can also fly from the major Scottish cities. After tourists have arrived at the ports and airports, smaller boats and planes can take them to the more remote islands. If you're planning to visit the Scottish islands in the summer holiday season, it's important to book all your transport before you go. There are fewer flights and ferries in the winter because of the bad weather, but if you have enough money, you can pay for a private plane for your holiday!

The popular tourist islands in the south have good public transport, and they often ask visitors to leave their cars at home. On some islands, like the Isle of Man, you can find old-fashioned transport like trams and <u>steam trains</u>. Some quiet islands, like Sark in the Channel Islands, have actually <u>banned</u> the use of cars. Visitors walk or use bikes or <u>horse-drawn carriages</u>. The most remote islands, like Easdale in the Hebrides, do not even have roads. A lot of tourists visit these islands for a walking holiday. Islands like Tresco in the Scilly Isles are popular with walkers because of their beautiful <u>wildlife</u>.

Glossary

inhabited	abitate
Celtic	celtica
mainland	terraferma
steam trains	treni a vapore
banned	proibito
horse-drawn carriages	carrozze a cavalli
wildlife	animali e piante selvatiche

Reading comprehension

1 **S.092** Leggi il testo e completa la tabella sulle isole.

Name of island	Group of islands	Location
The Isle of Man	✗	
The Isle of Wight	✗	
Sark		
Easdale		
Tresco		

2 Completa le frasi con le parole corrette.

1. _____ British islands are inhabited.
2. The Orkney Islands are in _____.
3. The Scilly Isles usually have _____ weather.
4. You can travel by _____ to the Shetland Islands from the Scottish cities.
5. You need to book your transport before you visit the Scottish islands in the _____.
6. Many small islands ask tourists not to bring their _____.
7. On the Isle of Man you can travel on _____ and steam trains.
8. Walking round the islands is a good way to enjoy the beautiful _____.

3 Rispondi alle domande sul tuo quaderno.

1. How many British islands are there?
2. In which country can you find the largest number of islands?
3. How do most people travel to the Shetland Islands?
4. How long is the journey from Aberdeen to the Shetland Islands?
5. Why are there fewer flights and ferries to the Scottish islands in the winter?
6. Why are there no cars on the island of Sark?
7. How do tourists travel around Sark?
8. What is unusual about Easdale, in the Hebrides?

Culture note

L'Isola di Man e le isole della Manica hanno il proprio Parlamento e ufficialmente non fanno parte del Regno Unito anche se, in linea di massima, seguono la legge britannica. I Parlamenti di queste isole hanno una storia antica che predata quella del governo del Regno Unito. Il Parlamento dell'Isola di Man ha mille anni e si pensa che sia il più antico del mondo.

Listening comprehension

*

4 🔊 **S.093** Callum è in vacanza su un'isola. Ascolta e scegli l'alternativa corretta.

1 Callum is on holiday on the Isle of **Wight/Man**.
2 He travelled there by **ferry/plane**.
3 He thinks that **there's a lot/there isn't much** to do.
4 **He's already explored the island/hasn't explored the island yet**.
5 He's having a windsurfing lesson **tomorrow/later today**.
6 *Amazon World* is a **zoo/film**.

**

5 🔊 **S.093** Riascolta il dialogo e completa gli appunti. **P**

1 Callum's holiday – the Isle of _____
2 Accommodation: _____
3 On holiday with: _____
4 Callum's opinion: _____
5 Natalie's opinion: _____
6 Sister's favourite activity: _____
7 Tomorrow's activity: _____
8 Natalie's suggestion: _____

***

6 🔊 **S.093** Riascolta e rispondi alle domande.

1 How many times has Callum been on a ferry?

2 Has Callum tried any water sports yet?

3 What time is his windsurfing lesson?

4 What time is he getting up?

5 What prediction does Natalie make about tomorrow night?

6 What can you see at *Amazon World*?

7 What is Callum going to send to Natalie?

8 When does Callum go home?

Dictation

7 🔊 **S.094** Ascolta e scrivi le frasi che senti.

1 _____
2 _____
3 _____
4 _____
5 _____
6 _____
7 _____
8 _____

Writing

Writing skills

Scrivere una cartolina

8 Osserva la cartolina che Callum ha spedito a Natalie. Sottolinea la parte del messaggio in cui Callum:

1 descrive che cosa ha fatto in vacanza

2 descrive che cosa ha intenzione di fare nei giorni di vacanza che gli restano

3 descrive cosa sta facendo in questo momento

4 saluta Natalie e firma la cartolina

POSTCARD

Dear Natalie,

I'm having a much better time here on the Isle of Wight now! I'm relaxing in the hotel at the moment. I've had two windsurfing lessons now, and we've also been to Amazon World. It was really interesting.

Tomorrow we're going to have a boat trip.

See you next week,

Callum

Ora fai l'Esercizio 9.

9 Leggi le informazioni sull'Isola di Man qui sotto. Immagina di trovarti in vacanza lì. Scrivi una cartolina a Natalie (50–70 parole), usando quella di Callum come modello. Includi queste informazioni:
P T

* an opening greeting
* what you are doing now
* what you have done on your holiday so far
* what you are going to do tomorrow
* a closing greeting and your signature

The Isle of man

TOP TOURIST ATTRACTIONS

* Beautiful beaches
* Castle Rushen medieval castle
* Famous motorbike races in the summer
* Snaefell mountain, with its mountain railway
* Scuba diving lessons

Functions on film

Using public transport

A Bella è alla stazione. Completa il dialogo con le frasi nel riquadro.

> Oh, yes. I have. Here you are.
> OK. A ticket to Exeter, please.
> OK. Here you are.
> Single, please.
> What time's the next bus to Exeter, please?

Bella	1 _____
Man	At ten past four.
Bella	2 _____
Man	Single or return?
Bella	3 _____
Man	Have you got a student card?
Bella	4 _____
Man	A single fare with a student card is £8.40.
Bella	5 _____

B Completa il dialogo.

Leo	A ticket 1_____ Newport, please.
Man	2_____ or return?
Leo	A return, please.
Man	When 3_____ _____ leaving?
Leo	This afternoon 4_____ four o'clock.
Man	And 5_____ _____ you _____ back?
Leo	On Saturday morning 6_____ ten past eleven.
Man	7_____ _____ _____ a Railcard?
Leo	Yes, I 8_____. _____ you are.
Man	Thank you. The return 9_____ with a Railcard is £31.30.

C Scrivi il dialogo seguendo la traccia.

Polly	1Chiedi a che ora è il prossimo treno per Bournemouth.
Woman	2Di' alle una e un quarto.
Polly	3Chiedi un biglietto per Bournemouth.
Woman	4Chiedi se vuole un biglietto di sola andata o d'andata e ritorno.
Polly	5Di' d'andata e ritorno.
Woman	6Chiedi quando parte.
Polly	7Di' col prossimo treno.
Woman	8Chiedi quando torna.
Polly	9Di' domani mattina.
Woman	10Chiedi se ha una tessera ferroviaria.
Polly	11Di' di no.
Woman	12Di' che il biglietto d'andata e ritorno è £25.90.
Polly	13Dalle i soldi.

The Legend of Sleepy Hollow
Washington Irving

Start thinking

1 Read about Washington Irving. What ghost stories do you know?
2 Do you believe in ghosts? Why?

Author factfile

Washington Irving

Born: 1783 in New York City, USA
Died: 1859

Important works: *A History of New York* (1809), *The Legend of Sleepy Hollow*, *Rip Van Winkle* (1819)

Did you know? Washington Irving was one of the first Americans to earn a living only from writing and to be successful in Europe.
It was Irving who first used the nickname 'Gotham' for New York City, later made popular in the Batman comic stories. He is buried in Sleepy Hollow Cemetery. The ghost story, *The Legend of Sleepy Hollow*, has been the subject of various films and even a musical.

1 Read the Background to the story on p.269. Match the characters (1–4) to their descriptions (a–d).

1 ___ Brom Van Brunt
2 ___ Katrina
3 ___ The Van Tassels
4 ___ Ichabod Crane

a Katrina's family
b a teacher in Sleepy Hollow
c a local young farmer
d the girl Ichabod loves

2 Describe the pictures (1–4). What happens at the party?

🔊 **5.17** Read the extract, and check your answers. What is the Headless Horseman?

3 Read the extract again. True or false? Write T or F. Correct the false sentences. **P**

1 ___ There aren't a lot of people at the party.
2 ___ Brom is very popular.
3 ___ Brom is a good dancer.
4 ___ At the party people tell funny stories.
5 ___ Brom tells the best story.
6 ___ Ichabod is happy when he leaves.

Why does Ichabod leave the party early? What do you think happens next?

4 🔊 **5.18** Listen to the next part of the story. What happens to Ichabod while he's on his way home? Choose the correct answers. **P**

1 Who does Ichabod see behind him?
a Brom
b something frightening
c someone from the village on a horse

2 What does Ichabod do first?
a He asks the rider who he is.
b He hides in the church.
c He gets off his horse.

3 Then what does Ichabod do?
a He goes home.
b He goes to the church.
c He goes across the bridge.

4 What does the Headless Horseman do?
a He tells Ichabod to stop.
b He throws his head at Ichabod.
c He gets off his horse.

5 What do people find the next morning?
a Ichabod, his hat and a pumpkin
b the Headless Horseman and a pumpkin
c Ichabod's horse, Gunpowder, his hat and a pumpkin in pieces

What do you think?

5 In pairs. Ask and answer the questions.

1 Do you think the rider is a real ghost? Why?
2 What do you think happens to Ichabod?
3 Do you like ghost stories or films? Why?

Writing

6 Choose task A or B. Write 100 words. **T**

A Imagine you are a reporter for the local newspaper. It is the day after the incident. Write a report that Ichabod is missing. Include this information:

- who Ichabod is and what he looks like
- what people know about him
- where people think he is
- ask for information

Begin like this:
Ichabod Crane is missing...

B Write a short summary of a ghost story or film that you know. Include this information:

- title and who the main characters are
- what happens and how it ends

The Legend of Sleepy Hollow

Background to the story...

It is 1769. Ichabod Crane is a teacher in the valley of Sleepy Hollow. He likes listening to the old women of the village telling ghost stories. He is also in love with Katrina Van Tassel, the daughter of a rich farmer. Ichabod wants to marry Katrina, but Brom Van Brunt, another local farmer, loves her, too. Brom sees Ichabod with Katrina and he's jealous. He and his friends decide to play tricks[1] on Ichabod to make him frightened. At night they move chairs and tables in the classroom, but Ichabod thinks it is witches[2] at work. Then one day the Van Tassel family invite everyone to a party.

It is early evening when Ichabod arrives at Van Tassel's farmhouse. All the farmers from the neighbourhood[3] are at the party with their families. When Brom arrives, everyone is happy to see him. (Not Ichabod, of course!) Brom's horse is big and strong. His name is

5 Daredevil, and only Brom can ride[4] him.

Ichabod feels happy when he sees all the good things to eat and drink in the farmhouse. Then he sees Katrina talking with Brom and he feels angry again. Someone begins playing music in the next room. Ichabod knows Katrina loves to dance. He smiles when he remembers

10 Brom can't dance. Ichabod knows he sings well, and he also dances wonderfully! When the dancing finishes, people begin to talk about the ghosts in Sleepy Hollow.

Brom tells the most exciting story. 'Some nights when I ride through the village, the Headless Horseman follows

15 me,' he says.'When I get to the bridge[5] in front of the old church,' Brom goes on, 'the Headless Horseman always stops. His horse can't step on to the bridge! And the rider and horse disappear[6] in a flash of fire.'

20 Soon the party is over, and everybody begins to leave. Before Ichabod goes, he tells Katrina about his love for her.

But something goes badly wrong, and soon Ichabod leaves Van Tassel's farmhouse

25 quickly and quietly. Without looking left or right, he rides away through Sleepy Hollow. The night is very dark. Ichabod thinks about Katrina and he feels terrible. Then he hears a noise.

From *Rip Van Winkle & The Legend of Sleepy Hollow*, Oxford Dominoes. Text adaptation by Alan Hines.

Glossary

[1]play tricks	*fare scherzi*
[2]witch	*strega*
[3]neighbourhood	*vicinato*
[4]ride	*cavalcare*
[5]bridge	*ponte*
[6]disappear	*scomparire*

Five Canterbury Tales: The Wife of Bath's Tale
Geoffrey Chaucer

Start thinking

1 Read about Geoffrey Chaucer.
2 Read the Background to the story and look at the main picture on p.271. What do you know about the legend of King Arthur, the Knights of the Round Table, and the other people in his kingdom of Camelot?

Author factfile

Geoffrey Chaucer

Born: c.1343 in London, England (date and place uncertain)
Died: 1400

Important works: *Troilus and Criseyde*, *The House of Fame*, *The Legend of Good Women* and *The Canterbury Tales* – one of the great epic poems in literature.

Did you know? Chaucer worked for the royal court and his job took him to France and Italy, where he came into contact with the works of Dante and Boccaccio.
He was the first great poet to write in English, at a time when the literary languages in England were Anglo-Norman and Latin. Chaucer is buried in Westminster Abbey in London.

1 🔊 5.19 Look at the picture. Then read Extract 1. What are the names of the people (A–D)?

A _____ C _____
B _____ D _____

2 Read the extract again and complete the sentences with the correct name: *King Arthur*, *Queen Guinevere*, *Tarquin* or *Lucretia*.

1 _____ was a knight.
2 _____ didn't love Tarquin.
3 _____ locked Lucretia in an old house.
4 _____ wanted Tarquin to die.
5 _____ wanted to punish the knight in another way.
6 _____ left Camelot for a year.

3 Find these words and phrases in the extract. What do they mean? Write a translation in the spaces. (L.= line in text)

1 rode his horse (L.6) _____
2 carried her away (L.8) _____
3 treats (L.14) _____
4 felt sorry for (L.16) _____
5 punishment (L.17) _____

What do you think?

4 In pairs. Ask and answer the questions. Then compare your answers with the class.

1 Do you think the queen was right to change Tarquin's punishment? Why?
2 How do you think Tarquin will find the answer to the queen's question?
3 What do you think the answer to the question is?

5 🔊 5.20 Read Extract 2. Check your answer to Ex.4, question 2.

6 🔊 5.21 Now listen to the next part of the story. What is the answer to the queen's question?
Listen again. Match the people to what they say. Write *T* (Tarquin), *G* (Queen Guinevere) or *W* (the old woman).

1 ____ 'I can tell you the answer, but first you must promise me something.'
2 ____ 'Of course, old woman.'
3 ____ 'What do women want most of all?'
4 ____ 'To rule their husbands.'
5 ____ 'You are a free man.'
6 ____ 'And now you must pay me back.'
7 ____ 'How much money do you want?'
8 ____ 'You must marry me!'

7 How do you think the story ends?

1 Tarquin marries the old lady, but then he leaves her.
2 Tarquin kisses the old lady and she becomes a beautiful, young woman.
3 Tarquin learns to love the old lady and becomes a good knight.

🔊 5.22 Listen and check your answers.

Writing

8 Find out more about King Arthur and his knights, and write a short text. Write 100–150 words. Include this information: 🅣

- King Arthur: who he was, and how he got his sword, Excalibur
- The Knights of the Round Table: who they were, and why the table was round
- Merlin: who he was, and how he helped Arthur

Background to the story...

The Canterbury Tales is about a group of pilgrims[1] who are travelling to Canterbury, to visit the shrine[2] of Saint Thomas Becket. The pilgrims are a mixed group: some are rich and some are poor. They also have very different jobs and experiences. Each one tells a story to make the journey more interesting. This is the story told by a woman from Bath. It takes place in the kingdom of King Arthur, the legendary king of England.

Extract 1

King Arthur's time, the king and his knights[3] lived in the castle of Camelot. One of Arthur's knights – Tarquin – loved Lucretia, a beautiful young woman with long black hair. But she didn't love him. One day she sat under a tree by the river,
5   when suddenly Tarquin rode his horse out of the forest and took her in his arms.

'Help!' cried Lucretia, but Tarquin carried her away quickly on his horse to an old house on a hill far from Camelot. There he put her in a
10 dark room and closed the door behind her.

At once, King Arthur called his knights to him. 'Find Tarquin and Lucretia', he said, 'and bring them to me.'

They soon brought Tarquin and Lucretia to the king. He was angry with Tarquin. 'When a knight from Camelot treats a woman badly, he must die,'
15 said Arthur.

But Queen Guinevere felt sorry for Tarquin. So she asked her husband, 'Can I give a different punishment to him?'

'Of course,' said the king.

Then she said to Tarquin, 'Tell me the answer to this important question: what do
20 women want most of all?'

Tarquin didn't know. So he said nothing.

Then the queen said, 'Tarquin, you can leave Camelot now, but you must come back in a year with a good answer to my question, or you die.'

Extract 2

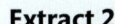

Tarquin went from village
25 to village and town to town. And always he asked different women Guinevere's question. In one village they answered, 'We want money.'
30 In the next village they said, 'We want to be happy.'

In one town, they told Tarquin, 'We want to hear nice things from our lovers.'

Days became weeks, and weeks became months. Soon
35 it was time for Tarquin to go back to Camelot. He felt bad because he didn't have a good answer to Guinevere's question.

On the road to Camelot, Tarquin rode his horse through a forest. It was dark and not easy to see there. After some time, he got off his horse and began to walk. Just then, he saw twenty-four beautiful young women in
40 front of him. They were all in green dresses, and they sang beautifully, laughed, and moved in and out of the trees. But when Tarquin came near, they suddenly left – and the only thing there in front of him was an ugly old woman.

Glossary

[1]pilgrim	*pellegrino*
[2]shrine	*santuario*
[3]knight	*cavaliere*

From ***The Wife of Bath's Tale, Five Canterbury Tales***, Oxford Dominoes. Text adaptation by Bill Bowler.

Sherlock Holmes and the Sport of Kings
Sir Arthur Conan Doyle

Start thinking

1 Read about Sir Arthur Conan Doyle. What do you know about Sherlock Holmes? Who is your favourite fictional detective? What are they like?
2 Read the Background to the story on p.273. Where does this story take place?

Author factfile

Sir Arthur Conan Doyle

Born: 1859, Edinburgh, Scotland
Died: 1930

Important works: Sherlock Holmes novels and collections of short stories, including *The Hound of the Baskervilles* (1902) and *The Lost World* (1912).

Did you know? Sir Arthur Conan Doyle was a doctor before he became a writer. His character Sherlock Holmes is one of the most famous fictional detectives of all time and the subject of many films, including *Sherlock Holmes* (2009), starring Robert Downey Jr.

1 ◀)) 5.23 Read the extract. What happens to the trainer, John Straker?

2 Read the extract again and answer the questions.

1 What time did John Straker get out of bed?
2 Why did he want to look around the stables?
3 What was the weather like?
4 Who or what was missing from the stables the next morning?
5 Did they find Silver Blaze?
6 What was in John Straker's hands?

3 Match the words and expressions from the extract (1–4) to their meanings (a–d).

1 ___ a servant (L.10)   3 ___ a cut (L.21)
2 ___ unlocked (L.12)   4 ___ a scarf (L.23)

a an injury made to skin with a knife
b someone who works for you in the house
c something that keeps your neck warm
d not closed with a key

What do you think?

4 In pairs. Ask and answer the questions.

1 Why do you think the staff were worried about a stranger at the stables?
2 Why do you think Silver Blaze wasn't there?
3 Who do you think killed John Straker? Why?

5 Read what happens next.

The local police think that the stranger, Fitzroy Simpson, killed Straker, but Holmes doesn't agree. There was blood on the knife they found at the scene of the crime, but Simpson hasn't got any injuries. Holmes decides that they need to find the horse in order to solve the case. He and his assistant Dr Watson walk across the moor[1] near King's Pyland to look for it.

[1]moor – brughiera

6 ◀)) 5.24 Listen to the next part of the story narrated by Dr Watson. Choose the correct alternative.

1 After the killing, Silver Blaze looked for a warm stable/another horse.
2 There is another stable far away/not far away at Capleton.
3 The two men easily follow/can't follow the horse's tracks down the hill to Capleton stables.
4 They find a man's tracks beside the horse's ones 20/200 metres from Capleton stables.
5 The man at Capleton stables is happy/unhappy to see Holmes and Watson.

7 Sherlock Holmes spoke to the man at the stables. He found Silver Blaze – he didn't steal him. So what happened that night? How did John Straker die if he was alone with the horse? Solve the mystery. The name of the 'murderer' and why he did it is in code (a = z).

Hroevi Yozav
Sv dzh uirtsgvmvw.

Why do you think Silver Blaze was frightened of his trainer?

Writing

8 Read the information below and read the extract again. Then write what you think happened minutes before John Straker died. Write 100–150 words. **P T**

Silver Blaze was the favourite to win the Wessex Cup. John Straker wanted to stop Silver Blaze winning because he could win a lot of money by betting against the favourite. He took the horse that night to cut one of his legs so it would lose. But Silver Blaze got frightened.

Begin like this:

It was one o'clock in the morning. John Straker got up, he went down to the stables to get Silver Blaze...

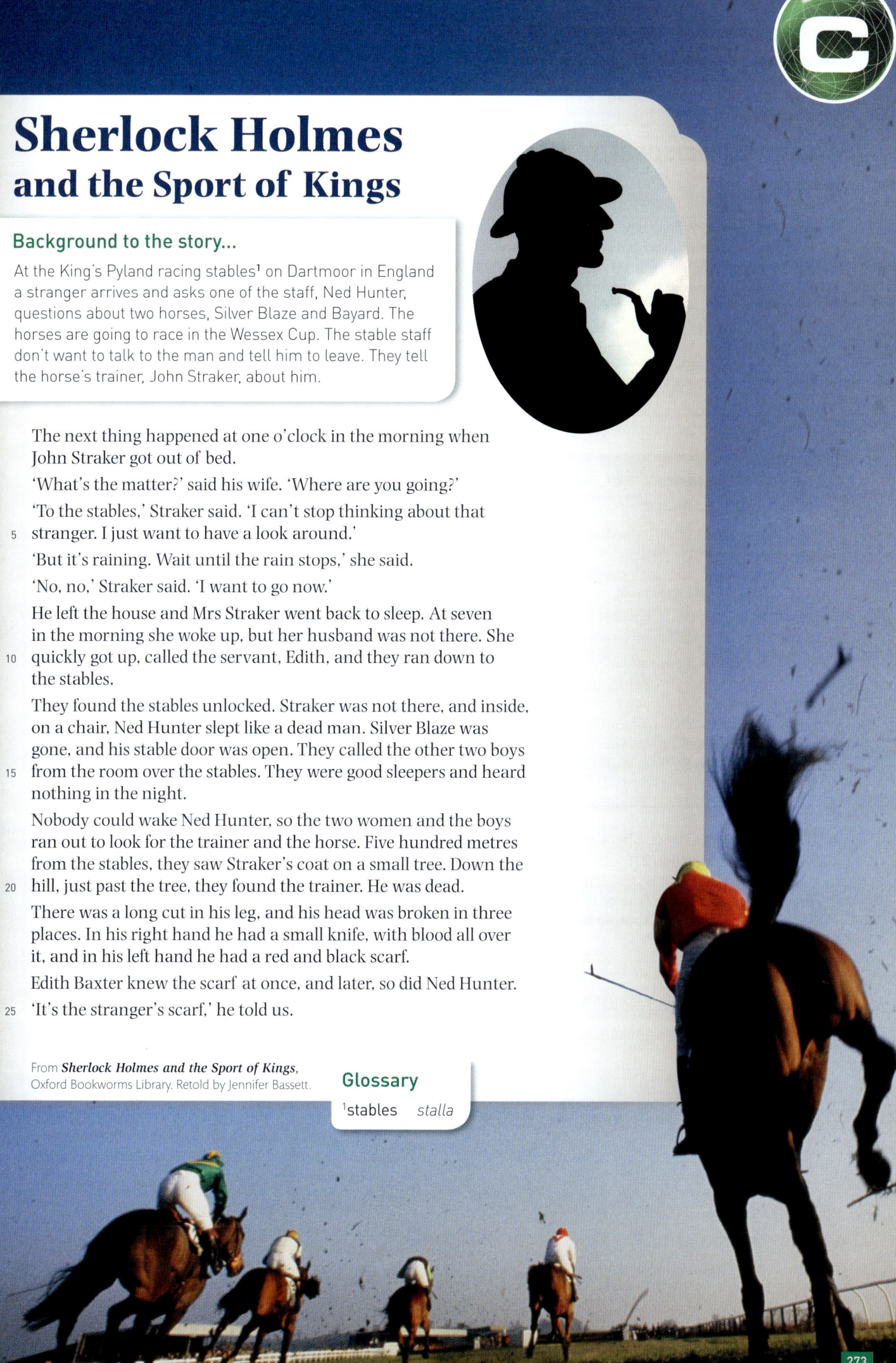

Sherlock Holmes
and the Sport of Kings

Background to the story...

At the King's Pyland racing stables[1] on Dartmoor in England a stranger arrives and asks one of the staff, Ned Hunter, questions about two horses, Silver Blaze and Bayard. The horses are going to race in the Wessex Cup. The stable staff don't want to talk to the man and tell him to leave. They tell the horse's trainer, John Straker, about him.

The next thing happened at one o'clock in the morning when John Straker got out of bed.

'What's the matter?' said his wife. 'Where are you going?'

'To the stables,' Straker said. 'I can't stop thinking about that
5 stranger. I just want to have a look around.'

'But it's raining. Wait until the rain stops,' she said.

'No, no,' Straker said. 'I want to go now.'

He left the house and Mrs Straker went back to sleep. At seven in the morning she woke up, but her husband was not there. She
10 quickly got up, called the servant, Edith, and they ran down to the stables.

They found the stables unlocked. Straker was not there, and inside, on a chair, Ned Hunter slept like a dead man. Silver Blaze was gone, and his stable door was open. They called the other two boys
15 from the room over the stables. They were good sleepers and heard nothing in the night.

Nobody could wake Ned Hunter, so the two women and the boys ran out to look for the trainer and the horse. Five hundred metres from the stables, they saw Straker's coat on a small tree. Down the
20 hill, just past the tree, they found the trainer. He was dead.

There was a long cut in his leg, and his head was broken in three places. In his right hand he had a small knife, with blood all over it, and in his left hand he had a red and black scarf.

Edith Baxter knew the scarf at once, and later, so did Ned Hunter.

25 'It's the stranger's scarf,' he told us.

From **Sherlock Holmes and the Sport of Kings**,
Oxford Bookworms Library. Retold by Jennifer Bassett.

Glossary
[1]stables   *stalla*

Macbeth
William Shakespeare

Start thinking

1 Read about William Shakespeare. Do you know anything about the plays mentioned? Are they comedies or tragedies? Can you name any other plays by Shakespeare?
2 Look at the words in the box. Read the list of characters and the Background to the story on p.275. What do you think the play is about?

future	Macbeth	witches
king	kill	Lady Macbeth

Author factfile

William Shakespeare

Born: 1564 in Stratford-upon-Avon, England
Died: 1616

Important works: Shakespeare wrote over 30 plays including *Romeo and Juliet* (1594), *A Midsummer Night's Dream* (1595), *Hamlet* (1600) and *Macbeth* (1606). He is also known for his poetry, particularly his sonnets.

Did you know? For many people, Shakespeare is considered the greatest writer in the English language. His plays are as popular today as in his time, and many have been made into films. Many popular expressions used in English come from Shakespeare, for example, *All's well that ends well*, *fair play*, *We have seen better days*, (Jealousy is) *a green-eyed monster*.

1 **◄)) 5.25** Read the extract. Check your answers to Start thinking, question 2.

2 Read the extract again. True or false? Write T or F. Correct the false sentences. **P**

1 ___ The witches know who Macbeth is.
2 ___ The witches' first prediction about Macbeth doesn't come true.
3 ___ Lady Macbeth doesn't believe the predictions.
4 ___ King Duncan is planning to visit Macbeth's house.
5 ___ Macbeth is pleased when his wife talks about him becoming king.
6 ___ Lady Macbeth wants her husband to kill King Duncan.

What do you think?

3 In pairs. Ask and answer the questions.

1 Why is Lady Macbeth excited about the predictions?
2 What are Macbeth and Lady Macbeth like?
3 What is their relationship like?
4 What do you think happens next?

4 Read what happens next.

> That night Macbeth kills King Duncan. The next morning, the king's friend Macduff finds him dead in his room. Macbeth says it was the servants. King Duncan's son, Malcolm, leaves Scotland because he is afraid, so Macbeth is made king. However, he isn't happy. He is sure that Banquo suspects that he murdered the king. He orders his men to kill Banquo and his son, Fleance. The men kill Banquo, but Fleance runs away. Macbeth is worried about Macduff as well and goes to see the witches again.

5 **◄)) 5.26** Listen to what happens when Macbeth visits the witches. Put the events (a–f) in the correct order (1–6).

a ___ Macbeth sees a baby over the pot.
b ___ The witches tell Macbeth not to speak.
c ___ Macbeth decides to kill Macduff.
d ___ Macbeth thinks he's safe from danger.
e ___ Macbeth sees a soldier's head above the witches' pot.
f ___ The soldier's head says Macduff is dangerous.

What do you think?

6 In pairs. Ask and answer the questions.

1 What do you think happens in the end?
   a Macbeth kills all his enemies and is king for a long time.
   b Macbeth and Macduff fight, and Macduff kills Macbeth.
2 What do you think the message of the play is?
3 Is Macbeth a bad character or a tragic one?
4 Why do you think the witches' predictions came true?

Writing

7 Find out about another Shakespeare play and write a short summary. Write 100–150 words. Include this information: **T**

- title and kind of play
- who the main characters are
- what happens, and how it ends

Macbeth

Background to the story...

The characters in this part of the play are:
Macbeth, a soldier in the Scottish army
Lady Macbeth, Macbeth's wife
Banquo, a soldier and a friend of Macbeth
King Duncan, the King of Scotland
Macduff, a friend of King Duncan

The story starts at the end of a battle between Norway and Scotland. Macbeth kills the Norwegian general and defeats his army. Duncan, the King of Scotland, wants to thank Macbeth. On their way to see the king, Macbeth and his friend Banquo meet three witches[1].

Suddenly they saw the three witches in front of them. 'Who are you? What are you doing?' asked Banquo. They didn't speak to him, but they looked at Macbeth. 'Macbeth!' cried the witches.

5   'What?! How do you know my name?' he asked. They spoke again, all at the same time: 'Macbeth, the soldier! Macbeth, the general! Macbeth, the king!' 'General? King? What are these women talking about?' Macbeth asked Banquo. 'I'm a soldier – nothing more!'

10 'Who are you?' asked Macbeth. 'Tell us more!' But suddenly the witches weren't there! Macbeth and Banquo looked here and there, but they could see nobody.

***

At Macbeth's home, his wife, Lady Macbeth, waited, day after day. But one day a letter arrived. It was a long letter
15 from her husband.

> *After the battle, Banquo and I met three women. They were witches, and they can see into the future! 'You're going to be a general,' they told me – and they were right! Next, they said: 'Macbeth, you're going to be king!' I can't stop*
> 20 *thinking about it!*

Lady Macbeth was excited[2]. Her husband ... King of Scotland! 'I want to be Queen of Scotland,' she thought. 'The witches are right. My husband is going to be king. Nothing can stop us!' She began reading again:

> 25 *King Duncan is coming to stay with us soon! His son Malcolm is coming too, and Banquo, and Macduff. We must be ready...*

Lady Macbeth cried excitedly. 'King Duncan! In our house? Good! He's king now, but things are going
30 to change. Scotland is going to have a new king!'

***

When Macbeth came home, his wife began to talk about their future. 'We're going to be rich and happy,' she said, 'when you are king.'

But Macbeth wasn't happy. 'What are you talking about?'
35 he cried. 'How can I be king? Scotland has a king!'
'Listen. You're a soldier, and you often kill men in battles,' said his wife. 'King Duncan is coming here tonight.'
'What are you saying?' asked Macbeth.
'You must be brave[3]. Remember the witches: you are
40 going to be king. Duncan must die here in our house. What's the matter? Are you afraid?'

Glossary

[1] witch   *strega*
[2] excited *elettrizzato*
[3] brave   *coraggioso*

From **Macbeth**, Oxford Dominoes.
Text adaptation by Alistair McCallum.

The Adventures of Tom Sawyer
Mark Twain

Start thinking

1 Read about Mark Twain.
2 Read the Background to the story and look at the first picture on p.277. What or who do you think the two boys can see through the holes in the floor? Look at the adjectives in the box. How do you think the boys feel?

frightened	bored	excited
happy	angry	interested/curious

Author factfile

Mark Twain (real name: Samuel Langhorne Clemens)

Born: 1835 in Missouri, USA
Died: 1910

Important works: *The Adventures of Tom Sawyer* (1876), *Adventures of Huckleberry Finn* (1884)

Did you know? The writer William Faulkner called Mark Twain 'the father of American Literature'. Mark Twain was a river-pilot on the Mississippi river before he became a writer. The name 'Mark Twain' came from this experience, and was a term used to indicate the depth of the water under the boat.
Mark Twain is famous for his humour and amusing cynical sayings, for example, *Always do right. This will gratify some people and astonish the rest.*

1 **5.27** Read the extract. Check your answers to Start thinking, question 2.

2 Read the extract again and answer the questions.
   1 Why do Tom and Huck go into the old house?
   2 What does Huck think the noise is?
   3 What do the boys see downstairs?
   4 Who is the old Spaniard?
   5 How did the men get the $650?
   6 What do the two men find under the floor?
   7 Where are the men going to put the money?
   8 Why do the two boys not follow them?

3 Find the words in the extract which mean the following:
   1 a lot of money, gold or jewellery (L.4) _____
   2 speak very quietly (L.12) _____
   3 steal money or property (L.26) _____
   4 make a hole in the ground (L.33) _____
   5 a tool used to cut things (L.34) _____
   6 a mark or an object formed by two lines crossing each other (L.45) _____

What do you think?

4 In pairs. Ask and answer the questions.
   1 What do you think the 'cross' is?
   2 What do you think Tom and Huck should do?
   3 What do you think they actually do?

5 Read what happens next and check your answer to Ex.4, question 3.

> The boys don't tell anyone about the treasure because they want to find it. Then Tom goes on a picnic with other children and they all go into a cave[1]. Tom and his friend Becky get lost. In the cave, Tom sees Injun Joe, but Injun Joe doesn't see him. After three days, Tom and Becky find their way out using some string[2]. Tom tells Becky's father that Injun Joe is still inside the cave. However, when they go back, they find Injun Joe dead. Tom thinks that Injun Joe was in the cave because the treasure is there.
>
> [1]cave – *caverna*
> [2]string – *spago*

6 **5.28** Listen to the next part of the story. Do the boys find the money?
Listen again. True or false? Write T or F. **P**
   1 ____ The boys take candles and some string to the cave.
   2 ____ They can't find the cross.
   3 ____ They find a different tunnel.
   4 ____ The money is in a small room.
   5 ____ The boys don't tell anyone about the money.
   6 ____ There are twelve hundred dollars in the box.

What do you think?

7 In pairs. Ask and answer the questions.
   1 In the extract Mark Twain says: 'When somebody finds treasure, everybody hears about it very quickly.' What do you think he means?
   2 Do you think Tom and Huck did the right thing? Why?
   3 What do you think Tom and Huck did with the money?
   4 What would you do?

Writing

8 Imagine you have just won a lot of money. Write an email to a friend. Write 100–150 words. Include this information: **T**
   • how much money you won
   • how you won it
   • what you did with it

The Adventures of
Tom Sawyer

Background to the story...

Tom Sawyer is 12 years old and lives with his Aunt Polly in St Petersburg, Missouri.

Tom's friend is Huckleberry Finn. Tom and Huck have adventures and often get into trouble[1]. During one adventure they see Injun Joe kill a young doctor, Dr Robinson. Injun Joe blames[2] another man, Muff Potter, and Muff is arrested. During Muff's trial[3] Tom tells the court[4] that Injun Joe was really the murderer. So Injun Joe escapes from the courthouse window. No one knows where he is. Later, Tom and Huck go looking for treasure.

Tom looked down at an old house at the foot of the hill[5].

'Hey, look!' he said. 'Nobody lives in that old house. Let's go there. Old houses are always good for treasure.'

5 'Good for ghosts, too!' said Huck.

They took the pick and shovel[6] with them, went down the hill, and into the old house. They looked in all the rooms downstairs, and then went upstairs. But there was no treasure, and no ghosts. Then they
10 heard a noise.

'*Sh!*' said Tom, suddenly. '*What's that?*'

'*Ghosts!*' whispered Huck.

There were holes in the floor, and through them the boys could see into the rooms downstairs.

15 '*No,*' Tom whispered. '*It's two men. One is the old Spaniard. He came to live in the village last week. I don't know the other man. Sh! Let's listen to them.*'

The two men sat down on the floor. The Spaniard had a green hat and long white hair; the other man was
20 small and dark. He took out a bag and began to open it.

'It's hot in here,' the Spaniard said. He took off his green hat – and then he took off his long white hair!

'*Tom!*' Huck whispered upstairs. '*That's Injun Joe!*'

25 'We took six hundred and fifty dollars when we robbed that house,' said the second man. He took some money out of the bag. 'We can take fifty dollars with us now. What are we going to do with the six hundred?'

30 'Leave it here,' said Injun Joe. 'We can come back and get it next week. Here, give me the bag.'

He walked across the room to the fireplace, moved two big stones[7] from the floor, and began to dig with his knife.

35 Upstairs, the two boys watched excitedly. Treasure! Six hundred dollars of wonderful treasure!

Injun Joe stopped digging. 'Hello. What's this?' he said. 'There's something here. It's an old box.'

Injun Joe put his hand into the box. 'There are
40 thousands of dollars here!'

We can't take it with us today,' said his friend. 'What can we do with it? Put it back under the floor?'

'Yes,' said Injun Joe. (Happy faces upstairs.) 'No!' (Very unhappy faces upstairs.) 'Let's put it under
45 the cross – nobody goes there. We can take it there tonight.'

When night came, the two men carried all the money away. The boys did not go after them because they were afraid of Injun Joe. But they
50 wanted very much to find that 'cross'.

From *The Adventures of Tom Sawyer*,
Oxford Bookworms Library. Retold by Nick Bullard.

Glossary

[1]get into trouble	*cacciarsi nei guai*
[2]blame	*incolpare*
[3]trial	*processo*
[4]court	*tribunale*
[5]hill	*collina*
[6]pick and shovel	*piccone e pala*
[7]stones	*pietre*

Emma
Jane Austen

Start thinking

1 Read about Jane Austen. Which Jane Austen stories do you know? Did you read the book or see the film? What are the main themes of her stories?
2 Read the Background to the story on p.279. What is Emma's family situation, and what is her main problem?

Author factfile

Jane Austen

Born: 1775 in Hampshire, England
Died: 1817

Important works: *Sense and Sensibility* (1811), *Pride and Prejudice* (1813), *Mansfield Park* (1814), *Emma* (1816), *Persuasion* and *Northanger Abbey* (both published after her death in 1817)

Did you know? Jane Austen started writing as a teenager. She often wrote about relationships and marriage, but she never got married herself. Jane Austen published her books anonymously during her lifetime and she remains one of the most popular English authors today. Her books are regularly serialized for TV and made into films, including *Pride and Prejudice* (2005) starring Keira Knightley.

1 🔊 **5.29** Read the extract. What does Emma plan to do for Harriet?

2 Read the extract again and correct the information in the sentences.

1 Emma talks to her father and Mr Knightley about Isabella.
2 Emma isn't interested in matchmaking.
3 Emma thinks Harriet is very beautiful and very clever.
4 The Martins are Harriet's cousins.
5 Emma thinks that Mr Robert Martin is an important person.
6 Mr Elton rarely visits Hartfield.

What do you think?

3 In pairs. Ask and answer the questions.

1 Why do you think Mr Knightley shakes his head? (L.17)
2 Do you think Emma is right to matchmake for her friends? Why?
3 Do you think Mr Martin would be the wrong husband for Harriet? Why?
4 How would you describe Emma?

4 Read what happens next. Why do you think Mr Knightley says Emma is not a friend to Harriet?

Mr Martin asks Harriet to marry him. Harriet is excited by his proposal, but Emma tells Harriet that she can't marry a farmer because she, Emma, could not be friends with a farmer's wife. So Harriet rejects Mr Martin's proposal. Mr Knightley hears about Emma and Harriet's conversation. He likes Mr Martin, and tells Emma she is not a friend to Harriet. Emma says that she is sure that Harriet can find a better man to marry – she means, of course, Mr Elton.

5 🔊 **5.30** Listen to the next part of the story. Complete the sentences with the correct name: *Emma*, *Harriet*, *Mrs Weston*, *Mr Elton* or *Isabella*.

1 _____ comes to stay at Hartfield for Christmas.
2 _____ invites everyone to dinner.
3 _____ can't come because she has a cold.
4 Mr Elton talks to _____ all evening.
5 _____ tells Emma he loves her.
6 Mr Elton says he doesn't love _____.

What do you think?

6 In pairs. Ask and answer the questions.

1 Why do you think Emma didn't know Mr Elton was in love with her?
2 How do you think Emma feels when Mr Elton tells her he loves her?
3 Mr Elton thinks to himself, 'It's true that Harriet is beautiful, but she isn't rich.' Why do you think he doesn't tell Emma this?
4 What do you think happens in the end?

Writing

7 Use your answers to Exs.3 and 6 to write a description of Emma. Write 100–150 words. Include this information: 🅣

- who she is, where she lives and her background
- her personality and her behaviour
- your opinion of what happened with Harriet

Emma

Background to the story...

Emma Woodhouse lives with her father in a house called Hartfield in the village of Highbury. Her father employs Miss Taylor to teach Emma and her sister, Isabella. Over the years Miss Taylor becomes a good friend of Emma's, but eventually she leaves to marry Mr Weston. Isabella also gets married and moves to London. Emma's father is rich and Emma has got everything she needs, but without her friend and her sister, she is bored. On this particular evening Emma is talking to her father and Mr Knightley, a friend of the family, in Hartfield.

'Poor Emma,' said her father. 'She misses Miss Taylor very much.'

'Of course Emma misses her friend,' said Mr Knightley, 'but I'm sure she is happy that Miss
5 Taylor has married.'

'Yes, I am,' said Emma smiling. 'And don't forget that they married because of me. I decided it four years ago when you all said that Mr Weston didn't want to marry again.'

10 'Oh, dear,' said Mr Woodhouse. 'Please don't matchmake¹ any more, Emma. Things always happen as you say they will.'

'But, Papa, I *love* matchmaking,' replied Emma, laughing.

15 'Mr Weston married Miss Taylor because he loves her and she loves him, not because he met her through you,' said Mr Knightley, shaking his head.

'But, Mr Knightley,' she said. 'I knew how they felt before they knew it themselves. That is the secret of a
20 good matchmaker!'

***

From **Emma**, Oxford Dominoes.
Text adaptation by Barbara Mackay.

Emma sometimes asked a group of her father's friends to spend the evening at Hartfield. On one of these evenings Emma felt very excited. A young woman of seventeen was coming to the party. She
25 had no friends or family but she was very beautiful. Her name was Harriet Smith.

Emma was interested in Harriet and they spent the evening talking. Harriet was not very clever, but she was friendly, kind, and had beautiful blue eyes.
30 When Harriet and her father's friends left, Emma made a plan. She wanted to teach Harriet, to be her friend, and to introduce her to the important people in Highbury.

Emma started to spend a lot of time with Harriet
35 and she soon knew all about her. Harriet told her about her friends, the Martins. She often stayed with them on their farm, and she liked Mr Robert Martin very much.

One day while the young women were out
40 walking, they met Mr Martin. Emma saw at once that Harriet liked him a lot, and she was very unhappy about it. A farmer was not the right husband for beautiful Harriet! Emma decided to be Harriet's matchmaker.

45 Emma soon thought of the right person for Harriet. It was Mr Elton – a handsome young clergyman² with a comfortable home who needed a wife. Emma started work at once. She spoke to Harriet about Mr Elton and to Mr Elton about
50 Harriet, and planned lots of ways for them to meet.

Mr Elton started to visit Hartfield often, and Emma was sure that her plan was working well.

Glossary

¹**matchmake**   *combinare matrimoni*
²**clergyman**   *ecclesiastico*

The Importance of Being Earnest
Oscar Wilde

Start thinking

1 Read about Oscar Wilde. Do you know any of the works mentioned? Have you seen any plays or films of his work? Which ones?

2 Look at the picture and read the Background to the story on p.281. Who is Jack visiting in London? Why has he come?

Author factfile

Oscar Wilde

Born: 1854 in Dublin, Ireland
Died: 1900 in Paris, France
Important works: *The Picture of Dorian Gray* (1891) – his only novel; *Lady Windermere's Fan* (1892), *The Importance of Being Earnest*[1] (1895) – both comic plays

Did you know? Oscar Wilde was a controversial and decadent figure, famous for his satire, often comic, of the hypocrisy of Victorian society, particularly the aristocracy. Although he was married, he was sentenced to two years in prison for having a relationship with a man, which was illegal at that time. When he got out of prison, his reputation was destroyed. He moved to Paris where he died penniless. Wilde is famous also for his clever sayings, for example, *I am so clever that sometimes I don't understand a single word of what I am saying.*

[1]**earnest** – *serio*

1  **5.31** Read the extract, and answer the questions.

1 What is Jack's other name?
2 When does he use his two names?

2 Read the extract again. True or false? Write T or F. Correct the false sentences. **P**

1 ___ Algy knows about Jack's two names.
2 ___ Cecily is Jack's aunt.
3 ___ Cecily lives in the country.
4 ___ Jack finds it easy to have fun in the country.
5 ___ Jack pretends to have a brother called Ernest in London.
6 ___ Algy has a friend called Bunbury.

What do you think?

3 In pairs. Ask and answer the questions.

1 Why do you think Jack doesn't want to invite Algy to his house in the country?
2 Why does Jack say 'I'm going to kill Ernest soon'?
3 Do you think it is right to invent another persona as Jack and Algy do? What does it tell us about Jack and Algy, and Victorian society? Do people still behave like this today?

4 **5.32** Listen to the next part of the play. Choose the correct alternative.

1 Gwendolen has always wanted to love a man called **Ernest/Jack**.
2 She says she loves Ernest **deeply/a little**.
3 Jack says the name 'Jack' is **boring/nice**.
4 Gwendolen says she **could never/could** love someone called Jack.
5 Gwendolen says she **won't/will** marry Ernest.
6 Lady Bracknell is **happy/unhappy** to hear that they are engaged.

What do you think?

5 In pairs. Ask and answer the questions.

1 Gwendolen says she loves Ernest because of his name. What do you think of this?
2 Lady Bracknell tells Gwendolen: 'When you are engaged, it is *I* who will tell *you*.' What does this tell us about the social conventions of the time?

Writing

6 Write a review of a play or film you have seen recently. Write 100–150 words. Include this information: **T**

- title and kind of play/film
- who wrote it/directed it, and who stars in it
- the main characters and what happens
- what you liked or didn't like about it, and why

The Importance of Being Earnest

Background to the story...

The characters in this part of the play are:

Jack Worthing, a young, country gentleman

Algernon Moncrieff (Algy), Jack Worthing's friend

Cecily Cardew, an 18-year-old girl looked after by Jack Worthing

Gwendolen Fairfax, Algernon's cousin

Lady Augusta Bracknell, Algernon's aunt and Gwendolen's mother

Jack Worthing is in London visiting his friend Algy (Algernon). He has come to London to ask Gwendolen, Algy's cousin, to marry him. Gwendolen and her mother, Lady Bracknell (Algy's Aunt Augusta), are coming to visit Algy this afternoon. After Jack's last visit Algy found a cigarette case[1].

ALGERNON (*Opening the case and looking inside*) Well, what do I see here? This isn't your cigarette case.

JACK Of course it's mine!

ALGERNON (*Reading*) 'From little Cecily, with love.' You
5   don't know anyone with that name, so it can't be yours.

JACK If you really want to know, Cecily is my aunt.

ALGERNON Your aunt! So why 'little Cecily'?

JACK Well, some aunts are tall, some are not.

10 ALGERNON Yes, but why does this small aunt say 'From little Cecily, with love to her Uncle Jack'? You aren't her uncle. And your name isn't Jack, it's Ernest.

JACK It isn't Ernest, it's Jack.

ALGERNON You've always told me that it was Ernest.
15   You answer to the name of Ernest. You're the most earnest-looking person that I've ever met. Look, your name's even on your cards. (*He takes a card from the case, and reads it.*) 'Mr Ernest Worthing, B4, The Albany.'

20 JACK Well, I'm Ernest in town and Jack in the country, and I got the cigarette case in the country.

ALGERNON Ah, I knew that you were a secret Bunburyist!

JACK Bunburyist? What does Bunburyist mean?

ALGERNON I'll tell you when you have explained why you
25   are Ernest in town and Jack in the country.

JACK Then give me my cigarette case first.

ALGERNON Here. (*He gives the case, but keeps the card.*)

JACK There's nothing strange about it. Cecily Cardew is the granddaughter of Mr Thomas Cardew, who
30   adopted[2] me when I was a boy. She lives at my house in the country.

ALGERNON Oh? And where is that house?

JACK I'm not going to ask you to visit me there, Algy, so that doesn't matter. Before Mr Cardew died he made
35   me Cecily's guardian[3]. That's why she calls me uncle.

ALGERNON Well, you still haven't told me why you're Ernest in town and Jack in the country.

JACK My dear Algy, I don't think that you'll understand this, but it's important for a guardian to be serious
40   about things. It's hard for me to be serious all the time.

ALGERNON That's true. Now, go on.

JACK I need to escape to London sometimes to enjoy myself. So I pretend[4] that I have a younger brother
45   here called Ernest, who gets into terrible trouble. That's all.

ALGERNON I was right. You are a Bunburyist!

JACK What *do* you mean?

ALGERNON You pretend to have a brother Ernest in town.
50   I pretend to have a very ill friend called Bunbury, in the country. You come to town when you want, to help Ernest, and *I* leave town when I want, to visit Bunbury.

JACK Well, I'm going to kill Ernest soon. Cecily is a little
55   too interested in him.

Glossary

[1] **cigarette case**	*portasigarette*
[2] **adopt**	*adottare*
[3] **guardian**	*tutore*
[4] **pretend**	*fingere*

From *The Importance of Being Earnest*,
Oxford Bookworms Library. Retold by Susan Kingsley.

Verb tables

1 Verbo *be*

Forma affermativa		Forma negativa		Forma interrogativa	Risposte brevi	
estesa	contratta	estesa	contratta		affermative	negative
I am	I'm	I am not	I'm not	Am I?	Yes, I am.	No, I'm not.
you are	you're	you are not	you aren't	Are you?	Yes, you are.	No, you aren't.
he/she/it is	he/she/it's	he/she/it is not	he/she/it isn't	Is he/she/it?	Yes, he/she/it is.	No, he/she/it isn't.
we are	we're	we are not	we aren't	Are we?	Yes, we are.	No, we aren't.
you are	you're	you are not	you aren't	Are you?	Yes, you are.	No, you aren't.
they are	they're	they are not	they aren't	Are they?	Yes, they are.	No, they aren't.

2 Verbo *have got*

Forma affermativa		Forma negativa		Forma interrogativa	Risposte brevi	
estesa	contratta	estesa	contratta		affermative	negative
I have got	I've got	I have not got	I haven't got	Have I got?	Yes, I have.	No, I haven't.
you have got	you've got	you have not got	you haven't got	Have you got?	Yes, you have.	No, you haven't.
he/she/it has got	he/she/it's got	he/she/it has not got	he/she/it hasn't got	Has he/she/it got?	Yes, he/she/it has.	No, he/she/it hasn't.
we have got	we've got	we have not got	we haven't got	Have we got?	Yes, we have.	No, we haven't.
you have got	you've got	you have not got	you haven't got	Have you got?	Yes, you have.	No, you haven't.
they have got	they've got	they have not got	they haven't got	Have they got?	Yes, they have.	No, they haven't.

3 Present simple

Forma affermativa	Forma negativa		Forma interrogativa	Risposte brevi	
	estesa	contratta		affermative	negative
I play	I do not play	I don't play	Do I play?	Yes, I do.	No, I don't.
you play	you do not play	you don't play	Do you play?	Yes, you do.	No, you don't.
he/she/it plays	he/she/it does not play	he/she/it doesn't play	Does he/she/it play?	Yes, he/she/it does.	No, he/she/it doesn't.
we play	we do not play	we don't play	Do we play?	Yes, we do.	No, we don't.
you play	you do not play	you don't play	Do you play?	Yes, you do.	No, you don't.
they play	they do not play	they don't play	Do they play?	Yes, they do.	No, they don't.

4 Present continuous

Forma affermativa		Forma negativa		Forma interrogativa	Risposte brevi	
estesa	contratta	estesa	contratta		affermative	negative
I am eating	I'm eating	I am not eating	I'm not eating	Am I eating?	Yes, I am.	No, I'm not.
you are eating	you're eating	you are not eating	you aren't eating	Are you eating?	Yes, you are.	No, you aren't.
he/she/it is eating	he/she/it's eating	he/she/it is not eating	he/she/it isn't eating	Is he/she/it eating?	Yes, he/she/it is.	No, he/she/it isn't.
we are eating	we're eating	we are not eating	we aren't eating	Are we eating?	Yes, we are.	No, we aren't.
you are eating	you're eating	you are not eating	you aren't eating	Are you eating?	Yes, you are.	No, you aren't.
they are eating	they're eating	they are not eating	they aren't eating	Are they eating?	Yes, they are.	No, they aren't.

5 *can*

Forma affermativa	Forma negativa	Forma interrogativa	Risposte brevi	
			affermative	negative
I can	I can't	Can I?	Yes, I can.	No, I can't.
you can	you can't	Can you?	Yes, you can.	No, you can't.
he/she/it can	he/she/it can't	Can he/she/it?	Yes, he/she/it can.	No, he/she/it can't.
we can	we can't	Can we?	Yes, we can.	No, we can't.
you can	you can't	Can you?	Yes, you can.	No, you can't.
they can	they can't	Can they?	Yes, they can.	No, they can't.

6 Past simple • Verbo *be*

Forma affermativa	Forma negativa		Forma interrogativa	Risposte brevi	
	estesa	contratta		affermative	negative
I was	I was not	I wasn't	Was I?	Yes, I was.	No, I wasn't.
you were	you were not	you weren't	Were you?	Yes, you were.	No, you weren't.
he/she/it was	he/she/it was not	he/she/it wasn't	Was he/she/it?	Yes, he/she/it was.	No, he/she/it wasn't.
we were	we were not	we weren't	Were we?	Yes, we were.	No, we weren't.
you were	you were not	you weren't	Were you?	Yes, you were.	No, you weren't.
they were	they were not	they weren't	Were they?	Yes, they were.	No, they weren't.

7 Past simple • Verbi regolari

Forma affermativa	Forma negativa		Forma interrogativa	Risposte brevi	
	estesa	contratta		affermative	negative
I walked	I did not walk	I didn't walk	Did I walk?	Yes, I did.	No, I didn't.
you walked	you did not walk	you didn't walk	Did you walk?	Yes, you did.	No, you didn't.
he/she/it walked	he/she/it did not walk	he/she/it didn't walk	Did he/she/it walk?	Yes, he/she/it did.	No, he/she/it didn't.
we walked	we did not walk	we didn't walk	Did we walk?	Yes, we did.	No, we didn't.
you walked	you did not walk	you didn't walk	Did you walk?	Yes, you did.	No, you didn't.
they walked	they did not walk	they didn't walk	Did they walk?	Yes, they did.	No, they didn't.

8 Past simple • Verbi irregolari

Forma affermativa	Forma negativa		Forma interrogativa	Risposte brevi	
	estesa	contratta		affermative	negative
I went	I did not go	I didn't go	Did I go?	Yes, I did.	No, I didn't.
you went	you did not go	you didn't go	Did you go?	Yes, you did.	No, you didn't.
he/she/it went	he/she/it did not go	he/she/it didn't go	Did he/she/it go?	Yes, he/she/it did.	No, he/she/it didn't.
we went	we did not go	we didn't go	Did we go?	Yes, we did.	No, we didn't.
you went	you did not go	you didn't go	Did you go?	Yes, you did.	No, you didn't.
they went	they did not go	they didn't go	Did they go?	Yes, they did.	No, they didn't.

9 could

Forma affermativa	Forma negativa	Forma interrogativa	Risposte brevi	
			affermative	negative
I could	I couldn't	Could I?	Yes, I could.	No, I couldn't.
you could	you couldn't	Could you?	Yes, you could.	No, you couldn't.
he/she/it could	he/she/it couldn't	Could he/she/it?	Yes, he/she/it could.	No, he/she/it couldn't.
we could	we couldn't	Could we?	Yes, we could.	No, we couldn't.
you could	you couldn't	Could you?	Yes, you could.	No, you couldn't.
they could	they couldn't	Could they?	Yes, they could.	No, they couldn't.

10 be going to

Forma affermativa		Forma negativa		Forma interrogativa	Risposte brevi	
estesa	contratta	estesa	contratta		affermative	negative
I am going to leave	I'm going to leave	I am not going to leave	I'm not going to leave	Am I going to leave?	Yes, I am.	No, I'm not.
you are going to leave	you're going to leave	you are not going to leave	you aren't going to leave	Are you going to leave?	Yes, you are.	No, you aren't.
he/she/it is going to leave	he/she/it's going to leave	he/she/it is not going to leave	he/she/it isn't going to leave	Is he/she/it going to leave?	Yes, he/she/it is.	No, he/she/it isn't.
we are going to leave	we're going to leave	we are not going to leave	we aren't going to leave	Are we going to leave?	Yes, we are.	No, we aren't.
you are going to leave	you're going to leave	you are not going to leave	you aren't going to leave	Are you going to leave?	Yes, you are.	No, you aren't.
they are going to leave	they're going to leave	they are not going to leave	they aren't going to leave	Are they going to leave?	Yes, they are.	No, they aren't.

11 Present perfect simple • Verbi regolari

Forma affermativa		Forma negativa		Forma interrogativa	Risposte brevi	
estesa	contratta	estesa	contratta		affermative	negative
I have danced	I've danced	I have not danced	I haven't danced	Have I danced?	Yes, I have.	No, I haven't.
you have danced	you've danced	you have not danced	you haven't danced	Have you danced?	Yes, you have.	No, you haven't.
he/she/it has danced	he/she/it's danced	he/she/it has not danced	he/she/it hasn't danced	Has he/she/it danced?	Yes, he/she/it has.	No, he/she/it hasn't.
we have danced	we've danced	we have not danced	we haven't danced	Have we danced?	Yes, we have.	No, we haven't.
you have danced	you've danced	you have not danced	you haven't danced	Have you danced?	Yes, you have.	No, you haven't.
they have danced	they've danced	they have not danced	they haven't danced	Have they danced?	Yes, they have.	No, they haven't.

12 Present perfect simple • Verbi irregolari

Forma affermativa		Forma negativa		Forma interrogativa	Risposte brevi	
estesa	contratta	estesa	contratta		affermative	negative
I have seen	I've seen	I have not seen	I haven't seen	Have I seen?	Yes, I have.	No, I haven't.
you have seen	you've seen	you have not seen	you haven't seen	Have you seen?	Yes, you have.	No, you haven't.
he/she/it has seen	he/she/it's seen	he/she/it has not seen	he/she/it hasn't seen	Has he/she/it seen?	Yes, he/she/it has.	No, he/she/it hasn't.
we have seen	we've seen	we have not seen	we haven't seen	Have we seen?	Yes, we have.	No, we haven't.
you have seen	you've seen	you have not seen	you haven't seen	Have you seen?	Yes, you have.	No, you haven't.
they have seen	they've seen	they have not seen	they haven't seen	Have they seen?	Yes, they have.	No, they haven't.

Pronunciation guide

Single vowels

/ɪ/	big	/bɪg/
/iː/	street	/striːt/
/i/	happy	/'hæpi/
/ʊ/	book	/bʊk/
/uː/	moon	/muːn/
/u/	situation	/ˌsɪtʃu'eɪʃn/
/e/	ten	/ten/
/ə/	around	/ə'raʊnd/
/ɜː/	girl	/gɜːl/
/ɔː/	horse	/hɔːs/
/æ/	hat	/hæt/
/ʌ/	up	/ʌp/
/ɑː/	car	/kɑː(r)/
/ɒ/	clock	/klɒk/

Diphthongs (Combined vowels)

/ɪə/	ear	/ɪə(r)/
/eɪ/	say	/seɪ/
/ʊə/	pure	/pjʊə(r)/
/ɔɪ/	boy	/bɔɪ/
/əʊ/	phone	/fəʊn/
/eə/	chair	/tʃeə(r)/
/aɪ/	why	/waɪ/
/aʊ/	now	/naʊ/

Consonants

/b/	bag	/bæg/
/k/	cat, key	/kæt, kiː/
/tʃ/	champion	/'tʃæmpiən/
/d/	dog	/dɒg/
/f/	fast	/fɑːst/
/g/	get	/get/
/h/	happy	/'hæpi/
/dʒ/	jazz, generation	/dʒæz, ˌdʒenə'reɪʃn/
/l/	live	/lɪv/
/m/	mouse	/maʊs/
/n/	number	/'nʌmbə(r)/
/p/	pen	/pen/
/r/	red	/red/
/s/	see	/siː/
/ʃ/	shop	/ʃɒp/
/ʒ/	pleasure	/'pleʒə(r)/
/t/	top	/tɒp/
/θ/	thin	/θɪn/
/ð/	that	/ðæt/
/v/	voice	/vɔɪs/
/w/	wear	/weə(r)/
/j/	yes	/jes/
/z/	zero	/'zɪərəʊ/
/ŋ/	song	/sɒŋ/

Punctuation guide

A	capital letter
a	lower case
.	full stop (AmE: period)
,	comma
;	semicolon
:	colon
'	apostrophe
?	question mark
!	exclamation mark (AmE: exclamation point)
-	hyphen
–	dash
...	dots/ellipsis
/	forward slash
\	back slash
" " ' '	quotation/speech marks (AmE: " " used more)
( )	brackets (AmE: parentheses; formal)
[ ]	square brackets (AmE: brackets; formal)
aaa	italics
aaa	bold
&	ampersand (= and)
*	asterisk
#	hash sign
@	'at'

Irregular verb list

Base form	Past simple	Past participle
be /bi/	was, were /wəz, wɒz, wə(r), wɜ:(r)/	been /bɪn, bi:n/
become /bɪˈkʌm/	became /bɪˈkeɪm/	become /bɪˈkʌm/
begin /bɪˈgɪn/	began /bɪˈgæn/	begun /bɪˈgʌn/
bet /bet/	bet /bet/	bet /bet/
bite /baɪt/	bit /bɪt/	bitten /ˈbɪtn/
bleed /bli:d/	bled /bled/	bled /bled/
blow /bləʊ/	blew /blu:/	blown /bləʊn/
break /breɪk/	broke /brəʊk/	broken /ˈbrəʊkən/
bring /brɪŋ/	brought /brɔ:t/	brought /brɔ:t/
build /bɪld/	built /bɪlt/	built /bɪlt/
burn /bɜ:n/	burnt, burned /bɜ:nt, bɜ:nd/	burnt, burned /bɜ:nt, bɜ:nd/
buy /baɪ/	bought /bɔ:t/	bought /bɔ:t/
can /kən, kæn/	could /kəd, kʊd/	been able to /bi:n ˈeɪbl tə/
catch /kætʃ/	caught /kɔ:t/	caught /kɔ:t/
choose /tʃu:z/	chose /tʃəʊz/	chosen /ˈtʃəʊzn/
come /kʌm/	came /keɪm/	come /kʌm/
cost /kɒst/	cost /kɒst/	cost /kɒst/
cut /kʌt/	cut /kʌt/	cut /kʌt/
deal /di:l/	dealt /delt/	dealt /delt/
do /də, du/	did /dɪd/	done /dʌn/
draw /drɔ:/	drew /dru:/	drawn /drɔ:n/
dream /dri:m/	dreamt, dreamed /dremt, dri:md/	dreamt, dreamed /dremt, dri:md/
drink /drɪŋk/	drank /dræŋk/	drunk /drʌŋk/
drive /draɪv/	drove /drəʊv/	driven /ˈdrɪvn/
eat /i:t/	ate /eɪt, et/	eaten /ˈi:tn/
fall /fɔ:l/	fell /fel/	fallen /ˈfɔ:lən/
feel /fi:l/	felt /felt/	felt /felt/
fight /faɪt/	fought /fɔ:t/	fought /fɔ:t/
find /faɪnd/	found /faʊnd/	found /faʊnd/
fly /flaɪ/	flew /flu:/	flown /fləʊn/
forget /fəˈget/	forgot /fəˈgɒt/	forgotten /fəˈgɒtn/
forgive /fəˈgɪv/	forgave /fəˈgeɪv/	forgiven /fəˈgɪvn/
freeze /fri:z/	froze /frəʊz/	frozen /ˈfrəʊzn/
get /get/	got /gɒt/	got (AmE: gotten) /gɒt, ˈgɒtn/
give /gɪv/	gave /geɪv/	given /ˈgɪvn/
go /gəʊ/	went /went/	gone, been /gɒn, bi:n/
grow /grəʊ/	grew /gru:/	grown /grəʊn/
hang /hæŋ/	hung /hʌŋ/	hung /hʌŋ/
have /həv, hæv/	had /həd, hæd/	had /hæd/
hear /hɪə(r)/	heard /hɜ:d/	heard /hɜ:d/
hide /haɪd/	hid /hɪd/	hidden /ˈhɪdn/
hit /hɪt/	hit /hɪt/	hit /hɪt/
hold /həʊld/	held /held/	held /held/
hurt /hɜ:t/	hurt /hɜ:t/	hurt /hɜ:t/
keep /ki:p/	kept /kept/	kept /kept/
know /nəʊ/	knew /nju:/	known /nəʊn/
lay /leɪ/	laid /leɪd/	laid /leɪd/
lead /li:d/	led /led/	led /led/
learn /lɜ:n/	learnt, learned /lɜ:nt, lɜ:nd/	learnt, learned /lɜ:nt, lɜ:nd/
leave /li:v/	left /left/	left /left/

Base form	Past simple	Past participle
lend /lend/	lent /lent/	lent /lent/
let /let/	let /let/	let /let/
light /laɪt/	lit /lɪt/	lit /lɪt/
lose /luːz/	lost /lɒst/	lost /lɒst/
make /meɪk/	made /meɪd/	made /meɪd/
mean /miːn/	meant /ment/	meant /ment/
meet /miːt/	met /met/	met /met/
pay /peɪ/	paid /peɪd/	paid /peɪd/
put /pʊt/	put /pʊt/	put /pʊt/
read /riːd/	read /red/	read /red/
ride /raɪd/	rode /rəʊd/	ridden /'rɪdn/
ring /rɪŋ/	rang /ræŋ/	rung /rʌŋ/
rise /raɪz/	rose /rəʊz/	risen /'rɪzn/
run /rʌn/	ran /ræn/	run /rʌn/
say /seɪ/	said /sed/	said /sed/
see /siː/	saw /sɔː/	seen /siːn/
sell /sel/	sold /səʊld/	sold /səʊld/
send /send/	sent /sent/	sent /sent/
set /set/	set /set/	set /set/
shake /ʃeɪk/	shook /ʃʊk/	shaken /'ʃeɪkən/
shine /ʃaɪn/	shone /ʃɒn/	shone /ʃɒn/
shoot /ʃuːt/	shot /ʃɒt/	shot /ʃɒt/
show /ʃəʊ/	showed /ʃəʊd/	shown /ʃəʊn/
shut /ʃʌt/	shut /ʃʌt/	shut /ʃʌt/
sing /sɪŋ/	sang /sæŋ/	sung /sʌŋ/
sink /sɪŋk/	sank /sæŋk/	sunk /sʌŋk/
sit /sɪt/	sat /sæt/	sat /sæt/
sleep /sliːp/	slept /slept/	slept /slept/
smell /smel/	smelt, smelled /smelt, smeld/	smelt, smelled /smelt, smeld/
speak /spiːk/	spoke /spəʊk/	spoken /'spəʊkən/
spell /spel/	spelt, spelled /spelt, speld/	spelt, spelled /spelt, speld/
spend /spend/	spent /spent/	spent /spent/
spill /spɪl/	spilt, spilled /spɪlt/	spilt, spilled /spɪlt/
split /splɪt/	split /splɪt/	split /splɪt/
spoil /spɔɪl/	spoilt, spoiled /spɔɪlt, spɔɪld/	spoilt, spoiled /spɔɪlt, spɔɪld/
spread /spred/	spread /spred/	spread /spred/
stand /stænd/	stood /stʊd/	stood /stʊd/
steal /stiːl/	stole /stəʊl/	stolen /'stəʊlən/
stick /stɪk/	stuck /stʌk/	stuck /stʌk/
swim /swɪm/	swam /swæm/	swum /swʌm/
take /teɪk/	took /tʊk/	taken /'teɪkən/
teach /tiːtʃ/	taught /tɔːt/	taught /tɔːt/
tell /tel/	told /təʊld/	told /təʊld/
think /θɪŋk/	thought /θɔːt/	thought /θɔːt/
throw /θrəʊ/	threw /θruː/	thrown /θrəʊn/
understand /ˌʌndə'stænd/	understood /ˌʌndə'stʊd/	understood /ˌʌndə'stʊd/
upset /ʌp'set/	upset /ʌp'set/	upset /ʌp'set/
wake /weɪk/	woke /wəʊk/	woken /'wəʊkən/
wear /weə(r)/	wore /wɔː(r)/	worn /wɔːn/
win /wɪn/	won /wʌn/	won /wʌn/
write /raɪt/	wrote /rəʊt/	written /'rɪtn/

Real talk

Starter

Am I right?	Giusto?
absolutely gorgeous	davvero bellissima
Careful!	Attenta!
Good luck!	Buona fortuna!
Honestly!	Insomma!
I'm in agony!	Mi fa malissimo!
I'm really sorry	Mi dispiace tantissimo
Of course	Certo
Oh dear!	Accidenti!
Pleased to meet you	Piacere (di conoscerti)
really cool!	ganzo!
Right	Allora
She's gorgeous!	È bellissima!
She's got a date	Ha un appuntamento
Sign here	Firma qui
Turn off your mobiles	Spegnete i cellulari
unfriendly	antipatico
Well done!	Bravo!
Wicked!	Bello!/Forte!
Your house looks amazing	la tua casa è bellissima

Unit 1

an only child	figlio unico
as usual	come al solito
Fancy a drink?	Ti va qualcosa da bere?
Give them a ring	Chiamali
Lucky you!	Beata te!
Who cares!	Che importa!
You're boring	Sei noioso
You're so messy!	Sei così disordinato!

Unit 2

By the way	A proposito
going to gigs	andare ai concerti
He's obsessed with...	È fissato con...
Hi, you guys!	Ciao, ragazzi!
I'll introduce you	Te li presento
I've got to go	Devo andare
Ignore him!	Non dargli retta!

Unit 3

Besides,...	E comunque,...
Come on!	Dai!
I'm fed up	Sono stufo
It's got to nothing to do with you	Non ti riguarda
It's worth it.	Ne vale la pena.
under pressure	sotto pressione

Unit 4

Come off it	Smettila
I see	Ho capito
I'm sorry to bother you	Mi dispiace disturbarLa
Is he getting on OK with..?	Va d'accordo con...?
It's just that...	È solo che...
What's the matter?	Che c'è?

Unit 5

Actually,...	A dire il vero,...
Don't be pathetic!	Non fare il patetico!
Hang on	Aspetta un attimo
I'm off!	Me ne vado!
See you later!	Ci vediamo dopo!
That's fantastic news!	Che bella notizia!

Unit 6

as far as	fino a
Check out	Dai un'occhiata a
I bet	Scommetto che
I think I've got that	Credo di aver capito
I'm dying to see you!	Non vedo l'ora di vederti!
Mind you,...	Però,.../Detto questo,...
You can't miss it	Non può sbagliarsi

Unit 7

Good point	È vero
I'm starving	Sto morendo di fame
One more thing	Un'ultima cosa
Shame about the weather	Peccato per il tempo
What do you fancy?	Che cosa ti va?
What's wrong with it?	Che cosa ha che non va?
You're right there	Hai proprio ragione

Unit 8

Here he comes	Eccolo
How did you get on...?	Come è andata...?
I'll have...	Prendo...
Poor thing	Poverino
What was Luca like?	Com'era Luca?

Unit 9

definitely the best	decisamente il migliore
I didn't hang around	Non sono rimasta
It was tough	È stato difficile
Not bad at all!	Mica male!
You're so lucky	Sei così fortunato

Unit 10

He's a good laugh	È divertente
I mean	Voglio dire
I'm gutted!	Sono distrutto!
loads of people	un sacco di gente
Oh, yes he is!	Sì che lo è!
What makes you think that?	Cosa te lo fa pensare?
What's up with him?	Che cos'ha?

Unit 11

a warm welcome	un benvenuto caloroso
Be honest	Dimmi la verità
Here you are	Ecco qua
I can't make my mind up	Non riesco a decidermi
It's a rip-off	Costa di più di quanto vale
Seeing as...	Visto che...
You haven't got a clue about...	Non hai la più pallida idea di...

Unit 12

Get off!	Giù le mani!/Vai via!
Here we go	Ci risiamo
What's going on?	Che cosa sta succedendo?
What's it for?	Per cos'è?
Where on earth...?	Dove diavolo...?

Unit 13

Get a move on!	Sbrigati!
I can't wait...	Non vedo l'ora...
...is really full	È veramente pieno
...is really getting me down!	... mi sta buttando giù di morale!
That's not fair!	Non è giusto!

Unit 14

Just joking	Stavo solo scherzando
on my own	da solo
Right! But like what?	Sì, ma che cosa?
Sounds like...	Sembra...
That's the whole idea	È proprio questo lo scopo
You can't be serious!	Non parli mica sul serio?
You look a bit upset	Sembri un po' giù

Unit 15

a bit shaken up	un po' scosso
That stupid dog	Quello stupido di un cane
What is it?	Che c'è che non va?
You've got ages	Hai un sacco di tempo

Glossary

A

- **(1) am** (abbr) /(ˌwʌn) ˌeɪ 'em/ (l'una) di mattina
- **(6) pm** (abbr) /(ˌsɪks) ˌpiː 'em/ (le sei) del pomeriggio; della sera
- **a (week)** (phr) /ə 'wiːk/ a/per (settimana)
- **abandon** (v) /ə'bændən/ abbandonare
- **about** (prep) /ə'baʊt/ circa
- **above** (prep) /ə'bʌv/ sopra
- **above all** (adv) /ə,bʌv 'ɔːl/ soprattutto
- **abroad** (adv) /ə'brɔːd/ all'estero
- **absolutely** (adv) /'æbsəluːtli/ assolutamente, decisamente
- **accent** (n) /'æksent, 'æksənt/ accento
- **accept** (v) /ək'sept/ accettare
- **access** (n) /'ækses/ accesso
- **access** (v) /'ækses/ accedere
- **accessory** (n) /ək'sesəri/ accessorio
- **accident** (n) /'æksɪdənt/ incidente
- **accommodation** (n) /əkɒmə'deɪʃn/ alloggio, sistemazione
- **according to** (prep) /ə'kɔːdɪŋ tə/ secondo, a detta di
- **accordion** (n) /ə'kɔːdiən/ fisarmonica
- **aches and pains** (phr) /ˌeɪks ən 'peɪnz/ avere dolori dappertutto, essere pieno di dolori
- **across** (prep) /ə'krɒs/ attraverso
- **action** (n) /'ækʃn/ azione
- **activity** (n) /æk'tɪvəti/ attività
- **actor** (n) /'æktə(r)/ attore
- **actress** (n) /'æktrəs/ attrice
- **actually** (adv) /'æktʃuəli/ effettivamente
- **administrative** (adj) /əd'mɪnɪstrətɪv/ amministrativo
- **admission** (n) /əd'mɪʃn/ ingresso
- **adult** (n) /'ædʌlt/ adulto
- **advance: in advance** (adv) /ˌɪn əd'vɑːns/ in anticipo
- **advantage** (n) /əd'vɑːntɪdʒ/ vantaggio
- **adventure** (n) /əd'ventʃə(r)/ avventura
- **adventure holiday** (n) /əd'ventʃə ˌhɒlədeɪ/ vacanza di avventura
- **adventure park** (n) /əd'ventʃə pɑːk/ parco avventura
- **advert** (n) /'ædvɜːt/ pubblicità, annuncio pubblicitario
- **advertisement** (n) /əd'vɜːtɪsmənt/ pubblicità
- **advice** (n) /əd'vaɪs/ consiglio
- **aerobatics** (n) /ˌeərə'bætɪks/ acrobazie aeree
- **after** (prep) /'ɑːftə(r)/ dopo

- **after: named after** (phr) /'neɪmd ˌɑːftə/ chiamato col nome di
- **afternoon: in the afternoon** (phr) /ˌɪn ðɪ ɑːftə'nuːn/ del pomeriggio, di pomeriggio
- **afterwards** (adv) /'ɑːftəwədz/ dopo
- **again** (adv) /ə'gen/ di nuovo
- **again and again** (phr) /əˌgen ən ə'gen/ più volte
- **against** (prep) /ə'genst/ contro
- **age** (n) /eɪdʒ/ età
- **agency** (n) /'eɪdʒənsi/ agenzia
- **aggressive** (adj) /ə'gresɪv/ aggressivo
- **ago: (a week) ago** (adv) /(ə 'wiːk) ə,gəʊ/ (una settimana) fa
- **agree (with)** (v) /ə'griː ˌwɪð/ essere d'accordo (con)
- **air** (n) /eə(r)/ aria
- **air transport** (n) /'eə ˌtrænspɔːt/ trasporto aereo
- **airport** (n) /'eəpɔːt/ aeroporto
- **alive** (adj) /ə'laɪv/ vivo
- **all** (pron) /ɔːl/ tutto
- **all over** (prep) /ˌɔːl ˌəʊvə(r)/ in tutto
- **all right** (phr) /ˌɔːl 'raɪt/ d'accordo
- **almost** (adv) /'ɔːlməʊst/ quasi
- **alone** (adj) /ə'ləʊn/ da solo
- **along: go along (High Street)** (phr) /ˌgəʊ ə,lɒŋ ('haɪ ˌstriːt)/ percorri (High Street)
- **already** (adv) /ɔːl'redi/ già
- **also** (adv) /'ɔːlsəʊ/ anche
- **although** (conj) /ɔːl'ðəʊ/ sebbene
- **altogether** (adv) /ˌɔːltə'geðə(r)/ in tutto
- **always** (adv) /'ɔːlweɪz/ sempre
- **amazing** (adj) /ə'meɪzɪŋ/ grandioso
- **amazingly** (adv) /ə'meɪzɪŋli/ sorprendentemente
- **ambitious** (adj) /æm'bɪʃəs/ ambizioso
- **among** (prep) /ə'mʌŋ/ tra, fra
- **and** (conj) /ænd, ənd/ e
- **angry** (adj) /'æŋgri/ arrabbiato
- **animal** (n) /'ænɪml/ animale
- **annoyed** (adj) /ə'nɔɪd/ seccato, irritato
- **annoying** (adj) /ə'nɔɪɪŋ/ seccante, irritante
- **anorak** (n) /'ænəræk/ giacca a vento
- **another** (det) /ə'nʌðə(r)/ un altro
- **answer** (n) /'ɑːnsə(r)/ risposta
- **answer** (v) /'ɑːnsə(r)/ rispondere
- **antenna** (n) /æn'tenə/ antenna
- **antique** (adj) /æn'tiːk/ d'antiquariato
- **anxious** (adj) /'æŋkʃəs/ in ansia, preoccupato
- **any** (det) /'eni/ nessuno; qualche; del
- **any more: not... any more** (adv) /ˌeni 'mɔː(r)/ non... più
- **anything: (I didn't say) anything** (pron) /(ˌaɪ ˌdɪdnt 'seɪ) ˌeniθɪŋ/ (non ho detto) niente
- **anyway** (interj) /'eniweɪ/ comunque
- **apart from** (prep) /ə'pɑːt frəm/ a parte
- **apologize** (v) /ə'pɒlədʒaɪz/ scusarsi
- **apology** (n) /ə'pɒlədʒi/ scuse
- **apparently** (adv) /ə'pærəntli/ apparentemente
- **appearance** (n) /ə'pɪərəns/ aspetto
- **apple** (n) /'æpl/ mela
- **applicant** (n) /'æplɪkənt/ candidato
- **application** (n) /ˌæplɪ'keɪʃn/ applicazione
- **apply** (v) /ə'plaɪ/ fare domanda
- **appointment** (n) /ə'pɔɪntmənt/ appuntamento
- **appropriate** (adj) /ə'prəʊpriət/ appropriato
- **approximately** (adv) /ə'prɒksɪmətli/ approssimativamente
- **April** (n) /'eɪprəl/ aprile
- **April Fool's Day** (n) /ˌeɪprəl 'fuːlz ˌdeɪ/ il primo d'aprile
- **archipelago** (n) /ˌɑːkɪ'peləgəʊ/ arcipelago
- **area** (n) /'eəriə/ area
- **argue** (v) /'ɑːgjuː/ litigare
- **argument** (n) /'ɑːgjumənt/ litigio
- **arm** (n) /ɑːm/ braccio
- **armchair** (n) /'ɑːmtʃeə(r)/ poltrona
- **around** (prep) /ə'raʊnd/ (in giro) per; intorno a, circa, verso (+ ora)
- **arrival** (n) /ə'raɪvl/ arrivo
- **arrive** (v) /ə'raɪv/ arrivare
- **art** (n) /ɑːt/ arte
- **art gallery** (n) /'ɑːt ˌgæləri/ galleria d'arte

- **arthritis** (n) /ɑː'θraɪtɪs/ artrite
- **article** (n) /'ɑːtɪkl/ articolo
- **as** (conj) /æz, əz/ come
- **as for** (conj) /'æz fə(r)/ per quanto riguarda, in quanto a
- **ask** (v) /ɑːsk/ chiedere
- **aspect** (n) /'æspekt/ aspetto; angolo, punto di vista
- **associate** (v) /ə'səʊʃieɪt, -sieɪt/ associare
- **astronomy** (n) /ə'strɒnəmi/ astronomia
- **at** (prep) /æt, ət/ a
- **at all** (adv) /ət 'ɔːl/ affatto
- **athlete** (n) /'æθliːt/ atleta
- **athletics** (n) /æθ'letɪks/ atletica
- **attachment** (n) /ə'tætʃmənt/ allegato
- **attendant** (n) /ə'tendənt/ addetto
- **attraction** (n) /ə'trækʃn/ attrazione
- **auction** (n) /'ɔːkʃn/ asta
- **audience** (n) /'ɔːdiəns/ pubblico
- **audition** (v) /ɔː'dɪʃn/ fare un provino
- **August** (n) /'ɔːgəst/ agosto
- **aunt** (n) /ɑːnt/ zia
- **auntie** (n) /'ɑːnti/ zia
- **authentic** (adj) /ɔː'θentɪk/ autentico
- **author** (n) /'ɔːθə(r)/ autore
- **authority** (n) /ɔː'θɒrəti/ autorità
- **autumn** (n) /'ɔːtəm/ autunno
- **average** (adj) /'ævərɪdʒ/ medio
- **avoid** (v) /ə'vɔɪd/ evitare
- **award-winning** (adj) /ə'wɔːd ˌwɪnɪŋ/ premiato
- **awareness: raise awareness** (phr) /ˌreɪz ə'weənəs/ sensibilizzare
- **away: Go away!** (phr) /ˌgəʊ ə'weɪ/ Va' via!
- **awful** (adj) /'ɔːfl/ orribile

B

- **B&B (bed and breakfast)** (n) /ˌbiː ən 'biː, ˌbed ən 'brekfəst/ bed and breakfast
- **baby: baby boy** (n) /'beɪbi, ˌbeɪbi 'bɔɪ/ maschietto, bambino, neonato
- **back (to the UK)** (adv) /ˌbæk (tə ðə ˌjuː 'keɪ)/ tornato (in Gran Bretagno)
- **background** (n) /'bækgraʊnd/ sfondo
- **bacon** (n) /'beɪkən/ pancetta
- **bad** (adj) /bæd/ cattivo
- **bad for you** (phr) /ˌbæd fə ˌjuː/ dannoso, malsano
- **badge** (n) /bædʒ/ simbolo, emblema
- **badly** (adv) /'bædli/ male, malamente
- **badly: do badly** (phr) /ˌduː 'bædli/ andare male
- **bag** (n) /bæg/ borsa
- **bagpipes** (n) /'bægpaɪps/ cornamusa
- **baked beans** (n) /ˌbeɪkt 'biːnz/ fagioli al forno in salsa di pomodoro
- **baker's** (n) /'beɪkəz/ panificio
- **ball** (n) /bɔːl/ palla
- **banana** (n) /bə'nɑːnə/ banana
- **band** (n) /bænd/ gruppo musicale
- **Bangladesh** (n) /ˌbæŋglə'deʃ/ Bangladesh
- **bank** (n) /bæŋk/ banca
- **bar** (n) /bɑː(r)/ bar
- **bar: chocolate bar** (n) /'tʃɒklət ˌbɑː(r)/ barretta di cioccolato
- **barman** (n) /'bɑːmən/ barista
- **barrier** (n) /'bæriə(r)/ cancello
- **basically** (adv) /'beɪsɪkli/ in pratica, praticamente
- **basics** (n) /'beɪsɪks/ alimenti di base
- **basis** (n) /'beɪsɪs/ base
- **basketball** (n) /'bɑːskɪtbɔːl/ basket, pallacanestro
- **bat** (n) /bæt/ pipistrello
- **bath** (n) /bɑːθ/ bagno
- **bath: have a bath** (phr) /ˌhæv ə 'bɑːθ/ fare il bagno
- **bathroom** (n) /'bɑːθruːm/ bagno
- **battle** (n) /'bætl/ battaglia
- **beach** (n) /biːtʃ/ spiaggia
- **beard** (n) /bɪəd/ barba
- **beautiful** (adj) /'bjuːtɪfl/ bello
- **because** (conj) /bɪ'kɒz/ perché
- **become** (v) /bɪ'kʌm/ diventare
- **bed** (n) /bed/ letto

bedroom (n) /'bedru:m/ camera da letto

beef (n) /bi:f/ manzo

beer (n) /bɪə(r)/ birra

before (prep) /bɪ'fɔ:(r)/ prima di

begin (v) /bɪ'gɪn/ cominciare

behind (prep) /bɪ'haɪnd/ dietro

believe (v) /bɪ'li:v/ credere

belong to (v) /bɪ'lɒŋ ,tu:, tə/ appartenere a

below (prep) /bɪ'ləʊ/ sotto

berry (n) /'beri/ bacca

Besides (interj) /bɪ'saɪdz/ E comunque

best (adj) /best/ (il) migliore

better (adj) /'betə(r)/ migliore

between (prep) /bɪ'twi:n/ tra

bicycle (n) /'baɪsɪkl/ bicicletta

big (adj) /bɪg/ grande

bike (n) /baɪk/ bicicletta

bill (n) /bɪl/ conto

Biology (n) /baɪ'ɒlədʒi/ biologia

birthday (n) /'bɜ:θdeɪ/ compleanno

biscuit (n) /'bɪskɪt/ biscotto

bit (n) /bɪt/ parte

bit: a bit (adv) /ə 'bɪt/ un po'

bizarre (adj) /bɪ'zɑ:(r)/ bizzarro

black (adj) /blæk/ nero

blackboard (n) /'blækbɔ:d/ lavagna

blazer (n) /'bleɪzə(r)/ giacca sportiva

blister (n) /'blɪstə(r)/ vescica, bolla

blond(e) (adj) /blɒnd/ biondo

blow (v) /bləʊ/ soffiare

blue (adj) /blu:/ blu

blueberry (n) /'blu:bəri/ mirtillo

boat (n) /bəʊt/ barca

body (n) /'bɒdi/ corpo

boiled (adj) /bɔɪld/ bollito

boiling hot (adj) /,bɔɪlɪŋ 'hɒt/ caldo infernale

bolt (n) /bəʊlt/ fulmine

book (n) /bʊk/ libro

book (v) /bʊk/ prenotare

bookcase (n) /'bʊkkeɪs/ libreria

bookshop (n) /'bʊkʃɒp/ libreria, negozio di libri

boots (n) /bu:ts/ stivali

bored (adj) /bɔ:d/ annoiato

bored: get bored (phr) /,get 'bɔ:d/ annoiarsi

boring (adj) /'bɔ:rɪŋ/ noioso; banale

born: be born (v) /,bi 'bɔ:n/ nascere

borrow (v) /'bɒrəʊ/ prendere in prestito

bottle (n) /'bɒtl/ bottiglia

bottom (n) /'bɒtəm/ fondo; sedere

bottom: at the bottom of (prep) /ət ðə 'bɒtəm əv/ nel fondo di

bowl (n) /bəʊl/ tazza, scodella

bowling: go bowling (phr) /,gəʊ 'bəʊlɪŋ/ andare a giocare a bowling

box (n) /bɒks/ scatola

boy (n) /bɔɪ/ ragazzo

boyfriend (n) /'bɔɪfrend/ ragazzo, fidanzato

brain (n) /breɪn/ cervello

brand (n) /brænd/ marca, marchio

Brazil (n) /brə'zɪl/ Brasile

bread (n) /bred/ pane

break (n) /breɪk/ pausa

break (v) /breɪk/ rompere

break down (v) /,breɪk 'daʊn/ guastarsi

breakfast (n) /'brekfəst/ colazione

bridge (n) /brɪdʒ/ ponte

brilliant (adj) /'brɪliənt/ fantastico; brillante

Britain (n) /'brɪtn/ Gran Bretagna

British (adj) /'brɪtɪʃ/ britannico

British Isles (n) /,brɪtɪʃ 'aɪlz/ Isole Britanniche

broadband (n) /'brɔ:dbænd/ banda larga

broken (adj) /'brəʊkən/ rotto

brother (n) /'brʌðə(r)/ fratello

brother-in-law (n) /'brʌðər ,ɪn ,lɔ:/ cognato

brown (adj) /braʊn/ marrone

brush (my) teeth (phr) /,brʌʃ (,maɪ) 'ti:θ/ lavar(mi) i denti

build (n) /bɪld/ costituzione

build (v) /bɪld/ costruire

building (n) /'bɪldɪŋ/ edificio

bully (n) /'bʊli/ bullo

bully (v) /'bʊli/ fare il bullo con

burger (n) /'bɜ:gə(r)/ hamburger

burn (v) /bɜ:n/ ustione

bus (n) /bʌs/ autobus

bus stop (n) /'bʌs ,stɒp/ fermata dell'autobus

bus/coach station (n) /'bʌs ,kəʊtʃ ,steɪʃn/ stazione degli autobus/dei pullman

bus: on the bus home (phr) /,ɒn ðə ,bʌs 'həʊm/ sul pullman/sull'autobus di ritorno a casa

busk (v) /bʌsk/ fare l'artista di strada

busker (n) /'bʌskə(r)/ artista di strada

busking (n) /'bʌskɪŋ/ fare l'artista di strada

busy (adj) /'bɪzi/ indaffarato; affollato

but (conj) /bʌt, bət/ ma

butter (n) /'bʌtə(r)/ burro

buy (v) /baɪ/ comprare

by the way (phr) /,baɪ ðə 'weɪ/ incidentalmente

by: go by (plane) (prep) /,gəʊ ,baɪ ('pleɪn)/ viaggiare in (aereo)

C

café (n) /'kæfeɪ/ bar

cake (n) /keɪk/ torta

call (v) /kɔ:l/ chiamare

calm (adj) /kɑ:m/ calmo

camera (n) /'kæmərə/ macchina fotografica

camper van (n) /'kæmpə ,væn/ camper

campsite (n) /'kæmpsaɪt/ campeggio

can (n) /kæn/ lattina

can/can't (v) /kæn, kɑ:nt/ potere/non potere

can't stand (phr) /,kɑ:nt 'stænd/ non sopportare

cancer (n) /'kænsə(r)/ cancro

canteen (n) /kæn'ti:n/ mensa

capsule (n) /'kæpsju:l/ cabina

car (n) /kɑ:(r)/ macchina

car boot sale (n) /,kɑ:(r) bu:t seɪl/ vendita all'aperto di oggetti usati

car park (n) /'kɑ: ,pɑ:k/ parcheggio

carbon dioxide (n) /,kɑ:bən daɪ'ɒksaɪd/ anidride carbonica

care: Who cares? (phr) /'hu: ,keəz/ Che importa?

carrot (n) /'kærət/ carota

carry (v) /'kæri/ portare, trasportare

carton (n) /'kɑ:tn/ cartone, confezione

cartoon (n) /kɑ:'tu:n/ cartone animato

case (n) /keɪs/ caso

cash desk (n) /'kæʃ ,desk/ cassa

cassette (n) /kə'set/ cassetta

cassette player (n) /kə'set ,pleɪə(r)/ mangiacassette

castle (n) /'kɑ:sl/ castello

casual (adj) /'kæʒuəl/ informale

cat (n) /kæt/ gatto

catch (a plane) (v) /,kætʃ (ə 'pleɪn)/ prendere l'aereo

cathedral (n) /kə'θi:drəl/ cattedrale

cause (n) /kɔ:z/ causa

cause (v) /kɔ:z/ causare

cautious (adj) /'kɔ:ʃəs/ prudente

ceiling (n) /'si:lɪŋ/ soffitto

celebrate (v) /'selɪbreɪt/ festeggiare

celebrity (n) /sə'lebrəti/ celebrità

cellar (n) /'selə(r)/ scantinato

central (adj) /'sentrəl/ centrale

centre (n) /'sentə(r)/ centro

century (n) /'sentʃəri/ secolo

cereal (n) /'sɪəriəl/ cereali

certainly (adv) /'sɜ:tnli/ certamente

chair (n) /tʃeə(r)/ sedia

chamber (n) /'tʃeɪmbə(r)/ camera

champion (n) /'tʃæmpiən/ campione

chance (n) /tʃɑ:ns/ possibilità

change (n) /tʃeɪndʒ/ cambiamento

change (v) /tʃeɪndʒ/ cambiare

changeable (adj) /'tʃeɪndʒəbl/ variabile

charismatic (adj) /,kæriz'mætɪk/ carismatico

charity (n) /'tʃærəti/ beneficenza

chat show (n) /'tʃæt ,ʃəʊ/ talk show

chat: have a chat (phr) /,hæv ə 'tʃæt/ chiacchierare, fare una chiacchierata

cheap (adj) /tʃi:p/ economico

check (v) /tʃek/ controllare

cheerful (adj) /'tʃɪəfl/ allegro

cheese (n) /tʃi:z/ formaggio

cheesy (adj) /'tʃi:zi/ al formaggio

chemist's (n) /'kemɪsts/ farmacia

Chemistry (n) /'kemɪstri/ chimica

chest (n) /tʃest/ petto

chicken (n) /'tʃɪkɪn/ pollo

child/children (n) /tʃaɪld, 'tʃɪldrən/ bambino, figlio/ bambini, figli

China (n) /'tʃaɪnə/ Cina

Chinese (adj) /tʃaɪ'ni:z/ cinese

chocolate (n) /'tʃɒklət/ cioccolata; cioccolatini

choose (v) /tʃu:z/ scegliere

church (n) /tʃɜ:tʃ/ chiesa

cigarette (n) /,sɪgə'ret/ sigaretta

cinema (n) /'sɪnəmə/ cinema

Citizenship (n) /'sɪtɪznʃɪp/ cittadinanza

city (n) /'sɪti/ città

civilized (adj) /'sɪvəlaɪzd/ civile

class: evening classes (n) /'i:vnɪŋ ,klɑ:sɪz/ corso serale

classroom (n) /'klɑ:sru:m/ classe

clean (adj) /kli:n/ pulito

cleaning product (n) /'kli:nɪŋ 'prɒdʌkt/ prodotto per le pulizie

clean (up) (v) /,kli:n ('ʌp)/ pulire

clear the table (phr) /,klɪə ðə 'teɪbl/ sparecchiare la tavola

clever (adj) /'klevə(r)/ intelligente

click (v) /'klɪk/ clic

climate (n) /'klaɪmət/ clima

close (adj) /kləʊs/ intimo, stretto; vicino

close (v) /kləʊz/ chiudere

cloth (n) /klɒθ/ stoffa

clothes (n) /kləʊðz/ vestiti

clothes shop (n) /'kləʊðz ,ʃɒp/ negozio di abbigliamento

cloudy (adj) /'klaʊdi/ nuvoloso

club (n) /klʌb/ club

coach (n) /kəʊtʃ/ pullman

coast (n) /kəʊst/ costa

coastline (n) /'kəʊstlaɪn/ linea costiera

coat (n) /kəʊt/ cappotto

coconut water (n) /'kəʊkənʌt ,wɔ:tə(r)/ acqua di cocco

coffee (n) /'kɒfi/ caffè

coke (n) /kəʊk/ cola

cold (adj) /kəʊld/ freddo

collect (v) /kə'lekt/ raccogliere

collection (n) /kə'lekʃn/ collezione

college (n) /'kɒlɪdʒ/ scuola, istituto superiore

colony (n) /'kɒləni/ colonia

colour (n) /'kʌlə(r)/ colore

colourful (adj) /'kʌləfl/ colorato, pieno di colore

come (v) /kʌm/ venire

come back (v) /,kʌm 'bæk/ tornare, ritornare

come from (v) /'kʌm ,frɒm/ venire da

come over (v) /,kʌm 'əʊvə(r)/ venire

comedy (n) /'kɒmədi/ commedia

comfort (n) /'kʌmfət/ comodità

comfortable (adj) /'kʌmftəbl/ comodo

comic (n) /'kɒmɪk/ fumetto

comment (n) /'kɒment/ commento

commit suicide (phr) /kə,mɪt 'su:ɪsaɪd/ suicidarsi

common (adj) /'kɒmən/ diffuso

common: in common (phr) /,ɪn 'kɒmən/ in comune

communicate (v) /kə'mju:nɪkeɪt/ comunicare

community (n) /kə'mju:nəti/ comunità

companion (n) /kəm'pæniən/ compagno

company (n) /'kʌmpəni/ società, azienda

competition (n) /,kɒmpə'tɪʃn/ competizione, gara

competitor (n) /kəm'petɪtə(r)/ concorrente

complain (v) /kəm'pleɪn/ lamentarsi

Glossary

complete (adj) /kəm'pliːt/ completo

completely (adv) /kəm'pliːtli/ completamente

comprehensive (adj) /kɒmprɪ'hensɪv/ tipo di scuola secondaria statale

computer (n) /kəm'pjuːtə(r)/ computer

computer game (n) /kəm'pjuːtə ˌgeɪm/ gioco al computer, videogioco

concentrate (v) /'kɒnsəntreɪt/ concentrare, concentrarsi

concentration (n) /kɒnsən'treɪʃn/ concentrazione

concentric (adj) /kən'sentrɪk/ concentrico

concert (n) /'kɒnsət/ concerto

condiment (n) /'kɒndɪmənt/ condimento

condition: weather conditions (n) /'weðə kənˌdɪʃnz/ condizioni atmosferiche

condition: working conditions (n) /'wɜːkɪŋ kənˌdɪʃnz/ condizioni lavorative

confident (adj) /'kɒnfɪdənt/ sicuro (di sé)

confused (adj) /kən'fjuːzd/ confuso

congestion (n) /kən'dʒestʃn/ congestione, ingorgo

congratulate (v) /kən'grætʃuleɪt/ congratularsi con

connection (n) /kə'nekʃn/ connessione

conscientious (adj) /kɒnʃi'enʃəs/ coscienzioso

consider (v) /kən'sɪdə(r)/ considerare

consist of (v) /kən'sɪst əv/ consiste di

construction (n) /kən'strʌkʃn/ costruzione

contact (n) /'kɒntækt/ contatto

contestant (n) /kən'testənt/ concorrente

continent (n) /'kɒntɪnənt/ continente

contract: recording contract (n) /rɪ'kɔːdɪŋ ˌkɒntrækt/ contratto di registrazione

control (n) /kən'trəʊl/ controllo

control: out of control (phr) /ˌaʊt əv kən'trəʊl/ ingovernabile

cook (v) /kʊk/ cucinare

cool (adj) /kuːl/ fresco

cool (adj, coll) /kuːl/ ganzo

coriander (n) /kɒri'ændə(r)/ coriandolo

corner: on the corner of (prep) /ˌɒn ðə 'kɔːnər əv/ all'angolo di

correct (adj) /kə'rekt/ corretto

correspond (v) /kɒrə'spɒnd/ corrispondere

cosmetic surgery (n) /kɒzˌmetɪk 'sɜːdʒəri/ chirurgia estetica

cosmetics (n) /kɒz'metɪks/ cosmetici

cost (n) /kɒst/ costo

cost (v) /kɒst/ costare

Could I (go home early)? (phr) /'kʊd aɪ (ˌgəʊ ˌhəʊm 'ɜːli)/ Posso (andare a casa prima)?

country (n) /'kʌntri/ paese

countryside (n) /'kʌntrisaɪd/ campagna

couple: a couple of (n) /ə 'kʌpl əv/ un paio di

courgette (n) /kɔː'ʒet/ zucchine

course (n) /kɔːs/ corso

course: of course (phr) /əv 'kɔːs/ certo, certamente

cover (v) /'kʌvə(r)/ coprire

crash (v) /kræʃ/ fare incidente

creative (adj) /kri'eɪtɪv/ creativo

creature (n) /'kriːtʃə(r)/ creatura

credit (n) /'kredɪt/ credito

credit card (n) /'kredɪt ˌkɑːd/ carta di credito

criminal (n) /'krɪmɪnl/ criminale

criticism (n) /'krɪtɪsɪzəm/ critica

criticize (v) /'krɪtɪsaɪz/ criticare

cross the road (phr) /ˌkrɒs ðə 'rəʊd/ attraversare la strada

crowded (adj) /'kraʊdɪd/ affollato

crucial (adj) /'kruːʃl/ decisivo, importante

cry (v) /kraɪ/ piangere

crystal (n) /'krɪstl/ cristallo

cup (n) /kʌp/ tazza

cure (v) /kjʊə(r)/ curare

curious (adj) /'kjʊəriəs/ curioso

curly (adj) /'kɜːli/ riccio

customer (n) /'kʌstəmə(r)/ cliente

cut (v) /kʌt/ tagliare

cut the grass (phr) /ˌkʌt ðə 'grɑːs/ tagliare l'erba

cycle (v) /'saɪkl/ andare in bicicletta

cycling (n) /'saɪklɪŋ/ ciclismo

D

dad (n) /dæd/ papà

daily (adj) /'deɪli/ giornaliero

dairy (adj) /'deəri/ caseario

dance (n) /dɑːns/ danza, ballo

dance (v) /dɑːns/ ballare

dancing: go dancing (phr) /ˌgəʊ 'dɑːnsɪŋ/ ballare, andare a ballare

danger (n) /'deɪndʒə(r)/ pericolo

dangerous (adj) /'deɪndʒərəs/ pericoloso

dark (adj) /dɑːk/ scuro

date (n) /deɪt/ data; appuntamento

daughter (n) /'dɔːtə(r)/ figlia

day (n) /deɪ/ giorno

December (n) /dɪ'sembə(r)/ dicembre

decent (adj) /'diːsnt/ decoroso

decide (v) /dɪ'saɪd/ decidere

decision (n) /dɪ'sɪʒn/ decisione

decisive (adj) /dɪ'saɪsɪv/ deciso

deduct (v) /dɪ'dʌkt/ dedurre

deep (adj) /diːp/ profondo

deep-fried (adj) /'diːp ˌfraɪd/ fritto

defend (v) /dɪ'fend/ difendere

definitely (adv) /'defɪnətli/ decisamente

degree (n) /dɪ'griː/ grado

delay (n) /dɪ'leɪ/ ritardo

delicious (adj) /dɪ'lɪʃəs/ delizioso

demonstrate (v) /'demənstreɪt/ dimostrare

dentist (n) /'dentɪst/ dentista

depend (v) /dɪ'pend/ dipendere

depressed (adj) /dɪ'prest/ depresso

description (n) /dɪ'skrɪpʃn/ descrizione

design (v) /dɪ'zaɪn/ progettare

designated (adj) /'dezɪgneɪtɪd/ designato

designer clothes (n) /dɪ'zaɪnə ˌkləʊðz/ vestiti firmati

desk (n) /desk/ scrivania

desperately (adv) /'despərətli/ disperatamente

dessert (n) /dɪ'zɜːt/ dessert

destination (n) /destɪ'neɪʃn/ destinazione

determine (v) /dɪ'tɜːmɪn/ determinare, decidere

devastate (v) /'devəsteɪt/ distruggere

develop (v) /dɪ'veləp/ sviluppare

developing (adj) /dɪ'veləpɪŋ/ in via di sviluppo

device (n) /dɪ'vaɪs/ apparecchio

dictionary (n) /'dɪkʃnri/ dizionario

die (v) /daɪ/ morire

diesel (n) /'diːzl/ diesel

diet (adj) /'daɪət/ dietetico

diet (n) /'daɪət/ dieta

diet (v) /'daɪət/ fare una dieta

difference (n) /'dɪfrəns/ differenza

different (adj) /'dɪfrənt/ diverso

difficult (adj) /'dɪfɪkəlt/ difficile

digital (adj) /'dɪdʒɪtl/ digitale

dining room (n) /'daɪnɪŋ ˌruːm/ sala da pranzo

dinner (n) /'dɪnə(r)/ cena

dinosaur (n) /'daɪnəsɔː(r)/ dinosauro

direct (v) /də'rekt, dɪ-, daɪ-/ dirigere

direction (n) /də'rekʃn, dɪ-, daɪ-/ direzione

dirty (adj) /'dɜːti/ sporco

disadvantage (n) /dɪsəd'vɑːntɪdʒ/ svantaggio

disagree (v) /dɪsə'griː/ non essere d'accordo

disappear (v) /dɪsə'pɪə(r)/ scomparire

disappointed (adj) /dɪsə'pɔɪntɪd/ deluso

disappointing (adj) /dɪsə'pɔɪntɪŋ/ deludente

disco (n) /'dɪskəʊ/ discoteca

discuss (v) /dɪ'skʌs/ discutere

disgusting (adj) /dɪs'gʌstɪŋ/ disgustoso

dish (n) /dɪʃ/ portata, pietanza; piatto

dissatisfaction (n) /dɪssætɪs'fækʃn/ insoddisfazione

distance (n) /'dɪstəns/ distanza

distant (adj) /'dɪstənt/ distante

distinct (adj) /dɪ'stɪŋkt/ distinto

district: the Lake District (n) /ðə 'leɪk ˌdɪstrɪkt/ la regione dei laghi

diving: go diving (phr) /ˌgəʊ 'daɪvɪŋ/ fare immersione

do (v) /duː/ fare

do (a sport) (v) /ˌduː (ə 'spɔːt)/ fare, praticare (uno sport)

doctor (n) /'dɒktə(r)/ dottore

document (n) /'dɒkjumənt/ documento

documentary (n) /dɒkju'mentri/ documentario

dolphin (n) /'dɒlfɪn/ delfino

dominate (v) /'dɒmɪneɪt/ dominare

Don't (worry)! /'dəʊnt (ˌwʌri)/ Non (preoccuparti)!

Don't sit around (complaining) (phr) /ˌdəʊnt ˌsɪt əˌraʊnd kəm'pleɪnɪŋ/ Starsene seduto (a lamentarsi)

donut (n) /'dəʊnʌt/ bombolone

door (n) /dɔː(r)/ porta

down: go down (High Street) (phr) /ˌgəʊ ˌdaʊn ('haɪ ˌstriːt)/ percorri (High Street)

dragon (n) /'drægən/ drago

dramatic (adj) /drə'mætɪk/ drammatico

dream (n) /driːm/ sogno

dress (n) /dres/ vestito

dried (adj) /draɪd/ essiccato

drink (n) /drɪŋk/ bevanda

drink (v) /drɪŋk/ bere

drive (v) /draɪv/ guidare

drop (of rain) (phr) /ˌdrɒp (əv 'reɪn)/ goccia (di pioggia)

drop (v) /drɒp/ far cadere

drugs: take drugs (phr) /ˌteɪk 'drʌgz/ drogarsi

drums (n) /drʌmz/ batteria

dry (adj) /draɪ/ asciutto

during (prep) /djʊərɪŋ/ durante

dust (n) /dʌst/ polvere

E

each (det) /iːtʃ/ ogni; ciascuno

each other: next to each other (pron) /ˌiːtʃ 'ʌðə(r)/ l'uno accanto all'altro

early (adv) /'ɜːli/ presto

earn (v) /ɜːn/ guadagnare

Earth (n) /ɜːθ/ terra

easily (adv) /'iːzəli/ facilmente

east (n) /iːst/ est

easy-going (adj) /ˌiːzi 'gəʊɪŋ/ calmo e rilassato

eat (v) /iːt/ mangiare

eat out (phr) /ˌiːt 'aʊt/ mangiare fuori

eating disorder (n) /'iːtɪŋ dɪsˌɔːdə(r)/ disturbo dell'alimentazione

economy (n) /ɪ'kɒnəmi/ economia

edge (n) /edʒ/ bordo

effect (n) /ɪ'fekt/ effetto

effective (adj) /ɪ'fektɪv/ effettivo

egg (n) /eg/ uovo

eighteenth (adj) /eɪ'tiːnθ/ diciottesimo

eighth (adj) /eɪtθ/ ottavo

either: not... either (det) /ˌnɒt... 'aɪðə(r), 'iːðə(r)/ né

elaborate (adj) /ɪ'læbərət/ elaborato, complesso

electric (adj) /ɪ'lektrɪk/ elettrico

electrical (adj) /ɪ'lektrɪkl/ elettrico

electrical goods shop (n) /ɪˌlektrɪkl 'gʊdz ˌʃɒp/ negozio di elettrodomestici

electricity (n) /ɪlek'trɪsəti/ elettricità

eleventh (adj) /ɪ'levnθ/ undicesimo

embarrassed (adj) /ɪm'bærəst/ imbarazzato

embarrassing (adj) /ɪm'bærəsɪŋ/ imbarazzante

emission (n) /i'mɪʃn/ emissione

emotion (n) /ɪ'məʊʃn/ emozione

encourage (v) /ɪn'kʌrɪdʒ/ incoraggiare

end (n) /end/ fine

end (v) /end/ finire

energetic (adj) /enə'dʒetɪk/ energetico

engineer (n) /endʒɪ'nɪə(r)/ ingegnere

English (n, adj) /'ɪŋglɪʃ/

enjoy (v) /ɪn'dʒɔɪ/ piacere; divertirsi

Enjoy! (coll) /ɪn'dʒɔɪ/ Divertiti!

enormous (adj) /ɪ'nɔːməs/ enorme

enough (det) /ɪ'nʌf/ abbastanza

enter (v) /'entə(r)/ entrare
entertainment (n) /entə'teɪnmənt/ intrattenimento
enthusiast (n) /ɪn'θjuːziæst/ appassionato
environment (n) /ɪn'vaɪrənmənt/ ambiente
epic (adj) /'epɪk/ epico
especially (adv) /ɪ'speʃəli/ specialmente
essential (adj) /ɪ'senʃl/ essenziale
ethical (adj) /'eθɪkl/ etico
ethnic (adj) /'eθnɪk/ etnico
Europe (n) /'jʊərəp/ Europa
European (adj) /jʊərə'piːən/ europeo
even (adv) /'iːvn/ perfino
even though (conj) /'iːvn ,ðəʊ/ anche se
evening: in the evening (phr) /,ɪn ði 'iːvnɪŋ/ della sera, di sera
event (n) /ɪ'vent/ evento
ever (adv) /'evə(r)/ mai
every (det) /'evri/ ogni
everybody (pron) /'evribɒdi/ tutti
everyday (adj) /'evrideɪ/ di ogni giorno
everything (pron) /'evriθɪŋ/ tutto
everywhere (pron) /'evriweə(r)/ dappertutto
exactly (adv) /ɪg'zæktli/ esattamente
exam (n) /ɪg'zæm/ esame
example: for example (phr) /fər ɪg'zɑːmpl/ per esempio
excellent (adj) /'eksələnt/ eccellente
excited (adj) /ɪk'saɪtɪd/ elettrizzato, eccitato
exciting (adj) /ɪk'saɪtɪŋ/ elettrizzante
excuse: there's no excuse (phr) /,ðeəz 'nəʊ ɪk,skjuːs/ non ci sono scuse
exercise (v) /'eksəsaɪz/ fare ginnastica
exhibit (v) /ɪg'zɪbɪt/ esporre
exhibition (n) /eksɪ'bɪʃn/ mostra
exist (v) /ɪg'zɪst/ esistere
expect (v) /ɪk'spekt/ aspettarsi
expensive (adj) /ɪk'spensɪv/ costoso
experience (n) /ɪk'spɪəriəns/ esperienza
experience (v) /ɪk'spɪəriəns/ provare, fare l'esperienza di
experiment (n) /ɪk'sperɪmənt/ esperimento
expert (n) /'ekspɜːt/ esperto
explain (v) /ɪk'spleɪn/ spiegare
express (v) /ɪk'spres/ esprimere
extraordinary (adj) /ɪk'strɔːdnri/ straordinario
extreme (adj) /ɪk'striːm/ estremo
extrovert (n) /'ekstrəvɜːt/ estroverso
eyes (n) /aɪz/ occhi

F

fabulous (adj) /'fæbjələs/ favoloso
fact (n) /fækt/ fatto
fact: in fact (phr) /,ɪn 'fækt/ anzi
fact: the fact that ... (phr) /ðə 'fækt ðət/ il fatto che ...
factory (n) /'fæktəri/ fabbrica
fair (adj) /feə(r)/ equo; chiaro
fall (off) (v) /,fɔːl ('ɒf)/ cadere (da)
fall asleep (phr) /,fɔːl ə'sliːp/ addormentarsi
family (n) /'fæməli/ famiglia
famous (adj) /'feɪməs/ famoso
fanatical (adj) /fə'nætɪkl/ fanatico
fancy (v) /'fænsi/ trovare attraente
fancy: Do you fancy (going to the cinema)? (phr) /də jə 'fænsi ,gəʊɪŋ tə ðə 'sɪnəmə/ Ti va (di andare al cinema)?
fantastic (adj) /fæn'tæstɪk/ fantastico
far (adj) /fɑː(r)/ lontano
far: as far as (prep) /əz 'fɑːr əz/ fino a
farmer (n) /'fɑːmə(r)/ agricoltore
fascinating (adj) /'fæsɪneɪtɪŋ/ affascinante
fashion show (n) /'fæʃn ,ʃəʊ/ sfilata di moda
fashion: in fashion (phr) /,ɪn 'fæʃn/ alla moda
fashionable (adj) /'fæʃnəbl/ alla moda
fashion-conscious (adj) /'fæʃn ,kɒnʃəs/ che ci tiene a seguire la moda
fast (adj) /fɑːst/ veloce
fast food (n) /'fɑːst ,fuːd/ pasto veloce

fat (adj) /fæt/ grasso
father (n) /'fɑːðə(r)/ padre
father-in-law (n) /'fɑːðər ,ɪn ,lɔː/ suocero
fault (n) /fɔːlt/ colpa
favour: I'm in favour of (phr) /'aɪm ,ɪn ,feɪvər əv/ sono a favore di
favourite (adj) /'feɪvərɪt/ preferito
February (n) /'februəri/ febbraio
feed (v) /fiːd/ dar da mangiare
feel like (v) /'fiːl ,laɪk/ sembrare, avere la sensazione di
feeling (n) /'fiːlɪŋ/ sensazione
female (adj) /'fiːmeɪl/ femmina
fencing (n) /'fensɪŋ/ scherma
ferry (n) /'feri/ traghetto
festival (n) /'festɪvl/ festival
few: a few (det) /ə 'fjuː/ alcuni
fifteenth (adj) /fɪf'tiːnθ/ quindicesimo
fifth (adj) /fɪfθ/ quinto
fight (v) /faɪt/ litigare
fill in (v) /,fɪl 'ɪn/ compilare
final (n) /'faɪnl/ finale
find (v) /faɪnd/ trovare
find out (phr) /,faɪnd 'aʊt/ trovare; scoprire
fine (adj) /faɪn/ che va bene
fine (n) /faɪn/ multa
finish (v) /'fɪnɪʃ/ finire
firmly (adv) /'fɜːmli/ fermamente
first (adj, adv) /fɜːst/ primo; prima di tutto
first class (adj) /,fɜːst ,klɑːs/ di prima classe
fish (n) /fɪʃ/ pesce
fishcake (n) /'fɪʃkeɪk/ crocchetta di pesce
fishing: go fishing (phr) /,gəʊ 'fɪʃɪŋ/ andare a pesca
fit (adj) /fɪt/ in forma
fixed (adj) /fɪkst/ fisso
flight (n) /flaɪt/ volo
flooding (n) /'flʌdɪŋ/ alluvione
floor (n) /flɔː(r)/ piano; pavimento
flower (n) /'flaʊə(r)/ fiore
fly (v) /flaɪ/ volare
foggy (adj) /'fɒgi/ nebbioso
follow (v) /'fɒləʊ/ seguire
food (n) /fuːd/ cibo
foot/feet (n) /fʊt, fiːt/ piede/piedi
foot: on foot (phr) /,ɒn 'fʊt/ a piedi
football (n) /'fʊtbɔːl/ calcio
footballer (n) /'fʊtbɔːlə(r)/ calciatore
for (prep) /fɔːr, fə(r)/ per
forecast (n) /'fɔːkɑːst/ previsioni del tempo
foreground (n) /'fɔːgraʊnd/ primo piano
foreign (adj) /'fɒrən/ straniero
foreigner (n) /'fɒrənə(r)/ straniero
forest ranger (n) /'fɒrɪst ,reɪndʒə(r)/ guardia forestale
forget (v) /fə'get/ dimenticare
form (n) /fɔːm/ modulo
form (v) /fɔːm/ formare
former (adj) /'fɔːmə(r)/ di un tempo
fortunately (adv) /'fɔːtʃənətli/ fortunatamente
forward: look forward to sthg/doing sthg (phr) /,lʊk 'fɔːwəd tə .../ non vedere l'ora di fare qualcosa
foundation (n) /faʊn'deɪʃn/ fondazione
fourteenth (adj) /fɔː'tiːnθ/ quattordicesimo
fourth (adj) /fɔːθ/ quarto
free (adj) /friː/ gratuito
free time (n) /,friː 'taɪm/ tempo libero
freedom (n) /'friːdəm/ libertà
freeze (v) /friːz/ congelare, gelare
freezing (adj) /'friːzɪŋ/ gelido
French (n) /frentʃ/ francese
frequent (adj) /'friːkwənt/ frequente
fresh (adj) /freʃ/ fresco, appena spremuto
Friday (n) /'fraɪdeɪ/ venerdì
fridge (n) /frɪdʒ/ frigorifero
fried (adj) /fraɪd/ fritto
friend (n) /frend/ amico
friendly (adj) /'frendli/ amichevole
fries (n) /fraɪz/ patatine fritte

frightened (adj) /'fraɪtnd/ spaventato
from (prep) /frɒm, frəm/ da
frozen (adj) /'frəʊzn/ congelato, gelato
fruit (n) /fruːt/ frutta
full (adj) /fʊl/ pieno
fun (n) /fʌn/ divertimento
funny (adj) /'fʌni/ divertente
further/farther (adj) /'fɜːðə(r), 'fɑːðə(r)/ più lontano
furthest/farthest (adj) /'fɜːðɪst, 'fɑːðɪst/ (il) più lontano
future (n) /'fjuːtʃə(r)/ futuro

G

gallery (n) /'gæləri/ galleria
games console (n) /'geɪmz ,kɒnsəʊl/ console di videogiochi
gap year (n) /'gæp ,jɪə(r)/ anno di pausa
garage (n) /'gærɑːʒ, -ɑːʤ, -ɪʤ/ garage
garden (n) /'gɑːdn/ giardino
garlic bread (n) /,gɑːlɪk 'bred/ fetta di pane spalmata di burro all'aglio e scaldata
general (adj) /'ʤenrəl/ generale
generally (adv) /'ʤenrəli/ generalmente
generation (n) /ʤenə'reɪʃn/ generazione
generous (adj) /'ʤenərəs/ generoso
genius (n) /'ʤiːniəs/ genio
genuine (adj) /'ʤenjuɪn/ autentico
Geography (n) /ʤi'ɒgrəfi/ geografia
German (n) /'ʤɜːmən/ tedesco
Germany (n) /'ʤɜːməni/ Germania
get (v) /get/ ottenere; procurarsi
get (the bus/train) (v) /,get (ðə 'bʌs, 'treɪn)/ prendere (l'autobus/il treno)
get dressed (phr) /,get 'drest/ vestirsi
get home (phr) /,get 'həʊm/ tornare a casa
get in (v) /,get 'ɪn/ entrare
get into (the car/taxi) (v) /,get ,ɪntə (ðə 'kɑː, 'tæksi)/ salire (in macchina/nel taxi)
get off (the bus/train) (v) /,get ,ɒf (ðə 'bʌs, 'treɪn)/ scendere (dall'autobus/dal treno)
get older (phr) /,get 'əʊldə(r)/ invecchiare
get on (the bus) (v) /,get ,ɒn (ðə 'bʌs)/ salire (sull'autobus)
get out of (the car/taxi) (v) /,get ,aʊt əv (ðə 'kɑː, 'tæksi)/ scendere (dalla macchina/dal taxi)
get up (v) /,get 'ʌp/ alzarsi
gherkin (n) /'gɜːkɪn/ cetrioli sottaceto
ghost (n) /gəʊst/ fantasma
giant (adj) /'ʤaɪənt/ gigante
gig (n) /gɪg/ concerto
girl (n) /gɜːl/ ragazza
girlfriend (n) /'gɜːlfrend/ ragazza, fidanzata
give (v) /gɪv/ dare
glass (n) /glɑːs/ bicchiere
glider (n) /'glaɪdə(r)/ aliante
gliding (n) /'glaɪdɪŋ/ volo a vela
global (adj) /'gləʊbl/ mondiale
gloves (n) /glʌvz/ guanti
go (v) /gəʊ/ andare
go back (v) /,gəʊ 'bæk/ tornare indietro
go out (with) (v) /,gəʊ 'aʊt (wɪð)/ uscire (con)
go shopping (phr) /,gəʊ 'ʃɒpɪŋ/ fare spese
go to bed (phr) /,gəʊ tə 'bed/ andare a letto
goal (n) /gəʊl/ obiettivo
good (adj) /gʊd/ buono
good for you (phr) /'gʊd fə ,juː/ che fa bene alla salute
good-looking (adj) /,gʊd 'lʊkɪŋ/ attraente
gorgeous (adj) /'gɔːʤəs/ bellissimo
got: have got (v) /həv 'gɒt/ avere
got: have got to (v) /həv 'gɒt tə/ dovere
government (n) /'gʌvnmənt/ governo
GPS (global positioning system) (n) /,ʤiː ,piː 'es (,gləʊbl pə'zɪʃənɪŋ ,sætəlaɪt)/ sistema di posizionamento globale (via satellite)
graffiti (n) /grə'fiːti/ disegni murali
grandad (n) /'grændæd/ nonno
grandfather (n) /'grænfɑːðə(r)/ nonno

grandma (n) /ˈɡrænmɑː/ nonna
grandmother (n) /ˈɡrænmʌðə(r)/ nonna
grandparents (n) /ˈɡrænpeərənts/ nonni
great (adj) /ɡreɪt/ grandioso
great-granddaughter (n) /ˌɡreɪt ˈɡrændɔːtə(r)/ pronipote (femmina, di nonni)
Greece /ɡriːs/ Grecia
Greek (n, adj) /ɡriːk/ greco
green (adj) /ɡriːn/ verde
green beans (n) /ˌɡriːn ˈbiːnz/ fagiolini
greengrocer's (n) /ˈɡriːnɡrəʊsəz/ fruttivendolo
greenhouse gases (n) /ˈɡriːnhaʊs ˌɡæsɪz/ gas serra
grey (adj) /ɡreɪ/ grigio
grilled (adj) /ɡrɪld/ grigliato
group (n) /ɡruːp/ gruppo
grow up (v) /ˌɡrəʊ ˈʌp/ crescere
grumpy (adj) /ˈɡrʌmpi/ scontroso, irritabile
guarantee (v) /ɡærənˈtiː/ garantire
guide (n) /ɡaɪd/ guida
guinea (n) /ˈɡɪni/ ghinea
guitar (n) /ɡɪˈtɑː(r)/ chitarra
guitarist (n) /ɡɪˈtɑːrɪst/ chitarrista
Guy Fawkes Night (n) /ˌɡaɪ ˈfɔːks ˌnaɪt/ Notte dei falò (5 novembre)
gym (n) /dʒɪm/ palestra
gymnastics (n) /dʒɪmˈnæstɪks/ ginnastica

H

hailstone (n) /ˈheɪlstəʊn/ chicco di grandine
hailstorm (n) /ˈheɪlstɔːm/ grandinata
hair (n) /heə(r)/ capelli
hair: get/have (your) hair cut (phr) /ˌɡet, ˌhæv (ˌjɔː) ˈheə ˌkʌt/ andare a tagliarsi i capelli
haircut (n) /ˈheəkʌt/ taglio (di capelli)
hairdresser's (n) /ˈheədresəz/ parrucchiere
hairdryer (n) /ˈheədraɪə(r)/ asciugacapelli
half (n) /hɑːf/ metà
half past (two) (phr) /ˌhɑːf ˌpɑːst (ˈtuː)/ (le due) e mezza
Hallowe'en (n) /ˌhæləʊˈiːn/ Halloween
hamburger (n) /ˈhæmbɜːɡə(r)/ hamburger
handle (n) /ˈhændl/ manico
handy (adj) /ˈhændi/ comodo, utile
hang (v) /hæŋ/ essere appeso
hang around (phr, coll) /ˌhæŋ əˈraʊnd/ passare del tempo insieme
happen (v) /ˈhæpən/ succedere
happiness (n) /ˈhæpɪnəs/ felicità
happy (adj) /ˈhæpi/ felice
hard (adj) /hɑːd/ difficile
hard (adv) /hɑːd/ duro, sodo
hardly ever (adv) /ˌhɑːdli ˈevə(r)/ quasi mai
harmonious (adj) /hɑːˈməʊniəs/ armonioso, ben proporzionato
harp (n) /hɑːp/ arpa
hash browns (n) /ˌhæʃ ˈbraʊnz/ patate lessate, tagliate a pezzettini e fritte
hat (n) /hæt/ cappello
hate (v) /heɪt/ odiare
have (v) /hæv/ avere
head (n) /hed/ testa
headphones (n) /ˈhedfəʊnz/ cuffie
healthy (adj) /ˈhelθi/ salutare
hear (v) /hɪə(r)/ sentire
heart disease (n) /ˈhɑːt dɪˌziːz/ malattia di cuore
heartbeat (n) /ˈhɑːtbiːt/ battito cardiaco
height (n) /haɪt/ altezza
helicopter (n) /ˈhelɪkɒptə(r)/ elicottero
help (n) /help/ aiuto
help (v) /help/ aiutare
here (adv) /hɪə(r)/ qui
hers (pron) /hɜːz/ suo (di lei)
hi-fi (n) /ˈhaɪ ˌfaɪ/ (impianto) hi-fi
high (adj) /haɪ/ alto
high definition (n) /ˌhaɪ defɪˈnɪʃn/ alta definizione
high wind (phr) /ˌhaɪ ˈwɪnd/ vento forte
high: (X metres) high (adj) /(… ˌmiːtəz) ˈhaɪ/ alto (X metri)

hill (n) /hɪl/ collina
hire (v) /ˈhaɪə(r)/ affittare
his (adj) /hɪz/ (il) suo (di lui)
his (pron) /hɪz/ suo (di lui)
historic (adj) /hɪˈstɒrɪk/ storico
historically (adv) /hɪˈstɒrɪkli/ storicamente
History (n) /ˈhɪstri/ storia
hit (v) /hɪt/ colpire
hi-tech (adj) /ˌhaɪ ˈtek/ a tecnologia avanzata
hockey (n) /ˈhɒki/ hockey
hold (v) /həʊld/ contenere
holiday (n) /ˈhɒlədeɪ/ vacanza
holiday village (n) /ˈhɒlədeɪ ˌvɪlɪdʒ/ villaggio turistico
home (n) /həʊm/ casa
homeless (adj) /ˈhəʊmləs/ senzatetto
homework (n) /ˈhəʊmwɜːk/ compiti
Honest! (interj) /ˈɒnɪst/ Davvero!
Honestly! (coll) /ˈɒnɪstli/ Ma insomma!
honour (n) /ˈɒnə(r)/ onore
Hooray! (interj) /hʊˈreɪ/ Urrà!
hoover (v) /ˈhuːvə(r)/ passare l'aspirapolvere
hope (v) /həʊp/ sperare
hopeless (adj) /ˈhəʊpləs/ senza speranza, una frana
horror (n) /ˈhɒrə(r)/ orrore
horse (n) /hɔːs/ cavallo
hospital (n) /ˈhɒspɪtl/ ospedale
hostel (n) /ˈhɒstl/ ostello
hot (adj) /hɒt/ caldo, molto caldo
hotel (n) /həʊˈtel/ hotel, albergo
hour (n) /ˈaʊə(r)/ ora
house (n) /haʊs/ casa
how (adv) /haʊ/ come
How about (going to the cinema)? (phr) /ˈhaʊ əˌbaʊt (ˌɡəʊɪŋ tə ðə ˈsɪnəmə)/ Che ne dici (di andare al cinema)?
How far …? (int) /ˈhaʊ ˌfɑː(r)/ Fin dove … ?
How much/many …? (int) /ˈhaʊ ˌmʌtʃ, ˌmeni/ Quanto/quanti … ?
however (adv) /haʊˈevə(r)/ comunque, in ogni caso
huge (adj) /hjuːdʒ/ enorme
Humanities (n) /hjuːˈmænətiz/ discipline umanistiche
humanity (n) /hjuːˈmænəti/ umanità
hundreds (n) /ˈhʌndrədz/ centinaia
hungry: be hungry (phr) /ˌbi ˈhʌŋɡri/ aver fame
hurry: (be) in a hurry (phr) /(ˌbiː) ˌɪn ə ˈhʌri/ aver fretta
husband (n) /ˈhʌzbənd/ marito
hypermarket (n) /ˈhaɪpəmɑːkɪt/ ipermercato

I

I think so. (phr) /ˌaɪ ˈθɪŋk ˌsəʊ/ Credo di sì.
ice (n) /aɪs/ ghiaccio
ice skating: go ice skating (phr) /ˌɡəʊ ˈaɪs ˌskeɪtɪŋ/ andare a fare il pattinaggio sul ghiaccio
icy (adj) /ˈaɪsi/ ghiacciato
idea (n) /aɪˈdɪə/ idea
idealism (n) /aɪˈdiːəlɪzəm/ idealismo
ignore (v) /ɪɡˈnɔː(r)/ ignorare
ill (adj) /ɪl/ malato
ill: become ill (v) /bɪˌkʌm ˈɪl/ ammalarsi
illegal (adj) /ɪˈliːɡl/ illegale
illusion (n) /ɪˈluːʒn/ illusione
image (n) /ˈɪmɪdʒ/ immagine
imagination (n) /ɪmædʒɪˈneɪʃn/ immaginazione
imagine (v) /ɪˈmædʒɪn/ immaginare
immediately (adv) /ɪˈmiːdiətli/ immediatamente
immigrant (n) /ˈɪmɪɡrənt/ immigrato
immigration (n) /ɪmɪˈɡreɪʃn/ immigrazione
imperfection (n) /ɪmpəˈfekʃn/ imperfezione
important (adj) /ɪmˈpɔːtnt/ importante
impossible (adj) /ɪmˈpɒsəbl/ impossibile
impression (n) /ɪmˈpreʃn/ impressione
improve (v) /ɪmˈpruːv/ migliorare
impulsive (adj) /ɪmˈpʌlsɪv/ impulsivo

in (prep) /ɪn/ in
in (two days' time) (phr) /ɪn (ˌtuː ˌdeɪz ˈtaɪm)/ tra (due giorni)
in front of (prep) /ˌɪn ˈfrʌnt əv/ davanti a
include (v) /ɪnˈkluːd/ includere
including (prep) /ɪnˈkluːdɪŋ/ incluso
increase (n) /ˈɪŋkriːs/ aumento
increase (v) /ɪnˈkriːs/ aumentare
incredible (adj) /ɪnˈkredəbl/ incredibile
incredibly (adv) /ɪnˈkredəbli/ incredibilmente
indecisive (adj) /ɪndɪˈsaɪsɪv/ indeciso
India (n) /ˈɪndiə/ India
Indian (n, adj) /ˈɪndiən/ indiano
indication (n) /ɪndɪˈkeɪʃn/ indicazione
individuality (n) /ɪndɪvɪdʒuˈæləti/ individualità
Indonesia (n) /ɪndəˈniːʒə/ Indonesia
Indonesian (n) /ɪndəˈniːʒn/ indonesiano
industrial (adj) /ɪnˈdʌstriəl/ industriale
industry (n) /ˈɪndəstri/ industria
information (n) /ɪnfəˈmeɪʃn/ informazione
informative (adj) /ɪnˈfɔːmətɪv/ informativo
ingredient (n) /ɪnˈɡriːdiənt/ ingrediente
inhabited (adj) /ɪnˈhæbɪtɪd/ disabitato
insecure (adj) /ɪnsɪˈkjʊə(r)/ insicuro
inspiration (n) /ɪnspəˈreɪʃn/ ispirazione
install (v) /ɪnˈstɔːl/ installare
instead (adv) /ɪnˈsted/ invece
instrument (n) /ˈɪnstrəmənt/ strumento
intelligence (n) /ɪnˈtelɪdʒəns/ intelligenza
intelligent (adj) /ɪnˈtelɪdʒənt/ intelligente
intend (v) /ɪnˈtend/ intendere, avere intenzione di
interact (v) /ɪntərˈækt/ interagire
interactive (adj) /ɪntərˈæktɪv/ interattivo
interactive whiteboard (n) /ɪntərˌæktɪv ˈwaɪtbɔːd/ lavagna interattiva multimediale
interesting (adj) /ˈɪntrəstɪŋ/ interessante
interview (n) /ˈɪntəvjuː/ colloquio
into: be (really) into (phr, coll) /ˌbi (ˈrɪəli) ˌɪntə/ interessarsi (davvero, molto) di
introduce (v) /ɪntrəˈdjuːs/ introdurre; presentare
introspective (adj) /ɪntrəˈspektɪv/ introverso
invent (v) /ɪnˈvent/ inventare
invention (n) /ɪnˈvenʃn/ invenzione
inventor (n) /ɪnˈventə(r)/ inventore
investigate (v) /ɪnˈvestɪɡeɪt/ indagare
invite (v) /ɪnˈvaɪt/ invitare
Ireland (n) /ˈaɪələnd/ Irlanda
ironing: do the ironing (phr) /ˌduː ðɪ ˈaɪənɪŋ/ stirare
irregular (adj) /ɪˈreɡjələ(r)/ irregolare
island (n) /ˈaɪlənd/ isola
IT (Information Technology) (n) /ˌaɪ ˈtiː (ɪnfəˌmeɪʃn tekˈnɒlədʒi)/ anche ICT (Information and Communication Technology) informatica
Italian (n, adj) /ɪˈtæliən/ italiano
Italy (n) /ˈɪtəli/ Italia
item: news item (n) /ˈnjuːz ˌaɪtəm/ una notizia
its (adj) /ɪts/ suo

J

jacket (n) /ˈdʒækɪt/ giacca
jacuzzi (n) /dʒəˈkuːzi/ vasca per idromassaggio
January (n) /ˈdʒænjuəri/ gennaio
Japan (n) /dʒəˈpæn/ Giappone
Japanese (adj) /dʒæpəˈniːz/ giapponese
jealous (adj) /ˈdʒeləs/ geloso
jealousy (n) /ˈdʒeləsi/ gelosia
jeans (n) /dʒiːnz/ jeans
jewellery (n) /ˈdʒuːəlri/ gioielli
job (n) /dʒɒb/ faccenda; lavoro
joke (n) /dʒəʊk/ scherzo
joke (v) /dʒəʊk/ scherzare
journalist (n) /ˈdʒɜːnəlɪst/ giornalista
journey (n) /ˈdʒɜːni/ giro; viaggio
judgement (n) /ˈdʒʌdʒmənt/ giudizio
juice (n) /dʒuːs/ succo di frutta
July (n) /dʒuˈlaɪ/ luglio
jumper (n) /ˈdʒʌmpə(r)/ maglione

June (n) /dʒuːn/ giugno
just (adv) /dʒʌst/ solamente
just: have just done sthg (phr) /ˌhæv 'dʒʌst/ aver appena fatto qualcosa
justified (adj) /'dʒʌstɪfaɪd/ giustificato

K

karate (n) /kə'rɑːti/ karate
keep sth cool (v) /ˌkiːp ... 'kuːl/ mantenere in fresco
key (adj) /kiː/ principale
kill (v) /kɪl/ uccidere
killer (n) /'kɪlə(r)/ assassino
kilt (n) /kɪlt/ gonnellino scozzese
kiss (n) /kɪs/ bacio
kitchen (n) /'kɪtʃɪn/ cucina
knock (v) /nɒk/ bussare
know (v) /nəʊ/ conoscere

L

lab (n, abbr) /læb/ laboratorio
label (n) /leɪbl/ etichetta
lake (n) /leɪk/ lago
lamb (n) /læm/ agnello
land (n) /lænd/ terra
land (v) /lænd/ atterrare
landline (n) /'lændlaɪn/ telefono fisso
language (n) /'læŋgwɪdʒ/ lingua
laptop (n) /'læptɒp/ computer portatile
large (adj) /lɑːdʒ/ grande
last (adj) /lɑːst/ ultimo
last (adv) /lɑːst/ ultimo
last (v) /lɑːst/ durare
last (night, year) (phr) /ˌlɑːst ('naɪt, 'jɪə)/ ieri (sera), (l'anno) scorso
late (adj) /leɪt/ in ritardo
later (adv) /'leɪtə(r)/ dopo, più tardi
latest (adj) /'leɪtɪst/ (il) più recente, ultimo
Latin (n) /'lætɪn/ latino
laugh (v) /lɑːf/ ridere
laugh: have a good laugh (phr) /ˌhæv ə ˌgʊd 'lɑːf/ divertirsi
launch pad (n) /'lɔːntʃ ˌpæd/ piattaforma di lancio
lazy (adj) /'leɪzi/ pigro
lead (n) /liːd/ guinzaglio
lead (v) /liːd/ condurre
lead singer (n) /ˌliːd 'sɪŋə(r)/ voce principale
leaflet (n) /'liːflət/ dépliant
learn (v) /lɜːn/ imparare
least: at least (adv) /ət 'liːst/ almeno
leave (school) (v) /liːv/ finire (la scuola)
leave (v) /liːv/ lasciare; uscire; partire
left (adv) /left/ sinistra
left-handed (adj) /ˌleft 'hændɪd/ mancino
legal (adj) /'liːgl/ previsto dalla legge
legally (adv) /'liːgəli/ legalmente
leisure centre (n) /'leʒə ˌsentə(r)/ centro sportivo
lend (v) /lend/ prestare
length (n) /leŋθ/ lunghezza
lens (n) /lenz/ lente
less (adv) /les/ meno
lesson (n) /'lesn/ lezione
let (v) /let/ permettere
let go (v) /let 'gəʊ/ lasciare, mollare
Let's go (to the cinema)! (phr) /'lets ˌgəʊ (tə ðə 'sɪnəmə)/ Andiamo (al cinema)!
lettuce (n) /'letɪs/ lattuga
level (n) /'levl/ livello
library (n) /'laɪbrəri/ biblioteca
licence (n) /'laɪsəns/ licenza
licensed (adj) /'laɪsənst/ che ha la licenza
life (n) /laɪf/ vita
light (adj) /laɪt/ leggero
light (n) /laɪt/ luce
lightning (n) /'laɪtnɪŋ/ lampo
like (conj) /laɪk/ come
like (v) /laɪk/ piacere

like: What is X like? (phr) /ˌwɒt ˌɪz '... ˌlaɪk/ Com'è X?
limit (n) /'lɪmɪt/ limite
limit (v) /'lɪmɪt/ limitare
line (n) /laɪn/ linea
list (n) /lɪst/ lista
listen to (v) /'lɪsn tə/ ascoltare
live (adj) /laɪv/ dal vivo
live (v) /lɪv/ vivere
live on (phr) /'lɪv ˌɒn/ perdurare, sopravvivere
lively (adj) /'laɪvli/ vivace
living room (n) /'lɪvɪŋ ˌruːm/ soggiorno
loads of (det, coll) /'ləʊdz əv/ molti
loaf/loaves of bread (n) /ˌləʊf, ˌləʊvz əv 'bred/ pagnotta/pagnotte di pane
local (adj) /'ləʊkl/ locale
logo (n) /'ləʊgəʊ/ logo
long (adj) /lɒŋ/ lungo
look (n) /lʊk/ aspetto
look (v) /lʊk/ guardare
look (= seem) (v) /lʊk/ sembrare
look at (v) /'lʊk ət/ guardare
look for (v) /'lʊk ˌfɔː(r), fə(r)/ cercare
look like (v) /'lʊk ˌlaɪk/ somigliare
lorry (n) /'lɒri/ camion
lose (v) /luːz/ perdere
lose (your) balance (phr) /ˌluːz (ˌjɔː) 'bæləns/ perdere l'equilibrio
lose (your) way (phr) /ˌluːz (ˌjɔː) 'weɪ/ smarrirsi, smarrire la strada
lose weight (phr) /ˌluːz 'weɪt/ perdere peso
lost property (n) /ˌlɒst 'prɒpəti/ oggetti smarriti
lot: a lot of (det) /ə 'lɒt/ molto/molti
lots of (det, coll) /'lɒts əv/ molti
lottery (n) /'lɒtəri/ lotteria
love (v) /lʌv/ amare
lovely (adj) /'lʌvli/ incantevole
loving (adj) /'lʌvɪŋ/ affettuoso
low (adj) /ləʊ/ basso
luck (n) /lʌk/ fortuna
luckily (adv) /'lʌkɪli/ fortunatamente
lucky (adj) /'lʌki/ fortunato
lunch (n) /lʌntʃ/ pranzo
lunchtime (n) /'lʌntʃtaɪm/ ora di pranzo
Luxembourg (n) /'lʌksəmbɜːg/ Lussemburgo

M

machine: ticket machine (n) /'tɪkɪt mə.ʃiːn/ distributore automatico (di biglietti di viaggio)
mad about (adj, coll) /'mæd əˌbaʊt/ andare pazzo per
made of (adj) /'meɪd əv/ fatto di
magazine (n) /ˌmægə'ziːn/ rivista
main (adj) /meɪn/ principale
main (= main course) (n) /'meɪn ˌkɔːs/ piatto principale
mainly (adv) /'meɪnli/ principalmente
maintenance (n) /'meɪntənəns/ manutenzione
majority (n) /mə'dʒɒrəti/ (la) maggior parte
make (v) /meɪk/ fare
make: make (your) bed (phr) /ˌmeɪk (ˌjɔː) 'bed/ rifare il letto
male (adj) /meɪl/ maschio
man/men (n) /mæn, men/ uomo/uomini
manager (n) /'mænɪdʒə(r)/ manager
manic (adj) /'mænɪk/ frenetico
manipulation (n) /mənɪpju'leɪʃn/ manipolazione
manufacturer (n) /ˌmænju'fæktʃərə(r)/ produttore
many (det) /'meni/ molti
map (n) /mæp/ mappa, cartina
marathon (n) /'mærəθən/ maratona
March (n) /mɑːtʃ/ marzo
mark (n) /mɑːk/ voto
market (n) /'mɑːkɪt/ mercato
married: get married (v) /ˌget 'mærid/ sposarsi
mashed potatoes (n) /ˌmæʃt pə'teɪtəʊz/ purè di patate
match (n) /mætʃ/ partita
mate (n, coll) /meɪt/ compagno, amico

material (n) /mə'tɪəriəl/ materiale
Maths (n) /mæθs/ matematica
matter: it doesn't matter (phr) /ɪt ˌdʌznt 'mætə(r)/ non importa
maximum (n) /'mæksɪməm/ massimo
May (n) /meɪ/ maggio
May Day (n) /'meɪ ˌdeɪ/ primo di maggio
May I (go home early)? (phr) /meɪ ˌaɪ (ˌgəʊ ˌhəʊm 'ɜːli)/ Posso (andare a casa prima)?
maybe (adv) /'meɪbi/ forse
me (pron) /miː/ me; mi; a me; io
meal (n) /miːl/ pasto
mean (adj) /miːn/ avaro
mean (v) /miːn/ significare
measure (n) /'meʒə(r)/ misura
meat (n) /miːt/ carne
media (n) /'miːdiə/ media, mezzi d'informazione
medicine (n) /'medsn/ medicina
medium (n, adj) /'miːdiəm/ media
meet (v) /miːt/ incontrare, incontrarsi
member (n) /'membə(r)/ membro
memorable (adj) /'memərəbl/ memorabile
menu (n) /'menjuː/ menu
mess (n) /mes/ pasticcio
mess around (phr) /ˌmes ə'raʊnd/ bighellonare perdendo tempo
message (n) /'mesɪdʒ/ messaggio
metereology (n) /miːtiə'rɒlədʒi/ metereologia
metre (n) /'miːtə(r)/ metro
Mexican (adj) /'meksɪkən/ messicano
middle: in the middle (prep) /ˌɪn ðə 'mɪdl/ al centro
mile (n) /maɪl/ miglio
milk (n) /mɪlk/ latte
million (n) /'mɪljən/ milione
mind (v) /maɪnd/ dispiacere (impers.)
mind: make (your) mind up (phr) /ˌmeɪk (ˌjɔː) 'maɪnd ˌʌp/ decidersi
mine (pron) /maɪn/ mio
mineral water (n) /'mɪnərəl ˌwɔːtə(r)/ acqua minerale
minimum wage (n) /ˌmɪnɪməm 'weɪdʒ/ salario minimo
minority (n) /maɪ'nɒrəti/ minoranza
minute (n) /'mɪnɪt/ minuto
mirror (n) /'mɪrə(r)/ specchio
miso soup (n) /ˌmiːzəʊ 'suːp/ misoshiru (zuppa giapponese)
miss (v) /mɪs/ perdere; saltare
missed: not to be missed (phr) /ˌnɒt tə ˌbi 'mɪst/ da non perdere
mistake (n) /mɪ'steɪk/ errore
mixture (n) /'mɪkstʃə(r)/ miscuglio
mobile (phone) (n) /ˌməʊbaɪl 'fəʊn/ (telefono) cellulare
modern (adj) /'mɒdn/ moderno
modest (adj) /'mɒdɪst/ modesto
moment (n) /'məʊmənt/ momento
moment: at the moment (phr) /ət ðə 'məʊmənt/ al momento, ora, adesso
Monday (n) /'mʌndeɪ/ lunedì
money (n) /'mʌni/ soldi
monkey (n) /'mʌŋki/ scimmia
monster (n) /'mɒnstə(r)/ mostro
month (n) /mʌnθ/ mese
monthly (adv) /'mʌnθli/ mensile
monument (n) /'mɒnjumənt/ monumento
Moon (n) /muːn/ luna
moor (n) /mɔː(r)/ brughiera
more (det) /mɔː(r)/ più
morning: in the morning (phr) /ˌɪn ðə 'mɔːnɪŋ/ del mattino, di mattina
most (det) /məʊst/ la maggior parte
mother (n) /'mʌðə(r)/ madre
mother-in-law (n) /'mʌðər ˌɪn ˌlɔː/ suocera
motion-ride simulator (n) /ˌməʊʃn ˌraɪd 'sɪmjəleɪtə(r)/ simulatore di viaggio virtuale
motorbike (n) /'məʊtəbaɪk/ motocicletta
motorised (adj) /'məʊtəraɪzd/ motorizzato
mountain (n) /'maʊntən/ montagna

mountain biking (n) /ˈmaʊntən ˌbaɪkɪŋ/ andare in mountain bike

move (v) /muːv/ trasferirsi; spostare; spostarsi

MP3 player (n) /ˌem ˌpiː ˈθriː ˌpleɪə(r)/ lettore MP3

much (adv) /mʌtʃ/ molto

muffin (n) /ˈmʌfɪn/ muffin (dolcetto soffice con pezzetti di frutta o cioccolato)

multi-level (adj) /ˈmʌlti ˌlevl/ a più livelli

mum (n) /mʌm/ mamma

museum (n) /mjuˈziːəm/ museo

mushroom (n) /ˈmʌʃruːm/ fungo

music (n) /ˈmjuːzɪk/ musica

musical (adj) /ˈmjuːzɪkl/ musicale

musician (n) /mjuˈzɪʃn/ musicista

Muslim (n, adj) /ˈmʊzlɪm/ musulmano

my (adj) /maɪ/ (il) mio

myth (n) /mɪθ/ mito

N

name (n) /neɪm/ nome

name (v) /neɪm/ chiamare; nominare

nasty (adj) /ˈnaːsti/ scortese

nation (n) /ˈneɪʃn/ nazione

natural (adj) /ˈnætʃrəl/ naturale

nature reserve (n) /ˈneɪtʃə rɪˌzɜːv/ riserva naturale

navigate (v) /ˈnævɪgeɪt/ guidare, procedere

near (prep) /nɪə(r)/ vicino

nearly (adv) /ˈnɪəli/ quasi

neat (adj) /niːt/ preciso, ordinato

necklace (n) /ˈnekləs/ collana

need (v) /niːd/ avere bisogno di

negative (adj) /ˈnegətɪv/ negativo

Neither do I. (phr) /ˌnaɪðə ˈduː ˈaɪ/ Neanch'io, Neanche a me.

Nepal (n) /nəˈpɔːl/ Nepal

nephew (n) /ˈnefjuː/ (il) nipote (di zii)

nerves (n) /nɜːvz/ nervosismo

nervous (adj) /ˈnɜːvəs/ teso, agitato

netball (n) /ˈnetbɔːl/ netball

network (n) /ˈnetwɜːk/ rete

never (adv) /ˈnevə(r)/ mai

new (adj) /njuː/ nuovo

New Year's Eve (n) /ˌnjuː ˌjɪəz ˈiːv/ vigilia di Capodanno

news: the news (n) /ðə ˈnjuːz/ telegiornale

newsagent's (n) /ˈnjuːzeɪdʒənts/ edicola

newspaper (n) /ˈnjuːspeɪpə(r)/ giornale

next (adj) /nekst/ prossimo

next (week/month/year) (phr) /ˌnekst (ˈwiːk, ˈmʌnθ, ˈjɪə)/ (la settimana, il mese, l'anno) prossimo

next to (prep) /ˈnekst tə/ accanto a

nice (adj) /naɪs/ bravo; carino

niece (n) /niːs/ (la) nipote (di zii)

night life (phr) /ˈnaɪt ˌlaɪf/ vita notturna

night: at night (phr) /ət ˈnaɪt/ della notte, di notte

nineteenth (adj) /naɪnˈtiːnθ/ diciannovesimo

ninth (adj) /naɪnθ/ nono

no: have no money (phr) /ˌhæv ˌnəʊ ˈmʌni/ non avere soldi, essere senza soldi

nobody (pron) /ˈnəʊbədi/ nessuno

noise (n) /nɔɪz/ rumore

noisy (adj) /ˈnɔɪzi/ rumoroso

non-motorised (adj) /ˈnɒn ˌməʊtəraɪzd/ non motorizzato

normal (adj) /ˈnɔːml/ normale

northern (adj) /ˈnɔːðən/ settentrionale

Northern Ireland (n) /ˌnɔːðən ˈaɪələnd/ Irlanda del Nord

Northern Irish (adj) /ˌnɔːðən ˈaɪrɪʃ/ dell'Irlanda del Nord

north-west (n) /ˌnɔːθ ˈwest/ nord-ovest

Norway (n) /ˈnɔːweɪ/ Norvegia

not (adv) /nɒt/ non

nothing (pron) /ˈnʌθɪŋ/ niente

novelty (n) /ˈnɒvəlti/ originalità

November (n) /nəʊˈvembə(r)/ novembre

now (adv) /naʊ/ ora

number (n) /ˈnʌmbə(r)/ numero

O

o'clock: (two) o'clock (phr) /ə ˈklɒk/ le (due)

obey (v) /əˈbeɪ/ obbedire

object (n) /ˈɒbdʒekt/ oggetto

observation (n) /ˌɒbzəˈveɪʃn/ osservazione

obsessed (adj) /əbˈsest/ ossessionato

obsession (n) /əbˈseʃn/ ossessione

obstinate (adj) /ˈɒbstɪnət/ ostinato

obviously (adv) /ˈɒbviəsli/ ovviamente

occasion (n) /əˈkeɪʒn/ occasione

occasionally (adv) /əˈkeɪʒnəli/ occasionalmente

occupied (adj) /ˈɒkjupaɪd/ occupato

occupy (v) /ˈɒkjupaɪ/ occupare

ocean (n) /ˈəʊʃn/ oceano

October (n) /ɒkˈtəʊbə(r)/ ottobre

of (prep) /ɒv, əv/ di

offer (v) /ˈɒfə(r)/ offrire

office (n) /ˈɒfɪs/ ufficio

off-peak (adj) /ˌɒf ˈpiːk/ non di punta

often (adv) /ˈɒfn, ˈɒftən/ spesso

Oh, I do. (phr) /ˌəʊ ˈaɪ ˌduː/ Io sì./A me sì.

Oh, I don't. (phr) /ˌəʊ ˈaɪ ˌdəʊnt/ Io no./A me no.

oil (n) /ɔɪl/ olio

old (adj) /əʊld/ vecchio

old-fashioned (adj) /ˌəʊld ˈfæʃnd/ fuori moda

olive oil (n) /ˌɒlɪv ˈɔɪl/ olio d'oliva

on (prep) /ɒn/ a; su

on time (adv) /ˌɒn ˈtaɪm/ in orario

once (adv) /wʌns/ una volta

one another's (houses) (phr) /ˌwʌn əˌnʌðəz (ˈhaʊzɪz)/ (a casa) di l'un l'altro

only (adv) /ˈəʊnli/ solo, solamente

only child (n) /ˌəʊnli ˈtʃaɪld/ figlio unico

onto (prep) /ˈɒntuː/ su

open (adj) /ˈəʊpən/ aperto

open (v) /ˈəʊpən/ aprire

openly (adv) /ˈəʊpənli/ apertamente

opera house (n) /ˈɒpərə ˌhaʊs/ teatro dell'opera

opinion (n) /əˈpɪnjən/ opinione, parere

opinionated (adj) /əˈpɪnjəneɪtɪd/ presuntuoso

opposite (prep) /ˈɒpəzɪt/ dirimpetto a

orange (adj) /ˈɒrɪndʒ/ arancione

orange (n) /ˈɒrɪndʒ/ arancia

orange juice (n) /ˈɒrɪndʒ ˌdʒuːs/ succo d'arancia

orangutan (n) /əˈræŋutæn/ orangutan

orator (n) /ˈɒrətə(r)/ oratore

order (n) /ˈɔːdə(r)/ ordine

order (v) /ˈɔːdə(r)/ ordinare

orderly (adj) /ˈɔːdəli/ metodico

organization (n) /ˌɔːgənaɪˈzeɪʃn/ organizzazione

organize (v) /ˈɔːgənaɪz/ organizzare

origin (n) /ˈɒrɪdʒɪn/ origine

original (adj) /əˈrɪdʒənl/ originale

other (adj) /ˈʌðə(r)/ altro

our (adj) /ˈaʊə(r)/ (il) nostro

ours (pron) /ˈaʊəz/ nostro

out of (prep) /ˈaʊt əv/ dal; fuori da

outdoor (adj) /ˈaʊtdɔːr/ all'aperto

outgoing (adj) /aʊtˈgəʊɪŋ/ estroverso

outlet centre (n) /ˈaʊtlet ˌsentə(r)/ negozio che vende articoli a prezzi scontati

outside (prep) /aʊtˈsaɪd/ fuori

over (prep) /ˈəʊvə(r)/ sopra; più di

over there (adv) /ˌəʊvə ˈðeə(r)/ laggiù

overnight success (phr) /ˌəʊvənaɪt səkˈses/ successo immediato

overtime (n) /ˈəʊvətaɪm/ (lavoro) straordinario

own (adj) /əʊn/ proprio

own (v) /əʊn/ possedere, essere il proprietario di

own: on (my) own (adv) /ɒn (ˌmaɪ) ˈəʊn/ da solo

owner (n) /ˈəʊnə(r)/ proprietario

P

pack (v) /pæk/ fare i bagagli, fare le valigie

package holiday (n) /ˈpækɪdʒ ˌhɒlədeɪ/ pacchetto vacanze

packed lunch (n) /ˌpækt ˈlʌntʃ/ pranzo al sacco

packet (n) /ˈpækɪt/ pacco

paint (v) /peɪnt/ dipingere

painting (n) /ˈpeɪntɪŋ/ pittura, dipinto

pair (n) /peə(r)/ paio

Pakistani (n) /ˌpækɪˈstɑːni/ pachistano

pancake (n) /ˈpænkeɪk/ crespella

panoramic (adj) /ˌpænəˈræmɪk/ panoramico

parents (n) /ˈpeərənts/ genitori

park (n) /pɑːk/ parco

Parmesan (adj) /ˈpɑːmɪˌzæn/ parmigiano

part (n) /pɑːt/ parte

participant (n) /pɑːˈtɪsɪpənt/ partecipante

particle (n) /ˈpɑːtɪkl/ particella

particular: in particular (adv) /ˌɪn pəˈtɪkjələ(r)/ in particolare

party (n) /ˈpɑːti/ festa

pass (v) /pɑːs/ passare

pass (a test/exam) (v) /pɑːs/ superare (un test/esame)

passenger (n) /ˈpæsɪndʒə(r)/ passeggero

passion (n) /ˈpæʃn/ passione

passion fruit (n) /ˈpæʃn ˌfruːt/ frutto della passione

passionate (adj) /ˈpæʃənət/ appassionato

passport (n) /ˈpɑːspɔːt/ passaporto

past (n) /pɑːst/ passato

past (prep) /pɑːst/ oltre

past: (ten) past (two) (phr) /(ˌten) ˌpɑːst (ˈtuː)/ le (due) e (dieci)

path (n) /pɑːθ/ sentiero

patient (n) /ˈpeɪʃnt/ paziente

pay (for) (v) /ˈpeɪ ˌfɔː, fə(r)/ pagare

pay (money) back (phr) /ˌpeɪ (ˌmʌni) ˈbæk/ restituire (i soldi)

PE (Physical Education) (n) /ˌpiː ˈiː, (ˌfɪzɪkl edʒuˈkeɪʃn)/ educazione fisica

peace: make peace with (phr) /ˌmeɪk ˈpiːs ˌwɪð/ fare pace con

peach (n) /piːtʃ/ pesca

peak-time (adj) /ˈpiːk ˌtaɪm/ ora di punta

pear (n) /peə(r)/ pera

peas (n) /piːz/ piselli

pen (n) /pen/ penna

pencil (n) /ˈpensl/ matita

penicillin (n) /ˌpenɪˈsɪlɪn/ penicillina

penny-farthing (n) /ˌpeni ˈfɑːθɪŋ/ biciclo

people (n) /ˈpiːpl/ gente, persone

pepper (n) /ˈpepə(r)/ pepe

perceptive (adj) /pəˈseptɪv/ percettivo

perfect (adj) /ˈpɜːfekt/ perfetto

perfect (v) /pəˈfekt/ perfezionare

perform (v) /pəˈfɔːm/ esibirsi

performance (n) /pəˈfɔːməns/ esecuzione, spettacolo

performer (n) /pəˈfɔːmə(r)/ artista

period (n) /ˈpɪəriəd/ ora (di lezione)

permission (n) /pəˈmɪʃn/ permesso

personal (adj) /ˈpɜːsənl/ personale

personality (n) /ˌpɜːsəˈnæləti/ personalità, carattere

pet (n) /pet/ animale domestico

phenomena (n) /fəˈnɒmɪnə/ fenomeni

phone (n) /fəʊn/ telefono

phone (v) /fəʊn/ telefonare

phone box (n) /ˈfəʊn ˌbɒks/ cabina telefonica

phone call (n) /ˈfəʊn ˌkɔːl/ telefonata

photo (n) /ˈfəʊtəʊ/ fotografia

physical (adj) /ˈfɪzɪkl/ fisico

physically (adv) /ˈfɪzɪkli/ fisicamente

Physics (n) /ˈfɪzɪks/ fisica

piano (n) /piˈænəʊ/ pianoforte

pick (sth) up (v) /ˌpɪk … ˈʌp/ raccogliere

picture (n) /ˈpɪktʃə(r)/ disegno, pittura; immagine

piece (n) /piːs/ pezzo

pilot (v) /ˈpaɪlət/ pilotare

pitch (n) /pɪtʃ/ posteggio

pity: (it's a) pity (that) … /(ˌɪts ə) ˈpɪti (ˌðət)/ (è un) peccato (che)

place (n) /pleɪs/ posto

plane (n) /pleɪn/ aereo
planet (n) /'plænɪt/ pianeta
plastic surgery (n) /ˌplæstɪk 'sɜːdʒəri/ chirurgia plastica
plate (n) /pleɪt/ piatto
play (v) /pleɪ/ giocare
play (a sport) (v) /ˌpleɪ (ə 'spɔːt)/ giocare a
play (the guitar) (v) /ˌpleɪ (ðə ɡɪ'tɑː)/ suonare (la chitarra)
playground (n) /'pleɪɡraʊnd/ cortile
please (phr) /pliːz/ per favore
pleased (to do sth) (adj) /pliːzd/ contento (di fare qualcosa)
pocket (n) /'pɒkɪt/ tasca
pocket money (n) /pɒkɪt ˌmʌni/ paghetta
poet (n) /'pəʊɪt/ poeta
point (n) /pɔɪnt/ punto
Pole (n) /pəʊl/ polacco
Polish (n) /'pəʊlɪʃ/ polacco
political (adj) /pə'lɪtɪkl/ politico
politician (n) /pɒlə'tɪʃn/ politico
polluted (adj) /pə'luːtɪd/ inquinato
pollution (n) /pə'luːʃn/ inquinamento
pool (n) /puːl/ piscina
poor (adj) /pɔː(r)/ scadente; povero
popular (adj) /'pɒpjələ(r)/ popolare
populated (adj) /'pɒpjuleɪtɪd/ popolato
population (n) /pɒpju'leɪʃn/ popolazione
pork (n) /pɔːk/ maiale
porridge (n) /'pɒrɪdʒ/ fiocchi d'avena con latte
port (n) /pɔːt/ porto
portable (adj) /'pɔːtəbl/ portatile
position (n) /pə'zɪʃn/ posizione
positive (adj) /'pɒzətɪv/ positivo
possible (adj) /'pɒsəbl/ possibile
possibly (adv) /'pɒsəbli/ possibilmente
post office (n) /'pəʊst ˌɒfɪs/ ufficio postale
pot (n) /pɒt/ vasetto
potassium (n) /pə'tæsiəm/ potassio
potato (n) /pə'teɪtəʊ/ patata
power (n) /'paʊə(r)/ potere
power station (n) /'paʊə ˌsteɪʃn/ centrale elettrica
practice: in practice (phr) /ˌɪn 'præktɪs/ in pratica
practise (v) /'præktɪs/ esercitarsi
prefer (v) /prɪ'fɜː(r)/ preferire
prescribe (v) /prɪ'skraɪb/ prescrivere
present (adj) /'preznt/ presente
present (n) /'preznt/ presente
pressure (n) /'preʃə(r)/ pressione
pretty (adv) /'prɪti/ piuttosto
prevent (v) /prɪ'vent/ prevenire
previous (adj) /'priːviəs/ precedente
price (n) /praɪs/ prezzo
principal (adj) /'prɪnsəpl/ principale
print (out) (v) /ˌprɪnt ('aʊt)/ stampare
printed (adj) /'prɪntɪd/ stampato
private (adj) /'praɪvət/ privato
probability (n) /prɒbə'bɪləti/ probabilità
probably (adv) /'prɒbəbli/ probabilmente
problem (n) /'prɒbləm/ problema
process (n) /'prəʊses/ procedimento
produce (v) /prə'djuːs/ produrre
product (n) /'prɒdʌkt/ prodotto
professional (adj) /prə'feʃənl/ professionale
profit (n) /'prɒfɪt/ guadagno
programme/program (AmE) (n) /'prəʊɡræm/ programma
project (n) /'prɒdʒekt/ progetto
project (v) /prə'dʒekt/ proiettare
pronounce (v) /prə'naʊns/ pronunciare
protect (v) /prə'tekt/ proteggere
protest (v) /prə'test/ protestare
proud (adj) /praʊd/ fiero
province (n) /'prɒvɪns/ provincia
psychologist (n) /saɪ'kɒlədʒɪst/ psicologo
psychotic (adj) /saɪ'kɒtɪk/ psicotico
pub (n) /pʌb/ pub
public (adj) /'pʌblɪk/ pubblico
publish (v) /'pʌblɪʃ/ pubblicare

push (v) /pʊʃ/ spingere
put (v) /pʊt/ mettere

Q

quality (n) /'kwɒləti/ qualità
quarter past (two) (phr) /ˌkwɔːtə ˌpɑːst ('tuː)/ le (due) e un quarto
quarter to (two) (phr) /ˌkwɔːtə tə ('tuː)/ le (due) meno un quarto
question: it's a question of (phr) /ˌɪts ə 'kwestʃən əv/ è una questione di, si tratta di
queue (n) /kjuː/ fila, coda
quickly (adv) /'kwɪkli/ velocemente
quite (adv) /kwaɪt/ piuttosto
quiz show (n) /'kwɪz ˌʃəʊ/ quiz show

R

race (n) /reɪs/ gara
race (v) /reɪs/ gareggiare
radio (n) /'reɪdiəʊ/ radio
railcard (n) /'reɪlkɑːd/ tessera ferroviaria
railway (n, adj) /'reɪlweɪ/ ferroviario
rain (v) /reɪn/ piovere
rainfall (n) /'reɪnfɔːl/ piovosità
rainy (adj) /'reɪni/ piovoso
raise money (phr) /ˌreɪz 'mʌni/ raccogliere soldi
range (n) /reɪndʒ/ gamma
rapper (n) /'ræpə(r)/ cantante rap
rare (adj) /reə(r)/ raro
rarely (adv) /'reəli/ raramente
rational (adj) /'ræʃnəl/ razionale
RE (Religious Education) (n) /ˌɑːr 'iː (rɪˌlɪdʒəs edʒu'keɪʃn)/ religione
reach (v) /riːtʃ/ raggiungere
reaction (n) /ri'ækʃn/ reazione
read (v) /riːd/ leggere
ready (adj) /'redi/ pronto
real (adj) /riːəl/ vero
realize (v) /'riːəlaɪz/ accorgersi
realistic (adj) /riːə'lɪstɪk/ realistico
reality (n) /ri'æləti/ realtà
reality show (n) /ri'æləti ˌʃəʊ/ reality (show)
really (adv) /'riːəli/ veramente
reason (n) /'riːzn/ ragione
receive (v) /rɪ'siːv/ ricevere
recently (adv) /'riːsntli/ recentemente
recommend (v) /rekə'mend/ raccomandare, consigliare
record (n) /'rekɔːd/ disco, vinile
record (v) /rɪ'kɔːd/ registrare
record: Just for the record (phr) /'dʒʌst fə ðə ˌrekɔːd/ Per la precisione
red (adj) /red/ rosso
red-haired (adj) /ˌred 'heəd/ dai capelli rossi
reduce (v) /rɪ'djuːs/ ridurre
redundant: make sb redundant (phr) /ˌmeɪk ... rɪ'dʌndənt/ licenziare per esubero di personale
refuse (v) /rɪ'fjuːz/ rifiutare
region (n) /'riːdʒən/ regione
registration (n) /redʒɪ'streɪʃn/ registrazione
regular (adj) /'reɡjələ(r)/ regolare
rehearsal (n) /rɪ'hɜːsl/ prova
reinvest (v) /riːɪn'vest/ reinvestire
relation: in relation to (phr) /ˌɪn rɪ'leɪʃn tə/ rispetto a
relationship (n) /rɪ'leɪʃnʃɪp/ relazione
relative (n) /'relətɪv/ familiare
relax (v) /rɪ'læks/ rilassare, rilassarsi
relaxing (adj) /rɪ'læksɪŋ/ rilassante
reliable (adj) /rɪ'laɪəbl/ affidabile
relief (n) /rɪ'liːf/ sollievo
relieved (adj) /rɪ'liːvd/ sollevato
religion (n) /rɪ'lɪdʒən/ religione
remember (v) /rɪ'membə(r)/ ricordare, ricordarsi
rent (n) /rent/ affitto
rent (v) /rent/ affittare
repair (v) /rɪ'peə(r)/ riparare

Republic of Congo (n) /rɪˌpʌblɪk əv 'kɒŋɡəʊ/ Repubblica del Congo
residential (adj) /rezɪ'denʃl/ residenziale
resource (n) /rɪ'zɔːs/ risorsa
responsibility (n) /rɪspɒnsə'bɪləti/ responsabilità
rest: have a rest (phr) /ˌhæv ə 'rest/ riposare
restaurant (n) /'restrɒnt/ ristorante
result (n) /rɪ'zʌlt/ risultato
result: as a result (phr) /əz ə rɪ'zʌlt/ di conseguenza
return (v) /rɪ'tɜːn/ restituire
return (ticket) (n) /rɪˌtɜːn ('tɪkɪt)/ (biglietto di) andata e ritorno
return fare (n) /rɪˌtɜːn 'feə/ tariffa (di viaggio) di andata e ritorno
reveal (v) /rɪ'viːl/ rivelare
revolution (n) /revə'luːʃn/ rivoluzione
rhinoceros (n) /raɪ'nɒsərəs/ rinoceronte
ribbon (n) /'rɪbən/ nastro
rice (n) /raɪs/ riso
rice ball (n) /raɪs ˌbɔːl/ polpetta di riso bianco (spuntino giapponese)
rich (adj) /rɪtʃ/ ricco
ride (n) /raɪd/ viaggio
ride a horse (phr) /ˌraɪd ə 'hɔːs/ andare a cavallo, cavalcare
ride a motorbike (phr) /ˌraɪd ə 'məʊtəbaɪk/ andare in moto, guidare la moto
ride: go for a ride (phr) /ˌɡəʊ fər ə 'raɪd/ andare a fare un giro
ridiculous (adj) /rɪ'dɪkjələs/ ridicolo
right (adj) /raɪt/ corretto
right (adv) /raɪt/ destra
Right (interj) /raɪt/ Va bene
right now (phr) /ˌraɪt 'naʊ/ adesso, in questo momento
ring (n) /rɪŋ/ anello
rise (v) /raɪz/ alzarsi
risk (v) /rɪsk/ rischiare
river (n) /'rɪvə(r)/ fiume
road (n) /rəʊd/ strada
roast beef (n) /ˌrəʊst 'biːf/ manzo arrosto
robot (n) /'rəʊbɒt/ robot
role model (n) /'rəʊl ˌmɒdl/ modello di comportamento
rollerblade (v) /'rəʊləbleɪd/ pattinare con i pattini in linea
rollerblades (n) /'rəʊləbleɪdz/ pattini in linea
rollerblading (n) /'rəʊləbleɪdɪŋ/ pattinaggio in linea
Roman (adj) /'rəʊmən/ romano
room (n) /ruːm/ stanza; spazio
rope ladder (n) /ˌrəʊp 'lædə(r)/ scala di corda
rose (n) /rəʊz/ rosa
rounders (n) /'raʊndəz/ rounders (gioco simile al baseball)
routine (n) /ruː'tiːn/ coreografia
royalty (n) /'rɔɪəlti/ i reali
rubbish (n) /'rʌbɪʃ/ spazzatura
rucksack (n) /'rʌksæk/ zaino
rugby (n) /'rʌɡbi/ rugby
rule (n) /ruːl/ regola
run (v) /rʌn/ correre
run away (phr) /ˌrʌn ə'weɪ/ scappare
run out in front of (phr) /ˌrʌn ˌaʊt ˌɪn 'frʌnt əv/ spuntare davanti all'improvviso
runner (n) /'rʌnə(r)/ corridore
running (n) /'rʌnɪŋ/ correre, corsa
Russia (n) /'rʌʃə/ Russia
Russian (adj) /'rʌʃn/ russo

S

sad (adj) /sæd/ triste
sailing: go sailing (phr) /ˌɡəʊ 'seɪlɪŋ/ andare in barca a vela
salad (n) /'sæləd/ insalata
sale: put sth for sale (phr) /ˌpʊt ... fə 'seɪl/ mettere qualcosa in vendita
salmon (n) /'sæmən/ salmone

297

salt (n) /sɔːlt/ sale

same (adj) /seɪm/ stesso

same: at the same time (phr) /ət ðə ˌseɪm 'taɪm/ allo stesso tempo

sandals (n) /'sændlz/ sandali

sandwich (n) /'sænwɪtʃ/ tramezzino

satisfied (adj) /'sætɪsfaɪd/ soddisfatto

satisfying (adj) /'sætɪsfaɪɪŋ/ appagante

Saturday (n) /'sætədeɪ/ sabato

sausage (n) /'sɒsɪdʒ/ salsiccia

save (v) /seɪv/ risparmiare

saxophone (n) /'sæksəfəʊn/ sassofono

say (v) /seɪ/ dire

say: have your say (phr) /hæv ˌjɔː 'seɪ/ dire la propria, dare il proprio parere

scared (adj) /skeəd/ spaventato

scarf (n) /skɑːf/ sciarpa

scary (adj) /'skeəri/ che fa paura, spaventoso

scene: music scene (n) /'mjuːzɪk ˌsiːn/ scena musicale

scenery (n) /'siːnəri/ paesaggio

schedule (n) /'ʃedjuːl/ programma

school (n) /skuːl/ scuola

schoolfriend (n) /'skuːlfrend/ compagno di scuola

Science (n) /'saɪəns/ scienze

score (v) /skɔː(r)/ segnare

Scot (n) /skɒt/ scozzese

Scotland (n) /'skɒtlənd/ Scozia

Scottish (adj) /'skɒtɪʃ/ scozzese

screen (n) /skriːn/ schermo

sculpture (n) /'skʌlptʃə(r)/ scultura

sea (n) /siː/ mare

seafood (n) /'siːfuːd/ frutti di mare

seaman (n) /'siːmən/ marinaio

seaside: go to the seaside (phr) /ˌgəʊ tə ðə 'siːsaɪd/ andare al mare

season (n) /'siːzn/ stagione

seaweed (n) /'siːwiːd/ alga

second (adj) /'sekənd/ secondo

second (n) /'sekənd/ secondo

secret (n) /'siːkrət/ segreto

section (n) /'sekʃn/ sezione

see (v) /siː/ vedere

seem (v) /siːm/ sembrare

self-catering flat (n) /ˌself 'keɪtərɪŋ ˌflæt/ appartamento con uso cucina

self-esteem (n) /ˌself ɪ'stiːm/ autostima

self-image (n) /ˌself 'ɪmɪdʒ/ immagine che si ha di sé stesso

selfish (adj) /'selfɪʃ/ egoista

sell (v) /sel/ vendere

send (v) /send/ mandare

send (sth) back (phr) /ˌsend ... 'bæk/ mandare qualcosa indietro

sense of humour (n) /ˌsens əv 'hjuːmə(r)/ senso dell'umorismo

sensible (adj) /'sensəbl/ assennato, saggio

sensitive (adj) /'sensətɪv/ sensibile

sensor (n) /'sensə(r)/ sensore

September (n) /sep'tembə(r)/ settembre

series (n) /'sɪəriːz/ serie

serious (adj) /'sɪəriəs/ serio

seriously (adv) /'sɪəriəsli/ seriamente

serve (v) /sɜːv/ servire

service charge (n) /'sɜːvɪs ˌtʃɑːdʒ/ coperto

service station (n) /'sɜːvɪs ˌsteɪʃn/ stazione di servizio

session (n) /'seʃn/ sessione

set (v) /set/ stabilire

seventeenth (adj) /sevn'tiːnθ/ diciassettesimo

seventh (adj) /'sevnθ/ settimo

severe (adj) /sɪ'vɪə(r)/ grave

Shall we go (to the cinema)? (phr) /ʃəl wi ˌgəʊ (tə ðə 'sɪnəmə)/ Andiamo (al cinema)?, Che ne dici di andare (al cinema)?

shame: it's a shame (phr) /ɪts ə 'ʃeɪm/ è un peccato

share (v) /ʃeə(r)/ condividere

sheep (n) /ʃiːp/ pecora

shellfish (n) /'ʃelfɪʃ/ crostaceo

ship (n) /ʃɪp/ nave

shirt (n) /ʃɜːt/ camicia

shocked (adj) /ʃɒkt/ sconvolto

shocking (adj) /'ʃɒkɪŋ/ sconvolgente

shoe shop (n) /'ʃuː ˌʃɒp/ negozio di calzature

shoes (n) /ʃuːz/ scarpe

shop (n) /ʃɒp/ negozio

shopping centre (n) /'ʃɒpɪŋ ˌsentə(r)/ centro commerciale

shopping: do the shopping (phr) /ˌduː ðə 'ʃɒpɪŋ/ fare spesa

short (adj) /ʃɔːt/ corto

shorts (n) /ʃɔːts/ calzoncini corti

shoulder-length (adj) /'ʃəʊldə ˌleŋθ/ all'altezza delle spalle

show (v) /ʃəʊ/ mostrare

shower (n) /'ʃaʊə(r)/ doccia

shower: have a shower (phr) /ˌhæv ə 'ʃaʊə(r)/ fare la doccia

shy (adj) /ʃaɪ/ timido

Siberia (n) /saɪ'bɪəriə/ Siberia

sick: be sick (v) /ˌbi 'sɪk/ vomitare

side (n) /saɪd/ lato

sight: love at first sight (phr) /ˌlʌv ət ˌfɜːst 'saɪt/ amore a prima vista

sightseeing: go sightseeing (phr) /ˌgəʊ 'saɪtsiːɪŋ/ visitare un luogo

silly (adj) /'sɪli/ sciocco

silver (n) /'sɪlvə(r)/ argento

similar (adj) /'sɪmələ(r)/ simile

simple (adj) /'sɪmpl/ semplice

simply (adv) /'sɪmpli/ semplicemente

since then (adv) /ˌsɪns 'ðen/ da allora

sing (v) /sɪŋ/ cantare

singer (n) /'sɪŋə(r)/ cantante

single (ticket) (n) /ˌsɪŋgl ('tɪkɪt)/ (biglietto di) sola andata

sink (v) /sɪŋk/ affondare

sister (n) /'sɪstə(r)/ sorella

sister-in-law (n) /'sɪstər ɪn ˌlɔː/ cognata

sit (down) (v) /ˌsɪt ('daʊn)/ sedersi

sitcom (n) /'sɪtkɒm/ situation comedy

site (n) /saɪt/ sito

situation (n) /ˌsɪtʃu'eɪʃn/ situazione

sixteenth (adj) /sɪks'tiːnθ/ sedicesimo

sixth (adj) /sɪksθ/ sesto

size (n) /saɪz/ misura, taglia; dimensione

skate (v) /skeɪt/ fare lo skateboard

skateboard (n) /'skeɪtbɔːd/ skateboard

skatepark (n) /'skeɪtpɑːk/ pista per skateboard

ski (v) /skiː/ sciare

skin (n) /skɪn/ pelle

skirt (n) /skɜːt/ gonna

sleep (v) /sliːp/ dormire

slice (n) /slaɪs/ fetta

slim (adj) /slɪm/ magro

slip (v) /slɪp/ scivolare

small (adj) /smɔːl/ piccolo

smart (adj) /smɑːt/ elegante

smoke (v) /sməʊk/ fumare

snack (n) /snæk/ spuntino

snorkelling: go snorkelling (phr) /ˌgəʊ 'snɔːkəlɪŋ/ nuotare con il respiratore

snow (v) /snəʊ/ nevicare

snowboarding (n) /'snəʊbɔːdɪŋ/ monosci (l'attività)

snowman (n) /'snəʊmæn/ pupazzo di neve

so (adv) /səʊ/ quindi

so (interj) /səʊ/ quindi

So do I. (phr) /ˌsəʊ ˌduː 'aɪ/ Anch'io, Anche a me.

so much/many (det) /ˌsəʊ ˌmʌtʃ, ˌmeni/ così tanto/tanti

soap (n) /səʊp/ telenovela

soccer (n, coll) /'sɒkə(r)/ calcio

social network (n) /ˌsəʊʃl 'netwɜːk/ social network

socks (n) /sɒks/ calzini

sofa (n) /'səʊfə/ divano

soft (adj) /sɒft/ morbido

solar power (n) /ˌsəʊlə 'paʊə(r)/ energia solare

solid (adj) /'sɒlɪd/ solido

solidify (v) /sə'lɪdɪfaɪ/ solidificarsi

solitary (adj) /'sɒlɪtri/ solitario

solstice (n) /'sɒlstɪs/ solstizio

solve (v) /sɒlv/ risolvere

some (pron, det) /sʌm, səm/ alcuni

somebody (pron) /'sʌmbədi/ qualcuno

someone (pron) /'sʌmwʌn/ qualcuno

sometimes (adv) /'sʌmtaɪmz/ a volte

somewhere else (adv) /ˌsʌmweər 'els/ altrove

son (n) /sʌn/ figlio

soon (adv) /suːn/ presto

sorry (phr) /'sɒri/ scusa

sort (n) /sɔːt/ tipo, specie

sort: all sorts of (phr) /ˌɔːl ˌsɔːts əv/ tutti i tipi di

sort out (v) /ˌsɔːt 'aʊt/ risolvere

sound great (phr) /ˌsaʊnd 'greɪt/ sembrare bello

soup (n) /suːp/ zuppa

south (n) /saʊθ/ sud

south-east (n) /ˌsaʊθ 'iːst/ sud-est

southern (adj) /'sʌðən/ meridionale

soy sauce (n) /ˌsɔɪ 'sɔːs/ salsa di soia

space station (n) /'speɪs ˌsteɪʃn/ stazione spaziale

spacecraft (n) /'speɪskrɑːft/ astronave

Spanish (n) /'spænɪʃ/ spagnolo

sparkling (adj) /'spɑːklɪŋ/ effervescente

speak (v) /spiːk/ parlare

special (adj) /'speʃl/ speciale

specialist (n) /'speʃəlɪst/ specialista

specialize (v) /'speʃəlaɪz/ specializzare; specializzarsi

specifically (adv) /spə'sɪfɪkli/ precisamente

spectacular (adj) /spek'tækjələ(r)/ spettacolare

speed (n) /spiːd/ velocità

spend (v) /spend/ trascorrere; spendere

spicy (adj) /'spaɪsi/ picante

spider (n) /'spaɪdə(r)/ ragno

sponsored blogging (phr) /ˌspɒnsəd 'blɒgɪŋ/ tenere un blog sponsorizzato

sports programme (n) /'spɔːts ˌprəʊgræm/ programma sportivo

sportsperson/people (n) /'spɔːtspɜːsn, 'spɔːtspiːpl/ persona/persone sportiva

spring (n) /sprɪŋ/ primavera

square (n) /skweə(r)/ piazza

squeezer (n) /'skwiːzə(r)/ spremitoio

stable (adj) /'steɪbl/ determinato

stadium (n) /'steɪdiəm/ stadio

stage (n) /steɪdʒ/ palco

stand (v) /stænd/ stare in piedi

standard (adj) /'stændəd/ comune, normale

star (n) /stɑː(r)/ stella

start (v) /stɑːt/ cominciare

starter (n) /'stɑːtə(r)/ antipasto

States: the States (n) /ðə 'steɪts/ gli Stati Uniti

station (n) /'steɪʃn/ stazione

statistics (n) /stə'tɪstɪks/ statistiche

stay (v) /steɪ/ pernottare

steam engine (n) /'stiːm ˌendʒɪn/ motore a vapore

stepbrother (n) /'stepbrʌðə(r)/ fratellastro

step-by-step (adj) /ˌstep ˌbaɪ 'step/ passo per passo

stepdad (n) /'stepdæd/ patrigno

stepfather (n) /'stepfɑːðə(r)/ patrigno

stepmother (n) /'stepmʌðə(r)/ matrigna

stepmum (n) /'stepmʌm/ matrigna

stepsister (n) /'stepsɪstə(r)/ sorellastra

stereotype (n) /'steriəʊtaɪp/ stereotipo

stereotypical (adj) /steriəʊ'tɪpɪkl/ stereotipico

still (adv) /stɪl/ ancora

still (water) (adj) /stɪl (ˌwɔːtə)/ (acqua) liscia

stop (v) /stɒp/ fermarsi; fermare

storm (n) /stɔːm/ temporale

story (n) /'stɔːri/ storia

storytelling tradition (phr) /'stɔːritelɪŋ trə,dɪʃn/ tradizione del raccontare storie

straight (adj) /streɪt/ liscio

straight on: go straight on (phr) /ˌgəʊ ˌstreɪt 'ɒn/ vai dritto

strange (adj) /streɪndʒ/ strano

street (n) /striːt/ strada

street dancing (n) /'stri:t ˌdɑːnsɪŋ/ street dancing

strict (adj) /strɪkt/ severo

strike (n) /straɪk/ attacco

strike (v) /straɪk/ colpire

stroke (n) /strəʊk/ colpo apoplettico, ictus cerebrale

strong (adj) /strɒŋ/ forte

strong-willed (adj) /ˌstrɒŋ 'wɪld/ che ha forte volontà

student (n) /'stjuːdnt/ studente

student exchange (n) /ˌstjuːdnt ɪks'tʃeɪndʒ/ visita di scambio di studenti

study (n) /'stʌdi/ studio

study (v) /'stʌdi/ studiare

stuff (n, coll) /stʌf/ cose

stunning (adj) /'stʌnɪŋ/ meraviglioso

stupid (adj) /'stjuːpɪd/ stupido, scemo

style (n) /staɪl/ stile

subject (n) /'sʌbdʒekt/ materia

suburb (n) /'sʌbɜːb/ periferia

success (n) /sək'ses/ successo

successful (adj) /sək'sesfl/ di successo

such as (phr) /'sʌtʃ əz/ come, per esempio

suffer (v) /'sʌfə(r)/ soffrire

sugar (n) /'ʃʊgə(r)/ zucchero

suggest (v) /sə'dʒest/ suggerire

suit (v) /suːt/ andare bene

suitcase (n) /'suːtkeɪs/ valigia

summer (n) /'sʌmə(r)/ estate

sun (n) /sʌn/ sole

suncream (n) /'sʌnˌkriːm/ crema solare

sunbathing: go sunbathing (phr) /ˌgəʊ 'sʌnbeɪðɪŋ/ andare a prendere il sole

Sunday (n) /'sʌndeɪ/ domenica

sunglasses (n) /'sʌnglɑːsɪz/ occhiali da sole

sunny (adj) /'sʌni/ soleggiato

suntan (n) /'sʌntæn/ abbronzatura

suntanned (adj) /'sʌntænd/ abbronzato

superficial (adj) /suːpə'fɪʃl/ superficiale

supermarket (n) /'suːpəmɑːkɪt/ supermercato

supervisor (n) /'suːpəvaɪzə(r)/ supervisore

support (v) /sə'pɔːt/ appoggiare, sostenere

suppose (v) /sə'pəʊz/ supporre

suppose: I suppose so. (phr) /ˌaɪ sə'pəʊz ˌsəʊ/ Immagino di sì.

sure (adj) /ʃʊə(r)/ sicuro

surf (the Internet) (v) /ˌsɜːf (ðiː 'ɪntənet)/ navigare (in internet)

surface (n) /'sɜːfɪs/ superficie

surfing: go surfing (phr) /ˌgəʊ 'sɜːfɪŋ/ fare surfing

surprise (n) /sə'praɪz/ sorpresa

surprised (adj) /sə'praɪzd/ sorpreso

survey (n) /'sɜːveɪ/ sondaggio

survive (v) /sə'vaɪv/ sopravvivere

sustainability (n) /səsteɪnə'bɪləti/ sostenibilità

sweatshirt (n) /'swetʃɜːt/ felpa

sweet (adj) /swiːt/ dolce

swim (v) /swɪm/ nuotare

swimming (n) /'swɪmɪŋ/ nuoto

swimming costume (n) /'swɪmɪŋ ˌkɒstjuːm/ costume da bagno

swimming pool (n) /'swɪmɪŋ ˌpuːl/ piscina

swimming: go swimming (phr) /ˌgəʊ 'swɪmɪŋ/ andare a nuoto

swipe card (n) /'swaɪp ˌkɑːd/ carta intelligente

symbol (n) /'sɪmbl/ simbolo

syrup (n) /'sɪrəp/ sciroppo

system (n) /'sɪstəm/ sistema

T

table (n) /'teɪbl/ tavolo

take (the bus/train) (v) /ˌteɪk (ðə 'bʌs, 'treɪn)/ prendere (l'autobus/il treno)

take a photo (phr) /ˌteɪk ə 'fəʊtəʊ/ fare una fotografia

take out (v) /ˌteɪk 'aʊt/ portare fuori

take part in (phr) /ˌteɪk 'pɑːt ˌɪn/ partecipare a, prendere parte a/in

take place (phr) /ˌteɪk 'pleɪs/ succedere, accadere

---

take sb to the doctor (phr) /ˌteɪk ... tə ðə 'dɒktə(r)/ portare qualcuno dal dottore

takeaway (n) /'teɪkəweɪ/ rosticceria

talent contest (n) /'tælənt ˌkɒntest/ concorso di talenti

talent show (n) /'tælənt ˌʃəʊ/ esibizione di dilettanti

talented (adj) /'tæləntɪd/ di talento

talk (v) /tɔːk/ parlare

tall (adj) /tɔːl/ alto

tan (v) /tæn/ abbronzarsi

tanning centre (n) /'tænɪŋ ˌsentə(r)/ centro per l'abbronzatura

tartan (adj) /'tɑːtn/ tessuto di lana scozzese a riquadri formati da righe di vari colori

taste (v) /teɪst/ assaggiare

tasty (adj) /'teɪsti/ gustoso, saporito

tea (n) /tiː/ tè

teacher (n) /'tiːtʃə(r)/ insegnante

team (n) /tiːm/ squadra

technology (n) /tek'nɒlədʒi/ tecnologia

Technology College (n) /tek'nɒlədʒi ˌkɒlɪdʒ/ scuola secondaria specializzata in materie tecniche e scientifiche

teenager (n) /'tiːneɪdʒə(r)/ adolescente

teeth (n) /tiːθ/ denti

television (n) /'telɪvɪʃn/ televisione

tell (v) /tel/ dire, raccontare

temperature (n) /'temprətʃə(r)/ temperatura

tenth (adj) /tenθ/ decimo

terrible (adj) /'terəbl/ terribile

terrifying (adj) /'terɪfaɪɪŋ/ terrificante

test (v) /test/ provare, testare, collaudare

text (v) /tekst/ mandare un SMS

text message (n) /'tekst ˌmesɪdʒ/ messaggino, sms

Thai (adj) /taɪ/ thailandese

than (prep) /ðæn, ðən/ di, che

thank you (phr) /'θæŋk ˌjuː/ grazie

thanks to (phr) /'θæŋks tə/ grazie a

that (adj, pron) /ðæt/ che; quello

that (conj) /ðæt, ðət/ che

that is (phr) /'ðæt ˌɪz/ cioè

thaw (v) /θɔː/ sciogliersi

theatre (n) /'θɪətə(r)/ teatro

their (adj) /ðeə(r)/ (il) loro

theirs (pron) /ðeəz/ (il) loro

them (pron) /ðem, ðəm/ loro, li

theme park (n) /'θiːm ˌpɑːk/ parco a tema

then (adv) /ðen/ poi, allora

there (adv) /ðeə(r)/ lì

there is/there are (v) /'ðeər ˌɪz, 'ðeər ˌɑː/ c'è/ci sono

these (adj, pron) /ðiːz/ questi

thick-skinned (adj) /ˌθɪk 'skɪnd/ insensibile

thin (adj) /θɪn/ magro; sottile

thing (n) /θɪŋ/ cosa

think (v) /θɪŋk/ pensare

third (adj) /θɜːd/ terzo

thirteenth (adj) /θɜː'tiːnθ/ tredicesimo

thirtieth (adj) /'θɜːtiəθ/ trentesimo

thirty-(first) (adj) /ˌθɜːti ('fɜːst)/ trentunesimo

this (adj, pron) /ðɪs/ questo

this afternoon (phr) /ˌðɪs ɑːftə'nuːn/ questo pomeriggio, oggi pomeriggio

this evening (phr) /ˌðɪs 'iːvnɪŋ/ stasera

this morning (phr) /ˌðɪs 'mɔːnɪŋ/ stamattina

those (adj, pron) /ðəʊz/ quelli

thousand (n) /'θaʊznd/ mille

through (prep) /θruː/ attraverso

throughout (prep) /θruː'aʊt/ durante tutto

throw away (v) /ˌθrəʊ ə'weɪ/ buttare

thunder (n) /'θʌndə(r)/ tuono

thunderstorm (n) /'θʌndəstɔːm/ temporale (con tuoni e lampi)

Thursday (n) /'θɜːzdeɪ/ giovedì

ticket (n) /'tɪkɪt/ biglietto

ticket office (n) /'tɪkɪt ˌɒfɪs/ biglietteria

tidy (adj) /'taɪdi/ ordinato

tidy (v) /'taɪdi/ riordinare

---

tie (n) /taɪ/ cravatta

tiger (n) /'taɪgə(r)/ tigre

tights (n) /taɪts/ calze

time (n) /taɪm/ epoca

times: (three) times (adv) /('θriː) ˌtaɪmz/ (tre) volte

tin (n) /tɪn/ lattina

tired (adj) /'taɪəd/ stanco

tiring (adj) /'taɪrɪŋ/ stancante

title (n) /'taɪtl/ titolo

to (prep) /tuː, tə/ a

to: (five) to (two) (phr) /(ˌfaɪv) tə ('tuː)/ le (due) meno (cinque)

toast (n) /təʊst/ pane tostato

today (adv) /tə'deɪ/ oggi

toilet (n) /'tɔɪlət/ bagno

tolerate (v) /'tɒləreɪt/ tollerare

tomato (n) /tə'mɑːtəʊ/ pomodoro

tomorrow (n, adv) /tə'mɒrəʊ/ domani

tonight (adv) /tə'naɪt/ stasera

too (adv) /tuː/ anche

too much/many (det) /'tuː ˌmʌtʃ, ˌmeni/ troppo/ troppi

toothpaste (n) /'tuːθpeɪst/ dentifricio

top (adj) /tɒp/ superiore

top up (v) /ˌtɒp 'ʌp/ ricaricare

topic (n) /'tɒpɪk/ argomento

tornado (n) /tɔː'neɪdəʊ/ tornado

torrential (adj) /tə'renʃl/ torrenziale

total (n, adj) /'təʊtl/ totale

tough (adj) /tʌf/ difficile, duro

tour (n) /tʊə(r)/ viaggio, giro

tourism (n) /'tʊərɪzəm/ turismo

tourist (n) /'tʊərɪst/ turista

tourist information centre (n) /ˌtʊərɪst ɪnfə'meɪʃn ˌsentə(r)/ ufficio informazioni turistiche

town (n) /taʊn/ cittadina, città

town council (n) /ˌtaʊn 'kaʊnsl/ comune

town hall (n) /ˌtaʊn 'hɔːl/ municipio

track (n) /træk/ binario

tracksuit (n) /'træksuːt/ tuta

trade (n) /treɪd/ commercio

tradition (n) /trə'dɪʃn/ tradizione

traditional (adj) /trə'dɪʃənl/ tradizionale

traffic (n) /'træfɪk/ traffico

traffic light (n) /'træfɪk ˌlaɪt/ semaforo

train (n) /treɪn/ treno

train (v) /treɪn/ addestrare; allenare, esercitare; allenarsi; esercitarsi

trainers (n) /'treɪnəz/ scarpe da ginnastica

training (n) /'treɪnɪŋ/ allenamento

translate (v) /træns'leɪt/ tradurre

translator (n) /'trænsleɪtə(r)/ traduttore

transport (n) /'trænspɔːt/ trasporto

trauma (n) /'trɔːmə/ trauma

travel (n) /'trævl/ viaggio

travel (v) /'trævl/ viaggiare

travelcard (n) /'trævlkɑːd/ biglietto/abbonamento integrato

tray (n) /treɪ/ vassoio

treat (v) /triːt/ trattare

treatment (n) /'triːtmənt/ cura

tree (n) /triː/ albero

trendy (adj) /'trendi/ di moda

trip (n) /trɪp/ escursione, gita, viaggio

tropical (adj) /'trɒpɪkl/ tropicale

tropics (n) /'trɒpɪks/ tropici

trouble (n) /'trʌbl/ problema

trouble: get into trouble (phr) /ˌget ˌɪntə 'trʌbl/ cacciarsi nei guai

troublemaker (n) /'trʌblmeɪkə(r)/ chi causa guai, piantagrane

trousers (n) /'traʊzəz/ pantaloni

true (adj) /truː/ vero

trumpet (n) /'trʌmpɪt/ tromba

try (v) /traɪ/ provare

try sth on (v) /ˌtraɪ ... 'ɒn/ provare, misurare

Tube (n) /tjuːb/ metropolitana

tube station (n) /'tjuːb ˌsteɪʃn/ stazione della metropolitana

Glossary

Tuesday (n) /ˈtjuːzdeɪ/ martedì
Turkey (n) /ˈtɜːki/ Turchia
turn (n) /tɜːn/ giro
turn into (v) /ˈtɜːn ˌɪntə/ diventare
turn left/right (phr) /ˌtɜːn ˈleft, ˈraɪt/ gira a sinistra/destra
turning: the (first) turning on the (left) (phr) /ðə (ˌfɜːst) ˌtɜːnɪŋ ˌɒn ðə (ˈleft)/ la (prima) traversa a (sinistra)
TV (n) /ˌtiː ˈviː/ TV, televisione
twelfth (adj) /twelfθ/ dodicesimo
twentieth (adj) /ˈtwentiəθ/ ventesimo
twenty-(first) (adj) /ˌtwenti (ˈfɜːst)/ ventunesimo
twice (adv) /twaɪs/ due volte
twin (n) /twɪn/ gemello
type (n) /taɪp/ tipo
typical (adj) /ˈtɪpɪkl/ tipico

U

ugly (adj) /ˈʌgli/ brutto
UK (United Kingdom) (n) /ˌjuː ˈkeɪ (juˌnaɪtɪd ˈkɪŋdəm)/ Regno Unito
umbrella (n) /ʌmˈbrelə/ ombrello
uncle (n) /ˈʌŋkl/ zio
uncomfortable (adj) /ʌnˈkʌmftəbl/ a disagio
under (prep) /ˈʌndə(r)/ sotto
underground (adj) /ˈʌndəgraʊnd/ sotterraneo
underground (n) /ˈʌndəgraʊnd/ metropolitana
understand (v) /ʌndəˈstænd/ capire
unemployed (adj) /ˌʌnɪmˈplɔɪd/ disoccupato
unfair (adj) /ʌnˈfeə(r)/ ingiusto
unfairly (adv) /ʌnˈfeəli/ ingiustamente
unfortunately (adv) /ʌnˈfɔːtʃənətli/ sfortunatamente
unhealthy (adj) /ʌnˈhelθi/ poco sano
uniform (n) /ˈjuːnɪfɔːm/ divisa
university (n) /juːnɪˈvɜːsəti/ università
until (prep) /ʌnˈtɪl/ fino a
untrue (adj) /ʌnˈtruː/ falso
unusual (adj) /ʌnˈjuːʒuəl/ insolito
up (adv) /ʌp/ sopra
up and down (prep) /ˌʌp ən ˌdaʊn/ su e giù
upset (adj) /ʌpˈset/ turbato, agitato
upstairs (adv) /ʌpˈsteəz/ sopra
uptight (adj) /ʌpˈtaɪt/ teso; permaloso
us (pron) /ʌs/ noi
USA (United States of America) (n) /ˌjuː ˌes ˈeɪ (juˌnaɪtɪd ˌsteɪts əv əˈmerɪkə)/ Stati Uniti d'America
use (v) /juːz/ usare
useful (adj) /ˈjuːsfl/ utile
usually (adv) /ˈjuːʒuəli/ di solito

V

Valentine's Day (n) /ˈvæləntaɪnz ˌdeɪ/ giorno di San Valentino
variety (n) /vəˈraɪəti/ varietà
veal (n) /viːl/ vitello
vegetables (n) /ˈvedʒtəblz/ verdura
vehicle (n) /ˈviːəkl/ veicolo, mezzo di trasporto
venue (n) /ˈvenjuː/ locale
verruca (n) /vəˈruːkə/ verruca
version (n) /ˈvɜːʃn/ versione
very (adv) /ˈveri/ molto
victim (n) /ˈvɪktɪm/ vittima
video (cassette) recorder (n) /ˈvɪdiəʊ kəˌset rɪˌkɔːdə(r)/ videoregistratore
view (n) /vjuː/ vista
village (n) /ˈvɪlɪdʒ/ paese
vinegar (n) /ˈvɪnɪgə(r)/ aceto
vinyl (n) /ˈvaɪnl/ disco, vinile
violent (adj) /ˈvaɪələnt/ violento
virtual (adj) /ˈvɜːtʃuəl/ virtuale
visit (v) /ˈvɪzɪt/ visitare
v-neck (adj) /ˈviː ˌnek/ con la scollatura a V
volleyball (n) /ˈvɒlibɔːl/ pallavolo
voyage (n) /ˈvɔɪɪdʒ/ viaggio

W

waffle (n) /ˈwɒfl/ cialda
wage(s) (n) /ˈweɪdʒ(ɪz)/ stipendio
waistcoat (n) /ˈweɪstkəʊt/ gilet
wait (for) (v) /ˈweɪt ˌfɔː, fə/ aspettare
waitress (n) /ˈweɪtrəs/ cameriera
Wales (n) /weɪlz/ Galles
wall (n) /wɔːl/ muri; muro
walk (n) /wɔːk/ camminata, passeggiata
walk (v) /wɔːk/ camminare
walk: go for a walk (phr) /ˌgəʊ fər ə ˈwɔːk/ passeggiare, andare a passeggio
want (v) /wɒnt/ volere
wardrobe (n) /ˈwɔːdrəʊb/ armadio
warm (adj) /wɔːm/ caldo; caloroso
wash: have a wash (phr) /ˌhæv ə ˈwɒʃ/ lavarsi
washing machine (n) /ˈwɒʃɪŋ məˌʃiːn/ lavatrice
washing: do the washing (phr) /ˌduː ðə ˈwɒʃɪŋ/ lavare i panni
washing-up: do the washing-up (phr) /ˌduː ðə ˌwɒʃɪŋ ˈʌp/ lavare i piatti
waste (v) /weɪst/ sprecare
watch (v) /wɒtʃ/ guardare
water (n) /ˈwɔːtə(r)/ acqua
water carrier (n) /ˈwɔːtə ˌkæriə(r)/ contenitore per il trasporto dell'acqua
water sports (n) /ˈwɔːtə ˌspɔːts/ sport acquatici
waterproof (adj) /ˈwɔːtəpruːf/ impermeabile
wavy (adj) /ˈweɪvi/ ondulato
wax model (n) /ˌwæks ˈmɒdl/ modello di cera
way (n) /weɪ/ modo
way: on (my) way (to school) (phr) /ˌɒn (ˌmaɪ) ˌweɪ (tə ˈskuːl)/ andando (a scuola)
wealthy (adj) /ˈwelθi/ ricco, agiato
wear (v) /weə(r)/ indossare
weather (n) /ˈweðə(r)/ tempo (atmosferico)
website (n) /ˈwebsaɪt/ sito web
wedding (n) /ˈwedɪŋ/ matrimonio
Wednesday (n) /ˈwenzdeɪ/ mercoledì
week (n) /wiːk/ settimana
weekend (n) /ˌwiːkˈend/ fine settimana
weigh (v) /weɪ/ pesare
weight (n) /weɪt/ peso
weight training (n) /ˈweɪt ˌtreɪnɪŋ/ allenamento con i pesi
weird (adj) /wɪəd/ strano
welcome (n) /ˈwelkəm/ benvenuto
well (adv) /wel/ bene
Well (interj) /wel/ Ebbene
well-balanced (adj) /ˌwel ˈbælənst/ equilibrato
well-known (adj) /ˌwel ˈnəʊn/ conosciuto, famoso
Welsh (adj, n) /welʃ/ gallese
west (n) /west/ ovest
Western (adj) /ˈwestən/ del west
wet (adj) /wet/ bagnato
what (pron) /wɒt/ ciò che
What...? (int) /wɒt/ Cosa... ?
What about...? (phr) /ˈwɒt əˌbaʊt/ Che ne dici di... ?
What time...? (int) /ˈwɒt ˌtaɪm/ A che ora... ?
What's the matter? (phr) /ˌwɒts ðə ˈmætə(r)/ Che c'è?
whatever (phr) /wɒtˈevə(r)/ qualsiasi
wheel (n) /wiːl/ ruota
wheelchair (n) /ˈwiːltʃeə(r)/ sedia a rotelle
when (adv) /wen/ quando
where (pron) /weə(r)/ dove
Where...? (int) /weə(r)/ Dove... ?
whether (conj) /ˈweðə(r)/ se
which (pron) /wɪtʃ/ che
Which...? (int) /wɪtʃ/ Quale... ?
white (adj) /waɪt/ bianco
Who...? (int) /huː/ Chi... ?
Whose...? (int) /huːz/ Di chi... ?
Why...? (int) /waɪ/ Perché...?
widescreen (adj) /ˈwaɪdskriːn/ schermo panoramico
wife (n) /waɪf/ moglie

wild (adj) /waɪld/ tempestoso
wildlife (n) /ˈwaɪldlaɪf/ animali e piante selvatiche
win (v) /wɪn/ vincere
wind (n) /wɪnd/ vento
window (n) /ˈwɪndəʊ/ finestra
windsurfing: go windsurfing (phr) /ˌgəʊ ˈwɪndsɜːfɪŋ/ fare il windsurf
windy (adj) /ˈwɪndi/ ventoso
wine (n) /waɪn/ vino
winning (adj) /ˈwɪnɪŋ/ vincente
winter (n) /ˈwɪntə(r)/ inverno
with (prep) /wɪð/ con
without (prep) /wɪˈðaʊt/ senza
woman/women (n) /ˈwʊmən, ˈwɪmɪn/ donna/donne
wonderful (adj) /ˈwʌndəfl/ meraviglioso
word (n) /wɜːd/ parola
work (n) /wɜːk/ lavoro
work (v) /wɜːk/ funzionare; lavorare
worker (n) /ˈwɜːkə(r)/ lavoratore
world (n, adj) /wɜːld/ mondo
worried (adj) /ˈwʌrid/ preoccupato, teso
worry (v) /ˈwʌri/ preoccuparsi
worse (adj) /wɜːs/ peggiore
worst (adj) /wɜːst/ (il) peggiore
worth: it's worth it (phr) /ˌɪts ˈwɜːθ ˌɪt/ ne vale la pena
would like (phr) /wʊd ˈlaɪk/ (mi) piacerebbe
write (v) /raɪt/ scrivere
wrong (adj) /rɒŋ/ sbagliato

Y

year (n) /jɪə(r)/ anno
yellow (adj) /ˈjeləʊ/ giallo
yesterday (adv) /ˈjestədeɪ/ ieri
yet, not... yet (adv) /ˌnɒt... ˈjet/ già, non... ancora
yoghurt (n) /ˈjɒgət/ yogurt
young (adj) /jʌŋ/ giovane
your (adj) /jɔː(r)/ (il) tuo
yours (pron) /jɔːz/ tuo
yourself (pron) /jɔːˈself/ tu stesso
youth club (n) /ˈjuːθ ˌklʌb/ circolo giovanile
youth hostel (n) /ˈjuːθ ˌhɒstl/ ostello della gioventù

Z

Zimbabwe (n) /zɪmˈbɑːbwi, -weɪ/ Zimbabwe
zone (n) /zəʊn/ zona
zoo (n) /zuː/ zoo

Literature lessons glossary

- **afraid** (adj) /əˈfreɪd/ impaurito
- **army** (n) /ˈɑːmi/ esercito
- **arrest** (v) /əˈrest/ arrestare
- **at once** (adv) /ət ˈwʌns/ subito, immediatamente
- **away** (prep) /əˈweɪ/ via
- **be in love with** (phr) /ˌbiː ˌɪn ˈlʌv ˌwɪð/ essere innamorato di
- **blood** (n) /blʌd/ sangue
- **bring** (v) /brɪŋ/ portare
- **character** (n) /ˈkærəktə(r)/ personaggio
- **classroom** (n) /ˈklɑːsruːm/ classe
- **courthouse** (n) /ˈkɔːthaʊs/ palazzo di giustizia
- **cross** (n) /krɒs/ croce
- **cut** (n) /kʌt/ taglio
- **dead** (adj) /ded/ morto
- **defeat** (v) /dɪˈfiːt/ sconfiggere
- **dig** (v) /dɪg/ scavare
- **easy** (adj) /ˈiːzi/ facile
- **employ** (v) /ɪmˈplɔɪ/ assumere
- **escape** (v) /ɪˈskeɪp/ scappare, fuggire, evadere
- **eventually** (adv) /ɪˈventʃuəli/ alla fine
- **excitedly** (adv) /ɪkˈsaɪtɪdli/ animatamente
- **face** (n) /feɪs/ faccia
- **farmhouse** (n) /ˈfɑːmhaʊs/ casa colonica, fattoria
- **feel** (v) /ˈfiːl/ sentirsi
- **feel sorry for** (phr) /ˌfiːl ˈsɒri fə(r)/ provare dispiacere per
- **fire** (n) /ˈfaɪə(r)/ fuoco
- **fireplace** (n) /ˈfaɪəpleɪs/ caminetto
- **flash** (n) /flæʃ/ bagliore
- **forest** (n) /ˈfɒrɪst/ foresta
- **general** (n) /ˈdʒenrəl/ generale
- **gentleman** (n) /ˈdʒentlmən/ gentiluomo
- **get** (v) /get/ arrivare, raggiungere
- **go after** (phr) /ˌgəʊ ˈɑːftə(r)/ seguire
- **good sleeper** (phr) /ˌgʊd ˈsliːpə(r)/ uno che dorme bene
- **have a look around** (phr) /ˌhæv ə ˌlʊk əˈraʊnd/ guardare in giro, guardarsi intorno
- **hole** (n) /həʊl/ buco
- **inside** (prep) /ɪnˈsaɪd/ dentro
- **interested** (adj) /ˈɪntrəstɪd/ interessato
- **invite** (v) /ɪnˈvaɪt/ invitare
- **jealous** (adj) /ˈdʒeləs/ geloso
- **king** (n) /kɪŋ/ re
- **kingdom** (n) /ˈkɪŋdəm/ regno
- **knife** (n) /naɪf/ coltello
- **leg** (n) /leg/ gamba
- **legendary** (adj) /ˈledʒəndri/ legendario
- **letter** (n) /ˈletə(r)/ lettera
- **look after** (phr) /ˌlʊk ˈɑːftə(r)/ accudire, badare a
- **lover** (n) /ˈlʌvə(r)/ amante
- **make** (v) /meɪk/ rendere
- **marry** (v) /ˈmæri/ sposare
- **matchmaker** (n) /ˈmætʃmeɪkə(r)/ chi combina matrimoni
- **matchmaking** (n) /ˈmætʃmeɪkɪŋ/ combinazione di matrimoni
- **miss** (v) /mɪs/ sentire la mancanza
- **mixed** (adj) /mɪkst/ assortito
- **most** (det) /məʊst/ il più
- **murderer** (n) /ˈmɜːdərə(r)/ assassino
- **next** (prep) /nekst/ accanto
- **night** (n) /naɪt/ notte
- **over** (adj) /ˈəʊvə(r)/ finito
- **particular** (adj) /pəˈtɪkjələ(r)/ particolare
- **party** (n) /ˈpɑːti/ festa
- **plan** (n) /plæn/ piano, programma
- **play** (n) /pleɪ/ opera teatrale
- **play music** (phr) /ˌpleɪ ˈmjuːzɪk/ suonare
- **punish** (v) /ˈpʌnɪʃ/ punire
- **question** (n) /ˈkwestʃən/ domanda
- **quietly** (adv) /ˈkwaɪətli/ silenziosamente
- **racing** (adj) /ˈreɪsɪŋ/ da corsa

- **rider** (n) /ˈraɪdə(r)/ fantino
- **rob** (v) /rɒb/ rubare
- **seat** (v) /siːt/ sedersi
- **servant** (n) /ˈsɜːvənt/ servo
- **shake** (v) /ʃeɪk/ scuotere
- **smile** (v) /smaɪl/ sorridere
- **soldier** (n) /ˈsəʊldʒə(r)/ soldato
- **step on** (v) /ˈstep ˌɒn/ mettere i piedi su
- **stranger** (n) /ˈstreɪndʒə(r)/ estraneo, sconosciuto
- **suddenly** (adv) /ˈsʌdnli/ improvvisamente
- **thank** (v) /θæŋk/ ringraziare
- **trainer** (n) /ˈtreɪnə(r)/ allenatore
- **treasure** (n) /ˈtreʒə(r)/ tesoro
- **unhappy** (adj) /ʌnˈhæpi/ infelice
- **unlocked** (adj) /ʌnˈlɒkt/ non chiuso a chiave
- **valley** (n) /ˈvæli/ vallata
- **wake** (v) /weɪk/ svegliare
- **whisper** (v) /ˈwɪspə(r)/ bisbigliare
- **wonderful** (adj) /ˈwʌndəfl/ meraviglioso
- **wonderfully** (adv) /ˈwʌndəfəli/ meravigliosamente

Student's Audio CD Contents:

- Starter and Student's Book storyline dialogues
- Student's Book *Skills and culture* reading texts
- Student's Book *Functions on film* model dialogues
- Student's Book *Culture network* reading texts
- Workbook Skills reading, listening and dictation
- Student's Book Literature lessons

  All audio tracks are in MP3 format.

Network 1
Paul Radley

OXFORD
UNIVERSITY PRESS
www.oup.com

Student's Audio CD
MP3 files • Tracks 001–110

Starter

Track

001	Introduction
002	Lesson A: p.4 Ex.1
003	Lesson B: p.6 Ex.1
004	Lesson C: p.8 Ex.1
005	Lesson D: p.10 Ex.1
006	Lesson E: p.12 Ex.1
007	Lesson F: p.14 Ex.1
008	Lesson G p.16 Ex.1
009	Lesson H p.18 Ex.1

Student's Book

Track

010	Unit 1: p.10 Ex.1
011	Unit 1: p.12 Ex.1
012	Unit 1: p.14 Ex.2
013	Unit 2: p.18 Ex.1
014	Unit 2: p.20 Ex.1
015	Unit 2: p.22 Ex.2
016	Units 1+2 Functions: p.25 Ex.2
017	Units 1+2 Culture network: p.26 Ex.1
018	Unit 3: p.28 Ex.1
019	Unit 3: p.30 Ex.1
020	Unit 3: p.32 Ex.3
021	Unit 4: p.36 Ex.1
022	Unit 4: p.38 Ex.1
023	Unit 4: p.40 Ex.2
024	Units 3+4 Functions: p.43 Ex.3
025	Units 3+4 Culture network: p.44 Ex.1
026	Unit 5: p.46 Ex.1
027	Unit 5: p.48 Ex.1
028	Unit 5: p.50 Ex.3
029	Unit 6: p.54 Ex.1
030	Unit 6: p.56 Ex.1
031	Unit 6: p.58 Ex.1
032	Units 5+6 Functions: p.61 Ex.2
033	Units 5+6 Culture network: p.62 Ex.1
034	Unit 7: p.64 Ex.1
035	Unit 7: p.66 Ex.1
036	Unit 7: p.68 Ex.2
037	Unit 8: p.72 Ex.1
038	Unit 8: p.74 Ex.1
039	Unit 8: p.76 Ex.4
040	Units 7+8 Functions: p.79 Ex.3
041	Units 7+8 Culture network: p.80 Ex.3
042	Unit 9: p.82 Ex.1
043	Unit 9: p.84 Ex.1
044	Unit 9: p.86 Ex.2
045	Unit 10: p.90 Ex.1
046	Unit 10: p.92 Ex.1
047	Unit 10: p.94 Ex.2
048	Units 9+10 Functions: p.97 Ex.2
049	Units 9+10 Culture network: p.98 Ex.3
050	Unit 11: p.100 Ex.1
051	Unit 11: p.102 Ex.1
052	Unit 11: p.104 Ex.3
053	Unit 12: p.108 Ex.1
054	Unit 12: p.110 Ex.1
055	Unit 12: p.113 Ex.4
056	Units 11+12 Functions: p.115 Ex.2
057	Units 11+12 Culture network: p.116 Ex.1
058	Unit 13: p.118 Ex.1
059	Unit 13: p.120 Ex.1
060	Unit 13: p.122 Ex.2
061	Unit 14: p.126 Ex.1
062	Unit 14: p.128 Ex.1
063	Unit 14: p.130 Ex.2
064	Units 13+14 Functions: p.133 Ex.2
065	Units 13+14 Culture network: p.134 Ex.2
066	Unit 15: p.136 Ex.1
067	Unit 15: p.138 Ex.1
068	Unit 15: p.140 Ex.3
069	Unit 15 Functions: p.143 Ex.3
070	Unit 15 Culture network: p.144 Ex.2

Workbook

Track

071	Units 1+2 Skills: p.159 Ex.1
072	Units 1+2 Skills: p.160 Exs. 4, 5, 6
073	Units 1+2 Skills: p.160 Ex.7
074	Units 3+4 Skills: p.175 Ex.1
075	Units 3+4 Skills: p.176 Exs. 4, 5, 6
076	Units 3+4 Skills: p.176 Ex.7
077	Units 5+6 Skills: p.191 Ex.1
078	Units 5+6 Skills: p.192 Exs. 4, 5, 6
079	Units 5+6 Skills: p.192 Ex.7
080	Units 7+8 Skills: p.207 Ex.1
081	Units 7+8 Skills: p.208 Exs. 4, 5, 6
082	Units 7+8 Skills: p.208 Ex.7
083	Units 9+10 Skills: p.223 Ex.1
084	Units 9+10 Skills: p.224 Exs. 4, 5, 6
085	Units 9+10 Skills: p.224 Ex.7
086	Units 11+12 Skills: p.239 Ex.1
087	Units 11+12 Skills: p.240 Exs. 4, 5, 6
088	Units 11+12 Skills: p.240 Ex.7
089	Units 13+14 Skills: p.255 Ex.1
090	Units 13+14 Skills: p.256 Exs. 4, 5, 6
091	Units 13+14 Skills: p.256 Ex.7
092	Unit 15 Skills: p.265 Ex.1
093	Unit 15 Skills: p.266 Exs. 4, 5, 6
094	Unit 15 Skills: p.266 Ex.7

Literature lessons

Track

095	Lesson A: p.268 Ex.2
096	Lesson A: p.268 Ex.4
097	Lesson B: p.270 Ex.1
098	Lesson B: p.270 Ex.5
099	Lesson B: p.270 Ex.6
100	Lesson B: p.270 Ex.7
101	Lesson C: p.272 Ex.1
102	Lesson C: p.272 Ex.6
103	Lesson D: p.274 Ex.1
104	Lesson D: p.274 Ex.5
105	Lesson E: p.276 Ex.1
106	Lesson E: p.276 Ex.6
107	Lesson F: p.278 Ex.1
108	Lesson F: p.278 Ex.5
109	Lesson G: p.280 Ex.1
110	Lesson G: p.280 Ex.4

OXFORD
UNIVERSITY PRESS

Great Clarendon Street, Oxford, OX2 6DP, United Kingdom

Oxford University Press is a department of the University of Oxford. It furthers the University's objective of excellence in research, scholarship, and education by publishing worldwide. Oxford is a registered trade mark of Oxford University Press in the UK and in certain other countries

© Oxford University Press 2012

The moral rights of the author have been asserted

First published in 2012
2016 2015 2014 2013 2012
10 9 8 7 6 5 4 3 2

No unauthorized photocopying

All rights reserved. No part of this publication may be reproduced, stored in a retrieval system, or transmitted, in any form or by any means, without the prior permission in writing of Oxford University Press, or as expressly permitted by law, by licence or under terms agreed with the appropriate reprographics rights organization. Enquiries concerning reproduction outside the scope of the above should be sent to the ELT Rights Department, Oxford University Press, at the address above

You must not circulate this work in any other form and you must impose this same condition on any acquirer

Links to third party websites are provided by Oxford in good faith and for information only. Oxford disclaims any responsibility for the materials contained in any third party website referenced in this work

ISBN: 978 0 19 427706 8

Printed in China

This book is printed on paper from certified and well-managed sources

ACKNOWLEDGEMENTS

The author would like to thank the Network *team for all their hard work on the project.*

The authors and publisher are grateful to those who have given permission to reproduce the following extracts and adaptations of copyright material: p.269 From Oxford Dominoes Starter: *Rip Van Winkle & The Legend of Sleepy Hollow* by Washington Irving, retold by Alan Hines © Oxford University Press 2010. Reproduced by permission; p.271 From Oxford Dominoes Level One: *Five Canterbury Tales* by Geoffrey Chaucer, retold by Bill Bowler © 2010 Oxford University Press. Reproduced by permission; p.273 From Oxford Bookworms Library Stage 1: *Sherlock Holmes and the Sport of Kings* by Sir Arthur Conan Doyle, retold by Jennifer Bassett © Oxford University Press 2008. Reproduced by permission; p.275 From Oxford Dominoes Level One: *Macbeth* by William Shakespeare, retold by Alistair McCallum © Oxford University Press 2010. Reproduced by permission; p.277 From Oxford Bookworms Library Stage 1: *The Adventures of Tom Sawyer* by Mark Twain, retold by Nick Bullard © Oxford University Press 2008. Reproduced by permission; p.279 From Oxford Dominoes Level Two: *Emma* by Jane Austen, retold by Barbara Mackay © Oxford University Press 2010. Reproduced by permission; p.281 From Oxford Bookworms Library Stage 2: *The Importance of Being Earnest* Playscript by Oscar Wilde, retold by Susan Kingsley © Oxford University Press 2008. Reproduced by permission.

Sources: pp.140–141 Source: http://boardfreebornfree.blogspot.com

Cover images by: Alamy Images (Gherkin skyscraper/Eddie Gerald), (Teen with tablet computer/Flint Images), (Belfast/Eye Ubiquitous); Getty Images (Teen girl with laptop/Paul Mansfield Photography), (Girl with headphones and laptop/Zero Creatives), (Teens with mobile/Oliver Rossi); iStockphoto (Tower Bridge/S. Greg Panosian), (World map/Will Evans); Oxford University Press (Durdle Door/Digital Vision), (Tate Modern/John Foxx), (Lloyds of London/Photodisc), (Edinburgh/Digital Vision), (Train/Martin Anderson), (Reading map/Dominic Burke), (Angel of the North/Digital Vision), (Newquay Harbour/Corel), (London buses/Stockbyte).

Commissioned photography: Chris King pp.8, 9, 10, 12, 18, 20, 28, 36, 38, 46, 48, 54, 56, 64, 65, 66, 72, 74, 82, 84, 90, 91, 92, 100, 108, 110, 118, 120, 126, 128, 136, 138.

With thanks to the following locations: Ferry Leisure Centre, Jericho Café, Kassam Stadium, Mamma Mia, Mind, Oxford Jewish Centre, Run Oxford, Shepherd and Woodward.

Film stills from Oxford University Press: pp.25, 43, 61, 79, 97, 115, 143

Illustrations by: Guy Atherfold/Advocate Art p.125; Humberto Blanco/Sylvie Poggio Artists Agency pp.11, 23, 29, 57, 148, 187, 188, 189, 197, 202, 218, 255, 256, 260, 264; Aaron Blecha pp.45, 49, 109, 130; Peter Bull p.8; Paul Daviz p.149 (ex4); Natalia Demidora p.271; Nicolas Gremaud pp.37, 99, 107, 149 (ex5), 164, 228 (ex2); Lisa Hunt pp.47, 121, 137; Joanna Kerr pp.65, 111, 154, 196 (ex4), 228 (ex1), 235, 237; Carol Liddimen/The Organisation p.277; Claire Littlejohn p.26; Gavin Reece/New Division pp.53, 67, 101, 196 (ex1); Keith Shaw pp.244, 246; Tom Sperling pp.268, 269.

The publisher would like to thank the following for permission to reproduce photography: Alamy Images pp.9 (globe/Hypermania Stock Illustration), 9 (Senior couple/Lisa F. Young), 15 (Francesco Totti with daughter Chanel/MARKA), 17 (Watching television/Kumar Sriskandan), 17 (Group of friends/Science Photo Library), 21 (Fashion show in New York/Rudy K), 23 (Necklace/Mathieu B.Morin/Jewellery), 27 (Man making knot in tie/Ted Horowitz), 32 (University students on campus/moodboard), 40 (The Earth Galleries at London's Natural History Museum/John Kellerman), 40 (BERTI robot/Marco Secchi), 41 (Stonehenge/kwhi02), 41 (Lake District National Park/Keith Taylor), 41 (Windsor Castle/Oleksandr Ivanchenko), 41 (Deep sea diving/AF archive), 43 (Bowling strike/Hypermania Images), 43 (Golden disco ball/MilsiArt), 44 (Student in science class/moodboard), 44 (Netball game/Laurie Strachan), 44 (Apple iPad/Hugh Threlfall), 49 (Basketball match/Bill Allsopp), 50 (Underground station/Andrew Fox), 51 (Busker/Keith Morris), 51 (Busking in Oxford/PhotoEdit), 58 (Millennium Stadium/Liquid Light), 59 (Food market stall/David Taylor Photography), 62 (Ballygally Castle/Design Pics Inc.), 62 (Film poster for *The Chronicles of Narnia*/AF Archive), 69 (English breakfast/Andrew Catterall), 69 (Breakfast/Morgan Lane Photography), 69 (Brazilian typical breakfast/Ricardo Junqueira), 69 (Overflowing litter bin/joefoxphoto), 71 (Hiking/moodboard), 75 (Man sailing a yacht/Shepic), 76 (Teen boy portrait/RubberBall), 77 (Four teenagers/MBI), 79 (Zebras/LUNA), 80 (Japanese sushi bar/picturesbyrob), 80 (Thai restaurant/Simply Signs), 80 (Indian restaurant/Manor Photography), 80 (Mexican diner/Leslie Garland Picture Library), 80 (Italian restaurant/Michael Kemp), 80 (Chinese restaurant/ColsTravel UK), 81 (Group of friends/Science Photo Library), (81 Basketball match/Bill Allsopp), 85 (TomTom One sat nav device/ICP), 85 (Sony Ericsson mobile phone/Jinx Photography Brands), 85 (Apple iPad with Times newspaper/Lourens Smak), 86 (Woman using an Apple iPad/Neil Frazer), 86 (Apple iPhone 3GS/Dave Bowman), 87 (Bush Bakelite television/Adams Picture Library t/a apl), 87 (Google maps on Apple iPhone/Alex Segre), 87 (Japanese athlete Yuko Matsumiya/Richard Wareham Fotografie), 94 (Woman in winter jacket/Somos), 105 (Fairtrade logo/Jack Sullivan), 105 (Emma Watson/Allstar Picture Library), 112 (Wedding in Sorrento/Barry Mason), 112 (Woman using laptop/Andy StJohn), 115 (Maternity trousers/mediablitzimages (uk) Limited), 115 (Trainers/mediablitzimages (uk) Limited), 115 (Maternity shirt/mediablitzimages (uk) Limited), 117 (Fog/Ireland Photography), 117 (Lighting thunderstorm/Ern Mainka), 122 (Hail stones/Vadym Kharkivskiy), 122 (Tornado/Steve Bloom Images), 123 (The four seasons/nagelestock.com), 128 (Adventure playground/Janusz Gniadek), 129 (Woman celebrating/Chris Rout), 129 (Swimming with a dolphin/Jeff Rotman), 129 (Horse trek in Kenya/John Warburton-Lee Photography), 131 (Tennis match/Wesley Hitt), 131 (Cyclists/BlueMoon Stock), 134 (Scottish piper/Ingolf Pompe 27), 134 (Urquhart Castle and Loch Ness/nagelestock.com), 135 (Cruise ship/Caribbean), 135 (Helicopter/Robert Convery), 135 (Car ferry/John Peter Photography), 135 (Plane/aerialarchives.com), 140 (Lands End sign/Bailey-Cooper Photography 3), 141 (Backpacker/Ray Evans), 160 (Man in karate uniform/Hunstock, Inc), 170 (Voting/Rob Wilkinson), 191 (Chinese New Year celebrations/M Itani), 192 (Sightseeing bus/The Photolibrary Wales), 192 (Cardiff Castle/Peter Titmuss), 192 (Outdoor cafe/Robert Harding Picture Library), 193 (Tourist information sign/Paul Thompson Images), 206 (Ice cream shop/ICP), 208 (Caramel latte/Bon Appetit), 211 (UK newspapers/ICP), 225 (Counselling/Catchlight Visual Services), 238 (Vintage clothes market stall/Bettina Strenske), 238 (1950's fashion/MARKA), 239 (1960's fashion/INTERFOTO), 239 (1970's fashion/ClassicStock), 254 (Surfer/Matthew Kirwan), 254 (Beach/doughoughton), 257 (Apple iPhone 4/Rob Bartee), 267 (Train ticket/Stuart Kelly); Bridgeman Art Library Ltd p.170 (*Portrait of Henry VIII* (1491–1547) aged 49, 1540 (oil on panel), Holbein the Younger, Hans (1497/8-1543)/Palazzo Barberini, Rome, Italy); Chris Boon pp.25 (London skyline), 27 (clock graphic), 44 (graphics on ipad screen) 61 (tourist information sign), 61 (map), 68 (plate and cutlery graphic), 68 (Emma headshot), 68 (Tom headshot), 81 (media illustrations), 81 (social network website), 83 (media collage), 97 (lost property form), 112 (website graphic), 113 (website graphics), 116 (wooden background), 117 (weather symbols), 121 (weather symbols), 122 (storm cloud), 128 (background) 140 (UK map); Corbis pp.14 (Gwyneth Paltrow with daughter Apple/epa), 17 (Teen using mobile phone/Randy Faris), 17 (Fencing duel/Inspirestock), 17 (Basketball/Mika), 17 (Swimmer/Stephen Frink), 17 (Beach volleyball/Kate Mitchell), 21 (Leona Lewis/Mark Savage), 21 (Espresso machine/Herbert Lehmann, Wien, Austria/the food passionates), 22 (Man with sailplane/Morgan David de Lossy), 22 (Man wearing hooded sweatshirt/Marcus Mok/Asia Images), 25 (Fish and chips/Foodfolio/the food passionates), 25 (The British Royal family/Daniel Deme/epa), 25 (Vivienne Westwood/WWD/Condé Nast), 25 (Robbie Williams/Kurt Krieger), 25 (1940 Packard Convertible Sedan/Car Culture), 26 (Justin Bieber wax figure/Wu Kaixiang/XinHua/Xinhua Press), 26 (Teen boy in city/Christian Green), 26 (Hyde Park boaters/Bob Krist), 27 (Teen girl in bed/Edith Held), 35 (Chemistry students/Eleanor Bentall), 43 (George Clooney/David Lefranc/kipa), 43 (concert/Ocean), 54 (Laganside, Belfast/Chris Hill/National Geographic Society), 54 (City Hall, Belfast/Chris Hill/National Geographic Society), 58 (Clifton suspension bridge/David Cheshire/Loop Images), 59 (Chocolate/Lutterbeck, Barbara/the food passionates), 62 (Giant's Causeway/Charles Bowman/Robert Harding World Imagery), 63 (Balsamic vinegar and grapes/Brauner, Michael/the food passionates), 63 (Oranges/Roulier/Turiot/photoscuisine), 63 (Mineral water/Arras, Klaus/the food passionates), 69 (Salad/Unangst, Andrew/Index Stock), 71 (Matira Beach, Bora Bora Island/Jose Fuste Raga), 73 (Lewis Hamilton/Rune Hellestad), 73 (Arctic Monkeys/Candice Lawler/Retna Ltd.), 75 (Man standing beside car/John-Francis Bourke), 81 (Justin Bieber wax figure/Wu Kaixiang/XinHua/Xinhua Press), 86 (Teens listening to cassette tapes/Roy Morsch), 87 (Couple with radio, ca. 1940s - 1950s/Bettmann), 89 (Giving a present/Strauss/Curtis), 91 (Matthew Bellamy of the band Muse/Jason Moore/ZUMA Press), 91 (Wimbledon final 2008/Ben Radford), 98 (Bottle of pills/Thomas Francisco), 98 (Houses of Parliament at night/Gregor Schuster), 102 (Hindu temples, Indonesia/Tibor Bognor), 102 (Komodo dragon/Nick Rains), 102 (Fish underwater/Stephen Frink/Science Faction), 117 (Windy day/Sandy Felsenthal), 119 (The Hollywood sign/Kurt Krieger), 127 (Matira Beach, Bora Bora Island/Jose Fuste Raga), 131 (Race starting position/Ocean), 131 (Cross country running/PCN), 158 (Venus and Serena Williams/Susan Mullane/NewSport), 159 (NFL players Eli and Peyton Manning/Chris Faytok/Star Ledger), 170 (Albert Einstein/Bettmann), 190 (Old Trafford stadium/Matthew Aston/AMA), 190 (The Lowry and Salford Quays Millennium Footbridge/Atlantide Phototravel), 192 (Millennium Stadium/Skyscan), 192 (Wales Millennium Centre/Chris Warren/Loop Images), 208 (Spaghetti Bolognese/Parque), 212 (African elephant/Anup Shah), 229 (Woman sitting on beach/Kevin Dodge), 240 (Second hand clothes/David Vintiner), 264 (Steam locomotive/Colin Garratt; Milepost 92 ½), 264 (Sark Island/James L. Amos), 264 (Tresco Abbey Gardens/Ashley Cooper); Getty Images pp.14 (David Beckham with his sons/Jordan Strauss/Getty Images for Xbox), 17 (Teen boy wearing headphones/Maria Teijeiro), 21 (Keira Knightley/Venturelli), 21 (Luca Fainello And Diego Fainello/JC Olivera/LatinContent), 21 (The Jonas Brothers/WireImage), 21 (Robert Pattinson/WireImage), 22 (Dancing woman/Miroslav Georgijevic), 25 (Frank Lampard/Jamie McDonald), 27 (Teen girl eating breakfast/Elle Bernager/Taxi), 30 (Teen boy laughing/Annabelle Breakey/Taxi), 32 (Teen boy smiling/Jenny Acheson/Riser), 33 (Bored teen girl/Walstrom, Susanne/Johner Images), 35 (School computer class/

Jetta Productions), 40 (Apollo 11 capsule/Dan Kitwood), 43 (Design elements/Che McPherson), 50 (Design elements/Che McPherson), 50 (Man rapping/Ian Spanier/The Image Bank), 51 (Teenage girl portrait/Radius Images), 58 (Edinburgh Castle and Ross Fountain/Fraser Hall), 58 (The Albert Memorial Clock/Gallo Images), 59 (Postcard showing Titanic/Bob Thomas/Popperfoto), 62 (Footballer George Best/Hulton Archive), 67 (Boy eating chocolate eclair/Donna Day/Riser), 73 (Russell Crowe/Munawar Hosain), 73 (Jessica Alba/FilmMagic), 76 (Graffiti on wall/Tim Franco/Flickr), 81, (Teen girl eating breakfast/Elle Bernager/Taxi), 84 (Bodrum, Turkey/John Elk III/Lonely Planet Images), 85 (Personal stereo cassette player/Monique le Luhandre), 86 (Personal stereo cassette player/Monique le Luhandre), 89 (Confident man/Markus Bernhard/The Image Bank), 89 (Man playing air guitar/Betsie Van der Meer), 93 (Rihanna/Steve Granitz/WireImage), 93 (Tom Cruise/Fred Duval/FilmMagic), 93 (Simona Ventura/Vittorio Zunino), 93 (Will Smith/WireImage), 94 (Portrait of man smiling/Peter Mason/Stone), 98 (Flat screen TV/Jorg Greuel/Photographer's Choice), 98 (Girl in the rain/Photographer's Choice), 98 (Riding a penny farthing bicycle/Hulton Archive), 102 (Indonesian woman with basket of flowers/Martin Puddy), 104 (Shoe factory production line/Adek Berry/AFP), 105 (Asian teen boy/Nacivet/Photographer's Choice), 112 (Hairdresser washing customer's hair/Reza Estakhrian), 113 (Teenage boy with laptop and phone/Bruce Lawrence/Riser), 116 (Eton College students/Christopher Furlong), 117 (Rainy day in London/Alan Copson), 117 (Sydney Opera House/Michael Dunning), 119 (Cable car in San Francisco/Mitchell Funk), 128 (Rope bridge/Ghislain & Marie David de Lossy), 128 (Zip line cable ride/Kate Powers), 134 (Celtic v Rangers football match/Julian Finney), 140 (Skateboarding/Stanislav Solntsev), 140 (Long and winding road/Peter Chadwick LRPS/Flickr), 141 (Happy teen girls/Cultura/Zero Creatives), 167 (English breakfast/Bob Thomas/Popperfoto), 170 (Plant shoots in test tubes/Geir Pettersen), 171 (College students/Emma Innocenti), 171 (Walking a dog/Bambu Productions), 174 (Bored teen/Franklin Lugenbeel/Vetta), 175 (Teen girl consoling friend/Stockbyte), 176 (Young woman sitting/Rubberball/Alan Bailey), 176 (Portrait of young man/Vicente Alfonso/Flickr), 176 (Orchestra/Hill Street Studios), 217 (Teen girl with corn row hairstyle/Arnos Morgan/Photodisc), 217 (Girl outside at beach/Alexa Miller/Digital Vision), 217 (Teen on school bus/Siri Stafford), 220 (Teen girl laughing/Hutch Axilrod/Riser), 230 (Teenage boy with fedora hat/Ron Levine), 238 (Teen girl with earrings/Daniel Arsenault), 240 (Shopping at market stall/Briony Campbell), 255 (Surfer/LaCoppola-Meier), 264 (Isle of Wight cliffs/Christopher Hope-Fitch), 266 (Windsurfing lessons/Karl Johaentges), 273 (horse racing/Dan Smith); Image Source pp.171 (Teen boys playing football/Surfacia), 217 (Teen girl wearing sunglasses); iStockphoto pp.9 (Abstract background/Aleksandar Velasevic), 30 (Sunbeam background/Roman Okopny), 43 (ice skating icons/Taras Livyy), 59 (Belfast River Lagan/James O'Neill), 69 (Hamburger in a box/JackJelly), 86 (3D glass arrows/Olena Marina), 94 (Rainbow flow design/Jamie Farrant), 94 (Abstract rainbow design/Jamie Farrant), 140 (Skateboard deck/makkayak), 150 (DVD cases/Doug Cannell), 150 (Mobile phone/artcyclone), 150 (Music player/Andrey Pokomeda), 170 (Globe in classroom/graphixel), 170 (Calculus/David Elfstrom), 174 (Chemist/blackwaterimages), 174 (Blue rays/Sergey Smirnov), 230 (Teen wearing suit/Stephanie Phillips), 251 (Speedy scooter/Radu Razvan), 275 (sword/supertee), 277 (wooden planks/Skip ODonnell); Kate Evans p.98 (LightSleeper/Quincom Ltd), 98 (Kate Evans with LightSleeper/Quincom Ltd); Kobal Collection pp.91 (Avatar/Twentieth Century-Fox Film Corporation), 278 (Emma 1996/Matchmaker/Miramax); Oxford University Press pp.17 (Skateboarder/Image Source), 17 (Snowboarder/Chad Riley), 25 (two students/Oxford University Press Video/MTJ), 25 (English tea/Creatas), 26 (London/Justin Kase), 27 (Teen boy sleeping/Rubberball), 27 (Doing homework/PhotoAlto), 27 (Students at school/Chris King), 31 (Rollercoaster/Purestock), 43 (two teenagers talking/Oxford University Press Video/MTJ), 43 (Shakespeare play/Stan Fellerman), 58 (Portrait of girl/Radius Images), 58 (Teen boy with backpack/Imageshop), 58 (Happy teen girl/Image Source), 61 (tourist information centre/Oxford University Press Video/MTJ), 63 (Wine/Digital Vision), 63 (Decanter of olive oil/Fancy), 63 (Bread/Photodisc), 63 (Pouring salt/BananaStock), 63 (Potatoes/Westend61), 63 (Apples/Photodisc), 63 (Peas/Stockbyte), 63 (Roast chicken/MIXA), 68 (Asian teen boy/Photodisc), 68 (Woman relaxing/Eyecandy Images), 68 (Teen girl in hammock/Corbis), 69 (Jogging/Mike Harrington), 79 (teens in a restaurant/Oxford University Press Video/MTJ), 80 (Japanese chopsticks/Photodisc), 81 (Weather forecast/Stockbyte), 81 (TV presenter/Digital Vision), 87 (Big Ben, London/Digital Vision), 94 (Teen male/Digital Vision), 97 (lost property office/Oxford University Press Video/MTJ), 97 (Train/Andrew Bell), 98 (Internet/1Apix), 104 (Trainers/David Cook/blueshiftstudios), 115 (clothes shop/Oxford University Press Video/MTJ), 115 (Jacket/Leonid Nyshko), 123 (Lightning/Photodisc), 127 (Hiker/Zen Shui), 127 (Skiier/Photodisc), 130 (Man with books/Westend61), 130 (Teen boy in library/Brand X Pictures), 130 (Teen girl in classroom/Digital Vision), 131 (Portrait of teen girl/Westend61), 133 (teen on phone/Oxford University Press Video/MTJ), 134 (Portree, Skye/Stephen Emerson), 134 (Tartan fabric/Corel), 135 (Businessman with bike/Digital Vision), 135 (Motorcyclist/Joe Fox Motorsport), 139 (Teen boy reading/PhotoAlto), 143 (ticket office/Oxford University Press Video/MTJ), 143 (Liverpool Street station/Dominic Burke), 144 (London underground sign/Photodisc), 144 (Underground station/Hisham Ibrahim/Photov.com), 151 (Portrait of girl/Gareth Boden), 155 (Portrait of teenage boy/Image Source), 156 (Cinema audience/Moodboard), 180 (Ducklings/Photodisc), 180 (Sunflowers/Photodisc), 180 (Pumpkins/Photodisc), 180 (Snowflake/Photodisc), 198 (Cake), 241 (Clothes shopping/Somos), 245 (Football goalkeeper/PhotoAlto), 256 (Lightning/Digital Vision), 262 (Passport stamp/Photodisc); Photolibrary pp.9 (Couple in ski gear/Juice Images), 9 (Children with dog/OJO Images), 15 (Family portrait/OJO Images), 15 (Woman with dog/Cultura), 17 (Teens playing computer game/I Love Images), 17 (Girl using laptop/Blend Images), 17 (Teenage boy band/Corbis), 17 (Woman shopping/Tetra Images), 17 (Mountain biking/Westend61), 17 (Girls playing football/Image Source), 21 (Carton of popcorn/Amanaimages), 27 (Boy washing face/White), 30 (Group of friends/White), 33 (Friends dancing/Juice Images), 33 (Music festival crowd/Image Source), 35 (School hiking trip/Cultura), 39 (Mother helping son with homework/Cultura), 58 (O'Connell Bridge over River Liffey/Tetra Images), 63 (Salt and pepper shakers/Kate Kunz/Fancy), 69 (Grilled saury/Mixa), 69 (Logging/Photodisc), 75 (Teen girl hiking/Moodboard), 76 (Geek and rebel/Image Source),

77 (Geek and skater girl/Image Source), 89 (Bored office worker/Image Source), 89 (Woman applying makeup/OJO Images), 89 (Businessman/Corbis), 94 (Woman in wooly hat/Radius Images), 94 (Woman in yellow/Image Source), 116 (High school student/Corbis), 116 (School students walking/Mixa), 117 (Quebec in winter/White), 160 (Judo/Peter Olive), 172 (Girl with football/Juice Images), 175 (Woman consoling friend/White), 177 (Teenage couple in school yard/Blend Images), 204 (Baby/FStop), 204 (Swimming pool/Radius Images), 206 (Close up of pizza/Radius Images), 207 (Coffee and cake/Radius Images), 208 (Takeway pizza/Stockbroker); Press Association Images pp.14 (Sir Bob Geldof and daughter Peaches/Zak Hussein/PA Archive), 122 (Flooding at Ottery St. Mary/Ben Birchall/PA Archive), 159 (Rugby players Alesana and Manu Tuilagi/Tony Marshall/EMPICS); Rex Features pp.25 (Sherlock Holmes, 2009/c.Warner Br/Everett), 161 (Singer Jessie J/NBCUPHOTOBANK), 176 (Chetham's School of Music/Sefton Samuels), 176 (Rudolf Steiner School sign/Jon Santa Cruz), 191 (The Lowry Theatre/Bruce Adams/Associated Newspapers), 215 (Dancing on Ice/Ken McKay/ITV), 222 (Coronation Street/ITV), 222 (Dynasty/Everett Collection), 222 (Emmerdale/ITV), 224 (Emmerdale/ITV), 224 (Coronation Street/ITV), 252 (The Saturdays/David Fisher), 266 (English beach/Paul Darrah), 273 (Sherlock Holmes statue/Anders Good), 279 (Emma 1996/c.Miramax/Everett), 280 (The Importance of Being Earnest 1952), 281 (The Importance of Being Earnest film still); Ronald Grant Archive p.275 (Macbeth 1971); Ross Parry Agency pp.98 (Solar fridge in Africa), 98 (Inventor Emily Cummins with solar fridge); SuperStock p.217 (Portrait of teen boy/age fotostock).

Although every effort has been made to trace and contact copyright holders before publication, this has not been possible in some cases. We apologize for any apparent infringement of copyright and if notified, the publisher will be pleased to rectify any errors or omissions at the earliest opportunity.

The author and Publisher would like to thank the following teachers who contributed to the development of this course: Margherita Accardi, Enzo Aceto, Cristina Amadei, Donata Andraghetti, Doretta Ardu, Annalisa Attento, Vanina Baldo, Fabia Baschenis, Maria Grazia Beltrame, Graziella Bentivegna, Raffaella Beole, Romana Bertini, Sandra Biagini, Ivana Bollea, Laura Bonello, Eleonora Brero, Diana Bruni, Celinda Campomori, Cecilia Carasso, Cinzia Caratti, Daniela Carignano, Eleonora Carbonati, Ivana Careri, Raffaele Carozza, Mara Casamassima, Paola Cattani, Susanna Cecchi, Ester Cerruti, Andreana Chiappone, Irene Chiribola, Anna Cicciotti, Antonietta Clemente, Sara Coccolo, Sara Corio, Luisa Cotti, Anna Cremonini, Maria Grazia Crisci, Monica Cristiani, Carla Cucinotti, Pierangela Cutillo, Maria Angela Dal Bianco, Franca Dal Pino, Eve-Marine Dauvergne, Maria Dei Fiori Zingarello Pasanisi, Francesca Delaini, Sofia Dell'Accia, Patrizia Depalma, Maria Di Donato, Teresa Flavia Di Lucia, Alessandra Fabbri, Francesca Falcone, Mirella Fanizzi, Paolo Fazzino, Marcella Ferrarini, Daniele Ferraris, Maria Chiara Ferretti, Sabrina Angela Ferri, Veronica Fiorillo, Lorenza Fogagnolo, Claudia Fontana, Monica Gaidolfi, Angela Gardin, Isabella Gargiulo, Alessandra Gattai, Anna Gliottone, Giuseppe Graceffa, Brunella Guerri, Olimpia Guitto, Flaviana Iantorno, Petronilla Ieracitano, Massimo Laria, Milena Lato, Daniela Lavagno, Carmelo Liaci, Anna Lopez, Cesare Luschi, Ermanno Maggi, Nicoletta Maglia, Maria Grazia Maglione, Alessandra Magno, Pierpaolo Maiorani, Maria Maltoni, Maria Pia Mangia, Silvia Manini, Nives Mantovani, Arianna Mastrogiacomo, Elena Mazzucco, Cristina Melchiorre, Rita Mellone, Maria Minelli, Ida Caterina Mugnone, Daniela Napoleone, Angela Negro, Francesco Oliva, Marina Orioli, Serenella Ospite, Mariateresa Pallone, Maria Letizia Peliti, Giulia Pelizzetti, Maria Elena Pellini, Mariella Petrollini, Flavia Pini, Raffaele Polichetti, Nadia Prioni, Michele Riccio, Sonia Rigari, Elena Rignani, Ileana Romano, Marta Ronzoni, Riccardo Rota, Emilia Salomone, Paola Santantonio, Carla Santini, Addolorata Santoro, Luigi Savinelli, Bruna Scornito, Maria Chiara Serrali, Concetta Silvestre, Mariella Sommovigo, Ester Spagnolo, Barbara Summa, Gigliola Tarabella, Anna Maria Tuba, Donatella Vailati, Gabriella Vicari, Anna Zagni, Francesca Zero, Patrizia Zizzari.

The author and Publisher would like to extend a special thanks to the following teachers: Monica Brondi, Cristina Oddone, Gabriella Silvano, and also Francesca Paola Brienza, Liviana Castellari, Marta Ceccarelli, Mary De Rosa, Simona Fefè, Fabio Macherelli, Daniela Trausi, Silvia Zalla.